THE *MONEY* BOOK OF MONEY

THE *MONEY* BOOK OF MONEY

Your Personal Financial Planner

Robert J. Klein

and the editors of

Money Magazine

LITTLE, BROWN AND COMPANY · BOSTON · TORONTO

Library of Congress Cataloging-in-Publication Data

Klein, Robert J.
The money book of money.
1. Finance, personal—United States. I. Money (Chicago, Ill.) II. Title.
HG179.K57 1987 332.024 86-33777
ISBN 0-316-49840-8

The author is grateful for permission to reprint excerpts from previously copyrighted material:

Chapter 33 is adapted from *Gaining on the Market* by Charles J. Rolo. Copyright © 1982 by Charles J. Rolo. Reprinted by permission of Little, Brown and Company (Inc.) in association with The Atlantic Monthly Press.

Figure 15 is from *Stock Market Strategy* by Richard A. Crowell. Copyright © 1977 by Richard A. Crowell. Used with permission of the author.

RRD VA

Designed by Patricia Dunbar

Published simultaneously in Canada by Little, Brown & Company (Canada) Limited

PRINTED IN THE UNITED STATES OF AMERICA

To Easy, in part payment for
fifty-two lost weekends

CONTENTS

List of Figures xi
Acknowledgments xiii
Foreword: *The Wisdom of Fifteen Volumes* xv

I. The Economy and You

1. The Financial Revolution 3
2. Getting Your Finances Together — At Last 7
3. Your Net Worth 9
4. Setting Your Goals 16
5. Creating a Budget 21
6. Leaving a Trail 32

II. You Don't Have to Go It Alone

7. Choosing and Using a Financial Planner 43
8. Paying Others to Invest for You 50
9. Letting Mutual Funds Do It 56

III. The Financial Life Cycle

10. The Economics of Being Single 63
11. Living Together 68
12. Prenuptial Agreements 75
13. The Two-Paycheck Life 81

14. The Best Companies for Working Parents 93
15. What Price Children? 96
16. The ABCs of Selecting Child Care 100
17. Buying Your First House 104
18. Paying for Baby's B.A. 111
19. An Educated Parents' Guide to College Financial Aid 116
20. How to Become Financially Independent 126
21. Sensible Divorce Settlements 134
22. Blended Families 143
23. When Aging Parents Need Help 148
24. Retirement Planning 156
25. The Taxing Choices of Retirement 175
26. Saving Widows (or Widowers) from Still More Losses 184
27. Estate Planning: How to Keep Your Money in the Family 190
28. Estate Planning: Avoiding Death Taxes 203
29. Where There's a Will 213

IV. The First and Last Word on Investing

30. Fearless First-Time Investing 223
31. Where to Put Your Savings 234
32. Strategies: Value Investing 242
33. Strategies: Going for Growth 249
34. Strategies: Timing the Market 258
35. Strategies: Takeover Targets 269
36. Strategies: The Best Defenses 277
37. All About Bonds 287
38. Real Estate: Ginnie Mae and Kin 305
39. Real Estate: REITs, FREITs, and Partnerships 311
40. Real Estate: Backyard Investing 316

41. An Investor's Guide to IRAs and Keoghs 322

42. Finding a Stockbroker to Suit Your Taste 334

V. Living with the Income Tax

43. Learning the Code 348

44. Your Tax-Advantaged Dwelling 362

45. Finding a Tax Adviser or Preparer 365

46. Coping with the IRS: How to Complain 370

47. Coping with the IRS: How to Handle an Audit 373

VI. The New World of Banking and Borrowing

48. Do You Still Need Your Bank? 381

49. How to Save on Checking 385

50. Shopping for Loans 389

51. Getting the Best Mortgage 398

52. How to Keep a Well-Polished Credit Image 405

53. The Debt Monster 412

VII. Insuring Against the Unkindest Cuts

54. The Best Auto Policies 419

55. Guarding Your Castle Against Calamity 425

56. Excess Liability: Your Last Bastion Against Damage Suits 431

57. Life Insurance: Enough Is Enough 435

58. A Health Insurance Checkup 455

59. Income While You Are Down 465

VIII. The Consummate Consumer

60. Secrets of Black-Belt Shoppers 474

61. A Car Shopper's Guide 480

62. Gaining Through Complaining 485

Appendix: Seventy Essential Addresses 492

Index 505

LIST OF FIGURES

1. Personal Balance Sheet 13
2. How Much to Set Aside toward a Goal 18
3. Your Cash-Flow Statement 23
4. Four Model Budgets 29
5. Your Financial File 34
6. How Much to Save Each Year for a College Education 112
7. A Crib Sheet for Collegiate Credit Seekers 122
8. How Far a Company Program Can Take You 129
9. A Less Taxing Divorce Settlement 138
10. Estimating Your Social Security Benefits 161
11. Retirement Planning Worksheet 164
12. Annuity Payments with Different Guarantees 177
13. Totting Up Your Estate 204
14. Valuing a Stock by the Numbers 245
15. Adding Up the Buy and Sell Signals 262
16. Mergerspeak 272
17. Finding the Lowest Fees for Your Trades 340

18. Projecting Your Next Tax Bill 357

19. Your Self-Imposed Debt Limit 391

20. The 10 Largest Car Insurers and Their Primary Discounts 420

21. Life Insurance Planning Worksheet 447

ACKNOWLEDGMENTS

THIS BOOK IS dedicated to the people who created it: the more than 100 men and women who have worked on the editorial staff of *Money* magazine since its inception in October 1972. Collectively, as writers, reporters, correspondents, and editors, they have amassed and put in print a body of knowledge about personal finance that surely is unmatched in journalism or, for that matter, in the financial and legal professions. On every working day, the current staff adds to that store, devoting itself to producing not only 12 issues of *Money* each year but also two special *Money Guides* on single topics and an imaginative list of other projects to advance the fine art of managing and enjoying one's money. Every word you are about to read derives from these labors.

In an especially heroic effort late in the summer of 1986, just about everybody on the masthead helped to produce a 50-page special report on the elemental tax reform legislation then emerging from a Senate–House conference committee. At the newsstands, checkout counters, and bookstores of America when President Ronald Reagan signed the tax bill that October, *Money* was the only magazine to publish a complete account of the new law, including a remarkably useful analysis of how taxpayers can best adjust to it. That issue serves as a standard reference in the households of 5 million *Money* readers. It was an indispensable tool in the creation of this book.

The idea for a *Money* book came to several minds at different times, but it went from idea to working project through the efforts and negotiations of William S. Rukeyser, the magazine's founding managing editor, and Keith R. Johnson, its first executive editor. I am indebted to

Marshall Loeb, managing editor from 1980 to 1986 (and now editor of *Fortune*), for assigning me the task of getting the project off a slow back burner, and to Landon Y. Jones, who succeeded Marshall as managing editor and saw to the project's completion. It was Lanny who, first, lightened my regular chores and, later, liberated me from them so that I could complete the book on schedule.

Special thanks for their hands-on work go to Susan Siegler, whose research helped vastly to bring the facts up to date, and Linda Schmidt of *American Ceramics* magazine, who typed my clip-paste-and-scribble manuscript on the word processor. Susan's work often became a hunt for missing persons who had been interviewed years earlier and whose pungent observations had been quoted in the magazine. Linda not only typed skillfully but also tutored me in the mysteries of writing and editing on a computer. Patiently enduring it all, prodding and encouraging me, while keeping the project alive with his colleagues in Boston, was Ray Roberts, my editor and counselor at Little, Brown. Susan, Linda, and Ray get much credit for the accuracy and quality of this book. The errors and gaucheries belong to me.

Robert J. Klein
March 1987

FOREWORD: THE WISDOM OF FIFTEEN VOLUMES

WHERE SHOULD I put my money now? Can I afford a house? How can I save enough to pay for the kids' college? Are bonds really safe? Is this a good time to invest in stocks? Which bank is best? How can I cut my taxes? What's the best way to get into real estate? What's the smartest way to save for retirement? Which investments will beat inflation?

The mission of the reporters, writers, and editors of *Money* magazine since its first issue in October 1972 has been to answer those questions and hundreds like them about personal finance. The questions must be readdressed from year to year because the answers change with the times. There being no eternal wisdom about how to conduct one's financial affairs, a pure anthology of *Money* articles would be perishable indeed. Yet an astonishing amount of the published material contains enduring truths. A reader who sat down to Volume 1, Number 1 of the magazine and plowed through to Volume 15, Number 12 (December 1986), the span of this book, would arise exhausted, it's true, but in possession of much valuable and usable information.

The Money *Book of Money* spares you the trouble while giving you the essence. It includes a few articles virtually as written, but in the main each chapter takes from two or more of the most recent articles on the same or related subjects. In addition to regular issues of the magazine, material comes from single-topic *Money Guides,* which we publish twice a year, and from other projects still in preparation. The style of the magazine follows the journalistic principle of finding out what's new and pertinent about a topic — whether it is divorce or financing a house or investing for income — and reporting from that perspective. Few articles simply survey the field and teach it textbook fashion. That would grow dull and untimely. It surely would have doomed *Money* magazine to a short life. In book form, however, the wedding of words, sentences, and paragraphs from several articles creates a more nearly comprehensive report on each subject treated.

Where possible, the conversational tone, actual human experiences, and personality that give *Money* its character are preserved. Further research has brought each chapter up to date. At the heart of the book is a sequence of chapters that corresponds to the ages of man and woman, a financial life cycle marked by certain predictable events. The cycle begins for most of us when we are single and fresh out of school. It ends five to eight decades later, on the day we put our affairs in order for what we assume is the last time.

In between come such milestones as financing our first house, paying off college loans, making our first investments, sharing property and financial plans with a potential mate, making the most of fringe benefits, having children, taking advantage of tax breaks available to families, providing for financial emergencies, insuring our lives and our property, developing long-term investment goals and strategies, putting children through college, looking toward retirement, planning our estates, and possibly — quite possibly — negotiating a divorce.

Throughout life's tour there are basics to be learned: about investing, taxes, banking, borrowing, insuring our lives and property, and being smart all-around consumers. In addition to the life-cycle section, the book has seven other major parts, each devoted to one of those aspects of personal finance. Part I, after some preliminaries, provides instructions and tools, in the form of worksheets, for taking the measure of your current financial condition. Throughout the book, wherever it seems useful, other worksheets appear, along with charts and tables of applicable data. What you will create by taking advantage of these fill-in-the-blank opportunities is a personal financial log, a snapshot of your present or recent condition. By reusing the forms you can reexamine your situation periodically.

You may have to retain, from time to time, professional advisers to help you do your taxes, write your will, revamp your insurance program, do your securities trading, or design a complete personal financial plan. This book prepares you to deal with accountants, bankers, brokers, insurance agents, lawyers, and financial planners from a position of knowledge and strength, which is always better than placing yourself blindly or passively in their care.

For longtime readers of *Money* magazine, *The* Money *Book of Money* is a ready reference and refresher course. For new and recent readers and for nonreaders of *Money,* it is a book to go straight through or to turn to for speedy aid and reliable advice. Revised editions are planned so that as the world changes, you can always turn to this book and ask, ''Where should I put my money now?'' And a thousand other questions.

I

THE ECONOMY AND YOU

In the 1960s Ralph Nader made Americans more aware of themselves as consumers, and baby boomers declared their sexual freedom. In the 1970s feminists and environmentalists raised our consciousness of women's rights and polluted surroundings. All the while, spontaneously and ungoaded by the propaganda of special interests, we have undergone a financial consciousness-raising. When *Money* magazine polled about 2,500 randomly selected Americans in 1985, one of the questions asked was this: Do you think more often about money or sex? The winner, by 37 percent to 24 percent, was money. This was no big news to marketers of financial services. Sensing that financial awareness was rising to new heights and raising along with it a public demand for new "products" as yet undreamed of, purveyors of investments, insurance, consumer credit, and bank accounts took aim at what they call the retail market — namely, us. The financial supermarket was born, and perhaps stillborn. A profession suddenly materialized: financial planning.

At its most basic level, financial planning dates back to Benjamin Franklin. The inventor of the public library, the fire department, and the wood stove listed among his 13 behavioral virtues four methods of enhancing one's economic well-being:

3. Order. Let all your things have their places. Let each part of your business have its time.

4. Resolution. Resolve to perform what you ought. Perform without fail what you resolve.

5. Frugality. Make no expense but to do good to others or yourself; i.e., waste nothing.

6. Industry. Lose no time. Be always employed in something useful. Cut off all unnecessary actions.

Franklin's other nine virtues were temperance, silence, sincerity, justice, moderation, cleanliness, tranquillity, chastity, and humility. He explained in his autobiography why he gave so high a priority to the above-mentioned: by freeing himself from debt and gaining affluence and independence, he would be more likely to achieve the genteeler virtues.

***The* Money *Book of Money* is essentially a handbook of do-it-yourself financial planning. For openers, here is a look at the economic and political forces that have brought us to our present pass and a set of beginning exercises in Franklin's fourth virtue, order.**

1

THE FINANCIAL REVOLUTION

Five major political events since 1970 unloosed a torrent of economic change in the lives of Americans and the rest of industrialized society: the devaluation of the dollar by President Richard M. Nixon on August 14, 1971; the embargo of oil shipments to the United States by the Organization of Petroleum Exporting Countries on October 19, 1973; the abrupt shift to strict control over the growth of the money supply by the Federal Reserve Board on October 6, 1979; the series of changes in income taxes and retirement accounts legislated under the rubric of Reaganomics starting in 1981; and the total overhaul of the income tax signed into law on October 22, 1986, by President Ronald Reagan and phasing into effect from 1987 to 1990 — the most radical revision of the tax system in half a century.

Nixon's dollar devaluation gave recognition at last to a decline in this nation's world economic might, a decline that probably began with Sputnik but manifested itself around 1960, when the Belgians began selling steel here at less than the American price. In a postwar world starving for raw materials and goods of all sorts, the U.S. dollar had become almighty. Inflation raged through Europe, but middle-class American tourists could live like royalty in Paris and London and on the Riviera, while a student's stipend on the G.I. Bill afforded veterans a comfortable bohemian existence on the Left Bank.

Then came the reckoning. Unchallenged by international competition, U.S. production and labor costs grew fat, and the quality of our output deteriorated. The dollar, although pegged to gold at $35 an ounce, began losing ground as the world's standard currency. Overheated by the Vietnam war, consumer prices began to inflate. By the time Nixon acted, the consumer price index was rising at a 6 percent annual rate. In addition to devaluation, the President took the dollar off the gold standard and stunned the nation by freezing prices, wages, and dividends. Americans sustained a great blow to their economic confidence.

OPEC's oil embargo, although short-lived, set energy prices on a skyward course. The effect of that disruption on prices in general may even now be underestimated. Double-digit inflation came and, finally, went. But it may take a generation before Americans again permit themselves to believe in a stable dollar; an inflation mentality has become part of our financial heritage.

A second round of crude-oil price increases in 1978 had the worse effect of paralyzing industrial growth by instilling in corporate planners an unshakable suspicion of the merits of capital expansion. Hindered by those doubts, corporate investments lagged behind in the business recovery that began in 1982.

One of high inflation's severest consequences is its impact on interest rates. While our savings sat in bank accounts paying the federally imposed ceiling rate of 5½ percent, government and corporate bond yields pushed toward 20 percent; even short-term rates in that then-mysterious place called the money market briefly exceeded 15 percent. The best that banks could offer in response was long-term certificates of deposit. At one point in the early seventies CDs were paying 7 percent — "magic sevens," we called them. Who would have suspected that he might be locked into sevens when a few years later bank certificates were paying 13 and 14 percent?

Against the inflation psychology that was paralyzing the economy, the Federal Reserve pitted monetarism. To combat inflation with tight money requires an interim period of still higher prices and interest rates. For a time, the cost of money became second only to the cost of energy in lifting the price of things. High interest worked its way through home mortgages into the cost of housing and through the financing of business inventories into the cost of such things as autos and appliances. The huge volume of debt carried by utility companies compounded rate increases in gas and electricity. In countless ways, interest rates percolated throughout the economic subsoil.

All during the bouts of hyperinflation, wages had managed almost to keep pace with prices. In the process, a new term gained currency — "bracket creep." Progressive income tax rates had been designed to nibble gently at the lower- and middle-income groups while taking a decent bite out of high salaries. But now those rates chewed at average taxpayers, who found themselves in the 30 and 40 percent brackets. Factory foremen, office managers, plumbers, and schoolteachers began using tax shelters that until recently had been the province of the wealthy. An underground economy of unreported income put waiters and moonlighters in the same league with bookies, prostitutes, drug peddlers, and other traditional tax dodgers.

The stage was set for Reaganomics and the Economic Recovery Tax Act of 1981. Congress cut taxes 25 percent in three yearly steps. The brackets would now rise in step with inflation so that wage increases intended merely to preserve an employee's buying power would no longer be taxed away as though he had been enriched. To emphasize its act of contrition toward the taxpayer, Congress turned a retirement plan for the pensionless into a universal benefaction. People who earned income by working could now put as much as $2,000 a year of the fruits of their toil into an Individual Retirement Account and deduct the money from their taxable income. From then until they withdrew funds from the IRA, the earnings from their investments in the account also went untaxed. In the next four years, 40 million of us tucked $170 million into IRAs, and projections showed the total passing the half-trillion-dollar mark by 1990.

All that tax cutting meant revenue cutting as well. With Congress and the White House unable to agree on offsetting budget cuts, the federal deficit ran completely out of hand. In an irony appreciated mainly by followers of John Maynard Keynes, archvillain of the Reaganite scenario, deficit spending helped turn the worst recession since 1929 into the prolonged economic recovery promised in the title of the tax act of 1981. In August 1982 the stock market shook off its disbelief in Reaganomics and began an ascent that lofted the Dow Jones industrial average in the next 54 months from below 800 to above 2200.

The Federal Reserve Board, under its dauntless chairman, Paul Volcker, stood resolutely with its successful monetarism until the inflation rate leveled off below 3 percent in 1985. Interest rates, however, remained high until the Fed at last relented and unleashed the money supply. Soon after the start of Reagan's second term, the yield on long-term Treasury bonds was under 8 percent, and short-term money was available for less than 6.5 percent.

The cataclysmic economic events since 1970 did more than change the tax system. They caused the dismantling of government controls on banking and interest rates. They opened the way for creative investments that the public badly needed. Whole new financial industries blossomed. A short list of the innovations would include money-market mutual funds, tax-free-bond mutual funds and unit trusts, investments in home mortgages called Ginnie Maes, junk-bond funds, publicly traded stock options, limited-partnership tax shelters for small investors, discount brokerage firms, many forms of investment in gold and silver, bank accounts paying money-market rates, salary reduction pension plans, tax-sheltered annuities, adjustable-rate mortgages, and universal life insurance.

The gyrations of the inflation rate, the enactment of tax-break opportunities, and the deregulation of financial institutions forced middle-income America to grapple with an immensely more complicated world of money. Despite all those tax cuts, many millions of people were paying 35 to 50 percent of their highest earnings to the Internal Revenue Service. Form 1040 kept growing longer and less fathomable. As the great monument to his second term as President, Ronald Reagan called for and fought for what he believed would be a simpler and fairer tax code. Having deregulated banking and stock brokerage, his administration now decreed that the lives of all taxpayers should be deregulated — that tax consequences should no longer govern their behavior as savers, investors, and consumers. Reagan found instant allies in both political parties and in the chairmen of the tax-writing committees of both houses of Congress.

The Tax Reform Act of 1986 flattens personal income tax rates from 14 progressively rising brackets to three: 15, 28, and 33 percent. It rolls back the number of people eligible for fully deductible Individual Retirement Accounts, eliminates or curtails many other tax deductions and shelters, takes a stingier view of tax-free fringe benefits, removes the preferential tax treatment of long-term capital gains realized by investors, shifts much of the direct tax burden from individuals to businesses, and alters the tax code in hundreds of its details. The same legislation also changes pension rights and estate taxes. No one can predict the impact of all this on the economy or human behavior, but it will be huge.

And inexorably it will bring still more changes to our lives and require new solutions to our financial problems. No generation is blessed with knowing what lies ahead. But the torrent of economic change — and new opportunities — goes roaring on.

2

GETTING YOUR FINANCES TOGETHER — AT LAST

To the money-haunted, the difference between night and day is one of degree: about 90 degrees, to be exact. During the day, you worry sitting up; at night, you fret lying down. Fear creeps over you: fear of the avalanche of unpaid bills that starts with helter-skelter record keeping, nonexistent or stagnating savings, and a budget that is all bull and a yard wide. Fear of finance takes many forms — all costly to the victims. Sometimes it masquerades as the fear of assuming responsibility. Psychiatrists call this hypengyophobia, but you can think of it as inertia. The burdensome consequences almost always include ugly mountains of unpaid bills and the specter of collection agents hammering at the door. There is also the fear of risks, the conviction that any bold action will end in disaster. The practical result of an overly cautious attitude is a depressing accumulation of missed investment opportunities. W. C. Fields, the comedian who played the role of confidence man in many of his flicks, in real life so distrusted people and so feared dying that he hid cash away in bank accounts across the country. Some of the money was still unaccounted for nearly 40 years after his death. Fields's ostrichlike behavior is a common sign of a person so petrified of risk that he does nothing with his money for fear of doing the wrong thing.

Then there is the oddest of all phobias: fear of wealth, which often disguises a low self-image. It costs you assurance and self-esteem that come from knowing you can handle the money you have rightfully earned. Fear therefore looms as the greatest obstacle to getting your financial act together. Climbing this barrier takes three giant steps. *Step one:* Replace nameless fears with numerical hard facts, recorded in a personal or family balance sheet of what you own and what you owe — a snapshot of your present position. *Step two:* Set yourself some important financial goals, starting with the establishment of a ready-cash fund for emergencies and stretching ahead to such aspirations as a down payment on a house, the money to send children to college, and a retirement nest egg. *Step three:* Develop a budget that will allow you to control your spending and free up money for the savings and investments you will need to achieve your goals.

Facing up to fears and foibles about money and then putting the family's finances in order is the only way that most Americans can afford the things they consider their birthright: a home of their own, a college education for their children, and perhaps financial independence at an early age. In a world where so much seems to be sliding out of control, you can still determine your own financial destiny.

3

YOUR NET WORTH

If you were fabulously rich or famous, you might never have to figure out how much you were worth. Other enterprising people would do it for you — and publish the results as Minnesota's Most Marriageable Men or Ten of Wyoming's Well-Heeled Widows. But if you are like most people, you probably have no notion of your true wealth and therefore no base from which to measure your financial progress. Just as analysts pore over the balance sheets of public corporations, individuals should analyze their personal balance sheets year by year. Without an itemized list of your assets and liabilities, you are adrift without a compass. For example, you cannot accurately plan your life insurance (see Chapter 57), map out your retirement savings (Chapter 24), or steer clear of the estate-tax collector (Chapter 28).

The financial picture you are about to take of yourself may surprise you pleasantly. You are probably richer than you think. But even if the bottom line is tinged with red ink, remember that this is only the first photo in a lifelong album of your financial accomplishments. To start this album, use the balance sheet provided in Figure 1 for the first two years. After that, you can prepare fresh forms or get more elaborate ones from your bank, which probably keeps a supply for loan applicants. If you are married or living with someone, you should involve your partner in the preparation of this net worth statement. List how your assets are owned — individually or in common — and which of you is responsible for what debts. Putting ownership status on paper can greatly ease the division of property in the unfortunate event of a death or the breakup of your relationship.

Filling in the assets and liabilities sides of the balance sheet takes only a short time. But first you must assemble the necessary documents, make some phone calls, and perhaps consult a few people who specialize in the value of things. On the asset side of the ledger there's good reason to sort out your possessions under five headings:

Cash

Itemizing deposits that can be turned quickly into currency at fixed value — bank accounts, money-market funds, and such — tells you how much cash you can lay hands on in an emergency. Your checkbooks and bankbooks speak for themselves. But you will need to phone the bank to learn the current value of your certificates of deposit and U.S. Savings Bonds. Whole life insurance policies have a table of cash values per thousand dollars of coverage for each year the policy has been in force. Find the value for the years you have owned the policy and multiply that amount by the number of thousands of dollars of coverage you have. For universal life and other variable policies, check your last bill or call your agent.

Liquid Investments

You can convert these holdings readily into cash by selling them on organized stock and bond markets, where prices are quoted at least once a day. But because securities prices go sharply up and down, you do not list these investments as cash, and you should not count on selling them on short notice to raise money for emergencies. There is too much risk of taking big losses. You can look up the prices of most stocks, mutual funds, and bonds in newspapers with complete financial sections. If the listing for a mutual fund has two prices, use the lower one. It is the redemption value for shareholders; the higher price includes an unredeemable sales charge paid by purchasers. To get the market value of unlisted stocks and bonds, unit trusts, and other securities not in the paper, call the brokerage house where you bought them. Ask a coin dealer the worth of your gold and silver coins or bars. For the cash value of an annuity, first look in your latest annual statement; if it doesn't show the cash value, call your insurance agent.

Nonliquid Investments

You can't count on cashing in these holdings on short notice even if you are willing to take a loss. Real estate takes time to sell, and the price is uncertain. If you own your home or other properties, estimate the market value by consulting a real estate broker or scanning the real estate ads for similar buildings in the same neighborhood. Most limited partnership shares can be sold only with great difficulty. Phone the sponsoring company for a current appraisal or list the shares at their purchase price. The value of retirement funds such as IRAs and employee savings plans appears in quarterly statements you receive from the sponsor or at work. If you are vested in a pension, ask your benefits office whether it has a lump sum value for people who leave the firm. Many plans cannot be cashed in, but they have a survivor's value — the amount your beneficiary would get if you died while still working. Money withheld from your salary for deposit in a thrift, profit-sharing, or stock ownership plan should be listed among your nonliquid investments; you cannot count on withdrawing your contributions or your employer's on short notice. Even if company savings plans were liquid, it would be wise to view them as untouchable retirement funds.

Personal Property

Face facts: most of your furnishings and clothing would bring small change at auction or in a tag sale. List them at knockdown value, not what you paid for them. Keep a record, but not on your balance sheet, of the purchase prices of the contents of your home for insurance purposes. As you will learn in Chapter 55, good homeowners policies pay replacement values for things lost in a fire or burglary. Value your autos, unless they are wrecks, at the trade-in prices listed in the National Automobile Dealers Association blue book. The loan department of your bank probably subscribes to this monthly service. If you own valuable art, antiques, jewelry, or other prized collectibles, have them appraised — mainly so that you can insure them properly in a floater on your homeowners policy. Ask a dealer to recommend an appraiser or get names by writing to the American Society of Appraisers or the Appraisers Association of America.

Under the heading of Liabilities, most of the entries are self-explanatory. List the amounts of unpaid bills only if they have arrived; it's not necessary here to anticipate, say, your next quarterly estimated income tax installment or the property tax bill due next month. The big items on the liabilities side of the ledger are likely to be balances you have let pile up on credit cards, education loans, car loans, and of course mortgages. You may have to phone lenders to get the unpaid balances of car loans and other big-ticket installment purchases. Don't just count the number of payment coupons left and multiply by the monthy payment. You would be overcharging yourself for interest that the lender has not yet earned.

You arrive at the bottom line of your personal balance sheet by subtracting total liabilities from total assets. The result, your net worth, may or may not thrill you. Either way, analyze the figures more closely. Are most of your assets expensive possessions such as BMWs and fur coats? As much as you treasure them, they are wasting assets, which will not get you any closer to your financial goal (except, of course, the goal of owning a luxury car and furs). To improve next year's balance sheet you will have to boost your holdings in securities or real estate, which have a fair chance of increasing in value.

The mix of liquid and nonliquid assets on your balance sheet is another key to your condition. The total cash holdings and liquid investments should amount to 20 to 50 percent of your assets. Not only can liquid funds provide money to get you past a rough patch, but you also can use them to take advantage of new investment opportunities. If most of your money has gone into real estate and other nonliquid holdings, you may want to channel future savings toward more marketable investments.

Your statement of assets may reveal a need for diversification. You take grave risks when you tie up a large chunk of money in a single type of investment. For instance, anyone who has most of his funds sunk in his own small business or his employer's stock might think about putting new savings elsewhere.

Finally, turn to your liabilities. Subtract the total of your unpaid bills from the total of your cash holdings. The result is your cash reserve. It should be enough to cover at least three months of living expenses if you lose your job or run into some other emergency.

Figure 1. Personal Balance Sheet

ASSETS

	This year ______ (date)	Next year ______ (date)
Cash and cash equivalents		
Cash on hand	$______	______
Bank accounts	______	______
Money-market funds	______	______
U.S. Savings Bonds	______	______
Certificates of deposit	______	______
Treasury bills	______	______
Loans to others	______	______
TOTAL CASH	______	______
Liquid investments		
Mutual funds	______	______
Stocks	______	______
Bonds	______	______
Treasury securities	______	______
Life insurance cash value	______	______
Precious metals	______	______
Other ______	______	______
______	______	______
______	______	______
TOTAL LIQUID INVESTMENTS	______	______
Nonliquid investments		
IRAs and Keogh plans	______	______
Annuities	______	______
Employee savings plans	______	______
Pension lump sum	______	______
Real estate investments	______	______
Your home	______	______
Limited partnerships	______	______
Your own business ______	______	______

Assets

	This year ______ (date)	Next year ______ (date)
Other ______	______	______
______	______	______
______	______	______
TOTAL NONLIQUID INVESTMENTS	______	______
Personal property		
Cars	______	______
Furnishings	______	______
Clothing, furs, jewelry	______	______
Art, antiques, collectibles	______	______
Other ______	______	______
______	______	______
TOTAL PERSONAL PROPERTY	______	______
TOTAL ASSETS	$______	______

Liabilities

	This year ______ (date)	Next year ______ (date)
Unpaid bills		
Taxes	$______	______
Mortgage or rent	______	______
Insurance premiums	______	______
Utilities	______	______
Alimony, child support	______	______
Charge-account balances	______	______
Other ______	______	______
______	______	______
______	______	______
TOTAL BILLS	______	______

	This year ______ (*date*)	*Next year* ______ (*date*)
Loans		
Home mortgage	______	______
Vacation home mortgage	______	______
Home improvements	______	______
Cars	______	______
Education	______	______
Other installment loans	______	______
Life insurance loans	______	______
Margin accounts	______	______
Home equity loan	______	______
Second mortgage	______	______
Other ______	______	______
______	______	______
______	______	______
TOTAL LOANS	______	______
TOTAL LIABILITIES	$______	______

SUMMARY

TOTAL ASSETS	______	______
minus		
TOTAL LIABILITIES	______	______
NET WORTH	$______	______

4

SETTING YOUR GOALS

If you know what your goals are and their order of importance to you, you will never lack inspiration for doing the nettlesome little things, such as budgeting, that help you get to your objectives. So fantasize for a moment. What would you do if you had, say, $10,000 more income each year? To what ends, present and future, would you direct the money? A power boat? A summer place? A change of career? Early retirement? This is no idle exercise. It's the pleasurable beginning of a process that will put your working life into a clear, purposeful focus by making you decide just what you want your earnings to do for you and your dependents. "Most people have very hazy goals," says Lewis Walker, a financial planner with Walker Cogswell & Company in Atlanta. "They've never bothered to think out in detail what they want to accomplish with their money."

Unless you are totally unattached, don't go through this exercise alone. Setting goals is a family affair. With the exception of young children, anyone in your household who might be affected by the goals you set should participate in the process. Betty D. Jones, a financial planner with Integrated Resources Equity Corporation in Wichita, Kansas, observes: "Each partner in a marriage, for example, might have different ideas about his or her financial future. There has to be give and take if you want to avoid problems later on." Setting goals means taking stock of your financial responsibilities — and your prospects. Perhaps you can foresee a situation that would make you suddenly responsible for an aging parent. Contrariwise, your parents may be wealthy enough to have put money in trust for your children's educations. That would seem to relieve you of an enormous responsibility. But don't count too heavily on others. Many a financial plan has gone awry when such money did not materialize. Your great-aunt could write you out of her will at the last minute.

Rate your goals for relative importance and set deadlines for reaching them. Write them in descending order of importance in the spaces provided in Figure 2. Now the question begins to take shape. How do I get there from here? How much do I start putting aside now to have the money I need when I need it? Discovering the answer involves a computation that would seem beyond the mathematical skills of the average person. But it is not. Our worksheet lets you hurdle the math with long division or, better still, a pocket calculator.

You do have to make some realistic assumptions about three unknowables: the return on your investments, the course of inflation, and your tax bracket. Taxes and inflation both will demand a cut of your investment profits and could also nibble into your principal unless you invest well.

Investment Returns

Probe your psyche to decide how much risk you are willing to take with your money. The answer will suggest the kinds of investments to consider in working toward your goals. You have to take greater risks in pursuit of larger profits, whether you are investing for interest, dividends, or capital gains. Everyone should respect his or her own tolerance for risk and not let passion or desperation sweep aside native caution. But circumstances should influence the degree of risk that's worth taking. If your money has to support an elderly parent, sacrifice high yields in exchange for assured income and safety of principal. If you don't have to worry about anybody but yourself, you can feel freer to put spare cash in riskier but potentially more profitable securities. Whatever your risk tolerance, in general make modest assumptions about the rate of return you expect to earn.

Inflation

With democratic impartiality, inflation guarantees that everyone's dollars will buy less next year than they do today. If the cost of living were to rise an average of 7 percent for the next decade, your dollar would be worth 50 cents; a 3 percent inflation rate would leave you with 74 cents; a 10 percent rate would grind it down to 38.5 cents. Therefore, the cost of all the goals you set now inevitably will rise. Pessimists will plan on high inflation, optimists on low. Realists will try to err on the high side.

Figure 2. How Much to Set Aside toward a Goal

1. *Goal*	2. *Amount needed*	3. *When*	4. *Years to goal*	5. *Rate of return*	6. *Divisor*	7. *Savings per month (col. 2 ÷ col. 6)*

Years to goal	*Divisors (by rate of return)* 2%	4%	6%	8%
1	12.1	12.2	12.3	12.4
2	24.5	24.9	25.4	25.9
3	37.1	38.2	39.3	40.6
4	49.9	51.9	54.1	56.4
5	63.1	66.2	69.8	73.6
6	76.5	81.1	86.4	92.1
7	90.2	96.6	104.1	112.3
8	104.2	112.7	122.8	134.1
9	118.4	129.5	142.7	157.7
10	133.0	146.9	163.9	183.4
11	147.8	165.1	186.3	211.1
12	163.0	184.0	210.1	241.2
13	178.5	203.6	235.4	273.7
14	194.2	224.0	262.3	309.0
15	210.4	245.3	290.8	347.3
16	226.8	267.4	321.1	388.7
17	243.6	290.4	353.2	433.6
18	260.7	314.3	387.3	482.2
19	278.2	339.2	423.6	534.9
20	296.1	365.1	462.0	592.0
21	314.2	392.1	502.9	653.8
22	332.8	420.1	546.2	720.8
23	351.8	449.3	592.2	793.4
24	371.2	479.6	641.1	872.0
25	390.9	511.2	693.0	957.2

Taxes

Here, everyone is at the mercy of Congress and his or her own potential earning power. Suppose you are now in the 28 percent bracket, meaning that every dollar of additional income up to a certain point includes 28 cents for the Internal Revenue Service. If you are planning to put money in a taxable investment paying 9 percent a year, the IRS will leave you with 6.5 percent. If that gripes you, you can look for tax-sheltered investments. Cutting taxes is a crackerjack idea. Indeed, it sits highest on many people's lists of financial priorities. But reducing taxes is not a goal in itself. The goal, rather, is to have more money left after taxes that you can devote to truly important objectives.

While investment returns and inflation are eternal question marks, you do not have to base your planning on shaky predictions. Since 1978, the income from rock-solid U.S. Treasury bills has exceeded our inflation rate by at least two percentage points and often more. This inflation-adjusted, or real, rate of return runs higher on securities involving more risk: longer-term government and corporate bonds. It runs still higher on stocks. Your taste for risk will tell you how high a real rate of return to shoot for. Then, to account for taxes, you should slice off for Uncle Sam a percentage of that return equal to your bracket. If you are in the 28 percent bracket and expect to earn a 4 percent real rate of return on your investments, your real after-tax yield will be 2.9 percent.

This exercise in educated expectations helps you to discover how much money you have to put aside each month to reach your financial destinations on time. You are grappling with three variables: the amount you are trying to save, the number of years before you will need the money, and your assumed real after-tax rate of return. In Figure 2, write down the first two variables for each of your goals. Then, in the table of conversion factors, find the divisor for the number of years ahead at your assumed real after-tax rate of return. The table covers 25 years. (Retirement, most people's longest-term goal, gets special attention in Chapter 24.) Dividing your dollar goal by the appropriate conversion factor gives you the monthly savings needed to reach that goal.

Example: You need a $50,000 down payment to buy a house in 10 years. Your assumed real after-tax return is 4 percent. Look down the 4 percent column to the ten-year line. The conversion factor is 146.9. Divide $50,000 by 146.9. You have to save $340 a month.

Welcome to the real world. Few people can afford everything on their wish list. That doesn't mean you have to give up on one goal to reach another. Adjust your deadlines according to your priorities and keep in mind that your objectives won't be static. At age 25, saving for retirement may be the farthest thing from your mind. Twenty years later, however, you may feel it is imperative to be able to retire at age 55. Remember, too, that over the years your income will rise, allowing you to invest more cash toward your aims. The message: periodically reevaluate your goals and the amount of money you are committing to them.

5

CREATING A BUDGET

At the office, you are the very model of a money-minded manager. Your department always shows an operating surplus. Your suppliers love you because you pay in 30 days. Few emergencies stymie you. When the crucial Poindexter project ran way over budget last year, you rescued it with funds from the contingency reserve. When your faithful aide, Mrs. Gruber, took early retirement, you found the cash to present her with a top-of-the-line Bells & Whistles telephone answering machine. So why is it that at home you are in a constant financial scramble? That you have no idea where you will find the funds to see the kids through college, much less to buy that 36-foot sailboat you have always coveted? Alas, you need a household budget.

As any successful administrator knows, the key to controlling cash flow is a budget that really works. It is a useful tool even if your head is well above water. It can help you capture money that just seems to trickle away and sluice it into savings and investments. Well-ordered households need not make a federal case out of putting a budget together. The whole project can be as simple as the advice given to clients by Judith Headington McGee, a Spokane financial planner. "Pay yourself first," she says. "Put the top 10 percent of each paycheck into savings." If you're not sure you can spare 10 percent, try reverse budgeting. It works like this: you add up the debit figures from your past 12 checking-account statements, subtracting any checks written for investments. If you deposit only part of your paycheck and keep the rest for your pocket money, add that cash amount to checkbook debits. Subtract the grand total from your annual take-home pay. What is left is surplus income. If it amounts to 10 percent or more of your gross income, congratulations. If it is between 3 and 7 percent, you have still got the upper hand on spending.

People whose expenditures have gone out of control have to take a thornier path. For them, shaping a budget is as difficult as that perilous journey undertaken by wayfarers from the land of destruction to the Celestial City in *Pilgrim's Progress*. They have to navigate the Abyss of Accounting, slog through the Slough of Debt, struggle up the Peak of Savings, run the Rapids of Retrenchment, and cross a Chasm of Conflict. Ah, but the pilgrimage will not be futile. Financial ease of mind lies ahead.

First, you must examine your income and how you have spent it in the past. This is the Abyss of Accounting. You don't have to exhume all records dating back to the Year One. Your income and expenses for the past six months will suffice to pick up all routine monthly costs, as well as those lump sums and irregular expenses — insurance, school tuition, gifts, and such — that keep you scrambling.

Start with your check register, where you (supposedly) have recorded every transaction. If it is virginal white, take out the actual canceled checks. Label separate sheets of paper or pages in a ledger with expenditure categories: Housing, Utilities, Food, Transportation, Clothing and Personal Care, Financial and Legal Services, Medical Care, Recreation, Insurance, Child Care, and Miscellaneous (see Figure 3, Your Cash-Flow Statement).

Also dig out the past six months' billing statements from credit-card companies and stores where you have charge accounts. The checks you wrote to Visa, MasterCard, American Express, Sears, and the rest don't tell you what you bought, but your bills do. Place each purchase in its proper category. Cash purchases will be harder to pin down. Budget experts say you should record them all in a notebook for at least one month. However, you can safely estimate your cash expenditures by totting them up for the past week. They might include commuting, lunches out, children's allowances, gasoline, tolls, and dry cleaning.

After you have sorted all your expenditures into categories, get out your pocket calculator. Total each spending category, double it to get full-year sums, and enter the amount on the proper line of Figure 3. Then add up your total 12-month outlay for everything and write it down in the space provided.

Next comes the calculation for your disposable income — the amount you take home after taxes. Since this is an exercise in looking backward, refer to your most recent federal and state income tax returns. To the income you reported for the past calendar year, add interest from tax-free

Figure 3. Your Cash-Flow Statement

Estimated disposable income for the past 12 months	
Gross income	
Husband's wages or salary	$______
Wife's wages or salary	______
Dividends and interest	______
Child support and alimony	______
Annuities, pensions, Social Security	______
Rents, royalties, fees	______
Other	______
TOTAL GROSS INCOME	______
Taxes	
Federal, state, and local income taxes withheld	______
Estimated quarterly income tax payments	______
Social Security tax withheld	______
TOTAL TAXES PAID	______
Estimated disposable income	
Total gross income	______
minus	
Total taxes paid	______
DISPOSABLE INCOME	______

Estimated living expenses for the past 12 months		*Subtotal*	*Percent of your disposable income*	*National average*
Housing				
Rent or mortgage	$________			
Property tax payments	________			
Insurance	________			
Furniture, appliances	________			
Maintenance and repair	________			
		$______	________	22.7%

Estimated living expenses for the past 12 months		*Subtotal*	*Percent of your disposable income*	*National average*
Utilities				
Electricity	______			
Gas and/or oil	______			
Telephone	______			
TV cable	______			
Other ______	______			
		______	______	6.5%
Food				
Meat and groceries	______			
Meals and snacks out	______			
		______	______	19.4%
Transportation				
Car payments	______			
Car insurance and registration	______			
Gasoline	______			
Maintenance and repair	______			
Public transportation: cab, bus, plane, train	______			
Tolls	______			
Other ______	______			
		______	______	10.4%
Clothing and personal care				
Clothes and shoes	______			
Linens	______			
Cosmetics	______			
Toiletries	______			
Hair care	______			
Other ______	______			
		______	______	7.7%

Estimated living expenses for the past 12 months		*Subtotal*	*Percent of your disposable income*	*National average*
Financial and legal services				
Lawyers	________			
Bank and broker fees	________			
Interest on loans (other than house and cars)	________			
Tax preparer	________			
Financial planner	________			
Investment information	________			
Other ____________	________			
		______	______	6.8%
Medical care				
Doctors	________			
Dentists	________			
Medication	________			
Other ____________	________			
		______	______	5.0%
Recreation				
Entertainment	________			
Sports	________			
Hobbies	________			
Vacations	________			
Fitness	________			
Other ____________	________			
		______	______	4.8%
Insurance (other than car and home)				
Life	________			
Disability	________			
Health	________			
Excess liability	________			

Estimated living expenses for the past 12 months		*Subtotal*	*Percent of your disposable income*	*National average*
Other ________	________			
		________	________	1.7%
Child care				
Day care	________			
Tuition	________			
Allowances	________			
Special activities				
________	________			
________	________			
		________	________	1.4%
Miscellaneous				
Pocket money	________			
Gifts	________			
Contributions	________			
Other ________	________			
		________	________	7.8%
TOTAL ANNUAL LIVING EXPENSES		________	________	________

Funds available for savings and investments				
Disposable income		$________		
	minus			
Total living expenses		________		
FUNDS AVAILABLE		________		5.8%

bonds, which you reported only on your state return, and the interest from any municipal bonds issued by your home state, which you didn't have to report on either return. Also add any capital gains that you earned on investments. (If you cheated on your taxes by failing to report some taxable income, you had better report it to yourself for budgeting purposes — and set up a reserve for back taxes and penalties in case you get caught.)

Enter each item of income separately on the cash-flow form in Figure 3 and take the total. Then enter your federal and state tax bill for the year, including withholdings. Separately, write in your Social Security taxes; they are listed on your W2 forms, which should be kept with your copies of federal and state tax returns. Add up all taxes paid, and subtract the total from your income, reportable and unreportable. The difference is your disposable income.

Now for the moment of truth. Subtract your total expenditures from your disposable income. Did you have an operating surplus or a deficit? A deficit indicates that you either borrowed money or drew from savings to get by. But don't automatically don sackcloth and ashes. Some of your salary may have gone automatically into a company savings, stock purchase, or pension plan or into an Individual Retirement Account. Check your paycheck stubs or company benefits statements for the amounts of pay withheld for such investments. You may have operated in the black after all; if so, your budget is still out of whack, but not as badly as your cash-flow statement indicates. Another and more frequent explanation of family deficits is illness, unemployment, or some other crisis that forced you to tap into your reserves temporarily.

The most dreadful trouble spot is the Slough of Debt. Was last year's deficit unusual or just one in a series of chronic deficit years? You could have blundered into boggy turf. If you suspect so, give yourself the financial examination outlined in Chapter 50. You will find a handy worksheet called Your Self-Imposed Debt Limit (Figure 19). Revolving credit is what gets most people mired in excessive monthly payments, especially when the monthly payments pile atop those for car loans, home improvement loans, education loans, and other installment debt. Budget specialists say you are carrying too much debt if installments exceed 15 percent of your after-tax income. Older people who have acquired most of their household goods should keep their loan commitments to 10 percent or less.

Do your debts fall within the acceptable range? Don't congratulate yourself just yet. You may be making minimum payments on tremendous credit-card balances each month and kidding yourself that you are handling debt well. If you are in that spot, your first goal ought to be reducing debt. To get out of the swamp, allocate a set amount each month for debt repayment — as much as you possibly can afford without suffering starvation or eviction. Use your savings, too. You will never get rich earning, say, 6 percent in a money-market account while paying creditors 18 percent. Until you are debt-free, avoid using your credit cards.

Next you must scramble up the Peak of Savings, where your first foothold will be an emergency fund. Two or three months of take-home pay should cover all but the most staggering setbacks. If you lack the discipline of thrift, use payroll savings plans. Or arrange with your bank or mutual fund to remove a set amount from your checking account each month for automatic deposit in an investment account. How much should you set aside? Again, be realistic. People who feel too strapped tend to give up saving. It is often better for them to take nothing from current income but, for example, to bank each raise until the next one comes along or to sock away bonuses, gifts, tax refunds, capital gains, and other windfalls. Whatever trail you take up the mountain, build savings into the budget instead of treating them as what's left over after you have run up bills all over town.

With so much money going into debt repayment and savings, you are going to feel as though you barely have enough to live on. So you will have to run the Rapids of Retrenchment. Budgets always have leaks you can plug. The most obvious ones in your case should pop out on your cash-flow statement when you compare your spending habits with the national average. For example, if 15 percent of your disposable income has been going into clothing and personal care, you are spending twice as much as most people do.

What's that you say? You don't want to be average? You're dressing for success? That's precisely why you need your own special budget. The average American does not exist. Each person and household has unique wants, depending not only on personal style but also on age, income, marital status, geography, and stage of life. If you live in New York City, your housing costs on average will be 32 percent higher than those in Des Moines. If you are a wife just returning to the work force, you may balloon your family's expenses by pushing household income into a higher tax bracket while spending more for clothes, child care, and household help.

To get you closer to reality than the national average, *Money* asked Financial Strategies Inc., a Washington, D.C., financial planning company, to shape reasonable spending ranges for people at four points in the life cycle. You will find these budgets in Figure 4. Using the family situation closest to your own as a model, do another analysis of your current cash flow for comparison. The spending categories change a bit. There is a new one, loan payments, that requires recalculation of other expenditures to screen out purchases made on credit. Savings become a category because now you are budgeting them into your plans.

Figure 4. Four Model Budgets

Financial planners recommend keeping each major spending category within a certain range, as a percentage of your disposable income. Here are four realistic budgets, each for a different stage of life. In shaping your own spending and savings, model them on the situation closest to your own, adjusting for special circumstances and balancing your percentage allocations to equal 100 percent.

Single, Age 25
Income: $25,000

Young singles are likely to go heavy on car payments and entertainment and fairly light on housing.

	Ideal range (%)
Housing	20–25
Loan payments	13–15
Food	10–15
Entertainment	7–14
Out-of-pocket expenses	8–12
Transportation	7–10
Clothing, personal care	4–8
Education	5–7
Utilities	4–7
Gifts, contributions	2–7
Savings	5–7
Insurance	1–3

Married, in Their Mid-Thirties, Childless
Two Incomes: $40,000

Even without children, many couples at this stage of life take on the responsibilities of home ownership.

	Ideal range (%)
Housing	25–30
Loan payments	15–17
Food	10–15

	Ideal range (%)
Clothing, personal care	8–10
Out-of-pocket expenses	7–10
Transportation	7–10
Utilities	7–9
Savings	5–7
Vacations	3–7
Insurance	3–5
Hobbies, entertainment	2–4
Gifts, contributions	1–3

Married, in Their Forties, Two Children
Two Incomes: $60,000

Budgeting gets stricter for working couples with children to raise and educate. Saving takes discipline.

	Ideal range (%)
Housing	30
Loan payments	13–15
Food	10–15
Child care	8–10
Out-of-pocket expenses	5–8
Education	5–7
Savings	5–7
Clothing, personal care	4–10
Utilities	4–7
Vacations	3–7
Hobbies, entertainment	3–7
Insurance	3–5
Gifts, contributions	2–5

Married, in Their Sixties
Retirement Income: $35,000

With the mortgage paid off, housing costs ease, to be replaced by higher recreation and medical expense.

	Ideal range (%)
Housing	10–15
Food	15–20
Utilities	15–18
Clothing, personal care	1–5
Transportation	10–12
Insurance	1–5
Vacations	10–15
Gifts, contributions	1–7
Out-of-pocket expenses	7–10
Hobbies, entertainment	2–4
Savings	1–5
Medical expenses	15–20

You probably will have to take some austerity measures to bring your expenses into line. But first look for ways to cut your taxes, thus increasing disposable income. (Chapter 43 offers plenty of ideas for using all your legitimate deductions.) Second only to taxes as a major expense is housing. If you bought your home a few years ago, when mortgage rates were 12 percent or higher, you may be spending as much as 40 percent of your income on the loan. That is too much. Compare today's mortgage rates with yours; if they have fallen at least two percentage points, try to renegotiate your loan. That could reduce your monthly expenses by $100 or more. Transportation is another budget breaker. If it burns up more than 15 percent of your budget, ask yourself whether you could dispense with one of your cars.

For married couples, especially those with two incomes, putting the budget in operation can seriously strain a relationship. To sidestep a Chasm of Conflict, you and your mate should devise an oversight system that keeps everybody in the family on a budget without loss of mutual respect and affection. Allow each member of the family to have some mad money. The fighting comes when you have to account for every nickel. Someone in the family will have to keep books for a few months to see that the budget stays on target, and as time passes, fine-tuning may be needed to make room for expenses you had not considered. Annual checkups should be enough. The secret of setting a budget you can live with is doing it your own way. After all, your goal is the Promised Land of Financial Ease. How you get there is your own business.

6

LEAVING A TRAIL

If you are like many people, your financial files are scattered about in a dozen different places. "Well, yes," you sheepishly admit. "But," you add defensively, "I know where everything is. The wills are right where they belong, in the strongbox in the hall closet. The investment records are where they've always been, in the middle drawer of the secretary in the living room. Copies of our tax returns, dating back to 1959, are — where else? — in the cardboard boxes under the bed in Junior's room."

Keeping your financial papers in several places is acceptable, so long as you know they are secure — and so long as you are not the only person who knows where everything is. But if key information about your financial affairs is stored in your head and only there, you have got a problem.

What you need is a device that would serve as a guide to whoever took over your finances if you became incapacitated or died. In some households one person handles most money matters, and in many others the financial chores are divided, with each adult familiar only with his or her area of responsibility. Then, too, in quite a number of two-income families, each spouse may be fuzzy about the other's company benefits and how to claim them in an emergency.

By writing down in one place the identity and whereabouts of all your financial documents and accounts, you will create a road map that can guide your survivors to your assets, alert them to your liabilities, and inform them of the professionals who handle your affairs — your lawyer, for example, and your stockbroker. And you will aid yourself at least as much as your survivors. The inventory you construct will make accessible, all in one place, such dispersed data as the account numbers of your credit cards in case you have to report them stolen, the names of your insurance agents in case of a claim, and the contents of your safe-deposit box in case of a lapse of memory about where securities are stored. Compiling such a record should involve both you and your spouse or other responsible adults in your household.

The importance of most of the information requested in Figure 5 is self-evident, but in some cases it is not. Military discharge papers and marriage certificates, for instance, can be crucial to collecting certain death benefits. Under the heading of Life Insurance you might include information about, say, mortgage insurance or the easily forgotten travel coverage you get with many credit cards.

Attach an extra page for explanatory remarks. In them, you might want to detail the Social Security or veterans' benefits that would be available to a survivor. Or you may wish to remind a survivor that he will need to purchase his own life, health, or disability insurance. If you have been the family's investment manager, you will want to let your survivors in on your strategies, pointing out what they probably should sell soon and what they should hold on to.

Once you have completed this financial file, keep it in a secure place at home, and make a copy to put in your safe-deposit box. Let family members know where your summary is, and if your children are very young, give a copy to their potential guardian. You will have created an indispensable, easily updated archive. Make sure you keep it up to date.

Figure 5. Your Financial File

Family member	*Birth date and place*	*Social Security number*	*Location of birth, baptism, marriage, and military discharge certificate and passport*

Wills

Family member	*Lawyer (address, phone)*	*Executor (address, phone)*	*Where kept*

Safe-Deposit Boxes

	Depository and address	*Owner*	*Person with power of attorney*	*Where contents are listed*
Box No. 1				
Box No. 2				

Life Insurance: Group and Individual Policies

Name of person insured	Face value	Insurance company	Policy number	Beneficiaries	Where kept

Burial Plot

Family member	Cemetery (address)	Where documents are kept (deed, instructions for burial, organ donations)	Preferred undertaker

Health Insurance: Hospital, Major Medical, Accident, Disability

Persons insured	Type of coverage	Amount of benefits	Insurance company	Policy number	Where kept

Casualty Insurance: Homeowners, Tenants, Auto, Excess Liability

Policy owner	Type of coverage	Insurance company	Policy number	Policy limit	Agent (phone)

Employee Savings and Stock Plans

Family member	Employer	Type of plan	Value	Date of valuation	Beneficiary

Credit Cards

Family member	Name of card	Issuer (bank, merchant, broker, gasoline, etc.)	Account number	Phone number to report its loss

Income Tax Records

Members of the family filing	*Current estimated quarterly payment*	*Location of: Latest full-year return and its supporting documents*	*Earlier returns and documents*	*Records for the current year*

Real Estate Records

Description of property (address)	*Location of: Purchase records*	*Deed*	*Receipts for capital improvements*	*Inventory of contents*	*Property tax receipts*

Children's Accounts and Trusts

Child's name	*Type of account or trust*	*Where funds are invested*	*Custodian or trustee (address)*	*Recent value/ date*

Adults' Savings Accounts

Family member	Name and type (checking, pass book, CD, money market, Treasury bills, etc.)	Special purpose if any (Keogh, IRA, etc.)	Account number	Where documents are kept

Adults' Investments

Family member/ company	Type: (stock, bond, mutual-fund, etc.)	Special purpose (Keogh, IRA, etc.)	Cusip or account number	Number of shares or units	Where documents are kept

Financial Advisers

	Address	*Phone*	*Client in family*
Lawyers			
Stockbrokers			
Tax preparers			
Employee benefits counselors			
Life insurance agents			
Financial planner			
Investment manager			
Other			

11

YOU DON'T HAVE TO GO IT ALONE

In an age when future shock has yielded to financial shock, you no sooner master one corner of your economic life than the ground suddenly teeters under your feet. Inflation surges, then ebbs. Interest rates swing mercurially. Tax-law changes are harder to follow than the subplots of "Dallas." Sensing the wits' end confusion of all this, professional would-be guides beckon to lead you out of the maelstrom. Some financial advisers have well-defined missions: an accountant's is to help you with your taxes; a lawyer's is to counsel you about wills or divorces; a broker's is to execute your buy and sell orders for securities. But what about the claims of others, sometimes more clamorous, who say they can manage a great swath of your financial affairs? Can anybody really simplify it all for you or at least put it all in perspective?

To a considerable extent, yes. For people who want help of the broadest nature, a class of advisers who call themselves financial planners has sprung up. Financial planners offer holistic medicine to cure not only your investment sinking spells but also any alarming symptoms they detect in your cash flow, insurance, retirement, and estate planning.

For people who are concerned mainly with investing their money and who want no part in the decisions about where to

put it, specialists called investment managers stand ready to take complete charge. They promise to design a strategy consistent with your goals and the degree of risk you are willing to take. If you have less than $200,000 to invest, many financial planners and most investment managers will probably recommend mutual funds as substitutes for personal investment services. Mutual-fund managers do what other investment managers do: run large portfolios of securities. Fund managers, however, do not tailor their strategies to any single person's needs. You have to seek out a mutual fund with a fixed strategy that resembles yours as closely as possible.

The next three chapters tell you how to choose and use the services of financial planners, investment managers, and mutual funds.

7

CHOOSING AND USING A FINANCIAL PLANNER

In a perfect world, a financial planner would indeed be a kind of physician for your money — a highly trained and impeccably objective practitioner who can heal an ailing pocketbook, prescribe a regimen to nurture your assets, and monitor your fiscal fitness with regular checkups. But in the real world, even the most basic questions about planners bring answers that frequently do more to confuse than illuminate.

Ask, for instance, what a financial planner is, and you learn that it is anyone who claims to be one. No license is required, no state or federal laws define qualifications of any sort. Try to find out what financial planners do, and you discover that they sell everything from advice to zero-coupon bonds. Check into the cost, and the estimates run from $150 to $5,000. Inquire about how useful planners are, and you hear raves, hisses, and every opinion in between. All of that makes for grave uncertainty. But first-rate financial planners are increasingly available if you know how to identify them.

Before you start sizing up planners at all, though, you owe yourself a heart-to-heart chat about whether you in fact need their help. If you have a single problem to solve — picking stocks or doing your tax return, for instance — chances are you don't need a grand strategy so much as you do a set of tactics from the appropriate financial specialist. The proper mission of a planner is to help you sew together your economic bits and pieces. The person best qualified to do that is a skillful generalist who knows the rudiments of household money management, insurance, investing, taxes, retirement, and estate planning.

Credentials

Most of the stripes on financial planners' sleeves mean little by themselves, but when you add them up you get a measure of experience and reliability. The two main courses of study, which most candidates take by mail, are the Certified Financial Planner (CFP) program administered by the College for Financial Planning in Denver and the Chartered Financial Consultant (ChFC) curriculum of the American College, a school for insurance professionals in Bryn Mawr, Pennsylvania. To earn either set of initials, a planner must pass a series of rigorous written exams. A planner who has not bothered to get at least this much financial training probably should be crossed off your list.

If you cannot find a planner nearby, the Institute of Certified Financial Planners (2 Denver Highlands, 10065 East Harvard Avenue, Suite 320, Denver, Colorado 80231-5942; 303-751-7600) can refer you to members in your area. To keep their affiliation, CFPs must take at least 45 hours of continuing education a year. Another source of referrals is the Registry of Financial Planning Practitioners, a subgroup of the International Association for Financial Planning (2 Concourse Parkway, Suite 800, Atlanta, Georgia 30328; 800-241-2148). Those listed in the registry must have at least three years of planning experience and a CFP, ChFC, or some other proof that they have studied the needed specialties.

Most practitioners in this fairly new profession come to it from other pursuits — mainly accounting, law, or the selling of insurance, stocks, or mutual funds. A planner's background identifies his specialty as well as his possible biases. He should be willing to furnish references from clients or such professionals as bankers and lawyers with whom the planner has worked to coordinate clients' affairs. Most planners also are willing to show sample plans (with clients' names removed to protect their privacy).

The planner you hire should have one more credential: registration with the Securities and Exchange Commission as an investment adviser. The law requires anyone to register who sells financial advice, no matter how general. While registration does not signify competence or training, SEC rules require planners and other registrants to tell you in writing their education and experience, the types of work their firms do, and how they are paid. If a planner works as an agent for an insurance company, for example, that fact has to be in the disclosure statement.

Compensation

Financial planners earn a living in one of three ways: by charging fees for advice, by giving free advice but taking commissions on whatever life insurance or securities they sell, or by combining fees and commissions. In point of fact, however, most planners receive commissions for practically everything they recommend, from stocks and mutual funds to limited partnerships and life insurance. Says Orestes Mihaly, chief of the Securities Bureau of the New York State Attorney General's office: "The worry is that planners may recommend certain financial products just to get commissions while neglecting better investments that aren't so rewarding to them."

Sure enough, an epidemic of collapsing tax shelters promoted by planners is intensifying concern about how they earn their money. Michael Unger, director of the Massachusetts Securities Division, reported in 1985, "Our check of 20 states turned up $20 million of fraud and abusive practices, and there is every indication that this is just the tip of the iceberg." Considering the volume of such abuses, the largely unregulated atmosphere of this business, and the confusion of fees and commissions charged, investors need to know much more about planners than about such other financial advisers as brokers and accountants.

Planners who charge only a flat fee for their advice and take no commissions argue that they have already resolved this potential conflict of interest. They claim that besides being untainted by temptations to fatten their income, they do a better job than their commission-taking brethren. One reason: without the pressure to sell products, they can devote most of their time to developing the plan.

Furthermore, a fee-only planner is less likely to recommend an investment as a solution to every problem, asserts Randy Hedlund, owner of Financial Management Consultants in Overland Park, Kansas, which was one of the first fee-only firms in the business. "I tend to use tools and techniques — custodial accounts for children and deferred compensation or Keogh plans for people with their own businesses — rather than high commission products like shelters to cut tax bills," Hedlund says.

While the fee-only approach may seem the ideal, it does not always fit the client. For one thing, fee-only planners are still relatively few in number. The membership of the National Association of Personal Financial Advisers, the only trade organization that requires planners to take a vow of fee-onlyness, was a mere 170 in 1985. (For a free list of members, write to the association c/o Leonetti & Associates, 125 South Wilke Road, Suite 204, Arlington Heights, Illinois 60005.) For another thing, common sense indicates that disinterested advice is not necessarily competent advice.

Perhaps most important of all, fee-only planners tend to be the most expensive, precisely because they get no income from commissions. Some will not take clients unless they have a net worth and income high enough to justify fancy planning advice. A typical client of John Sestina and his colleagues at SMB Financial Planning, a fee-only firm in Columbus, Ohio, might be a family with $250,000 to invest. Their fee would run about $7,500 the first year and 10 percent less annually for follow-ups. In 1986, planner Randy Hedlund charged $90 an hour, with the average plan running from $2,500 to $4,000. There are low-fee exceptions: for example, Richard T. McNellis, a St. Paul, Minnesota, planner, was charging $75 an hour, with a minimum fee of $300.

Some fee-only planners shy away from specifics in their plans. McNellis makes generic recommendations such as growth mutual funds or term life insurance policies. If you cannot find them on your own, he will suggest reputable companies that sell them. He will refer you to a brokerage firm but will not provide the names of particular brokers. "In fact, I tell my folks to interview several brokers at the same company. That way, I can freely criticize a broker or agent," he says. Once a client decides to buy a specific product, McNellis insists on seeing the prospectus or policy to make sure that it has the features he recommended.

Above the $200,000 income level, many planners believe, is the true territory of the fee-only practitioner, who can develop strategies to meet the complicated financial needs of the rich. For most other people, the services of a fee-only planner may be too sophisticated and pricey. They probably will have to take their chances with someone who gets most of his compensation from commissions. One planning industry insider estimates that 70 percent of the average fee-plus-commission planner's revenues comes from commissions. In a typical case, that might turn a $1,200 plan into a $4,000 total bill, including $2,800 in commissions. Such planners in effect dig twice into a client's pockets, first for a fee to develop an elaborate financial plan and then for commissions to carry out that plan. That is fine unless, say, a planner begins recommending a certain high-commission limited partnership deal because it is time for his kids to go to college.

In this imperfect situation, the best mix of commission and fee depends heavily on how much help you need. People with incomes up to $35,000 usually are best off going to commission-only planners, most of whom represent mutual-fund or insurance companies. Explains David Bugen, a partner in Individual Asset Planning Corporation, a fee-plus-commission firm in Morristown and Princeton, New Jersey: "Such clients probably can afford and need no more planning services than simple recommendations for a mutual fund, an Individual Retirement Account, an annuity, or term life insurance."

For those who earn between $35,000 and $75,000, Bugen suggests prefabricated financial plans sold for up to $750 by major brokerage houses and insurance companies. A serviceable example: Merrill Lynch's Financial Pathfinder (25 Broadway, New York, New York 10084; $250). Such plans provide simple strategies to help people meet their goals. You are not obligated to purchase investments, insurance, or other financial goods, but expect some sales pressure.

Those with incomes of $75,000 to $200,000 require tax and estate planning; they might hunt for planners who charge a fee for a relatively complex plan but may also from time to time collect commissions. Many fee-plus-commission planners have another advantage. Generally they charge a set fee for the plan, allowing clients to buy their own mutual funds or other investments at a discount brokerage house if they like. Otherwise, the clients can let the planner recommend specific investments.

How can you make sure that the recommendations of a commission-collecting planner are not colored by sales charges? The best way is to ask the planner to disclose fully the exact amount of money he will make on each investment he sells. Sales charges usually range from less than 1 percent on stocks bought through a discount broker to 10 percent for collectibles such as stamps and coins. Of the 30 percent load on limited partnerships in real estate, a planner may get as much as a third. Another useful question to ask: Is there a way to accomplish a particular objective without buying an investment or other product? If so, why hasn't the planner recommended it?

Content

A financial plan can be anything from a hundred leather-bound pages describing your entire economic life to back-of-the-envelope calculations of what you will need to send your budding Madame Curie to MIT. Specifics are more critical than mass: the advice you get can be put into action only if it is concrete and molded to your needs.

Long or short, a plan should be put in writing, with explanations of all assumptions made — such as the rate of inflation used to estimate your retirement needs, the rate of return assumed on your investments, and your tolerance for risk. Working with a list of your assets and a summary of your cash flow, the planner should produce an analysis of your financial status that pinpoints such trouble spots as too much exposure to estate tax or excessive life insurance. Says Malcolm A. Makin, a practitioner in Westerly, Rhode Island, "This part of the plan tells you where you are. The next part should spell out alternatives for getting where you want to go, giving the pros and cons of each approach."

So the planner who says he can make you rich should have more to offer than a once-in-a-lifetime chance to invest in the next Xerox. Watch out for the guy who tells you something like "Your biggest asset is your tax liability." Whether you are trying to support an elderly parent or dreaming of a Maserati, a planner should consider your goals sacred. Attempts to dissuade clients from their goals often are not high-minded efforts to save wastrels from themselves; they are sales pitches.

Commitment

Planners spend three or four hours with most clients, half in gathering facts and the rest, a few weeks later, in discussing the plan. The more money you have and the more complex your affairs, the more time you will need. Once written, your plan should be explained to you in person, and you will need time to consider the ideas before you decide which, if any, financial wares to buy.

Equally critical is an understanding of the support the planner can marshal from other professionals. Since no one person can master all the technicalities of taxes, banking, insurance, investments, retirement benefits, and estate planning, you need to know where this knowledge will come from. If you already have a competent lawyer and accountant, a planner should be willing to work with them. For those without such advisers, some large planning firms have lawyers and accountants on their staffs, while others call on whomever they deem best for the client. If possible, the planner should arrange for you and all your advisers to sit down together at least once. That way, everyone will know what everyone else is doing on your behalf.

Finally, what will happen after you get your financial plan? Even if you are assured of help in carrying it out, you need to know what the planner will do — and at what cost — when circumstances change. For most people, a yearly update will suffice, and planners generally charge by the hour for this service. But a sizable raise, a major illness, or the sale of a home can undo the best-laid plans overnight.

Even if your finances stay the same, the rest of the world probably won't. New tax laws, a sudden turn in the stock market, or a jump in interest rates may necessitate a change of course. Because of that, no financial plan can ever be more than a starting point. As Denver planner Eileen Sharkey puts it, ''Good planners don't try to imitate Moses coming down from the mountain with stone tablets.'' Still, they are well qualified to lead you out of the financial wilderness.

8

PAYING OTHERS TO INVEST FOR YOU

Until recently the ablest of professional money managers kept their profiles low, and almost all of them kept their account minimums high. Unless you had a significant six-figure sum to invest, you were about as welcome in their lives as a bear market. The number of investment managers is on the rise, however, intensifying competition for the accounts of pension funds and superrich individuals. Some managers with impressive records are at last courting customers who have as little as $25,000 to work with.

At the same time, a growing number of potential clients — particularly two-career couples — are accumulating five- and even six-figure bankrolls. What they don't have is the time or the skill or the confidence to invest the money for themselves.

Investment managers, also known as investment advisers, operate in accordance with their clients' goals and tolerance for risk. In signing up with such a professional, you normally give him full power to buy and sell whichever securities he chooses for your account, whenever he thinks the trade will be timely, and without consulting you or getting your permission. Those powers go with what is called a discretionary account. A few advisers, however, are willing to consult with their clients, or even get their consent, before making major moves.

Some money managers come from the ranks of brokers and financial planners. Many handle investments for bank trust departments. But the majority — about 8,000 — belong to independent firms that specialize in portfolio management. There is no official count of how many of these companies accept accounts with less than $100,000, but the number is still not large. Those that do take less charge a fairly wide range of fees. Buying professional investment management is like borrowing money — the more you have, the less it costs. Fee schedules are percentages of the assets under management, scaled downward from about 3 to 1 percent as assets rise. On a $50,000 account you might typically pay $1,000 a year.

How They Have Done

The top investment managers — the ones who have consistently outperformed their peers as well as the market — are found among the independents. Even so, not many are worth their fee. CDA Investment Technologies, a Silver Spring, Maryland, company that follows 250 large money-management firms, reported that for the five years through mid-1985 the value of their total stock investments, with all dividends reinvested, rose 112 percent. That was a shade less than the 114.4 percent gain in Standard & Poor's 500-stock index, a measure of the market as a whole.

No honest investment manager promises to beat the market. In fact, it is wise to avoid hustlers who boast that they will do better or make other outrageous claims. Thomas Putnam, president of Fenimore Asset Management in Cobleskill, New York (minimum account, $250,000), recently was hired by a client whose previous manager made the improbable claim of having an inside line to the Federal Reserve and knowing what it was going to do about interest rates. "No one piece of inside information can make that much difference anyway," Putnam says. "A conglomeration of things affects stock prices." James Kalil, Sr., president of Compu-Val Management Associates, a Wilmington, Delaware, investment firm (minimum, $100,000), adds, "Be wary of any manager who gives you guarantees. We are not in the get-rich-quick business."

Sound performance may mean nothing more than preserving the better part of a client's capital during bear markets and beating the broad averages by a couple of points during bullish times. A fair number of amateurs can do that for themselves if they are prepared to spend time reading intensively about the market and watching over their investments. But most people don't think they can.

Where to Look

The search for the best professional to run your money might start with your broker. But whether to hire him or any other broker for the job is problematical. Some brokerage firms have investment advisory subsidiaries that are worth considering, and there may also be a few scrupulous customers' men who handle discretionary accounts in addition to their normal duties without letting brokerage commissions influence investment decisions. However, the potential for conflict of interest is just too great. The more that brokers trade for their clients, the more they earn. Some financial planners also have investment-management affiliates as adjuncts to their practices, but they usually want you to buy their full package of financial services.

Bank trust officers used to do most of the investment advisory chores for monied families. So conservatively did they perform their responsibilities that they still bear a stigma of fuddy-duddyism. But trust officers generally do at least as well with your money as independent managers. In the five years through June 1985, for example, the stock holdings of trust funds were up 114.4 percent vs. the big advisory firms' 112 percent. What's more, over the 10 years to that same point, CDA found that bankers' aggressive growth-stock portfolios rose 333 percent, compared with 290 percent for mutual funds with similar objectives.

Until recently, this winning performance would not have made you any richer unless you had a spare $250,000 or more to invest. But now, banks are often willing to reduce their minimum to $100,000 in accounts held in trust. The trust departments of most large banks charge a minimum fee that runs to $1,000 a year. And that is just for pooled accounts. If you want individual attention, the minimum fee is about $2,500 a year.

You can ask your lawyer, accountant, or stockbroker for the names of able advisers as well as for referrals to consultants who specialize in evaluating money managers. Such consultants are rather new on the financial scene. Some are affiliated with brokerage houses and charge no fee; others are pricey independent scouts. Explains one self-employed consultant, Norma Yaeger of Los Angeles, "We select money managers the way managers select stocks." Many of these talent scouts are brokers who have found that they serve clients best by sending them to skillful advisers. In exchange for matching a client with a manager, they expect to get the trading commissions on the account. As an added incentive, they may slash their commissions on large accounts by as much as 50 percent.

Other such matchmakers charge flat fees for their services. They tend to be expensive and to cater to corporate customers. One consultant who specializes in individual clients with $100,000 or more to invest is Michael Stolper. His firm, Stolper & Company of San Diego, charges a finder's fee of $1,500. To watchdog your account, Stolper charges $500 a year. To evaluate your investment manager, he gets $200. Consultants connected with brokerages charge no fee for this monitoring. George Daniels, who matches clients and managers for Investment Directions Associates, an affiliate of Robinson-Humphrey/Shearson American Express in Birmingham, Alabama, says, "This system creates a balance of power. Everyone wants the client's money to grow, and we all watch each other to make sure that happens."

Screening potential advisers yourself will be necessary if you are starting small. Your task is definitely not simple. Almost anyone who has not been caught seriously violating a securities law can legally sell financial advice by applying to the Securities and Exchange Commission to become a registered investment adviser and paying a one-time fee of $150.

The SEC is a lax cop. While Congress has charged it with monitoring advisers' activities, it does not set performance standards or educational requirements, and it hardly ever chastises advisers for anything short of flagrant mismanagement of funds. Registered investment advisers, however, are required to tell prospective clients their fees, services, method of market analysis, and strategies, as well as their educational and business backgrounds.

To appraise a money manager, first look at his or her performance. Jeremiah Milbank III of the top-rated investment firm Milbank Tanaka & Associates in New York City (minimum account, $500,000) advises, "It's crucial to make the distinction between a good manager who has had a bad year and a bad manager who has made fortuitous choices." Most professional evaluators will not recommend an investment manager unless he has attained an average annual return of 15 percent or better for as long as he has been in business. "History is the only real hope you have, the only evidence of skill," says Michael Stolper. Note in particular how the adviser did in down markets as compared with the S&P 500 or the Dow Jones industrial average. "If he earned a respectable return in the bad years, the good years generally take care of themselves," Stolper says.

Even if a manager's record covers only a brief time, he may have left some footprints at an earlier job. For example, Robert McElwain started North American Capital Management in Overland Park, Kansas (minimum account, $80,000) only in 1983. But as an investment manager at Paine Webber, McElwain earned an average of 27 percent for his clients in 1981, when the S&P was down 5 percent. He showed a gain of 37 percent in 1982, when the S&P was up 21.4 percent.

If the manager you plan to hire has done well in down markets, ask him how he did it. Most consistently successful investors follow a strategy of selling stocks and switching to cash early in a declining market rather than buying so-called defensive stocks — those that ordinarily fall less than the market as a whole. The potential for a sizable gain is slight with defensive stocks, while the risk of a loss is great.

Ideally, the performance figures offered by investment managers in their own behalf should be audited by an independent accounting firm and should include all accounts under management. That way you know the figures are not based on some possibly meaningless model portfolio. The figures should be net results after payment of management fees and brokerage costs. You can easily compare the performance figures with the quarterly total return of the Dow, which is published at the end of each quarter in *Barron's*.

It is essential that your investment goals and your risk tolerance square with the philosophy of your adviser. Some managers will modify a nerve-racking approach — adding a few government bonds to a portfolio of undervalued stocks, for instance — to appease a nervous client. But other managers invest only one way. If you are uncomfortable with it, look elsewhere.

Investment company evaluators agree that most people should shun firms that manage more than $500 million. Companies that large usually are not owned by individual money managers, who are likely to have a larger stake than you do in their own success. Furthermore, firms with, say, $20 million under management have flexibility to buy and sell stocks of companies too small for giant portfolios.

Cementing Your Relationship

When you do retain an investment adviser, take pains to understand and shape the contract you enter into. It should stipulate not only fees but also cancellation provisions. Ask for a clause that gives you the right to fire your adviser immediately by telephone rather than after a 30-day notice by letter. While you can authorize trades through any broker, your adviser may recommend one with whom he can negotiate discounts on your behalf. He will designate a third party, usually the broker or a bank, to serve as the custodian of your securities. Clients receive confirmations from the broker of all trades. Advisers send quarterly statements of the securities in the account and how well they have performed. At the end of each year expect a more detailed statement summing up the account.

Even though you are turning over the responsibility of managing your investments to others, it is up to you to monitor them. When Mark Lohman, a commercial photographer, gets a statement from his manager,

Gary Goodman, head of G.J.G. Inc. in Los Angeles (minimum account, $50,000), listing a new stock, he telephones Goodman for the lowdown. "I like to pick his brain, to find out why he bought it and what his expectations for it are," says Lohman.

Measure the performance of your account against your objectives. "If your goal is growth via common stocks, then consider your account doing well if it's giving you an after-tax return at least a few points higher than the rate of inflation," says George Daniels, the Birmingham consultant. Give a manager at least a year to prove himself. "Patience is important," manager Jeremiah Milbank counsels, "but don't stand by patiently and watch your account being butchered." If the value of your holdings drops 20 percent from the high of the previous quarter and the adviser does not move into cash or take other remedial action, it may well be time to fire him. On the other hand, an uneasy and untutored investor may want to cash in at the wrong time. A wise counselor will talk him through the bad periods.

9

LETTING MUTUAL FUNDS DO IT

When it comes to investing, mutual funds can simplify your life. What you get from a mutual fund, at relatively low cost, is professional management of your money by people who devote their full time and attention to investment decisions. Even a pro sometimes gets poor results, of course, but the average fund does better than you probably can do for yourself, according to studies by Marshall Blume, chairman of the finance department at the University of Pennsylvania's Wharton School and a distinguished student of securities markets.

The mechanics of mutual funds make them easy to use. For a small investment — typically no more than $1,000 — they relieve you of the exacting, time-consuming chore of researching and assessing the outlook for companies whose securities you might buy. And you get a portfolio that usually consists of 50 or more securities. With that kind of diversification, a disaster in one stock or bond won't deliver the knockout punch that it might if you owned only a few.

Whereas stock prices can change from minute to minute, those of mutual fund shares remain the same for a full day at a time. All trades are made at the price at the end of that day, a figure that reflects the composite value of the securities held by the fund at the stock market's close. The fund is the only market for its own shares. It stands ready to redeem them on demand.

Once your money is invested, you receive dividends quarterly and capital gains annually, if the fund has earned either. Almost all funds offer to reinvest your earnings automatically in additional shares, and all funds send you periodic statements of your holdings. You can use mutual funds for Individual Retirement Accounts and Keogh plans. If your fund belongs to a family of funds, you can switch money from one to another, often with a simple phone call. That makes it easy to move money out of stocks or bonds and into a safe-haven money-market mutual fund whenever you are convinced that securities prices are in for a bad time.

Types of Funds

Investing in mutual funds is like buying a suit or a dress off the rack compared with the custom tailoring you get when you hire your own investment manager. Each fund has a clearly defined style, and you select the one that matches your investment goals.

Broadly speaking, there are five different types of funds:

Aggressive growth. Aggressive funds strive for maximum capital gains, buying the flighty shares of fast-growing companies.

Long-term growth. These funds own the less erratic issues of better-known and still smartly growing firms.

Growth and income. To achieve this combination, funds buy bonds and the stocks of large companies that are big dividend payers and also offer some prospect for capital gains.

Income. Funds with this objective attract investors seeking high yields.

Sector. In recent years, a type of fund that specializes in stocks of one industrial sector or several related industries, such as health care, high tech, or energy, has become popular.

Even within the same category, management styles differ markedly. One long-term growth fund will try to protect investors' capital by switching to Treasury bills when the manager foresees turbulence in the stock market; another will stay fully invested in stocks at all times.

The mutual funds you choose will depend on your investment goals. Are you a young person trying to amass capital as quickly as possible? Are you middle-aged and buying funds to supplement a corporate pension? Before you invest, you should weigh your financial prospects and commitments, determine how long the money is likely to stay invested, and make an honest assessment of how much of a chance you are willing to take. The last is the hardest: everyone wants a whale of a return at a minnow-sized risk.

Money you will need within a year for college tuition or some other crucial commitment should not be risked at all. Keep it in a money-market fund compounding interest. But savings you know you won't touch for 10 years or more should go at least partially into stocks — where greater gains can compensate you for greater risks. Over the 60 years from 1925 to 1985, the average annual total return — that is, dividends plus capital gains — from stocks was 9.7 percent compared with 4.6 percent for corporate bonds, according to a study by Ibbotson Associates of Chicago.

Mutual fund investors who want to keep it simple should heed the advice of Burton Berry, whose *NoLoad Fund*X* newsletter in San Francisco keeps tabs on mutual-fund performance. "Avoid the more speculative funds," he says. The least complicated strategy is to invest in growth and income or growth funds whose managers have a history of doing relatively well in both strong and weak markets. Among such funds are Fidelity Equity Income (82 Devonshire Street, Boston, Massachusetts 02109); Mutual Shares (26 Broadway, New York, New York 10004); Neuberger & Berman Partners Fund (342 Madison Avenue, New York, New York 10173); Nicholas Fund (312 East Wisconsin Avenue, Milwaukee, Wisconsin 53202); and Twentieth Century Select (P.O. Box 200, Kansas City, Missouri 64141). All are called no-load funds because you pay no brokerage commission to buy their shares. Therefore, all your money gets invested.

Another type of low-anxiety fund buys more speculative shares and attempts to protect your capital by switching to Treasury bills or other money-market investments when storm clouds for stocks appear. Successful funds of this type include Strong Total Return (815 East Mason Street, Milwaukee, Wisconsin 53202) and Janus (100 Fillmore Street, Suite 300, Denver, Colorado 80206) — both no-loads — and American Capital Pace, which is sold through brokers and charges an 8.5 percent commission. Market timing is the most difficult investment decision, so it makes sense for most people to invest in a fund that will do the switching for them.

Portfolios of Funds

If you have $5,000 or more to invest, you should consider owning a portfolio of mutual funds with different investment objectives. The bulk of your money — say, 80 percent — might be in growth and income funds, which are good at protecting against bear market losses. Then you could allocate 20 percent to aggressive funds, which invest in fast-growing companies.

When interest rates on bonds are running high, as they did in the first half of the 1980s, mutual funds that invest in bonds offer a combination of high yields and potential capital gains. You can get many bond varieties in mutual funds: high-grade corporates, lower-grade so-called junk bonds, tax-free municipals of either quality level, Treasury bonds, and government-backed GNMA mortgage certificates called Ginnie Maes (see Chapter 38). A well-diversified, closely managed junk-bond fund gives you extra-high yields while taming the additional risk of owning bonds of companies with middling credit ratings. Especially when forecasters think interest rates will be coming down, people who want a nice flow of income should include bond funds in their portfolio.

How to Choose Funds

Once you have decided on the categories of funds you want in your portfolio, it is time to choose specific funds. Make your first cut on the basis of whether the fund has a sales charge. Paying commissions of up to 8.5 percent on load funds can make sense if the fund's performance is spectacular. Load funds also make sense if you are buying through a trusted broker or other adviser who will choose a fund for you, monitor its performance, and advise you if you need to switch. Otherwise, stick with no-loads.

Next, you should look at performance. That is easy enough to check out. *Money,* among a number of other magazines and newspapers, publishes mutual-fund rankings periodically. Our monthly "Fund Watch" column shows which funds have gained the most, with all dividends and capital gains reinvested; which income and bond funds are paying the highest yields; and which funds have done the best for the least risk over long periods. We call the last category All-Weather Funds. Twice a year *Money* publishes complete rankings in tables that also give you such details as risk ratings, loads, and phone numbers, most of which are toll-free.

Although turning your money over to a mutual fund lets you bypass many of the time-consuming complexities of investing, it does not permit you to ignore your holdings. You should check on your fund at least quarterly. To keep closer track, you can subscribe to a specialized monthly newsletter. Two that follow only commission-free funds are *NoLoad Fund*X* at $87 a year (235 Montgomery Street, Suite 839, San Francisco, California 94104), and the *No Load Fund Investor* at $79 a year (P.O. Box 283, Hastings-on-Hudson, New York 10706). If you own a load fund, your broker can get performance figures from Lipper Analytical Distributors, which ranks all mutual funds each week.

Don't switch funds every time yours lags a few percentage points behind the leader in its category. But if most of the funds in that category had big gains when the market was rising and your fund fell wearily behind, move to another in the same group that is doing better.

How to Switch Funds

Large families of funds let you switch among their offerings with just a telephone call, but they can be positively obstructive when you want to move to another fund sponsor. You are usually required to fill out forms with signature guarantees from a bank or broker and then endure delays of 10 to 15 days before your money is transferred. To get around these obstacles, open a money-market fund account with checking privileges in the same family that runs your mutual fund. Then you can move assets by telephone from the stock or bond fund to the money-market fund and write a check to the new sponsor, bypassing most of the red tape.

There is an even easier way to move money from sponsor to sponsor, but you have to pay commission charges to do it. Charles Schwab & Company, a discount brokerage firm, offers telephone buying and selling among 250 different funds in its Mutual Fund Marketplace account. There is no minimum investment, but to move $2,000, for example, costs $28 in commissions. Burton Berry says, "For people who hate to do paperwork, the Schwab account can be very convenient."

The ultimate in simplicity, of course, would be a fund of funds, an idea that fell into disrepute in 1972 because of its association with the fallen fund empire of Bernard Cornfeld. Now Michael Hirsch, a portfolio manager at Republic National Bank in New York City who invests his clients' money in mutual funds, has revived the idea and is managing a no-load mutual fund that invests in other funds. Known as FundTrust (sold through Furman Selz Mager Dietz & Birney, 230 Park Avenue, New York, New York 10169), it requires a minimum investment of $2,500 for ordinary accounts and $250 for IRAs. All an investor has to do is choose among four objectives: aggressive growth, growth, growth and income, and yield. Hirsch puts the money into appropriate funds and moves it as he thinks warranted.

Hirsch's fund is too new to have proved itself in competition with the run of funds with similar objectives. Until it has compiled a superior performance for several years, those who invest in it should watch the results as closely as they would in any other fund. For now, the best to be said of FundTrust is that it might become the ultimate in simplicity.

III

THE FINANCIAL LIFE CYCLE

Rites of passage make handy metaphors for the rhythm of life's seasons. As Ecclesiastes recites them: a time to be born, and a time to die; a time to plant, and a time to pluck up that which is planted; a time to get, and a time to lose; a time to keep, and a time to cast away. Over the millennia these seasons pass in biblical order. In personal lives, only the beginning and the end always follow in sequence. Even so, a logical order of financial milestones suggests itself: setting up your first household, living with someone, preparing for marriage, handling two incomes, rearing children, financing their college education, reaching for financial independence, salvaging the most you can from a divorce, planning for retirement, handling your finances as a widow or widower, preserving assets for your heirs.

In real life, the sequence comes far less predictably than that. You may marry in college or in mid-career, middle age, or later. You may have kids early, late, before marriage, or with no thought of marrying. You may lose your spouse through death or, much more likely, divorce while you are still young. Retirement or independence may preoccupy you from an early age or never. Drawing up a prenuptial agreement may make more sense in December than in May. All the

same, here we will follow the conventional order of events.

One strand seems to connect life's passages like the thread that Theseus followed through the labyrinth. It is called the Internal Revenue Code. No one ever accused congressional tax writers of being evenhanded. In the Tax Reform Act of 1986, which was enacted in the name of fairness and simplicity, they embedded in a bias against living alone or being a single parent. Yet, naughtily, they continued to give a somewhat better break to couples living together out of wedlock than to those who marry. They made it less profitable to bestow large gifts of money on your children, but they agreed to pick up part of the tab if you hock your house to put the kids through college. They left openings in the estate and gift tax law large enough to drive a Brink's truck through.

You will read much in the next 20 chapters about the tax implications or consequences of financial decisions at various stages of family development and dissolution. But this section is not a tax primer. You get to the basics in Part V, Living with the Income Tax. If you are just in from Mars or Lhasa, skip first to that section; but if you have ever put your signature to Form 1040, you should have no trouble understanding what is to come.

10

THE ECONOMICS OF BEING SINGLE

In the 1950s, said anthropologist Margaret Mead, Americans suffered ''an attack of matrimony — an absolute panic, with everyone getting married.'' Now the United States has a severe case of the singles. People are marrying later, divorcing more often, and waiting longer to remarry, if they remarry at all. Just look at the census figures: in 1985, some 63.5 million adults were unmarried. They represented 37 percent of all Americans over 18, compared with 28 percent in 1970. Many singles lived with their parents or shared digs with friends or lovers. But one-person households are increasing fast. By 1990, the Census Bureau estimates, they will account for one household in four, up from one in six in 1970.

The single life should be blissfully free of financial woes. After all, the young, unattached, and childless have few of the nagging responsibilities borne by married couples. A childless person saves the $14,000 a year that, according to recent government studies, it costs on average to raise a son or daughter. Favorable joint-return tax rates and extra tax exemptions for children hardly suffice to offset those burdens.

Nevertheless, singles who collect large salaries may well fall victim to buying binges that eat up income they should be saving and investing. If their wages are lean, their problem is the reverse: how to pay their bills and still have money left for fun. In either case, they may have nothing to fall back on if their health or bank account gives out. Restraint would be their salvation, but few young people know how to begin. The short answer: find a system for accumulating savings that, over time, will produce investable funds. Invest those funds smartly.

Unattached men and women do seem to have special financial needs. The largest chunk of their after-tax dollars often goes to what they call "meeting people," by which they mean circulating among potential husbands and wives. Getting into circulation costs more than the tab for drinks at a singles bar. Take housing, for example. Rarely do unmarried people choose to live in unpretentious low-cost neighborhoods. Instead, if they can afford to, they cluster in high-rent colonies like Marina del Rey in Los Angeles and the Upper West Side of Manhattan. When the Bureau of Labor Statistics compiled its last Consumer Expenditure Survey (for 1982–1983), housing accounted for 29 percent of singles' income, compared with 25 percent for couples.

When singles leave their expensive housing, they keep doing expensive things. They spend half their food dollar eating out, while Americans as a whole keep the figure to 36 percent. In 1985, when Rick Bolandz of Alexandria, Virginia, was 29 and unwed, he earned nearly $3,600 a month as a management consultant and routinely shelled out $500 of it on restaurant meals.

Polishing an image that appeals to the opposite sex is another costly business. Kindness and strength of character should be enough to attract a suitable mate, but they usually are not. In Westchester County, New York, and neighboring Fairfield County, Connecticut, a recent survey of 1,000 single people aged 30 to 50 confirmed that men look for women who are young and beautiful, while women want men with money and social status. Consequently, women invest tremendous sums in grooming. "I call it marketing. I am my most important product," said Lorel Kish when she was 34 and single in Palo Alto. Three times a year, Kish, a real estate consultant, descended on the designer boutiques on Beverly Hills's Rodeo Drive. In one two-hour visit she managed to part with $3,000. "I was racing to catch a plane," she explained.

To simulate an aura of money and social status, many young men feel compelled to own cars that announce their success in life. For that purpose, a Mercedes, a BMW, a Jag, or a Saab conveys more than passengers. On dates, the single male must have cash or credit cards at the ready. Women's liberation has prompted some women to share the expenses of an evening out, but as one Chicago bachelor says, "They usually offer to pay for parking — not dinner."

When bouts of heavy spending have failed to corner the quarry, single men and women are inclined to retreat to their lairs and nurse their damaged egos. "Loneliness can be expensive," says Judith Langer, a New York City market researcher. She finds that it is not unusual for a single person to buy several TVs, VCRs, radios, and phones to make up for the company and friendship commonly found within a family. If they still feel uncompensated, many unmarrieds go into psychotherapy at $80 a session or, better yet, group therapy.

An Honest Budget

The single spender's first step back to financial sanity is an honest attempt at a budget. Add up the amounts spent in a month on meals out and entertainment, advises Fred Williams, a banker who used to do volunteer work as director of a 1,300-member singles group in Houston. The totals are usually discouraging but loaded with shock value. You begin to see the value of free or cheap activities, such as going to beaches, dollar movies, parks, and college lecture series.

In addition to spending $500 a month at restaurants, Rick Bolandz, the Arlington, Virginia, management consultant, was putting $1,140 a month into mortgage payments and maintenance fees on his two-bedroom condo, as well as several thousand dollars a year into clothes. His good life left him only $200 a month for savings and investments. A panel of financial advisers assembled by *Money* at that point in his life advised him to control his spending enough to save three times as much, thereby reserving 30 percent of his income for his future welfare. Bolandz accepted that advice by convincing himself that disciplined saving was the only way to realize his most passionate goal: to start an international yacht-brokerage business in the Caribbean.

Coping with the Tax Penalty

All but the highest-salaried people pay an income tax penalty for being single. If you are earning $36,000 a year, your federal income tax bill after 1987 is likely to exceed $6,000. If you are married and filing jointly, you won't pay more than $4,065. The singles penalty: about 50 percent. The difference narrows as your income climbs. Also, using 1988 rates, a single can reach the 33 percent pinnacle — the highest marginal tax bracket in the 1986 tax law — with a gross income a bit over $48,000; a couple don't get there until their gross hits at least $81,000. State and local income taxes sometimes compound the penalty.

To increase your deductions, as well as your standard of living, consider buying a place to live instead of renting. You will get write-offs for the interest on your mortgage and for your property tax. Ease of maintenance is important to singles, which is why many of them pick condominiums instead of houses with yards to keep up and exteriors to paint.

Another opportunity to slash your high-bracket tax as a single often comes on the job. Take fullest advantage of whatever forms of tax-deferred income your company offers. Many large corporations have salary deferral plans under Section 401(k) of the tax law. By holding back as much as 25 percent of your salary and putting it in an investment trust, your company can save you taxes in your present bracket and perhaps drop you into a lower one. Rick Bolandz became eligible for a 401(k) in 1985. His employer, Management Logistics International, was contributing 75 cents for every dollar he invested, up to 6 percent of his income. All of the earnings on his contributions and his employer's matching ones were tax-deferred — up to $7,000 a year.

Because childless singles have neither a spouse nor children to depend on in their old age, they have greater need for careful retirement planning than almost anyone else. In the absence of a company pension plan — or in addition to one if your income is less than $35,000 — you can deduct as much as $2,000 of each year's paychecks by putting that much into an Individual Retirement Account, which has tax advantages resembling those in a 401(k) plan, though on more limited contributions. Working people with self-employment income can grab the much larger tax benefits of a Keogh plan. For details about tax-deferred retirement plans of various kinds, see Chapter 24.

Singular Insurance Problems

Discrimination against singles is unintentionally built into many fringe benefits of employment, particularly at companies with unusually generous plans. Free group life insurance is of little use to single people without dependents. Such workers rarely need more than enough death benefits to pay funeral expenses. They do need health insurance, but here, too, fringe benefits usually are designed for families. Hospital and major medical coverage in a typical company's employee group policy is worth a lot more to a family with six kids than it is to an unmarried worker. Fortunately, a growing number of corporations are offering flexible benefits, also called cafeteria plans, so that employees can match what they get with what they need.

One neglected coverage is disability-income insurance. Choose the largest amount you can get as a fringe benefit. In case of extended illness, disability insurance kicks in with monthly payments equal to a percentage of your salary. The plan should be one that continues paying benefits for the rest of your normal working life if you are stricken with a permanent injury or a chronic or degenerative disease. If your company doesn't offer this coverage, you can buy it in the commercial arena.

Single men between the ages of 17 and 29 find themselves in a high-risk and expensive category of customers for automobile insurance. They have more accidents than women in the same age group and cost more in claims than the average driver. As a result, young single men pay from 50 to 250 percent extra in premiums. If they live in a densely populated urban area and especially if car theft is rife there, they sometimes have to get insurance from their state's assigned risk pool. Birthdays eventually cure this problem, but another succeeds it. Single people who live alone develop a special need for health insurance that covers extended hospital or nursing home care, or at least home care. If they cannot fend for themselves after an illness, they will have trouble getting along without outside help.

11

LIVING TOGETHER

Mention that you know a couple living together without benefit of clergy and you are likely to raise more yawns than eyebrows. Some 2 million couples now fit the Census Bureau description of POSSLQ (persons of the opposite sex sharing living quarters) — more than triple the 1970 figure. Add to that a sizable but unknown contingent of same-sex couples and the total could be millions more.

Although sheer numbers have helped render unconventional relationships more socially acceptable, unmarried couples still live in a cloudy and unpredictable legal climate. State courts are recognizing their rights, but New York City attorney Doris Jonas Freed, an authority on family law, says, "The country still is riddled with old-fashioned judges."

Until the law catches up with the facts of unmarried life, couples who by choice or necessity leave the knot untied will operate at a distinct disadvantage compared with married partners. Among the major problems:

Inheritance. When a husband or wife dies without a will, state laws typically assume that the bulk of the person's property will pass to the surviving spouse. But when an unmarried person leaves no will, all of his or her earthly goods can be claimed by the next of kin. Even a loathsome great-aunt thousands of miles away stands ahead of a POSSLQ (pronounced *poss*-ul-cue) in the inheritance line.

Health insurance. Plans that cover a spouse almost never extend to an unmarried mate.

Children's rights. To protect their children's future claim to financial support and inheritance, both unmarried parents have to take the extra step of acknowledging in writing the paternity of the child.

Separation. In a divorce, state laws offer guidance for dividing property, but unmarried couples who split up are left to slug it out on their own.

Spread over these difficulties is a crazy quilt of state laws ranging from outright bans on cohabitation to various shades of permissiveness. In Georgia, unwed cohabitants risk a $1,000 fine and a year in jail. Although such laws rarely are enforced, they can tilt the way judges settle other legal problems. In a court dispute with a landlord, for instance, an unmarried couple with a entirely justified gripe may find themselves out on the sidewalk because their living arrangement is against the law.

Archaic statutes can stymie other seemingly just claims. Some years ago, the Illinois Supreme Court denied a woman's plea for an equal share of the assets accumulated by the man with whom she had lived for 15 years — even though she had borne him three children while he was establishing a dental practice. The court ruled that their relationship amounted to common-law marriage, which the state had outlawed back in 1905.

It is usually possible for couples to plug the holes in a legal system that predated POSSLQs and gay lib, but the remedies they have to take will mock their deliberately casual way of life. These involve drawing up contracts or agreements — precisely the kind of thing that the resounding majority of such couples finds odious. "Contracts just don't go with moonlight and roses," sighs San Francisco lawyer Melvin M. Belli. And Elliot L. Evans, a lawyer in New York City, observes, "People who live together often do so because they don't want to define their relationship. They think that if they don't write things down, they won't lock themselves in."

Alas, by not writing things down, unmarried couples may inadvertently lock themselves *out*. Without written contracts, they often forfeit the legal protections of married couples. If disputes arise over an inheritance, ownership of property, or financial obligations, POSSLQs may end up in court, where the outcome could have scant relation to what either wants done. And the absence of written agreements leaves the door wide open for the spurned lover to go to court to argue the existence of an unwritten contract. Michelle Triola established that precedent in California (but failed in her own claim) when she sued her ex-lover, actor Lee Marvin, for "palimony."

Mere utterance of the word *contract* calls up visions of inflexibility (ironclad, written in stone) and complexity (party of the first part and party of the second part). But contracts don't have to be complicated or, for that matter, permanent. In one common type of agreement, couples simply waive all financial claims on each other: what's his is his and what's hers is hers, period.

Contracts also can provide for revisions. When Mary Gannaway of Raleigh, North Carolina, decided to return to college, she borrowed the tuition from her companion, Dick Merritt. In an amendment to their cohabitation agreement, she guaranteed to repay him whether or not they continued living together. Two years later the couple broke up. Not only did Mary fully intend to start paying off her debt to Dick three months after she graduated but also, in lectures she was giving at the time on the business of living together, she strongly advocated cohabitation contracts.

Instead of drawing up a single comprehensive contract, many couples write several agreements, each one focused on a specific bit of business. That is how Ralph Warner and Toni Ihara, two lawyers living together in Berkeley, California, in the early 1980s handled ownership of their house and their interests in Nolo Press, which publishes *The Living Together Kit* ($14.95 at bookstores or from the publisher, 950 Parker Street, Berkeley, California 94710) and other self-help legal material. Warner explained: "She and I have a written agreement covering the house. And every time we do a book together, we write that down."

Many lawyers say that couples with little money and no major assets usually can get by with fill-in-the-blanks legal forms found in such books as *The Living Together Kit.* If the financial picture is more intricate, you should see an attorney — but first you should compose a rough draft as a way of clarifying financial expectations of each other. When serious questions arise over individual interests, each partner should consult a different lawyer.

Whether prepackaged or tailor-made, contracts between unmarried couples generally are recognized by courts so long as they violate no laws and both parties enter into them freely. Leave out of the contract the nature of your relationship, especially in states where cohabitation and homosexuality are illegal. Never put in writing any words that could be construed as an agreement to exchange money for sex, lest you run afoul of prostitution laws. Living-together documents should be signed, witnessed, and notarized in triplicate: one copy for each of you and the third entrusted to a relative or lawyer.

With or without contracts, unmarried couples make dozens of decisions that can have legal reverberations. Here are the major considerations.

Day-to-Day Finances

As soon as two people set up housekeeping, they begin accumulating possessions — from video rigs to Cuisinarts. For unmarried couples who split, the best protection against a needlessly bitter end is separate ownership. He buys the car, she buys the computer. "They should acquire as little as possible together and keep receipts or other records of what each of them buys," says New York City matrimonial lawyer Raoul Lionel Felder. Unmarried couples should not have joint bank accounts or joint credit cards. Each person is 100 percent responsible for debts incurred by the other in joint charge accounts, and creditors can seize bank assets that are deposited in both names.

The tidiest way to split household expenses is down the middle, which many POSSLQs do quite simply by initialing receipts, tossing them into a drawer and squaring accounts once a month. But if one person falls ill, quits work, or is fired, the situation may call for a written agreement. "Couples need to plan what financial support they will provide each other," says Merle Horwitz, a Los Angeles lawyer and author of *Love Is Love But Business Is Business: The Essential Guide to Living Together* (William Morrow, $4.95). "These plans should be part of their written contract. It's fine to make promises, but feelings change when there's stress on a relationship."

In prince-and-pauper partnerships, a proportional sharing of expenses may feel more comfortable than a fifty-fifty split; but the American Bar Association cautions that the law generally respects cash more than services. So if the prince contributed mostly money and the pauper mostly elbow grease, a judge might well view the toil as a gift — and deny the toiler's claim to any possessions paid for by the prince. In a written contract, however, the pair could spell out their intentions for sharing the fruits of their individual contributions.

Housing

So many unmarried couples buy homes together that builders have coined a name for these customers — *mingles*. Even so, legal hazards remain. They range from shared leases to disagreements over jointly acquired real estate. Roberta Springer and Michael Spitalnik leased an apartment together a few years ago, hoping to make a profitable investment if the building was converted to a co-op or condo. The building eventually was converted, but by then the couple had broken up and Springer had moved out. Since her name was still on the lease, though, the landlord insisted that the two of them would have to buy the apartment jointly to get the favorable price available to existing tenants. When he and she each pressed for the individual right to buy at the insider price, Spitalnik asked a New York State court to rule that he alone, as the occupant, should be allowed to buy the apartment. Their legal tiff might have been avoided had they spelled out each person's share of any profit in case the place was bought and later sold.

"Business partners make these buy-sell agreements all the time," says Judith Zabalaoui, head of Resource Management, a financial planning firm in New Orleans. "The idea is that you negotiate the exit as you're making the entrance. That's when everybody has a nice, rosy glow and a concern for each other's interests."

Taxes

One positive inducement for living together unwed is that the tax code still requires many two-career married couples to pay more than their unmarried counterparts. Whereas singles are taxed more heavily than marrieds with the same income, two singles filing separate returns are likely to pay more of their income tax at 15 percent, the lower of the two basic rates in the 1986 tax law, than if they had to combine their incomes — or file separately — as a married couple.

Take the case of a couple who each earn $30,000, for a combined income of $60,000. Assuming their deductions amount to 15 percent of their earnings, they would owe $9,321 in federal income tax at 1988 rates ($9,610 in 1987) as a married couple filing a joint return. But if they were single, their combined tax bills would be only $8,548 ($8,704 in 1987). The $773 marriage penalty for them after the 1987 tax phase-in period comes to 9 percent. For couples earning disparate incomes, the penalty gets worse. For instance, if one of them earns $100,000 and the other $30,000, their penalty is three times as high as it was under the old tax law.

But the rules turn against unwed couples if just one partner works. You can claim your POSSLQ as a dependent only by passing a stiff IRS test. Among the conditions for the exemption: the state does not ban cohabitation, the tax-paying partner furnishes more than half of the other's support, and the dependent earns less than $500 a year. Your state income tax laws might not look on unmarried couples even that tolerantly.

Children

The rights of children, especially to inheritances and financial support, are the same whether their parents marry or not. And child custody disputes usually are not decided on the basis of marital status. But parents should write a statement acknowledging the father's parenthood to ensure that neither a parent nor a child will have to go to extravagant lengths to prove paternity.

A divorced mother who moves in with another man should know that her cohabitant's contributions to the household may cost her the loss of child support from her ex-husband. "If the unmarried couple have a written contract stating that the man does not contribute to the children's support, that would be a helpful piece of evidence in court," says lawyer Merle Horwitz.

Insurance and Wills

Unmarried couples' problems with most types of insurance are minimal as long as they tell the truth on application forms. Homeowners and tenants policies should carry both names so the possessions of both are clearly covered. One temptation to resist: registering his car in her name to escape the high premiums paid by young unmarried men. Bill Malcolm, past president of the Professional Insurance Agents Association of Connecticut, says, "If there's an accident, she'll be liable even if he's driving. Judgments these days can be enormous, and any such award would stay on her insurance record even if she left him and married someone else." Settlement of a negligence claim would sharply raise her premium or cause the insurance company to cancel her policy.

Because employer-provided family health insurance does not extend to POSSLQs, unmarried couples have to buy their own protection against catastrophic medical costs if either of them is not covered by a group plan. One advantage of unmarrieds over marrieds: they are not liable for each other's medical bills. One disadvantage: if an unmarried person is hospitalized with a serious illness, the hospital may grant visiting privileges only to kin. To get around such rules, draft a medical power of attorney that permits an unrelated person not only to visit but also to make medical decisions for a totally incapacitated patient.

Don't neglect to name your POSSLQ as the beneficiary of your life insurance policies. Also arrange for your partner to receive the death benefits if you die before you collect your pension or profit-sharing proceeds. You should hit no obstacles with pension and profit-sharing plans, but life insurers have balked at making one unmarried person the beneficiary of another. An easy, perfectly legal way out is suggested by Bill Malcolm: ''Name a family member when you take out the policy, and change the beneficiary later.''

Pension plans frequently offer a joint-and-survivor annuity, which allows the widow or widower of a pensioner to continue collecting retirement benefits. But POSSLQs don't qualify for the joint-and-survivor option. An unmarried pair's only safe passage through the pension maze is to explore with the company's employee-benefits counselor other annuity options that provide a survivor benefit.

While money from life insurance and pensions goes directly to the beneficiaries, most other assets acquired over a lifetime are destined for the owner's estate. That is the domain ruled over by his or her last will and testament. To make sure your wishes are carried out in probate, each of you had better write a will. A few years ago, when a New York writer died intestate, the apartment that he owned went to his co-op association instead of to his male live-in lover of 10 years.

Social Security

Although individual retirement benefits earned while you are working are the same for unmarrieds as for marrieds, the Social Security system generally favors those who wed. When a husband or wife is the only one getting retirement benefits and then dies, the spouse gets survivor's income: a POSSLQ has no such right.

For example, if one spouse worked for a short time and accrued only a small individual benefit, the law allows that person the option of drawing a pension equal to half of the other spouse's benefit. So a 65-year-old wife who is entitled to $200 a month and is married to a man receiving $700 could raise her benefit to $350. Unmarried couples do not get this option. But children under 18, whether their parents marry or not, are entitled to monthly income if a parent dies or is totally disabled.

12

PRENUPTIAL AGREEMENTS

For many modern courting couples, only one subject is still taboo: money. It seems indelicate if not downright greedy to ask, ''What's your net worth? How much do I get if we split?'' Nevertheless, a frank discussion of your finances helps to build a strong foundation for marriage. More and more about-to-be-married couples are going further: they are swallowing their inhibitions and writing contracts that specify who owns what property and what becomes of it in various contingencies. Prenuptial agreements are gaining legal status, too; courts in more than half of the states now recognize a contract that tries to head off a battle in case of divorce. A few states have even opened the door to financial agreements made after you marry.

A Money Talk

By no means everyone needs a prenuptial agreement. A premarital money chat often suffices. If you marry young, for instance, you probably don't have sufficient assets or obligations to justify the expense of drawing up a contract. But before cutting the cake, find time to sit down together and talk money. Here is what to do:

Take inventory of your separate assets and liabilities. The purpose of this goes beyond an exchange of information about who owns what and who owes how much. It encourages you to decide what property each of you wants to keep in his or her own name and what you want to merge. For example, most advisers suggest separate as well as joint bank accounts.

Familiarize yourself with the law. Each state has its own laws governing marital and separate property and on what happens if the two are mingled. This can keep you from putting under both names something — a car, for instance — that you meant to keep separate. If you want to put property in your spouse's name, avoid the gift tax by transferring ownership after the marriage. The marital gift deduction is unlimited.

Discuss the advantages and disadvantages of joint ownership. An accountant or other financial adviser can explain the nuances. In joint tenancy with right of survivorship, the title specifies that when one of you dies, the property goes automatically to the other. In another form, tenancy in common, you each own half, and you can leave your half to whomever you wish, such as a child from an earlier marriage.

Make or update your wills. If you die without a will, your spouse generally receives one-third to one-half of your separate property. The rest is distributed among other relatives.

Consolidate or coordinate medical insurance. If you both have group plans where you work and you are paying part of the premiums, you may be able to save money by dropping one plan and having the other cover you as a family. Or you may be able to keep both policies, naming each other as dependents, and get more of your medical costs covered.

Don't forget the obvious. Change the beneficiary on your life insurance, pension, profit sharing, and annuity.

Prenuptial Contracts

In the past, prenuptial agreements were Hollywood-style devices typically used by sugar daddies about to marry possible gold diggers. A millionaire would make a compact with, say, a waitress to prevent her from getting half of his money if the union did not last. The man was rich, the woman was eager to marry, and an inequitable but acceptable bargain was struck. That is still the model for many agreements. "Usually, one party wants an advantage over the other," says Chicago attorney Marshall J. Auerbach.

There is now a different reason behind the growing number of contracts: modern couples are trying to forge covenants that will be fair. In part this is because, increasingly, the bride as well as the groom has a career, with her own income, assets, and obligations. Also, full-time homemakers are asking to have the economic value of their contributions recognized. Concern for children's inheritances is another leading motive.

No doubt prenuptial contracts take some of the romance out of marriage. If drawn carefully, however, such agreements also can take the litigation out of divorce, saving hundreds of hours of fact finding and testimony and thousands of dollars in fees. More important, a prenuptial agreement can help you set the financial ground rules for a lasting marriage and resolve ahead of time any mismatched expectations over money.

Each of you should have your own lawyer review the agreement and be prepared to pay legal fees of $500 to $2,500, depending on the depth of your problem. But first work out the details yourselves.

Broadly, prenuptial contracts should have one or more of three goals:

To protect the inheritances of children by an earlier marriage.

To clarify who owns what property and how pooled assets would be split if the marriage broke up.

To pin down how much a working spouse contributes to the future earnings of a husband or wife who is studying for a profession.

A contract can safeguard the interests of children by a first marriage, not by serving as a substitute for a will but by reinforcing an existing one. If your spouse agrees to your intentions, he or she probably won't try to overturn a will that leaves the bulk of your property to someone else. Written evidence that your partner approved of the bequest also can minimize tension between grown children and a new stepparent.

When Californians Annette Kelleher and John Travis decided to marry some years ago, both were parents of grown children. Kelleher foresaw potential complications. "I had reared my children essentially by myself," she explained later. "They had helped me many times, so the assets I accumulated came partly from their labors. It was important to me to ensure that these assets would go to my children should I die." With Travis's consent, she asked her attorney to draw up an agreement assuring her of control over the assets she had built up — real estate and a portfolio of stocks and bonds. Her husband retained control of his money-market accounts and stamp collection. Their respective children will inherit these separate assets.

Ownership Rights

Without a prenuptial contract, you let state law dictate, in general terms, what property each of you owns separately and what you share. You can manage and bequeath separate property as you wish; you must divide pooled assets if you divorce. In most states, what you own before marriage is yours, along with anything you later inherit or receive as a gift from anyone but your spouse.

Nine states (Arizona, California, Idaho, Louisiana, Nevada, New Mexico, Texas, Washington, and Wisconsin) merge everything else that you and your spouse accumulate during the marriage as community property, jointly owned by both of you. Neither of you can dispose of the property without the other's consent. In most of the other 41 states, whatever you earn after the wedding is yours to do with as you please — spend it, invest it, or put it into jointly owned possessions. But when a marriage ends, the law views this accumulated wealth as "marital property," to be divided "equitably."

If you do have a prenuptial contract, it can supplant these property rules in various ways. In about half the states, you can legally anticipate the possibility of divorce and decide together what property is separate and what is shared. The other states refuse to recognize any contract that looks ahead to division of property if a marriage comes apart, on the ground that smoothing the path to divorce is against public policy. But even in those states, a written pact might offer compelling evidence of your original intentions if a dispute over property was taken to court.

When separate property grows in value during marriage, a postnuptial contract can define each spouse's potential interest in the increase. Attorney Gloria Allred faced this situation in California, one of the states where it is possible to write a marital-property agreement during as well as before a marriage. Ten years after Allred's wedding, her husband's aircraft-parts business had grown in value, and she believed that under California law some portion of that increase was community property. To define the size of her interest, she and her husband decided to work out an agreement. "It took us a year and a half," she reported, "but we finally compromised on a formula that determines my share, based on a percentage of the appreciation of the business."

Some compacts made before marriage provide for progressive sharing of a growing asset. For instance, you might agree that for the first five years any income or appreciation in the value of your property will be yours alone, after which 30 percent becomes marital property, and that after 10 years you and your spouse share a joint interest in 100 percent of the value.

A Stake in Future Earnings

It is more difficult to hit on a fair percentage when you are dividing something less tangible than a house or business — for example, the value implicit in a medical license or a law degree. Nevertheless, couples who marry with the understanding that one will earn a living while the other prepares for a profession should recognize in writing their joint investment in future earnings.

The lack of an agreement often leads to stormy relationships. In a 1984 Michigan divorce case, Henry Griffin sued his psychiatrist wife for half of her practice; he placed its value at $1.3 million. Griffin, whose income of about $30,000 as a market analyst at General Motors at the time of their separation was considerably less than his wife's, worked while she was in school and argued that he had contributed substantially to her earning power. Dr. Griffin countered that since she earned money and got fellowships during her schooling, she would have managed to earn the degree whether or not she had wed. The court eventually ruled that she owed him nothing; but while the case was pending, her lawyer, Henry Baskin, acknowledged that he wished she had signed a protective contract. "I used to be against prenuptial agreements. Now I'm not," he said.

Children

The most painful issue in a divorce, the fate of the children, cannot be resolved by a contract beforehand. Some states allow you to make prenuptial provisions for custody and support, but in the end it is the court's judgment of a child's best interests, not a contract between his parents, that rules. For George Davis, an account executive at a Wall Street brokerage, it barely mattered that his agreement sheltered his finances in case of a divorce. "I protected my flanks but lost the war — my wife and child."

Dos and Don'ts

Some contracts stray beyond their proper scope. In Chicago a woman insisted on a stipulation that she could keep her cat even though her husband was allergic to it. Another woman tried to require her husband to accompany her whenever she went to the opera. No court would attempt to enforce such provisions. In some states, even the much more serious question of alimony cannot be legally predetermined. Since one shaky provision can upset an entire contract, you may want a severability clause. This provides that if one portion of the agreement proves illegal or unenforceable, the rest remains valid.

Avoid trying to turn a prenuptial contract into a roommates' agreement, with every penny accounted for. Attorneys report that couples who try to negotiate which of them will pay each bill are often all too successful in preventing a messy divorce — they wind up calling off the marriage. In the worst case, a prenuptial agreement can infinitely complicate a divorce. What results, says Boston attorney Gerald L. Nissenbaum, is in essence two trials: one to decide whether the agreement was fairly made, the other to consider the issues of the divorce.

Don't try to pressure your prospective spouse to sign a prenuptial agreement, and never present your fiancé with a document at the eleventh hour. Anything less than unhurried mutual consent may bring down a contract in court. You also can wreck a contract by not revealing to your spouse all your assets. As proof of full disclosure, notarized statements of net worth should accompany the covenant.

Finally, don't try to write your own contract. It is almost certain to topple in court. Judges suspect that without an attorney to protect the interests of each side, one party may too easily sway the other. In reality, not many prenuptial contracts have been tested in court. The reason, according to attorney Anthony R. Daniele of New York City, is that "people who draw them up tend to stay married."

13

THE TWO-PAYCHECK LIFE

In the 1970s, married couples with two paychecks looked like a new elite, with boundless self-confidence and mobility, extraordinary buying power, and freedom to pursue distinctive goals. As that decade drew toward its end, an economist at the Urban Institute, a Washington, D.C., research center, said, "We call it a subtle revolution. With two full-time adult earners, it's very hard for most families to be poor. They have to be considered at least middle class." Back then, two out of every three families in the richest 20 percent of the nation had at least two wage earners. And the trend has proceeded, making wives who work the social norm instead of the exception.

The two-paycheck revolution changed the basics of community life: marriage, child raising, work, spending, and saving. With their liberal incomes, working couples moved into expensive new subdivisions and commuted to their jobs, turning residential neighborhoods into something like ghost towns five days a week. They helped make Sunday the busiest day at the shopping mall. They choked major thoroughfares with fast-food franchises dishing up quarter-pounders and tacos to multitudes of kids whose mothers were too tired to cook. Whatever provisions they made for child care, they spurned the advice of a previous generation's gurus that, for mothers, working was incompatible with raising children. Phyllis Wertz, who as a young mother in 1979 earned more selling real estate in Muncie, Indiana, than her husband, Terry, earned selling Pontiacs, voiced a brave new attitude toward the upbringing of their four-year-old son, Christopher: "I enjoy working a lot more than being home all day with a small child, and Chris will be more outgoing and self-confident for it. We were overmothered; he won't be. Besides, how could my child be happy if I'm not happy, too?''

The Wertzes were going for it all. They wanted not just marriage but equality within marriage, not just jobs but careers, and perhaps most demanding of all on top of the other two, a third career: parenthood. But having it all may mean having too much — too much work, too many responsibilities, and more anxiety than nerves can stand. Can any parent adequately meet the rigid demands of two workplaces while satisfying the limitless needs of children? With so many calls on your time and energy, can you settle for doing everything — from breadwinning to housework — all at once, while kids, for all practical purposes, raise themselves? The old division of labor — Mom's at home, Dad's at the office, and all's right with the world — may have been junked. But it has not been replaced — not satisfactorily, anyway. Some who have delved professionally into the new work ethic find it basically wanting. ''I have the heretical view that parents should not both pursue fast-track, nonstop careers when they have kids,'' says Pat Libbey, codirector of the Career and Family Institute, a nonprofit Minneapolis organization that advises corporations on the needs of working parents.

To relearn how to raise kids, couples may have to reshuffle their goals and make compromises. They may also have to relearn thrift. In many cases they are richer than they ever dreamed — yet poorer than they think. For when wives work, the family's finances undergo a range of adjustments that few households are adequately prepared for or even explicitly aware of. Costs tend to be higher, spending freer, and time at a premium. In such an atmosphere, debts can accumulate far more easily than savings or investments, and the future is too often left to fend for itself.

It all comes down to what two-career parents should do about various profound or mundane questions: timing their childbearing, redividing the household responsibilities, rejiggering their budgets and financial defenses, resetting their occupational goals, and choosing lines of work or employers that throw the fewest impediments in their path. Psychologists, sociologists, doctors, early-childhood development specialists, financial advisers, and other all-knowing experts stand ready with easy advice. Wise couples will listen carefully, but, in the last analysis, provide their own answers.

When to Have Babies

Some couples act as if the rest of their lives revolves on a single question: how do we time the births of our children so that neither of our careers suffers too much?

The decision to create a new life is an instinct of body and spirit. It would be a cold pair indeed who thought of nothing but net worth and cash flow before succumbing to the urge. Still, you do have to decide whether you are going to have your first child when you are young and just starting out or older and more established in your jobs. What really scares mothers and fathers is the thought that they may be neglecting children just to chase the almighty buck. Will their progeny wind up in therapy groups 20 years hence, pounding pillows and flooding Kleenexes because their parents were too involved with business appointments, quarterly reports, and a selfish search for success? The concern is deep and pervasive — especially among women. Judith Langer, the New York City market researcher, who has observed discussion groups of first-time moms, many of whom had or wanted careers, reports, "They mention the word 'guilt' almost as often as the word 'baby.' "

The fact is, both youth and maturity have parental advantages and drawbacks. It is easier to conceive in your twenties, and you have more energy then to cope with kids and jobs. Also, since younger people earn less money, the opportunity costs of taking a leave from the work force are lower than they would be when you have become high earners.

"By the time you are in your early thirties," says the personal finance columnist and commentator Jane Bryant Quinn, "you have already built two incomes into your life-style. If you're going to have a housekeeper, you wonder how you'll afford one. You've been living to the hilt on your two incomes." Quinn also argues that the demands of a career in full stride, such as traveling and working nights and weekends, are incompatible with having a baby in the house. Her advice: "In the old-fashioned way, which is the way I did it, you get married and have a baby right away. Then you have built the cost of child care immediately into your budget. The child just comes along the way the mortgage, the furniture payments, and the car payments come along."

There's a contrary argument, of course. The older couple have had time to build greater financial security. They have had their trips to Europe and nights at the opera and are ready to settle down uncomplainingly to the routine of child rearing. "Highly valued professionals may be better able to negotiate flexible schedules with employers,'' says Kristin Moore, senior research associate with Child Trends, a Washington, D.C., research organization.

The Redivision of Labor

Most parents debate long and hard about whether one should take off several months from work — or even a year or two — after their child's birth. Childhood development specialists have sold Americans on the idea that the first two years are absolutely crucial. Supposedly, if kids don't get enough love, attention, and stimulation from Mom and Dad in those early days, everything from their math scores to their future sex lives will suffer.

Yet many experts now assert that what they call ''good substitute care'' — read baby-sitter or day-care center — can more than adequately supply the needs of infancy and toddlerhood. The problematical word is ''good''; much of the caretaking that U.S. parents must choose from is anything but. Mothers and fathers shopping for day-care centers worry about the much-publicized incidents of child sexual abuse. More commonly, young children in group care suffer from simple neglect. (For guidelines to shopping for day care, see Chapter 16.)

Couples who find their local child-care market unpromising may decide that they would be most comfortable having one parent stay at home during a child's first year or so. Whether it is Mom or Dad may depend on a number of factors: whose career will sustain the lesser setback from dropping out of the work force for a while; which parent's job can provide the family with more financial security; and last, who is willing to take on the job of full-time homemaker.

When two parents are working full time, they face the no-win challenge of divvying up infinity — housework and child care. A 1982 study conducted by F. Thomas Juster, director of the Institute for Social Research at the University of Michigan in Ann Arbor, showed that although husbands do 14 hours worth of housework a week — three hours more than a decade earlier — wives are still stuck with most of the drudgery.

Oddly, many working women are resigned to being exhausted, overstressed Superwomen. According to Joseph H. Pleck, associate director of the Wellesley College Center for Research on Women, surveys indicate that only 42 percent want their husbands to help more with child care and only 36 percent would like the men to do more housework. Pleck speculates that some women may fear losing their feminine identity if they yield their turf — especially child care. But if they can lick that fear, they may do well to pass off some of the child raising to their husbands. A study of a small number of families undertaken by the Child Study Center at Yale University has shown that fathers adapt readily to the task of full-time parenting and may even help their children achieve somewhat higher levels in social and analytical skills than other kids.

James Morgan, an economist who studies household work at the Institute for Social Research in Ann Arbor, asserts that household and child-care tasks require management more than sheer back-breaking labor. Inevitably, one member of a two-career couple serves as the family anchorperson, a manager responsible for the overall well-being of home and children. That spouse sees to it that children have doctors' appointments and camps to attend, that someone takes them to piano lessons, that a substitute is available for a sick baby-sitter, that the larder contains food, and that the housecleaner has enough detergent to do the laundry. Without a competent manager to delegate responsibilities, husband and wife usually wind up squabbling about them every day.

Who, then, usually becomes the anchorperson? The one with the less demanding job, the more regular hours, and the flexible vacation days. Sometimes geography dictates the choice. Whose office is closer to home? There is, of course, a dark underside to this arrangement. The family manager usually suffers a slowdown in career advancement until the time when roles can be switched.

Spending Problems

Many two-income families delight in indulging themselves and not having to keep track of their money. Truly prosperous couples may be able to afford this, but many who cannot afford it give it a go anyway — typically in the first six months after the wife goes to work. Debt counselors point to that period as the most dangerous of all. Inevitable costs materialize when both husband and wife work all day. Since time is scarce, housekeeping shortcuts become necessities. Frozen prepared foods, microwave ovens, family dinners out, and frequent trips to the high-priced convenience store at the corner can, by even the most conservative estimate, inflate food bills by $20 a week or more. The better clothes a working wife must buy add perhaps $30 a week, lunches out $25, transportation to work $15, and once-a-week housecleaning service $40 or more. Last but sometimes most costly, child care can come to $55 a week or far more.

These extra expenses can quickly add up to $9,000 a year. If a woman earns the working wife's median income of $15,500, her net after-tax contribution to the household is marginal at best and, if all extra costs are unflinchingly totted up, perhaps even a fiscal extravagance.

There is one other prime budget buster to consider: two-income families' well-charted propensity to overdo it. They are twice as likely to eat out regularly as families in which the mother stays at home. They spend a third more on transportation and 100 percent more on education — their own and their children's. Other indications of heavy spending: their total assets are less, and their gifts to charities are more meager than the one-earner household's.

Working couples not only spend more, they also monitor their spending less. For marketers of all kinds of products, the working woman is the hottest news since credit. Studies show, for instance, that she is the least economy-minded of her sex, the biggest impulse buyer, and the least apt to shop for bargains.

Expanded credit opportunities fan spending. Almost inevitably, many two-income couples are in over their heads. Credit counseling services, many of whose clients are middle- and upper-income two-earner families, report soaring business. The average family seeking help tends to think it has three times as much discretionary income — what's left over after paying for essentials — as it actually has. While fewer and fewer wives work for bread alone, there are plainly better ways to slice the loaf.

For some couples budgeting can come naturally and informally. Try pooling your incomes and working with one joint checking account. Ideally, you should be able to save 10 percent of your gross income. Then figure out each month's fixed expenses, including rent or mortgage payments, utilities, commuting costs, and car payments. Use what's left for day-to-day spending. If you still have money in your pocket, you can use it for play. When it is not there, cancel your weekend away.

That kind of simple self-discipline comes hard to most people, however. If you are among the majority, you may need to get a more formal grasp on your fiscal affairs. In short, draw up a budget. Begin by keeping track of all expenditures for a few months and filling out the cash-flow statement in Chapter 5 (Figure 3). You'll learn exactly where your money is going. Only then can you redirect it. You may discover that eating out and buying small gifts for yourselves claim 10 percent of your take-home pay. If this is at the expense of security or basic goals, it is time for belt tightening.

But squeezing too hard does not help. Rules, such as banking all of one salary or never eating out, are easy in theory but unreasonable in practice. Be realistic. Convenience foods, for instance, may cost more than other supermarket items, but they are a big economy over restaurants.

Economists, those dismal scientists, are worrying their calculators more and more over the record-breaking debt loads of two-income families. What happens, they fret, if a deep recession blows away many of those second salaries? Consequently, many a financial adviser is pressing traditional credit strictures with fresh fervor on two-income clients.

The first commandment: don't commit more than 15 percent of after-tax income to monthly payments — not counting the mortgage. Safe is the family that can liquidate its short-term debts in one year.

The second commandment: liquidate as many of those debts as you can right now. Your credit-card and charge-account balances probably are costing you 18 or even 20 percent interest. Until those balances are gone, it makes little sense to put money in savings accounts paying one-third as much.

Make systematic savings your third commandment. Since two-income families tend to spend at two-income rates, financial planners often advise keeping reserves equal to three to six months of after-tax income of both spouses. Alexandra Armstrong, a Washington, D.C., financial planner, goes that rule one better: "I recommend that my clients have three to six months of expenses put aside — expenses, not income, because so many people live beyond their income." If one member of a two-career family loses a job, the reserve can be the difference between frantically taking the next offer that comes along and waiting for the right one.

Tax Strategies

The second earner used to be the most heavily taxed American. Since the first dollar of a wife's income was taxed at the rate of the last dollar of her husband's, she was propelled into a high bracket when she added, say, her $25,000 to his $50,000. As of 1988, when the highest tax bracket becomes 33 percent, down from 50 percent in 1986, and the highest rate on total income flattens out at 28 percent, this marriage penalty is much more bearable. However, working couples still cannot avoid paying Social Security taxes twice even though the wife is likely to add no retirement benefits beyond those she would get if she never worked. Nor is the income tax penalty entirely wiped out. As explained in Chapter 11, two-income couples living together unmarried get a better break than those who are wed.

The first defensive measure you can take when you enlist in the two-income ranks is to rough out the coming year's tax bill. Then confer with your payroll departments about boosting withholding tax. Better still, save up the impending deficit in a bank or money-market fund, which at least pays interest to you instead of the U.S. Treasury.

Two-income tax planning turns next to ways of cutting the April 15 bill. The search should begin at home. Financial planner Alexandra Armstrong says, "If clients don't already own a house or condominium, I tell them to buy one as soon as they can and then come back and talk to me about other investments." The immediate tax advantage of owning your home — deductibility of mortgage interest and property taxes — also applies to a second home. But the 1986 tax law is phasing out deductions against your ordinary income for paper losses on investment property that you own as shares in real estate limited partnerships.

Many two-income couples can still find ample tax shelter in company-sponsored savings and profit-sharing plans. Better still, in many companies they can escape immediate taxation of as much as $7,000 of salary each year by signing up for a salary withholding plan, also known as a 401(k) plan, which is described in Chapter 20.

If either or both of you work for an employer who has no pension plan or a plan you are not yet eligible for, take advantage of Individual Retirement Accounts. If you are self-employed or operate a business together, a whole vista of tax-saving retirement plans comes into view: Keoghs, corporate pension funds, and others. (You can learn more about tax-sheltered pensions in Chapter 24.) If you are parents who plan to send children to college, a bit of tax sanctuary can be had in special accounts established in the children's names on their fourteenth birthdays. (See Chapter 18.)

Two-Income Investors

In an age of increasing financial enlightenment, couples face more complex investment choices than ever before. What percentage of your income should you put aside to achieve your goals? Do you need tax shelters? Will you be able to withdraw money without paying the IRS a penalty? You need to be nimble enough to change course suddenly when baby makes three and disciplined enough to forget about that new sports car or realistic enough to stop dreaming about retiring at 45. Yet many young couples forging a life together have considerable assets. Whatever your goal, by undertaking the challenge together you are twice as likely to reach it.

Any investment strategy should conform to your own special hopes and fears. However, a look at someone else's fairly adventurous experiences gives you an idea of the thought process. In 1985, *Money* asked a panel of financial advisers to make recommendations for a Minneapolis couple, Craig Johnson, then 41 and a printing company salesman, and his wife, Susan Shearer, 37, a staff manager for AT&T Information Systems. While many of their generation were buying houses and having families, Johnson and Shearer had stayed single and lived singles' lives, spending money on cars, clothes, and vacations. "We were having a good time," Susan said somewhat ruefully. But after marrying in 1981, they decided to make an effort to catch up.

At a time when the rise in property values was slowing, the couple bought a one-bedroom condominium in downtown Minneapolis for $66,000. Three years later, after getting a real estate agent's estimate that their home was worth $74,000, they were emboldened to become landlords. Purchasing a lot near the University of Minnesota, they built two adjoining townhouses, occupied one, and put the other on the market. Instead of selling their old place, they rented it out, as a hedge against possible inflation. The income, $600 a month, just about covered expenses on the property.

The second townhouse, for which they were asking $102,000, attracted no buyer, leaving Craig and Susan in something of a hole. Supporting all three pieces of real estate was costing them $41,500 a year — 41 percent of their combined $100,000-plus salaries. All too literally, they had mortgaged their future. Nevertheless, our financial panel advised them to keep seeking a buyer for the empty building rather than rent it out. "It will sell better as a new property than a used one," said Margaret Starner, a financial planner with Raymond James & Associates in Coral Gables, Florida.

If the condo was sold, Craig and Susan's total real estate payments would be reduced by 37 percent, to $26,300 a year. Then they could increase and diversify their investment portfolio. They had saved $27,500, primarily in IRAs and company thrift plans. The money was spread among stocks, government securities, and a tax-sheltered limited partnership. Panelist Malcolm Makin, a Westerly, Rhode Island, financial planner, said, "The next critical step should be to build an emergency reserve of at least $10,000 in a money-market fund. Then begin buying growth mutual funds." He recommended Fidelity Magellan and Massachusetts Capital Development, which had performed unusually well over the previous five years, rising at average annual rates of 30 and 16 percent, respectively.

Insurance

Working couples are likely to have two complex sets of company benefits, and that is where any inventory of insurance coverages should begin. For many childless couples, that is also where it should stop. They usually do not need additional life insurance and can use the dollars saved to build up their investments or emergency fund. Only in rare instances would the death of one working spouse mean a much-reduced living standard for the other.

Couples with children, however, often have too little insurance. "Chances are the surviving parent won't be able to manage on one income," says Charles G. Hughes, Jr., a Bay Shore, New York, financial planner. How much insurance do you need? You will find detailed instructions for figuring that out in Chapter 57. One shortcut is to see how much money each of you brings home after deductions and personal expenses such as commuting, lunches, and clothing. Then buy enough insurance on each of your lives so that, assuming a 10 percent yield, your survivors could invest the principal and live off the interest. Say you bring home $20,000. You would need to leave about $200,000 to replace that salary, but probably not nearly that much insurance. First subtract your net assets and, if you have children under 18, about $1,000 a year in Social Security for each one. Which kind of life insurance is best? Annual renewable term. "It's flexible, simple, and dirt cheap," says planner Dick Knight of Bellevue, Washington. Even a $200,000 policy for a 30-year-old woman should cost no more than about $310 a year; add $40 for a man the same age.

If you think you also need mortgage insurance — which automatically pays off the existing mortgage in the event of the insured's death — think again. It is a better idea not to tie insurance to specific purposes. Give your spouse the choice of whether or not to pay off the mortgage. Another waste of funds is insuring a child's life. Frequently parents buy whole life policies for their children as a way of saving for college. Although the objective is laudable, the tactic is not. It violates a strict financial principle: insure the breadwinner, not the dependent.

When it comes to health insurance, working couples often have more than they need. They can do little about it if employers are paying the cost, and that may be for the best. The partner who elects to drop health coverage may regret it if the one who stays covered dies or loses his or her job.

Ideally, the time to evaluate your health insurance is before you conceive your first child. But in any blessed event, don't wait until your baby is born. If your policy pays less in maternity benefits than the customary two-thirds of hospital costs and physicians' fees, you may want to set aside extra money in your emergency fund. That is almost always more cost-effective than trying to buy a separate policy to boost your coverage. Besides, if the woman is already pregnant, she won't be able to get such a policy.

If both you and your spouse have group coverage, compare policies. Use the policy that offers the more generous benefits or that pays the hospital directly rather than the one that reimburses you after you have coughed up the cash. While you won't be able to collect double by filing a claim against your other group policy, it may pick up where the first one leaves off.

Disability insurance is as important as life insurance for young couples, but much more often overlooked. At all working ages, you are much more likely to be disabled by sickness or injury for at least 90 days in a row than you are to die. Almost everyone has the disability-income insurance provided by Social Security, but the top benefit is not likely to meet your needs. Check with your company to find out how much disability coverage, if any, it provides you as a fringe benefit. Such a policy, together with Social Security, should replace about 60 percent of your pretax salary. If you have to buy disability coverage on your own, consult Chapter 59 for guidelines on choosing the right policy at the least cost.

Dividing the Spoils

The protocol for dividing the ownership of real estate, securities, bank accounts, and other valuables between spouses used to be rather tightly governed by the need to fend off the estate tax or the divorce court. Greatly simplified treatment of marital property for tax purposes has taken much of the financial pain out of death and some out of legal separation. Whatever property one spouse inherits from the other, whether through joint ownership or bequest, is exempt from death taxes (though attorneys and financial planners have good reason to caution well-endowed couples against making fullest use of the marital deduction). Amendments to the federal tax code take the capital-gains-tax onus off a spouse who gives his or her half of the family residence to the other in a divorce settlement. (Estate planning is discussed in Chapter 27 and divorce in Chapter 21.)

Nevertheless, a certain amount of individual ownership of assets and separation of financial identities is advisable. The motivation for this applies more often to wives than to husbands. Working wives, according to academic research, seek compensation in psychic fulfillment at least as much as in money; nevertheless, they should think beyond feeding their souls. If current divorce rates prevail, roughly half of all marriages made in the 1980s will self-destruct. Wives will then discover that courts have become stingy in granting them maintenance and child-support payments. If married women don't keep careers going full blast, they risk eventually supporting two or three kids on so small an income that it barely keeps them above the poverty level.

In addition, financial planners universally advise working wives to assume their full share of family debt instead of letting all borrowing be in the husband's name. By borrowing in her own name, a wife establishes a separate identity with credit bureaus. Separate credit cards also make sense. Even a wife who does not take particular pride in being her own economic boss could someday — in case of divorce or widowhood — sorely need a credit history of her own.

14

THE BEST COMPANIES FOR WORKING PARENTS

The careers most compatible with raising children are those that allow you maximum control of your work schedule. It is no coincidence that sales representatives, real estate agents, civil servants, and lawyers in private practice often seem disproportionately represented at afternoon ballet recitals and early-evening Little League games.

Unless you determine that child rearing is to be your main career, your choice of occupations had better be based on your own interests and ambitions, not on secondary considerations, even if they are as exalted as those of parenting. A wiser tactic may be to hunt for an employer in your chosen field whose benefits, programs, and flexible attitudes demonstrate sensitivity to the conflicting demands of working mothers and fathers.

Check out potential employers' attitudes by asking during employment interviews what management's policies are on such issues as giving maternity and paternity leaves and providing either on-site or company-subsidized day care. Some 500 major public and corporate employers operate either on-site or nearby day-care centers for employees' children; many more either help pay for or aid parents in locating independent child-care facilities. By interrogating potential supervisors and coworkers, you can get a feel for the length and flexibility of office hours and the amount and predictability of overtime.

A handful of employers stand out as leaders in making the unavoidable conflict between job and family easier to bear. You can use the kinds of benefits they offer as a yardstick in evaluating those of your own company or a prospective employer. *Money* surveyed career counselors, employee-benefits consultants, and executive recruiters to isolate major employers that can serve as your models. In alphabetical order, they are:

Control Data. This Minneapolis-headquartered computer manufacturer and computer services provider calls itself "the flexible workplace." Employees decide when their eight-hour workdays begin and end, except for a core period, from 10 a.m. to 2 p.m., when they must be at work.

Hewlett-Packard. H-P pioneered flexible working hours starting in 1971. Most employees may schedule their arrivals on a day-to-day basis at any time from 6:30 to 8:30 a.m., then leave eight hours later. This Palo Alto-based manufacturer of measurement and computation products also keeps listings of top-quality local day-care centers and counsels spouses of relocated workers on how to find jobs in the new city.

International Business Machines. Most of IBM's 239,000 U.S. employees choose their own hours. Some can customize their schedules with their supervisors; others are allowed to begin and end workdays half an hour earlier or later than their colleagues. In searching for child care, employees get free information and guidance from community organizations or local consultants. The firm's biggest drawback for dual-career couples is its reputation for relocating employees frequently. Three percent of IBM employees are transferred each year.

Merck. This pharmaceutical giant promises to rehire women employees for up to 16 months after the birth of a child and will grant an additional two months if a job at a similar level is available. For about $400 a month, employees at Rahway, New Jersey, headquarters can enroll their infants and toddlers, up to age five, in a nearby day-care center that the company helped start. Parents may drop off their tots beginning at 7:30 a.m., an hour before the main work force arrives; the center's lights go out at 6 p.m., an hour after the close of business.

Procter & Gamble. Employees at the Cincinnati home of this consumer products colossus can enroll their preschoolers in off-site day-care centers started by the company. The highest fee is $90 a week for children under three. What sets P&G apart is its six-month unpaid child-care leave for fathers. In addition, this is one of a growing number of companies providing financial assistance — up to $1,000 — to parents of adopted children.

Steelcase. This Grand Rapids, Michigan, office-furniture manufacturer made our list because of its job-sharing program. With their supervisor's approval, many factory hands and some office workers split their workdays or workweeks any way they wish with a colleague who agrees to the arrangement. Each collects a pro rata share of pay and benefits. The company also publishes a monthly newsletter of child-care tips and games and maintains a free family-counseling clinic staffed by psychologists.

Stride Rite. This shoe manufacturer opened an on-site day-care facility for its entire Boston community in 1971. By 1986 the company had two such centers — one at its Boston distribution center, the other at its nearby Cambridge headquarters. Parents pay $65 a week or less per child, depending on income. They also get substantial discounts on shoes for their children.

3M. At 3M's headquarters in St. Paul, Minnesota, an executive works full time coordinating child-care information services. These include referrals to the firm's list of state-licensed day-care providers and free seminars on child rearing. One especially innovative program is designed to keep parents working when their kids are sick. The company will arrange for a nurse or nurse's aide to care for the child at home, and it will foot one-half to three-quarters of the $8-an-hour bill. Employees on low salaries get the greatest reimbursement.

U.S. Navy. The military services rival the best corporations in dealing with the problems of two-income couples with children. Some career counselors consider the navy's family-assistance program the best of the lot. In addition to offering paid maternity — but not paternity — leaves, it operates child-care centers for children four weeks to 12 years old. Cost: about $40 a week. The navy also helps couples to locate licensed child-care providers. Psychologists, social workers, and counselors advise wives and husbands on coping when their spouses go to sea. The navy has established a spouse employment assistance program (SEAP) featuring a computerized job registry to pinpoint job opportunities at navy installations throughout the world.

15

WHAT PRICE CHILDREN?

Planned parenthood is more than just deciding when to have children. You also have to determine how to take care of your family's financial needs once you do. Especially if both of you have been working, your cost of living takes on a compelling new significance when you assume the responsibility of bringing children into the world.

"Whatever expenses you have planned for, they will be more," promises Kathleen Muldoon, a financial planner with Carter Financial Management in Dallas. Roberta Israeloff, a faculty member at New York University, commented in 1983, when her first child was 14 months old, "Everything surprised me: how much of a change it was; how much I was attached to Benjamin; how much I was angered by my role as mother—and how much it all cost financially."

Bringing up baby is more expensive than at any time in history, partly because the luxuries of your parents' era have come to be considered middle-class birthrights. Studies that tally the cost of kids produce totals ranging all over the playground. A research project by the U.S. Department of Agriculture concluded in the early 1980s that having and raising your child to age 18 would run from $81,000 to $117,000, assuming you lived in a city or suburb. The USDA found expenses even higher in most small towns and rural areas, largely because of transportation costs. Using more recent consumer expenditure data and a different economic model, a National Institutes of Health study put the figure, for a couple earning $50,000 a year, at $300,000.

That estimate did not include the special parenthood costs of two-income couples, who must choose to pay for day care or lose a paycheck while one parent stays home with the child. Child care can easily add $3,500 to $12,000 to the annual bill. Nor do the government's child-rearing projections include the towering burden of college. The average tab for a student rooming at a private university in 1986 exceeded $10,000, up 7 percent from the year before. If the rate of increase averages 5 percent during the next 22 years, a bachelor's degree for a child born in 1985 will exceed $100,000.

Should Mom stay home till Junior toddles off to kindergarten, her lost income could amount to $110,500, based on a salary of $20,000 and 5 percent inflation. That dollar cost might be compounded by atrophying skills and evaporating seniority. Whether they take long or short maternity leaves, women may have to overcome prejudiced attitudes of colleagues and bosses who question how serious they are about their careers.

Though the government estimates are the best that government money can buy, they are only estimates — an attempt to fit quirky patterns of consumer spending into tidy statistics. Raising kids, after all, is a highly individualized pursuit. You may spend less than is forecast for your child, and you might have spent much of it anyway, child or not. Gross estimates are of less use in planning family finances than the *patterns* of spending that emerge from the studies. So before you throw out the baby with the bathwater, take a look at the big-ticket stages in a child's life.

Newborns come into the world at considerable expense. Routine hospital and delivery fees, in 1986 dollars, average $2,300; an untroubled cesarean birth adds about $1,150. New procedures such as amniocentesis, a test given to mothers to detect birth defects, and ultrasound monitoring, a picture of the fetus made with sound waves for many purposes, including averting complications at birth, can add as much as $1,000 to the bill. Food, which becomes the largest expense in the child's life, costs little now if nursing moms produce their own and later on are willing to whip up purees in the Cuisinart for the baby gourmet.

Kids actually get cheaper after that until they go off to school. Then around the age of six or seven the expense curve starts to inch up, along with the child's increasing appetite for fast food, designer jeans, video games, and TV toys. The curve keeps climbing through age 12, roughly the end of childhood. These are the Wonder Bread years, when the bulk of the money goes to feeding and clothing your rapidly growing youngster. Weekly lessons in ballet, computer, piano, French, tennis, gymnastics, or the myriad other interests that today's overcultivated child can pursue also add up quickly. The cost of eight weeks of summer camp away from home, for example, ranges from $1,900 to $3,000.

The alpine ascent continues through the teenage years. Puberty is pricey, in part because of dating and all its accoutrements. Wear and tear on the family car, including gasoline and insurance — the annual premium can more than double with a 16-year-old son at the wheel — drive up the outlay for transportation. A championship season in high school sports is also costly. With budgets being cut in public schools, for example, athletes at Hutchinson High School, 60 miles west of Minneapolis, have to pay to play. The 1986 fees were $33 for basketball, $37 for baseball, $43 for football, and $48 for hockey. After age 17, the cost curve shoots toward the summit — a peak three times higher than in the birth year. Welcome to the groves of academe and the most expensive years of the child's life.

Knowing when to expect expenses to rise and fall can help parents prepare for them. For instance, more than half of the medical costs in a child's first year may be covered by insurance. A good maternity package in a group policy will pay two-thirds of the hospital and physicians' fees, including the mother's semiprivate room and board, labor and delivery charges, and anesthesia. Parents will have to come up with the rest. Many insurance policies do not cover the nursery, which can run more than $100 a day, or circumcision and routine tests for the infant. The medical needs of a healthy baby are not included in most policies. So you will probably have to budget at least $400 to cover routine monthly visits to the pediatrician during the baby's first year. When the two children of Mary Claire Bond of Bethesda, Maryland, were 15 months and five years old, she half-joked, "I'm in the doctor's office so often I am going to have a Bond memorial chair installed."

Past the first year, as child-related expenses decline and incomes rise, parents may be lulled into thinking that the financial strain went the way of the 2 a.m. feeding. This is the time to begin stashing cash in money-market funds, certificates of deposit, and other investments you can tap in the more costly teenage years. It is also the moment to start beefing up your emergency fund. Instead of settling for three months' living expenses, try to double that amount. When children enter your financial picture, expenses pop up unexpectedly. You should also have that extra cushion in case Mom — or Dad — decides to spend another few months at home with the baby after paid maternity or paternity leave has expired. The pressure on a mother to go back to her job soon grows insistent. According to a survey by Catalyst, an organization specializing in career women's issues, nearly 70 percent of new mothers are back on the job within four months after having a child. Some return for the satisfaction they find in their careers; most do so out of economic necessity. In either case, much of their earnings goes for day care.

More often than not, motherhood means taking a job with fewer responsibilities, working part-time or staying home while the kids are young. Depending on the company she works for or the career path she is on, a woman may be more or less penalized for time away from the job. To ease the eventual transition back to work, full-time mothers should lunch with former business associates, keep up with the periodicals in their field, and perhaps take on free-lance projects they can do at home.

Dad's dedication to work may also change, but in a different way. He may find himself more involved with his job. ''A father may feel a genuine responsibility to bring home the bacon, especially if the wife had worked before,'' says Georgia State sociologist Ralph LaRossa. ''But he may also spend more time on the job to get away from the racket and chaos at home.'' The breadwinner takes his work even more seriously when there's a second child.

What price children? In hard dollar terms, the answer has to be, a lot. But the figures are significant only to a government economist trying to arrive at a defensible figure for welfare payments or to a matrimonial lawyer attempting to win more alimony for a client or to a couple building a case for remaining childless. To those who have kids — or who want them — the cost is meaningless when compared with the first smile, the feel of arms clasped about your neck, or the sound of your child's name called out on graduation day. Kids certainly do cost a bundle, but most parents would readily agree that if you pay a lot for the priceless, you're getting it cheap.

16

THE ABCS OF SELECTING CHILD CARE

While growing demand by career families has fostered a better supply of day-care options, selecting the one that is best suited to your budget and your kids' upbringing is not child's play. Many couples no longer can count on the traditional solution — grandmother or another female relative — or afford a nanny. Nursemaids who work 45-hour weeks typically command $900 or more per month, exclusive of employer-paid vacations and Social Security taxes.

As a result, nearly 20 percent of working mothers must choose among competing types of group care — sole proprietorships, nonprofits, cooperatives, and commercial chains — that vary widely in size, staff qualifications, and requirements for state licenses. Although licensing may help to enforce minimum health, fire-safety, and staffing standards, it is no guarantee against incompetence — or worse.

Though unsettling, reported incidents of day-care-related neglect or physical abuse of children remain relatively rare, says Vivian Weinstein, a professor emeritus of pediatrics at Los Angeles's King Drew Medical Center. Her staff found that only eight of 661 child-abuse cases reported during a recent nine-month period could be traced to day-care centers or elementary schools.

Bear in mind that most group-care providers are unregulated. Licenses are held by only 10 percent of the estimated 1.4 million day-care centers in private homes, which take in two to six children per staff member. Most are informal operations that aren't subject to — or don't bother with — state requirements. Around 20,000 licensed day-care centers have enrollments of as many as 200 kids. Half of these operations are nonprofit centers sponsored by churches, universities, cooperatives, or employers. The rest are commercial ventures ranging from independents to major chains such as La Petite Academy, Kinder-Care, and Children's World.

Group day care is an issue of controversy among specialists in the field of child development. On the positive side, government studies suggest that preschoolers generally benefit from such care. According to Allen Smith, a spokesman for the U.S. Department of Health and Human Services, "Day-care children tend to be more social, assertive, and verbally advanced than kids of comparable ages raised at home." Harvard pediatrician T. Berry Brazelton adds, "Even infants thrive in centers where each one is played with sensitively."

Unfortunately, much of the caretaking that U.S. parents must choose from is anything but sensitive. Young children in group care too often suffer from simple neglect. Runny noses go unwiped, diapers don't get changed quickly, colds and flu are common.

The cost of group care depends largely on a child's age and the number and experience of the attending staff. The Department of Health and Human Services found that monthly fees for infants under age two averaged $325 nationally in 1985, compared with $275 for children three years or older. Day-care homes and employee-sponsored programs are usually less expensive than the national average. Centers that place their charges in small groups tended by specially trained teachers can cost considerably more. At Houston's Montessori Country Day School, where 80 percent of the staff have degrees in early childhood education, monthly tuition was $625 for infants up to 18 months, $475 for toddlers from 18 months to three years, and $350 for children aged three to five. The center employs one teacher for every three youngsters up to the age of one and for every eight to 10 older preschoolers. Uncle Sam helps to defray the cost of day care with a tax credit for working couples and single parents, which applies to children under 15 (see Chapter 43 for details).

The principal advantages of large day-care centers over intimate home-based proprietorships are greater flexibility of hours and broader programs. Chains and commercial centers may have more modern facilities than nonprofit providers, many of which operate in church basements. But nonprofits often allocate a larger percentage of their budgets to salaries to attract better-trained teachers and reduce staff turnover — a problem at chains that pay minimum wages. Couples who have time to get involved may want to consider joining a cooperative. The primary attraction is not cost savings but control: parents constitute the board of directors, hire teachers, and manage finances. They must also donate several hours a month to chores as menial as fixing seesaws and cleaning classrooms.

The following nine questions will help you to assess group care facilities. Pose them to care providers and fellow parents before you enroll your children.

1. How large are groups or classes at the center? The maximum number of infants under two years old should be eight per group, while toddlers aged two to three should not be placed in groups larger than 12. Bigger groups tend to be too confusing for the children.

2. What is the ratio of staff to children? This is especially important for infants, who need constant cuddling and attention. Look for at least one adult for every three or four babies or every five or six toddlers, advises Gwen Morgan, a professor of early childhood education at Wheelock College in Boston.

3. Are teachers readily accessible? Be wary of centers that don't encourage parents to drop by anytime for a chat. Formal conferences to evaluate a youngster's progress should be scheduled at least twice a year.

4. Is there a wide variety of toys designed to appeal to your child's age group? Infants like colorful mobiles, mirrors, and plastic boxes. Toddlers' short attention spans demand lots of books, puzzles, and modeling clay. With preschoolers, look for musical instruments, games, and costumes as well as slides and swings.

5. Does the center offer a reasonable mix of organized and free play? Group activities often make children "people weary," explains Gwen Morgan. If youngsters are wandering about aimlessly, however, you have to wonder how attentive the teachers are.

6. What kind of food is served? If your child has been raised on homemade soups and whole-grain breads, try to find a center that provides equally healthy fare. Make sure kids receive ample servings and can ask for second helpings.

7. Are teachers conscientious about sanitary conditions? Kids under age three in day care contract about 30 percent more diarrhea and other gastrointestinal ailments than those who stay at home, warns Larry Pickering, a professor of pediatrics at the University of Texas Medical School in Houston. Note whether employees wash their hands before and after changing diapers and feeding babies. Bottles and toothbrushes should have name tags to reduce mix-ups.

8. Have arrangements been made for medical emergencies? A nurse or doctor should be available nearby, if not on call. Parents should be

informed promptly about outbreaks of chicken pox, measles, and other highly contagious diseases.

9. Are the names of parents freely given as references? Get in touch with several and ask them some of these questions. Also double-check the center's reputation with your local department of health and social services.

Once you have settled on a day-care center, continue to monitor it for changes in programs or personnel. Your child's enthusiasm may be your best indicator. If the little dear sideswipes you as you try to kiss him or her goodbye at the center's door, chances are you made the right choice.

17

BUYING YOUR FIRST HOUSE

If young Americans have one thing going for them in their search for shelter, it is choice. The combination of new types of cost-efficient housing and flexible methods of financing has created more opportunities than ever to get your foot in the door of your own home.

There is no denying that being a homeowner puts a considerable strain on family finances. Prices went through the roof during the 1970s and early 1980s, and after they leveled off, mortgage rates still hovered between 8 and 12 percent. First-time buyers also had to hurdle a new obstacle. A rise in mortgage delinquencies caused lenders to impose stiffer qualifications on borrowers. Where once banks approved the applications of families who would have to devote as much as 35 percent of their after-tax income to housing, that limit was lowered to 25 percent.

Undaunted, most Americans still aspire to living in a single-family detached house with lots of space and a private yard. Higher prices, slower appreciation, and impossible mortgage payments may prevent you from making this dream come true the first time around. But you need not be fenced out altogether. Your options include condominiums, existing or new houses, and mass-produced dwellings. By choosing carefully, you can not only take pleasure in your home while you live in it but also parlay it into a more substantial spread later on.

Condominiums

Condos can be apartment buildings, attached townhouses, or clusters of detached houses in the heart of downtown or out in the suburbs. Owners have title to their own living space and share possession of such common areas as lawns, swimming pools, and tennis courts. Buyers have all the advantages of traditional home ownership. They qualify for mortgages just as easily as buyers of single-family houses; they are entitled to the same tax deductions; and they can sell their units at will. In New York City and other places where cooperative ownership is more the custom than condominiums, buyers own shares in the building corporation. They still can get mortgage financing and tax deductions, but the co-op's board of directors can restrict a member's right to rent out the apartment. If you decide to sell your digs, the directors can veto your choice of buyer.

Condos are somewhat less expensive than single-family houses but are not likely to appreciate as much. Overbuilding has glutted the condo market in some cities and has caused high vacancy rates. Moreover, as mortgage rates have eased, buyers have returned to their first love, the single-family house.

If you want architectural character for your limited money, though, a condo may win you over. The best projects have stylistic touches that often are missing from tract houses. Bay windows, balconies, and vaulted ceilings may strike you as a fair trade-off for getting less space. The median-sized condominium measures about 1,150 square feet, compared with 1,600 feet in the average new single-family house. For condo lovers, minimal upkeep chores are valuable compensation. You leave the grass cutting, snow shoveling, repairs, and other nuisances to the maintenance crew. The management does not do this out of gratitude, of course. You pay a monthly maintenance fee, and it is likely to be higher than the monthly expenses of running a house. This fee includes the cost of recreational facilities whether you use them or not and the price of any embellishments approved by the condo board.

Existing Houses

If a house is a machine for living, as the French architect Le Corbusier once said, nowhere is the machinery as fine-tuned as in a dwelling with a past. After standing for 10 years it has probably settled on its foundations about as much as it is going to. If no major cracks have appeared in the plaster and concrete, you can be fairly certain that none is likely to develop. The neighborhood probably has settled, too. The condition of other houses on the block testifies to how well the owners are caring for them. As real estate industry analyst Sanford Goodkin of La Jolla, California, says, "You can observe an older house in action."

The quality of materials and construction in many houses built before World War II surpasses that of new dwellings. You will find thicker walls, solid doors, hardwood floors, elaborate moldings, higher ceilings, and often larger rooms.

Houses that have been sold at least once before tend to be less expensive than new homes. The differential, using houses of median price for comparison, is about 10 percent. There are other financial advantages to older houses. You may be able to assume the seller's low-interest mortgage, and you can estimate the cost of running the house by asking the owner to show you his bills for heating, electricity, and water. Property taxes in established neighborhoods, where streets, public utilities, schools, and sewers are in place, may be lower than in new developments where everything must be built from scratch.

However, you can't automatically assume that older is better. The electric wiring may be inadequate for the heavy load of contemporary appliances. Vintage cast-iron water pipes may be sclerotic, and drains may be clogged. The heating system may be archaic and inefficient; repairing it will be expensive but essential for comfortable living. Skimpily insulated exterior walls and attic floors may multiply heating and cooling costs.

New Houses

In recent years, new houses have gone up in value twice as fast as old ones, doubtless because everyone has become energy-conscious. It is widely known that local building codes now require the installation of efficient heating and electrical equipment, adequate insulation, and weatherstripping. You also get the latest fixtures and appliances.

A trend to bigger houses has resumed. The median-sized new single-family dwelling gained 85 square feet of living space between 1982 and 1984 — the area of one small room. Victor Mirontschuk, an architect in Houston, observes, "The problem with some of these small homes is that no sooner do people move in than they outgrow them." Builders who continue to streamline their houses are compensating for the shrinkage by creating the illusion of spaciousness. Walls have come tumbling down to create so-called great rooms, which combine the living room, dining room, family room, and even part of the kitchen into one multipurpose open area. "What we've taken away in square footage we've given back in design," asserts Barry Berkus, a prominent architect in Santa Barbara, California.

The biggest drawback to buying a new house is that you are not sure how well everything will work. You don't know whether the house will settle or how expensive it will be to maintain. One way to protect yourself is to look for signs of high-quality construction. For example, double-glazed windows with a sealed air space between the two panes allow less heat to escape and less noise to enter your house. The carpentry should be neatly finished; uneven wall surfaces and ill-fitting moldings are signs of shoddy workmanship. A builder warranty against structural flaws is another sign that the house is well constructed. About 25 percent of new houses come with warranties.

Factory-Built Houses

Was it built in a factory or on a foundation? These days only your contractor knows. Once assembled, factory-built houses look exactly like those built from the ground up on the site and appreciate just as fast — or slowly. One-third of all new housing units are partially or totally fabricated in factories and assembled on their lots. The advantages are obvious: lower cost and speedier construction.

Industrialized homes, as factory-built dwellings are also called, are usually sold through builder-dealers. But you can hire your own contractor or put the dwelling together yourself. There are four categories of industrialized housing: precut, prefabricated, modular, and mobile homes.

Precut houses are built with two-by-fours and other basic components sawn and marked in a factory. The pieces of a prefabricated house are cut and assembled into wall, roof, or floor panels at the factory. Panels can be ordered with only studs, wallboard, and insulation, or builders can get them complete with wallpaper hung and windows installed. Depending on how nearly finished the panels are, on-site construction takes two weeks to two months, as opposed to three months or more for a precut house and six months or more stick by stick. Modular houses arrive on the site as preassembled rooms or groups of rooms. They are clamped together or piled up to make the house. Once shipped to the site, a modular house can go up in a week, but you cannot do much about modifying the design.

The more work that can be done on a house at the factory, the less expensive it should be in the end. The savings may be illusory, however, or at least hard to pin down. Instead, hope for higher quality. "Workmen don't cut corners building modular homes at the factory," says builder Tim German of AMCOL Development Group in Annandale, Virginia. "They never have to rush the job because the weather is bad."

Cathedral ceilings, pitched roofs, cedar siding, and bay windows have enhanced the look of permanency in mobile homes, which now conform to a national building code set by the Department of Housing and Urban Development. As a result, buyers can qualify for conventional 30-year mortgages instead of having to finance their purchases with installment loans. The average price of a mobile home in the mid-1980s was only $21,500. Alas, though, these dwellings are not likely to appreciate as fast as other factory-built houses; their reputation still suffers from decades of shabby construction and careless trailer-park development.

The Down Payment

The biggest hurdle facing you as a first-time home buyer is not finding a house you can afford. It is finding the cash for a down payment on a house you can just barely afford. Lenders prefer lots of cash up front; your substantial investment in the house reassures them that you will not default on your mortgage. But you shouldn't automatically assume you have to raise 10 or 20 percent of the purchase price in cash. It may be possible to buy a home with little or nothing down. (Mortgages are discussed in detail in Chapter 51.)

The easiest terms come with a mortgage backed by the Veterans Administration. If you have served in the armed forces, you may be able to get a loan for 100 percent of the cost of the house. You can apply for a VA–guaranteed loan at banks, mortgage companies, and some savings and loans just as you would for any other type of mortgage. You must borrow the money at a fixed rate set by the VA. When that is below the market rate, however, a lender will demand points. Each point amounts to 1 percent of your mortgage. That is a big piece of change paid up front, when you take title to your house. In a VA loan, the buyer is allowed to pay just one point. The seller has to pick up any additional front-end interest, and you should assume that it has been added to the purchase price of the house.

You don't have to be a veteran to qualify for the Federal Housing Administration's mortgage program. An FHA-insured loan, which you apply for through a conventional lender, can cover up to 95 percent of the entire outlay for a house — including closing costs such as points, title insurance, mortgage taxes, and legal fees. The law sets a limit, however, on the size of an FHA mortgage. In most cities you can't borrow more than $67,500.

You can also get a 95 percent loan without government backing. Some lenders will write you a mortgage for that much as long as your income is high enough to meet the payments and your credit rating is impeccable. Your closing costs would be higher than for comparable VA and FHA loans, which can include those expenses and mortgage insurance as part of the mortgage principal. Thus you might have to lay down an additional wad of cash that could equal or even slightly exceed the down payment.

When you are making a minimal down payment, the lender will comb your credit history for the slightest blemish. "A good record on auto and student loans is important," says Jane Greenstein, president of Mortgage Clearing House Inc., an advisory service for borrowers in New Hyde Park, New York. "If you are constantly late with your payments, that looks bad. If you haven't begun repaying a student loan that's due, you will give a lender the idea you're trying to stiff the government."

Once you know that you can qualify for 95 percent financing, you can start hunting for the cash to cover both the down payment and closing costs. One possible source is your Individual Retirement Account. You will pay ordinary income tax on the money you withdraw early from an IRA or other previously untaxed retirement plan, plus a 10 percent penalty, but those costs may be outweighed by the tax deductions the house will generate. You can usually borrow as much as $50,000 against a profit-sharing or salary-reduction account where you work. The 1986 tax law requires your employer to charge you the going interest rate for commercial mortgages. But loans to help finance the purchase of your primary residence can be repaid in small installments spread over many years.

The advantage of borrowing your down payment from a corporate plan is that the loan probably will not show up on any credit bureau report because you are borrowing your own money. Lenders look at the size of your long-term debts as reported by a credit bureau to figure out whether you can afford the mortgage you want. They will usually refuse your application if more than 36 percent of your after-tax income is going to debt repayments, including the mortgage.

After you have exhausted your own resources, you will probably turn to your family for help; most first-time buyers do. Even if you have every intention of repaying your folks, you may have to give the lender a letter from the family stating that the money is a gift, not a loan. Rather than ask your parents for the down payment, you could suggest that they become co-owners of the house in return for making the down payment and paying some or all of the closing costs. That way you could buy a more expensive place than you could afford on your own. As co-owners, your parents could take annual tax deductions for property taxes in proportion to their stake in the house.

If you are contemplating an arrangement in which your parents take sole title to the property, you may want to consider hiring a firm to help you with the paperwork. These deals are complex because your parents become your landlords. If they expect to claim tax write-offs for depreciation and other expenses of property ownership, they will have to charge you rent at what the IRS will accept as a fair market rate. And they won't be able to claim tax losses unless they conform to tricky new rules best interpreted by a certified public accountant.

In yet another way around a large down payment, the seller of the house you want to buy can lend you the up-front money. You are most likely to get his help when interest rates are rising and a seller is quite desperate to unload his property. But it never hurts to ask, according to Andrew C. Levine, a New York City real estate lawyer. ''If the seller doesn't need the cash right away, you may be able to negotiate terms that are better for both of you,'' Levine says.

You may be able to negotiate a noncash down payment with the seller. If the house is dilapidated, offer to make needed repairs or improvements in lieu of at least part of the cash. If you later default on your loan, the former owner can foreclose on a property that is more salable than it was before you bought it. Consultant Donna Milling of Real Estate Investors Inc. in Thornton, Pennsylvania, recommends that you talk with the seller at length to find out what his real needs are. ''All sellers think they must have cash, but some would rather just be rid of the property,'' she says.

18

PAYING FOR BABY'S B.A.

Newlyweds often bring to their marriages a liability the likes of which they swear not to pass on to their children — the burden of unpaid student loans used to finance tuition their parents couldn't handle. But as the years pass, young families learn that vowing to finance a child's education is one thing, while keeping the vow is quite another. College costs have been ratcheting far beyond most families' ability to pay. No wonder that Stephen Leightman, national sales manager of Prudential-Bache Securities, can persuasively say, "Parents of a six-month-old who haven't started saving for college yet are already six months late."

In laying long-term plans for financing college, you should establish a realistic goal. Find out the current cost of tuition, room, board, personal expenses, fees, and transportation at a target college, then pick the rate at which you think those bills will swell in the years ahead and compute the projected total outlay for educating your child. Such projections, illustrated in Figure 6, look staggering. But they are much less intimidating if you reduce them to the annual amounts you would have to put away, starting now, to have the cash on hand when it is needed.

For several years in the 1970s and 1980s, college costs grew far faster than general inflation, and most educators believe the pace won't slow much. The best estimate for the years through 2000 is for annual increases in the 4.5 to 6 percent range. In 1986, the average tab for one year at a public college was about $5,700. Assuming costs rise 5 percent a year, a four-year education at such a school for a child born in 1987 would total $65,500. At an average private university, the bill would be

Figure 6. How Much to Save Each Year for a College Education

Parents who start saving and investing now for a child's college expenses have to grapple with three unknowables in deciding how much money to put away each year: How expensive a school will your child attend? How much will the school's tuition, room, and board have risen by the time your child enters the senior year? What rate of return will your investments earn until then?

The annual savings goals below are based on projected annual costs in 1987 for three types of institutions: the average state or community college, shown in the table as the average public college; the average private college; and an Ivy League school, representing the most expensive type of institution. Estimates of future costs assume that expenses will rise 5 percent a year indefinitely.

The amounts shown are for children born in several different years, but all entering college at age 18. The rate of return used to reduce future costs to present values is 8 percent, a reasonable return to expect from high-yield tax-exempt bond funds in the mid-1980s.

	Average public college	*Average private college*	*Ivy League college*
Annual cost starting in 1987	$6,300	$10,700	$16,800
Four-year cost starting in			
1987 (child born in 1969)	27,000	46,000	72,500
1990 (child born in 1972)	31,500	53,500	84,000
1995 (child born in 1977)	40,000	68,000	107,000
2000 (child born in 1982)	51,000	87,000	136,500
2005 (child born in 1987)	65,500	111,000	174,500
Annual savings needed for a child starting college in			
1990	$3,950	$6,709	$10,533
1995	2,370	4,026	6,321
2000	1,701	2,889	4,536
2005	1,321	2,244	3,523

Source: R. Philip Giles, Ph.D., statistical consultant.

around $111,000. In the top reaches of academe — the Ivy League, for example — you would have to amass $174,500.

Even as gargantuan a sum as that can be domesticated by breaking it down into annual payments starting at a baby's birth and continuing for the next 21 years, by which time the child would normally be entering the last year of college. If you had the baby in 1987 and immediately began funding an investment that yielded 8 percent after taxes, the yearly payments for an Ivy League education would come to a little over $3,500 a year.

Until the tax code was changed in 1986, your children could help you put them through college starting the day they were born. By transferring capital from your name to theirs, whether as outright gifts or by means of a temporary device such as a short-term trust called a Clifford trust, you could make them the payers of income tax on the investment earnings. Since their tax rate on this comparatively low income lingered around 11 percent, it took only a 9.8 percent investment return to net 8 percent after taxes, whereas earnings on investments in your name might be subject to taxes as high as 50 percent.

The short-term trust can no longer be used, however, to transfer investment earnings to a child's lower tax bracket until the child reaches the age of 14. The only way you can shift any tax at all to a child's lower bracket is by giving the child money outright and investing it for him. Even then, only the first $1,000 of earnings enjoys tax breaks. Until children are 14, their first $500 of investment income is tax-free, the next $500 is taxed at the child's rate, and any additional returns are taxed at the parents' rate. This rule applies whether the invested funds are a gift from parents or come from grandparents, other relatives, or friends.

Still, it takes an investment of between $10,000 and $20,000 to generate the $1,000 that a young child can earn before using up the tax advantage of income shifting, and you can shelter that much for each child. Furthermore, the tax brackets established in the 1986 tax code narrow the gap between the top and bottom rates. Instead of ranging from 11 to 50 percent, after 1987 the gulf becomes the difference between 15 and 33 percent, with most parents who file joint returns or head-of-household returns as single parents taxed no more than 28 percent. (For a full description of the new tax structure, see Chapter 43.)

To take advantage of the remaining tax breaks for children, parents and others must make direct gifts to their offspring or put the money in custodial accounts conforming to the Uniform Gifts to Minors Act. This device allows you to give funds to your child while keeping control in the hands of an adult custodian. Most banks, mutual funds, and brokerages can supply the needed forms at little or no cost. Usually the only requirements are a listing of the names of the donor, the custodian, and the child, along with his or her Social Security number (which you now must apply for at your local Social Security Administration office anyway when a child is five years old to claim him or her as an exemption).

The custodial role can be filled by a family member, the child's legal guardian, or any trusted adult. Donors should avoid acting as custodians themselves. If they were to die before the youngster came of age, amounts they gave the child might be returned to their estates and subjected to death taxes.

You can put as much as $10,000 a year per parent into a Uniform Gifts to Minors Act account for each child without running afoul of the gift tax. But such gifts could disappoint the giver's intentions. One drawback to Uniform Gifts to Minors accounts is that at the age of majority — 18, 19, or 21, depending on the state you live in — a child can withdraw the money without the custodian's permission and spend it freely. This leads Eileen M. Sharkey, a financial planner in Denver, to observe, ''Junior may decide to follow a guru to the ends of the earth in search of the meaning of life — and take his college savings with him.''

If you have already established a Clifford trust or a variant of it called a spousal remainder trust, its tax treatment will depend on when you set it up. Income from trusts created before March 1, 1986, will be taxed at your rate until your child reaches age 14. Then his tax rate will apply. But if you set up the trust after that date, the income will be taxed at your rate even after your child hits 14. You probably won't be able to dissolve an existing trust, so if yours predates March 1, 1986, load it with tax-deferred investments such as U.S. Savings Bonds. If it is newer than that, your best option is tax-exempt municipal bonds.

Happily, you can still shoot for an 8 percent after-tax return in tax-exempts. In the first half of the 1980s they were paying even more than that. For convenience and the safety of diversification, use a tax-free-bond mutual fund, where you can add as little as $100 at a time to your investment. The ''Fund Watch'' department of *Money* magazine reports on tax-free-fund yields every month. In early 1987, for instance, two funds paying about 8 percent or above were Venture Muni Plus (800-545-2098) and Value Line Tax Exempt High Yield (800-223-0818).

The greatest risk in municipal bonds or any other fixed-income security is a drop in its market value because of a rise in prevailing interest rates. One way to get around this problem is to buy a zero-coupon municipal bond, which carries a fixed return and maturity date. As with other zero-coupon securities, you pay a fraction of what you will receive when it matures, and the difference between the two prices is considered interest. You can buy zero-coupon municipal bonds through stockbrokers.

One traditional piece of advice you probably won't want to follow is to put all of your college money into long-term bonds timed to mature with your child. The wisdom was that you won't need the money sooner, so you can take advantage of the higher rates that long-term investments usually command. But the volatility of interest rates in recent years has called that approach into question. Any interest rate you nail down now could seem woefully small when tuition bills start turning up. Clair Longden, a financial planner in the New York City office of the Butcher

& Singer brokerage firm, tells parents to look toward a much shorter investing horizon. Her advice is to buy bank certificates of deposit and interest-bearing bonds with maturities of no more than eight years. "Looking ahead, you don't know which years are going to be the high-inflation ones," Longden points out. "But wherever rates are, you will get part of your money back each year and can reinvest it at prevailing levels."

There are other ways to postpone taxes while you build savings in a young child's account. One is to buy supersafe Series EE U.S. Savings Bonds. In 1987 they were paying 6 percent annually if held for a minimum of five years. You can usually leave savings bonds uncashed beyond their maturity date and let the interest keep piling up. It won't be taxed until you cash in the bonds.

Still another device is a universal life insurance policy (see Chapter 57). The policy's cash value will increase over the years with no taxes due on the earnings until withdrawal. Eventually you could borrow at low rates from the policy to pay school bills without owing any tax at all. For example, you might pay annual premiums of $5,100 for a $250,000 policy that netted, in 1987, 7.25 percent a year. If that rate held up, after 18 years a child born in 1987 would have as much as $178,000 to borrow against for college at rates lower than those offered by banks.

19

AN EDUCATED PARENTS' GUIDE TO COLLEGE FINANCIAL AID

While some families get a proper fix on college costs before their children are out of diapers, most Americans are going to need some kind of financial aid: grants, scholarships, loans, or student part-time jobs. Relief in one or more of those categories sometimes is available in fuller measure than you might expect. Don't assume you are too well-off to qualify. Even people with incomes exceeding $70,000 get caught in the budget supersqueeze.

Don and Sandy Neu, of Bellevue, Washington, thought they had an airtight plan for their three sons' educations. The parents would pay for room and board while the sons paid for tuition. Then, in 1980, the Neus' middle son, Brian, precociously wrecked the plan by getting himself skipped two grades, from eighth to tenth. That brought him academically even with his brother Ken. It did not take advanced calculus to figure out that Brian's accelerated schooling would overtake the family's education fund. Yet the Neus were coping five years later, with Brian and Ken in college. Though the parents had a combined income of $74,000, Brian was paying part of his $8,080 tuition at Macalester College in St. Paul, Minnesota, with student loans and scholarships.

About half of all undergraduates receive financial aid. Despite a 19 percent pinch in federal aid to students during the Reagan Administration, the average amount of assistance per recipient in 1985 was around $2,000 at public colleges and $4,000 at private schools, according to the American Council on Education in Washington, D. C., which represents 1,500 colleges. Of public-college students receiving aid, 10 percent were from families earning more than $30,000 a year. At private colleges — where costs are typically double those at public institutions — the figure was 27 percent. If you have more than one undergraduate to support at the same time, your income might run as high as $80,000 or so before you are expected to pay for everything.

So generous and widespread is aid, in fact, that it can give your youngster a chance at a college that may seem too expensive to you. Indeed, the costlier schools are often the best equipped to provide support. Bowdoin, the University of Chicago, and other schools costing more than $10,000 a year regularly give grants of $5,000 and up to families with $60,000 incomes and more than one child in comparably priced colleges. But aid, on average, covers only about half of a family's total college bill. And whether or not you qualify, you will probably have to write a hefty check to the registrar at the beginning of each semester. Even then, you usually can obtain help in the form of loans at below-market interest rates from the government, the colleges, and private lenders.

Nearly half of the average award is so-called gift aid: grants or scholarships that can amount to a sizable discount on a college's sticker price. Most gift aid has nothing to do with your youngster's academic merit. It is your family's financial need that counts. Aid other than scholarships or grants is known as self-help, which consists of part-time jobs and loans at below-market rates.

Most aid originates with the government and is intended, of course, for students whose families earn too little to cover college costs. The federal aid pool flows mainly through six programs. Three give money to the colleges, which pass it on to the students. These college-based programs, as they are called, are Supplementary Educational Opportunity Grants ranging from $200 to $2,000 a year; College Work-Study in the form of part-time employment, usually paying a student $600 to $1,000 a year; and Carl D. Perkins National Direct Student Loans worth up to $9,000 over four undergraduate years at a bargain rate of 5 percent.

The other federal programs require you to apply on your own to the government or a lender. Pell Grants range from $200 to $2,100 a year. Guaranteed Student Loans (GSL) provide up to $13,250 over four years at 8 percent interest for four years, starting six months after graduation, and 10 percent after that. Supplemental Loans for Students and Loans for Parents (formerly called Parent Loans for Undergraduate Students, or PLUS) are worth up to $4,000 a year at a variable interest rate pegged

3.75 percentage points above the one-year Treasury bill rate, with a maximum, or cap, of 12 percent.*

Next to Uncle Sam, the biggest aid providers are the colleges, which supplement the federal programs with $3 billion of their own funds. It is often from the colleges that middle-income families receive the most help. The states contribute an additional $1 billion. And $700 million comes from corporations, communities, labor unions, and other outside sponsors whose generosity may include grants, scholarships, and interest-free loans. Wherever else you search, your principal source of extra money will be the college of your choice.

Applying for Aid

The first step toward getting your share of benefits is to learn the basics of the financial aid system that almost all colleges use. This system subjects your finances to a standardized process called need analysis. After January 1 in the year your child heads for college, you fill out a need-analysis form that records your family size, income, assets, household expenses, and other information. The two big private need-analysis services are sponsored by the College Scholarship Service and the American College Testing Program. Using an elaborate formula, both arrive at virtually the same reckoning of a pivotal figure known as your family contribution — the amount of money the custodians of the system believe you can "reasonably" afford to pay out of pocket for a year of college.

Chances are you won't find the family contribution all that reasonable, because the need-analysis formula is designed for a family with no children in college and frugal spending habits. If your standard of living is higher than the low-budget model, the formula underrepresents your costs and raises your family contribution to an amount that may startle you.

Say you are a family of four with one child in college; the sole breadwinner, age 48, earns $40,000 before taxes; and the family's assets — home equity, savings, and investments, for example — are $40,000. Your family contribution in 1986, by the need-analysis formula, would have been a stiff $5,250. (When both children are in college, the amount is halved.)

Your $5,250 contribution would have remained roughly the same at most colleges where your youngster applied, though each would have

*A comprehensive booklet about college-student subsidies, *Free to All,* can be obtained by writing to The Student Guide: Federal Financial Aid Program, P.O. Box 84, Washington, D.C. 20044.

adjusted the figure after taking a look at your finances. At a school whose annual cost — tuition, room, board, personal expenses, and travel — exceeded $5,250, the financial aid system said you had need. Therefore, you were eligible for aid, which aims to fill the gap between your family contribution and the total cost of the college of your choice. Many colleges have a policy of meeting most or all of a student's needs.

The Aid Package

In March of the college entrance year, if you are like hundreds of thousands of other parents of high school seniors, you are scanning the mail for the results of the need-analysis form you filled out earlier in the year — your own family-contribution computation. Those results are also on the way to the various schools where your child applied the previous fall. Now each school's financial aid officer will assemble an aid package custom-tailored to your youngster.

Most colleges have their own method of "packaging" applicants, as the financial aid officers say. Generally, your child's achievements will affect the amount and kind of aid in your package. The University of Southern California, for example, usually meets the first $1,000 or so of any applicant's need with gift aid — grants from the government or the university. The next $1,500 comes from self-help — loans and jobs. The actual proportion of gift aid and self-help may depend on how eager USC is to land your offspring.

Such favoritism in the aid process may make you wonder whether your need, or lack of it, can affect your child's chances of admission. Ideally, admission is "need-blind" — made without regard to your financial status. At almost all colleges, the ideal is still standard practice. Once the admissions office makes its choices, however, the financial aid office may try to recruit promising students by sweetening their aid packages.

In shopping for schools, then, you would be wise to know as much as possible about your financial situation — and theirs. You can get a rough idea of your family contribution by filling out a need-analysis form in any of several financial aid guidebooks, such as Robert and Anna Leider's *Don't Miss Out: The Ambitious Student's Guide to Financial Aid* (Octameron Press, P.O. Box 3437, Alexandria, Virginia 22302; $4.75). This pamphlet, among others in the Leiders' series on aid, contains sample forms, worksheets, and tables that can help guide you through the maze of options.

For information about aid at the various schools on your child's wish list, the quickest reference may be *The College Money Handbook*

(Peterson's Guides, $14.95). It gives financing profiles of 1,700 colleges. An important entry to compare is the average percentage of need met at each school.

The first application for aid is only the beginning of an annual rite. Between a student's senior year of high school and last semester of college, there should be ample opportunity to lighten the family's debt load. Here are three tactics to improve your child's aid package.

1. Pick a school that considers your kid a catch. A brain, an athlete, or an otherwise exceptional student probably will get more gift aid and less self-help.

2. Substitute a job for a loan. Colleges, concerned about student debt, are expanding work-assistance programs. At Cornell, alumni have raised $7 million to supplement student wages for part-time work during the school year and full-time work in the summer. Some 1,000 schools offer cooperative education, which alternates semesters of school work and employment in an off-campus job related to the student's field of study. For 200,000 collegians a year, the experience and the chance to earn a substantial part of their college bills seem worth the longer wait for a degree.

3. Tap new state-aid resources. In response to federal budget cuts in the 1980s, many states expanded their aid programs. Among the most generous are Alaska, Illinois, Maryland, Massachusetts, Minnesota, New York, and Pennsylvania. Students apply for state loans at their college or a state education agency. For many states, the fund-raising tool of choice has been the sale of tax-exempt bonds. Sometimes such bonds are floated on behalf of colleges in the state. A 1982 New Hampshire issue for Dartmouth yielded a $13 million war chest from which needy students could borrow a four-year total of $7,000 at 10.9 percent. Wesleyan University, in Connecticut, uses bond revenues to lend parents up to $5,000 a year at 9.5 percent. A Massachusetts bond-financed program is providing loan funds for as much as 75 percent of total college costs at 11.5 percent a year at Boston College, Wellesley, and some 25 other participating schools.

Often state programs are limited to in-state colleges. But if you are from New Hampshire or Pennsylvania, your children can take a state loan with them wherever they enroll. The Pennsylvania Family Partnership Loan, for instance, is designed mainly for families earning $30,000-plus. The loan maximum is $5,500 a year at 8 percent for students and 12 percent for parents. The amount is divided equally between parents and offspring, who pay their respective rates. Check with your state education agency.

Where the Loans Are

The final component in a college aid package often takes the form of a federally financed low-interest Guaranteed Student Loan, for which your youngster can apply only after choosing a school. (The terms of this and other education loans are compared in Figure 7.) A Guaranteed Student Loan obliges the student to borrow from outside lenders such as banks or credit unions. Because Uncle Sam gives them an interest subsidy and an extra allowance, lenders aren't scarce. Checks go directly to the school. Repayments, spread over 10 years, don't begin until six months after completion of studies.

If a student's family income is more than $30,000, his family must pass a remaining-needs test to qualify for a Guaranteed Student Loan. The test calls for the school to add your family contribution — the amount you supposedly can afford — to the assistance in your financial aid package, then subtract the sum of the two from your total college cost. The difference is the amount of money the student can borrow. In practice, many aid officers limit the amount of other aid in your package to enable your offspring to get the maximum Guaranteed Student Loan.

Once a student's aid package has been put together, the parents' next problem is paying their portion of the college bill. Most of the cheaper financing options are shown in Figure 7. The government-sponsored Supplemental Loans for Students and Loans for Parents require no test of need. Payments start 60 days after the loan has been consummated. One problem: lenders are sometimes hard to find because of the low interest subsidy Uncle Sam gives them. Ask the college or state higher-education authority for help in finding a bank.

In the unsubsidized loan market, pension plans, credit unions, and employers sometimes extend credit to parents at below-market rates. But the best deal under the 1986 tax overhaul is a home-equity loan. The interest is pegged one to two points above the prime rate, which probably compares favorably with state-subsidized loans. More important, the interest on home-equity loans used for education is fully tax-deductible unless you are taking too much advantage of other loopholes (see Chapter 43). The deduction is not allowed for any other type of education loan. You can borrow against your home at banks and stock brokerages (see Chapter 44).

Banks rarely make other types of unsubsidized college loans. However, parents of students needy or otherwise at the University of Rochester (New York) may borrow up to $5,000 a year at below-market interest from the Chase Lincoln First Bank. The university guarantees the

Figure 7. A Crib Sheet for Collegiate Credit Seekers

Here is a sampling of the best college loans. Unless otherwise specified, the parents are the borrowers. Likeliest to vary are the loan rates, which may be pegged to such factors as the prime rate. "Need" means that you can get the loan only if you qualify for financial aid.

	Interest rate	*Term (years)*	*Maximum per year*	*Restrictions*
FEDERAL LOANS				
Carl D. Perkins National Direct Student Loan	5%	10	$2,250	Students get the loans but their families must prove need; generally reserved for families with incomes of less than $30,000
Guaranteed Student Loan (GSL)	8% for the first four years; then 10%	10	$2,625 in each of the first two years, $4,000 in years 3 and 4	Students get the loans but their families must prove need; families with incomes over $30,000 must pass an additional test
Supplemental Loan for Students and Loans for Parents	3.75 points above 1-year Treasury bill rate; 12% cap	10	$4,000	Open to all
STATE LOANS				
Connecticut Family Education Loan	10.98%	11.75	$10,000	Student must attend a Connecticut school
Iowa Higher Education Loan	11%	10	$5,000	Student must attend an Iowa private school
Louisiana Association of Independent Colleges and Universities Loan	10.8%	12	$4,000	Student must attend one of six participating private schools

	Interest rate	*Term (years)*	*Maximum per year*	*Restrictions*
New Hampshire Alternative Loan for Parents and Students	12.6%	12	$15,000	Student must be a New Hampshire resident or attend a New Hampshire school
COLLEGE LOANS				
Emory University Student-Parent Loan	7%	10	$9,250	Student must be ineligible for scholarships
Stanford University Parent Loan	9.25%	8	$15,908	Family must have income over $25,000
Northwestern University Parent-Student Loan	8.25%	6	$11,000	Family must have income under $100,000
COMMERCIAL LOANS				
Knight Insurance Agency Extended Repayment Plan	10.25%	10	100% of college costs	None
Tuition Plan	15.95%	10	100% of college costs	Borrower must be a resident of one of 38 participating states
Mellon Bank Edu-Check Program	12.4%	8	100% of college costs	None

loans. One commercial firm in Figure 7 specializes in college financing at fairly low rates: the Knight Insurance Agency at 53 Beacon Street, Boston, Massachusetts 02108. It accepts applications by mail.

Many colleges allow you to pay off a year's bill by the month, but as a rule installment privileges require that you start payment several months before the term begins. At the opposite extreme, you can hedge against tuition increases at about 25 colleges by paying in advance for all four years at the going freshman price. For example, at the University of Detroit, a private institution, the four-year cost for a student who enters in 1990 is expected to be $35,618. But if his family paid the full four-year tuition in 1986, the tab would have been only $17,836. The further the child is from college age, the deeper the discount. The cost at birth for a child born in 1986 and therefore likely to start college in 2004 was $6,412, compared with a projected $91,841 if payments began at enrollment. The difference amounts to a 22 percent rate of return on the advance payment.

Such deals have pitfalls, though. The most serious hazard is that your child might never attend the school you have invested in. Colleges that give these discounts can do so not only because they invest the advance payment but also because they assume that some of the kids won't enroll. When that happens, the college keeps the earnings on the money and returns only the original payment.

Finding Scholarships

The race for scholarships is not always won by the best and the brightest, the neediest, or even the sweatiest. Every year thousands of students pick up outside scholarships — those sponsored by a variety of noncollege organizations — that together are worth some $100 million a year before taxes. Some scholarship money has to be reported to the IRS as income under the new tax law. The grants excluded from taxation are those covering tuition, fees, books, and equipment; the ones taxed are those covering room, board, or other living expenses.

The search for scholarships should begin at home, or at least near it. Your best hope may be your family's professional or business connections. Some 420 companies, unions, and trade organizations sponsor National Merit Scholarships worth up to $2,000 a year over four years of college. Many other organizations have their own scholarships. For labor union programs, consult the listings in the *AFL-CIO Guide to Union Sponsored Scholarships, Awards and Student Financial Aid,* which high school guidance counselors may have on hand.

Guidance counselors also should be your best sources of information on other local scholarship programs. If you are a veteran, inquire at the local American Legion post about awards available for your children. A comprehensive reference to the thousands of military-service–related scholarships is the legion's *Need a Lift?* The legion itself has 7,500 programs that annually give away more than $1 million worth of awards from $25 to $8,000.

Be prepared to seek out money from local civic, religious, and fraternal groups, especially those to which your family belongs. The Knights of Columbus, for example, has 12 four-year scholarships, each worth $1,000 a year for children of members. Even a nonmember's child is eligible for scholarships from the Elks ($1,500 on average) and the Soroptimists ($1,250).

Though a student's chances are better in local scholarship competitions, the nationals tend to have the richest prizes and the most prestige. The Army, Navy, and Air Force Reserve Officer Training Corps pay full tuition, fees, and $100 a month at any of 600 participating colleges. Each year at least 46,000 students apply for 10,665 places. The winner's obligation usually is to put in four years of postcollege military service plus two or more years in the reserves.

The lure of riches has spawned dozens of computerized search services around the country. They charge up to $60 for a list of scholarships selected to jibe with the customer's qualifications. But comparable information is free at high school guidance offices and public libraries. Of the several thick guidebooks charting the scholarship territory, the most useful is Oreon Keeslar's frequently updated *Financial Aids for Higher Education* (William C. Brown, 2460 Kerper Boulevard, P.O. Box 539, Dubuque, Iowa 52001; $32.95). To help narrow a search among the 3,200 entries, Keeslar includes a "program finder," which matches a student's background, talent, or interests with appropriate awards.

Choosy benefactors sometimes bequeath special-restriction scholarships to colleges. The student in your family who happens to have the characteristics to match the criteria may be in for a small bonanza. At Harvard, needy collegians named Murphy may be eligible for aid from the William S. Murphy fund.

20

HOW TO BECOME FINANCIALLY INDEPENDENT

Independence means having the wherewithal to say to yourself, "If I wanted to, I could quit what I'm doing today and live comfortably for the rest of my life." Or in the words of Dale E. McClelland, a Flint, Michigan, financial planner, "You have enough money working for you so you don't have to." Millions of Americans can reach that enviable position a decade or more before normal retirement age. It may take some luck, but what you mainly need is self-discipline and the flexibility to adjust course as the years unfold.

Financial independence is as much a state of mind as of pocketbook. Nobody this side of Robinson Crusoe can claim absolute self-sufficiency. If you are like most people, you won't fancy yourself to have achieved it until you can reasonably expect to pay off the mortgage, put the kids through school, see to your parents' well-being, provide for your own retirement, and earmark funds for future investments. But one fine day you might just review your net worth and find these things within your reach. At that moment the choices are yours — and delectably varied. You might stay at your job, or pack it in for a second career, perhaps in community service, or intersperse vacations and stints of work, or hit the beach.

One pathway to independence calls for the courage to join a start-up company and be present at the creation of an Apple, a Genentech, or a Federal Express. You accept a lean salary but a fat wad of stock options, work like a pack mule for a few years, and come into clover — *if* the promise pays off. Never mind that a start-up is about the toughest, riskiest business there is. Turning your back on one would seem vaguely un-American.

Your chances of realizing the dream may be greater than you think. Businesses are being minted in the United States today with frontier-era fervor. More entrepreneurs than ever are offering stock incentives to employees they consider essential to a new enterprise. Even a small piece of the action can sprout into a fortune. For the lucky employee shareholders, the date of their company's initial public offering becomes Financial Independence Day.

Starting a business of your own is the front line of independence if you have the drive, the temperament, and the right plan for success. Most businesses, like fruit flies and New Year's resolutions, have short life spans. Only a fraction of the hundreds of thousands of firms born each year will survive for even five years. Some will fail outright, but many will fall prey to a subtler scourge: unfulfilled expectations. As their owners discover, many businesses turn into treadmills instead of springboards to independence.

Take heed of those risks if you contemplate launching an enterprise. Then consider the rewards. In 1979, Robert Kniffin left a secure job at a New York City advertising agency to start Computer Pictures Corporation, a software company. With $50,000 borrowed from friends, he and three colleagues drew up a business plan outlining their idea for a program to display business data graphically on desk-top computers. They then convinced venture capitalists to invest $2 million in exchange for a one-third interest in the business. The combination of capital and a timely idea proved a superb success. In 1982, another software company bought Computer Pictures for $14 million. Kniffin's share of the pie was more than $1 million.

That is one variation of the independence seeker's dream. Another is to build a company that may not be as salable but pays you so well for your own expert services that you will get rich on your income.

Gaining Independence the Company Way

If your father didn't tell you, your uncle or grandfather surely did: you will never get rich working for someone else. Happily, that handed-down advice is wrong. Without realizing it, millions of diligent employees of American companies can get on a medium-fast track to affluence. For most people, in fact, the main chance of piling up a liberating stake comes from their regular workaday jobs.

Your dream of independence might go like this. You are 30 years old and hope to have it made by 50. Your present salary is $35,000, and in 20 years, allowing for inflation and raises, it will be $100,000. At that point, if you assume that your investable assets will return 10 percent a year, you can replace your salary and declare your independence only by socking away the spectral sum of $1 million.

You may not have pictured yourself as a future millionaire, but all it takes is time, discipline, and a bit of luck. To become a millionaire on a $35,000 salary, you will need to save an amount equivalent to at least 10 percent of your earnings for the next 20 years. Compound interest is on your side. If you deposit $2,000 a year in a company savings plan and it faithfully earns 10 percent, in 20 years you will have $126,000 — a leg up on your million. If your spouse does the same, make that $252,000. By regularly investing an additional $100 a month in a more aggressive fashion and realizing, say, 15 percent on it, you will produce $150,000 before taxes. Boost your systematic savings to $200 a month and you'll have $300,000. (Investment strategies for achieving high returns are laid out in Chapter 33.) Inflate those monthly investments to match your rising income, and independence can be yours. Even without counting Social Security or possible pension benefits, your million should see you nicely through your nineties.

Along the way, though, other on-the-job benefits may come to you. Management-level posts often lead to stock options, for example, but you don't have to be an executive to approach your goal. Anyone working for a firm with a strong profit-sharing or savings plan can go a long way toward liberation. At most salary levels, everything the company tosses into the pot, plus all the earnings, will get the huge extra boost of tax deferral. And what the company won't do for you, you can do for yourself by contributing from your salary over a long period. "That takes an unusual degree of self-control," cautions Peter Egan, a partner at Hewitt Associates, a benefits consulting firm in Lincolnshire, Illinois. "Usually you get a couple of promotions and then improve your life-style. But if you want to be well-off some day, you have to have the discipline to keep driving your old clunker when your peers are buying BMWs."

Under the tax law passed in 1986, all the contributions made by you and your employer to profit-sharing plans, savings plans, pension funds, and other retirement programs may not exceed 25 percent of your pay or $30,000 a year, whichever is less. That limitation won't squeeze you until you are earning more than $120,000, an amount that will rise along with the cost of living.

Now that you know what sacrifices lie ahead, let's go back to our earlier hypothesis, the one in which you are making $35,000 and would need $1 million to bid farewell to your office in 20 years or so. Figure 8 gives you a look at how far the savings programs at beneficent companies

Figure 8. How Far a Company Program Can Take You

You can make excellent progress toward financial independence by working for a company with a generous employee savings or profit-sharing plan. The table shows how much someone now earning $35,000 a year would amass in 15, 20, and 25 years with the same company. We have assumed annual pay increases of 7 percent and an investment return from the plan of 10 percent a year. We have also assumed that independence requires a capital fund large enough to produce income, at a 10 percent return, equal to your final salary. The employers' contributions shown are the highest that are likely to be offered by U.S. corporations.

Length of service	*% of salary contributed yearly by*	*Final salary*	*Total fund*	*% of goal*
SAVINGS PLANS				
15 years	Employee — 6 Company — 3	$96,500	$156,227	16
	Employee — 10 Company — 3		225,662	23
20 years	Employee — 6 Company — 3	135,500	314,811	23
	Employee — 10 Company — 3		454,727	34
25 years	Employee — 6 Company — 3	190,000	595,668	31
	Employee — 10 Company — 3		860,410	45
PROFIT-SHARING PLANS				
15 years	Employee — 6 Company — 10	96,500	306,658	32
	Employee — 6 Company — 15		402,489	42
20 years	Employee — 6 Company — 10	135,500	608,475	45
	Employee — 6 Company — 15		798,623	59
25 years	Employee — 6 Company — 10	190,000	1,140,686	60
	Employee — 6 Company — 15		1,497,151	79

Sources: savings plans, Buck Consultants; profit-sharing plans, Towers Perrin Forster & Crosby.

could take you toward that goal — at best, nearly 80 percent of the way. Here are some of the best corporate benefits:

Salary Reduction Plans

The increasingly popular 401(k), or salary reduction, plan is now offered by thousands of companies, including two-thirds of the Fortune 500 firms in 1986. It is "simply the best tax shelter going," says Philip Alden, a vice president at benefits consultant Towers Perrin Forster & Crosby in New York City.

The 401(k) plan's unique advantage over other types of company thrift and profit-sharing programs is that all contributions up to $7,000 are excluded from your taxable income and grow untaxed until you withdraw them. (Until 1987, however, the maximum was $30,000.) You can usually direct your money into stock, bond, or money-market funds or fixed-income investments chosen by your employer. Firms typically permit employees to set aside up to 10 percent of their paychecks. Moreover, many employers match all or part of your contributions, which makes it easier to stash away the full $7,000 yearly maximum.

Profit Sharing

More than 350,000 U.S. companies put a portion of their earnings into profit-sharing accounts assigned to their employees. The yearly contribution is determined by a formula based on corporate earnings. On average, companies contribute about 10 percent of each worker's pay. A few firms, such as Deluxe Check Printers of St. Paul and Fisher-Price Toys of East Aurora, New York, have been kicking in 15 percent year after year.

Most programs also allow employees to put in money of their own, generally ranging from 1 to 10 percent of their salary. A typical limit is 6 percent. The money usually can be invested in a variety of stock and bond funds or in a guaranteed income contract, which carries a fixed interest rate. As Figure 8 shows, anyone who puts his money into a generous plan and gets a decent return can pile up assets in the high six figures.

Stock Plans

Similar to profit sharing but less widespread is a type of savings program known as an ESOP, for employee stock-ownership plan.

Here, the company buys you shares of its own stock, and sometimes you can purchase additional shares automatically with money withheld from your paycheck. David Beckerman, vice president of advertising for Tandy Corporation, which owns the Radio Shack chain, has been an avid participant in his company's ESOP and an earlier plan since 1965. He was recently investing 15 percent of his salary, which was enhanced by a 12 percent company contribution. With Tandy's stock flourishing, in 1986 Beckerman had a net worth of more than $2 million. ''The point of our plan,'' he exults, ''is to give employees a feeling of security — and it has certainly done that for me.''

Savings Programs

In a fairly typical savings plan, the company adds 50 cents to each dollar you invest, to a maximum of 6 percent of your salary. You can usually put away the equivalent of another 4 to 6 percent unmatched. There is a choice of fixed-income and diversified stock portfolios in which you can put all or part of the contributions.

One of the best savings plans is Conoco's, in which employees can invest as much as 16 percent of their pay and the company, a subsidiary of DuPont, matches the first 6 percent. There is a choice of five investments, ranging from a stock fund to government bonds. At Coastal Corporation, a Houston oil and gas concern, workers' investments are matched dollar for dollar to a limit that climbs to 8 percent of salary after an employee has been with the company for seven years. At Bankers Trust in New York City, the company chips in $2 for each $1 that an employee contributes, up to 6 percent of his income. By participating to the maximum in one of these plans and getting solid returns on investments, an employee can close in fairly fast on financial independence. A Bankers Trust staffer who contributed the maximum for 25 years would have 70 percent of the capital he needed to replace his salary with investment income.

Withdrawal Penalties

Need to raise cash quickly? Well, don't count on withdrawing it from one of these retirement plans. The 1986 tax overhaul puts stringent tax penalties on withdrawals before age 59½ and also puts limits on the amount you can borrow from your fund.

The most stringent provisions apply to 401(k)s. You cannot take out even your own contributions unless you plead hardship. What's more, you have to pay a 10 percent tax penalty on such withdrawals, as well as regular income tax. The penalty is waived only if you use the money to pay medical expenses that exceed 7.5 percent of your adjusted gross income. The same penalties and exception apply to withdrawals of company contributions from profit-sharing and other company-sponsored plans.

You can pull out your own previously taxed contributions made before 1987 without tax or penalty. But later contributions will get nipped. As far as the Internal Revenue Service is concerned, each withdrawal will be viewed as consisting of tax-deferred contributions by your employer and earnings on your account, as well as your own pretaxed contributions. If half of your account balance has not been taxed, half of each withdrawal will be taxable. Withdrawals of more money than you contributed will be penalized 10 percent.

The least painful way to get cash out of retirement plans is to borrow it. As Allen Steinberg of Hewitt Associates puts it, "Congress has stacked the deck in favor of borrowing because there's no 10 percent penalty on loans." The most you can borrow at any one time, however, is $50,000 minus your highest outstanding loan balance from the plan over the previous 12 months — even if you have already paid off that loan. Your company must charge you a market rate of interest, and you must repay each loan within five years, in at least quarterly installments. But as mentioned in Chapter 17, the five-year rule does not apply to loans toward the purchase of your principal residence.

The Job-Hopping Penalty

In the quest for independence, it seldom pays to flit from job to job. Profit-sharing programs, for instance, often have a one-year waiting period. Pension plans — yes, you will need a pension plan, too — typically won't vest you for five years. The one program that job hoppers can sometimes negotiate is a stock plan, especially with high-tech firms. They rely heavily on incentive compensation to attract and motivate talent. Often the benefit they have in best supply is a reserved seat on the spaceship to prosperity. In Silicon Valley a senior engineer might say to a prospective employer, "The salary sounds fine, but I'd also like 3,500 shares," a headhunter there reports.

If you don't attain independence just when you planned, there is no shame in pushing your timetable back. You are likely to reconsider the goal, anyway, as you get older. Once you reach age 62 you can count on an infusion of benefits kicking in. Social Security will pay working people now in their thirties $10,200 a year on average in 1985 dollars, according to an estimate by Sophie Korczyk, director of benefits research at Peat Marwick Mitchell in Washington, D.C. She also figures that 75 percent of workers in this age group will get pensions, which will average $12,400.

Even if a high salary gives you hope of better benefits than these, do not be lulled into investing overcautiously. Some extremism in the pursuit of your liberty is no vice, says Korczyk. "Being financially independent means being financially aggressive. You've got to save but you've also got to take chances."

21

SENSIBLE DIVORCE SETTLEMENTS

When it comes to divorce, the scales of justice these days are weighing mostly dollars and cents. In a subtle revolution now sweeping the country, state laws and family courts are coming to regard marriage less as a sexual union than as an economic partnership. Gone are the private detectives who ambushed blondes in motel rooms; taking their place on the witness stand are accountants and appraisers, who evaluate art collections and pension plans, and economists, who calculate the cost of living apart. Harry Fain, a Beverly Hills lawyer and a past president of the American Academy of Matrimonial Lawyers, sums it up this way: "The divorce itself is a two-minute affair. All the rest is money and property."

Divorce, as pointed out in Chapter 13, has become a fifty-fifty possibility for couples now marrying. Those who contemplate it should prepare by learning the particulars of the law in their state and by getting their own financial house in order. They should try, against all emotional odds, to reach a settlement out of court. Not only is lengthy litigation expensive, but also the outcome is highly unpredictable and sometimes inequitable. For example, judges may overlook tax implications, thereby unwittingly awarding Uncle Sam — the third party in any divorce — too much of the spoils.

When it became clear that divorce laws needed modernization, the legal profession developed a model state statute called the Uniform Marriage and Divorce Act. The authors took into account two important social realities: that marriage doesn't necessarily last a lifetime, and that women are increasingly able to support themselves. The act calls for lump-sum settlements and, when practical, temporary alimony to assist a dependent spouse just long enough for her to complete an education or find a job. Moreover, the courts are instructed no longer to use the division of property to punish sexual misconduct.

Although the model statute has not unified divorce laws or caused judges to think alike, 47 states now aim to divide property either "equally" or "equitably." The two terms have vastly different definitions. "Equal" means fifty-fifty. Thus in community property states (Arizona, California, Idaho, Louisiana, Nevada, New Mexico, Texas, Washington, and Wisconsin) judges require that the value of a house, cars, stocks, and other assets be split down the middle. "Equitable," the operative word in most other states, means that if a couple cannot agree on who gets what, judges decide what is fair. It is not unusual for a court to give one spouse 70 percent of the assets and the other 30 percent.

The laws do provide a certain amount of guidance. For example, while justice is supposed to be blind to misconduct, judges in some states can still reduce the share of assets awarded to a spouse whose drinking, gambling, or carrying-on depleted a couple's wealth. In deciding what is equitable, courts may still weigh age and health, how long the couple have been married, and who has custody of the children. But they can also take into account employability and the effort each spouse put into building their net worth.

Enlightened though the thought behind it may be, this focus on finances is inflicting new pain and confusion on the parties to many divorces — and raising the price of separation. Proceedings are taking longer than they used to as lawyers and judges sift through the fine points of the new laws, and the process can be financially as well as emotionally draining. "A simple case can become a Rube Goldberg. What you end up with is two bankrupt persons," says Charles J. Fleck, formerly presiding judge of the Cook County divorce court in Chicago, one of the nation's busiest.

One crucial test of equitable distribution laws is how the courts treat wives in deciding on their fair share of marital assets — in particular, wives who work as homemakers or who take home far lower wages than their husbands. Women in most states have been receiving about one-third of the assets. That is nowhere near the fifty-fifty splits required in community property states. Still, it is an advance over the situation until the 1970s, when a woman could not count on getting anything unless it was in her own name. Now most states hold that all assets earned during a marriage, no matter by whom or in whose name the assets have been held, go into a common pot to be divided in whatever way a judge decides is fair. The only exception is anything that a spouse owned before marriage or received as an inheritance or gift during the marriage; such property continues to belong to the one who owned or received it.

At the same time, though, women are getting less support. Courts no longer are burdening a husband with an ex-wife's maintenance for years and years. It is expected that most women will work and support themselves. So alimony usually is awarded just long enough for them to reenter the work force or train for a better job. Support of the children is considered both parents' responsibility.

Thus, despite the trend toward equitable distribution, women everywhere still tend to fare far worse than men after a divorce. Their salaries are usually lower, and they wind up with fewer assets. A study by Lenore Weitzman, a sociologist at Stanford University, found that on average a woman's standard of living plummeted 73 percent in the year following a divorce, while a man's typically increased by 42 percent.

Because of that inequity, and the flux that divorce laws are in, anyone thinking of dissolving a marriage is well advised to do some serious financial planning first. The place to begin is with your lawyer, who can help you get the best possible agreement. He will have a keen appreciation of the tax implications of various settlements and the resources for pinning down the value of things.

Alimony and Child Support

"If the wife's attorney can save the husband money," observes Edward I. Stein, a Chicago divorce lawyer, "it follows that the husband will have more money available to give the wife." The key strategy for saving the husband money is to have him pay the optimum mix of alimony and child support.

For tax purposes the two are markedly different. Alimony is tax-deductible by the person who pays it and taxable to the person who receives it. Money designated as child support, on the other hand, provides no deduction for the parent paying it and is tax-free to the recipient. For example, if an ex-husband takes $1,000 a month of his earnings and pays it as alimony to his ex-wife, she pays taxes on it; if the same payment is called child support, he pays the taxes.

At first blush, it would seem to the ex-wife's advantage to receive most of the payments in the form of tax-free child support, while the ex-husband would want his contributions labeled alimony. It is not that simple, though. If a man is in a higher tax bracket than his ex-wife, both of them may benefit from having most or all of the payments labeled alimony. The money that he pays to her would otherwise be taxed (at 1988 rates) 28 or 33 percent; when reported on her tax return, all or most of it would be taxed only 15 percent. As illustrated in Figure 9, he can kick in larger monthly payments and still come out ahead.

Another tax advantage goes to the recipient. Although the Tax Reform Act of 1986 cuts way back on deductions for contributions to Individual Retirement Accounts, it leaves untouched the privilege of a former spouse to put a tax-deductible $2,000 of her alimony income into an IRA each year. Result: a double deduction. The payer of alimony takes the $2,000 off his adjusted gross income; the contributor to the IRA takes it off hers, too.

While the new tax code was taking shape, divorce lawyers predicted that the slash in the number of brackets from 15 to three and the huge reduction of the top rate from 50 percent to 33 percent would dilute the argument in favor of paying alimony. As before, however, the best blend of alimony and child support, for tax purposes, depends in large part on the size of the gap in tax brackets between the two parties. As a head of household, starting in 1988 a divorced woman with a child pays the bottom rate of 15 percent on taxable income up to $23,900. Her ex-husband, filing as a single taxpayer, starts paying 28 percent on every taxable dollar from $17,850 to $43,150. On additional income above that level, and all the way up to $100,760, he will be in the 33 percent bracket. In states with their own high income tax, his alimony payments give him additional tax relief.

Despite its possible advantages, alimony plays a diminishing role in the drama of divorce. Even housewives with long marriages can expect no guarantee of permanent maintenance payments. Courts generally reserve long-term payments for women who are over 50, disabled, or in poor health. Nationally, a mere 14 percent of divorced women still receive alimony, and the percentage is declining.

One type of arrangement, called rehabilitative alimony, has resisted the trend. The general idea is for the former husband to help pay for the further education or training that his ex-wife needs to get a job, then scale down his support as her earning power grows. His payments to her are likely to be large but to continue for only a short period — usually two to five years. For two years, 1985 and 1986, Congress put a crimp in rehabilitative alimony by taking away the payer's tax deduction on payments of more than $10,000 a year unless they continued for at least six consecutive years. But the 1986 tax law went back to the older definition.

Figure 9. A Less Taxing Divorce Settlement

By designating most of his monthly payments as alimony instead of child support, an ex-husband often can give his ex-wife and children more money, yet add to his own after-tax income. In this illustration, using 1988 tax rates and exemptions, the man earns $70,000 and itemizes $10,000 of deductions. The woman earns $15,000 in addition to what she gets from him and takes the standard deduction of $4,400 as the head of a household. She has custody of their two dependent children and, by agreement under their divorce settlement, claims them as exemptions. At first he offers to contribute $15,000 a year toward the support of his children and ex-wife. But her lawyer shows him how he can raise his contribution to $18,000 and, by designating most of it as alimony instead of child support, net $300 more instead of $3,000 less. His ex-wife and children get to keep $1,500 more. The only loser is the U.S. Treasury, which comes up $1,800 short.

Ex-husband's Annual Divorce Payments:

	Option 1	*Option 2*
Alimony	$3,000	$13,000
Child support	12,000	5,000
Total	15,000	18,000
Ex-husband's earnings	$70,000	$70,000
Adjustment for alimony paid	−3,000	−13,000
Itemized deductions	−10,000	−10,000
Exemptions (1)	−1,950	−1,950
Taxable income	55,050	45,050
Federal income tax	13,689	10,389
Gross income	$70,000	$70,000
Divorce payments	−15,000	−18,000
Income tax	−13,689	−10,389
Net income	41,311	41,611
Ex-wife's earnings	$15,000	$15,000
Alimony income	+3,000	+13,000
Standard deduction	−4,400	−4,400
Exemptions (3)	−5,850	−5,850
Taxable income	7,750	17,750
Federal income tax	1,163	2,663
Earnings	$15,000	$15,000
Divorce payments	+15,000	+18,000
Income tax	−1,163	−2,663
Net income	28,837	30,337

Pensions and Other Marital Assets

In preparing yourself and your attorney for the tedious negotiations so often necessary in hammering out a divorce settlement, you should compile a list of all the family's assets. In addition to bank accounts and investments, include credit union accounts, pensions, the cash value in life insurance policies, IRAs and Keoghs, royalties, income tax refunds, stock options, and any other pools of income the family has had. Don't forget nonliquid assets. Jewelry, cars, boats, vacation time shares, and collectibles — no matter in whose name — are considered part of the pie to be divided. (For further guidance and a handy worksheet, turn to Chapter 3.)

Divorcing couples can apportion between them property that has appreciated in value, such as their house, shares of stock, and art objects, without having to pay an immediate tax on the capital gain. That was not always true. Only in 1984 did Congress enact tax relief. Before then, the spouse who gave up his or her share of the family residence had to pay the tax that year on any capital gain even if the property was not being sold. In devising a divorce settlement, you should nevertheless weigh the eventual tax consequences of transferring appreciated property. The spouse taking possession of it will face a tax when the time comes to sell it. What's more, the bill may be staggering, because long-term capital gains lost their preferential tax treatment as of 1987.

Though retirement may be many years away, pension rights are the largest asset in many households. In the past, some states did not allow courts to divide retirement benefits. But the Retirement Equity Act, a federal law passed in 1984, makes it easier to claim your share. You can start collecting as soon as your former mate reaches early-retirement age, normally 55. Or you can demand a lump sum if the company pension plan allows it. Making an appraisal of a pension's current value may require the services of an actuary, who will charge anywhere from $300 to $2,000, depending on the pension's complexity.

A limited-partnership tax shelter has worth, too, even though the spouse who owns it may insist that, since it generates no income, it is valueless. What you will need then is a recognized authority to set the shelter's worth. The Liquidity Fund Investment Corporation (1900 Powell Street, Emeryville, California 94608) regularly evaluates public real estate partnerships — those registered with the Securities and Exchange Commission — and will buy your partnership share if you want to liquidate the investment. Appraising private (unregistered) shelters usually requires an accountant's or investment banker's help.

Now that marriage is more of an economic partnership in the eyes of the law, women are claiming — and sometimes getting — a share of their husbands' professional practices or businesses. Couples are splitting royalties from books and music written or recorded by one of them during the marriage. In rarer instances, judges have compensated wives for working to put their husbands through school.

The changing nature of divorce settlements has grafted a new branch onto the appraisal industry, the evaluation of everything from family heirlooms to family businesses. Putting a price on a business can cost thousands of dollars. Female clients of Dallas lawyer William Koons pay as much as $10,000 for appraisals of the worth of corporations their husbands own. Academics are also selling their services as expert witnesses.

Armed with expensive guidance tailored to their conflicting interests, opposing sides in a divorce can disagree on their net worth by hundreds of thousands of dollars. The wife's lawyer may allege that the husband has been socking money away in a Swiss bank or keeping two sets of books to make his business appear less thriving than it is. But judges usually find such allegations hard to believe. In 1977, Claire and Ronald Puorro bought a Carvel ice-cream franchise in Kenilworth, New Jersey, for $63,000. In divorce court, she asserted that he was skimming 20 percent of sales — some $30,000 a year — into his own pocket. She also claimed that he fixed the books so that the business appeared to be losing money. The judge found her evidence unpersuasive and awarded her only $33,000, to be paid in monthly installments of $216.

Coldhearted as it sounds, even the most loving couples should take steps to head off the acrimony and financial pain of a possible divorce. One way is to draw up and sign a prenuptial agreement, a document that spells out the rights and obligations that the couple will honor till divorce them do part. (See Chapter 12.) While such contracts are not necessarily legally binding, most courts take them into consideration.

Attorneys and Mediators

Instead of acting as adversarial litigators, divorce lawyers now mostly orchestrate settlements, calling in appraisers, accountants, tax-shelter specialists, and the like. Says Joseph N. DuCanto, a Chicago attorney, "We have to keep a whole stable of specialists to help us, and they are expensive — very expensive." It easily can cost $5,000 for a middle-class couple with children, a house, and a variety of other assets to get divorced, and that is when they settle out of court. If the couple insist on going to trial, fees can double or triple.

Typically, the spouse who controlled the family's purse strings is reluctant to share with his or her partner all of the financial information needed to arrive at a settlement. In a bitter divorce, a spouse may try to hide assets that are held in his or her name alone. A skilled lawyer has the means of uncovering most deceptions. He will look over joint tax returns from the past several years and check out all banks, brokers, and financial advisers with whom the couple have done business. If need be, he will examine check registers. By counting how much money has been flowing out, he can reckon how much has been flowing in — and from where. Using just such a reverse audit, Saul Edelstein, a New York City divorce attorney, discovered that a high school teacher who sold socks at flea markets on weekends was making an astounding $50,000 a year from his sideline — an asset that otherwise might not have been fully valued.

Because the costs of thrashing out divorce settlements run so high, another kind of specialist — the mediator — is helping to ease the financial and emotional blow. Mediators, whose training may be in law, psychology, social work, or the ministry, aid in negotiating settlements, typically for $75 to $150 an hour. Most mediators can bring couples to agreement in six to eight sessions of an hour or longer.

Courts in California, Florida, and 20 other states have set up free divorce-mediation programs. But they generally are limited to such child-related issues as custody and visiting rights. For help with tax problems you can turn to private practitioners, who are at the forefront of this young profession. Typically, a mediator in private practice asks the couple for a complete accounting of their assets and debts. Then he meets with the husband and wife together and separately to help them resolve such basic questions as who takes the kids and who gets the house.

Mediators do not replace attorneys; indeed, a conscientious mediator encourages clients to hire lawyers as soon as negotiation begins. Nor is mediation necessarily less expensive than a lawyer-negotiated settlement. Observes Ann Milne, a practitioner in Madison, Wisconsin, "I don't sell mediation on the basis that it's cheaper. I say it's better. Often couples can resolve their disputes better for themselves than others can do it for them." She adds, however, that not every spouse has the peacemaking temperament that can help make mediation a success. "Some couples only want to fight," she says.

An actual separation agreement must be drafted by a lawyer and should be gone over by lawyers for both husband and wife. Only attorneys can ensure that the settlement meets prevailing court standards and that your interests are protected. Because the mediation profession is unregulated, couples should take pains in deciding whom to see. For reliable referrals, try the Academy of Family Mediators (P.O. Box 4686, Greenwich, Connecticut 06830; 203-629-8049) or one of the 29 offices of the American Arbitration Association (see the Yellow Pages under ''Mediation Services'').

22

BLENDED FAMILIES

Dennis Butler and Veda Weeks were wed in 1981 at the Paramount Terrace Christian Church in their hometown of Amarillo, Texas. Flanking them were three children from their first marriages; Dennis's son, Ryan, 6, and Veda's daughters, Dondi, 11, and Amber, 8. Veda's white poodles, Peaches and Misty, rounded out the menage. "Dennis took all five of us," Veda says. Ever since, the Butlers have constituted a so-called blended family.

But the Butlers' marriage resulted in the merger of more than two households. It immediately created a new, extended family embracing four sets of grandparents and the Butlers' ex-spouses, each of whom maintains close ties with the children. And two families' budgets blended into a complex new one.

The Butlers are one of an exploding number of blended families in the United States created by high divorce and remarriage rates. The Census Bureau estimates that 10 to 12 million people live in step relationships, some 6.4 million of them children. They even have their own fast-growing organization, the Stepfamily Association of America, with headquarters at 28 Allegheny Avenue, Towson, Maryland 21204, and chapters in 28 states. At meetings, members air such vexing issues as spouses' differing standards for discipline, who pays which child's expenses, the influence on the children of absentee biological parents, and friction between stepsiblings. The Butlers began visiting their local chapter three months before they married. Dennis says, "We wanted to learn what was in store for us, to head off problems before we had them."

Life is unusually hectic for stepparents, and their time with their children comes at a premium. Like all parents, they worry about paying bills, financing college, and preparing for eventual retirement. But stepparents cope with especially delicate, emotion-laden financial issues. For example, the Butlers' first Christmas was painful because Dennis's son got so many more presents than Veda's daughters. The boy's mother and maternal grandmother sent him a total of nine gifts, while the girls' father didn't send them any. He was liable for $350-per-month child-support payments but had paid only $200 in almost two years. The Butlers debated taking legal action, largely out of concern over raising all three kids' future college expenses. In addition, the couple were perplexed about how to protect the children in the event that Dennis or Veda died.

The solutions to these kinds of issues are seldom neat. Ideally, couples about to enter a second marriage ought to talk out money matters ahead of time. At the top of the agenda should come such ticklish subjects as how much each spouse should contribute to joint expenses, whether assets should be held together or separately, and what financial provision each should make in case of death.

Once the issues have been framed, you can cope with the tough ones in a variety of ways. One approach is to negotiate a prenuptial agreement that spells out each partner's financial privileges and responsibilities (see Chapter 12). This is almost never a matter-of-fact undertaking. People who want a financial understanding worked out before marriage have a specific reason: to make sure their assets go to their children rather than to their new spouse if they die. Without such a prior contract, a spouse in most states has a legal claim to between one-third and one-half his or her mate's assets.

For most people, a prenuptial agreement is probably an unnecessary expense — and one fraught with you-don't-trust-me-enough danger. What partners need above all is to clarify their roles and thereby prevent misunderstandings later on. Choosing where you will live is one of the first orders of financial business. It is usually a mistake for one spouse to move into the other's place. Ghosts of the past can bedevil both of them, and the children will probably feel uncomfortable.

Purchasing a house or condo together doesn't mean that each of you has to have enough money to contribute precisely half the down payment, nor does it mean that you must bisect the monthly mortgage bill. You will minimize potential resentments, though, if each of you has some stake in the place. If you want to leave your share of the property to your children, be careful how you and your spouse share ownership. Usually couples buy a home as joint tenants with what's called a right of survivorship. That means when one dies, the survivor automatically becomes the sole owner. Stepparents are better advised to take title as tenants in common. Then, by specifying their wishes in their wills, both partners can leave their shares to anyone they choose.

There is a drawback to leaving your stake in the house to your kids. If you die, they will be part owners of the place. An awkward moment might arise if, for example, they wanted to sell the house to get cash. Tulsa financial planner William Morris and his second wife, Lu Ann, solved the problem by purchasing life insurance. Each took out a $100,000 policy on the other so that in case Lu Ann died, for instance, William would have sufficient funds to buy her share of the house from her heirs — her two sons — if they wanted to sell.

Paying household bills is the next big obligation. Because of the husband's responsibility to his first family for child support or alimony, money is often in short supply in stepfamilies. Sacrificing luxuries is the customary solution. When Diane Beal, a product development manager for an Omaha computer company, married Dick Beal in 1981, she suddenly became the stepmother of three boys. The family's finances were pinched because her husband was starting his own consulting firm. While he was pressed for cash, a substantial portion of her $40,000 annual income went toward supporting her stepsons. "I used to travel and buy myself just about whatever I wanted. Now I really have to watch it," she said at the time.

The spending strategy that a couple in a second marriage work out says a lot about their relationship. One of the best approaches, notes Barbara Fishman, a family therapist in Bala-Cynwyd, Pennsylvania, is to create an overall plan for the new family and to be equal partners in it. For example, the couple might have three bank accounts — his, hers, and theirs. That gives both spouses a sense of independence and autonomy; yet they can collaborate on family expenses. The common pot might go for food, utilities, household maintenance, joint savings, recreation and entertainment, insurance, and major purchases. Individually, the partners would attend to their own responsibilities: alimony and child support, each one's share of the mortgage, auto expenses, clothing, medical bills, and allowances for their children.

In general, Fishman advises, your goal in allocating family resources should be to work toward less separation and more unity. That requires both of you to be sensitive to every family member's needs, which is tough enough to begin with and more difficult if a couple with kids of their own also have children together. When a prickly financial situation confronts you, it is reassuring to realize that all stepparents make mistakes — and all have successes. Fishman notes that in one stepfamily she has counseled, a teenage girl who sufferd badly from her parents' divorce was doing poorly in school and hanging out with a bunch of rough kids. Then the girl discovered modern dance. A special program proved an excellent outlet, but it was expensive. When her natural father refused to help bear the cost, the teenager's mother and stepfather, with whom she lived, decided to sacrifice other things and undertake the entire expense. "That sort of joint decision brings a stepfamily close together," Fishman says.

Because of the greater separation they typically maintain in their finances, however, couples in second marriages face another sticky issue: taxes. The problem was worse under the old tax system than it is now. For example, a husband who earned $50,000 and a wife who earned $25,000 might be in the 38 percent federal income tax bracket. Were they single, however, the woman could easily have been in the 20 percent bracket while the man was in the 42 percent bracket. So he would gain by filing a joint return, while she would be penalized by having her smaller income piggybacked on his. However, the new three-bracket tax code pretty much irons out this disparity. Starting in 1988, both the $25,000 and the $50,000 earner pay the same marginal rate: 28 percent. As joint filers, too, their rate is 28 percent.

Being in the same bracket does not mean that one single taxpayer earning twice as much as another pays the same amount of tax. Far more of the husband's $50,000 will be taxed at 28 percent than of the wife's $25,000. His tax bill as a single filer would exceed $10,000; hers would be about $3,200. Nevertheless, by filing jointly as a married couple, they would pay about $1,400 more than their combined bill as singles.

If a couple are trying to maintain separate financial identities, how do they divide their joint tax payments? Chicago attorney Leon Fieldman and his wife, Mary, a bank trust officer, have faced this problem annually since they were married in 1979, he for the second time, she for the third. Fieldman says, "The simplest method is to apply the ratio of the couple's income to their share of the taxes." If the man makes twice what the woman does, he should shoulder at least two-thirds of the final tax liability. But since the income tax system is still progressive, simple proportioning may not be equitable. You can make the arrangement fairer by stipulating that the spouse with the lower income need never pay more than he or she would have paid by filing as a single person. The same logic can be applied to divvying up an income tax refund.

The last thing to be blended in a stepfamily is usually the two partners' financial assets. Stepparents, eager to make sure that their natural children are provided for, generally keep separate some or all of the holdings they brought to the marriage. To make doubly certain that your desires for disposing of your estate are observed, you should write new wills almost as soon as the ink is dry on your marriage certificate. Expect this to be a rougher exercise than the simple will you wrote during your first marriage. Stepparents have to decide on the proportions they want to leave to their new spouse, to children the couple have had together, and to the children from their prior marriages. If you already have children, it is probably unwise to leave everything to your second spouse. Your estate might be used against your wishes to support your spouse's kids. If your spouse remarried after your death, your assets could come into the possession of a stranger.

Wealthy people sometimes get around this problem by immediately establishing trust funds for their children. But it is more economical for most stepparents to write into their wills a provision called a testamentary trust (see Chapter 27). In it, you can designate the assets you want to leave to your kids and also decide how and when they will get them. For example, you could instruct your trustee to provide a child with income to pay for college and get started in a career but to hold back the balance until the child is older and probably better equipped to handle a large sum. Wills containing trust provisions are more complex than the wills most people write during first marriages. So expect to pay more for one. The typical charge is $500 to $1,500 per will.

The assets you have accumulated may not provide sufficiently for both your spouse and your children if you die. To bolster your estates when you are starting a second marriage, you may want to increase life insurance coverage. You can do so fairly inexpensively with term insurance. (Life insurance is fully discussed in Chapter 57.)

Life insurance has other advantages. The death benefit is not subject to federal income or estate taxes if a husband and wife buy policies on each other's lives. Furthermore, it is not subject to the expense and public exposure of the probate process. The executor of your estate needs to know about the money so that he or she can file the federal estate-tax return. But no one else has to know. That could head off possible resentment on the part of a child about his parent's leaving a large sum to the stepparent.

23

WHEN AGING PARENTS NEED HELP

Nobody has a pat formula for resolving the wrenching dilemma that confronts husbands and wives when aging parents need money. Should you help your parents at the expense of your children's educations? To the detriment of your own retirement fund? Religious precepts don't do much to clarify your obligations. The fifth commandment says "Honor thy father and thy mother." But the matrimonial service from the Book of Common Prayer admonishes, "And, forsaking all others, keep thee only unto her, so long as ye both shall live."

Modern-day clergymen's answers also vary. Monsignor Charles Fahey, a former chairman of the Federal Council on Aging and a Vatican delegate to the United Nations World Assembly on Aging, says, "There is a strong responsibility to care for and love your parents, but that does not equate with economic support. Your primary responsibility is to your own children, not your parents." At the opposite extreme, Rabbi Stanley Schachter, former vice chancellor of the Jewish Theological Seminary of America, notes that financial responsibility for elders is deeply embedded in Jewish culture and religion. "Children have an obligation to maintain their parents at a level of their highest dignity, ideally in the manner to which they are accustomed," he advises. The Reverend John Rhea, a Presbyterian minister who is a staff member of the denomination's office on aging, takes a midway position: "Each time you give in to an unreasonable demand, the expectations become greater. The top priority for an adult child is not to make the parents happy but to make them comfortable, to be sure their basic needs are met."

People are living longer — those 65 and older will make up 13 percent of the U.S. population in the year 2000, up from 11.3 percent in 1980 — and thus are increasingly susceptible to the chronic, debilitating illnesses that wipe out savings fast. Therefore more and more families are likely to be asked for aid. The call may not even come from the parent. It may come from the government. Federal regulations permit states to demand that adult children contribute, along with Medicaid, the funds needed to pay their indigent parents' bills. In addition, more than half the states have laws that could require children to help support their parents before the parents can collect state welfare payments.

Even without government prodding, almost everyone would want to step in to help his or her aging parent. Given the emotional content of this situation, the worst time to address ways of giving is when the crisis is upon you. It is better by far to have a plan in place before the moment arises. Indeed, some ways of giving care cut the burden for you while sharing it with Uncle Sam. But careful thinking must be done to ensure the security of three generations: aging parents, children, and grandchildren.

Questions of when, how, and how much to give cannot be answered unilaterally in a marriage. While at least two people, you and one of your parents, have the largest emotional stake in the decision, your spouse and children also have a financial interest in it. Try to get everyone involved in the planning, especially the elderly parent, so that the parent's assets can be made to work to the maximum.

What to Ask

By asking the difficult questions now, you may be able to protect not only your parents' financial well-being but also the estate that eventually may pass to you, your spouse, and children — a goal that few loving parents would fault. The questions that follow are crucial.

Do you have assets or liabilities that I don't know about? Older people can be especially tight-lipped about the details of their financial lives. Still, you need an understanding of your parents' affairs in the event that you will be called on to manage them. Some assets, like the house, are obvious; others can be easily overlooked. For example, you may be aware of Dad's pension but not of the lump-sum settlement that is one of his death benefits. One of your parents might have a bank account in another state — or even another country. Lawrence A. Krause, a financial planner in San Francisco, says, ''Billons of dollars are lost to survivors because assets remain hidden.''

Ask your parents to make a list of their assets and liabilities, including any debts they may owe to relatives. Ask how their assets are held — in joint tenancy, tenancy in common, or in one person's name alone. Even if your parents steadfastly refuse to discuss their finances, they may agree to compile such a list and keep it in a sealed envelope or a locked box at home. Make sure that you know where the list is and that you will have access to it when you need it.

Are you getting enough income now and have you considered ways you could get more? Your parents should work out a cash-flow statement like the one in Chapter 5, telling them how much money is coming in and whether it is enough to meet their retirement needs. If they are struggling, you may be able to advise them, for example, that they can swap their passbook savings account for higher-paying bank CDs or corporate-bond mutual funds. You may want to point out to them that their home, perhaps the largest asset they have, can be a source of income for them even while they live in it. Ways to unlock this equity include so-called reverse mortgages, sale-leasebacks, Grannie Maes, charity life agreements, and home equity credit lines. Banks, brokerage houses, and financial planners can provide information on these relatively new methods. As Eileen Sharkey, a financial planner in Denver, says, "Owning a house free and clear is a goal your parents are likely to have had for years. Still, it may be reassuring for them to know that in an emergency they can write a check against it."

Are you properly insured? If your parents are 65 or older, they qualify for Medicare. But they also need supplementary health insurance, a so-called medigap or wraparound policy that pays deductibles and the burdensome portions of doctor and hospital bills not covered by Medicare. "Buy the best medigap policy you can afford from a reputable company," says Nancy Chasen, author of *Policy Wise,* a guide to insurance for older consumers (American Association of Retired Persons, 400 South Edward Street, Mount Prospect, Illinois 60056; $7.40). The package of retirement benefits supplied by large corporate employers often includes adequate medigap insurance. Failing that, Blue Cross/Blue Shield offers some of the most comprehensive plans at costs that range from $200 to $800 a year, and Blue Cross hospital plans in 17 states have health maintenance contracts for as little as $10 a month.

You should discourage queasy parents from piling on one policy after another; they cannot usually be reimbursed more than once for the same bill. Similarly, they should avoid insurance that covers only one type of illness, such as cancer. Medical insurance should be as comprehensive as possible.

To offset the extra cost of medigap coverage, most retired people can stop paying for life insurance. As long as neither spouse is dependent on the other's wages and no estate-tax bills are anticipated, they can convert whole life policies to paid-up smaller contracts, or they can surrender the policies for cash and invest the money for current income.

Have you each appointed someone to take care of your affairs if you are incapacitated? Senility, illness, or accident could leave either of your parents unable to manage. Unless they have designated someone to handle their financial affairs, the court will appoint a guardian or conservator — even if one partner is still competent. These legal proceedings can be time-consuming and costly. Moreover, the appointed person may not be the one either parent would have chosen.

To make sure people whom your folks trust will take over for them, they need durable power-of-attorney agreements. Each parent should give that power to the other and a successor, probably one of their children. They can make the powers as broad or narrow as they like. The appointed individual can manage all their finances or simply have check-writing privileges. Attorneys' fees for drawing up the documents might amount to $150 or $200.

The assets of elderly couples often cannot be adequately protected from the brutal costs of prolonged illness. With bills averaging $65 a day in 1986, or $23,725 a year, two-thirds of all nursing home patients who start out paying their own way are impoverished within a year. The difference between a parent's income and his or her uninsured upkeep may be more than even the most willing child can bear. Medicare picks up the total tab for only the first 20 days in a Medicare-certified home and a varying percentage of the cost for the next 80 days. Moreover, benefits are restricted to skilled care, not custodial or home care. Many elderly people erroneously believe that so-called medigap policies issued by private companies to supplement Medicare will pay most of their nursing home bills. But those policies, too, pay only for skilled care and don't pay at all after the hundredth day.

Fortunately, a growing number of insurance companies offer nursing home policies that pay as much as $120 a day toward the cost of skilled nursing home care, meaning care provided by a nurse or other medical professional, or custodial care — primarily help in dressing, bathing, eating, and walking. You can also find plans that cover medical and nonmedical care in a patient's home.

Annual premiums vary enormously — from $175 to $4,460 in one recent survey, depending on the age of the person insured, the benefits he chooses, and other provisions. For example, a Fireman's Fund policy that pays $80 a day for skilled and custodial care and $40 for home care costs a 65-year-old man or woman $730 a year. A 75-year-old would pay $1,095. AGI Life offers a much more generous policy, one paying $120 a day for skilled and custodial care and $60 for home care. But the premium is far steeper: $1,241 for a 65-year-old and $2,776 for a 75-year-old. In some policies there is a choice of how long a stay in a nursing home triggers insurance benefits. This "waiting period" may be 15 days, 20 days, or as long as 100 days. The longer the wait, the lower the premium.

The best way to shop for nursing care policies is through an independent insurance agent. Ask how long the benefits continue. Skilled and intermediate care is usually covered for three or four consecutive years, which should be adequate. Custodial care may be covered for as few as 60 days, however, or as long as five years. The longer the better. Most insurers require that nursing home care be preceded by a hospital stay of at least three days. Policies differ in the maximum number of days that may elapse between hospital discharge and nursing home admittance. The range is 14 to 90 days. Again, the longer the better.

Don't buy a policy that excludes nursing home stays for mental or nervous disorders, such as senility or Alzheimer's disease, a devastating brain disorder that causes progressive loss of memory. Applicants who have recently suffered serious illnesses such as heart disease, cancer, or stroke will find it hard to buy insurance. If they can get a policy, it will not pay anything for the aftermath of those illnesses for as long as one year.

Two government programs in particular are designed to supplement income and cover the medical costs of the elderly and needy—Supplemental Security Income (SSI) and Medicaid. But to qualify for these locally administered benefits, a married couple cannot own more than $2,550 in real and personal property plus the family home, auto, and a specified amount of life insurance. In short, people have to be nearly destitute to get Medicaid, and permanent disability from a stroke or bone disease, for example, can quickly cause just such destitution.

To prevent it, lawyers used to advise older people to establish a living trust, designating their children as trustees, and to put most of their liquid assets, such as stocks, bonds, and money-market funds, into the trust. But in 1985 Congress passed a law empowering welfare officials to deny financial aid to people until the assets of a living trust are consumed.

Another kind of trust, known as a testamentary trust, may permit children to provide in their wills for their parents' well-being while protecting the legacy from invasion by federal and state social-service programs. The trust agreement should instruct the trustees to provide luxuries, not to pay for basic support. According to Sanford Schlesinger, a New York City attorney and author of *Estate Planning for the Elderly Client* (John Wiley & Sons, $75), your parents then may remain eligible for public assistance and your assets will be out of the state's reach. (For greater detail, see Chapter 27.)

How do you feel about life-prolonging measures? Medical science increasingly has the ability to extend life, often at reduced levels of competence and consciousness. Life-prolonging measures can quickly exhaust an estate and postpone a death that may be desired by the terminally ill individual. Ending an artificially sustained life is a wrenching decision for relatives, so it is best to know what your parents prefer. By writing down their wishes in a document called a living will and attaching it to a durable power of attorney, they can ensure that no extraordinary steps will be taken to keep them alive. They must explicitly give the appointed person decision-making responsibility for their health care and should outline their wishes in a letter. One copy of a living will ought to be given to the doctor, and another should be kept with the person's actual will.

Have you any preferences with respect to your funerals? Funerals can be cheap or expensive. Typically, they range from $1,500 to $5,500, but $15,000 is not unheard-of. Your parents should get what they want, not what you find suitable. Thomas C. Nelson, author of the funeral planning guide *It's Your Choice* (American Association of Retired Persons, $4.95), suggests that children focus the discussion on practical considerations. "Most people are quite comfortable to approach it as a consumer purchase," Nelson says. You will need to know whether your parents prefer burial or cremation and whether they have arranged for organ donations. Once you have had the conversation, encourage them to outline their plans in their living wills.

Are your wills up to date? If your parents wrote their present wills before revisions to the estate-tax law went into effect starting in 1981, or if they moved to another state after signing their wills, a lawyer should review these important documents. Bequests should take into account such changes as the 100 percent marital deduction and the boost in the unified gift and estate tax exemption. (For more about wills and estate planning, see Chapters 27 through 29.) Such events as a divorce or the birth of a grandchild also may suggest changes.

Where are your important papers? The best place for wills is in your parents' attorney's office. They and the executor should have copies as well. Financial planners suggest parents keep all important papers in triplicate with one copy in their safe-deposit box, another in a fireproof box at home, and the third at one of their children's homes.

When It Is Too Late to Plan

It is understandable but unfortunate that most families prefer not to think about potential catastrophes. Parents whose health is failing tend to cling to their eroding status as autonomous and sometimes autocratic family heads. Most are reluctant to accept help because of its implications of dependency, while some fail to acknowledge their ebbing power, yet increasingly demand assistance when aid becomes essential. You may have to piece together their financial picture by yourself.

You can find out fairly easily about your parents' Social Security, pensions, and at least the more obvious assets: house, car, and so forth. Then tally their yearly living expenses plus day-care help or specialized medical expenses. Don't be surprised if you uncover an acute deficit. "Families wait for a crisis — and then there is no time to plan," says James C. Mulder, a Houston attorney who specializes in estate planning and trusts.

Therapy for Embattled Couples

Sometimes financial aid is not the only way to go. A whole new network of services has begun to provide care and support for the aged and their families. Good sources of information on these services are your city or state department of aging, listed in most phone books. Family Service Association of America, a nonprofit group representing 300 social agencies, will direct you to its local chapter, which lists other services. They include day-care centers, foster homes, and Meals on Wheels. Write to the association at 44 East 23rd Street, New York, New York 10010.

Making what Monsignor Fahey calls "an ethical choice between two goods" — the welfare of your spouse and children versus that of a parent — can put a severe strain on your own marriage. Francine and Robert Hatfield of Petaluma, California, found themselves running two households when his 69-year-old father was committed to a nursing home and his mother could no longer manage because of failing eyesight. As Robert recalls, "I was moody, and my wife and I were always tired." The Hatfields stuck it out, but weaker marriages may collapse. A well-to-do Long Island, New York, couple battled over the wife's insistence that her mother be cared for in their home. The mother, a victim of

Alzheimer's disease, required constant attention. Their 25-year marriage dissolved over this issue.

So much emotion is spent on deciding questions of family loyalty that people are turning to self-help groups and individual family counseling. Typical fees are $15 to $25 for group sessions and $35 to $65 for a private hour. In a group, you can vent common fears and frustrations with people in similar situations. Groups are often set up by social agencies and religious organizations. In individual counseling, a trained professional helps you deal with the circumstances unique to your family. A hospital, nursing home, or senior-citizen center can refer you to such a counselor. Or you can consult the National Association of Social Workers' *Clinical Register* at a public library. It lists the names of counselors in your area.

Private counseling can take as little as one or two hours but requires the cooperation of all family members. First, a social worker or a team of professionals — usually including a doctor, a physical therapist, and a psychologist — assesses the parent's condition and needs. Then the counselor helps relatives come to terms with their financial and emotional limits.

24

RETIREMENT PLANNING

The need to prepare carefully for retirement has always been great, and the much-extended life expectancy of people approaching retirement age has made preparations more important than ever. The average American life expectancy was 47 years in 1900. In the 1980s it was 71 for men and 78 for women. And it will become even greater. If you are now 40, you can look forward to another 35 to 40 years of life. Clare Corbett, a past president of the International Society of Preretirement Planners, concludes: "Chances are, you will live after retirement as many years as before you entered the workplace. That takes a lot of planning."

In a happy link of circumstances, the resources for financing a long post-working life have vastly improved along with the expectation of one. Individual Retirement Accounts and Keogh plans were unknown to retirees of earlier generations. The number of company pensions and savings plans doubled between 1974 and 1984, and the benefits have become far more generous. Social Security pensions have never been higher. Developments such as these lead Peter Stearns, a Carnegie-Mellon University retirement scholar, to say, "This is one of the best times to retire in American history."

Not only do pensioners stand a greater chance of living well, but they are freer to choose when to call it quits. Although the standard retirement age in the United States is 65, both early and late retirement are catching on. Contributing to an early departure from work are attractive financial packages that growing numbers of companies offer to older employees. Working longer is on the upswing for quite different reasons. Since 1978, federal law has prohibited companies from making retirement mandatory for anyone except top-level executives.

Career switching and part-time work late in life are more acceptable than before. They are also more available. Albert Myers, author of *Success Over Sixty* (Simon & Schuster, $8.95), attributes job opportunities for older people to the national swing from a manufacturing economy to a service economy. ''Now the opportunities to start a business in your sixties are infinite because you can take advantage of your lifetime of experience and skills,'' he says.

It is never too late to start planning for your retirement, but ideally the process begins soon after you go to work. You will be laying the foundation by saving for goals nearer at hand, such as buying a house and raising children. By getting into the habit of saving at least 5 percent of your salary, you do more to prepare for the future than you would by worrying specifically about pensions and such. The time to begin concerning yourself with a specific retirement fund is when you enter your forties. The aim then is to put aside 10 percent of your income, including maximum contributions to company savings or retirement plans. It is also time to hesitate about changing employers unless you are vested in your present company's pension plan — that is, guaranteed a pension even if you resign.

Retirement planning begins in detail at 50. You are near enough to the event to get a fix on how much income it will take to live well without a salary. You can also make realistic estimates of the income you will be getting from pensions and Social Security. That will tell you how much additional you will have to provide out of your savings. Raise your savings target at this stage to no less than 15 percent of gross income. If you have been putting much of your money in stocks or mutual funds with high-growth objectives, start shifting gradually into blue-chip stocks, conservative mutual funds, and fixed-income investments.

Sizing Up Your Company's Plan

Unless you are young and intend to flit for a few years from job to job, take a keen and analytical interest in the retirement benefits you can accumulate as an employee. To evaluate your pension and savings plans, you will have to roll up your sleeves and start picking apart their often tangled features. A good primer to help you penetrate the thicket is the booklet *A Guide to Understanding Your Pension Plan* (Pension Rights Center, 1701 K Street N.W., Washington, D.C. 20036,

$3.50). It clearly defines pension terms and explains how benefits are calculated. Your company's summary plan description, often contained in employee-benefits handbooks, is must reading as an introduction to your pension. New employees automatically receive this report, and updated versions are distributed to all employees from time to time. The summary plan description notes how soon you will be vested and at what age you can get full benefits. In addition, it describes eligibility requirements for participating in the pension plan, how to calculate your benefit, and how time off is counted for vesting. Ask your benefits office for a statement of your pension earned to date. Many employers issue personalized employee-benefit statements, which show not only your accrued benefit but also an estimate of what will become payable on retirement.

Armed with these Baedekers to your pension plan, you will be equipped to spot any rough roads ahead. Start by assessing your prospects for getting a pension. This question splits in two: Will you work for the company long enough to vest, and will there actually be a company pension when you retire?

Starting in 1989, companies must vest you in their retirement plans either fully after you have participated in their plan for five years or gradually over your third to seventh years. You cannot be docked vesting rights for taking maternity or paternity leaves of a year or less. If the company won't let you participate in a pension plan until you have been on the payroll for two years, it has to vest you after four years on the job. Once you are vested, some plans let you walk off with employer's contributions as a lump sum when you leave the company. More likely, though, the money won't be accessible all at once; you will receive it as pension payments at retirement age.

It is possible that your company will scrap its pension plan someday. Thousands of firms have done so, usually replacing one type of pension with another. For example, Celanese and Occidental Petroleum shut their pensions and opened new ones, not because they couldn't afford to pay benefits but because they were flush with pension fund surpluses and wanted to scoop up the extra cash.

Of course, if your pension plan is underfunded, there may be nothing for you when the time comes to retire. For a tip-off to this, consult the plan's tax return, Form 5500 or 5500c, which your employer must furnish on request. Look on the front of Schedule B for a ratio of the plan's assets to liabilities. The current value of assets should equal or exceed the value of vested and nonvested accrued benefits. "If the ratio has declined from, say, 160 percent to 110 percent over the past few years, I'd worry that the plan will be underfunded soon,'' says Jerry Kalish, president of National Benefit Services, a Chicago consulting firm.

Once you feel confident that you will get a pension, the next step is to figure out how large it will be. Companies typically arrive at your yearly pension benefit by multiplying the number of years you have participated in the pension plan by 1.4 to 1.7 percent of your average salary during your last several years at work. For example, an employee covered by his pension for 15 years whose final years' salary averaged $50,000 might get a $10,500 annual pension (15 × .014 × $50,000).

Most companies base their pensions on a salary that is the average of your last five years at work or longer. The best plans count only your last three years, when your earnings usually are at their peak. Poorer plans use your career-average salary, producing meager benefits because of your early, low-earning years. A career-average pension can often be less than half the size of one based on final pay. But many companies that use career-average formulas, such as IBM and AT&T, increase accrued benefits every few years or so to keep pace with rising salaries.

One other variable in the pension formula deserves scrutiny. Check the summary plan description to see if the company will shave your pension by a percentage of what you get from Social Security. Most companies reduce pensions through this method, known as Social Security integration. Typically, pensions are offset by up to 50 percent of your Social Security benefit. The higher your pay, the smaller the portion of income Social Security will replace and the less integration will pinch.

Your pension could well be chopped by 10 percent or more if you are married. Companies must give married people the option of taking a pension in the form of a joint-and-survivor annuity — a guarantee of monthly income to the worker and, upon his or her death, to the worker's spouse. The employer pays an insurer more for a joint annuity than for a single one, and the employee usually shares this extra cost by accepting a reduced retirement benefit. The younger your spouse, the more your pension is likely to be trimmed. If you retire when your spouse is 60 and accept a joint annuity, your benefit could be cut by 12 percent; if your spouse is 45, your pension might be three-quarters of your full benefit.

Anyone considering working past 65 should find out whether those extra years on the job will count in the company's pension calculations. Most plans stop accruing benefits for employees who work past the company's normal retirement age, usually 65.

Your pension almost certainly will be reduced if you retire early. About half of large U.S. companies scale back pensions for workers who quit at 62 after 30 years of service, and 90 percent do so for employees retiring at 55. Typically, a company cuts pensions by one-third for employees who retire at age 60 and halves them for workers who pack up at age 55, no matter how long they have worked for the company.

It is much easier to size up a company savings plan than a pension. All the information you will need appears in either the summary plan description or the quarterly and annual statements of investment performance given to plan participants. Look for six pieces of data: how soon you can participate, when you will vest, how much you can and must put in, how much the company will contribute, which of your contributions are pretax, and how the plan has done compared with similar investments.

Typically, you can enroll in a savings plan after working for the company for a year regardless of your age. The better vesting schedules let you claim the employer's contributions after three years. The more you can invest pretax, the more attractive the plan. If your company matches your contributions, you have an automatic profit. If the fund is a diversified stock portfolio, track its previous six-month and five-year performance against Standard & Poor's 500-stock index. A bond fund should measure up to the top corporate-bond funds tracked monthly in *Money* magazine's "Fund Watch."

Factoring In Social Security

Despite a persistent fear that the government's retirement program will fold, Social Security is here for the long term. True, the system might need a little bolstering to ensure benefits for workers who were nearing retirement in the 1980s. But things will be on firm footing again between 1990 and 2010. After that is when trouble could set in. Theoretically, Social Security could go bankrupt when people born in the first 15 years after World War II reach retirement age. But the political power of those baby boomers should head off any such debacle. Instead, the rules will change. No one can predict the alterations with absolute certainty, but they are likely to include higher payroll taxes, later retirement ages, and cutbacks in the percentage of your pay replaced by Social Security benefits.

The system as it stands pays upper-middle-income people ($45,000 a year or so) nearly 25 percent of their preretirement wages. As Figure 10 shows, a person who retires at 65 in 1990 will get as much as $9,324 a

Figure 10. Estimating Your Social Security Benefits

To find out how much you will get from Social Security when you retire, you can write to your Social Security office when you reach the age of 60. Ask for Form 7004, Request for Statement of Earnings. Fill out and mail in the form, and the government will send you an estimate of your future benefits. To get an idea of this figure before you are 60, request the free pamphlet *Estimating Your Social Security Retirement Check* from your local Social Security office. The figures below are annual benefits estimated by Social Security for two levels of income: that of the average recipient and that of someone eligible for maximum benefits. The amounts are given in current dollars; they will rise automatically after years with inflation rates higher than 3 percent.

Year you will retire	*Average earnings*		*Maximum earnings*	
	Age 62	*Age 65*	*Age 62*	*Age 65*
1990	5,520	6,900	7,464	9,324
1995	5,880	7,344	8,148	10,188
2000	6,324	7,908	9,120	11,400
2005	6,588	8,496	9,816	12,672
2010*	6,792	9,048	10,392	13,824
2015*	7,284	9,708	11,364	15,156

* Age for full benefits is 66.

year, not including automatic cost-of-living increases after any year in which the consumer price index rises more than 3 percent.

Generally, you must work 10 years before Social Security will pay you a retirement benefit. Any worker born after 1937 will have a slightly shorter vesting period. Not everyone who works long enough will get a Social Security check. Employees of nonprofit organizations such as museums and hospitals get no credit for their earnings before 1984 unless they have paid Social Security taxes all along. About one-third of employees of state and local governments are not covered, nor are any federal employees hired before 1984.

The Social Security Administration pays full benefits to employees who retire at 65 and cuts payouts for workers who quit earlier. You can't apply for your own retirement check until age 62, when it will be 80 percent of the amount you would get by waiting until age 65. In the year 2000 the minimum age for full benefits will begin to rise by two months a year, reaching 66 in 2005. From 2006 through 2016, the minimum age will remain at 66. After that, it will go up by two months a year until it reaches 67 in 2022. Also starting in 2000, and lasting through 2022, the early-retirement benefits for a 62-year-old will be nipped by about eight-tenths of a percent a year. So by 2022, early-retirement checks from Social Security will be only 70 percent of full benefits.

In the meantime, Social Security rewards workers who put off their benefits past 65 by adding 3 percent to their retirement checks for each year they delay taking full benefits between age 65 and 70. The delayed retirement credit will inch up a bit for anyone turning 65 in 1990 or later. But don't put off taking your Social Security benefit at 65 just to get a larger check later. The extra money you receive from the delayed retirement credit won't equal the Social Security income you could have been accepting since age 65. However, if you plan to work for pay to supplement your Social Security checks, you may be better off postponing your benefits, for the reasons described in Chapter 25.

If you are married but only one spouse worked for pay, Social Security will send you one monthly check equal to 150 percent of the worker's entitlement, provided the beneficiary does not start collecting until age 65. If the nonworking spouse is 62, the couple will get 137.5 percent of the worker's benefits. A working couple with only one spouse employed long enough to receive a full Social Security benefit at 65 will also get one monthly check of 150 percent of that spouse's entitlement. If the lower-earning spouse did not earn enough to get a Social Security benefit equal to more than half of the higher-earning spouse's, the couple will also get a single check of 150 percent of the bigger benefit. Couples entitled to two full benefits are mailed separate checks unless they request a single monthly payment. A divorced person can get the spouse's benefit at age 62 if the couple were married more than 10 years.

Women frequently have two choices. They can collect Social Security based on their own employment, or they can take a joint benefit based on their husband's earnings. Paula Toomey-Ryan, a financial planner with Equitable Capital Management in New York City, advises working women to send for a statement of their Social Security earnings record once they reach age 55. Then the woman will know if she has worked long enough to get a full benefit. "If she doesn't have enough credits to get her own benefit, she might want to work a little longer to qualify," Toomey-Ryan says. "After that, she can compare her own benefit with her husband's to figure out whether they will be better off getting one check based on his earnings or two checks based on both their salaries.

To get your earnings record, write to the nearest Social Security office and include your Social Security number, birth date, address, and signature. Ask explicitly for the number of quarters of coverage you have earned for Social Security.

Saving for What You Will Need

Even if your retirement is two or three decades off, you can get an idea right now of whether you will have enough money to enjoy your postemployment years. Coming up with cash-flow projections for your sixties and seventies will be an imprecise exercise. But when you are young, rough estimates are the best you can hope for. By age 55, the figures will become firmer, and you can adjust your savings targets accordingly. Then you will have a better idea of the size of your pension, Social Security benefits, and savings.

The arithmetic of retirement is laid out in Figure 11. To get the cash-flow machine moving, set your sights on retirement income based on your present earnings. But don't aim to replace every dollar of it. Few people have the financial resources to duplicate their salaries, and few need to. Your tax bill will almost certainly drop. At least half of your Social Security benefits will be tax-free, for instance, and you won't have payroll deductions for Social Security taxes unless you continue to work. Furthermore, you won't have work-related costs, which can eat up 5 percent of a household budget. Housing costs often fall as mortgages are paid off. You can cut back on life insurance coverage and take advantage of off-peak and senior citizens' discounts on entertainment and travel.

Certain other expenses will balloon, however. Poor health could consume many thousands of dollars in medical bills, especially if you retire early and fall ill before age 65, when Medicare kicks in. Inflation is sure to hurt. Corporations' pensions are rarely indexed to the cost of living. Nor do conservative fixed-income investments that retirees favor, such as Treasury bonds and bank certificates of deposit, appreciate in value as an inflation hedge. On the positive side, inflation's impact on a retiree's expenses is somewhat softened. People who own their homes free and clear are not affected by increases in house prices or mortgage rates. Rising costs of gasoline and car repairs don't hit you so hard when you no longer commute to work.

All told, the inflation rate of your living expenses in retirement is likely to be one-half to two-thirds the national rate. With that in mind, retirement counselors say you can expect to maintain your preretirement standard of living with about 70 percent of your former pretax earnings.

After arriving at a suitable retirement income, ponder your life expectancy. You don't want to outlive your retirement savings; yet if you are like most people, you won't be able to live off the interest on your earnings and investments without ever dipping into principal. At a min-

Figure 11. Retirement Planning Worksheet

By taking the 13 simple steps in the worksheet on the next page, you will know how much to save each year to reach the lifetime retirement income goal you set for yourself. Read the text of this chapter for help in setting that goal. Retirement planning is the roughest of approximations, subject as it is to such unknowables as your life expectancy, future tax and inflation rates, and the success of your investments. Nonetheless, you can cope with these uncertainties by making some conservative assumptions. For example, instead of guessing how long you will live, assume that you won't expire until the fine old age of 100. In the face of inflation and unpredictable investment results, the highly conservative assumption built into the multipliers in the tables below is that your net return, after inflation and taxes, will be a modest 2 percent. Most of the multipliers are spaced at five-year intervals to avoid putting too fine a point on your calculations. When in doubt, choose multipliers that fall this side of your retirement age and your remaining years on the job.

Life-span Table

Retirement Age	*Multiplier A*
85	13.1
80	16.7
75	19.9
70	22.8
65	25.5
60	27.9
55	30.1
50	32.1

Savings Table

Years until you retire	*Multiplier B*	*Multiplier C*
5	1.10	.192
6	1.13	.158
7	1.15	.135
8	1.17	.117
9	1.20	.103
10	1.22	.091
15	1.35	.058
20	1.49	.041

Years until you retire	*Multiplier B*	*Multiplier C*
25	1.64	.031
30	1.80	.025
35	2.00	.020
40	2.21	.017

WORKSHEET

Step 1.	Your current annual income	$________
Step 2.	Annual income needed after retirement, in current dollars	$________
Step 3.	Annual Social Security income (see Figure 10)	$________
Step 4.	Annual company pension (see text)	$________
Step 5.	Guaranteed annual retirement income (step 3 plus step 4)	$________
Step 6.	Annual retirement income needed from savings and investments (step 2 minus step 5)	$________
Step 7.	Amount you must save by retirement, in current dollars (step 6 times Multiplier A)	$________
Step 8.	Amount you have saved so far, including IRAs, Keogh plans, vested corporate profit-sharing, thrift, and salary-withholding plans	$________
Step 9.	What your savings to date will have grown to by the time you retire (step 8 times Multiplier B)	$________
Step 10.	Amount of savings still needed (step 7 minus step 9)	$________
Step 11.	Amount of savings needed each year (step 10 times Multiplier C)	$________
Step 12.	This year's employer contributions to your plans in step 8	$________
Step 13.	Amount you need to set aside each year (step 11 minus step 12)	$________

imum, use the national mortality tables that your insurance agent has. To be safer still, figure as we do in the worksheet that you'll live to be 100.

Multiplying your target annual income by your anticipated years in retirement will give you a workable idea of the amount of money you will need to have on hand to retire without a financial care in the world. That seven-digit figure also will give you the willies. Remember, though, that you won't have to come up with all the scratch personally. Social Security benefits and a company pension can easily make up two-thirds of your needed retirement income, leaving one-third of the funding to you.

Begin adding up your retirement income by estimating your Social Security benefit. If you are married and your spouse won't have earned enough to get his or her own Social Security benefit, count on one check for the two of you equal to 1½ times your benefit.

Then add your company pension if it looks as if you will be eligible for one. For an employee who works for the same company for 10 years, a pension will probably equal 10 to 15 percent of final salary; after 20 years it will replace 20 to 25 percent of pay, and after 30 years, 35 percent. Your company's employee-benefits counselor can tell you the size of your pension, but the figure will be very rough for employees in their twenties through forties. It assumes you will stay at the company until retirement and is based on a hypothetical salary you will get more than 20 years hence. To estimate your future annual pension benefit in current dollars, use the formula many large companies do; take 1.66 percent of your anticipated highest salary at the company. Multiply the result by the number of years you will have worked there, and subtract half the Social Security benefit you will get at age 65.

Your company benefits department will also supply, upon request, the anticipated size of your profit-sharing or savings-plan funds at retirement. This figure is also squishy for young employees. There is no telling how the fund's investments will perform, whether the company will turn a profit every year, or how much you will contribute to the plan.

After calculating how much money you will need in retirement and what's coming from the government and your employer, you will know how large a hole your savings must fill.

Where Your IRA Fits In

People who are not eligible to participate in a company pension plan definitely should start filling the gap between their retirement goal and their present resources with an Individual Retirement Account. The basic rules governing this tax shelter with the government seal of approval are fairly simple — though far from brief. Anyone who earns a paycheck is free to invest in an IRA as little as $1 or as much as $2,000 of his or her annual earnings; two-income couples can contribute up to $4,000; divorcees who get alimony can sock away $2,000 of it even if they have no job. In one-income families, the wage earner may chip in an additional $250 for his or her spouse. The couple may divide their $2,250 annual maximum in separate his and hers accounts and in any proportion they choose.

In some situations, every dollar invested in an IRA can be deducted on your income tax return. To take the full deduction, you must be ineligible for a company pension plan or you must be earning less than a specified annual wage — $25,000 if you are single, $40,000 if you are married or the head of a household as defined by tax law. People earning more can still deduct part of their IRA contributions until a single person's salary reaches $35,000 and a married person's or head of household's reaches $50,000. As your salary rises toward those ceilings, the $2,000 maximum yearly deduction is reduced proportionally.

A second tax benefit of IRAs is open to every wage earner. It is the postponement of taxes on investment earnings in an IRA until you withdraw money from your account. Under the 1986 tax overhaul, which clamped these strict conditions on tax-deductible contributions, everyone can still put as much into his or her IRA each year as before. So you can let the money compound tax-free until you make withdrawals, presumably at retirement.

You can make your IRA contribution for the year anytime from January 1 through the April 15 tax-filing deadline in the following year. You may tap your IRA anytime. Part of each withdrawal — or all of it — becomes taxable income for that year. For example, if half of your entire account consists of untaxed contributions and deferred investment income, half of the withdrawal will be taxed. You must pay an additional tax, in the form of a 10 percent penalty, for taking previously untaxed money from your IRA before the year you turn 59½ years old. After age 70½, however, you will be penalized if you *haven't* begun withdrawals.

You can open an IRA at any bank, credit union, mutual fund, brokerage house, or insurance company. Under many circumstances you will be charged an annual maintenance fee, usually $25 or less. In some cases you also will have to pay a start-up fee of $25 or so. There is no limit on the number of accounts you can maintain at different institutions, but sowing your cash in too many places can cause fees to add up and cut into growth — especially when you are starting out. Only a few investments are not permitted: life insurance, gemstones, art, stamps, collectibles, and investments that involve borrowing, such as stocks bought on margin and mortgaged real estate. You can even put precious metals in your IRA, in the form of gold and silver coins issued by the federal government. (See Chapter 41 for investment strategies tailored to IRAs and other tax-sheltered retirement accounts.)

The tax-deductible contributions and the deferred status of earnings in an IRA translate into powerful money builders. If you are in the 28 percent bracket — which applies in 1988 to taxable incomes above $29,750 for married couples, $23,900 for heads of households, and $17,850 for singles — and you make a $2,000 contribution, each investment would cost you $2,778 were it not for the tax deduction. Let's say you set aside $2,000 at the beginning of each year for 25 years and the account earns a steady 10 percent, compounded quarterly. Your grand total at the end of that period would be $216,364. But if you invest identically in a taxable account and withdraw enough each year to cover the taxes on your investment income, your grand total will dwindle to $139,563.

Where you stash an IRA will depend largely on what you hope to do with it. If you want the safety of principal offered by certificates of deposit, a bank, savings and loan, or credit union will do. A family of mutual funds is the place to go for professionally managed portfolios of stocks or bonds. Brokerage houses offer the widest choice of investments and the chance to open the most flexible IRA — a self-directed account in which you can trade individual stocks, bonds, CDs, options, and government securities. For a fee of $27.78 on a $2,000 transaction, the discount brokerage firm Charles Schwab & Company also allows investors to buy and sell more than 200 no-load and low-load mutual funds for their IRAs.

So far, banks cannot match brokers for variety, but some are taking the same supermarket approach. IRA customers at New York's Citibank, for instance, can choose from CDs, a money-market account, and four investment portfolios managed by the bank. Citibank also has self-directed IRAs sponsored by an affiliated discount brokerage service.

Whether you plan to keep all your IRA money under one roof or spread it around, ask about the cost of opening, maintaining, and closing accounts. For simple accounts, such as those with CDs only, many banks charge no fees. Some mutual-fund groups charge $5 to $10 to open an account, and most charge annual maintenance fees in the same range. You also pay their standard annual management fee and, for load funds, a sales or redemption charge. Brokerage firms charge start-up fees, maintenance fees, or both. When every worker could deduct IRA contributions, the tab came to about $50 a year. But to keep on attracting investors, brokerages may have to lower their fees. In any case, you also pay a commission on every trade.

The only investments that don't make sense for IRAs are those that already offer tax advantages — municipal bonds, for example. Because IRAs are sheltered from taxes, exemptions are wasted. Still worse, all income will be taxable when withdrawn, including otherwise tax-free yields. Similarly, the appeal of annuities rests partly on their tax-deferred earnings. It is better to buy annuities outside an IRA and devote the money inside it to investments that otherwise would be taxable as income accumulates.

Keogh Plans

One of the biggest fringe benefits of being self-employed, or even having an income-producing business on the side, is the chance to take complete control of your retirement plan. The basic, or defined-contribution, Keogh allows you to put away — and deduct from your taxable income — either $30,000 a year or 20 percent of net self-employment income, whichever is smaller. This is the same maximum that applies to all defined-contribution pension plans, whether you are in one or several.

Keoghs can be kept in any institution with qualified plans. That generally includes the same institutions that sponsor IRAs, from banks to brokers. (Except in certain states, a Keogh holder can bypass these institutions and act as his own trustee.) The deadline for annual contributions is the same as for IRAs, April 15 of the following year, but only if you opened your Keogh account by the previous December 31. In many cases, Keogh holders, like IRA holders, are penalized 10 percent for withdrawing funds before age 59½.

Another version of the Keogh is the defined-benefit plan, which lets the grasshoppers catch up with the ants. Say you are 55 and haven't saved a sou. At this age and after, you can save — and deduct — whatever it takes (up to $90,000 a year if you earn that much) to give yourself retirement income equal to the average of your earnings in your three consecutive highest-paid years. But every year, you must submit to the Internal Revenue Service a form on which an enrolled actuary has made the official calculations for your plan.

Keogh withdrawals are considered ordinary income, but they are eligible for five-year forward averaging on lump-sum withdrawals, while IRA withdrawals are not. The basic idea of averaging is to cut taxes by treating a withdrawal as though it were income received over five years. If your fiftieth birthday was on or before January 1, 1986, you can use ten-year forward averaging, a much better deal. But timing these moves, sorting out the consequences, and structuring a Keogh properly to begin with are all quite complicated — particularly if you have employees.

Only an accountant well versed in Keoghs can keep you from scrambling this nest egg.

Annuities

Insurance company annuities can play one or two roles in your retirement act. While you are working, you can stash cash in a so-called deferred annuity and watch it grow, unchecked by taxes. After you retire, you can use that money — or other funds — to buy an immediate annuity, which then starts paying you monthly income for the rest of your life.

You shouldn't buy an annuity for either purpose solely on the recommendation of an insurance agent or stockbroker. Shopping is essential, because returns on deferred and immediate annuities vary enormously from insurer to insurer. Also, your money is safer with some companies than with others. One clue to an annuity sponsor's financial stability is its rating, published in the life and health edition of *Best's Insurance Reports,* available at large public libraries. Deal only with insurers that are rated A+ or are licensed by New York State, which has a strong insurance and annuity guarantee fund.

You can buy a deferred annuity with a single premium, typically $5,000 or more, or you can pay in periodic installments. Deferred annuities come in two types, fixed and variable. Fixed annuities pay interest like a bank account. Your principal is guaranteed. Variable annuities produce fluctuating returns based on the performance of stock, bond, or money-market portfolios managed by the insurer or an outside adviser. More unusual funds are also available, including some that invest in real estate. Many insurers let you reallocate your cash in several funds. If a fund flops, however, you can lose principal.

Despite their moniker, fixed annuities guarantee a stable rate of return for only a few months or a year. After that, the rate changes at the insurer's discretion, though it cannot fall below a stated minimum, typically 3.5 percent. Fees can also affect your return. Insurers usually let you withdraw up to 10 percent of the money in your annuity each year without charge. If you take out more, the insurer imposes surrender fees that usually start at 7 percent of your excess withdrawal during the contract's first year and decline until they disappear in seven to 12 years. Some insurers offer a bailout clause under which you can get all your money at no charge if interest rates slip a point or two below what you were originally promised. But with any annuity bought after January 19,

1985, withdrawals before you reach age 59½ will cost you a 10 percent federal tax penalty, as well as income tax, on earnings withdrawn.

A heavy overlay of other fees can sap the annual return in annuities. One study of the fixed annuities of 45 companies, covering a 12-year period when interest rates were moderate, made the startling discovery that average annual returns ranged from 8 percent to less than half a percent. Under the circumstances, it is something of a scandal that insurers do not publish such data for shoppers. However, a firm in Albuquerque, New Mexico, Comparative Annuity Reports, compiles annual returns on annuities sponsored by 220 insurers and sells the results to insurance companies and the public at $75 per report (P.O. Box 8488, Albuquerque, New Mexico 87198). When you shop for an annuity, ask each agent how high his company ranked in the latest Comparative Annuity Reports survey; insist on getting data that take fees into account.

In a projection through the end of this century, Comparative Annuity Reports identifies eight companies rated A+ by *Best's* whose fixed single-premium annuities should post the highest net returns on the basis of 1985 interest rates and fee schedules:

Guarantee Security Life, Jacksonville, Florida
General American Life, St. Louis, Missouri
Unionmutual Life, Portland, Maine
Columbus Mutual Life, Columbus, Ohio
Great American Life, Los Angeles, California
Pan-American Life, New Orleans, Louisiana
Great American Reserve, Dallas, Texas
Life of Georgia, Atlanta, Georgia

All are worth including on your fixed-annuity shopping list.

It is easier to identify the top variable annuities, which closely resemble mutual funds, because Lipper Analytical Services, an investment advisory firm, monitors many of them. As a group, variable annuities that invest in common stock funds gained 84.4 percent in the five years through September 1985, versus 54.9 percent for Standard & Poor's 500-stock index. Three annuities available outside of IRAs from insurers rated A+ by *Best's* outperformed the pack. First Variable Annuity "A" gained 126.9 percent, National Life's Variable Annuity Account I gained 119.6 percent, and Aetna Life's Variable Fund gained 103.9 percent.

Because more insurers have just recently started to offer variable annuities invested in bond and money-market funds, Lipper has followed only a few such funds for more than a couple of years. Northwestern Mutual Life's Separate Account "C" Bond variable-annuity bond fund topped Lipper's charts for the 12 months through September 1985, with a rise of 23.6 percent.

Lipper's figures take investment management charges into account but not sales commissions, which range from zero to 8.5 percent. Insurers typically trim 1.5 percent off a variable-annuity account's balance annually for administrative expenses. Ask insurance agents where companies they represent currently rank on Lipper's lists.

Investment Strategies

Along with IRAs, Keoghs, company savings plans, variable annuities, and other tax-sheltered retirement funds has come a new and grave responsibility: the success of your investments. In old-style pension plans your employer or union or whoever serves as sponsor promises to pay you lifetime retirement income in an amount that is fixed by a formula in the plan. This is called a defined benefit. In the newer plans, all the boss promises is to put money into your retirement account under a set formula. This is called a defined contribution. How much of a retirement benefit you get depends partly on how well you invest the contributions — yours and your employer's — and partly on how well you invest and preserve the whole fund after you retire. No professional pension fund manager will be there to help you unless you hire one yourself. Considering that most people know little about managing money and absolutely nothing about the actuarial science of making it last a lifetime, the burden of having your financial fate entirely in your own hands looks awesome.

The art of pension management is to find the right combination of investments for the long term — and that depends largely on how old you are. Just as surely as you will weather physical and psychological passages in the decades that stretch between youth and retirement, your financial profile will undergo gradual — but ultimately dramatic — shifts. You will get the best results if you pursue a lifetime financial plan that reflects your changing needs for security, income, capital growth, and tax shelter as you grow older.

Youth offers the greatest opportunities to start working toward the distant goal of retirement. Since younger investors have many years in which to recoup any serious losses, they can afford to be daring. With an eye to greater rewards, most 30-year-olds are well-advised to put as much as 10 to 20 percent of their investment funds in such high-risk vehicles as aggressive growth-stock mutual funds and bonds with high yields but low safety ratings. The next 50 to 60 percent might go to buy moderate-risk growth stocks with solid long-term prospects. Those investments may take years to fulfill their promise, but young people have time to ride out short-term temporary losses if necessary. Meanwhile, they will avoid paying frequent brokerage commissions. The last 20 to 30 percent of their holdings can be divided evenly between two types of secure investments: cash equivalents such as Treasury bills, money-market accounts, and short-term certificates of deposit for easy access in case of emergencies; and blue-chip stocks for income and capital gains.

Younger investors actually increase their risk by concentrating too much of their money in the most conservative investments. For example, top-rated long-term bonds offer the assurance that you will receive all of your principal back if you hold the bond to maturity, but the principal you eventually retrieve may be deeply eroded by inflation. You can guard against such a setback by diversifying into riskier inflation hedges such as growth stocks and a mutual fund that invests in gold.

But never lose sight of the special charms of slow and steady profits. When retirement is still decades distant, even modest annual gains, consistently maintained, can add up to impressive growth. Compounding is the long-term investor's strongest ally.

As your temples gray and your career progresses, you should consolidate some of the gains of your youth. An investor age 45 or so might place half of his retirement money in blue-chip stocks, Ginnie Maes or other mortgage-backed securities, corporate bonds, and money-market accounts or funds. If promotions and raises have pushed up your taxable income, turn to high-quality municipal bonds for good after-tax returns combined with relative safety of principal. You will still need to take some risks to combat inflation. Growth-and-income mutual funds might account for 40 percent of your portfolio. You can still afford some aggressiveness by putting 5 to 10 percent of your money in high-risk stocks, precious metals, or lower-rated bonds.

If as you have aged you have fallen behind in your pursuit of retirement goals, you might be tempted to invest more in high-risk propositions in an attempt to make up lost ground. But whatever your age, ask yourself how large a loss you can stoically contemplate. While some gambles may offer you a chance to retire rich, a few costly mistakes can make it difficult to meet more modest objectives.

The nearer you are to retirement, the more care you should take to preserve the capital you have accumulated. You ought to begin shifting gradually to more conservative income-producing investments. A well-conceived portfolio for an investor age 60 might allot 70 percent of retirement savings to corporate bonds and Treasury issues. You might also consider an annuity.

At least 20 to 25 percent of your assets should remain in growth-oriented investments, although you are well advised to switch some of your stock-market allocation from high-fliers to blue chips with strong financial backing and high dividends. It may be too late to take big chances with your savings, but 5 percent or so invested in gold could offer a valuable shield against inflation.

25

THE TAXING CHOICES OF RETIREMENT

Free at last! Or are you? You have worked all your life, saved diligently, taken advantage of every tax-sheltered opportunity to build a retirement nest egg, earned a pension and a full ration of Social Security. But you are not through yet. Every dollar of tax-deferred money and Social Security benefits comes with a string on it. Hauling money out of those retirement shelters too rapidly or too slowly could cost you dearly in taxes or penalties, while earning money in a postretirement job could cost you part or perhaps all of your Social Security pension. Commercial insurance agents are waiting, too. They can entrap you with anemic annuities, or you can snag yourself by choosing the wrong lifetime option for your corporate pension. You have entered a phase of financial life full of new and unfamiliar terms and concepts: lump sums, rollovers, joint-and-survivor benefits, 10-year forward averaging, life-expectancy tables, and other bewilderments. Even if you never hired an accountant before, you are likely to need one now.

If you have invested on your own and also put in a decade or more with a reasonably munificent company, your retirement landscape should have at least one prominent topographic feature: a mountain of capital. And if you work for a company that permits you to take your pension in a single payment instead of in monthly checks, you will have yet another sum to add to the others. The total could run well into six figures.

Such largesse presents you with two critical and complicated choices. The first is whether to take your nest egg in one glorious lump sum or have it parceled out to you as an annuity — that is, in fixed monthly payments for the rest of your life. If you take the lump sum, you come to the second crossroads: whether to pay the tax on your lump sum now or postpone the reckoning by rolling over the money into an Individual Retirement Account.

Don't underestimate the importance of these decisions. You will be dealing with intricate tax regulations and probably the largest pile of money you have ever had. A wrong turn could prove disastrous.

If all you have coming is a pension, your employer may have made the decision for you. Most companies, concerned that retirees might squander a lump sum, insist that you take your pension as a lifetime annuity. With profit-sharing and thrift plans, however, it is up to you. Companies normally hand you this money all at once. You can manage it yourself or put it in an annuity.

Lifetime Annuities

An annuity, whether you fund it with your private savings or company retirement funds, offers one undeniable attraction: peace of mind. You will get monthly income for the rest of your life. You give up control of your retirement funds in an annuity, but you also relinquish the headache of managing them and the risk of seeing your principal erode because of bad markets or bad judgment. An annuity pays you a guaranteed amount, boom times or bust. Best of all, an annuity banishes fear. The guaranteed lifetime income may greatly comfort people who fret about outliving their savings — or squandering them in Las Vegas. But an annuity is a one-way street. After you sign a contract for lifetime income, there is no turning back.

You can choose from among four basic ways of receiving annuity income, all of which pay income for at least one person's lifetime. Monthly payments get increasingly smaller with each additional money-back guarantee, as illustrated in Figure 12.

A *straight-life* annuity pays you until you die. If you are unlucky enough to expire after cashing just one check, the insurance company keeps the rest of your capital.

An *installment-refund* annuity pays you or a beneficiary at least as much money as you invested.

A *period-certain life* annuity guarantees that you or a beneficiary will collect for at least a set number of years.

A *joint-and-survivor* annuity continues until both you and a beneficiary are dead.

Under any option, the size of your monthly check depends on how much you invested, how old you are, and whether you are male or

Figure 12. Annuity Payments with Different Guarantees

A single premium immediate annuity offered by New York Life Insurance Company recently presented the following income options to a 65-year-old couple investing $100,000.

Option	*Monthly Payment*
Straight life	$1,109
Five years certain	1,086
Installment refund	1,063
Ten years certain	1,043
Joint and 50% survivor	1,025
Joint and 2/3 survivor	999
Fifteen years certain	998
Twenty years certain	958
Joint and 100% survivor	952

female. It also varies from insurer to insurer in a hotly competitive and fast-changing market. In 1986, for example, a 65-year-old man could have bought a straight-life annuity for $25,000 from Federal Kemper Life and received monthly payments of $262.75. Alexander Hamilton Life would have paid him only $255.81. You just have to wait until you are on the verge of retirement and then shop around.

How to Handle Lump Sums

One distinct advantage of taking your pension and other accrued retirement funds in a lump sum is that the principal is yours and becomes part of your estate. If heirs are not the issue, you should weigh the lump sum against the annuity for investment value. "What you want to figure out is, can you take the pension money, invest it conservatively, and get a return equal to the annuity," says Gary Strum, head of pension services and tax strategy at E. F. Hutton. With its guarantee of undiminishing monthly payments, an annuity is a highly secure source of income, which only very safe lump-sum investments can match. "For me, the touchstone is long-term government bonds," says Strum.

When pension payments slightly exceed the return on government bonds, taking a lump sum may still make sense because you retain control of your investment. You can dip into principal if necessary to meet emergencies, whereas an annuity can never give you more than the monthly allowance. More important, the buying power of fixed annuity payments will decline because of inflation. There is some chance of managing a lump sum so that it will appreciate along with rising prices. But you have to take the risk that goes with investing in real estate, precious metals, or stocks, even the bluest of chips: that your capital may shrink.

If a lump sum makes sense for both your temperament and your investment plan, you come to a rather sophisticated question of tax planning. When you take your tax-deferred money out at retirement, the Internal Revenue Service will demand its long-postponed cut. With an annuity, previously untaxed income enters the IRS net gradually, without jacking up your tax bill very much. With lump sums, the law leaves you two ways to soften the blow. You can step back under the shelter of tax deferral by rolling over the money into an IRA within 60 days. Or you can pay the tax immediately but at a lower rate reserved for lump-sum distributions of Keogh plans and other funds that represent pretax income. The major exception is the IRA itself, which does not qualify for special treatment of lump-sum withdrawals.

The treatment is called forward averaging. To use it, you must have been a participant in your company's retirement plan for at least five years before the distribution, and the amount you receive must be all the money due you. You are allowed to use forward averaging just once. You can use it only after you pass age 59½ — with one exception. As part of the transitional process from the old tax law to the one passed in 1986, people who reached age 50 before 1986 can use 10-year forward averaging, which is being phased out and replaced by less generous five-year forward averaging. Also, if you turned 50 by that deadline, you don't have to wait until you reach 59½ to use this potential tax break.

What makes forward averaging advantageous is that you compute the tax as if you had received the lump sum in equal parts over the next five (or 10) years and as if it were your only income in each of those years. Even if you are married, you pay the tax rate of a single person. Nevertheless, starting in 1988, five-year averaging lets you hold down the tax on nearly $100,000 of retirement distributions to a flat 15 percent. The normal tax on such a lump sum, when combined with your other income, would range up to 28 percent or even 33 percent.

If you have pension rights dating to 1973 or earlier, the new tax law leaves open a second kind of tax treatment of retirement funds received all at once. Until 1992 — or with no deadline if you hit 50 before 1986 — you can pay a 20 percent capital-gains tax on the old money.

To all these options, the 1986 tax reform adds one further complication — and a potentially costly one for people with large assets stashed in tax-deferred plans. It levies a 15 percent tax on distributions from such plans in excess of $112,500 a year. The tax applies to pensions, company-sponsored savings plans, and tax-sheltered annuities available to teachers and employees of certain other nonprofit institutions. You can reduce the tax, but not eliminate it, on money put into a plan before August 1, 1986, and you can receive five times the amount ordinarily tax-free, $562,500, if you use five-year forward averaging. The penalty, though alas not the five-year averaging, also applies to distributions from IRAs.

Should you use forward averaging? Are you eligible for 10-year averaging or only five-year? Which would work out best in your case? Is your best choice to roll over all your untaxed retirement money into an IRA? As these questions suggest, people on the eve of retirement face one of the most complicated — and crucial — tax-planning decisions of their lives.

In general, people who can afford to let their nest egg grow untouched for five years or more probably will be best off in the long run with an IRA rollover. Those who intend to use up the distribution fairly quickly — to start a business, say, or take a world cruise — probably should choose forward averaging. However, the choice is seldom that obvious. Among the variables you will have to consider are the size of the distribution you will receive, the rates of return you can expect to get inside and outside the IRA, and how soon you will need the money. "The only thing to do then," says Greg Kushner, a senior tax manager of the accounting firm of Price Waterhouse in Los Angeles, "is to run the numbers and find out which option leaves you with the most after-tax money." Considering that a large portion of your life savings may be at stake, you would do well to seek advice from a tax lawyer or accountant before choosing one method over the other.

Unwinding Your IRA

Compared with the straightforward rules for opening and adding to IRAs (see Chapter 24), those governing withdrawals are positively Byzantine. The best way of coming to terms with these rules is to think of them as divided into three parts — one for the time before you reach age 59½, another for the period between 59½ and 70½, and a third for the years after 70½.

At each stage, these rules grow in complexity.

Before 59½, you can take out as much money as you want, but unless you are totally disabled, you must pay a 10 percent penalty (15 percent on amounts over $112,500) in addition to income tax on any withdrawals.

When you reach 59½, you are free to do whatever you wish with your retirement account. You can take out as much as $112,500 a year without penalty, or you can continue putting cash in. Indeed, you can make both withdrawals and deposits. You can also continue to exercise the valuable right to defer taxes on lump-sum distributions from qualified pension or profit-sharing plans by rolling them over into your IRA. Your main decision turns on whether you need to live on your IRA money. You can dip into it, of course, even if you are not retired — although it is generally wise to let your funds continue compounding tax-deferred if you can.

At 70½, your freedom to withdraw or not to withdraw ends. In this third IRA period, instead of paying a penalty for using your money — as you do prior to 59½ — you become subject to a penalty for *not* disgorging some of your hoard. To deter you from leaving a tax-sheltered bounty to your heirs, Uncle Sam takes a full 50 percent of any cash you were supposed to withdraw but didn't.

So how much must you withdraw? The answer draws you into Kafkaesque regulations and computations. To fathom them requires the assistance of an accountant or financial adviser or the trustees of your IRAs. Even so, it is a good idea to get the gist of the rules.

The average life expectancy of people your age and sex is the crux of the matter. The government allows you to draw down your IRA savings at a rate that matches your life span as projected on insurance industry actuarial tables. To determine your minimum annual withdrawal, you divide your life expectancy into the sum of all your IRAs. But how long is your life expectancy? The answer changes every year. The longer you live, the longer the tables expect you to live. For example, a man of 70½ can anticipate reaching 82; a woman the same age, 85. A man of 75, however, has a life expectancy of 85, and a woman of 75 can expect to hit 87. And people who attain those ages will live, on average, to 91 and 94.

To adjust for the actuarial facts, the IRS lets you recalculate your life expectancy annually so that you never outlive your Individual Retirement Account. What's more, you can reduce your minimum withdrawal further by using an actuarial number that takes into account your life expectancy and that of your spouse. For example, a 71-year-old man is likely to live 11.6 more years and a 70-year-old woman, 15 years. But the IRS figures that at least one of them will live for 18 more years. By using joint survivorship tables, the husband could elect to withdraw as little as one-eighteenth of his IRA total in his 71st year — not the roughly one-eleventh he would have to take out on the basis of his own life expectancy.

To spread your IRAs over both your expected life span and that of your spouse, you simply name your husband or wife as your beneficiary. When you must begin receiving distributions, you instruct the trustees of your IRAs to compute the minimum payout by using the joint survivorship tables.

Your beneficiary need not be your spouse for you to take advantage of the joint life-expectancy gambit. To slash to an absolute minimum the amount you are required to take out, you can name someone significantly younger than you. A 71-year-old woman and her 35-year-old son, for instance, have a joint life expectancy of 38.9 years. There is a catch, however. Each year you must withdraw at least half of the amount you would be expected to take out on your own, regardless of the joint life expectancy calculation. For example, if that 71-year-old woman had IRAs totaling $150,000, she would be required to take out at least $5,208 in the first year. That equals half of the $10,416 she would be forced to pull out if she used her own 14.4-year life expectancy.

After you pass 70½, your IRA trustees may alert you that you must make a minimum annual withdrawal. Some trustees will even compute the amount for you, and a few will give you the option of having a set percentage of your investments automatically withdrawn at intervals as frequent as monthly. Usually, though, you are on your own. Banks, brokerage firms, and mutual-fund companies reason that most of their customers have more than one IRA and that no single trustee can calculate how much you must take out of all your accounts each year to avoid being penalized.

Enrolling for Social Security

You become eligible for partial Social Security retirement income as early as age 62. To get full benefits, however, you must wait until you are 65. Social Security won't start sending you monthly checks until you notify the local office that you are ready. Go there and fill out an application three months before you want the first check to arrive and be sure to take with you a certified copy of your birth certificate. If you expect a check for your spouse's benefit, you also will need a certified copy of your marriage license. Divorcées filing for benefits have to present certified copies of marriage and divorce papers. To make certain that you get your full benefits starting with your first check, take along W-2 tax withholding statements for your final two working years.

Your check will arrive in your mailbox — or, if you prefer, it will be deposited directly to your bank account — no later than the third day of the month. Each January, Social Security benefits automatically rise by the percentage increase in the previous year's cost of living. If inflation is less than 3 percent, however, you won't get a raise unless Congress votes for one.

It is advisable every few years — no matter how far away from retirement you are — to ask your local Social Security office for a Request for Statement of Earnings form. Three or four weeks after you fill it out and mail it back, you should receive a statement listing your past earnings. Double-check the figures against your W-2 forms for each year to ensure that your taxable wages haven't been understated.

From Social Security's inception in 1937 through 1983, all benefits were free of federal, state, and local taxes. No more. Up to half your benefits are now subject to federal income tax if your income exceeds a certain level. Here is how it works. Add up your pension payments, investment income, and any job earnings. Subtract any exclusions you are entitled to. The amount left is your adjustable gross income. You must then tack on any municipal bond interest you have earned, even though it is exempt from federal income tax, and add to that figure half of your annual Social Security benefits. The special tax will hit you if you are married and filing jointly and the total exceeds $32,000 or if you are single and the total exceeds $25,000. You will be taxed on half of any excess above those limits or half of that year's Social Security benefit, whichever is smaller.

The Penalty for Working

Let's say you have started drawing your pension, the Social Security checks are arriving on schedule, and your investments are providing the comfortable level of income you expected. Nevertheless, you are not ready for the rocking chair, and you are tempted to boost your retirement income by taking a job at a salary of $20,000 a year. Before you put away the golf clubs and dust off the briefcase, consider this bleak news: between 65 and 70, you could pocket as little as $2,000 for working all year in that $20,000 job. Take into account commuting costs and other job-related expenses, and you might lose money by going back to work.

How does this dramatic disappearing act take place? First, until the month you reach 70, your Social Security check shrinks in proportion to growth in your job earnings above a certain limit, adjusted upward each year. In 1986 the limit was $7,800, and it is expected to rise to $8,800 by 1989. Whatever the limit, your Social Security payments will be cut one dollar for every two dollars you earn above that amount. Subtract the earnings limit from your retirement-job salary, divide the difference by two, and you arrive at the amount of Social Security benefits you will lose by working. There is a quick formula for calculating when you will eliminate all your benefits: double your annual Social Security income and add the current earnings limit. The result is the salary at which you will have canceled your Social Security check.

The earnings threshold is lower for people who start drawing Social Security before they are 65. In 1990, however, the penalty starts coming down. You will lose one dollar for every three dollars in earnings over the limit that year, and after that the level will rise annually.

Besides costing you Social Security benefits, going back to work may push you from the 15 to the 28 percent tax bracket. And you will keep on paying FICA tax on your earnings even if your past contributions to the Social Security system already entitle you to full benefits. In 1987, the rate was 7.15 percent of your salary up to $43,800. If you were self-employed, the rate was 12.3 percent. The employee rate rises in small steps to 7.65 percent and the self-employed rate to 15.3 percent in 1990. Social Security taxes are not deductible from your taxable income, but after 1989, one-half of a self-employed person's Social Security taxes will be deductible.

The question arises: Is working worth the effort? Probably not, if your motives are purely financial. Some retirees, however, continue working to satisfy other desires. "Many people seek postretirement jobs to retain the sense of identity and accomplishment that they got from working throughout their careers," says Paul Westbrook of Buck Consultants, a benefits consulting firm in New York City.

26

SAVING WIDOWS (OR WIDOWERS) FROM STILL MORE LOSSES

In finance, as in love, it is what spouses don't know or don't tell each other that hurts. The hazard of being poorly informed about your marriage partner's assets and liabilities — such as real estate holdings and mortgages, sideline business income and obligations, pension rights, and veterans' benefits — is that he or she may leave you permanently in ignorance. Every estate lawyer has a drawerful of stories about the expense and anguish bequeathed to clients by spouses who died without telling their mates everything they needed to know about the family's assets and liabilities.

Financial ignorance is all too common, especially among the nation's 11 million widows, who outnumber widowers by more than five to one. On average, new widows are 56 years old and, unless they remarry, face two decades on their own. Yet, rich or poor, most wives — as well as some husbands — are ill prepared to handle the family's assets. As psychologist Rosalind Barnett of Wellesley College's Center for Research on Women observes, "The overwhelming majority of widows have never thought at all about how their economic needs would be met in the future." Bryan M. Van Eaton, a Houston investment executive, adds, "Most widows haven't been taught anything beyond writing checks and managing a household budget."

A woman pays a heavy emotional price for her lack of knowledge. She also may put her economic well-being in jeopardy at a time when she is overcome by grief, confusion, and fear of the future. When James Purzer, a Houston geologist, died unexpectedly of a rare bone disease at 49, he left his widow, Janet, a small fortune in real estate and oil-well investments — and little inkling of how to manage them. To her dismay, Mrs. Purzer, then 43 and the mother of three teenage daughters, discovered that a $10,000 life insurance policy had lapsed because the monthly premium had not been paid. Worse, her husband owed $87,000 to banks and several thousand dollars to friends. Hoping to put off the creditors a bit, Mrs. Purzer, as executor of the estate, wrote polite notes to them explaining that her husband had died. They promptly slapped $45,000 in liens on the estate. Then American Express canceled her credit card without explanation, even though her account was separate from her husband's. "As far as what was really going on, I didn't have a clue," she said later.

Along with financial losses, secrecy between mates complicates the chore of settling an estate. For Edna Shaver, a homemaker and mother of four in Columbus, Ohio, the process dragged on for five years after her husband, a physician, died of a heart attack in 1978. He had provided well for his family, leaving $1 million, mostly in trust funds. But because Mrs. Shaver did not know much about her husband's finances, she had trouble appraising the estate and getting money from it. One of the problems was the discovery of investment real estate near Montreal that her husband had purchased. She was saved from temporary hardship only with the aid of the bank trust department and the immediate cash she received from insurance policies. It was a sobering experience. Looking back on it, she said, "I wish I had been in on the planning of things."

Catapulted into an unwelcome and unaccustomed role, a widow not only has to help settle her husband's estate but also has to decide which household bills to pay immediately and which ones can wait. She is faced with establishing her own credit with merchants, banks, and credit-card companies. She must fend off opportunists who prey on widows, such as shady businessmen offering speculative deals and con men posing as creditors of her husband. Often, one of her first decisions is whether to take the insurance payment in installments or in a lump sum. Since it is usually more money than she has ever handled, that lump sum can spark the impulse either to splurge or to conserve excessively. One widow was so confused that she stuck the check in her freezer for safekeeping.

A common reaction is to spend the money in a mistaken attempt to retain your old standard of living, according to Charlotte Kirsch, author of *A Survivor's Manual*. She warns, "If a new widow does not complete even a basic financial plan within six weeks of her husband's death, she is in grave danger of spending her entire inheritance."

The widows in the best financial shape do not necessarily have large inheritances. But they learned before their husbands died how to manage money. They regularly discussed family finances with their husbands and, more important, they rehearsed what to do with their potential legacies. These widows are a small minority. Kirsch has found that only one in seven husbands with annual earnings of $40,000 or more takes the "final step of telling his wife to invest her inheritance in vehicles that will give her monthly income." A husband who does not help his wife to plan for her years as a widow — or at least introduce her to his own financial advisers — forces her to seek help on her own. "He is turning her over to other men when he dies, and he has excluded her from meeting them while he is alive," Kirsch says.

Talking to your spouse about what you own seems a simple thing to do. What makes so many couples reluctant? For one thing, some husbands assume their wives don't understand finances or aren't interested in the subject. For another, some couples just don't trust each other. Partners who are fearful of divorce often think it necessary to conceal assets from their mates. But since there is an equal chance that the marriage will last, the more compelling fact is that 70 percent of wives outlive their husbands. James Dankenbring, an estate lawyer in Clayton, Missouri, concludes: "I suspect the foremost obstacle is that people just don't want to think about death. It's like pulling teeth to get clients to come in here and sign a will."

Financial planners and widows are united in their advice on how to deal with money in the event of a spouse's death: prepare beforehand and go slowly afterward. Lynn Caine, author of books on the family, suggests that a couple set aside an annual "contingency day" when they will assess what the surviving spouse would inherit and consider what he or she would do with it. Eugene Schorr, a partner in the accounting firm of Peat Marwick Mitchell in New York City, says you should ask each other a series of questions: "If either of you dies tomorrow, how much is there? Is that enough? And if it is not enough, how can it be increased?" If the answer is still "not enough," you should talk about ways the survivor could manage with less income and whether he or she ought to sell major assets that will be inherited — the house, an art collection, a business. You also should reexamine your wills and discuss where the survivor might go for financial advice.

Most important, you should update — and put in writing — all the information about your finances, records, and postmortem arrangements that is on the worksheet in Figure 5 of Chapter 6. Such a document will immensely help the survivor and the executor to settle the estate.

To begin preparing for the possibility of your spouse's death, both of you should learn the rudiments of money and investment. The wrong time to start asking the difference between money-market and stock funds is when you have to start managing the family assets alone. Nonetheless, a surprising number of women — even career women — show little interest until it is too late. As recently as 1981, Catherine W. Willis, then head of the Chase Manhattan Bank's financial advisory service for women, remarked, "We see young professional women who are unbelievably ignorant about money."

To make sure that both of you pay attention to the family's financial affairs, you should maintain separate checking accounts, take turns paying the monthly bills, and confer jointly with your broker, tax preparer, and other professional advisers. That way, each of you will know where to turn for counsel if the other dies first. Then you will be in less danger of turning to inexpert relatives for financial guidance. Relying on the well-intended but ill-informed advice of family friends a few years ago, a New York City widow invested in tax-free municipal bonds although her reduced income made the tax benefits worthless.

When It's Too Late to Plan

What if death has foreclosed on your opportunity to make plans together and take the necessary measures to understand your financial situation? Then you may be in for some detective work. Quite a few items of financial nitty-gritty won't show up on routine asset inventories — for example, the details of your spouse's work history. If your mate held a previous job long enough to earn a pension, you could be eligible for additional retirement income.

The only way to ferret out unsuspected assets is by systematically searching through your spouse's records. Start with checkbooks and canceled checks; they are mines of data about investments and insurance premiums. Next, dig out income tax returns. If you cannot find copies at home or at a tax preparer's office, you or the executor can get them from the regional office of the Internal Revenue Service. You may wait as long as 12 months for the returns to arrive, but the waiting can pay off. For example, Schedule B, which lists income from interest and dividends, should name each bank, stock, mutual fund, and bond that generated taxable income that year. Tax-free investments won't be entered on federal returns but may have been reported on state income tax returns, obtainable from your state tax department.

One benefit most surviving spouses are in line for is Social Security. It often pays benefits of more than $15,000 a year to a widow with young children. "Don't assume you aren't eligible just because no one ever told you so,'' says a spokesman for the Social Security Administration. Phone or visit the nearest SSA office within 30 days of the death and get the process started. Later you will need your spouse's Social Security number and death certificate, your marriage and birth certificates, and the birth certificates of any dependent children.

Military service often endows survivors with financial rights. If your husband or wife was in the armed forces, you might be in line for life insurance, a pension, burial expenses, even a VA mortgage loan. To apply for these benefits you will need the vet's discharge papers, which have a way of getting lost. After Alan Reese of Atlanta was killed in an auto accident in 1980 at the age of 46, his widow, Peggy, found a $15,000 serviceman's life insurance policy and learned for the first time that he had been in the navy. The Veterans Administration would not pay the insurance unless she could produce his discharge certificate, which was not among his papers. She had about given up hope of finding it until one day, while she was showing her son Chris, then 12, his father's picture in a college yearbook, the document fluttered to the floor.

Even without that bit of luck, Peggy Reese might have collected her husband's insurance if she had known what to do. You should apply for survivor's benefits while you are searching for the right paper — either the separation document or the discharge certificate. Start your inquiry at the state unemployment insurance office serving the town where the veteran lived after he left the armed forces. That is one of the first stops many service people make after their discharge. Next try the county clerk's office. Vets usually register their papers there. If all else fails, write to the National Personnel Records Center (Military Personnel Records, 9700 Page Boulevard, St. Louis, Missouri 63132). Even if the government has lost the discharge papers, this agency may be able to reconstruct the missing records.

As a last resort, some people use private investigators to sniff out hidden assets. This can be expensive — up to $100 an hour plus expenses — but worth the price if the suspected hoard proves to be substantial. Besides combing the obvious financial records, an investigator, often hired through an attorney, will scan phone bills and credit reports, check with the department of motor vehicles, and use contacts he has at whatever banks and other financial institutions the trail leads to.

Often the sleuth examines the subject's way of life for clues to what he or she owned. ''Older European families, for instance, may leave money in trust for the kids or grandkids but not tell them where it is,'' says Vincent Parco, who runs an investigation agency in New York City. Parco once tracked down a cooperative apartment that belonged to the estate of a man-about-town. He had bought it for his mistress — an expensive proposition in Manhattan. But because he had kept the property in his own name, the man's widow inherited it, not the lover.

Handling an Inheritance

As a widow or widower, your first priority should be to preserve your inheritance. Thoughtlessly converting assets such as a house into cash can be wasteful. Also, it may be possible to delay paying some bills so that money can earn bank interest. To guard against mistakes and con men, you would be well advised to double-check whether questionable bills have already been paid and whether the debt was actually incurred. You should also determine whether your spouse carried insurance policies specifically designed to pay off the mortgage or other loans.

Wait six months or a year before investing your inheritance in anything that is not safe and liquid. ''You won't be thinking straight before then,'' says Virginia Deaton, a widow who once taught courses in the San Francisco Bay area on coping with widowhood. Keep your cash safely in certificates of deposit, money-market mutual funds, or conservative stock funds until you are ready to absorb the counsel of professionals and decide how to diversify your investments.

To minimize a sense of helplessness in the meantime, you can turn to several books. Charlotte Kirsch's *A Survivor's Manual* and *Widow* by Lynn Caine are out of print but may be in your library. *Coping* by Martha Yates (Prentice-Hall, $9.95) is available in bookstores, or send for the pamphlet *What Do You Do Now?* ($1.30 from the Life Insurance Marketing and Research Association, P.O. Box 208, Hartford, Connecticut 06141). The Theos Foundation (Penn Hills Mall, Suite 410, Pittsburgh, Pennsylvania 15235; 412-243-4299) can suggest additional sources of financial and emotional counsel.

27

ESTATE PLANNING: HOW TO KEEP YOUR MONEY IN THE FAMILY

After a brush with death has moved Ishmael, the narrator in Herman Melville's *Moby Dick*, to write his will, he says with relief, "I felt all the easier; a stone was rolled away from my heart." In mid-nineteenth-century America, Ishmael's bequests, like most men's, would have been simple: a bit of money, a seabag of personal effects, perhaps a scrimshaw carved on whalebone by a fellow crewman of the *Pequod*. In the late twentieth century, more is likely to be at stake. It takes only a few successful investments, a small business, or a house to make you a candidate for comprehensive estate planning.

People who fail to make such provisions don't suffer; their heirs do. Those whom you love most may inherit the least — or nothing at all. The tax collector may help himself to a generous portion of your estate. If your heirs are very young, mentally handicapped, or lacking in financial acumen, the management of the money and property you left to them may fall into the hands of strangers. The cost of probate — the legal process of proving your will valid and taking inventory of your assets — may eat into the value of your estate and expose your survivors to embarrassing publicity.

To craft a solid estate plan, you need to know how to employ four basic tools: wills, trusts, lifetime gifts, and joint ownership. A will should be the cornerstone of your plan. (See Chapter 29.) If you have not written one, you have plenty of company. Only one-third of all adults have wills, and one can only guess how many of those people should have, but haven't, updated their documents to reflect changes in their lives or the law.

Many people who lack wills rationalize that joint ownership with right of survivorship can take the place of a will. But consider what would happen if a childless married couple who owned all of their major assets jointly were involved in an accident in which the husband was killed instantly and the wife survived for another day. The husband's half of the couple's joint property would automatically pass to his wife upon his death. Unless she managed to write a will on her deathbed, however, all of the couple's assets would go to her relatives after her death, leaving his family without a legacy.

Couples with young children also need wills, even though their jointly owned property would pass to their children under state laws of intestacy if they perished together. In a will, you can also pass along the responsibility for caring for your children and their inheritances should they be orphaned. If you die without a will, the court appoints guardians for your children and their inheritances.

The wisest strategy is for parents to write wills in which a trust is created to hold their children's inheritances. A guardian of your children's property, either named in your will or appointed by the court, must annually report major expenditures and investments on the children's behalf to a judge. That seems an excellent way to ensure that a guardian does not steal or dissipate an orphan's inheritance. But it requires cumbersome paperwork and gives the judge — a stranger — power over how your legacy is invested and spent.

A trust negates the need for you to name a guardian for your children's property. It also keeps a child's inheritance out of his reach for as long as his parents wish. Under guardianship rules, heirs gain control of their money at the age of majority, 18 in most states.

Naturally, you will also want to make sure that you will leave as much money and property as possible. Thanks to the generous provisions of the 1981 tax law, married couples can, as of 1987, bequeath estates worth as much as $1.2 million to their heirs without losing a cent to the federal tax collector.

Gift Tax

The 1981 law lumps gift and estate taxes into one "unified" amount at death. A tax exemption applies to the sum of taxable gifts you make while you live and the estate you leave behind. Every year, you are allowed to make tax-free gifts of as much as $10,000 each to as many people as you would like; married couples may give joint gifts of as much as $20,000. Amounts above those annual limits are taxable once their total exceeds the lifetime exclusion for federal gift and estate taxes. Since January 1, 1987, that exclusion has amounted to $600,000 per person.

Additionally, you may give limitless amounts and leave an estate of any value to your spouse tax-free. This unlimited marital deduction has proved to be a mixed blessing. As financial planner Marcia Elefant of Houston points out, "There's a misconception that the unlimited marital deduction does away with the need for estate planning when all it does is postpone taxes until the second spouse's death."

Shedding Assets

You can trim estate taxes by removing assets from your estate. One way is by giving money or valuables to friends and relatives during your lifetime. Another is by making charitable donations while you are alive as well as in your will. A third is by bequeathing property to your heirs through trusts. It is with the help of a trust, for example, that married couples with a $1.2 million estate can sidestep federal estate tax. Each spouse's will leaves $600,000 of assets to a trust from which the other spouse draws income during her or his lifetime. When the second spouse dies, the trust fund passes untaxed to their heirs, and the rest of the second spouse's assets up to $600,000 also go to their heirs tax-free.

Leaving Liquid Capital

When you tackle estate planning, you should make certain that your estate is liquid enough to pay taxes as well as debts and other expenses. If your estate is top-heavy with real estate, for example, your survivors may be forced to unload some of it at fire-sale prices to raise cash quickly. You can solve a liquidity problem by purchasing life insurance (see Chapter 57). As an added bonus, insurance proceeds are not taxable as part of your estate as long as you bought the policy at least three years before your death. The lesson: don't wait until you are on your deathbed to figure out that your heirs will face a liquidity crisis.

Bypassing Probate

Probate avoidance is not as crucial a concern as taxes, which can devour up to 55 percent of a very large estate. But probate has its own costs and problems. Lawyers' fees, court costs, and other expenses can consume as much as 5 to 10 percent of a legacy. Additionally, the probate process can delay the settlement of an estate for anywhere from two months to two or more years, depending upon the efficiency of your executor and attorney as well as the court in your jurisdiction. During that time, some of your heirs may not have access to their full inheritances.

Assets such as trust funds, life insurance, pension funds, and IRAs, for which you have designated beneficiaries, automatically bypass probate. Nevertheless, you should periodically review beneficiary designations to make sure that your plans have not been scrambled by recent tax-law changes or other legislation. Assume, for example, that a man who was widowed named his daughter as the beneficiary of his pension plan, then remarried in 1985. Despite his wishes, his pension would not go to his daughter. Under a law that took effect that year, pension plan proceeds must be paid to a surviving spouse unless he or she waives the right in writing.

Joint Property

In some cases, joint ownership is an ideal way to avoid probate. For example, if you reside in Massachusetts and own a vacation home in New Hampshire, your heirs will have to endure probate in two states. These and most other states don't recognize out-of-state probate. You can sidestep that problem, however, by establishing in the deed to your summer place that you and your intended heir are joint owners with rights of survivorship. Upon your death, the house passes to your co-owner. However, joint ownership can also cause legal hassles and create unnecessary estate-tax liabilities when it is used injudiciously.

People who live in one of the nine community property states (Arizona, California, Idaho, Louisiana, Nevada, New Mexico, Texas, Washington, and Wisconsin) must be wary of attempting to make someone other than a spouse the joint owner of community property. In those states, all income earned and property acquired by a couple during marriage, except for individual gifts and inheritances, is deemed community property and is owned equally by each spouse. When the first spouse dies, half of his or her share of community property passes to the surviving mate, and the other half goes to heirs named in the dead spouse's will. The surviving spouse may or may not be among them.

In other states, married couples who own everything jointly may bequeath to their heirs a hefty estate-tax bill. Say that a couple jointly own assets worth $800,000. On the husband's death, his half of the joint property passes to his wife without penalty because married couples may leave estates of any size to each other tax-free. When she dies, however, $52,200 of her $800,000 will end up in the federal treasury instead of her heirs' bank accounts. Had the couple held some of their property separately, each of them could have taken advantage of the $600,000 federal estate-tax exclusion.

Trusts

There is another way to dodge probate that is more costly than joint ownership but less likely to cause complications: establish a revocable living trust. This device would have proved useful to Alta Maeder, a Raytown, Missouri, widow who died in 1984 at the age of 84. Maeder wanted to make it easy for her six children and two grandchildren to divide her modest $48,000 estate, so she wrote a will, liquidated her small stock portfolio, sold her house, and invested in certificates of deposit at a bank where she had maintained a savings account for more than half a century. But when Vivian Brownell, one of Maeder's daughters, tried to close out her mother's bank accounts, she was told that she would have to wait until the probate process was completed. The bank's recommendation of an attorney to handle the probate chores was accepted by Maeder's son, who had been named executor but was not sure what the job entailed. Fifteen months later, the bank released Maeder's money — minus $5,000 in probate and legal fees. "You always hear that you need a will," says Vivian Brownell, "but no one ever tells you that sometimes a will isn't enough."

Had Maeder transferred her bank accounts to a revocable living trust, she could have received income from the trust for the rest of her life. At her death, her estate would have skipped probate, and her money would have been distributed as she wished. An attorney would have charged $400 to $1,000 to draft the trust, far less than probate cost. Revocable living trusts have a second advantage. If Maeder had ever been unable to take care of her own financial affairs because of illness, a successor trustee who had been named in her trust agreement could have managed her money for her.

To the uninitiated, trusts can seem hopelessly confusing, especially when attorneys tick off the names of dozens of different types, including such unlikely-sounding ones as sprinkle and QTIP. Trusts actually come in only two basic types, testamentary and living (sometimes called *inter vivos*). A testamentary trust is created in your will and takes effect upon your death. A living trust starts to operate during your lifetime.

Quite simply, a trust is a legal instrument that holds assets contributed to it by one person, called the grantor, for the benefit of one or more others, called the beneficiaries. The grantor sets down instructions for the management of a trust and the disbursement of its income and principal. This is done in a document called a trust agreement, which an attorney draws up. The grantor also chooses a third party, called a trustee, to hold title to the trust property and carry out the grantor's wishes.

Many people mistakenly believe that trusts work only for rich families, who can afford to tie up large chunks of cash for long periods. But as the Maeder estate demonstrates, trusts can solve the estate-planning problems of middle-income families as well. Best of all, a trust can be as flexible as the individual who establishes it. Or as Bernard Finkelstein, a New York City attorney, puts it, "A trust is like a big bolt of cloth that can be cut in almost any style to suit your needs."

Instead of going through probate upon your death, assets in a living trust automatically pass to your chosen heirs or remain in trust for their benefit. That is because a living trust is a private legal agreement between grantor and trustee. By contrast, property in a testamentary trust is included in your probate estate because such trusts are created in wills, which are public records. Testamentary trusts are usually established to minimize taxes or to appoint a financially astute trustee to manage the inheritances of youthful, wasteful, or incompetent heirs.

Living trusts may be revocable or irrevocable. With a revocable trust, you continue to enjoy complete control over trust property, meaning you can change the trust's provisions, terminate it, or even serve as trustee. Once you establish an irrevocable trust, however, you cannot control assets in it or tinker with its provisions. As a result, assets in an irrevocable trust are removed from your taxable estate, but assets in a revocable trust are not. While testamentary trusts become irrevocable upon your death, property in them is still included in your taxable estate because you controlled the assets during your lifetime.

Here, then, are the major types of trusts designed to safeguard your heirs' inheritances, protect your assets should you fall ill, and avoid probate.

Revocable Living Trusts

You can spare your heirs the costs and delays associated with probate by transferring all or most of your assets to a revocable living trust during your lifetime. Probate courts operate more efficiently in some locales than others, but it is not unusual for lawyers' fees and probate costs to shave about 5 percent off a $200,000 estate. As in the Maeder case, costs consume even greater percentages of smaller estates. Some of your heirs may not have access to their full inheritances for a few months, if probate is swift, or for two or more years, if it drags on. If you own property in more than one state, your heirs will have to contend with multiple probate procedures. Finally, probate court records are open to anyone who cares to look at them, from nosy neighbors to newspaper reporters.

With a revocable living trust, you may retain any or all income the trust produces, act as trustee, change the trust's provisions, or even terminate it. As a result, such trusts lack tax advantages: you have to pay income tax on trust income, and trust assets are included in your taxable estate. After your demise, the trust can remain intact for the benefit of your heirs or can terminate, with assets distributed to those same beneficiaries.

Revocable living trusts provide a second advantage that is less publicized than probate avoidance. You can act as trustee while you are in good health, but a successor trustee of your choice can take over if your doctor ever certifies that you are no longer physically or mentally capable of handling your own affairs. The arrangement is superior to the alternative, a court-appointed conservatorship. If you lack a living trust, your friends or relatives must ask a judge to declare you incapacitated and name a conservator (sometimes called an administrator) to handle your investments and pay your bills. The conservator's annual fee can equal three-quarters of 1 percent of your assets. Additionally, critics of the conservatorship system charge that it is marred by political patronage and unscrupulous appointees. In a widely publicized scandal, real estate investor John Zaccaro, the husband of 1984 Democratic vice-presidential candidate Geraldine Ferraro, was removed as conservator of an elderly New York City woman's estate after improperly borrowing $175,000 from it for his own real estate deals.

The major disadvantage of a revocable living trust is the inconvenience of transferring everything you own to it. You must change the titling documents of stocks, bank accounts, and real estate to show that your trust, not you, owns the assets. If you establish a living trust but neglect to alter your titling documents, the property in your name at your death will be subject to probate.

While a revocable living trust performs the same functions as a will, you should also write a so-called pour-over will, in which you can bequeath personal belongings of sentimental value and name a guardian for your minor children. You could stipulate that any property you did not have time to place in your trust should go there after your death, but these assets will be subject to probate.

Standby or Convertible Trust

If you don't want to bother transferring title of all your assets to a trust while you are healthy, you can set up a variation of the revocable living trust called a standby or convertible trust and leave it empty. At the same time, your attorney draws up another legal document that gives a friend or relative durable power of attorney over your assets. Unlike a standard power of attorney, the durable variety remains in effect if you are incapacitated. At that time, the person with power over your assets transfers them to your standby trust. All goes as planned if you suffer a lingering illness. But if you die suddenly, the person to whom you gave durable power of attorney may not have time to place your assets in the standby trust; then your property will be subject to probate.

Minors' Trust

You can protect your young children by creating a testamentary trust in your will to hold property that you bequeath to them. The trust becomes irrevocable upon your death, but since you controlled the trust property during your life, such an arrangement will not reduce or eliminate estate taxes. (A spouse who handles the family finances can establish the same sort of trust for a mate who lacks the skill or inclination to manage money.)

A minors' trust safeguards your children's property from con artists or ne'er-do-well relatives who might stake it on high-risk ventures. If you fail to establish a trust, the guardian you appoint in your will must make an annual accounting to the court of major expenditures and investments on the children's behalf. Some state laws set strict limits on a guardian's spending. In Delaware, for example, guardians must obtain the court's approval to spend more than $1,200 a year on a child's private school or college.

Additionally, a guardian and the court can control a child's money only until he reaches majority. At that time, Junior is free to spend his inheritance as he pleases — on the college education that you saved for or the Las Vegas sabbatical you had not intended to sacrifice for.

If you establish a minors' trust, the trustee must follow instructions you set down in your trust agreement, not the orders of a judge. You can also keep the trust principal out of your beneficiary's hands until he is older and presumably more mature. Parents often stipulate that one-third of a trust's assets should go to a child at age 25, with the other thirds distributed five and ten years later.

You can also maintain control over how your legacy is spent for the trust's duration. For example, if you want your offspring to develop a strong work ethic, you can direct that a percentage of trust income be used for necessities while the rest can be withdrawn only to cover medical emergencies, private school tuition, or the cost of launching a business. You can even include an incentive provision in your trust document. Its terms might stipulate that the more money your children earn on their own, the more trust income they are entitled to. Spendthrift clauses that prohibit beneficiaries from assigning future trust income to their creditors are also popular.

There is a chance, however, that your children will successfully challenge your trust's provisions in court if you try to run their personal lives from beyond the grave. Court decisions vary from state to state, but trust agreements that prohibit children from marrying are usually easy to overturn.

To strike the right balance, it is often advisable to give your trustee discretionary powers, including the right to tap trust principal in case of an emergency. A trust with two or more children as beneficiaries can also include a so-called sprinkling provision, which allows the trustee to allocate income and principal to beneficiaries in accordance with their changing needs. If one heir wins the lottery while another is permanently disabled in an accident, the trustee can give the less fortunate heir a bigger share.

Trusts for the Handicapped

It may sound paternalistic, but it is only practical: if you want to leave all or part of your legacy to a disabled beneficiary, don't give him control of his inheritance. Leaving property directly to a disabled individual may disqualify him from federal and state social-service programs designed for the indigent. The main financial support system — Medicaid to pay for hospitalization and Supplemental Security Income to pay for food and shelter after or between hospital stays — may be cut off until he has used up his inheritance. Hospital fees alone quickly will drain away money you may have willed to a handicapped child to make his life easier.

One way of sidestepping this trap is to bequeath your estate to an obliging relative or friend along with a letter instructing him to spend some of the money on your heir. Then, according to Sanford Schlesinger, a New York City attorney and the author of a legal text on estate planning for the elderly, your heir will still be eligible for public assistance and your assets will be out of the state's reach. Unfortunately, if your informal trustee decides to keep your money all to himself, no law can stop him.

A formal testamentary trust offers protection from a corrupt relative but not necessarily from institutional predators. Social-service agencies have gone to court and succeeded in seizing the contents of trusts set up for disabled beneficiaries to compensate for services. A philosophical debate is going on between those who believe that everyone has a right to state services and those who think that families should expend their own funds before society has to pay. Both sides have won skirmishes in court, so it is essential to have your trust drafted by an attorney who is familiar with the case law in your state. Most state and local bar associations have committees that address the legal problems of the disabled and may be able to refer you to an experienced lawyer.

You can probably keep the government at bay by inserting certain provisions in a trust for a retarded child or a bedridden parent. First you must make it clear in your trust agreement that trust income should be used to supplement, not replace, public assistance. You should underscore that intention by including in the trust agreement a sprinkling provision, which gives your trustee the power to distribute income and principal not only to your disabled heir but to other beneficiaries as well. Likewise, stipulate that the principal should pass to your other relatives or to a charity when the trust ends.

As with other types of trusts, you may name a family member, friend, bank, or trust company to serve as trustee. Name a guardian, too, who may double as trustee.

You may want to add an escape clause that provides for the trust to terminate if it is challenged in court. Again, principal should not go to your disabled heir but to other beneficiaries. During your lifetime, you can ask these secondary beneficiaries to spend some of their inheritance on your handicapped heir. But if your trust for him terminates, Schlesinger warns, formalizing such a request in a letter just might invite another legal challenge by the state of your heir's right to receive government benefits.

The Right Trustee

Choosing a trustee is probably the toughest part of establishing a trust. You are searching for someone who is both financially savvy and sensitive to the needs of your beneficiaries — a tall order. Even if you intend to act as your own trustee for a revocable trust, you should name a successor trustee to take over if you become too ill to manage your money.

People with modest trusts probably should select a relative or friend. Unlike professional trustees, whose fees usually are determined by state law, friends and relatives may agree to serve without compensation. Annual fees for professional trustees can range from about three-quarters of 1 percent to 1 percent of a trust's assets up to $300,000. Above that amount, the larger the trust, the smaller the percentage of assets lost to fees.

Not surprisingly, professional trustees reserve the right to reject trusts that would bring in paltry fees. Large banks and trust companies in major metropolitan areas generally snub trusts worth less than $200,000 or $300,000. Small-town banks may be willing to accept trusts worth $50,000 or even less. John Fitzgerald, an attorney in Glens Falls, New York, who specializes in estate planning, offers this advice: "If your trust contains only a couple of life insurance policies, a savings account and your house, ask yourself whether there is someone in your family who can act as trustee."

People shopping for an institutional trustee should ask trust officers how their funds have performed recently, as well as over the past five and 10 years, so that bull and bear markets are both taken into account. Trust departments have lately shed their stodgy image, but returns vary tremendously from bank to bank.

The reputation of bank trust departments was tarnished in 1984, when the U.S. Comptroller of the Currency warned 100 large banks to stop parking uninvested trust monies in their own savings accounts, which were then earning just 5.5 percent interest. These banks were supposed to invest funds in the highest-yielding, safest short-term investments available.

No matter what their investment performance may be, all banks and trust companies hold an important advantage over individual trustees: continuity. Barring a bank failure, a professional trustee will always be around when you need him, unlike friends or relatives, who may move, go on vacations, become preoccupied with their own affairs — or die.

If you fear that an institutional trustee will not be sensitive to your family's needs, you can appoint a family member or friend to act as cotrustee. The two trustees make decisions together. If you appoint an individual to serve as a sole trustee, you should also name a backup in case your first choice is unable to serve. You may also wish to insert a clause in your trust document that gives adult beneficiaries the right to change trustees by majority vote.

You should leave the original of your trust agreement with your trustee, keeping copies for yourself and your attorney. As a service, some large banks and trust companies automatically notify you every couple of years to make certain that there is nothing you would like to change in a revocable or testamentary trust. But it is usually your responsibility to review your arrangements whenever tax laws are revised, your financial situation changes, or a birth, death, marriage, or divorce alters your family.

Should You Do It Yourself?

People with simple estate-planning needs may consider saving on legal fees by writing their own wills and trusts. The cult of self-sufficiency was born a generation ago, when Norman Dacey's *How to Avoid Probate!*, a how-to book with fill-in forms for living trusts, was number 1 on the best-seller list, topping even Masters and Johnson's *Human Sexual Response*. Today, do-it-yourself will-making kits are hawked on TV, and blank wills are sold in office supply stores.

Chances are that you do not need to hire an attorney, accountant, or financial planner to advise you on estate planning unless you are self-employed, have a potentially taxable estate, or cannot fathom the basics about wills, trusts, gifts, and joint ownership. But it is advisable to hire an attorney to draft the legal documents necessary to carry out your plan, no matter how simple that seems.

If Otto Holmok were alive today, he would probably agree. Holmok was a physicist in Hayward, California, who died of cancer in 1983. Without consulting an attorney, he had written a will that left $10,000 to his sister, and $800,000 to "all universities in California that does [*sic*] research work on human cancer." His sister received her inheritance immediately, but a probate court judge ruled that Holmok's executor was obliged to notify every institution of higher learning in California of the $800,000 bequest. That sparked a raging battle among a dozen universities and research institutions. Nearly three years after Holmok's death, not a cent of his legacy, by then worth about $1.2 million, had been used to find a cure for cancer. In fact, Holmok's sloppily worded will does not even stipulate that the money should eventually be used for that purpose. Since it is unclear whether the gift was meant to be restricted to cancer research or unrestricted to a university that conducts cancer research, the money could conceivably be spent to re-sod Stanford's lawns.

Any competent attorney could have stated Holmok's intentions clearly. If your estate plan calls for complex bequests or a trust agreement, you may be wise to hire an estate specialist. You can obtain referrals from your local bar association or by writing to the American College of Probate Counsel (10964 West Pico Boulevard, Los Angeles, California 90064).

Finally, if you feel that procrastination is preferable to contemplating your own mortality, remember that an estate plan not only secures your family's future but also pays a dividend during your lifetime. It forces you to organize your financial affairs. As Laura Connon, a Seattle attorney, puts it, "An estate plan makes it easier for you to see where you are financially and decide where you want to be." When you get there, like Ishmael, you will doubtless be possessed of a lightened heart.

28

ESTATE PLANNING: AVOIDING DEATH TAXES

Would you include in your will a debt-ridden spendthrift who already has taken more of your money than you can begin to add up? Probably not, especially if he is the Uncle Sam we all know and, well, respect. But unless you plan carefully, the old moocher could end up with a big share of your life's savings after you are gone.

Fortunately, the federal tax code contains an assortment of opportunities for you to protect your estate from the government's grasp. To review them: the most generous is the marital deduction, which lets you leave as much as you want to your spouse, tax-free. In addition, you and your mate each can pass to other heirs a total of as much as $600,000 in assets, minus any taxable gifts you make during your lifetime, without owing federal estate taxes. Those rules mean that if you have a net worth — counting the value of any life insurance proceeds you would receive upon your spouse's death — of $600,000 or less, you won't have to do a thing to shield your estate from federal taxes, although you still may be exposed to nasty state death taxes. Even if you are married and, as a couple, are worth as much as $1.2 million, you can arrange your affairs so that the Internal Revenue Service cannot haunt your heirs.

The essence of estate-tax planning is to arrange your assets so that the taxable estate of each spouse can claim as much as possible of the full $600,000 exemption. The first step toward accomplishing that goal is to take a rough tally of whether you would leave anything to the IRS if you shuffled off tomorrow — or how close your estate now stands to the taxable threshold. Figure 13 takes you through the calculation.

Figure 13. Totting Up Your Estate

To their heirs' dismay, many people incorrectly assume that their estates are too modest to be taxed. Instead of guessing, you can determine your estate's federal tax liability by completing the worksheet on page 205.

First, estimate the value of your gross estate by adding up these assets (if you haven't already done so in Chapter 3, Figure 1):

- Stocks, bonds, real estate; cash in money-market funds, checking, and savings accounts.
- Household furnishings, automobiles, jewelry, and other collectibles.
- Your share of jointly held property. If you own an asset with your spouse that he or she will automatically inherit upon your death, half of its value ends up in your estate. If your co-owner is not your spouse and you received property as a joint gift or inheritance, half of its value is included in your estate. When such co-owners purchase property together, the portion of the property you paid for is part of your estate. People who live or have lived in a community property state should be aware of another rule. All income earned and assets acquired by a couple while married and living in these states — except for individual gifts and inheritances — are considered community property. Half of that property is included in each spouse's estate.
- Proceeds from life insurance policies and annuities.
- Retirement benefits, including Individual Retirement Accounts and employer-sponsored pension, profit-sharing, and stock-purchase plans.
- Gifts you have made with strings attached. For example, if you gave your house to your daughter but retained the right to occupy it, the tax collector could declare that you still own it.
- Assets over which you hold general power of appointment. Say your father put stock in a trust and gave you general power of appointment over it, meaning you would be allowed to distribute the stock to anyone, including yourself. Because you have this right, the law says that stock is yours, even if you never touch it.

Enter your total assets on line 1 of the worksheet. Next, add up your outstanding debts (line 2), including mortgages, liens on your real estate, income and property taxes, credit-card balances, and loans.

Then estimate funeral expenses — the average is about $2,500 — and the cost of settling your estate (line 3). Court costs, executors', attorneys', accountants', brokers', and appraisers' fees can devour 5 to 10 percent of your gross estate.

The marital deduction (line 5) equals the amount you are leaving to your spouse. You can leave your entire estate to your spouse tax-free. You needn't do this, of course, but if you choose to, your spouse should fill out a photocopy of this worksheet to determine whether federal tax will be due later on his or her estate.

Subtract charitable bequests (line 6) from your adjusted gross estate.

Skip line 7 unless you have been very generous. It applies to people who have made large gifts that don't qualify as charitable donations. Only such gifts given after 1976 are taxable, and then only if the amounts given in any one year exceeded the tax-free-gift limit. You may make tax-free gifts of up to $10,000 a year to as many people as you like; married couples giving jointly may bestow as much as $20,000 a year. (Before 1982 the limits were $3,000 for individuals and $6,000 for married couples.) You also may make unlimited tax-free gifts in the form of medical expenses or educational expenses paid directly to hospitals or schools on behalf of people who are not your dependents for income tax purposes. Add up the amounts you gave that exceeded the annual limits. Subtract from this total the gift taxes you have already paid. To figure out quickly how much tax you paid, check the gift-tax returns (Form 709) that you filed the year after making taxable gifts. Any net taxable gifts go on line 7 and are added to your taxable estate.

Finally, refer to the table below the worksheet for the estate closest in size to yours to find out roughly how much federal tax, if any, your estate would owe. For example, before credits are taken into account, the federal tax line (line 9) on a $1 million taxable estate is $345,800. The estate would be entitled to a credit against that amount for paying state death taxes (line 10). In this case, $33,200 is subtracted from $345,800 to get $312,600. The credit for federal gift and estate taxes (line 12) is deducted from $312,600 to determine the IRS's share of the estate (line 13).

WORKSHEET

1. Gross estate	$__________
2. Outstanding debts	$__________
3. Administrative and funeral expenses	$__________
4. Adjusted gross estate (line 1 minus lines 2 and 3)	$__________
5. Marital deduction	$__________
6. Charitable bequests	$__________
7. Taxable gifts made after 1976 (minus gift taxes paid)	$__________
8. Taxable estate (line 4 plus line 7 minus lines 5 and 6)	$__________
9. Federal estate tax before credits (find the amount on line 8 in column A of the table below and read across)	$__________
10. Maximum credit for state death taxes (column C)	$__________
11. Federal estate tax less state death taxes (column B minus column C)	$__________
12. Federal unified credit for gift and estate taxes	$ 192,800
13. Federal estate tax due (line 11 minus line 12)	$__________

Col. A Taxable estate	*Col. B* Federal estate tax before credits are applied	*Col. C* Maximum credit for state death taxes	*Col. D* Federal estate tax less state death tax credit
$50,00	$10,600		$10,600
100,000	23,800		23,800
200,000	54,800	1,200	53,600

Col. A Taxable estate	*Col. B* Federal estate tax before credits are applied	*Col. C* Maximum credit for state death taxes	*Col. D* Federal estate tax less state death tax credit
300,000	87,800	3,600	84,200
400,000	121,800	6,800	115,000
500,000	155,800	10,000	145,800
600,000	192,800	14,000	178,800
700,000	229,800	18,000	211,800
800,000	267,800	22,800	245,000
900,000	306,800	27,600	279,200
1,000,000	345,800	33,200	312,600
1,200,000	427,800	45,200	382,600
1,500,000	555,800	64,400	491,400
2,000,000	780,800	99,600	681,200
3,000,000	1,290,800	182,000	1,108,800

The State's Bite

What the IRS leaves to your heirs, your state tax collector may take away. Twenty-nine states and the District of Columbia impose taxes that could eat into your bequests even if you are not liable for federal estate or gift taxes. Before making any plans for your estate, find out what the rules are where you live.

State death taxes won't be a problem if you live in any of the following states: Alabama, Alaska, Arizona, Arkansas, California, Colorado, Florida, Georgia, Hawaii, Illinois, Missouri, Nevada, New Mexico, North Dakota, Texas, Utah, Vermont, Virginia, Washington, West Virginia, Wyoming. Except for Nevada, which doesn't collect death taxes, these states impose so-called pickup taxes, which are levied only on estates subject to federal tax. With pickup taxes, the state collects part of what the federal government would otherwise get, so your estate won't owe additional tax.

The laws in the 29 other states vary tremendously. Each imposes either an estate tax or an inheritance tax, but not both. An estate tax is levied on the value of your estate — just like the federal tax — while inheritance taxes are based on each heir's share of your assets. Both are collected by the state where you are considered to be a legal resident when you die. Other states, however, may tax the value of such assets as real estate, cars, and boats if the property is located there.

Of these 29 states, nine collect their own death taxes. Minnesota, Mississippi, Oregon, and South Carolina have exemptions ranging from $120,000 to $500,000. Taxes on the remainder range from 1 to 16 percent, depending on the estate's size. Massachusetts, New York, Ohio, Oklahoma, and Rhode Island offer larger exemptions and charge lower rates if you leave property to your closest relatives. In Rhode Island, for instance, the exemption is $200,000 for the surviving spouse but only $20,000 for all other heirs, including children. The rest of the add-on-tax states and the District of Columbia collect inheritance taxes. Spouses and children are usually subject to the least onerous inheritance tax.

The same tactics for getting around the federal estate tax apply to state death taxes. But be careful in making gifts if you live in one of the nine states — Delaware, Louisiana, New York, North Carolina, Oregon, Rhode Island, South Carolina, Tennessee, and Wisconsin — that impose gift taxes. You may not be able to give away as much tax-free in these states as federal law permits.

When to Untie Joint Property

If you find that your estate is anywhere near the taxable level or even if you just have expectations of getting there, consider transferring ownership of jointly held property, wherever possible, to just one spouse. Avoiding probate gets a back seat now, because all jointly owned assets automatically pass to the surviving spouse, which means that the survivor could end up with a lot more than $600,000 if the couple kept both their names on most of their property. In changing ownership of joint assets, it is best in most cases to divvy them up as evenly as possible. That gives both spouses the flexibility to make the most of the $600,000 exclusion when they pass along their estates.

Another reason for rearranging ownership of your assets is that jointly held property cannot be placed in a trust that benefits a spouse. And irrevocable trusts are the key to keeping your combined estates free of taxes when they exceed $600,000.

Testamentary Trusts

If you are too asset-rich to take shelter behind the $600,000 exclusion, you will want to consider testamentary trusts — the kind that you specify in your will.

Bypass Trust

Suppose a couple own $1.1 million worth of assets, $700,000 of which are in the husband's name and $400,000 in the wife's. Instead of leaving all his property to his wife, dooming her estate to hefty taxes later on, the husband could arrange in his will to create a bypass trust. Upon his death, no more than $600,000 of his estate would go into the bypass trust. His widow would receive all, part, or none of the trust's income, depending on the provisions he includes in his will. Those provisions might also entitle her to some of the trust's principal — as much as 5 percent or $5,000, whichever is greater, each year.

When the widow died, the trust would dissolve, and the remaining assets would go to heirs other than the wife whom the husband named in his will. Assets left in a bypass trust do not qualify for the marital deduction because the spouse has limited access to its income and principal. No estate taxes would be due on the trust, however, since the amount contributed was within the husband's $600,000 exemption. The $100,000 of his property that he didn't put into the bypass trust would go directly to his wife tax-free, since it would qualify for the marital deduction. She would then have $500,000, with plenty of room to spare before her estate crossed the $600,000 tax-exempt threshold.

Marital Deduction Trust

If an estate tax doesn't seem likely but you want someone to keep a rein on your spouse's inheritance, have a look at a marital deduction trust. In contrast to a bypass trust, it requires that the spouse receive all the income that the trust produces. The surviving partner also would be entitled to withdraw much more sizable portions of the principal than he or she could get from a bypass trust. Even though the survivor doesn't directly control the money, he or she receives enough benefit to qualify the trust assets for the marital deduction.

One reason to set up such a trust rather than leave assets directly in your spouse's hands is that an experienced trustee might manage the money more skillfully than your spouse could. You can also rest in peace knowing that if your spouse remarries, the new partner won't be able to abscond with the assets. In addition, if you pass along stock in a closely held company that goes bankrupt after you die, your spouse will be protected from creditors as long as the shares remain in the trust.

You have two main types of marital deduction trusts to choose from:

General power of appointment trust. This arrangement lets your spouse decide who will inherit the trust's assets after his or her death.

QTIP trust. Short for a qualified terminal interest property trust, a QTIP enables you but not your spouse to select who will ultimately get the money. The most common motive for establishing a QTIP trust is to prevent your spouse from cutting off your children born of a previous marriage. In other respects, QTIPs and general power of appointment trusts are essentially identical in that they both qualify for the marital deduction, are included in the surviving spouse's estate, and produce income that must go exclusively to the surviving spouse.

It is generally wisest to put assets that are likely to appreciate substantially in a bypass trust, while leaving less promising investments in a marital deduction trust, according to Julian Bush, a senior estate partner with the New York City law firm Shea & Gould. The reason is that no matter how large the assets in a bypass trust may grow, they remain tax-exempt as long as they were worth $600,000 or less when the trust started. But because the investments you place in a marital deduction trust become part of your spouse's estate upon his or her death, they are taxable if their value, when combined with other assets, climbs above $600,000. "You are usually better off putting your high-flying investments in the bypass trust while leaving more conservative, income-producing assets to your spouse," Bush says.

Irrevocable Life Insurance Trust

Ordinarily, the proceeds of insurance on your life go into your taxable estate. Couples with insurance policies sizable enough to push the surviving spouse's estate over the $600,000 mark can elude the estate tax by transferring ownership of the policies to an irrevocable life insurance trust. This removes the value of your insurance from the estates of both you and your mate. Upon your death, the proceeds go into the trust untaxed, and in most cases your spouse receives all the income the trust earns for the rest of her or his life, as well as any principal your spouse might need to cover living expenses. After your spouse dies, the trust terminates, and its remaining assets go to beneficiaries named in your will.

A much simpler way to remove insurance proceeds from your estate is to give the policy to someone else. If your wife, say, owns all rights to the policy, including the right to change the beneficiary, the death benefit won't be taxed in your estate (though it may be in hers). It costs nothing to change policy ownership (unless you have paid enough into the policy to incur a gift tax); all you do is ask your agent for a change-of-ownership form and send it to the company.

A couple of technicalities, however, can snag attempts to protect life insurance from death taxes. One is that if you die within three years of transferring ownership of a policy to an individual or a trust, the proceeds will be included in your estate anyway. For that reason, an irrevocable life insurance trust document should include a clause stating that if you die within three years the insurance should go directly to your spouse or into a marital deduction trust. That way, because of the marital deduction, you can still postpone the estate tax until after your mate's death.

The second snag may lurk in your state's laws. Just eight states — Massachusetts, Minnesota, New York, North Carolina, Rhode Island, South Carolina, Tennessee, and Wisconsin — adhere to the federal rule of counting insurance as part of your estate if you own the policy. Most of the others tax insurance proceeds only if they are paid to your estate, a common practice to provide the estate with liquidity. In those states, you can avoid tax by having the insurance paid directly to a named beneficiary. You run into unique rules in some states. Pennsylvania never touches life insurance, for example, while Oklahoma taxes all insurance that doesn't go to the spouse.

Giving Away Taxable Assets

Like trusts, gifts you make during your lifetime can shave the size of your estate, helping you to avoid estate taxes. But remember that the surviving spouse will have no access to the money you give away, which is not the case with trusts. It is therefore wise to make gifts only when you are sure of two things: that the survivor will have enough income to live on after you die and that your estate will be taxable unless you make gifts.

As long as a gift is no larger than the $10,000 tax-free limit, you don't have to report it to the IRS, but individuals and couples who bestow more than that must file Form 709, the gift-tax return. If you make gifts in excess of the tax-free benchmarks, you won't have to pay the IRS right away. But after you die, the IRS tallies up the taxable gifts you made during your lifetime and subtracts the total from your $600,000 estate tax exemption. Let's say a single person gave $60,000 to his brother in 1987 and then died in 1988. After allowance for the tax-free $10,000, he made a $50,000 taxable gift, leaving him only a $550,000 estate-tax exclusion.

From a tax-planning standpoint, it is best to give away property that is likely to grow in value. Someone who bestows an investment worth $10,000 today and then dies in five years will have removed from his estate the $10,000 plus all the investment's subsequent appreciation.

Besides giving away cash or investments, you can transfer ownership of your life insurance policy to one of your children. In computing whether the policy will be subject to gift tax, figure its value as the total premiums you have paid so far or its current cash surrender value, depending on the type of policy. The proceeds that the beneficiaries would receive upon your death are not a factor in calculating gift-tax liability.

You can also remove assets from your estate by making charitable contributions, which are not subject to gift tax and are deductible on your income tax return. Very wealthy people who are unable to avoid estate tax entirely may want to try to minimize the government's take by setting up charitable trusts in addition to making outright donations. There are two main types.

Charitable Remainder Trust

By means of this trust you can give assets to a charity, receiving deductions along the way, while allowing you or members of your family to receive all the income that the trust throws off. After a specified time, often upon the death of your surviving spouse, the trust terminates and the charity gets outright ownership of the assets. You can create such a trust while you are alive or in your will. In a testamentary trust, the donated property is considered part of your estate, but a portion of its value is deductible before estate taxes are taken out. If you start a charitable remainder trust while you are alive, you will probably get an income tax deduction in the year you open it.

Some charities operate pooled income funds that provide income and tax benefits similar to remainder trusts without requiring donors to go through the process of setting up a trust. These funds operate much like income-oriented mutual funds, investing assets contributed by a group of donors and passing along a share of the returns to them.

Charitable Lead Trust

Your estate will get a bigger tax deduction, in some cases up to the full value of your contribution, if you arrange in your will for a charitable lead trust. The inverse of a remainder trust, it donates its income to a charity until the trust ends. Then the assets are distributed to your heirs. In exchange for the larger estate tax write-off, however, your heirs have to forgo income they would receive from a remainder trust or pooled income fund. IRS tables base the size of your estate-tax deduction for the trust on the amount you contribute, the investment's projected rate of return, and the trust's specified life.

29

WHERE THERE'S A WILL

The will of Charles Collingwood, the CBS correspondent who died in 1985, was in part a reflection on a life well lived. Though much of Collingwood's estate went into a trust for his wife, he saved special gifts for his friends. It is easy to picture his satisfaction as he imagined his former boss, William S. Paley, sipping a goblet of Château Ausone from Collingwood's wine cellar, or presidential chronicler Theodore White browsing through Collingwood's 13-volume set of the *Oxford English Dictionary*.

Drafting your will can be an opportunity to savor friendships and relive shared pleasures, although lawyers quibble that property bequests like Collingwood's are better made outside the will in a letter of instruction. Such a document lets you change your mind without going through the legal rigamarole of changing your will. The main point of making a will, everyone agrees, is not remembrance of things past but avoidance of future problems for your family and friends.

Even if you put most of your assets in trusts, you will need a will to ensure that the rest of your property is distributed the way you want it to be. Instead of following a rigid legal formula, a will can apportion your assets according to what you see as your children's needs or merits. It can bestow gifts on friends, lovers, charities, stepchildren, and grandchildren or put money into trusts. If you die without a will, such people and institutions will receive nothing. In addition, you need a will to appoint an executor who will wrap up your financial affairs and a guardian who will take custody of your minor children.

In most cases, failure to prepare a will stems from unreadiness to contemplate one's own mortality or from mistaken notions about the workings of the law. Many people believe, wrongly, that writing a will is unnecessary because their surviving spouse will automatically inherit everything. This is true in five of the nine states with community property laws (California, Idaho, New Mexico, Nevada, Washington), provided the assets are acquired during the marriage and are not gifts or inheritances to one spouse. In the other 45 states, the law makes your spouse share your estate with your children, siblings, or parents. Intestacy laws can create sticky situations for childless couples, too. In New York State, your spouse gets $25,000 plus half of your remaining estate, but your parents get the rest. Most people therefore should have separate wills.

Resist the temptation to write your own will by following a recipe in some how-to book or using official forms published by some states. Technical slipups could make your homemade testament worthless. It is far wiser to spend a little money on legal fees. Hiring a lawyer to draw up a simple will costs only $50 to $200, although when your estate is large or complicated, the fee can escalate to four or even five digits. The less time your lawyer has to spend on research, the lower his bill will be. Thus you will save money by preparing detailed, accurate lists of your assets, debts, and beneficiaries and indicating who holds title to your property — you alone, you jointly with someone else, or a trust. Such lists, regularly updated and left with your lawyer, will also simplify your executor's task.

Reciting your bequests on videotape is not a substitute for a written will. But videotaping the witnessing and signing can help thwart future contests in which a disgruntled heir argues that you were incompetent. After completing and signing your will, leave the original with your lawyer or in a will depository provided by some county probate courts for a small one-time fee. Putting the will in a bank safe-deposit box can cause delays in settling your estate, since most banks seal the boxes at death and will not open them without a court order. Your spouse's safe-deposit box is a poor choice, too, since the two of you may die together.

Disinheritances

It is hard — but not impossible — to cut out of your estate people who would be considered your natural heirs. Most state laws will not allow you to disinherit a spouse, but you can convey your hard feelings by putting the legal minimum in trust and giving your spouse access only to the income from that trust. After his or her death, the principal will go to whomever you have specified.

If you are dead set — as it were — on leaving your spouse as little as possible, you must do so outside the will, and with a little finesse. The best tactic is to shrink the estate by gradually moving assets into trusts and gifts to relatives, friends, and charities. Spouses can also sign prenuptial agreements, in which each of you waives your share of the other's estate in the event of death or divorce. But prenuptial agreements, although increasingly common, can be difficult to enforce. Jacqueline Kennedy signed such a contract with Aristotle Onassis in 1968, in which she gave up her entitlement to any share of his estate in return for $3 million in cash after the wedding. Yet after Ari's death, Jackie got his daughter, Christina, to increase the widow's mite to $26 million, reportedly to avoid a court fight over the will.

You should mention your children by name in your will, but you are not obliged to leave them anything — except in Louisiana, where the law forces you to do so. Elsewhere, children and other blood relations can receive as little as you choose. "But be sure that your will shows that you know who's out there," warns Charles W. Ufford, Jr., trusts and estates partner at Skadden Arps Slate Meagher & Flom, a New York City law firm. "Without such an indication, the have-nots can contest the will with a claim that you simply overlooked them," Ufford explains. In disinheriting someone, use this language: "I make no provision for so-and-so because he is otherwise provided for." But don't say that the person is "amply" provided for or that you have done the providing. "The fewer the details," says Ufford, "the less opportunity there will be to contest the will."

If you do disinherit someone, be thorough about it. By leaving, say, a nickel as an insult, you could provoke the disappointed heir into spitefully delaying signature of the necessary receipt, creating problems for your more favored heirs.

The Importance of Naming Names

Make sure your lawyer inserts a clause to cover children born or adopted after the will is drawn up. In many states, failure to mention such children is construed as an unintentional oversight, and they would inherit under the state intestacy laws for children. In some states these laws entitle such children to receive one-third to one-half of your assets, which means they might get more than their siblings and conceivably as much as your spouse.

Even when you have addressed every possible contingency, the language in your will can create ambiguities that open the door to a contest.

For example, if you bequeath $10,000 to your niece, specify her relationship to you. There could be several people with the same name as hers, and each could insist that she was the one you meant. These construction problems, as they're called, are usually decided by the probate judge. They don't invalidate wills, but they can rob someone of a legacy. For the same reason, when you leave gifts to charities, be exact about the names.

Playing the Percentages

When you are leaving money, you can earmark percentages of your estate or dollar amounts, with an unspecified remainder directed to one or more beneficiaries. But bequests in dollars would effectively disinherit other beneficiaries if your assets were to dwindle between the time you wrote your will and the day you died. If your $500,000 dwindled to $100,000 at your death, the $50,000 you left to a charity would constitute half of your assets, not the 10 percent it represented when you wrote in the bequest. So percentages almost always are preferable. In the happy event that your $500,000 estate grew to $1 million by your death, your three kids would thank you twice as much for the 10 percent shares you left each of them.

Naming contingent or backup beneficiaries allows you to decide who is to inherit your property if your first choice cannot be located, refuses to accept your gift, or dies before you do. In addition to leaving gifts of property or cash, you can use a will to forgive debts.

Avoiding Squabbles

Don't burden your will and leave it open to contest by trying to rule your beneficiaries from the grave. Most vulnerable to attack are clauses that make a legacy conditional upon something that might reasonably destroy an heir's health, wealth, or happiness. You can leave your niece $5,000 for finishing college but not for marrying a particular man or serving as a volunteer in a war-torn land. And do not leave any parting shots. If you bequeath your Nautilus machine to your overweight sister "in the hope that she will cease to resemble a blue-ribbon sow," the injured party may be able to sue your estate for defamation and get a fat chunk of your fortune to pay legal expenses.

A letter with your will instructing your executor to make gifts of jewelry, furniture, and other personal items, not only can be changed as often as you like but also can head off trouble. "Personal possessions cause all the terrible fights, especially nowadays with so many second marriages,'' says Ellen Harrison, a lawyer at Morgan Lewis & Bockius in Washington, D.C. ''Nothing causes as much trouble within families.'' Some lawyers recommend discussing your intentions with your family to smooth any ruffled feathers.

When you make specific bequests, you can avoid ambiguity, arguments, and hurt feelings by being as detailed as possible in your description of each gift. Don't say, ''I leave my emerald ring to my daughter Susan'' but ''I leave my two-carat marquise-cut emerald in the platinum setting . . .'' A ring with a smaller stone may turn up among your possessions, and Susan could inherit the wrong rock.

Letters of instruction are also the proper place for directions concerning organ donations and funeral arrangements. Make sure that your doctor and your family have copies of such letters. By the time your will is found and read, it may be too late to follow your wishes. Letters spelling out property distributions are legally binding in many states, but burial instructions have only moral force.

Choosing an Executor

The executor you name in your will must combine the tact of a diplomat with the administrative skills of an executive. He or she should be close enough to you and your family to do as you would wish, yet be able to act decisively, calmly, and fairly if conflicts break out among beneficiaries.

The executor first must identify and determine the value of the assets that are part of your estate — trusts, life insurance policies, pension plans, and some kinds of jointly owned property fall outside the executor's purview. This often requires hiring an appraiser, whose fee comes out of your estate, as do expenses for lawyers, accountants, and other professionals. An executor pays all your remaining debts, files tax returns, and distributes whatever is left to your heirs. Throughout, he or she must keep careful records; most probate courts will demand a detailed account of all money received, spent, or held by your estate.

Almost any person you trust can be your executor. For most people the best choice is their spouse or best friend, who may also be a beneficiary. Large estates may need two executors: someone to interpret your wishes and another person or institution, such as a bank, to make business or investment decisions, pay taxes, and keep records. Whomever you pick as executors, inform them of your decision and make sure they are willing to accept the responsibility. It is often advisable to go over your will with them to clear up any ambiguities about your intentions, but you need not give them copies.

Choosing a Guardian for Your Children

Providing for the upbringing of children is one of a will's most important functions. If you and your spouse die without appointing a guardian in your wills, the court may appoint someone whom your children dislike or whose views and values are disturbingly different from your own. ''Very rarely do both parents die. It's an actuarial blip,'' says Atlanta attorney Ann Salo. Even so, just as you wouldn't leave young kids home alone without a baby-sitter, you shouldn't leave them without making provisions for their future if anything happens to you and your spouse.

Naming a guardian is easy — and hard. The easy part is the mechanics. You just nominate someone in your will. Although the court actually appoints the guardian, the judge usually follows the will's instructions. About the only time he might not is when a natural parent is contesting the guardian or the guardian is obviously unfit to raise a child. A guardianship lasts until the orphan reaches the age of majority, which in many states is 18.

The court's first choice as guardian is usually a family member. If, for example, you name a friend over a sister or brother, spell out your reasons. Indeed, if your will contains any instructions that might be construed as out of the ordinary, it generally is advisable to explain yourself. That can forestall attempts to overturn the document on the ground that you didn't realize what you were doing.

Financing your children's upbringing can be done in one of two ways. You can leave your property to the kids, with their guardian or someone else as conservator of the assets. But a conservator must often get court permission to pay the children's expenses from their legacy, must account to the court for the assets' management, and often has to post a bond, the cost of which comes out of your estate. To give the guardian greater flexibility, put your assets in trust for the children, with their guardian as trustee or cotrustee.

The hard part about choosing a guardian is selecting the right person. Choose someone who is about your age; grandparents are usually not suitable candidates to raise young children. Younger relatives often are, because of what Richard A. Gardner, a psychiatrist who practices in Cresskill, New Jersey, calls ''the psychological power of biological ties.'' When the child is your sister's or brother's or cousin's, Gardner says, everyone benefits from the family link. If you are not close to your family, pick a person who would bring up your children the way you would.

Psychologists urge that you appoint couples rather than single people, so that the kids will be raised in a household with adults of both sexes. (Lawyers, however, advise you to name only one spouse the actual guardian, in case the couple divorce later on.) But a single person who has a close relationship with the children and values similar to yours can be a better choice than a married sister with a different life-style who lives half a continent away. If your children are young, placing them in a family with teenagers may reduce sibling rivalry, but two sets of kids who are close in age get the benefits of companionship. Whatever you decide, satisfy yourself that the guardian is bringing up his or her own children in a way you approve of.

Make sure you ask the people you have in mind whether they would be willing to take on the responsibilities of guardianship. Discuss with them the financial arrangements you have made and how you want the children brought up. Apart from the simple courtesy of letting someone know you want him to inherit your children, there is another reason to tell him. A guardian named in a will is under no legal obligation to accept the responsibility. If the person designated refuses to serve, the court will appoint someone else — perhaps a person you would not have wanted chosen. For that reason, attorneys recommend that you also name a backup guardian in your will.

Children, too, have the right to know who their guardian is going to be. Consult older children before you make a decision. You may be surprised to hear one of them say, "I've never told you, but I can't stand Aunt Sally." In many jurisdictions, a child of 14 or older can challenge your nominee and ask for a substitute. Courts listen to children but tend to abide by the wishes of the parents as expressed in the will.

Keeping Your Will Current

Every few years, or whenever personal or financial circumstances change, review all the provisions in your will. Even the best-drawn document can go awry if left without periodic monitoring. The brother you have named as guardian may have been divorced, or your best friend may now run a head shop in Malibu. If you replace a guardian in your will, inform the former guardian of your change of mind right away. If you don't, you run the risk of embarrassing that person when the document is probated.

Marriage or divorce automatically invalidates an existing will. You should also look over your will's provisions if you move to another state — legal requirements may be different there — or if you become a lot richer or poorer. And even if your personal circumstances remain the same, give your will a checkup every three years or so to keep pace with tax-law changes.

You don't have to write a new will every time you want to make small changes, such as substituting a beneficiary or changing the size of someone's bequest. These alterations can be done in codicils, which should be drawn up by a lawyer and, like the rest of the will, must be witnessed. But if your codicils are complicated or begin to resemble the tail on a kite, revising the entire document will help to preserve its validity. Whatever you do, don't write on the will itself. Such changes may invalidate it, reducing all your careful planning to ashes and handing your estate over, willy-nilly, to the court for distribution.

IV

THE FIRST AND LAST WORD ON INVESTING

In the big book of *things that people more often do wrong than right,* investing must certainly top the list, followed closely by wallpapering and eating artichokes. Where do investors err? They buy on hot tips, they sell too quickly or hold on too long, they lack a well-defined goal and a strategy for reaching it, they don't diversify.

Often they don't even try. "I was burned once," they plead, or "I haven't got the time," or "I just don't know anything about investing." Then the capper, "It's too late — everyone who could make money in this market already has."

Let us now praise wiser investors. They do their homework, deal with compatible brokers, invest for a longer-term purpose without being unnerved by day-to-day market fluctuations. They expect to make mistakes, but they know that investing can help them achieve a goal, whether it is to pay the kids' college costs, amass the down payment on a house, build a retirement fund, or just put away enough money to live well — and securely. They have discovered that you *can* find an investment strategy to match your spare time and your willingness to devote it to the task. They are smart enough to realize that there is always more to learn.

Whether you are an investor already, an ex-investor, or a rank beginner, assess your position from three perspectives:

1. Define your financial goals and how you plan to reach them (see Chapter 4).

2. Take an inventory of your resources. Before tying up money in securities, buy enough life and disability insurance to protect your dependents and yourself (see Chapters 57 and 59). Also put aside emergency cash where you can retrieve every dollar on demand — for example, in a bank account or money-market mutual fund.

3. Test your tolerance for risk. Some people enjoy watching their investments behave like Tarzan, swinging wildly from limb to limb, as long as they think they will be rewarded with long-term gains. Others cannot bear the uncertainty. Where conventional wisdom doesn't apply to you, ignore it. The usual advice tells young or single people to aim for maximum capital gains and older investors to focus on stocks that move somewhat slowly but pay generous dividends. But if you are a 25-year-old bachelor who hates to risk losing money, forget your age and adopt a conservative approach. If you are a 70-year-old swinger with no financial worries, go ahead and have a speculative ball.

After finding your comfort level, you will know better how to shape your portfolio for regular income and longer-range capital gains. You probably need a mix of the two. If interest rates rise again into double digits, you should consider not only stocks but also Treasury bonds and top-grade corporate bonds. Then, when rates next fall, you can sell your bonds at a profit because declining rates mean rising prices.

Whether you try bonds or stocks, don't get too caught up in the race for profits. You may be tempted to draw $5,000 out of a bank account and sink it into the latest wonder stock. You would almost always be wiser to pick several stocks as a way of cushioning your losses. Some of your choices figure to be flops, so go by the rule of five, says Kenneth Janke, president of the National Association of Investment Clubs: for every five stocks you own, one will be a loser, three will do nicely, and one will do much better than you expected.

30

FEARLESS FIRST-TIME INVESTING

The hardest part is getting started. Beginners intimidated by unfamiliar terminology and afraid of looking foolish have trouble mustering the confidence to take the plunge. They will be reassured to learn that anxiety is not limited to investment novices. The savviest bond trader may quiver at the prospect of investing for the first time in commodities or real estate.

Success hinges in part on confidence — not mindless bravado but a realistic faith in your own judgment, born of a solid understanding of investment fundamentals. Genuine self-assurance will enable you to move decisively when you spot opportunities.

Investment Clubs

Granted, few newcomers are confident enough to venture forth totally alone. Investment clubs can be excellent sources of guidance and support. They typically consist of a dozen or so individuals who pool modest monthly contributions in a common fund used to buy securities. Typically, investment clubs meet once a month, and each member spends several hours a week doing assigned research. Some people prospect for investments while others follow stocks already bought. The membership makes buy and sell decisions by majority vote.

It is usually tough to get into an existing club. Groups tend to develop an esprit that they may be reluctant to extend to newcomers. But the National Association of Investment Clubs (1515 East 11 Mile Road, Royal Oak, Michigan 48067) stands ready to help you start a club, as it has done for 6,400 existing groups with nearly 90,000 members. For a yearly fee of $30 per club plus $7 a member, the association gives assistance — primarily in the form of manuals and a monthly magazine on investment technique. A dozen confederates who can ante up $20 to $30 a month for the joint portfolio are all you need — that and a consensus on what you are trying to accomplish. As an undergraduate a few years ago, Robert Silverstone was president of the Quincy House Investment Club at Harvard College. He said sensibly at the time, "As a group we are not in this to make a lot of money. That would be nice, but mainly we are here to learn." Many investment-club members use their organization's broker for their own trading. Though their transactions may be small, their link with the club makes them seem much bigger — and more important — customers to the broker.

Seminars and Courses

If the committee approach sounds too limiting, try joining the American Association of Individual Investors (612 North Michigan Avenue, Suite 317, Chicago, Illinois 60611). For a $48 annual fee, you get a rather scholarly monthly financial journal, a yearly guide to no-load mutual funds, and the opportunity to attend meetings arranged by the association's 30 chapters. You may hear an economist lecture on the economy's impact on the stock market or a tax lawyer discuss passive income and losses.

Courses given by brokers, whether free through their firms or at modest tuition when sponsored by adult schools, often illuminate specific aspects of investing. The quality of the teaching can be spotty, however, and the content self-serving if the lecturer cares more about recruiting clients than enlightening students. John Feeney, a broker who used to teach in the Boston area and who cares about enlightenment, gives this advice: "When you shop for an investing class, sit in on one session first. Then ask yourself, 'Am I being pitched?' If you are, get out."

Continuing-education programs taught in colleges by professors or executives of financial firms can be more objective and certainly are more comprehensive than the classes taught by brokers. You find such courses increasingly at distinguished institutions — Brown University in Providence, Rhode Island, for example, and the University of Washington in Seattle. Johns Hopkins in Baltimore offers a 10-week evening course that can serve as a model of what to look for. Once-a-week lectures cover every aspect of investing from the economy and the mechanics of the marketplace to the various kinds of securities. For only $115 tuition, you are likely to learn vital truths about yourself. One student, Arlene Coppel of Columbia, Maryland, reported, "I found out what kind of investor I am — I'm very conservative."

Successful investing, as you will be told by worthy instructors, starts at the bookshelf, not on the phone to your broker. In its quiet way, your public library is anticipating your needs by stocking up on financial publications and perhaps opening a special room to contain them. The Seattle Public Library now has files on several thousand corporations in the Pacific Northwest and conducts group tours of its business section to familiarize users with its 67,000 volumes and 250 periodicals.

The first books to check out are a pair of classics, *The Intelligent Investor* by Benjamin Graham (Harper & Row, $18.45) and *The Battle for Investment Survival* by Gerald M. Loeb (Fireside Books, $8.95). A modern companion to Graham and Loeb, much of it first researched and written for *Money*, is *Gaining on the Market* by Charles J. Rolo (Atlantic–Little, Brown, $16.95).

Among the indispensable resources in any first-rate business library are the *Value Line Investment Survey,* with its detailed coverage and ratings of 1,700 stocks, and Standard & Poor's *The Outlook,* which sizes up the market and recommends specific issues. Both are published weekly. S&P's *Stock Reports,* regularly updated loose-leaf sheets describing 3,500 companies, are a prime source of financial data.

Mutual Funds

Mutual funds (described fully in Chapter 9) offer fledgling investors instant diversification. Ideal for many beginners are growth funds, which aim for higher long-term earnings than stocks in general will produce, and growth and income funds, which pay more attention to the cash dividends that well-established companies usually pay their shareholders. Most mutual funds require initial investments of only $1,000 and let you invest as little as $50 at a time in additional shares.

Besides getting you into the stock market, mutual funds can educate you about it. When quarterly reports arrive in the mail, scan them for stocks that the manager has added to his portfolio or has sold. Then look up the companies in the Value Line or Standard & Poor's publications for news that might have influenced his decision. In the second quarter of 1983, for example, many aggressive funds were loading up on high-tech stocks. But before long, alert fund managers began fleeing Silicon Valley. Sure enough, by early August such high-tech favorites as Apple and Tandy had fallen 40 percent from their 12-month highs.

Tiptoeing into the Market

After a year or so in mutual funds, you may get the itch to start investing on your own. "Funds are fine, but why let them have all the fun? It's your money," says Louis Rukeyser of TV's "Wall Street Week." Little guys (you) have several advantages over big guys (mutual funds and other financial institutions). You can choose from a universe of 7,000 actively traded stocks. Mutual-fund managers generally stick to a much smaller galaxy of 500 or so medium-size and large corporations that are followed by brokerage houses. Most funds buy such large blocks of stock that they can't trade small companies without driving prices up or down. And most fund managers, like pachyderms, follow the herd. When a few decide it is time to buy AT&T or Xerox, the jungle cry sounds and the rest buy it.

So now comes the biggest question: how do you pick winning stocks? Answer: very carefully. Many first-time investors are attracted by the razzle-dazzle of highly active issues. When Michael Partington, a real estate broker in Sacramento, made his first foray into stocks, he bought 100 shares of TeleVideo Systems, a computer maker, at $20 each. A volatile stock, TeleVideo climbed to $27 in a few days, then fell back to $21. "I got so nervous that I phoned my broker eight times in one day," he said. The stock quickly recovered to $28, and Partington cashed in. Although he made $689 after commission, the experience convinced him that he lacked the temperament for active trading.

Penny stocks — low-priced shares issued by newly public companies — are particularly seductive to novice investors. Because a small amount of money will buy thousands of shares, many first-timers erroneously conclude that they are risking less. In reality, these stocks can double their worth or lose half their value in a single day. Few investors have the luck or skill or inside knowledge to buy and sell penny stocks at the opportune time.

For the most part, you will increase your chances of success by sticking to conservative issues and holding on to them. Much of a stock picker's time goes into hunting for undervalued issues. "Using present and future earnings as a guide, IBM selling for $150 a share could be cheap compared with a $20 stock that is overpriced for its actual value," says Bernard Van der Linden, a broker and senior vice president at Howard Weil Labouisse & Friedrichs in New Orleans.

To escape impulse buying, try a stock-selection system and stay with it long enough to see if it works. When Chris Wysock, a construction industry consultant in Longmont, Colorado, entered the stock market in 1982 at the age of 30, he decided to restrict himself to issues selling near their 12-month lows. One was Quanex, a maker of steel tubing, whose shares were then $7 on the New York Stock Exchange. Wysock invested $2,800 and watched the price sink to $5.25. But he held on and was rewarded. When Quanex reached his target price of $10 in 1984, he took a $1,200 profit. He bought other stocks near their lows and doubled his initial stake.

Anyone with more than $2,000 to invest should put it in two or more companies. You will want to diversify by industry as well. If interest rates rise, for instance, and all your shares are in six housing stocks, you will be pummeled. So adopt a serviceable formula. A good one for people investing less than $15,000 is to put the money in three to five companies. If you have more than $75,000, buy stocks in a minimum of four industries.

Deciding when to sell your shares is as important as choosing the right ones. Do you intend to buy and hold stocks indefinitely or to become an active trader? Both approaches are valid, and you probably will employ them at various times. But a buy-and-hold strategy requires the least time and skill. You just have to keep an eye on each company you own. While you might want to sell it if it hits hurricane weather, don't rush to dump a long-term growth stock just because it has sunk along with the market. That is the time to consider buying more shares. In the market tumble of 1974, McDonald's hit a low of $14; by 1985 it sold above $80.

Securities and Their Uses

As the basic implements of investing, securities are often misused. Stocks, though primarily for making your money grow, also can be appropriate for generating regular income. Bonds, while basically for income, can reward you with capital gains. For precision work in tight corners, you can choose among such specialized equipment as puts, calls, and convertibles. For diversification and professional craftsmanship, you can employ a mutual fund. Here is a shop manual explaining the financial tools.

Common Stocks

While you may feel a shiver of pride in being the part owner of a corporation, never forget that your main motive for buying shares is to increase your wealth. Stocks can deliver in two ways: with dividends and capital gains. Some investors, intent on getting the most gains for their money, are wary of dividends. For their purpose, the company should be plowing all its profits back into the business. Others look for a combination of dividends and capital gains. Still others, in need of income now, care less about the price of a stock than about the chance that its dividend will keep rising. Nonetheless it is growth, not dividends, that gives stocks their investment edge.

Taxes no longer should influence your choice between dividends and appreciation. The reformed Internal Revenue Code has done away with the special blessing previously given to long-term capital gains, which used to be defined as profits made by selling stocks held more than six months. In 1987, long-term gains are taxed like dividends except that the top rate on gains is 28 percent, while that on dividends is 38.5 percent. In 1988 and beyond, all earnings from investments are taxed the same. Capital losses still can be used, however, to offset capital gains. If you have more losses than gains in the same year, you can deduct as much as $3,000 of your net loss from dividends or other income.

To help investors match their goals to appropriate stocks, securities analysts try to sort the merchandise into bins labeled *growth* and *income*. By definition, growth stocks are shares in companies that are expanding faster than the economy. Often they are fledgling companies exploiting new technologies or innovations in marketing. Their earnings may be meager or nonexistent, and their dividends surely will be negligible. But their prospects strike some analysts and investors as dazzling.

In rising markets, the stocks of young and growing companies tend to do at least one-third better than the basic stock indexes. And to tantalize you all the more, there are the incredibly high fliers. From its introduction on the stock market in 1982 to its peak in 1983, Convergent Technologies went from $8 to $40 a share, a 400 percent rise. No wonder the stock became a favorite of high-tech mutual fund managers. Alas, issues that shoot up faster than the market also are likely to plunge faster. Two years later, Convergent hit bottom at $3.88.

For a little peace and quiet — maybe — you can try income stocks. Their emphasis on dividends instead of growth makes their prices more stable. Utility stocks are usually cited as a foremost example. State regulatory commissions are empowered to raise electricity and gas rates to ensure that utility company shareholders receive a fair rate of return. But when an electricity company blows billions of dollars on a nuclear generator and then is forced to abandon the project, as several utilities did in recent years, state regulators seldom dare heap all the cost on the public.

Instead, the shareholders pay for the company's folly in lost dividends — and squashed share prices.

You might want to try for the best of both worlds: the stout and steady dividends of an income stock with the potential for sustained price appreciation. Those are the attributes of blue chips, the stocks of the well-established, financially sound companies that are household names in American industry — American Express, General Electric, IBM, Merck, and their peers — with records of long-term profits and dividend growth. Bank trust departments and life insurance companies revere them. Executors put them in the portfolios of dowagers. Blue chips don't pay the highest dividends or lead the growth rankings and they can turn gray. For instance, you no longer can count on the big farm-equipment makers to pay dividends, let alone raise them. But blue chips will always represent a compelling compromise.

Warrants

As an added inducement to buy new issues of stocks or bonds, called initial public offerings, companies sometimes attach warrants to them. This prize in the Cracker Jack box is a security with little present value but possibly great potential. Warrants give their owners the right to buy more shares at a fixed price until an expiration date, usually several years away. If the stock rises above that fixed price, the warrant takes on value. Warrants trade independently at prices that move with the value of the underlying shares. If the stock goes up or down, the warrants are likely to move much faster. All kinds of companies have issued warrants, from upstarts to AT&T.

Options

Even if a major company doesn't issue warrants, you probably can get a similar deal in the options market. Options trade in the form of *calls* — contracts giving the owner the right to buy a particular stock at a set price for a limited time. They also trade as *puts* — contracts conferring the right to sell stock at a set price. It is possible to trade puts and calls on more than 400 stocks. The latest wrinkle is an option not on one stock but on the whole market, as represented by a stock index.

Buyers of options are taking long shots that the price of a stock — or the market as a whole — will go in a particular direction. The contracts they buy are called wasting assets, because their value ebbs as time runs out. Since option buyers lose money on most of their contracts, it stands to reason that the sellers of options usually make money. If you are holding 100 shares of some blue-chip stock for income, you can tell your broker to sell a call on the stock — a nice safe call giving some speculator the right to buy your shares for more than their current price. For example, when General Electric is selling at $60 a share, a call to buy the stock at $65 for the next six months might be worth $1.75. Say you bought 100 shares that day and sold a call on them. After paying a commission on the option, you would net about $150, a dandy supplement to the $220 of annual dividends you would earn on the shares. Your only risk would be that the stock might shoot far higher than $65. But if it did, you could solace yourself with your extra income — and a $500 capital gain.

Professional investors and postgraduate amateurs use options as insurance against market reverses. Buying a put on a stock you own, for instance, gives you a hedge against the stock's decline. In case the price does fall, the put will shoot up because it represents the right to sell shares for more than the market price.

Preferred Stocks

This crossbreed of debt and equity pays more dependable, generally more generous dividends than the same company's common shares but yields less income than its bonds. The dividend on a preferred stock usually is fixed, so you do not share in higher profits if the company prospers. The price of the stock responds mainly to changes in bond yields. With preferred shares, you are strictly interested in getting decent income from your investment. When USX (formerly U.S. Steel) preferred yields 11 percent, the common may be paying only 4.5 percent.

Bonds

Long the cornerstone of any income-oriented portfolio — a widow's best friend, bankers once dubbed them — bonds have undergone something of a character change. The unruly inflation of the 1970s undermined the appeal of their fixed interest payments. A $1,000 corporate bond yielding $70 a year may have looked attractive in 1973. But you would still be getting 7 percent on it today, although the same bond or one like it might be yielding 9 percent or more to new buyers because its price has sunk. As sure as sunrise and sunset, bond prices fall when interest rates climb, and climb when interest rates fall.

Fears of renewed inflation, higher interest rates, or both give the bond market extreme price jitters. Still, as we will see in Chapter 37, carefully chosen bonds in one form or another — corporates, tax-free municipals, or governments — can be attractive for income-minded investors.

Convertibles

Corporate bonds and preferred stocks that are convertible into common shares are the fence sitter's delight. Choose either type of convertible for current income and the chance of a capital gain. If the underlying common stock ascends to a trigger price, you can swap your convertible for shares worth considerably more than you paid for the bond or preferred stock. Accordingly, the convertible security rises in price. You can't expect as much current income as from a nonconvertible bond of similar type and quality, nor can you reap as large a gain as you might have if you had owned the common. But the yield is substantial enough to bolster the market price of a convertible when its underlying stock has a sinking spell. Investment advisers recommend convertibles for clients who have to earn income on their money yet hate to forfeit all chance to share in the company's success.

Real Estate

The tangibility of property is one of its main appeals to first-timer investors. Another is its familiarity — most investors have bought or rented a home. Investing in one or more pieces of property had quite a vogue when real estate prices were scooting ahead of the inflation rate, mortgage interest was knocking against state usury ceilings, and tax write-offs turned apparent losses into pocketable profits. The interest ceilings are gone now, except on Veterans Administration and Federal Housing Administration loans; when mortgage costs are high, they take the wind out of sprinting prices. The number of people shopping for houses also is falling as family formation slows. And the tax losses that after-hours dabblers in real estate can claim are sharply limited. In such a climate, the buy-and-fix-up investor can succeed only by finding truly profitable properties.

If you are not interested in sweat equity, you can buy shares in real estate investment trusts. They invest in real estate and mortgages, and their shares are traded like stocks. Another option: real estate partnerships. Once synonymous with tax shelters, they now devote themselves to the wholehearted pursuit of income.

Precious Metals

Gold and silver tend to gain in value during times of political and economic turmoil. The price can multiply in a hurry when inflation saps public confidence in the value of currencies. You therefore invest in precious metals as either a speculation or a hedge against that sleeping dragon, inflation. Folks with political fears prefer to buy and take possession of gold bars or coins. Serener souls tuck away shares of mutual funds that specialize in mining stocks.

Futures

Like options, futures are used to speculate on the direction of the price of an asset or to protect a current asset from a harmful price change. Novices and most other amateurs should shun the futures markets. The odds against making a profit are nearly insurmountable. Remember that, because you may get a phone call anytime from a persuasive stranger who tells you his deal is different. The only difference is that he is selling sure losers.

All the more reason to understand commodity basics. Futures are contracts pledging you to buy or sell a standard amount of a tangible commodity or a stock-market index or a government security or a foreign currency. The contract sets a date on which the other party to the contract can demand delivery and a price at which the sale will be made. Before the contract expires, you will sell it at a profit or loss. You can trade contracts on soybeans, pork bellies, orange juice, heating oil, Japanese yen, Treasury bills, and Standard & Poor's 500-stock index, among other things.

To make an investment in futures, you place an order with a commodity broker, either at a firm that handles commodity transactions exclusively or at a major stock brokerage. Contracts usually range in value from $10,000 to $65,000, although one commodity exchange — the MidAmerica in Chicago — trades minifutures with values as low as $2,000. The broker will ask for a cash deposit of 10 to 15 percent of your contract as "margin." If the price of the commodity begins to move against you, he will demand more money — sometimes much more. Most brokers insist that futures investors have easily liquidated assets to back up their trades. If you lack the required resources, you can invest in professionally managed futures funds (minimum: $5,000). It would be wise to check thoroughly the past performance of the fund managers, however. Many have dismal records.

Buying on Margin

Futures trading is a form of margin trading: the investor puts up a fairly small sum compared to the value of the securities or commodities on which he gets a piece of the action. When you buy stock on margin, your broker lends you as much as 50 percent of the price. He charges interest and takes your shares as collateral. If the stock goes up 25 percent and you sell it, you will get a 50 percent gain on your money, less interest and brokerage commission costs. But if the stock drops by 25 percent, your broker will worry about his collateral and probably demand more cash.

Stock-market prodigies may want to plunge right into margin buying and other exotica: stock-index futures, commodities, options, and the like. But there is no rush. Even for beginners who stick to plain old stocks and bonds, investing is, as Louis Rukeyser says, ''about the most fun you can have legally in America.''

31

WHERE TO PUT YOUR SAVINGS

In the old days the rate of interest that you could earn on your savings, before paying taxes on the income, usually was no more than two or three percentage points above the rate of inflation. With the deregulation of bank-account interest ceilings, however, savers have been able to reap as much as a 5 percent inflation-adjusted, or real, rate of return. What broke the regulatory logjam was the advent of the money-market mutual fund. It gave the general public access to the unfettered arena of short-term money, a rarefied market where corporations and the federal government borrow and lend in units of $1 million or more. When people discovered during the double-digit inflation of the 1970s that they could get more than 10 percent interest in a money-market fund, where their principal was safe from defaults and retrievable at full value by writing a check, they began draining their bank accounts in a hurry. Congress had little choice but to let banks, savings and loan associations, and credit unions offer their own versions of money-market accounts. By April 1986 the last vestiges of federal control over the rates and terms of bank-deposit interest had been swept away.

Keep clearly in mind the difference between saving and investing. Savings accounts promise to preserve your capital as well as offer steady income. Investing, by contrast, involves accepting the risk of losing some — or all — of your capital in exchange for a chance of a much greater total return. People save, or should save, for a specific purpose such as the creation of an emergency fund.

Once you decide to save, your first concern is where to put the money. Since the safety of your capital is paramount, federally insured banking institutions come quickly to mind. At any bank, savings and loan association, or credit union that belongs to the Federal Deposit Insurance Corporation, the Federal Savings and Loan Insurance Corporation, or the National Credit Union Share Insurance Fund, accounts containing $100,000 or less are fully guaranteed by the U.S. government.

Although only one account in your name in a given institution is covered, you can have an unlimited number of fully insured accounts in different institutions. You can also set up multiple accounts in one place. Each depositor, for example, can have an account for ordinary deposits and another, also insured for $100,000, that is designated as an Individual Retirement Account. People with joint accounts can share a third $100,000 umbrella. Thus a two-income couple with two IRAs can protect as much as $500,000 in a single federally insured institution; if they have offspring, each child is entitled to a fully insured account in his or her own name. But if only one person's name is on more than one ordinary account in the same establishment, the limit applies cumulatively. So if you have, say, $70,000 in a money-market savings account and $40,000 in a certificate of deposit, both under your name, your combined $110,000 exceeds the insurance limit by $10,000.

Sometimes banks that don't belong to the federal insurance system offer higher interest than member banks. To get you that extra income, they take extra risk. Insolvencies at institutions whose deposits were guaranteed by state-government-sponsored privately run insurance funds have set off massive withdrawals in recent years, forcing government officials to suspend withdrawals not only at shaky banks or S&Ls but also at scores of healthy ones. Deposits in one big Maryland S&L that went belly-up in the spring of 1985 were still frozen in 1987. Temporary loss of access to their cash by thousands of depositors in Maryland and Ohio had one positive result: many privately insured institutions signed up with federal insurance agencies.

Money-market mutual funds are not insured. Their assets are invested in the short-term borrowings of institutions with high credit ratings — major corporations, billion-dollar banks, and the U.S. Treasury. Only one money fund out of 357 has ever failed to repay on demand 100 cents on the dollar, and even that one redeemed 97 percent of its investors' original share value. If those odds disturb you, stick with federally insured banks.

Treasury securities are the safest of all places for your savings in that you are assured of repayment when a security matures. But be careful: if you have to cash in a Treasury bill, note, or bond before it is due, you could get back less cash than you put in. (See "Treasuries," below, for the differences among these.) For however long you tie up your cash — whether a few weeks or several decades — you run the risk that interest rates will rise. Then nobody will take the security off your hands for as much as you paid for it. You can still consider Treasuries as savings deposits, but only by limiting yourself to short-term issues: three-month or six-month T-bills for money you might need at any time and one-to-five-year Treasury notes if the maturity coincides with an expected near-term need.

Banks offer a smorgasbord of savings accounts and certificates of deposit. When the demand for money intensifies in a particular city, rate wars can erupt. In New Orleans, for example, a 1985 skirmish between Hibernia National Bank and Gulf Federal drew several other bayou banks into an all-out donnybrook, boosting interest rates to nationwide highs. At about the same time, Coast Savings & Loan of Los Angeles began luring out-of-state depositors with CD rates that were higher than those for California residents. Robert K. Heady professionally monitors these goings-on in a weekly newsletter called *100 Highest Yields* (P.O. Box 088888, North Palm Beach, Florida 33408; $84 a year); he ranks federally insured banks paying the most on money-market accounts and CDs.

Brokerage firms have elbowed into the competition with $100,000 CDs that they buy from money-hungry banks at above-market yields and parcel out in thousand-dollar denominations to the public. At brokerages and mutual-fund houses, money-market funds have blossomed into varieties to suit almost all tastes and needs. Even retail chains and finance companies have entered the savings business. Here is a closer look at your choices.

Bank Money-Market Deposit Accounts

Money-market deposit accounts pay rates that vary from month to month but seem to hover about half a point below the national average yield on money-market funds. After the accounts were deregulated in 1986, some banks stopped requiring depositors to maintain a minimum balance of $1,000 or more to qualify for money-market rates. Money-market accounts now often double as checking accounts.

Money-Market Mutual Funds

You can write any number of checks on a money-market fund, but the smallest check you can issue is usually for $250 or $500. The funds are likely to maintain their yield advantage over bank money-market accounts, according to Glen King Parker, publisher of *Income & Safety*, a monthly newsletter covering money-market and fixed-income mutual funds (3471 North Federal Highway, Fort Lauderdale, Florida 33306; $100 a year). "Banks and S&Ls have found they can scale back their rates and still hold deposits," Parker says.

Despite the enviable safety record of money funds, people who wish to add a belt to their suspenders can use lower-yielding government-only funds, which restrict themselves to Treasury bills, or they can choose privately insured money funds — the insurance guaranteeing your return of capital. For a money fund with unlimited checking privileges, you can open an asset management account at a brokerage firm. You will pay $30 to $100 a year for this and other services — a credit card, a securities and margin account, and a comprehensive monthly statement (see Chapter 48). Most asset management accounts require you to stock the account with several thousand dollars worth of cash, shares, bonds, or other securities.

Tax-Exempt Money-Market Funds

Tax-exempt funds usually pay yields that exceed what a high-bracket investor would earn after taxes from a regular money-market fund. To judge whether you are in that elite class, use the following formula:

$$\frac{\text{Tax-exempt yield}}{\text{(1 minus your decimalized tax bracket)}}$$

If you are in the 28 percent bracket and can get 4.5 percent from a tax-exempt money fund, the calculation will look like this:

$$\frac{\text{4.5 percent}}{1 - .28 = .72} = \text{6.25 percent}$$

If regular money-market funds are paying less than 6.25 percent, you are better off in a tax-exempt fund. Most large mutual-fund organizations and brokerage firms have tax-exempt funds. If your state income tax rate is high, you may be able to find a fund that also qualifies for the state tax exemption by investing only municipal securities of your home state.

Bank Certificates of Deposit

Banks and S&Ls let you squirrel away money in certificates of deposit at rates that are guaranteed for periods of seven days to 10 years or so. The minimum investment depends on the institution but might typically be $500 or $1,000. By and large, the longer the term of the certificate, the higher your return. When you buy a CD, you preserve liquidity. If you have to pull out your cash early, the most you will probably lose is three months' interest. The penalty may vary from bank to bank, though, so shop around. Some banks waive even this penalty for customers who have CDs in their IRAs and need to withdraw savings for retirement income.

To attract your savings, banks are trying to make their CDs more adaptable to your needs. Some institutions let you decide when you want your CD to mature — in two years and seven months, for instance, if that's when you will need the money for college tuition. Some banks offer variable-rate CDs, whose interest rate changes weekly or monthly. Don't sign up for one unless you expect a huge jump in interest rates soon.

If you sleep better at night knowing your money is locked up in the vault at the corner bank, forget about searching the United States for higher-paying CDs. But if you couldn't care less whether you ever see a banker again, here are two rules for playing the new rate-chasing game:

Quantify your return. In bank ads trumpeting high returns, what you see is not necessarily what you get. One accurate way to compare deals is to ask an officer at each prospective bank exactly how much money you would get back when, say, a one-year certificate of deposit matures. Robert Heady of *100 Highest Yields* gives this warning: ''Look out for the so-called tiered-rate account, where your money earns different rates depending on how much you have deposited with the bank.''

Understand the mechanics of investing. Each bank has its own rules on how you get your money to it and when you start earning interest. Most banks will assign you an account number by telephone. Ask for the mailing address of the branch of the institution with which you will be doing business. Then open the account with a check made out to that account number and endorsed ''for deposit only.'' Make sure the institution sends you a form that puts your name, address, and Social Security number on record. Inquire whether your money starts earning interest as soon as the bank receives your check or only after it clears. Also ask an officer about the bank's other rules — for example, the penalty for early withdrawal of a CD.

Then determine how you will be notified when your CD comes due. The bank should send you a reminder a few weeks before you have to make a decision about where to roll over the money. A few banks just mail you your check, while others may not notify you at all. Unless you instruct them otherwise, they automatically invest your money in another

CD. Some banks even put your money on hold in a measly-interest passbook account.

Brokered CDs

Most brokers sell certificates of deposit issued by federally insured banks or S&Ls, which pay a fee to the broker for bringing in funds. The yields on ''brokered'' CDs usually exceed those available from your local bank. Buying from brokers gives you one other valuable advantage: you will not have to pay any early-withdrawal penalties. Brokers, unlike regular banks, maintain an active secondary market in CDs. They will sell yours as they sell bonds — at a price that reflects current interest rates. You still may take a loss, but you have a fair chance of breaking even or perhaps making a profit.

A problem with brokered CDs is that their high rates are often accompanied by high risks. So far this has been a problem for the feds but not for investors. For instance, Bell Savings & Loan Association in San Mateo, California, with up to $400 million of its $1.7 billion of assets provided by brokers, collapsed in July 1985 after suffering a projected loss of $60 million on bad loans. Bell was immediately reorganized under new management, but its CD owners would have been protected anyway by the Federal Savings and Loan Insurance Corporation. The FSLIC and FDIC have tried to limit the growth of the brokered-CD business, but the courts have overruled them. In any case, you needn't worry about the safety of individual accounts of $100,000 or less.

Treasuries

U.S. Treasury securities are the quintessentially safe investment because Uncle Sam can print new dollars to repay old debts. As a sweetener, interest on Treasuries is exempt from state and local taxes. With the national debt in the trillions, there is never a shortage of new issues.

Treasury offerings come in tempting arrays ranging from savings bonds that you can buy for $25 to cash-management bills requiring a minimum of $1 million. Maturities span a few days to 30 years. But savers should stick to basic black — Treasury bills and notes — because they are easy to buy and cash in. Three-month and six-month bills are auctioned every week and require that you put up at least $10,000. Twelve-month bills are offered every four weeks, also in $10,000 minimums. Two-year and three-year notes are issued in $5,000 minimums, four-to-10-year issues in $1,000 units. One-to-10-year notes go on sale every four weeks or so.

You can buy newly issued Treasury securities through a bank or broker at a sales charge of $25 or more. Or you can save that expense by sending your money to the Treasury with a form that you can pick up at Federal Reserve banks and branches. Three- and six-month bills are auctioned every Monday, one-year bills every fourth Thursday. For more information, write for a free booklet, *Buying Treasury Securities at Federal Reserve Banks* (The Federal Reserve Bank of Richmond, Public Services Department, Box 27622, Richmond, Virginia 23261).

You won't know what interest rate you are getting on a T-bill until after you have bought it. But rates rarely change dramatically from day to day. You can get a good idea of what the new securities will pay by checking yields of similar securities in your newspaper's financial pages or under the "Money Rates" heading deep inside the *Wall Street Journal*.

Treasury notes are sold at face value and pay cash interest every six months. Bills are sold at a discount and are redeemed at face value. Here's how that works. Say you send in $10,000 to buy a six-month bill paying 7 percent. A week or so later, the government will send you a check for $350, the amount of the discount; it will pay back your $10,000 in six months. You have only $9,650 invested in the bill, so your annualized yield is not 7 percent but 7.25 percent.

Plan on holding your Treasuries until they mature. You can borrow against them or sell them in the secondary market, where you may get more or less than you paid, depending on whether interest rates have fallen or risen since you bought them. If you are selling less than $100,000 worth, brokers consider that an "odd lot" and nick you a bit on the commission.

U.S. Savings Bonds, once the ugly ducklings of the Treasury, have turned prettier. Nevertheless and despite their name, they are the wrong place for money that you want to keep handy for early use. Their several beauties are discussed in Chapter 37.

Department Stores and Finance Companies

Banks owned by department-store chains such as Sears and J.C. Penney are offering increasingly attractive savings plans. Sears's Discover card account is designed for savings as well as credit-card usage. Cardholders should be able to earn a competitive rate of interest on a full range of money-market and CD accounts, including IRAs. Beneficial Finance and Household Finance have entered the savings market, too. Household Financial Services has added consumer banking to its more familiar lending and insurance lines. Household banks in California, Colorado, Illinois, Kansas, Maryland, and Ohio sell flexible CDs — you set the amount and maturity. Beneficial markets CDs by mail and over a toll-free telephone number (800-841-8000) from its insured Delaware banking subsidiary at yields right up there with the highest.

32

STRATEGIES: VALUE INVESTING

When securities analysts forecast favorable earnings for a company, the managers of pension funds, mutual funds, and other financial institutions sometimes bid up the company's stock to unreasonably high prices. Predicting earnings is a risky business. Unforeseen problems in the company or a recession in the economy can upset such projections. When profits fall short of estimates for a popular stock, portfolio managers are likely to bail out en masse, causing the price to nosedive. At that point, fallen institutional favorites become prime pickings for investors in search of value, who conclude that little risk remains of serious further price declines. Value seekers also do their prospecting in fairly small companies that are followed by only one or two analysts. In poorly lit corners of the market, undervalued stocks may gather dust until foraging investors belatedly discover their worth.

Value-minded investors are followers of the late Benjamin Graham, coauthor with David Dodd of the 1934 classic, *Security Analysis* (McGraw-Hill, $41.95). Graham, a professional investor and Columbia University finance professor who died in 1976, originated modern methods of assaying the value of companies. He believed that the only sound investment strategy is to buy stocks while they are priced below their intrinsic value, which eventually will be recognized by other investors.

The most notable Graham disciple is preeminent stock picker Warren E. Buffett, who in the early 1950s earned an M.S. in economics at Columbia and an A+ in the professor's course. A person who put $10,000 into a private investment partnership organized by Buffett in 1956 would have pocketed $300,000 in 1969, when the venture was dissolved. Buffett is now chairman of Berkshire Hathaway, an Omaha holding company that owns primarily insurance firms and invests a sizable portion of corporate funds in stocks. Buffett sums up his investment approach in characteristic understatement: "If a business is worth a dollar and I can buy it for 40 cents, something good may happen to me."

To find the stock-market equivalent of 40-cent dollar bills demands discipline, patience, and a willingness to go against prevailing opinion. You will find the most opportunities during bear markets, when all stock prices are down, and progressively fewer great buys as stocks rise during bull markets. But even then bargains usually can be found, says Michael Metz, an Oppenheimer & Company analyst. Along with a growing contingent of colleagues, Metz programs his computer to identify potentially high-value stocks that other investors have overlooked.

As with any kind of investing, you should diversify your portfolio of undervalued stocks so that your gainers can outdo the inevitable losers. You also should be prepared to wait out the market, which may be slow in recognizing the merits of your discoveries. As Metz says, "If you buy value stocks right, your chief risk is boredom." Many value-minded investors hold stocks for five years or longer. Graham was not that patient; his counsel was to consider selling if nothing good happened in the next three years.

The chances of quicker rewards have been enhanced by the epidemic in recent years of corporate mergers, takeovers, and leveraged buyouts initiated by companies or individuals with an eye for undervalued assets. Walt Disney's fall from institutional favor in 1983 produced a storybook ending for some value hunters. When an earnings drop that autumn sent Disney from around $60 a share to $47, analysts such as Metz and his partner, Norman Weinger, began to look at the company's assets. They decided that the balance sheet underappraised real estate near Disney's California and Florida theme parks and a library of famous films. As a result, the analysts concluded, the company's book value (total assets minus total liabilities) was closer to $70 a share than the $40 cited in the annual report.

The Oppenheimer analysts recommended Disney to their clients as a buy at $47 in November 1983. Takeover artists soon agreed. Financiers Saul Steinberg and Irwin Jacobs both bought large stakes in the company. But after complicated maneuvering, the Bass brothers of Fort Worth controlled 28 percent of Disney's shares and helped install new management. While all that was happening, the Oppenheimer asset players took a 28 percent profit by selling the stock at $60. A few months later, with the price at $75.50, other analysts began touting Disney as a growth stock.

Stories in the *Wall Street Journal* or your local newspaper may alert you to prominent stocks like Disney that have tumbled. Opportunities may also surface in the daily stock-page tallies of stocks whose prices have hit their lowest levels in 52 weeks.

Once you have spotted an interesting company in the newspaper, you need to do further research to ascertain why the stock has been hammered down and whether the company is financially strong. Does it have appealing cash hoards, real estate, oil reserves, or other natural resources that might cause the market assessment to brighten? For answers, start with the *Value Line Investment Survey* (711 Third Avenue, New York, New York 10017; $395 a year), which is available in well-stocked libraries. Value Line gives you most of the necessary information for 1,700 companies in a format that is accessible once you have become familiar with the fact-crammed layout. With a little extra work, you can derive even more information from a company's annual report (see Figure 14).

If you own an Apple II, IBM PC, or IBM-compatible personal computer, you can buy software that allows you to screen out the most attractively priced of the 1,700 Value Line stocks. The program, called Value/Screen or Value Screen Plus, costs $348 and includes a year's subscription to monthly updated data disks. A competitor, Standard & Poor's Stockpak II (25 Broadway, New York, New York 10004), contains essential information on 1,500 or more companies. The basic package costs $275, plus a one-time $30 registration fee; you get the software and 12 monthly disks. At prices ranging as high as $980 a year, you can get data on thousands of additional companies. For the computerless, James B. Rea (10966 Chalon Road, Los Angeles, California 90077), a money manager who worked with Benjamin Graham in the early 1970s, publishes computer-screened analyses of stocks that appear to be undervalued in terms of net current asset value. Rea charges $300 for 12 monthly reports and $40 for a single computer run.

The Graham Guidelines

Here is a closer look at the best ways to evaluate stocks under guidelines laid down by Graham or his disciples.

Debt Ratios

Companies worthy of consideration should be fundamentally sound. One measure of soundness is the debt-to-equity ratio: long-term debt divided by total capitalization (the sum of all long-term obligations and share-

Figure 14. Valuing a Stock by the Numbers

Before sizing up a stock on this worksheet, see whether the company's long-term debt is less than 40 percent of its total capitalization, as explained in the accompanying text. All the data needed here can be found in the company's annual report or derived from figures there. A handier source, because it makes many of the calculations for you, is the *Value Line Investment Survey,* available at your library or broker's office. Refer to the text for explanations of the fundamentals. To help you along, the worksheet analyzes a company whose value sparkled in 1985, Gordon Jewelry of Houston. Disappointing 1984 earnings had depressed the stock, which trades on the New York Stock Exchange. Before investing in a company you have analyzed, ask your broker for late news about it and probe its annual report for unsettling problems that don't show up in the numbers.

The Stock Data

	Gordon Jewelry (2/85)	*Your stock now*		*Gordon Jewelry*	*Your stock*
Latest share price	$16	______	Earnings per share	$2.32	______
52-week range	$14–$20	______	Annual dividend	$0.46	______

The Fundamentals

	Gordon Jewelry	*Points*	*Your stock*	*Points*
Dividend yield (3 points if above 5%)	2.9%	0	______	______
Price/earnings ratio (4 points if below 7)	6.9	4	______	______
Current ratio (5 points if 2 or more)	2.8	5	______	______
Book value per share (6 points if above stock price)	$22.13	6	______	______
Price to free cash flow per share (6 points if ratio is less than 10)	12.7	—	______	______
Return on equity (7 points if above 18%)	10.4%	—	______	______
Net current asset value per share (10 points if above stock price)	$17.20	10	______	______
Total points		25		
(15 points or more signal a possible buy)				

holders' equity). A company whose debt is less than 40 percent of its equity is in good shape. A second measure of soundness is called the current ratio: total current assets (cash, marketable securities, accounts receivable, and inventories) divided by total current liabilities (all debts payable within a year). If the current ratio is 2 or more, the company probably has ample capital to cover its expenses and run its business effectively in the coming year.

Book Value

The most common measure of a company's intrinsic worth is book value per share, computed by subtracting total liabilities from total assets and dividing the result by the number of shares of common stock outstanding. But the book-value figure includes a company's plant and equipment, which are often hard to appraise. Graham preferred to look for stocks selling below their net current asset value, a computation that excludes the value of plant and equipment. A stock's net current asset value is total current assets minus three balance-sheet items: current liabilities, long-term debt, and the aggregate redemption value of any preferred stock. Divide the result by the number of common shares. Stocks selling below their net current asset value are an almost automatic buy for value hunters.

Hidden Assets

Stocks that fit the net-current-asset-value measure may become harder to find as more and more investors discover them with computer screens and bid up prices, says asset hunter Mark Boyar. Boyar, who publishes *Asset Analysis Focus,* a $10,000-a-year advisory letter for money managers, believes investors should look for such assets as real estate, which companies often undervalue on their balance sheets. For accounting purposes, the value of buildings is depreciated over the years, but land must be carried on the books at the original cost.

The accounting procedure used by a company to appraise its inventory sometimes hides the true value of assets. The traditional FIFO (first in, first out) method assumes that items are sold in the order in which they entered the inventory. In periods of rising prices, FIFO accounting exaggerates profits because the items just sold cost considerably less to make than their replacements in the inventory. During the high inflation of the late 1970s and early 1980s, many companies switched to LIFO (last in, first out) accounting. By assuming that each item sold was the last to enter the inventory, LIFO lowers earnings but cuts taxes and provides a more accurate picture of the company's profits.

While stating profits more realistically, LIFO undervalues readily marketable inventories, such as consumer goods. This extra worth can give a company added financial strength. If it needs to borrow money, banks will count as collateral the true value of inventories. These LIFO reserves, as analysts call them, are also attractive to takeover specialists who want to finance the acquisition of a company by borrowing against its assets. Gordon Jewelry, the company used to illustrate value analysis in Figure 14, switched to LIFO in 1981. The hidden inventory value of its diamonds, jewelry, and watches was $28 million more than shown on its books and added more than $2 a share to the company's net current asset value.

Cash Flow

In addition to assaying assets, you should check out cash flow. To get this figure, tally the firm's net income with the amounts it has allowed for depreciation, amortization, depletion (if it is a natural resource company), and extraordinary charges against reserves. All these are bookkeeping deductions that aren't really paid out in dollars. Cash flow is an important measurement of a company's health, especially during periods of high inflation. Charles Royce, manager of the Pennsylvania Mutual and Royce Value funds, explains why: "In an environment of rising prices, cash flow determines your ability to replace plant and equipment and makes a significant difference to your capital needs."

The number that is of particular interest to value hunters is the so-called free cash flow, which is adjusted for dividend payments and capital expenditures. This figure is easily calculated from the Value Line company summary, which breaks out the per-share values for cash flow and the other items. A positive free cash flow demonstrates that a company should have capital to expand its business or buy back its stock. Oppenheimer's Michael Metz feels that when takeover activity is intense, a stock is appealing if its price is less than 10 times free cash flow. That is one good indication of sufficient borrowing power to finance a takeover or buyout of the company.

Return on Equity

Sometimes a company can have low earnings but still be healthy for the long term. One way to spot such strength is to look at the firm's five-year average return on shareholders' equity, sometimes called return on net worth. This figure is usually included in annual reports; if not, compute it by dividing net income by shareholders' equity. With a 10.6 percent median return on equity for Fortune 500 companies, a return of more than 18 percent is considered very strong.

When coupled with robust earnings growth, a high return on equity tends to result in an elevated price/earnings ratio (P/E), a measure of stock value obtained by dividing the share price by the latest 12-month earnings per share. Value investors shun high P/Es, but they come to attention when a decline in a company's earnings or problems for its industry produce high returns on equity from a stock selling at a low P/E. They will glance at the P/E as a quick indicator of whether the stock is in or out of favor with investors. If the P/E of the S&P 500 is hovering around 10, a P/E below 7 for an individual stock suggests that it is sufficiently out of favor to merit consideration. Various studies have shown that in the long run the lowest P/E stocks at a given time will consistently outperform the stocks with the highest ratios. Some proponents of high value, low P/E stocks also look for a 5 percent or greater dividend yield so that they can collect income while they wait for the stock to go up.

One such investor is Leonard Heine, who left a Wall Street job in 1970 to go out on his own as a value-conscious money manager. From 1981 to 1985, his firm in Westport, Connecticut, was ranked seventh among pension fund managers by financial scorekeepers at Computer Directions Advisers. Heine says the problem with trying to forecast the course of the market — and which stocks will move along with it — is that you have to grapple with too many unknowns: ''What are interest rates going to do? What is the economy going to do? What is the weather going to do? What will be the mood of the American people?'' Instead, Heine has boiled down his approach to a cardinal stock-picking rule: ''Buy value and it will out.''

33

STRATEGIES: GOING FOR GROWTH

As the 1960s merged into the 1970s, the Wall Street crowd flocked to what they called the Nifty Fifty. These were stocks that managers of pension funds and mutual funds believed capable of rising almost indefinitely because there was no limit in sight to the growth of profits in the companies behind the shares. And so the likes of Avon, Kodak, IBM, and Xerox became institutional darlings, which rose and rose — until their bubble burst. A few years later, as the 1970s merged into the 1980s, the spotlight shone on smaller "emerging growth" companies, most of them in high technology. The Silicon Valley followers of high tech poured their money into the likes of Apple Computer, Commodore, and scores of other fledgling makers of computers and computer-related products or services. That bubble burst in 1983, in the midst of a rampaging bull market.

Obviously, the pursuit of growth stocks is speculative, nerve-racking, and faddish. Yet investors who make the most money in the stock market often are those who can spot promising companies before others do and have enough conviction to buy shares when no one else will. These same growth businesses typically can maintain annual earnings increases of 15 percent or more during economic recessions as well as booms. Some very large companies — General Electric for one — still qualify. But with armies of Wall Street analysts and institutional investors following such issues, the rest of us are not likely to find undiscovered bargains among them.

Private investors therefore are apt to assume they can't compete in the growth-stock market. But the record dispels that notion. It is in the nature of professional investing to move millions of dollars in and out of various issues every day. Big money managers can do that only by investing in companies with a large number of shares outstanding. Otherwise they would push up the prices of stocks they were trying to buy and depress the prices of stocks they were trying to sell. Portfolio managers also are constrained in their choice of stocks by the fierce competition among them for corporate pension fund clients. The law requires the managers of such funds to invest prudently, and that usually means shunning out-of-fashion or unknown stocks. Yet those are the issues that can make the greatest gains.

Individual investors do not have to worry about causing market turbulence or justifying their stock picks to a fickle clientele. They can go prospecting in a market of 6,000 or so stocks that most of the institutions ignore and few, if any, analysts bother with. Recent history suggests that those are the shares that, as a class, produce the biggest profits. Two finance professors, Avner Arbel of Cornell University and Paul Strebel of the State University of New York at Binghamton, tracked the market behavior of 510 stocks between 1970 and 1980. They discovered that issues with virtually no institutional ownership rose an average of 20.8 percent a year vs. 10.4 percent for institutional favorites. They have confirmed their findings in more recent studies, and Arbel elaborates on his neglected-stock hypothesis in *How to Beat the Market with High-Performance Generic Stocks Your Broker Won't Tell You About* (William Morrow, $16.95).

In the stock market, the prices of small and medium-sized growth companies are almost bound to take giddier turns, both up and down, than those of big firms. The giddiest of all in recent years — and the hardest to analyze — have been the shares of computer and other high-technology companies. In fast-changing markets, some miracle microchip can suddenly make yesterday's hot product obsolete. Even if the technology is unchallenged, the original companies in a glamorous, lucrative business can lose market share as rivals move in. You may be able to assess companies in high-tech fields if you work in a related area or understand a particular technology. Otherwise, it is probably wisest to concentrate your search in more mundane but understandable businesses. In either case, if you have been diligent in your research and courageous enough to buy when the stock was unpopular, you will have cut your risk.

Growth Industries

Demographic and economic trends suggest much about the profit centers of tomorrow. By the end of the twentieth century, for example, 35 million Americans will be over the age of 65, up from 28.6 million in 1985. Working women will edge close in number to men in the work force. Fifteen years before the turn of the century, economists believed that inflation would average around 5 percent annually through the year 2000, low enough to allow for relatively steady business growth. It seemed evident that the United States would continue to swing toward a predominantly service economy as manufacturing moved to lower-wage nations.

Such trends presage tremendous growth potential in long-term health care for the aged and private day-care centers for the preschool population. Technology-based companies in such fields as telecommunications and plastics will continue to thrive at the expense of basic industries that depend more on brawn than brains.

For every prosperous new business, one or more others face decline or extinction. Examples probably will include leather goods, apparel, and textiles, which for the most part will be imported. Defense spending went on a roll during the Reagan presidency but could slip into a decline, dimming the allure of aerospace and arms manufacturing.

The following industries show particular promise for the rest of the century.

Child Care

Huge encampments of day-care centers will be required to satisfy the armies of working mothers who already are or will be holding down jobs outside the home. As early as 1990, some 10 million women with young children will be working for pay, almost double the number in 1980. Yet professionally managed child-care centers are in short supply, and waiting lists often exceed enrollment.

Because of highly publicized safety concerns, day care is abandoning its backyard beginnings. At least five publicly traded companies that own or franchise centers have sprung up, and their numbers are growing. Some, like La Petite Academy, a nationwide chain based in Kansas City, Missouri, sell their services to corporations. La Petite centers operate almost like private schools, providing instruction for children up to the age of 12 in such subjects as math, music, and computers.

Computer Systems

The computer as corporate decision maker and troubleshooter instead of just compiler and collator is beginning to take command, thanks to new systems hand tailored to help businesses operate more efficiently. DM Data, a consulting firm in Scottsdale, Arizona, estimates that one specialty, artificial intelligence technology, will generate sales of products and services worth more than $4 billion in 2000, up from $719 million in 1985.

In addition, special-purpose computer systems will find an increasingly large and important role in medicine, where they will help doctors diagnose illnesses and recommend treatment. William R. Baker, former head of artificial intelligence in medicine for the National Institutes of Health, predicts that by the turn of the century "every physician will be dealing with a computer." The market for such systems, which attempt to put volumes of medical knowledge at the user's fingertips, is expected to reach $100 million by the year 2000.

Another growth area is computer-integrated manufacturing, or CIM. Pioneering firms such as the privately held Consilium Inc. in Mountain View, California, are starting to supply software that monitors and controls factory production to prevent waste and extra work. Dave Hanks, Consilium's director of marketing, reports: "We can reduce a factory's inventory of partly finished goods by as much as 40 percent, improve the quality of the product and increase the amounts that are produced."

Fiber Optics

The growing needs of information-hungry businesses will keep the telecommunications industry humming. Among the developments to watch is the changeover of the nation's communications system from copper wire to fiber optics. The United States is replacing more than a billion miles of copper wire in telephone cables with optical fibers — thin strands of glass that use pulses of light flashed from a laser to carry voices or computer data. Why the switch? To speed the flow of data. It would take more than two weeks to transmit the telephone books of the 20 largest cities in the United States over copper telephone lines; with fiber optics the time could be reduced to less than a second.

Fiber optics also promises vast increases in capacity. A pair of strands have the potential to carry at least 300,000 times the number of telephone conversations that two copper wires can convey. Businesses will therefore transmit information over great distances faster and more efficiently. This will nearly quadruple fiber-optics sales.

Consumers also will get a payoff from communications advances. Cellular telephone technology will make car telephones as common as tape decks, according to Stan Feldman, senior vice president and chief economist in the industry and regional analysis division of Data Resources Inc., a research firm. Since cellular communications is a capital-intensive business requiring as many as 25 high-rise antennas for each city, companies that will dial into tomorrow's cellular growth are ones that have already made a substantial investment in it.

Geriatric Care

As the number of aged grows, long-term care becomes a critical need. Among the promising alternatives are residential-care communities and group living centers. To provide such facilities for merely 5 percent of the nation's over-75 population near the end of the century will require almost five times the number of facilities that exist today. According to W. Robert Friedman, Jr., a partner at Montgomery Securities in San Francisco, ''Quality geriatric care in a warm environment is the wave of the future. People want to live where they aren't constantly watched by nurses but where they can secure medical care if they need it.'' Payment for such services will come from the increasingly affluent elderly. The U.S. Census Bureau reports that only 12 percent of those aged 65 and over were living below the poverty level in 1984. Back in 1959, the number in poverty was 35 percent.

Health Services

With employers, insurers, and the government all cracking down on rising medical costs, patients are spending less time in hospitals. Not only are they going home sooner than usual, but they are also choosing to undergo treatment at home rather than in the hospital. Patients who require kidney dialysis or chemotherapy, for instance, will need less frequent hospital treatments. What was recently a $7 billion home health-care business is expected to grow to $30 billion by 2000. Companies that will pocket these revenues are the diversified medical and drug concerns that have already targeted the home-care industry, as well as medical-equipment manufacturers whose devices can be used away from hospitals.

While products created through biotechnology have been slow to reach the market, their potential remains enormous. Researchers hope eventually to find treatments for the various forms of cancer that afflict three in 10 Americans at some time in their lives. One treatment with promise involves attaching toxins to monoclonal antibodies that seek out cancer cells and destroy them.

Homemaker Helpers

Growing numbers of working parents will stimulate demand for service firms that do household chores. For example, Lisa Dorfman's Woman for Rent, in New York City, performs such tasks as supervising home renovations, planning parties, and dealing with landlords, at $25 an hour.

The success of small personal-service firms may generate chains and franchised operations. By 1985 an organization called Services Unlimited had opened two branches in New York City. The company, which at that time charged $10 to $125 a job, dispatches helpers to do such chores as wait in line for theater tickets, passports, and auto registrations.

Semiconductors

U.S. semiconductor makers, if they can stave off Japanese rivals, will experience dramatic growth because of a still-expanding market for integrated circuits. As early as 1992, domestic demand for memory chips alone could balloon to $9 billion — nearly 4½ times larger than it was in the mid-1980s. The impetus for growth will come from increasingly powerful devices that can be used in a wide variety of products. W. J. Sanders III, president of Advanced Micro Devices, calls them "the crude oil of the twenty-first century." Chips that hold 100 double-spaced typewritten pages will soon be replaced by ones capable of holding 1,600 pages. Because of their greater usefulness, according to some experts, chips that find their way into electronic devices like stereo receivers and computers will have 16 times their former capacity.

Specialty Polymers

The good advice that Dustin Hoffman got from his father's friend in the 1967 film *The Graduate* — "I want to say just one word: plastics" — still seems valid. Plastics remain out in front, finding their way into unexpected applications. Stronger yet lighter materials called specialty polymers can replace metals, wood, glass, and paper in everything from semiconductor chip mountings to automobiles. Specialty polymers are expected to generate some $30 billion in sales in the year 2000, up from $7 billion in 1984.

The growth of plastics in electronic components will be most dramatic. Polymers resistant to flame, heat, and chemicals will replace metals in microchips, computer connectors, and data storage disks. More visible to consumers will be the growing use of polymers in automobile bodies. The percentage of plastics in autos is expected to triple by the turn of the century, making the family car lighter and more fuel-efficient than ever.

Assembling a Portfolio

Before venturing into growth stocks, make up your mind to hang on for two or three years — or longer if necessary — until other investors recognize the company's merits and push up the price. John Rogers, editor of the *Patient Investor* newsletter (9307 North Michigan Avenue, Chicago, Illinois 60601; $125 a year), puts it this way: "We try to get people to think in terms of buying into a business instead of playing the market." Don't own growth stocks one at a time, though. If you value your nerves, you should invest in five to 10 companies. Diversification is essential to investing successfully in small companies.

Investment ideas are everywhere. Items in financial newspapers and magazines may spark your interest in a company. Or your five-year-old fast-food expert may rave about a new restaurant chain on the highway to Grandma's. Specialized investment advisory newsletters beat the bushes for little-known growth situations. Perhaps the outstanding newsletter is *Growth Stock Outlook* (P.O. Box 15381, Chevy Chase, Maryland 20815; biweekly plus a weekly telephone hotline, $175 a year). The editor, Charles Allmon, includes basic balance-sheet information on all the companies that he recommends. Taking an essentially long-term approach, he constructs a model portfolio and weights it according to how much of your money he thinks each stock deserves.

To maximize the small investor's natural edge, you have to do what does *not* come naturally: shrug off what most people are saying and doing, overcome your own doubts, and rein in your enthusiasm. Discipline is one of the dirty little secrets of successful investing. Andrew Lanyi, a broker with Ladenburg Thalmann & Company in New York City, who has engineered big gains for his clients by avoiding the institutional favorites, gives this advice: "Get into the habit of going against the consensus because any consensus is most wrong just when it matters most — at major turning points."

Cornell professor Avner Arbel compares institutional investors to "giraffes that nibble on the tall trees in the investment forest and ignore the underbrush." Since he believes that the biggest potential winners lie hidden in that underbrush, he strongly favors stocks that the institutions have ignored. How many institutional owners are too many? Arbel draws the line at four to a stock. Lanyi, who specializes in firms with sales of less than $25 million, prefers no big stockholders at all. John Rogers of the *Patient Investor* looks for medium-size companies with no more than 20 percent institutional ownership. Standard & Poor's *Stock Guide,* which all brokers and many libraries have, gives you the number of shares owned by pension funds and other large investors.

The denizens of the underbrush are likely to be companies with less than $100 million worth of shares outstanding and, of course, the promise of swift earnings growth. Lanyi turns up candidates by searching the earnings reports in newspapers for companies with big spurts in revenues over the previous quarter. When he spots a likely candidate, he does what anyone can do: he calls the company for its annual and quarterly reports and any other available information, and he looks up the issue in the *Value Line Investment Survey,* Standard & Poor's *Corporation Records,* or Moody's *OTC Industrial Manual.* Here is what to look for:

Low price/earnings ratios. Stocks with low P/Es typically produce better long-term results than high P/E stocks do. Just as investors overpay for the earnings potential of stocks with high P/Es, so do they underestimate the prospects of low ones. Therefore, if you find a solid company selling at a lower multiple than others in its industry or at the low end of its own P/E range, the situation may warrant investigation. Newspaper stock tables show the P/E based on the previous 12 months' earnings. But the ratio based on analysts' estimates of future earnings is a better indicator of a stock's potential. You can find such estimates in the *Value Line Investment Survey* or Standard & Poor's stock reports. Value Line also publishes a weekly low P/E list.

Sound, simple finances. A growth company should have little or no long-term debt. Money should go into business expansion, not interest payments. Furthermore, firms with low debt are best able to ride out rough times. You can find the long-term debt figure in the consolidated balance sheet published in a company's annual report.

Look also for a return on shareholders' equity of 20 to 25 percent, a sign of healthy profitability. If this figure is not stated in the annual report, you can quickly figure it by dividing net income by stockholders' equity, a number in the balance sheet. Beware the company that seems to be doing creative accounting. For a tip-off, look at the footnotes at the back of successive annual reports. If a concern has been routinely including in its earnings such nonrecurring items as special tax credits or proceeds from the sale of a divested division, move on to your next stock.

A strong competitive position. An impressive record of earnings can evaporate if rivals start taking business away from a company. The annual report is likely to give an upbeat view of the competitive situation, but common sense can help you figure out whether the grounds for optimism are realistic. They are probably solid, for example, if the company has spent several years building a chain of outlets or a complicated distribution network; no competitor could quickly replicate that kind of foundation for long-term profitability.

Indicators of earnings growth. Andrew Lanyi looks for such telltale signs as a large volume of unfilled orders. As long as the backlog is not the result of production problems, it will translate into increased revenues and then into future earnings. In service companies, he wants to see repeat orders from a high and growing percentage of customers. Fast-rising earnings will eventually push up the stock price, and he is willing to wait two or more years for that to happen.

Prospecting among Larger Firms

You can apply many of the same criteria for growth potential to companies with $100 million to $300 million in sales that you use to discover profitable smaller concerns. But a corporation with revenues in nine figures is likely to be known to institutional investors. Therefore, you need to find companies whose stock has staggered because of a drop or pause in earnings after several years of strong growth. The trick is to spot a situation where the earnings slowdown is only temporary — for example, losses that come from closing down unprofitable plants.

When to Sell

Successful growth-stock investing calls for shrewd selling as well as deft picking. Since you can't predict how long it will take other investors to recognize the value you saw in the shares, you should set your own target price for selling them. When John Rogers of the *Patient Investor* buys shares in a medium-size company at less than 10 times earnings, he considers selling at a P/E of 15. He will wait five years if necessary for the stock to get there. One handy formula is to part with a stock when its P/E is double the earnings growth rate.

There is a limit to everything, however, including patience. The time comes when you will have to root out losers. The prospects for a company sometimes do deteriorate, and there is no point hanging on while the shares are skidding toward an apparently unavoidable crash.

34

STRATEGIES: TIMING THE MARKET

Of all the qualities that contribute to success in investing, the most important is a sharp sense of timing. Keeping all your money in the stock market throughout sharp slumps can be a brutally punishing experience. It is even worse, of course, if you finally panic, sell out near the bottom, and then fail to get back in again until stock prices have had a big rebound. To avoid such disasters and yet profit from major upswings, you don't need uncanny foresight. What you do need is a plausible system for anticipating major market moves — and the will to buy and sell on cue.

Your timing need be only partially right to improve your investment results substantially. That is, you can do well if you sell some or all of your stocks within a few months of the peak of a bull market and then move back into stocks not too long before or after prices have hit bottom. This doesn't entail frequent trading and heavy commission expenses. In fact, if you invest in no-load mutual funds, the cost of making switches is negligible.

The period from 1960 through 1982 presented just six definitive market bottoms, which of course are the ideal occasions to buy stocks, and six distinct tops, the ideal times to sell. That averages roughly one buy or sell decision every couple of years. If your timing had been partially right on those occasions — if you had caught, say, 70 percent of each upswing and you had been out of stocks during 70 percent of each downswing — you would have fared nearly three times as well as by following a buy-and-hold policy. This assumes that you invested in a no-load stock fund that did no better than the Dow Jones industrial average.

Haphazard attempts at market forecasting can do more harm than good. For any hope of success, you need to develop a system that is not too complex and time consuming — and stick with it. Such a system appears in Figure 15. It consists of two parallel checklists on the state of the economy and the market. By answering 15 questions on each list, you get a serious indication of whether it is time to buy, sell, or wait.

The system combines four different but complementary disciplines in market forecasting. They are known among investment professionals as the fundamental, the psychological or contrary opinion, the technical, and the election cycle investing approaches. Here is a closer look at all four and how they can help you to anticipate major moves in the stock market.

The Fundamental Approach

A fundamentalist is guided primarily by his expectations for the economy and such components of it as company earnings and interest rates. The trend in overall corporate profits is the most important fundamental influence on stock prices; profits in turn are closely related to the ups and downs of the economy. Because investors try to anticipate the future, major declines in the stock market usually start while the economy is still booming, and major advances usually begin in the depths of a recession. In recent business cycles, stock prices peaked and started to decline six months on average before the onset of the next recession; the shortest lead time was one month, the longest 12 months. Prices then bottomed and started to rise, on average, about five months before the economy showed definite signs of recovery.

Another market fundamental, interest rates, has become critically important in recent years. Exceptionally high interest yields, both short and long term, made fixed-income investments formidable competitors of common stocks. Turning points in the trend of interest rates are useful signals of market bottoms: stocks usually hit low points either shortly before or not long after interest downtrends get under way. But interest rates tell less about market tops. Since World War II, upturns in rates have begun anywhere from seven to 44 months before stock prices hit major peaks.

The trouble with interest rates as a market-timing tool is that their course is extremely hard to predict. When the celebrated economist Milton Friedman was asked where interest rates would be three months hence, he answered, "I haven't got the faintest idea." However, one interest-rate indicator has predicted the market perfectly for half a century. It is based on the Federal Reserve Board discount rate, the lending rate charged by Federal Reserve District banks to their member commercial banks. Except on the eve of the Great Depression, whenever the Fed has lowered its discount rate twice in a row — without raising it in between —Standard & Poor's 500-stock index was higher 12 months after the second cut; the gains at these points have averaged nearly 32 percent.

With rare exceptions over the past century, high inflation has been bad for stock prices, and diminishing inflation has been bullish. One reason is that rising inflation pushes up interest rates, causing the Fed to pursue tight-money policies that eventually slow business activity.

The Psychological Approach

Success in investing often comes from acting contrary to the herd. When panic prevails in the stock market and the outlook couldn't be darker, prices are close to a bottom and it is time to buy. But when euphoria reigns, the market is approaching a peak and the time has come to sell. The theory's leading modern exponent was Humphrey B. Neill, a successful stock-market trader who died in 1977. Neill's basic premise is that investors swayed by crowd psychology become totally irrational, succumbing to extremes of greed, fear, and gullibility. His conclusion: "When everyone thinks alike, everyone is likely to be wrong."

Contrary opinion theory has a twofold rationale. It holds, first, that because the future is largely unpredictable, an overwhelming consensus on where stock prices are heading usually ignores many uncertainties and thus is probably wrong. Typically, consensus forecasts extrapolate current trends into the future and fail to take into account forces at work that could bring change. For example, the general conviction in 1980 that oil prices assuredly would continue to rise ignored the possibility that conservation measures, energy substitutes, and new sources of supply would create a worldwide oil surplus.

Exponents of the contrary opinion approach also believe that a market trend expected by almost everyone is not likely to occur because investors act in anticipation of it, thereby changing the course of the market. By the time an overwhelming bullish consensus has taken shape, most investors have already done their buying, and there is not enough purchasing power left to sustain a further advance. Similarly, by the time pessimism has become ubiquitous, scared investors have dumped their stocks, and the selling pressure that has driven prices down is abating.

The psychological approach can be a big help to long-term investors in judging whether the market is far from a major turning point. Since a contrarian is not a trend follower, he will usually do his buying and selling a bit too early. But as Humphrey Neill sagely remarked, "If you're not early, you'll probably be late."

The Technical Approach

Technical analysts base their forecasts on patterns they detect in the past behavior of stocks and the volume of trading. While much about technical analysis smacks of abracadabra, its underlying premise is one that common sense can readily accept: the behavior of investors tends to repeat itself, so past trends in buying and selling can provide valuable clues to future price movements. Technical analysts don't deny that economic factors such as earnings, interest rates, and prospects for business influence the actions of investors. Where technicians depart from fundamentalists is in claiming that everything that influences investors — including fear, greed, and crowd psychology — is precisely reflected in patterns of stock prices and trading volume discernible on charts.

While the best policy for most amateur investors is to rely mainly on fundamentals in their choice of investments, some of the tools of technical analysis can be of considerable help to them in deciding when to buy and when to sell. Of the 50 or more indicators that technical analysts study, five key ones are used in the forecasting system in Figure 15.

The advance/decline line. Joseph E. Granville, a pioneer of technical analysis, has called this indicator "the single most important technical tool." It is a chart line that periodically signals changes in the market's direction that are masked by the day-to-day behavior of the popular averages. For example, the Dow Jones industrials often rise even when a majority of stocks are declining and fall when a majority are rising. That is because the Dow is strongly influenced by the behavior of a few high-priced stocks. But the A/D line, an average based on the ratio of stocks advancing to stocks declining, reveals whether the overall market is turning up or down. Thus, while the Dow was soaring to its 1973 peak of 1052, the A/D line was warning that the general market was in a menacing decline — one that later culminated in the appalling crash of 1973–1974. Any good broker can tell you whether the A/D line is diverging from the popular averages.

The mutual funds' cash/assets ratio. This reveals whether mutual funds as a group have plenty of buying power, which is bullish, or whether their cash reserves are low, which is bearish. The ratio is expressed as a percentage of the total assets of mutual funds — excluding money-market funds — that are currently in cash or so-called cash equivalents (Treasury

Figure 15. Adding Up the Buy and Sell Signals

One of the best market timing systems was presented in 1977 in a book, now out of print, called *Stock Market Strategy* by Richard A. Crowell, president of Boston Company Advisors, an investment consulting firm. The system doesn't try to forecast short-term fluctuations, which are highly unpredictable, or even intermediate-term swings, which can last several months and also are difficult to forecast with enough accuracy to produce consistent profits. But the system does help anticipate major turning points.

All you are required to do is answer two parallel sets of questions, primarily about various indicators of the market and the economy. The accompanying text explains them and tells you where to find the needed data. Keep your answers current with frequent updating, ideally once a month. If most of the answers in one of the questionnaires are "yes," the chances are that this is an excellent time to make your move.

The questionnaires give you a sell signal when the economy is still booming, the market is still rising (or close to a peak), and public sentiment is optimistic. And they give you a buy signal when the economy is in the doldrums, the market seems to be in deep trouble, and public sentiment is pessimistic. But most of the time neither checklist will give a clear-cut go-ahead signal, since turning points occur infrequently.

The Time-To-Buy Checklist
("Yes" answers are favorable.)

	Yes	*No*
The business cycle		
1. Is business activity in a down trend, and if so do you foresee the end of that down trend?		
2. Is inflation decelerating?		
3. If corporate profits have declined from their previous peak, do you expect them to start turning upward soon?		
Monetary policy and interest rates		
4. Are short-term interest rates starting to decline?		
5. Has the Federal Reserve Board given indications that it will ease restraints on growth of the money supply?		
Stock valuations		
6. Has the price/earnings ratio of the Value Line composite index fallen near or even below its level at the market's last cyclical low point?		
Sentiment indicators		
7. Are mutual funds heavily in cash?		

	Yes	*No*
8. Is the odd-lot short-sales ratio very high?	____	____
9. Is the specialists' short-sales ratio exceptionally low?	____	____
10. Are your friends and business associates pessimistic or apathetic about the market?	____	____
State of the market		
11. Has the market been declining for many months since its previous cyclical high?	____	____
12. Has the market registered a large percentage drop from its previous cyclical high?	____	____
13. Has the market recently accelerated its rate of decline, as it typically does in the final stages of a bear market?	____	____
14. Has the market rebounded from its last major low point, dropped back to that low once or twice, and then advanced?	____	____
The presidential election cycle		
15. Is the next presidential election not much more than two years from now?	____	____
TOTAL CHECKS	____	____

THE TIME-TO-SELL CHECKLIST
("YES" ANSWERS ARE WORRISOME OR BEARISH.)

	Yes	*No*
The business cycle		
1. Is evidence mounting that the business cycle has reached a peak?	____	____
2. Is inflation accelerating?	____	____
3. If corporate profits are rising, does the current rate of increase appear too strong to last?	____	____
Monetary policy and interest rates		
4. Are short-term interest rates rising and are they as high as they were at the corresponding stage of the previous upturn?	____	____
5. Has the Federal Reserve Board started to tighten monetary policy?	____	____
Stock valuations		
6. Has the P/E ratio risen near or above its level at the market's last cyclical peak?	____	____

	Yes	No
Sentiment indicators		
7. Are the cash reserves of mutual funds low?	____	____
8. Is the odd-lot short-sales ratio very low?	____	____
9. Is the specialists' short-sales ratio exceptionally high?	____	____
10. Are your friends and business associates talking about their winners and feeling euphoric about the market?	____	____
State of the market		
11. Has the market been advancing for many months since its previous cyclical low?	____	____
12. Has the market registered a large percentage gain from its previous cyclical low?	____	____
13. Is the advance/decline line underperforming the popular averages—an indication of deteriorating market strength?	____	____
14. Has the market dropped below its recent high and climbed back to it a couple of times or more, only to retreat again?	____	____
The presidential election cycle		
15. Is this the year following a presidential election?	____	____
TOTAL CHECKS	____	____

bills, commercial paper, and other short-term securities). This key figure is compiled from mutual-fund balance sheets on the last day of each month by a trade association, the Investment Company Institute. The information is made public three weeks later; it appears in the *Wall Street Journal* or you can get it by phone from the institute (202-293-7700).

From the mid-1970s to 1987, the cash/assets ratio fluctuated between 7 and 14 percent. Typically, it stood near 9.5 percent, of which about 4 percent is the cash reserve required to meet expenses and redemptions of fund shares. When interest rates are steep, fund managers sensibly tend to maintain high cash/assets ratios because they can get big returns on money-market securities.

The odd-lot short-sales ratio. A measure of bearishness among the smallest speculators, who deal in lots of fewer than 100 shares, this ratio is a contrary opinion indicator. It tells you to do the opposite of what odd-lot short-sellers are doing: buy when they are exceptionally bearish and sell when they are highly bullish.

In short selling — a sale of borrowed stock — the seller thinks the price will decline, giving him the opportunity to buy back the stock and return it to its owner for less than was realized on its sale. The odd-lot short-sales ratio is closely watched, because amateur speculators who sell short invariably have been wrong at major turning points in the market. Their selling has been heaviest when bear markets were about to end and lightest when prices were about to peak.

To compute the odd-lot short-sales ratio you divide the volume of odd-lot short sales by the average activity of all odd-lotters — the total purchases and sales, including short sales, divided by 2. These figures are published weekly in *Barron's,* but you probably can get the actual ratio from your broker. Over a period from the 1970s to the mid-1980s, the ratio averaged 0.6 percent. Whenever it rises above 1.25 percent — indicating that odd-lot short selling is exceptionally large — there is a strong chance that stocks will advance. When it has dropped to 0.5 percent, it has signaled a market decline.

The specialists' short-sales ratio. This tells you whether floor specialists — the people responsible for maintaining orderly markets on the floor of the stock exchanges — are bullish or bearish. The ratio is the number of shares sold short by specialists divided by the total volume of short sales; it is calculated weekly. The figures are published on Mondays in the *Wall Street Journal* and on *Barron's* "Market Laboratory" page.

Specialists constantly do short selling to help bridge the gaps that occur when buyers outnumber sellers. Because they make their living in part from profits on short selling, it is almost axiomatic that specialists are, as a group, the most knowledgeable of short sellers. During periods of intensive corporate takeover activity by arbitrageurs, the specialists' short-sales ratio loses its usefulness as a market timing tool. Normally, however, when specialists' shorting is unusually heavy in relation to total short sales — an indication that they are bearish — the strong probability is that prices will decline. The smaller the specialists' share of total short selling, the likelier it is that prices will rise. When the ratio gets close to 50 percent, it is giving a bearish signal; when it falls below 40 percent, it is sending off a bullish one.

The Political Approach

The connection between presidential elections and recurring tendencies of the stock market is rooted in the interaction of politics and economics. For any President — and for investors — a quadrennial cycle of economic policy making begins with the approach of midterm congressional elections. To hold or win a majority's support, the incumbent Administration, regardless of party, veers then toward economic policies that will please or placate the voters. For example, it supports generous increases in federal spending and measures to fatten real disposable income — even though these policies may run counter to the best judgment of White House economists. Such concessions to expediency, which tend to be inflationary, are usually greatest in presidential election years. But some time after the presidential election, the economy usually has to pay the price for policies designed to win votes. Often that price is tighter monetary and fiscal policies that bring on recession.

Such tactics tend to create a correlation between presidential terms and business cycles. The average duration of business cycles has been about 48 months — the same as the election cycle. Since 1948, the economy has peaked seven months, on average, after the presidential Election Day and has sunk to its low 11 months later. At that point, the Administration has had an average of 30 months before the next election to put through expansionary policies that increase the public's sense of well-being.

The stock market usually anticipates changes of trend in the economy by about six months, and its recovery phases have tended to start about 30 months before the next presidential election. With similar perceptiveness, the market has tended to top out early in the first year of a President's term; it is anticipating the contraction that is apt to start some months later. Bear markets began under Hoover in 1929, Roosevelt in 1937, Eisenhower in 1957, Nixon in 1973, Carter in 1977, and Reagan in 1981.

Obviously, the behavior of the economy and the stock market in any particular four-year political cycle can vary widely from the post–World War II average. Nonetheless, the historical record shows clearly which political periods are best for buying stocks, for selling them, and for staying out of the market.

A timing strategy geared to the presidential election was formulated in 1973 by David W. MacNeill, an investment specialist for banks. The strategy could not be simpler: you put your money into a growth-oriented mutual fund or a well-diversified portfolio of common stocks on November 30 of the second year after a presidential election, and you keep it there for exactly two years. Then you sell and park the proceeds in money-market funds or Treasury bills. After the subsequent presidential election, you go back into the market. MacNeill's strategy between November 1962 and November 1984 would have boosted a $10,000 investment in the Standard & Poor's 500-stock index to $196,000, better than triple the gain you would have made by staying in the S&P stocks.

Professional Timing Services

The demand for advice on when to get in and out of the stock market has brought forth a thriving business in market-timing advisory services. By 1986, there were 50 or more of them managing people's money in mutual funds and in many cases publishing newsletters for investors who wished to make their own moves. A few services were organizing mutual funds of their own with authority to use stock funds, bond funds, and money-market funds in whatever proportions seem best suited to market conditions.

If you want a professional to manage your money, here is a way to hire one who won't sniff at small sums. Some of these services accept as little as $2,000 in a regular account or $500 to seed an Individual Retirement Account. Most mutual-fund timing services devote equal time to picking the most promising stock and bond funds and to forecasting market turns. Depending on the service and your own preference, you can select mutual funds from a list of those used by the management or let it decide which funds to put your money in. Either way, you buy and own the fund shares but turn over to the timing service the power to move your money between stock, bond, and money funds. For this type of management, you pay a yearly fee equal to 1.5 to 2 percent of your investment. Usually there is also a one-time setup fee and a small fixed charge per annum — perhaps $35 or so.

Timing firms use the technical approach, sometimes augmented by such fundamentals as interest rates and the state of the economy. In the end they may switch your money less than once a year or several times in the same month.

Switching between mutual funds got its impetus in the 1970s with the introduction of money-market funds. After that, quite a few mutual-fund companies began letting investors transfer capital back and forth between stock, bond, and money funds. You can switch by telephone or by writing a letter. The charge, if any, is generally $5 or less.

Are timers worth their fees? "About 75 percent of the market-timing services we look at add no value in a bull market," says Phillip R. Verrill, president of Pallas Financial Services, a Nashville firm that evaluates timers for brokerage firms and financial planners. But he adds, "The value of timers comes during market corrections. On those occasions, the statistics are almost the reverse — in favor of timers. They are a defensive mechanism and should be viewed as insurance against major market declines."

Market Timing Newsletters

It is possible, of course, to switch your mutual-fund investment back and forth without employing a timer. Ambitious do-it-yourselfers can turn to newsletters for guidance. They include *Fundline* (P.O. Box 663, Woodland Hills, California 91365; semimonthly, $97 a year); *Fund Exchange* (1200 Westlake Avenue N., Suite 507, Seattle, Washington 98109-3530; monthly, $99 a year); *Growth Fund Guide* (P.O. Box 6600, Rapid City, South Dakota 57709; monthly, $85 a year); *Mutual Fund Specialist* (P.O. Box 1025, Eau Claire, Wisconsin 54702; monthly, $79 a year); *No-Load Fund Investor* (P.O. Box 283, Hastings-on-Hudson, New York 10706; monthly, $79 a year); *Switch Fund Advisory* (8943 Shady Grove Court, Gaithersburg, Maryland 20877; monthly, $135 a year); and *Telephone Switch Newsletter* (P.O. Box 2538, Huntington Beach, California 92647; $117 a year).

To keep in touch with their readers between issues, some letters send out midmonth updates or provide telephone hotlines. They also give you comprehensive information about the universe of mutual funds. The *Mutual Fund Specialist,* for example, publishes performance data on more than 500 stock funds and ranks those that allow exchanges by phone. The *Telephone Switch Newsletter* provides four types of timing programs — for funds that are invested in domestic stocks, foreign stocks, or gold-mining stocks, and for sector funds, which invest in a single industry.

35

STRATEGIES: TAKEOVER TARGETS

Like those mousy girls in old movies who finally fling off their glasses, let down their hair, and undo the top button of their schoolmarm blouse, many humdrum corporations conceal voluptuous charms. For years, investors pass these wallflowers by. Then suddenly a financial Lothario peeks under the balance sheets and — wow! It's takeover time. The stock rises 20 percent, 30 percent. Perhaps even 50 percent.

What the suitor has discovered is heady earnings potential, highly valuable assets, and lots of cash, all muffled in a depressed stock price. Acquisition artists with designs on the profits or the assets can dangle the coveted cash before their bankers as potential collateral for loans needed to buy up the stock.

Sensing that its endowments are being ogled, the company's managers may try to defend its virtues and fend off unwelcome suitors. Some antitakeover tactics are good for the stock. If the management uses its cash to buy back shares, the price probably will go up. If the decision is made to take the company private with borrowed money — a leveraged buyout — the price also will rise. But if management's reaction is to make the company financially less attractive, the stock may fall.

For private investors the game is to find potential takeover targets before major acquisitors start lusting after them. Having discovered truly alluring companies, your next problem is to use the best tactics once the bidding starts.

Balance Sheet Analysis

Since balance sheets are public property, anyone can identify companies that might catch a financier's fancy. But it takes much more than casual scanning to single out the ripest prospects. The process of elimination might best begin with a look at book value — a company's net assets after subtracting depreciation, corporate debts, and preferred stock. To be an irresistible merger candidate, the firm should be buyable for less than its net worth in terms of book value per share.

A test of corporate debt further narrows the field. Cast out companies whose shareholders' equity — the value of the stock and retained earnings — is less than its debts. In analysts' parlance, demand a debt/equity ratio no higher than 1. Takeover specialists smack their lips over plentiful untapped borrowing power to finance a leveraged buyout. In search of the revenues to repay such loans, they get out their calculators and add up the latest year's cash flow — sales revenues and other income.

Stock price and earnings should pass a couple of other tests. The shares of a nubile firm should be selling at less than eight times the cash flow per share. It is fine, too, if outside analysts agree that earnings will rise smartly. Look for predictions of at least a 20 percent profit gain in the current year. Moreover, the price you pay for that potential growth should be attractively low — less than 10 times predicted earnings.

Ask your broker to help in your search. His research department probably riffles regularly through databases for just such companies. Better yet, if you have a personal computer and really are getting up to speed on it, learn to do your own stock screening by subscribing to one of the monthly disk services described in Chapter 32. But don't invest in a takeover prospect on the strength of your research alone. Get the latest analysts' reports and tell your broker to scan the news for signs of any basic weaknesses that would repel takeover investors.

Reacting to Takeover Offers

Picking likely takeover stocks is only half the battle. The other half is knowing which moves to make if, sure enough, you get merger action. How you handle a bid for your now coveted stock can mean the difference between a tidy profit and a galling loss. All such bids, whether welcomed or decried by the targeted firm, give stockholders a shot at a windfall. But the flashes, bongs, and ratcheting of scores in this corporate pinball game can end just as easily in a "tilt," leaving investors with no profit or with shares that are worth less than before.

Despite the 1986 insider-trading scandal involving Ivan Boesky, the arbitrageur, and growing suspicions about the safety of the bonds (called "junk bonds") used to finance takeovers, the pace of acquisition activity is likely to continue to be as hectic as it was in the mid-1980s. If so, you will have to be ready to act fast. Your response should depend mostly on whether the managers of your company view the bid as friendly or hostile. The terms of the offer, such as whether or not it applies to all outstanding stock, should also influence your decision. Toughest of all, you must try to judge the bidder's chance of success.

The acquisition game takes several forms, and your strategy will be different for each one. In 1984, for example, Saul Steinberg, a daring and ruthless tactician, was said to be resorting to greenmail in buying up huge blocks of Walt Disney stock. Greenmail, a word play on blackmail and an example of the colorful language of mergers and acquisitions (see Figure 16), refers to the hold that an attacker puts on his corporate victim by buying enough shares in the open market to show his financial muscle. To save itself, the target company buys back its freedom. Only the greenmailer wins this game. The other stockholders get no premium for their shares, which typically deflate in a hurry.

Other variants of corporate conquest spread profits more evenly among shareholders. Sincere tender offers — direct solicitations for your shares — usually tempt you with a steep premium over a stock's market value. Sometimes a company's management makes a tender offer for its own shares, in which case the deal is known as a buyback. Veterans of takeover pinball have developed winning strategies for each type of game.

Friendly Offers

The terms of an unopposed takeover — the commonest type — rarely change much from those outlined in the initial announcement and therefore give least cause for anxiety or for mapping a defensive strategy. In friendly mergers, the management of the company for which the bid is being made approves the offer and agrees on an acquisition price. Payment may be in cash, securities, or a combination of the two.

The Beatrice Companies acquired Esmark on amicable terms in 1984, though not before a lively auction. Kohlberg Kravis Roberts, a private investment partnership, looked like the winner with a $55 bid until Beatrice suddenly jumped in with an offer of $56. Beatrice's second bid, $60, clinched the deal. Before the action began, Esmark had been trading around $45.

Another form of takeover, the leveraged buyout, has become increas-

Figure 16. Mergerspeak

The record number of corporate takeover battles in recent years has added to the dictionary of financial jargon. To learn whether you are fluent in acquisition argot, answer the following questions.

Q. Should a company welcome the attentions of a *white knight?*
A. Yes, if it is confronted with an otherwise unpreventable takeover. A white knight is a company that will block such a merger, usually at the invitation of the targeted firm, by taking over the corporation itself on terms more favorable to current management.

Q. Suppose it's a *gray knight?*
A. Wait until it shows its true colors. A gray knight gallops uninvited to the scene of a hostile merger, offering to buy the besieged firm. It may be hailed as a hero or challenged, depending on its terms.

Q. Who eats *porcupine provisions?*
A. An unfriendly buyer. Porcupine provisions—also known as *shark repellent*—are corporate bylaws designed to put obstacles in the way of taking over and running the company. Examples: USX has staggered its directors' terms in such a way that an acquiring company can't quickly pack the board.

Q. What does a *poison pill* do?
A. It can boost the cost of acquiring a company. A poison pill is a new issue of preferred stock that gives holders the right to redeem it at a premium price after a takeover.

Q. Can a *scorched-earth policy* help?
A. Perhaps, if the takeover target can survive the self-destructive ploys that such a strategy calls for. With a scorched-earth policy, a company takes extreme steps to become unattractive to the buyer. For instance, it might schedule all debt to come due immediately after a merger.

Q. How can a company use its *crown jewel?*
A. A takeover target can sell the crown jewel—often its most profitable subsidiary—as a scorched-earth tactic. In a battle between retail titans, Carter Hawley Hale, the retailing firm, fended off The Limited by giving another firm the option to buy Carter Hawley Hale's Waldenbooks division.

Q. Should directors of a takeover target ever play *Pac-Man* on the job?
A. Yes. In the Pac-Man maneuver, the company bites back by trying to swallow its attacker. That is how Houston Natural Gas defeated a buyout attempt by Coastal Corporation.

Q. Would management at a takeover-target company like to receive a *bear hug?*
A. Probably not. A bear hug is an offer so generous that directors can't refuse it without facing shareholder ire.

Q. Is a *teddy bear hug* any better?
A. Yes. A teddy bear hug is an overture that can be fended off.

Q. Do white knights wear *greenmail?*

A. Not unless it is St. Patrick's Day. Greenmail is a strategy in which a single shareholder or group acquires a large interest and threatens to take over the company unless the directors buy out the greenmailer at a premium.

ingly popular. Such acquisitions are most often set in motion by a company's own management as a way of taking the firm off the stock market. The managers or their allies borrow heavily to pay for the shares, then retire the loan with a hoard of cash from the till of the company or with money obtained by selling off some of its assets. Heavy borrowing makes leveraged buyouts fragile, raising your risk as an investor if you wait for the deal to go through.

Whether the merger is friendly, hostile, or internally generated, you must make a choice: either sell your shares at less than the full takeover price or wait for the eventual settlement, which generally takes three to six months. The spread between the market and takeover prices narrows as the deal nears completion, but always reflects the betting on whether the merger will go through. The announcement of an agreement between the parties provides a clue to the outcome. So-called definitive agreements, which put the deal in the form of a contract, have at least an 85 percent chance of success. Agreements in principle, which are less formal, go through about 75 percent of the time. Because even a definitive agreement can collapse, the stock at first will typically sell at a 20 to 25 percent discount from the proposed acquisition price. An agreement in principle creates a discount of 25 percent or more.

The discount is heavily influenced by arbitrageurs — professional traders who speculate on takeover issues. Arbitrageurs, unless they are illegally in on the deal, as Boesky often was, buy shares after a bid has been announced, hoping that a successful merger or a bidding war will push the price higher. The best way to play a friendly merger as a small shareholder, says Janet Clarke, an arbitrage analyst at Greenspan Advisory in New York City, is to sell as much as half of your stock upon announcement of the takeover. This protects your gain on the off chance that an antitrust ruling or some other snag spoils the agreement. Hold your remaining shares, says Clarke, until the market price gets to within 10 or 15 percent of the acquisition bid. After that, it may not be worth holding out for the extra dollars you would get a few months later from a completed deal.

When the merger involves an exchange of stock, you may do best by selling all your shares right away, rather than take the risk that the value of the offered securities will fall. A swap may be preferable, though, for investors who want to avoid a capital gain for tax reasons. You pay no tax on an exchange of shares in a merger.

Hostile Bids

The takeover game heats up when an offer to buy is unwelcome. ''With a hostile bid, the risks and rewards are both greater,'' says George A. Kellner, a managing partner at Kellner DiLeo & Company, an arbitrage firm in New York City. Animosity may drive up the bid. It may also blow the deal apart, as in the rejection by Carter Hawley Hale of The Limited's 1984 bid. Carter Hawley's stock peaked at $32, up 34 percent. When the offer of $35 was spurned, the stock sank to $20 — lower than before the fracas.

Hostile bids are usually as easy to detect as your neighbor's blaring stereo. Full-page ads mined with innuendos about the bidder's motives may appear in major newspapers. But you can not always be sure whether the message signifies outright rejection or a coy invitation for higher bids. Therefore, arbitrageurs advise selling one-third to one-half of your shares. In many cases, rejection of a hostile bid leads to an offer from a more acceptable suitor or a sweeter price from the original swain.

Trying to guess how far a stock's price might rise during a hostile takeover try is a game for skillful speculators. A safer way to determine when you should sell is to compare how much you may make with the amount you stand to forfeit. Say you bought a stock at $30 and it went to $42 on a takeover bid. There is talk of a further rise to $48. You already have a paper profit of 40 percent and a possible additional gain of 15 percent — but a potential loss of $12 a share if the stock falls back to $30. Holding out for the extra $6 probably is not worth the risk. When a stock in an unfriendly takeover try has risen 20 to 30 percent beyond its normal trading range, sell at least half of your position.

The price action of a target company's stock can provide clues about how arbitrageurs expect the situation to turn out. The stock sells at a discount that often amounts to 3 percent of the offering price for every month that traders expect to wait before the deal is completed. Four months before the anticipated close, for example, stocks that have an acquisition price of $50 per share will typically sell for around $44. When the price is almost equal to the merger bid and there has been no shortening of the waiting period, the market is telegraphing a message. ''It is telling you that the smart money expects a better bid soon,'' says Sharon Kalin, publisher of Risk Arbitrage Monitor, a news service for stockbrokers. ''You can go along for the ride or not.'' A decline in a stock's price and trading volume, by contrast, often reflects a conviction by the smart money that the deal will fall through.

Tender Offers

As the fastest way to take over a company, the tender offer has long been a favorite technique of hostile bidders. If successful, it takes about a month to complete, compared with three to six months for merger agreements. Shareholders often find tender offers hard to resist because they are under time pressure to respond. Nevertheless, tendering your shares is not always the right move. Sometimes you will do better by selling them on the market or just waiting.

Target companies must reply to a tender offer within 10 days, telling shareholders whether the offer is friendly or hostile. Wait at least that long before tendering or selling. Douglas Austin, president of Douglas Austin & Associates, a merger and acquisition specialist in Toledo, Ohio, advises, "Never tender unless you are confident that the deal will go through." If you tender and the takeover bid fails, your stock will often be lower than it was before the offer.

In evaluating a tender, first read the offer-to-purchase statement that the bidder must send to all shareholders. The document, which resembles a prospectus, will reveal these important facts:

Whether the bid price applies to "any and all" shares tendered or only to some of them. Any-and-all offers are more lucrative than partial offers.

When the offer expires. Note, too, if you tender your shares, how many weeks the company will give you to change your mind and retrieve them.

How the deal will be financed. In a section titled "Source and Amount of Funds" you may find, for example, that the bidder has set aside more money than is necessary to pay for the shares at the announced price. When American Stores bid successfully for Jewel Companies in 1984, American had $100 million more than it needed to buy all outstanding shares at the initial bid price. This was a tip-off that American was prepared to raise its bid. Indeed, Jewel agreed to the merger after the offer went from $70 to $75 a share.

What if you don't tender and the deal goes through? You will still get the offering price, but the acquisitor may decide to give its own securities in exchange for yours. Eric Rosenfeld, chief arbitrageur at Oppenheimer & Company, offers this counsel: "Unless you want to avoid capital-gains taxes, tender your shares when it looks as if the deal will work out." Alternatively, says Rosenfeld, sell up to half your stock and tender the rest.

The decision whether to sell or tender is often a toss-up, but in some situations it is usually wiser to sell. One is when the bidder seeks only a percentage of the outstanding stock; that leaves you in ignorance of how many of your shares will be accepted. Selling will bring a surer, though possibly smaller, profit. Another occasion to consider selling is when you get a two-tier offer, which pays cash for part of the shares and securities for the rest.

Whether you tender all or some of your shares, wait as long as possible before relinquishing them. Seemingly, you would have nothing to lose by responding right away because you are assured of getting the highest price if the bidder raises its price. The hitch is that a rival company may win the takeover battle. If so, you will get the second-class treatment reserved for holdouts. You will probably wait one or two months for payment and may have to accept securities instead of cash.

To play for time in a tender offer without any risk of missing the deadline, Donald C. Carter, president of the Carter Organization, a proxy solicitation and takeover consulting firm in New York City, advises having your broker tender your shares. Individuals must mail in their responses at least a week before the expiration date to ensure that the bidder receives them in time. But brokers can wait until the last day.

Buybacks

One type of tender almost never fails. This is the buyback, in which a company offers to purchase its own stock from shareholders. In a maneuver typical of buybacks, Teledyne announced in June 1984 that it would retrieve 25 percent of its outstanding shares. By reducing the public's holdings, Teledyne accomplished two aims: it used up cash that might have attracted a hostile bid, and it increased per-share earnings. On news of the offer, Teledyne rose 20 percent. Your decision in such a case should rest on your confidence in the company's long-term prospects. ''If you liked a company before a buyback, you will like it afterward,'' says Sharon Kalin of Risk Arbitrage Monitor. ''Don't be in a hurry to get rid of your shares.''

36

STRATEGIES: THE BEST DEFENSES

Professional investors safeguard huge positions in securities by using insurance strategies to counter their own follies. If the market or a particular stock backfires, they make sure that part of the loss will be offset by another investment that would profit from the reversal. Guarding against investment mistakes is called hedging. For many cautious people, hedging is a way of life. For those with a bolder temperament, judicious but limited countermeasures suffice. For still others, hedging means having a strategy for selling every stock they own. The first line of defense in personal investing, however, is to buy conservative stocks.

Trusting in Dividends

Even the most courageous investors are unnerved by share prices that go up a dollar one day and down two the next. But your stockholdings need not give you frequent anxiety attacks if at least some of the shares provide you with a calming stream of income. Those quarterly dividend checks can mitigate the effects of a gyrating stock market. Not only does the income help cushion losses, but it can also generate growth should you choose to reinvest your dividends. Moreover, share prices tend to rise when dividends do. Thus companies that offer generous income have long been the trenches to which experienced investors repair during periods of stock market uncertainty.

You have to pick your defensive position carefully, however. Electric utilities — once the most stable of all high-yield issues — have in recent times felt the shock of dividend cuts or skipped payments. Initially, you may be attracted to the loftiest yields listed in newspaper stock tables. But you can't afford to base your share buying on dividends alone. For example, the 15 stocks in the Dow Jones utility average were yielding around 8.5 percent in early 1986, but shareholders of Central Maine Power were receiving 9.7 percent. Central Maine had a stake in a costly and incomplete nuclear generating plant at Seabrook, New Hampshire. The difference in yield instantly highlights the risks that its hardy stockholders were taking.

Serious problems lurk beneath the surface of many high-paying concerns. When the investing public becomes aware of a crisis in a company, the stock price usually drops, increasing the effective yield from the current dividend. Yield buyers, being naturally more averse to risk than investors in growth stocks, should guard against becoming yield hogs. Richard Evans, editor of the *Dow Theory Forecasts* newsletter in Hammond, Indiana, says, "If you see a stock that yields substantially more than others in its industry group, be very wary."

That said, many lower-yielding utility companies continue to reward investors with uninterrupted dividend payments and stock price stability. And if you are willing to sacrifice a little income on your shares, you can sometimes make it up in capital appreciation. Certain blue-chip companies offer moderate amounts of income and appreciation potential. Examples are international and domestic oil companies, consumer goods manufacturers, and food producers.

When you invest for income, you want to be as sure as possible that the company will continue to make those quarterly payments. Beverly S. Jacobs, senior vice president of AFA Financial, an investment firm in Cleveland, watches corporate management for clues to an imminent cut in the payout. "If a firm changes from a quiet, unaggressive approach to one that goes heavily into new-product development," she says, "then you may be witnessing action that will ultimately result in a reduced dividend." Although the new policy could benefit the company's stock later on, the initial reaction to it is usually negative.

Such was the case when ITT executives began funneling so much money into research and development that the company could barely cover its $2.76 per share annual payout. ITT wanted to make the transition from a conglomerate tortoise into a high-growth hare, and one of the first casualties was the dividend. After directors cut it to $1 on July 11, 1984, the stock plunged more than 30 percent in one day.

How can you protect yourself from such a cut? There are signs to look for. Are known executives retiring and being replaced by unknowns? Is the usually staid chief executive of your favorite cosmetics concern talking animatedly about entering the computer software field? Getting into exciting new businesses can cause a hemorrhage in the cash that would otherwise pay the dividend.

As prudent as anticipating dividend cuts before they bleed you is being able to identify companies that are most likely to increase their payouts soon. That way you benefit from higher income and the rising stock price that usually accompanies it. Robert Cardwell, editor of *Indicator Digest,* a semimonthly investment letter out of Palisades Park, New Jersey, offers this simple method of spotting prospects for dividend increases: "Look for a firm with a long history of raising its dividends but one that has not yet done so in the current fiscal year." Unless profits have taken a tumble, you can figure on another increase coming.

At AFA Financial, Beverly Jacobs follows almost as simple a strategy. She seeks out companies that have maintained or increased quarterly dividends for 10 years and have a satisfactory current yield. In 1986 "satisfactory" meant at least 6 percent, one-fifth higher than the yield on the Dow Jones industrials.

To minimize steep declines in price, Jacobs avoids issues whose prices jump around more than usual. This is called high volatility. She limits her portfolio to stocks with a beta, or volatility rating, between 0.9 and 1.1. Betas are listed in the *Value Line Investment Survey*. As a measure of financial strength, she looks for a debt-to-equity ratio of 50 percent at most. If debt rises to outweigh equity, or if the dividend is cut or the yield falls to 4 percent, she sells the stock. But in the absence of any serious deterioration in the financial fundamentals, a drop in the price of a high-yield stock usually is a signal to buy more shares. "If I like a stock at 8 percent, I'll love it at 10 percent," she says.

A conservative yield strategy can be rewarding. Jacobs's total return over the five years 1981 through 1985 averaged 22.9 percent.

Automatic Dividend Reinvestment

Many companies that appeal to the income investor work hard to retain his fealty by offering dividend reinvestment plans. You can authorize the corporation to reinvest your payout automatically each quarter in more of its stock. A few companies charge a small fee — usually under $3 — for the shares or fractions of shares you buy this way. (By crediting you with full and fractional shares, the company reinvests every penny of your dividends.) And sometimes you get a special incentive to reinvest: a 5 percent discount from the market price of the shares. If you reinvest $100 of dividends, for example, you are credited with $105 worth of stock. Most plans let you start reinvesting the dividends from even a single share, providing an ideal opportunity to interest children in the stock market.

One of the virtues of dividend reinvestment plans is that your dividends buy more shares when the stock price is dragging around in the cellar than when it is high. Another advantage is that you can send in extra money every month or quarter — usually up to a maximum of $12,000 a year — and get additional shares through the company free of brokerage commissions. When you add in the discount on reinvested dividends — as you could in 1986 at 50 or so companies — this seemingly modest practice can build up your holdings significantly over the years. "These plans have become popular because they really give the investor something for nothing," comments Robert D. Ferris, an executive vice president of Investor Access Corporation, an investor-relations consulting firm in New York City.

More than 900 companies offer dividend reinvestment plans to common-stock shareholders, according to Duane E. Frederic, who keeps track of dividend reinvestment plans. Frederic publishes monthly lists of these companies and indicates which ones reinvest at a discount ($10 per issue, 8908 E. Pilgrim Drive, Chagrin Falls, Ohio 44022). He says that exploitation of discounts by arbitrageurs and other large traders has caused many companies to stop giving shareholders this edge.

To enroll in a dividend reinvestment program, you must register the stock in your own name. Shares your stockbroker holds in his firm's "street" name are not usually eligible. Once you are on record as a shareholder, you simply sign a form authorizing the company to open an account for you and put all your dividends in additional shares. When you decide to sell, the transaction is typically made commission-free or at a small fee.

Some companies allow you to split your dividends between cash and stock. You just tell the transfer agent, usually the bank that services the stockholders, what portion of the dividend you want to receive by check and how much you want to reinvest in stock. You send your money to the dividend reinvestment plan administrator in advance of the dividend payment date, so that the shares can be bought at the same time dividends are reinvested. If you have firm faith in a company's future, here is your chance to become a bargain-basement believer.

Cost-Averaging Techniques

Enrolling in a dividend reinvestment plan is a modest way of using a strategy called dollar-cost averaging. By investing relatively stable amounts at regular intervals, you get more shares when the price is low and fewer when the price is high. As a result, the average price you pay over the years probably will work out to be lower than if you tried to time your stock purchases.

In much more general applications, dollar-cost averaging serves as a classic defense mechanism. It won't make you the Wizard of Wall Street, but it will usually protect you from disaster. Investing a fixed sum each month in a no-load mutual fund with a strong performance record gives you an excellent chance of doing better than the popular averages without taking inordinate risks. Dollar-cost averaging also can be used to buy shares of individual stocks, but that is much riskier than using a no-load fund and also costly in brokerage commissions. Mutual funds, with their diversified portfolios, bounce back from disasters when the market recovers, whereas an individual stock can fall through the floor and languish for years in the cellar. Moreover, no-load funds, by definition, charge no commissions (for details about the mechanics of mutual funds, see Chapter 9).

Think of dollar-cost averaging as investing on the installment plan. Some versions of this approach are mercifully easy, while others are so daring and complex that they are suitable only for investors with strong nerves and home computers. The simplest version, in which you put the same amount every month into the same investment, may seem about as exciting as watching grass grow. Nevertheless, there is a lot to be said for it. The discipline of dollar-cost averaging helps you avoid two common errors: overenthusiastic investing when prices are high and panic selling when prices are deeply depressed.

It is true that if the market advances for several years with only minor setbacks, a lump-sum investment made at the very beginning of that rise will produce much larger profits than dollar-cost averaging. As a defensive policy, however, buying on the installment plan is well suited to periods of wild up-and-down swings, such as those of the past 25 years.

If you find the standard method of dollar-cost averaging too tame, you might prefer a variation: increase the sums you invest when the market drops and reduce them when the market climbs. The rationale is that you will profit significantly by having stepped up your buying when prices are down, because the shares will ultimately rise again and you will own a lot of low-priced stock. Also, in a roller-coaster market, it pays to buy less when stocks are advancing; before too long they will come down again.

The formula for this variation is rather complex but worth knowing: divide your average cost per share by the current price and multiply that result by the amount you invest monthly. Let's say, for example, you have been investing $100 a month, that your average cost per share is now $9, and the current market price is $8. Divide 9 by 8, which gives you 1.125; then multiply that by $100. Your next investment will be $112.50. If your average cost is $9 and the market price is $10, the arithmetic is 0.9 × $100, or $90. In periods when stock prices recurrently soar and plummet, this formula can produce superior profits.

Hedging Sizable Gains

In contrast to the buy-and-hold nature of dollar-cost averaging, investors who venture into the game of buying their own stocks and are fortunate enough to earn a large capital gain may have mixed feelings about taking a profit just then. Perhaps they are reluctant to give as much as one-third of their gain to the tax collector; perhaps they expect the stock to keep riding up. The dilemma is that the price of the stock may fall while they wait.

With a rather modest outlay, you can hedge against a major setback and protect profits now in hand. The hedging can be done with a simple options strategy. When used by themselves, options — contracts giving you the right to buy or sell shares at a fixed price for a limited time — are speculative investments. But when used in conjunction with stocks that you already own, they can greatly reduce risks. Options trade in units of 100 shares, so they cannot be used to hedge smaller holdings. For round lots of 100 shares, however, they can counteract the loss you would suffer if one of your stocks gave ground.

Selling Calls

One way to offset a possible paper loss is to sell a *call,* an option giving someone else the right to buy your shares. In return, you get money now — the price, or premium, for the option. But the protection you get is quite limited. Say you own 100 shares of a $40 stock and you sell a call against them for $500. You are fully protected only against a drop in price to $35 a share. To get the biggest hedge, you must sell at a low strike price — the price at which the owner of the call can buy your stock. Option brokers usually recommend selling calls with a strike price that is lower than the present market price of the stock. The call is said to be "in the money." But don't worry. The owner of your call cannot exercise his option profitably until the stock rises more than he paid you. The farther the strike price is below the stock's value, the more you can get for a call.

When you sell calls, you are forfeiting part or all of the potential gain on a rise in the price of your stock. That potential now belongs to the call buyer; he bought the option to speculate on just such a gain. In the case of your $40 stock with the $5 option, the danger begins if the stock rises above $45 a share. At that point, you can cancel the deal by *buying* a call on your stock. Such an option will now cost you more than the one you sold, but you can claim the difference as a capital loss.

Buying Puts

You can get a lot more protection for your profits from a *put* than from a call. A put gives you the right to sell the underlying security at a fixed price. The put itself becomes ever more valuable as the price of the security falls. Then you can sell the put at a profit, offsetting most of the paper loss on your stock. The advantage of using puts is that they cut your losses to a relatively small, predetermined amount — the price of the put itself. You probably will want to buy a put with a strike price close to the stock's current price. If the stock sinks much below that level, the price of your put will soar. You can either sell it then to offset most of your paper loss or sell the underlying stock at the predetermined higher price. If your stock doesn't fall, you write off the cost of the put as a tax loss.

Using Index Options

For protecting individual stocks, options have their limitations. They are available on only 400 or so issues, almost all of them on the New York or American stock exchange. If you own a diversified portfolio, you cannot easily hedge profits on each stock. But you can hedge on broad sections of the market by trading one of several index options. If you own shares in many major companies in different industries, choose Standard & Poor's 100 index, which trades on the Chicago Board Options Exchange (the CBOE). For a bundle of blue chips, use the American Stock Exchange's Major Market index.

To see how the process works, assume that you have a diversified portfolio that has appreciated magnificently in a few months and is now worth $60,000. You don't want to cash in your profits just yet; still, some pundits have been saying they expect the market to drop 10 percent. To guard against the possibility that they are right, you buy puts on the S&P 100.

Brian Abdoo, an index-options specialist at Paine Webber, suggests that you choose a put with a strike price close to the index price. That way, if you are correct in anticipating a drop, your put immediately starts to gain in value; but you won't have paid an arm and a leg for it. Abdoo recommends a put giving you the right to sell a mythical 100 shares of the S&P 100. When the index stood at 200 after the record-breaking market streak of 1985's fourth quarter, such a put cost $600 and would have hedged $20,000 worth of shares for the next three months.

If the market had declined 10 percent during those three months, your portfolio would have shown a $6,000 loss, but each put would have risen nearly $1,400 in value, Abdoo calculates. So he would have advised buying three contracts at the 200 strike price for a total cost of $1,800 ($600 × 3) to protect your $60,000 portfolio. On a 10 percent market drop, the puts probably would show a $4,200 profit — enough to offset all but $1,800 of your $6,000 loss. If, on the other hand, the index had held steady or risen, you would have been out the price of your puts, $1,800, but could have claimed that amount as a loss on your next tax return. In pursuing such a strategy, Abdoo warns: "It is very important to make sure that your portfolio is diversified and that it mirrors the action of the index."

Reasons to Sell

For many investors, selling stock is like shaking some bad habit — it is a painful step you know is good for you, but you keep putting it off. As Justin and Robert Mamis point out in their book *When to Sell* (Pocket Books, $6.95), buying a stock is an act of hope, but selling — especially at a loss — is an act of surrender. When you part with a winner, you end the dream of reaping heady profits, and dumping a loser means accepting a loss. As long as you continue to hold the stock, hope is alive, no matter how horrifying your losses. When you sell, hope dies.

Investment professionals agree that deciding when to sell a stock is harder — and more important — than deciding when to buy. If you don't own a stock and its price rises, you have lost nothing but an opportunity. If you fail to sell a stock and it falls, you lose real money. Here are four guidelines that will help you to set the alarm on your time-to-sell clock.

Cut your losses. Never hesitate to sell because you are behind — you could wind up further behind. Some investment managers would consider dumping New York Stock Exchange issues if they declined 15 percent and American Stock Exchange or over-the-counter issues, which are more volatile, if they fell 20 to 25 percent. By selling when a stock drops a predetermined amount, you may miss a rebound, but you limit your loss. If you ride a stock down 50 percent — and such plunges are common — you will need a 100 percent increase in its price just to break even.

Sell if you bought a stock expecting a favorable development that does not occur. It might be a proposed takeover by another company, a fat increase in earnings, or the unveiling of a new product with extraordinary profit potential. If the blessed event doesn't come to pass within a reasonable time, get out. If the expected does happen and the price of the stock doesn't go up, unload promptly.

Sell on a sharp rise in the price/earnings ratio. Set your P/E ceiling 50 percent above the present level — unless you or your broker has strong reasons for believing that the company's prospects have improved dramatically.

A stock's P/E is a basic yardstick of valuation. (The P/Es in newspaper stock tables are based on the most recent 12 months' earnings, but analysts substitute their estimates of earnings for the current year.) If two companies are expected to earn $1 a share this year and their stocks sell for $8 and $16 a share, the valuation of the $16 stock is twice that of the other. Common sense is all it takes to recognize that if either stock's valuation rapidly goes up 50 percent, the chances are that the stock is no longer cheap. It is highly likely, in fact, that the company has become overvalued. By selling your shares at that price and reinvesting in an issue that seems undervalued, you stand to increase your profit potential and reduce your risk as well. Stocks whose P/E has become overgrown are likely to sag the next time the company reports disappointing earnings or the market drops.

Sell on any significant deterioration in a company's fundamentals. This means keeping close watch on sales growth, profitability, financial health, competitive position, and the prospects for the industry your firm is in. A company can lose its investment allure, for instance, if its technological edge becomes eroded by competitors. Take Xerox, which pioneered photocopying. The company's profit growth was so rapid until the early 1970s that the stock soared from below $2 in 1960 to $172 in 1972. But as competition intensified, Xerox's growth rate slowed, and the stock's P/E — once over 70 — sank as low as 5.

Investors should also be alert to the serious problems that can arise from a heavy burden of debt. A company that can operate profitably with tremendous debt when times are good is liable to get in deep trouble when its industry sinks into an exceptionally severe slump.

The stock market is a cruel place, with no sympathy for losers. Aunt Minnie may have loved Polaroid when she left you her shares in 1972. But Polaroid didn't love you when it dropped from $149.50 to $18.50 in the next 10 years. In volatile markets, once a stock or industry group falls from favor, the way down can be steep and long. Quipped Richard Yashewski, a distinguished analyst at the Butcher & Singer brokerage firm until his death in 1986: "On Wall Street, when the affair is over, there is no such thing as 'Let's be friends.' "

37

ALL ABOUT BONDS

What most people want from a bond is steady income and minimum risk to their capital. That doesn't come as easily as it once did. Jagged rises and falls in interest rates since the mid-1970s have caused bond prices to plunge and leap. And fluctuating rates are just one of four types of risk in the bond market. The others are financial adversity for the bond issuer, which threatens your interest payments and perhaps your principal; a call for early redemption, which can cut short a high rate of return; and inflation, which can severely erode the value of your investment. Even so, if you are an income seeker, you can still find ways to get a touch of the old-time safety and also lock up high income yields. Moreover, the Tax Reform Act of 1986 has put you on equal footing with growth seekers for the first time since 1921, because capital gains are no longer eligible for a tax break.

A bond is a long-term IOU from the U.S. Treasury, a foreign government, a corporation, or a municipality, usually paying a fixed amount of interest every six months. Your capital is repaid when the bond comes due. Far-off maturity dates and fixed interest rates are what make bonds both attractive and risky. Say you buy a new 30-year corporate bond at its $1,000 face value and it has an 11.5 percent "coupon," paying $115 a year. If long-term interest rates subsequently slip to, say, 10 percent, your bond will go on paying its promised sum, and in the market that bond will be worth more than you paid for it. But if interest rates rise to 15 percent, your bond will be worth less than you paid for it and will yield less than new bond buyers are earning. To make your bond's yield competitive, buyers will bid only $767 for it — the amount that would make its $115 return equal a 15 percent yield. You could then either sell and take your loss or resign yourself to accepting an inferior yield.

There is no limit to how low a bond's value can fall — until it reaches zero. But the sky is far above the limit to which it may rise. To guard against having to pay much more than the current interest rate for years to come, the issuer customarily includes a call date in the bond agreement. This heads-I-win-tails-you-lose clause lets him redeem your bond in a few years at face value plus a modest premium — no more than a year's interest. If interest rates sink much below the coupon rate, the borrower will invoke his privilege and refinance his debt at a lower cost.

If you want to speculate — that is, bet that interest rates will fall, pushing prices up — you can choose a bond with a sharply limited call provision: a U.S. government issue, for example. But a better strategy is to buy a bond selling far below face value — a "deep discount" bond — and maturing many years from now. Even if this kind of bond is called, you will make a handsome gain.

If you believe in revival of that old-time bond-market religion — a faithful return without much risk — buy a highly rated bond that is selling below face value and has only a few years to maturity. Price fluctuations won't plague you because the assurance of a capital gain on a definite date fortifies the bond against market assaults.

Bonds are rated for safety by Standard & Poor's and Moody's. Ratings range from AAA, which is as safe as you can get, to D, for a bond that is in default. But the people who judge bonds are not infallible; International Harvester debt issues that Moody's initially rated A sank to a perilous Caa when the company went to the brink of bankruptcy in the early 1980s. (Harvester later dusted itself off, sold its farm equipment operations and changed its name to Navistar International. In 1985 Moody's raised the rating on Navistar debentures to B3.)

Taxable Bonds

Corporate bonds generally provide the highest current yields among fixed-income securities. That high income is fully taxable, but pension funds, life insurance companies, and other tax-sheltered financial institutions make good use of corporates, and so can you. Consider corporates for an Individual Retirement Account or Keogh plan and for income after you retire, if you find yourself with a low effective tax rate.

Corporate bonds divide broadly into two groups, utilities and industrials. The torrent of utility bonds that engulfed the market while electricity companies were building new capacity during the energy crisis of the

1970s lowered their quality and raised their yields. In 1987, you still could get a 9 percent yield from a Pacific Gas & Electric issue maturing in about 20 years, nearly a percentage point higher than from a Procter & Gamble bond of roughly the same maturity. The P&G issue had the higher rating, AAA against the utility's A, because bond buyers and rating services were leery of power companies with large nuclear generating plants. Even so, Alvin Markle, director of fixed-income research at Butcher & Singer in Philadelphia, advised, "In times like these, people seeking maximum yields should buy utility bonds and use industrials for diversification purposes."

Taxable Junk

Junk bonds — corporate issues rated below BBB and paying very high interest — were enjoying a heady vogue in the 1980s. Otherwise conservative investors were attracted by the yields on such issues, which were running four to five percentage points above those of AAA-rated bonds. Furthermore, statistics show that losses due to default reduce yields on junk-bond portfolios by only about 1.6 percentage points in typical years and 4 to 4.5 points during major recessions. The result: low-quality bonds consistently outperform high-grade paper over time, and high yields on junk debt more than make up for the risk of default. A much-noted study by Marshall Blume and Donald Keim at the University of Pennsylvania's Wharton School concluded that from January 1980 through June 1984, a portfolio of low-quality bonds returned an average of 13.5 percent a year, while AAA-rated bonds returned a comparatively dour 8 percent.

But there's a hitch. The junk-bond market turned treacherous in the 1980s for unwary small investors. The problem was a boom in low-quality debt created by megadeals in which outsiders took over huge corporations or insiders captured control of them by means of leveraged buyouts. Many corporations whose borrowing power was thus exploited became weighed down with more debt than their cash flows could safely support. If there were a recession or a miscalculation by the deal makers, some of these corporations could take a dive — and drag down their bondholders with them.

This caused Wall Street professionals to muse that the new junk bonds could prove riskier than the flakiest growth stocks. In a major bankruptcy, a defaulting junk bond could lose more than half of its value overnight. "The past record of very few defaults is not indicative of what the risk may be in the current crop of bonds," said Steven Leuthold, a Minneapolis investment adviser. "In some cases, the bonds from takeovers and buyouts are of much poorer quality than past issues." Indeed, the rate of default for junk bonds in 1985 doubled the average number of failures over the previous decade.

Given all this, should small investors consider buying junk bonds? The answer is a qualified yes. There are more terrible bonds than ever before, but plenty of sound high-yield bonds also are being issued. You have to know how to separate the junk from the toxic waste. Indeed, Richard Omohundro, manager of the high-yield bond group at Merrill Lynch Capital Markets, observed: "While some large deals are dangerous, the average quality of the other new issues has actually increased."

To stay on the safe side, small investors attracted to junk bonds should always observe a couple of rules. The first is to avoid debt issued in connection with takeovers and leveraged buyouts. Some of that debt may be of fairly good quality, but it is almost impossible for an amateur to evaluate. The second and more important rule is to diversify. Richard C. Young, president of Young Research & Publishing, investment advisers in Newport, Rhode Island, puts it emphatically: "When an individual owns fewer than 10 issues, it's speculation, not investment. Ideally, you ought to own 40 or more positions."

But who can afford as many as 40 bonds? Even buying minimal positions of $5,000 per issue, you would need $200,000 to assemble such a portfolio. Brokerage houses offer a solution for small investors in the form of unit investment trusts, which are large assemblages of bonds, units of which are sold to small investors for around $1,000. This solution may be far from ideal. The Drexel Burnham Lambert High Interest Trust Shares (HITS), a series of unit trusts sold through many brokers, has consisted of portfolios of 17 to 24 new issues — considerably fewer than the optimum. Further, unit trusts have the shortcoming of not being actively managed. After a trust is set up and the units have been sold, the sponsor will cull issues from the portfolio only if they have run into severe financial difficulties. Drexel's trusts have also tended to include leveraged, deal-related issues.

The most troubling aspect of the Drexel trusts may well be that this firm has been far and away the dominant force in the junk-bond market, particularly for less active issues. As a consequence, if you wish to sell your unit back to the sponsor before it matures — as is your right — the price you get will ultimately depend on the actions of the sponsor's own trading department. Michael O'Brien, manager of the high-yield bond department at Oppenheimer & Company, said in 1985, "For many issues, you can't find a market unless you call Drexel, and then the market is what they make it.''

For determined junk-bond investors, the best choice is to purchase shares in a high-yield bond mutual fund. With portfolios of 70 to 140 issues, bond funds offer broad diversification and active management. They are discussed later in this chapter.

Convertibles

Convertible bonds give you a way of earning fixed income while still playing the stock market. These hybrid securities — part stock, part bond — offer a higher profit potential than conventional bonds and a lower risk of losses than common stocks. Thus a convertible provides, in addition to income, the possibility of growth and a good measure of principal protection. The primary attribute of this type of security is that you can convert the bond to a specific number of shares of the company's common stock. This becomes profitable if the stock reaches what is called the conversion price — usually 15 to 30 percent above its price when the bond is offered for sale.

A convertible's price therefore swings not only with interest rates but also with the value of the company's underlying shares, making this kind of bond more speculative than a plain bond of similar credit quality. If share prices rise or fall, convertible prices rise or fall in tandem. Companies issue convertibles because they carry lower interest rates than straight bonds and because the debt will magically vanish from the corporate balance sheet if the bonds are converted to stock. For the investor, the fixed income acts as a cushion under the bond's price. Should the stock price slump, the value of the convertible probably won't drop as far — unless the company is so shaky that it may have to default on its bond interest. Convertibles pay higher yields than most common and preferred stocks do but not as much as ordinary corporate bonds.

Treasuries

At the opposite extreme from junk bonds are U.S. Treasury bonds. Backed by the full faith and credit of the U.S. government, Treasuries are impregnable to default. They also have excellent call protection; yet their yields may be no more than one point below those of the highest-quality corporate bonds. Along with top quality, you get a tax break: your income from Treasuries is exempt from state and local income taxes.

While you can buy Treasuries with maturity dates as far ahead as 30 years, long-term investors who believe that safety of principal is the highest priority should stick with 20-year issues. They can be bought directly from Federal Reserve banks for as little as $1,000. Commercial banks and brokerages will buy them for you at Treasury auctions for a $25 fee or on the bond market for a commission that varies with the broker and the size of your order. Treasury notes, which have maturities of 10 years or less, require a minimum investment of $5,000 and can be purchased in the same ways.

Treasuries' call provisions offer about the best defense against having a high-yield bond snatched away from you. Most other types of bonds issued in recent years are callable after five or 10 years. The risk of a call is heightened in times of go-go interest rates. It is after rates have dropped steeply that the holder of a high-yielding bond most cherishes his fixed-income payments. Treasuries lock the government into a fixed rate for as long as 25 years.

One way to limit the loss potential if you have to sell a bond during periods of rising interest rates is to buy a Treasury issued in 1981 or 1982, when interest rates roamed from 14 to 16 percent. Unless those unprecedented rates return, you will have to pay more than face value for such a bond, but the high yield will bolster its market value if rates rise. Another safeguard is to buy intermediate-term notes, particularly those maturing in one to five years. The no-load Scudder Target Fund (175 Federal Street, Boston, Massachusetts 02110) offers an easy way to do so. The bonds in its five U.S. government portfolios all pay off on a specific date. You can choose maturities of one year or more.

Savings Bonds

Once the wallflower at the Treasury ball, the Series EE U.S. Savings Bond was turned into a belle in 1982. It was then that Congress decreed that this bond must pay 85 percent of the average yield on five-year Treasury bonds and must be adjusted every six months to maintain that relationship. Furthermore, the Treasury sets a minimum interest rate below which EE Bond interest can never drop. Until November 1986 the floor was 7.5 percent; then the Treasury lowered it to 6 percent.

Savings bonds are sold at a discount from their face value. You cannot resell them on the open market, but you can always redeem them at the bank for their accrued value. The only catch is that if you redeem in less than five years, the interest is calculated at a lower rate. EE bonds are designed to mature in 10 years, but the Treasury may well extend their lives as it has for the old Series E savings bonds, which don't expire until they are 25 to 40 years old, depending on the date of issue. So you may be able to keep piling up interest almost indefinitely. Best of all, your income is not taxable until you take your money out and is never taxable by your state or city. At your pleasure, you can transform EE bonds worth $500 or more, tax deferment and all, into an HH Bond, whereupon the Treasury will send you interest checks every six months for at least 10 years. You do pay taxes on this income, but the value that accumulated in your old EE Bonds remains inviolate until you cash in the HH Bond.

Tax-exempts

Until quite recently, individuals bought as few as 15 percent of all newly issued municipal bonds, which states and localities use to finance public works and subsidized home mortgages and industrial developments. The rest were purchased by banks, insurance companies, and other institutions. More recently, though, nearly 80 percent of fresh tax-exempts were being snapped up by private investors.

The enthusiasm for munis is easily explained. First, the income is exempt from federal income tax and, if you live in the state where the bond was issued, from state and local income taxes as well. Second, yields on tax-exempts reached extraordinarily high levels compared with the after-tax income available from taxable issues. In late 1986 a long-term utility bond yielded about 9.5 percent. For an unmarried investor earning $36,000 a year in a high-tax state like New York, 50 cents of each dollar of interest income could go for federal, state, and local taxes. With an income above $58,000, an investor might keep less than 43 cents of each dollar. The result: a 9.5 percent taxable yield might really be worth only 4.1 to 4.75 percent, while a comparable tax-exempt issue could offer 7 percent or higher.

Lower tax rates under the overhauled 1986 revenue code would seem to have weakened the case for municipals because the tax exemption is now worth less than before. But in fact, tax-exempt bonds remained the most attractive choice for middle- and upper-income investors. Yields were exceptionally high by any historical standard, with some municipals paying more than taxable Treasuries. Although new restrictions on tax-exempt bond issuers were expected to halve the number of new bonds coming to market each year, sharp limitations on the tax exemption of interest earned on municipals by banks and insurance companies were likely to cut the demand along with the supply.

The new tax code shrouds the future of municipals in uncertainty. But at any given time you can easily enough figure out whether you can benefit from the tax exemption on bond interest. With only three tax brackets to contend with, your task is even simpler. Depending on your top rate, you divide current tax-free yields by one of the following numbers to find the equivalent taxable yield:

If you are in the 15 percent bracket: 0.85.
If you are in the 28 percent bracket: 0.72.
If you are in the 33 percent bracket: 0.67.

Thus for an investor in the 28 percent bracket, the arithmetic might look like this:

$$\frac{\text{tax-exempt interest}}{0.72} = \text{taxable equivalent}$$

If the current rate on a tax-exempt bond is 7 percent, the breakeven point is as follows:

$$\frac{7.0}{0.72} = 9.72$$

If good, safe corporate bonds were paying less than 9.72 percent, this investor would do better in a high-quality muni.

Most investment advisers recommend that individual investors buy munis rated A or better. Low-rated bonds, although they may pay enticingly higher interest rates, are best left to professionals, who can spot signs of trouble in time to unload shaky bonds before trouble hits.

If you want the higher yields — but not the risks — of a lower-rated issue, confine yourself to insured bonds. They are guaranteed by groups of insurance companies, which agree to pay the interest and principal in the event of default. Insured bonds can be excellent buys. Although Standard & Poor's automatically rates most of them AAA because of the insurance, these securities at times have yielded half a percentage point *more* than uninsured AAAs. This seeming inconsistency has a rational explanation: bond insurance has never been tested by a major claim. But most analysts believe that the insurers could handle all but a long series of defaults.

Call provisions of tax-exempts usually give you a poor chance of locking in a high yield for very long after rates have dropped sharply. Most munis let issuers redeem them after five or 10 years. While the call price is, as a rule, the face value plus a small premium (usually 2 to 3 percent), it is invariably less than the bond's recent market value. Furthermore, you will have to reinvest the proceeds at a lower rate.

Unless you decide to buy only insured bonds, find some way of diversifying your muni holdings. Some advisers urge that your portfolio contain no fewer than five different securities. With munis typically issued in $5,000 denominations, that kind of advice is useless to most investors. But if you buy discounted bonds, diversification requires less capital than you might think. For example, you can create a small portfolio by purchasing three $5,000 face-value bonds trading at 65 percent of face value, or $3,250 apiece. Then your total cost will be less than $10,000.

Owning just three issues doesn't constitute broad diversification, but a high-quality bond portfolio need not be as diversified as a stock portfolio. "If you go out and buy one AAA-rated bond, you will probably be better off than with 10 A-rated bonds," says Hildy Richelson, coauthor of *Income Without Taxes* (Carroll & Graf, $16.95). She suggests that a sound portfolio can be constructed from three or four of the highest-quality issues, provided that their maturities are 10 years or less; longer-term bonds leave their owners vulnerable to a resurgence of inflation and rising interest rates. Diversification by maturity is just as important as diversification by issuer. An optimum small portfolio, according to Richelson, might consist of four bonds with different maturities, such as four, six, eight, and 10 years.

Tax-free Unit Trusts

In large part, the 80 percent of municipal bonds owned by private investors have been acquired in the form of shares in unit trusts. These prefabricated portfolios address the problem of diversification by permitting investors with as little as $1,000 to buy into a package of 12 to 35 issues. Annual sales of unit trusts grew from less than $1 billion in 1974 to $15 billion in the 1980s. Yet for all their popularity, unit trusts have drawbacks. Cost, for one. The sponsors who assemble trusts nick you twice — with a sales commission and also a markup on the price they pay for the bonds. Unsuspected risk, for another. Investors often shop for the highest rate without considering other important criteria, such as the quality of the securities in the trust and the number of years before the bonds mature and the principal is repaid.

To figure out whether a trust is your best investment choice, you need to know a bit about the way the municipal bond market works and how trusts are put together. Typically, a brokerage or bond dealer acquires the bonds for a trust from its own inventory, new issues, or other dealers. Sponsors often get extremely good prices because of their knowledge of the market and their bulk buying power. Moreover, they analyze the credit ratings of the issuers of all bonds selected for the portfolio.

Once the package is put together, a third-party evaluator such as Standard & Poor's sets the offering price of the units on the basis of what the bonds could be sold for. This gives most of the advantage of bulk buying to the sponsor. In addition, muni dealers quote two prices: a bid price (what they will pay for a bond) and a higher asked price (what they will sell it for). These two quotes can differ by as much as four percentage points. Since it is the asked, or selling, price that serves as the basis for figuring a unit's value, sponsors make a profit on every bond that goes into a trust. For example, if a bond was quoted at 98 bid–100 asked, the sponsor of a unit trust would pay $980 per $1,000 worth of bonds — or more likely $970 each for a block of bonds with face values of $200,000 or more. He would value each bond at $1,000 for the purpose of pricing a trust unit. The unit price also includes a sales fee, usually 4 to 5 percent and known as the load, which the sponsor charges for having put the trust together.

As the bonds earn interest, a trustee collects the payments. After annually deducting small service fees that add up to about 0.2 percent of a unit's face value, the trustee sends a prorated share of the interest to each unit holder either once a month or twice a year. If, as occasionally happens, the issuer of one of the bonds in a trust runs into financial trouble, the sponsor may decide to sell the bond. The unit holders get the proceeds because unit trusts are not permitted to add issues after a portfolio has been packaged and sold. This makes trusts slow to respond when a bond's creditworthiness begins deteriorating.

The assumption behind a unit trust is that the investor intends to buy and hold it. After a stated time, sometimes as long as 30 years, the trust terminates, the securities are sold or redeemed, and the original investment is repaid in full. It is possible for an investor to sell his units back to the sponsor before the trust terminates. But sponsors do not refund the load; nor do they redeem at the current asking price of the bond, but at the significantly lower bid price. In short, you buy units at retail but redeem them early at wholesale. That spread, together with the 4 or 5 percent sales charge, makes early redemptions quite costly.

Redemptions, however, make it possible to buy old trusts. These are available through brokers and dealers and are priced the same way new trusts are. An investor who needs to have principal returned at a specific time and who is unable to find a newly issued trust with a suitable term to maturity may be better served by purchasing an old one.

All in all, if you want convenience and don't mind paying for it, unit trusts may be for you. Jim Lebenthal, chairman of Lebenthal & Company, a firm that specializes in tax-exempt bonds and unit trusts, says, "Buying a unit trust is like going to a Mexican restaurant and ordering the combination plate instead of staring at the menu trying to figure out the difference between an enchilada and a burrito." Even so, you still have some menu reading to do. The following guidelines should help.

Avoid maturities of more than 10 years. Many new trusts are made up of bonds with 20- to 30-year terms. If you can't find an attractive new intermediate-term trust, ask the broker or dealer whether any older trusts are available.

Check the bond ratings listed in the trust's prospectus. If you see bonds rated A by Standard & Poor's or Moody's but not by both, or if the trust contains a lot of Puerto Rican tax-exempts, be careful. The sponsor may have included issues of borderline quality to boost the yield.

Look for call protection of at least 10 years. If interest rates fall, bonds without call protection may be redeemed by their issuers. You will have failed to lock in your high yield.

Be especially careful about buying old unit trusts at premiums above their face value. The current yields will look high, but when the bond matures you will get back less than you invested. For example, a trust selling at $1,100 per unit that matures at $1,000 in 10 years is, in effect, losing $10, or 1 percent, of its principal value each year.

Don't automatically buy a trust containing only debt issues of your own state. It is true that these so-called triple-tax-free trusts give you income exempt from state and local as well as federal levies, but sometimes yields on national trusts — those holding bonds from assorted states — are a lot higher. So much so, in fact, that you may be better off buying one and paying some state and local taxes.

Bond Mutual Funds

Small investors are discovering bond mutual funds in a massive way. In the mid-1980s, nearly two-thirds of all mutual-fund sales were bond funds. By far the most popular were government income funds, which manage portfolios of Treasury bonds, issues of other government agencies, and federally guaranteed mortgage certificates. But all other kinds of bond funds were selling briskly, too: those specializing in corporate bonds, national municipal bonds, and single-state municipals. You can start investing in most bond funds with $1,000 and in some with as little as $250.

Because a mutual fund will always redeem its shares at the present worth of the underlying bonds — the net asset value per share — any appreciation in the fund's portfolio is immediately reflected in its share price, which is the amount you would get by selling the fund just then. However, bond funds never come due, as individual bonds and unit trusts do. No matter how long you hold them, you take a chance that when you want to sell your shares they won't bring as much as you paid for them.

Brokers sell bond funds at commissions up to 8.5 percent. Or you can buy commission-free no-load funds by mail. (For a free directory of such funds, write to Schabacker Investment Management, 8943 Shady Grove Court, Gaithersburg, Maryland 20877.) With many bonds in its portfolio, a fund can take more risk for the sake of yield than you could afford to take yourself. Here's a closer look at the types of funds.

Corporate Bond Funds

The income from them is taxable. But if you are investing in an IRA, these funds may improve the income on your investments. As a rule, corporate funds pay better yields than government funds. You cannot assume that, though. Sometimes the difference is so small that you might as well bask in the complete safety of government securities.

The largest mutual-fund groups usually offer two types of corporate bond funds, one consisting of high-rated bonds and the other dipping down into the lower grades and labeled as a high-yield fund. Since you can usually switch money between funds with a phone call, it is easy to choose the high-yield portfolio when it is paying a significantly higher yield than the high-rated fund, then retreat to the safer fund when the yield differential narrows. From 47 high-yield corporate bond funds available in 1986, the three no-loads that had the highest compound annual total returns (interest plus appreciation) for the three years to August 1, 1986, were Hutton Bond & Income Series, which returned 18.7 percent (800-334-2626; in New York State 212-742-5000); Fidelity High Income Fund, which returned 17.8 percent (800-544-6666; in Massachusetts 617-523-1919); and Fidelity Flexible Bond, which returned 16.1 percent (same phone numbers as Fidelity High Income).

You can get extra zip from closed-end bond funds, which are bought and sold on stock exchanges. Although nobody really knows why, the market often prices their shares at a discount from net asset value. One closed-end fund specialist, Thomas Herzfeld, who has his own firm in South Miami, Florida, observes that when bond prices rise, bond fund discounts tend to shrink, giving you a double gain. But when bond prices fall you can get stuck with a double loss. A table of closed-end bond funds with their discounts or premiums — many sell *above* their net asset value when bond prices are on the rise — appears every Wednesday in the *Wall Street Journal*.

Government Bond Funds

The airtight safety of the securities held by government bond funds doesn't necessarily preserve your investment from spoilage. At any given moment, the yields from various funds may differ widely. Current yields in August 1986 ranged from 8.5 to 10.5 percent or higher. The lower yields came from intermediate-term portfolios. The highest came from so-called yield-enhanced government funds, which trade bond futures and options to generate extra income. However, that strategy can undermine the value of your assets.

For the highest safe yields from government bonds, look into Ginnie Mae funds, which specialize in Treasury-guaranteed mortgage certificates issued by the Government National Mortgage Corporation (GNMA). (For details about Ginnie Maes and other mortgage securities, see Chapter 38.) The Vanguard Fixed Income — GNMA fund (800-662-7447) was yielding 10.4 percent on August 1, 1986, and had achieved a compound annual total return over the previous three years of 16.4 percent, making it the highest performer in the U.S. government bond fund category.

Tax-exempt Bond Funds

These funds provide an alternative to tax-exempt unit trusts. If you aren't sure that you can hold a municipal bond or unit trust until maturity, a tax-exempt fund is probably a better choice. For one thing, funds generally calculate the value of a share the same way whether you are buying or selling, while trusts give you the low end of the bid-asked spread. For another, a no-load mutual fund saves you the 4 to 5 percent trust sales charge. But you do pay a yearly management fee equal to around 1 percent of your assets; this fee is deducted from interest payouts. If you hold unit trusts for eight years or more, they typically turn out to be cheaper than mutual funds; for less than eight years, funds are cheaper.

Unlike trusts, which are intended to hold all securities until they mature, funds buy and sell bonds as market conditions change. By the time a trust matures, it will have returned your original investment. With bond funds, the value of your investment depends partly on how well the fund's portfolio managers do their job. In theory, active management should mean that a fund's principal value will fluctuate less than a trust's, particularly in a declining bond market. Some funds have superior records. Among them: Stein Roe Managed Municipal (no-load; 800-621-0320; in Illinois 312-368-7826); Hutton National Municipal (4 percent load; 800-334-2626; in New York State 212-742-5000); and Safeco Municipal (no-load; 800-426-6730; in Washington State 800-562-6810). But the available evidence suggests that funds as a group have not performed significantly better than trusts.

Steady-State Bonds

Because bond prices fall when interest rates rise, most bonds expose you to the risk of a loss if you have to sell at a bad time in the financial markets. To keep you in the lending game, big borrowers have devised bonds that help to insulate you from the vagaries of the market.

Put Bonds

One way of protecting your principal is with something called a put bond. It is a bond that can be cashed in for its full face value well before it matures. That shields you against unfavorable changes in interest rates. No matter how high rates rise, you are promised the right of redemption on specified dates. Because of this unusual feature, the price of a put bond tends to be much more stable than that of a conventional long-term bond.

Some put bonds can be cashed in on only one or two dates a few years after they were first floated. You can redeem others on a specified date each year after they have been in circulation for, say, five years. Tax-exempt put bonds pay interest and principal from revenues generated by the projects financed; the bond's safety is sometimes buttressed by letters of credit from major banks. For example, a 9 percent Marietta, Georgia, Housing Authority issue maturing in 1999 gets its revenues from rental income; a letter of credit from Cardinal Federal Savings Bank of Cleveland guarantees payment. This AAA-rated bond is redeemable in 1990 and once a year after that.

The trade-off for capital preservation in put bonds is a lower yield. The closer you are to the first redemption date and the more often those dates come, the lower your return will be. Just as these bonds are "putable" by the buyer, most are also callable by the issuer. Fair enough; both the bondholder and the issuer are hedging. You will exercise your right if you can get a higher return elsewhere, and the borrower will pay you off early if he can get cheaper financing on a new bond.

Floating-rate Bonds

For even more impervious armor against loss of principal, buy a bond with a floating interest rate. Since rates tend to climb along with consumer prices, floaters may also offer inflation protection. Floating rates rise and fall in line with some predetermined index or standard rate. For example, Citicorp adjusts the yield every week on its 1992 bond so that it always pays a percentage point more than 13-week Treasury bills. Because the investor gets the current market rate, resale value should be stabilized — unless the issuer's credit rating sours. Some floaters also have put privileges every two or three years.

Floating-rate municipals typically are tied to the highest of two or three different indexes. A Prince George's County, Maryland, pollution-control bond maturing in 2010 adjusts weekly to 66 percent of the 13-week Treasury bill rate or 72 percent of the 30-year Treasury bond rate. From 1981 to 1986 the return ranged from 7 to 10 percent. All floaters set a floor and ceiling on adjustments — 6 and 12 percent for the Prince George's bond.

Corporate floaters trade actively on major exchanges. Muni floaters can be a bit harder to find. E. F. Hutton makes a market in them but sometimes has a long waiting list of small investors. Merrill Lynch groups them in unit trusts at around $1,000 a share.

Zero-Coupon Bonds

To get the idea of a zero-coupon bond, think of a Series EE Savings Bond. You buy it at a discount and redeem it several years later at a far higher worth. Meantime, you get no interest. Zero-coupon bonds don't enjoy tax-sheltering of interest the way EE Bonds do unless the zero happens to be a tax-exempt municipal issue. But zeros usually have a fixed interest rate and always have an immutable maturity date. That means you can put a padlock on the rate of return for almost as long as you wish — from six months to 30 years. A $1,000 investment in a 15-year zero paying 9.5 percent, for example, would be worth more than $4,025 at maturity.

Merrill Lynch unleashed a loony-sounding zooful of zeros in 1982. The brokerage giant stripped the interest coupons from the principal portion of Treasury bonds and sold the bonds as TIGRs (for Treasury investment growth receipt). Other brokerages whelped LION and CATS. In 1985 a powerful new competitor appeared: Uncle Sam himself. With the introduction of the U.S. government's STRIPS (for separate trading of registered interest and principal of securities), the government zero has become an even safer choice for investors. By 1986, investors had plunked more than $100 billion into acronymic zeros. Their chief drawbacks are twofold: you owe immediate federal income tax on interest you usually won't receive for many years; and as interest rates fluctuate, market prices of zeros rise and fall more dramatically than those of full-coupon bonds.

The difference between brokerage zeros and STRIPS is that Merrill Lynch's TIGRs and Salomon Brothers' CATS (certificates of accrual on Treasury securities) are certificates issued by custodian banks —Manufacturers Hanover for TIGRs and Morgan Guaranty for CATS — which hold in an irrevocable trust the federal government bonds that the brokers have stripped of their interest coupons. STRIPS, on the other hand, are bonds the government itself has stripped and delivered directly to brokers and banks, which in turn sell the bonds to the public. Because STRIPS are direct obligations of the U.S. government to the individual bondholder, they yield up to a tenth of a percentage point less than TIGRs or CATS.

Zeros, despite their allure, aren't for every long-term investing need. They are ideal when you want to build up a certain amount of money by a particular date. That's why many investors use them to fund IRAs and Keoghs or to produce college tuition money when it is needed. But unless you put them in a tax-favored account, you must pay tax on the interest you are *not* collecting.

If you shop for a zero, make sure you are getting the best price by asking several brokers to supply you with three figures: the total amount of money you have to invest now (including all fees and commissions), the total amount of money you will receive when the bond matures, and the effective yield to maturity that this growth represents. The yield you receive depends, as usual, on the risk you are willing to take on interest rates. In general, the longer you commit your money, the higher your yield. You will also boost your return if you can live with a slightly less stellar credit risk than the U.S. government. Brokerage firms are pushing a variety of such securities, as follows.

Corporate Zeros

Corporates, being riskier than Treasury-based issues, usually offer a higher return. All that ultimately backs them is the reliability of the corporation issuing them; if it goes under, you could lose your investment. Many non-Treasury taxable zeros have been issued by quasi-public corporations. For instance, the World Bank, rated AAA by Standard & Poor's, has floated a $1.3 billion zero issue, the largest ever.

Mortgage-backed Zeros

One brokerage house, Kidder Peabody, is creating a zero secured by collateral that in turn is guaranteed by federal agencies such as the Government National Mortgage Association (Ginnie Mae), Federal National Mortgage Association (Fannie Mae), and the Federal Home Loan Mortgage Corporation (Freddie Mac). The bonds, secured by mortgages on single-family houses, are rated AAA because of the creditworthiness of the federal agencies. Nevertheless, their comparatively high yield reflects a risk factor, says Peter Cooper, chief of bond marketing at Kidder Peabody, where these bonds are called ABCS (agency-backed compounded securities). ''Because you are never sure when homeowners will prepay the underlying mortgages in these securities, the bonds could be redeemed before you expect,'' Cooper explains.

Zero Certificates of Deposit

Some banks and savings and loans offer attractive yields on zero CDs sold through brokerage firms or by the banks. Such CDs are insured up to $100,000 by the Federal Savings and Loan Insurance Corporation or the Federal Deposit Insurance Corporation.

Municipal Zeros

These are the kind best suited to college funds because returns are tax-free. On an after-tax basis, it may be tough to beat the yields available on muni zeros. They are only as safe, however, as the municipality backing them, so remember to check the credit rating. If you are particularly concerned about safety, find an insured municipal zero and expect to sacrifice about half a percentage point of yield.

There is still one serious uncertainty in most municipal zero offerings: the possibility of early redemption. As John O'Brien, the head of the municipal trading department at Salomon Brothers, cautions: "Even though the yields are attractive, investors must be wary of early-call features, which are not widely understood." Callability is a problem with zeros issued by state and local housing finance agencies, which use the proceeds for below-market mortgage loans to home buyers. After about 18 months, bondholders may get some of their capital back. Therefore, look for nonhousing-related municipal bonds that cannot be called in early. For example, an issue of zero-coupon Manatee County, Florida, hospital bonds is not callable until 1995 and a University of Illinois issue is safe from call until 2001. At 1986 prices, both these bonds were yielding around 7.25 percent.

Zero-Coupon Unit Trust

If the preceding varieties of zero-coupon bonds are not enough for you, E. F. Hutton is packaging a series of 10-year unit trusts called the high-yield and zero-coupon Treasury series. Investors in this trust (minimum investment: $225 for IRAs and Keoghs, otherwise $1,000, with a 4.25 percent load) own units of a portfolio combining Treasury zeros and corporate junk bonds with credit ratings of B or better. William Addiss, a Hutton bond specialist, explains: "In the worst of all possible worlds, if every junk bond in the portfolio defaulted, a unit holder would still get his original investment back because the zeros will have tripled in value by the time the trust matures."

38

REAL ESTATE: GINNIE MAE AND KIN

They sound like a hillbilly clan straight out of Dogpatch. Fact is, Ginnie Mae and her kissin' cousins Freddie Mac and Fannie Mae do constitute a family of sorts — an investment family. They are related not to Li'l Abner but to Uncle Sam, since these bonds and bond-like securities are usually backed by pools of home mortgages guaranteed by government agencies. Ginnie Mae and her relatives have made brokers happier than they could get on a gallon of Kickapoo Joy Juice, but that doesn't necessarily mean that these securities are right for you.

To be sure, Maes and Macs have considerable charms, particularly for safety-conscious investors seeking income rather than capital gains. Although there are significant differences between these similarly named securities, they generally have in common yields that can run as much as two percentage points higher than those on Treasury bonds of comparable maturities. Not all carry the same explicit backing by the federal government that Treasury issues do. But Maes and Macs are guaranteed by agencies closely tied to the government, making them virtually as safe as Uncle Sam's own notes and bonds. Maes and Macs are also just as affordable as Treasury issues. The minimum investment is as little as $1,000.

Maes and Macs are similar to bonds in that they bear interest and carry maturity dates. But they are more complex. Being mortgage securities, they return part of your principal in monthly installments, along with interest payments, and they frequently mature long before their stated due date. Mae and Mac securities trade in a secondary market in a manner similar to conventional bonds, with prices tending to rise when interest rates fall. But the prices of these securities rise less than those of bonds because investors are not willing to pay much of a premium for certificates that regularly return their principal to them at face value. When rates go up, however, the prices of Maes and Macs will drop just as sharply as bond values.

Because even brokers admit to confusion about the nuances of the Mae and Mac investments they sell, you cannot rely on your financial adviser to explain all the advantages and drawbacks. Yet just because Maes and Macs are complex doesn't mean that they are bad investments. In fact, it is partly because these securities are so difficult to understand that they must carry such temptingly high yields and stellar guarantees. So if you are an income-oriented investor willing to take the time to learn about the Mae and Mac clan, you may find yourself well compensated for your effort. The following family tree will help you with your homework.

Ginnie Maes

When you invest in a mortgage-backed security, you are buying a share in a package of fixed-rate home mortgages. In the case of Ginnie Maes, securities issued by the Government National Mortgage Association, the mortgages are insured by the Federal Housing Administration or the Veterans Administration. Ginnie Mae then guarantees the securities, and Uncle Sam in turn backs Ginnie Mae. That makes Ginnie Maes the only securities in the mortgage market that carry the same unconditional federal government guarantee as Treasury bonds.

As homeowners make their mortgage payments, your share of those payments is passed along to you in monthly checks. Hence, these securities are also known as pass-through certificates. Part of the amount you receive reflects interest payments on the mortgages, and the rest represents paydown of the principal.

Getting a share of your principal back at monthly intervals can be either a benefit or a disadvantage, depending on your needs and the direction in which interest rates are moving. If you require a sizable monthly cash flow to meet living expenses and don't mind eating into your capital, you will appreciate the larger amounts you receive from a Ginnie Mae than from an interest-only security. Otherwise, deciding every month where to reinvest that cash can be a pain in the neck — and a pain in the pocketbook when interest rates are dropping, because you will get a lower rate of return on that newly invested capital. When rates are rising, however, the system works in your favor.

Another problem with Ginnie Maes is that you can never know exactly how much money you will receive in a given month or how long your payments will last. With a regular bond, interest payments always remain the same, and they usually continue until the issue matures. Then you get all your capital back. But inevitably, some people sell their houses and pay off their mortgages ahead of schedule. And when interest rates have fallen sharply, many homeowners find it profitable to refinance their mortgages at a lower rate. Thus one month you might receive an unexpectedly large check, reflecting an unscheduled payoff of principal. When that happens, subsequent checks will be smaller because you are earning interest on a diminishing investment.

Mortgage prepayments are so common that Ginnie Maes backed by 30-year mortgages have an average life of 12 years and those backed by 15-year mortgages expire after an average of about seven years. To give you a more realistic idea of the return you will get on your investment, the yields to maturity quoted for Ginnie Maes are calculated on the basis of this average life rather than on the stated term of the underlying mortgages. But it is difficult to predict how fast any particular pool will be paid off. The return you end up with may bear little resemblance to the yield originally quoted. Ginnie Maes in effect compensate investors for this uncertainty by paying a higher interest rate than Treasury issues.

You can participate in the Ginnie Mae market in various ways. If you can afford a $25,000 minimum initial investment, you can buy a newly issued certificate from any broker or government securities dealer. Older certificates, in which much of the debt has been paid off, may cost as little as $10,000. You can also invest in Ginnie Mae unit trusts or mutual funds for a minimum of $1,000. Trusts sometimes yield slightly more than certificates because trust portfolios may contain some older, premium-priced issues bearing a higher-than-market rate of interest. But you run a risk of a loss with these trusts. If interest rates drop sharply, many homeowners are likely to prepay the high-rate mortgages in the older pools, which the trust bought for more than their face values. That deprives investors of a slice of their high yields and a sliver of their capital.

Ginnie Mae mutual funds usually make sounder investments. They are actively managed, and a few entail no commissions. Mutual-fund portfolio managers can make adjustments in their holdings to reflect changing market conditions — for example, selling high-coupon certificates to avoid a sudden rush of mortgage prepayments if interest rates seem poised for a sharp decline. You don't have to reinvest returns of principal from a GNMA fund. The managers automatically plow it into new mortgage pools. No-load Ginnie Mae funds include the Vanguard Fixed Income–GNMA Portfolio in Valley Forge, Pennsylvania (800-662-7447; $3,000 minimum) and the Lexington GNMA Income Fund in Saddle Brook, New Jersey (800-526-7443; $1,000 minimum).

You also can buy Ginnie Mae securities backed by adjustable-rate mortgages. The interest rate on these securities is adjusted once a year, with the adjustment pegged to movements in the rate on one-year Treasury bills but limited to one percentage point a year and five percentage points over the life of the investment.

Freddie Macs and Fannie Maes

The Federal Home Loan Mortgage Corporation, known as Freddie Mac, and the Federal National Mortgage Association, Fannie Mae, both issue mortgage-backed securities similar to Ginnie Maes. Both are pass-through certificates representing shares in pools of fixed-rate home mortgages, but the pools are made up primarily of conventional home loans rather than mortgages insured by the FHA or VA. Like Ginnie Maes, Freddie Macs and Fannie Maes pass along to investors the monthly interest and principal payments made by homeowners on mortgages in the pools. Fannie Mae guarantees, just as Ginnie Mae does, that you will receive your fair share of interest and principal every month even if homeowners do not meet their obligations. Freddie Mac, however, only guarantees timely payment of interest and the ultimate payment of principal. If homeowners do not make their mortgage payments on time, you will still receive your interest payments every month, but you might have to wait as long as a year to receive your rightful share of principal.

As with Ginnie Maes, newly issued certificates from Freddie Mac and Fannie Mae require a minimum investment of $25,000. Likewise, you can buy the agencies' older certificates, whose principal has been partially paid off, for as little as $10,000. You probably won't find any unit trusts or mutual funds that invest solely in Freddie Mac and Fannie Mae pass-throughs. Some mutual funds, however, keep a portion of their money in these securities. In 1986, for example, the USAA Income Fund in San Antonio, Texas (800-531-8181; $1,000 minimum) had nearly 60 percent of its portfolio in Maes and Macs and the rest in high-yield common stocks, preferred stocks, bonds, and commercial paper.

Both Freddie Mac and Fannie Mae are corporations chartered by Congress, though they are not officially part of the federal government. While the securities that they issue lack the unconditional guarantee that Ginnie Maes carry, it is unlikely that Uncle Sam would refuse to bail out these corporations should they run into financial difficulties. Their securities, however, typically yield from one-fourth to one-half of a percentage point more than Ginnie Maes to compensate investors for the marginally higher risk.

The advantage of Freddie Mac and Fannie Mae pass-through certificates is a steadier flow of income and principal. Each certificate is backed by thousands of mortgages, compared with only 40 or 50 in a typical Ginnie Mae pool. The greater the number of mortgages in a pool, the more accurately you can apply the law of averages to predict how fast the principal will be paid back. ''If you can afford them, always invest in the larger pools like Freddie Macs,'' advises Dexter Senft, managing director of fixed-income research at First Boston. ''It's the only way to get some measure of consistency in your returns.''

Real Estate Mortgage Investment Conduit

An offspring of Ginnie Mae called the real estate mortgage investment conduit (REMIC for short) was introduced in 1987 under a provision of the Tax Reform Act. The REMIC pays you interest and principal in a more predictable manner than an ordinary pass-through certificate does. Issues are divided into four classes of maturity, each called a tranche (after the French word for slice). There are tranches of two, five, 10, and 20 years. Investors get interest payments from the mortgages that back the REMIC. Mortgage prepayments, however, are assigned to the shortest tranche, usually assuring you of getting your original yield for the full term you have chosen. Once that class of investors has been paid off in full, prepayments are channeled to investors in the next shortest maturity. The process continues until all tranches have been retired.

The first issue of REMICs, put together by Salomon Brothers for sale in January 1987 and sold in minimum amounts of $1,000, yielded one or two percentage points more than Treasury securities. For example, the two-year tranche paid 7.2 percent, compared with 6.2 percent for the two-year Treasury note, and the 20-year tranche paid 9.7 percent, compared with the Treasury's 7.7 percent. REMICs are rated AAA because of their backing by the federal government. More speculative issues were being contemplated, however. Bernard Carl of Salomon, one of the architects of the REMIC, said at the time of introduction, ''We might design riskier but higher-yielding REMICs that contain commercial mortgages.'' He speculated that such ''junk REMICs'' might yield as much as five percentage points more than comparable Treasuries.

Sonny Mae et al.

Officially known as the State of New York Mortgage Agency, Sonny Mae issues bonds backed by fixed-rate single-family-home mortgages and uses the proceeds to subsidize below-market-rate mortgages for first-time home buyers. These are ordinary bonds — that is, securities that pay only interest until they mature. Rated AA by Moody's, they are exempt from federal taxes for all investors and from state and local taxes for New York State residents.

Although their names may not end in Mae or Mac, many other state housing agencies issue mortgage-revenue bonds similar to the ones sold by Sonny Mae. The after-tax yields on these bonds may be hard to beat, but the Tax Reform Act of 1986 will make them harder to find. A new formula, which limits the dollar volume of new issues of this tax-exempt financing under a formula based on the state's population, is expected to reduce the supply. Nevertheless, unless you are in the lowest bracket, it is worth checking to see if your state offers double- or triple-tax-exempt issues.

39

REAL ESTATE: REITS, FREITS, AND PARTNERSHIPS

Real estate investment trusts, better known as REITs, raise money in the stock market with which to buy income-producing properties, to write mortgages on existing buildings, or to do both. When you buy shares in a REIT, you are buying a stock that trades on an exchange or over the counter just as any other stock does. Rental income from the properties or interest on the mortgages is paid to you in the form of dividends. When properties are sold, capital gains are passed to you as special dividends or increased earnings per share, which are likely to boost the price of the stock.

The combination of generous dividends and price appreciation rewarded REIT holders with average total returns of 16 percent annually from 1982 through 1985, compared with 15.3 percent for Standard & Poor's 500-stock index. REITs almost always sell at a discount from the appraised value of their properties, and the size of the discount can boost or lower your profits. In 1982, most REIT shares were selling at discounts of 25 to 30 percent, but a couple of years later, the discounts narrowed to 10 to 15 percent. Even so, says Alan Crittenden, publisher of the *Crittenden Report,* a newsletter that monitors real estate trends for commercial developers, "The stock market is still the cheapest place to buy real estate."

Curbs on the tax advantages of investing in real estate have little impact on REITs, which are prohibited from using accelerated depreciation and passing along tax losses to investors. REITs do have a significant tax advantage, however. They pay no corporate income tax because they distribute 95 percent of their income in dividends. Some REITs are also able to shelter part of the income they pay out with offsetting deductions for depreciation and mortgage interest.

The chief virtue of REITs is that they are a liquid way of investing in a traditionally illiquid asset because you can sell your REIT shares in the stock market. Be sure to ask your broker how actively traded your trust is, however; a dozen or so over-the-counter REITs change hands infrequently.

The value of REIT shares fluctuates with investors' expectations for earning and capital gains. Poor dividend prospects, for example, are bad news on the market. In addition, says Martin Cohen, who manages the National Securities Real Estate Stock Fund, a New York City mutual fund with REIT holdings, "The slow-moving nature of the real estate business puts a limit on how fast REIT shares can rise. In a strong market they will not keep up, although their high yields give you some protection when the market sinks."

In selecting the right REIT, you have to decide whether you want a reliable old profit retriever or a frisky young pup that may grow fast. And with so many underwriters trying to teach an essentially old dog new tricks, you have to be careful that you are not the one who jumps through the hoop. A rundown of the advantages and disadvantages of the various types of trusts follows.

Finite-Life REITs

Nicknamed FREITs, these self-liquidating trusts own commercial and residential rental properties or a mix of properties and participating mortgages, which give the lenders a share of the profit when a building is sold. FREITs attempt to solve the perpetual discount problem. Conventional trusts keep buying and selling properties, but they never entirely liquidate their portfolios. For that reason, investors treat a trust's appraised value as a promise instead of a reality and refuse to pay face value for the holdings. FREITs, however, have a deadline, usually 10 to 15 years, for selling all their properties and distributing any capital gains to the shareholders. As the trust nears its liquidation date, the market value of the stock should rise to reflect the true value of the properties about to be sold.

Analysts are skeptical of FREITs, however, suspecting that they are merely marketing gimmicks designed to attract investors who have been scared away from tax shelters. Liquidation dates can be changed with the approval of the trustees to keep the trust from having to sell in a bear market for real estate. Thus the shares may keep selling at a discount, and investors could be locked in or have to liquidate at a loss. FREITs are also expensive to buy; the average price/earnings ratio is significantly higher than for ordinary equity trusts. That leads Martin Cohen to say, "It doesn't make sense to pay more for FREITs when they offer no assurances of selling their properties on schedule."

Equity REITs

These trusts own shopping centers, office buildings, apartment houses, and warehouses. Dividend yields don't come up to those on mortgage REITs, but as much as 50 percent of the cash distributions may be sheltered by deductions for depreciation passed on to shareholders.

Many equity REITs begin as blind pools, which do not own any properties at the time of the offering. The trusts take at least a year to complete their acquisitions, keeping shareholders' dollars in a money-market fund until then. The interest may be paid to shareholders or added to the pool to buy more real estate. Declining interest rates work against blind pools, so pass up new issues with blind pools in favor of those that have specified or already bought their properties. Older REITs can be attractive because they sell at the deepest discounts from their appraised values, which means you are buying properties for substantially less than their resale value.

Single-Purpose REITs

A recent variation on traditional equity trusts is the single-purpose REIT. A company whose business requires it to own real estate sells its properties to the REIT and leases them back at a fair market rent. Single-purpose portfolios invest entirely in one type of property, whether it is steakhouses, tire stores, or nursing homes. Yields are quite high, and some of the rental income is sheltered by deductions for depreciation, mortgage interest, and operating expenses. Lack of diversification is a major worry, though, when a REIT is dependent on the success of one business. If sales lag, rents may not even cover expenses. Yet shareholders won't be able to write off the losses for tax purposes. Thus Robert Frank, senior analyst for real estate research at Alex. Brown & Sons in Baltimore, foresees only modest price appreciation for single-purpose REITs.

Mortgage REITs

The high yields on mortgage trusts are attractive to income investors. There are no deductions for depreciation to offset dividends, however, so these trusts are probably best for Individual Retirement Accounts and Keogh plans (see Chapter 41). Most older mortgage trusts own some properties acquired through foreclosure during the real estate bust of the mid-1970s. Newer entries are building in an inflation hedge by writing second mortgages that are tied to participation agreements giving the REIT a share of increased rental income.

Limited Partnerships

Until tax reform, brokers and financial planners used the terms ''limited partnership'' and ''tax shelter'' interchangeably. A new passive investment rule instituted as part of tax reform invalidates that second name. If you own less than 10 percent of a piece of property or leave the management to someone else, you can write off losses only up to the amount of your income from that real estate and other so-called passive investments — ones in which you do not take a direct managerial role. In real estate, the limited partnership is the classic passive investment. Only property bought before President Reagan signed the Tax Reform Act on October 22, 1986, can generate losses that you can deduct from your ordinary income. Those deductions phase out gradually and disappear in 1991. You can deduct 65 percent of your partnership losses for 1987, 40 percent for 1988, 20 percent for 1989, and 10 percent for 1990. You can write off other passive losses only up to the amount of your income from other passive investments. For most people that means income from other limited partnerships. Therefore, partnership promoters and sponsors have shifted the emphasis to the production of real estate profits from their investments.

There are two basic types of real estate partnerships: public and private. Public programs are registered with the Securities and Exchange Commission and usually pool money from thousands of investors. The minimum investment is $2,000 to $5,000, with a special $2,000 floor for Individual Retirement Accounts. Private programs, which are not registered with the SEC, are designed for wealthier investors, who can ante up $10,000 to $100,000.

Real estate partnerships usually operate for five to 12 years. Then the properties are sold and the proceeds are divided between the outside investors, who are the limited partners, and the general partner. Dividends paid by REITs are often higher than the cash distributions from partnerships, making REITs more attractive to investors who need current income. But over the life of a limited partnership the average annual return, including capital gains as well as cash distributions, is often as good as or better than that of a REIT. A major reason is that partnerships have a free hand in buying and selling properties, while trusts are required by law to hold most of their properties for at least four years.

Tax reform should add to the attractions of income-producing limited partnerships. In 1987, sponsors of new programs may find prices of apartment and commercial buildings depressed. Leanne Lachman, president of Real Estate Research Corporation in Chicago, forecasts that well-run partnerships will yield between 8 and 11 percent. To protect yourself from brokers and financial planners hawking shaky programs, stick with general partners whose managers have been in the real estate business for at least 10 years and stay away from new types of deals, such as parking lots, that lack a record of success.

The only worthwhile surviving tax shelter in passively owned real estate is the rehabilitation credit, which amounts to 10 percent of your investment in a limited partnership that restores buildings erected before 1936 and 20 percent of the cost of restoring certified historic structures. A tax credit reduces the bottom line on your tax return dollar for dollar, whereas the deduction of losses was worth only a fraction of its dollar amount. Most rehab deals are offered in the private partnership market.

40

REAL ESTATE: BACKYARD INVESTING

What is a backyard real estate investor? Someone who is willing to go out and study nearby neighborhoods, talk to property owners, and size up dozens of prospective real estate investments to find undervalued properties that can grow in worth. Someone, too, who is committed to managing those properties with utmost efficiency. The backyard investor has to build a real estate empire brick by brick. Nevertheless, says John T. Reed, editor and publisher of *Real Estate Investors' Monthly* (342 Bryan Drive, Danville, California 94526; $96 a year), "if you are looking to start out in real estate, this could be the window of opportunity."

Being a hands-on landlord demands a special temperament. One day during office hours, Thomas R. Kuhns, a New York City ophthalmologist, got an urgent call from a tenant in his East Side townhouse. Water was flowing down the inside wall of the tenant's apartment. With patients in the waiting room, Kuhns slipped out a side door of his office, unchained the bike he rides to work, and swiftly pedaled the 18 blocks to his building. There he discovered that debris left by a roofing crew had blocked the gutter, causing snowmelt to spill onto the facade and through an open window. Kuhns cleared the drainage system, hopped back on his bike, and was seeing patients just 35 minutes after the call.

If you tend to become unhinged by this sort of interruption of your day, put your money in T-bills or blue chips and stay away from bricks and mortar. Before you tackle such tantalizing challenges as equity sharing and positive cash flow, face up to the backyard investor's key questions. Do you really want to be a landlord? Can you fix a leaky faucet? Would you regard a Sunday morning complaint about a lack of heat as an unpardonable intrusion? Would you cringe at evicting a tenant who had stopped paying the rent? Ruth Phiel, a veteran Chicago real estate agent and 1984 Illinois Realtor of the Year, quit investing because, she said, "I was always nervous about the way my tenants were caring for the property. You have to know how to handle late payments and things like that. I wasn't tough enough."

The travail of being a landlord is just one of the prices you must pay. Owning investment property is a management-intensive job, and there is no substitute for involvement. Your first task is to mesh your objectives with your resources. If your cash and credit situation is strong but the time you can devote to your investment is scant, buy real estate that is in ready-to-rent condition. If you have time to spare and are handy with saw and paintbrush, look for properties that can profit from a moderate amount of fix-up.

While individual investors and small partnerships have done well with commercial properties, managing them requires the kind of skills — finding suitable tenants and writing business leases, for example — that few novices possess. Most real estate specialists advise beginners to stick with residential properties. The consensus on the ideal investment: a three-bedroom, one-and-a-half-bath house. It is large enough for a small family — the most stable tenant — and, if need be, it is the easiest property to liquidate.

Professionals also recommend properties with one or more of the following characteristics:

A structurally sound house in a solid, stable neighborhood.

The worst house on the best block. A property that can be pulled into rentable condition with a fresh coat of exterior paint could be an excellent investment.

A deteriorating house in a turnaround neighborhood. Locating this property requires an intimate knowledge of your area. You also need a sharp sense of timing. If you are too early, rentals from the house will not support its upgrading.

One of the deterrents facing first-time investors is the size of the asset: $40,000 to $50,000 for inexpensive houses, $300,000 and more for luxurious ones. But borrowing makes the price of entry much more manageable. The typical down payment for houses financed with bank mortgages is 10 to 20 percent, or $10,000 to $20,000 on a medium-priced house — one you can get for, say, $100,000. Bear in mind that you must pay other charges when you take title to your property: points (a surcharge, normally 2 or 3 percent of the face value of the mortgage, levied by the lender), title search, lawyer's fees, prepayment of property taxes and insurance. Altogether, these closing costs can total $3,000 to $5,000 on a medium-priced house, depending on its location.

Scraping up the initial stake certainly paid off for Mary Boyd of Syracuse, New York. To supplement her income some years ago as a music teacher and pianist for the Syracuse Symphony, Boyd borrowed $5,000 from her father and made a down payment on an $18,000 two-family rental house in a blue-collar neighborhood. Seven years later, she and her husband, Frederick, a trombonist with the symphony, were performing their theme and variations on 37 residential and commercial properties worth about $2.5 million. To find time for their music, they employed a full-time manager and a second employee. The properties were generating $400,000 of rental income and around $70,000 in profits.

Look for Positive Cash Flow

In negotiating the total price of an acquisition, you should aim to avoid properties with a negative cash flow — those on which the mortgage, tax, utilities, and maintenance payments, plus necessary rehab costs, exceed the rental income. Such deals are dangerous in low-inflation periods. Some investments with negative cash flow in the early years can be justified if your down payment is 10 percent or less or if a close analysis indicates that rents can soon be raised to meet costs. Unless real estate values are rising fast, you should build a big enough cushion into your financial plan to run a building for at least five years.

Once you have determined what kind of property is most suitable for you, there is a natural desire to put your money immediately to work. Resist any such impulse. Instead, immerse yourself in a study of real estate as you would for any business venture. Chicago lawyer Jeffrey Bunn admits that his biggest mistake was his first: ''Overestimating what I knew about investing. Since I wanted to get the deal together too fast, I didn't spend enough time looking for the right investment.'' His initial purchase, a six-unit, $200,000 apartment house in Chicago's Lakeview area, appreciated a mere 5 percent in the first six years.

Pockets of Growth

You can avoid a poor performer like Bunn's by concentrating your search in pockets of economic growth. Cities such as Denver, Houston, and Oklahoma City suffered from oversupplies of housing and commercial space in the mid-1980s, but even in those locales opportunities could be seized by those close to the scene. Keep an eye out for neighborhoods that have begun to gain favor among young householders. Determine whether the district has a strong infrastructure: transportation, local retail establishments, and good schools. Most important, look for a strong employment base. In 1985, for example, Howard Green, a Birmingham, Michigan, shopping-center consultant, was bullish on certain Detroit suburbs near new auto plants and related businesses. "I'm having the last laugh on developers who look around the map for nice climatic amenities," Green said. "It is jobs that cause growth, not the sun."

Sizing Up a Piece of Property

When you have pinpointed a locale for your investment, you can begin to look at specific properties. Your best ally is likely to be a broker who is knowledgeable about your chosen area. Real estate agent Ruth Phiel recommends checking the broker's reputation with local bankers and attorneys. Take time to discuss with broker candidates your debt limits and the kind of building you are looking for. Above all, choose someone with whom you feel you can develop a rapport. Impatience and misunderstanding will only thwart your investing program. There are other obvious but fruitful sources of sale properties: listings by owners in your newspaper's real estate section, FOR SALE signs posted on front lawns, city auctions of buildings in tax arrears, word of mouth. Plan to inspect dozens of buildings before you make a bid.

Investigate thoroughly any property that approaches your standards. Unless you are versed in structural matters, take along a construction engineer whose judgment you trust. He will be well worth his $100 to $200 fee. Things to look for include a modern furnace and a water heater with at least 40 gallons of capacity for each family unit. Water stains on ceilings are symptoms of plumbing or roof leaks, sagging floors hint at structural defects. One fast way to confirm the stated age of a house is to look inside the tank of a toilet that seems to be part of the original plumbing. You will probably find the date of manufacture engraved in the ceramic wall.

Jot down all deficiencies together with any thoughts you may have about improvements that might boost the value of the property — a deck, for instance, or the conversion of basement space into a bedroom — and return with a tradesman to get estimates of the work. But don't take the quotes too literally. Typically they will be 40 percent below the actual price of the job, according to experienced rehabilitators.

Rental income and operating expenses supplied by the owner of a building or his broker all too often are optimistic approximations of the true cash flow. Ask to see utility and property tax bills and bear in mind that buildings are often reassessed for tax purposes after they change hands. If the place is currently rented, inspect tenant leases to confirm the income claimed. Before you decide that the rent could easily be raised, scan the classifieds to see what other landlords are charging.

Financing

In real estate investing, you normally seek the largest possible mortgage at the lowest possible interest rate. In many localities you can find mortgage consultants, who specialize in finding loans that will meet your needs and who have an affiliation with a lending institution. A consultant's services are usually paid for by the bank that makes the loan, so check around for yourself to confirm whether your consultant has found the best deal for you — and not just for the bank.

Quite often, the best source of financing is the seller, who, depending on his urgency to unload his property, can offer far more attractive terms than the banks will. Bernard Hale Zick, author of *How to Make Your Real Estate Fortune* (Real Estate Investor's Training, P.O. Box 12085, Overland Park, Kansas 66212; $29), describes a broad array of seller financing that he has negotiated for buildings he has bought. Some real estate ads will mention the availability of owner financing. In others a tip-off may be the phrase "owner being transferred." To avoid carrying two mortgages, this seller may be sufficiently motivated to offer financing. Brokers often know of such sellers, too.

A relatively new financing twist allows an investor and an occupant to split the costs and obligations of owning a house. Shared equity, as it is called, combines two incomes to qualify for a loan, so it can be an especially attractive strategy for investors who would not qualify on their own or who choose not to tie up a large amount of their credit. The law authorizing shared equity, a 1981 clarification of the tax treatment of vacation homes, requires only that the two owners sign an agreement and that the occupant pay fair market rent for living in the house (with the proportion of the rent that represents his ownership going into his own pocket). In the typical agreement, one of the investors is given an option to buy out the other at the end of a specified period at the then-appraised value of the house.

Shared equity alleviates potential tenant problems. "Who is likely to take better care of a property than an owner?" asks Benny L. Kass of Kass & Skalet, a Washington, D.C., law firm that specializes in real estate. If you are looking for a shared-equity partner, alert brokers in your area to the amount of down payment and credit you are willing to offer. Then check out candidates with special care. You will be getting not only a tenant but also a business partner.

Screening Tenants

Once you have become a landlord, the hours you spend selecting and rejecting tenants can save days of grief later on. "You don't manage buildings," says Thomas O'Dea, a real estate consultant in the Washington, D.C., area, "you manage tenants. A bad tenant is worse than no tenant at all." Adds real estate author Bernard Zick, "Don't screen tenants, sieve them."

Everyone in the business emphasizes the importance of checking references. Confirm job tenure with employers. Get an appraisal of the applicant's desirability as a tenant from his or her present landlord. Donna Milling of Thornton, Pennsylvania, a veteran investor with more than 50 single-family houses in her portfolio, runs a credit check on applicants and informs those she rents to that she never accepts personal checks after one has bounced. To minimize the annoyance of minor repairs, Milling discounts the rent $75 a month to tenants who don't call her but undertake these chores themselves and pay by the first of the month.

Landlords can duck such problems by handing them over to a management company, which collects rents, interviews prospective tenants, and maintains the property for fees ranging from 5 to 10 percent of rentals. However, hiring an agent will undermine any claim you make for losses under the new tax law. Furthermore, a managing agent's compensation can spell the difference between a profit and a loss. So you should probably plan to handle these duties yourself.

41

AN INVESTOR'S GUIDE TO IRAS AND KEOGHS

An Individual Retirement Account or Keogh plan may flourish or flop, depending on the investments you choose for each year's contribution.* For starters, consider this overarching principle: when you are evaluating any investment, whether it is as simple as a certificate of deposit or as complex as a real estate limited partnership, you should first study how it measures up in four fundamental areas. They are:

Preservation of principal. Think of it as a question. How great a chance is there that I could lose a portion, or even all, of the money I put into the investment? IRA and Keogh investors who have a low tolerance for risk or are planning to withdraw income soon should probably confine themselves to assets that guarantee they won't lose a penny. Safety has its price, however. Ultrasafe Treasury notes, for instance, generally deliver lower returns than securities that put principal at risk.

Liquidity. The more quickly and easily you can convert an investment into cash, the more liquid it is. Penalties for cashing in bank certificates of deposit (CDs) before they mature, for example, make them less liquid than, say, money-market mutual funds. Since IRAs and Keoghs are by nature long-term investments, liquidity is of greatest concern when it is nearly time to start withdrawing income. At any stage, however, illiquid investments hamper your ability to alter the mix of your portfolio in response to economic changes.

* Maximum contributions are $2,000 in an IRA, 20 percent of self-employment income in a defined-contribution Keogh, and $90,000 in a defined-benefit Keogh. For details on how they work, see Chapter 24.

Volatility. The key question here is how often and how sharply the value of your investment will rise and fall. Investments such as stocks in small companies and gold mining operations move up and down repeatedly and often in great leaps, gaining or losing as much as 50 percent of their value in a matter of weeks. Other alternatives, such as CDs, are as docile as a sleepy kitten. Note that high volatility can be an impediment to liquidity because there is a greater chance that your investment's value will have plunged just at the time you need to cash in. If you are going for long-term growth and don't plan to tap your retirement fund within the next 10 years or so, you needn't steer clear of an investment solely because it is volatile. By contrast, if you will be dipping into your fund soon, or if the thought of riding a broncolike investment makes your palms moist, play it safer.

Inflation protection. Getting a 7.5 percent yield on a CD is admirable when inflation is only around 3 percent, but that locked-in rate would lose its glitter if inflation shot back toward the double-digit levels that prevailed as recently as 1981. As your IRA or Keogh grows and you begin to diversify, it is important to add investments that tend to increase in value when inflation is on the rise.

To help you choose the components that best suit your objectives, *Money* rated the eligible investments as to how strongly they exhibit each of the four characteristics just described. The ratings are on a scale of 1 to 5, with 5 being the strongest representation of a particular investment characteristic. For example, a score of 5 for inflation protection means the investment offers the highest degree of protection, while a score of 1 indicates the lowest. We also included estimates of the average annual returns you might expect during the next 15 to 20 years — estimates based on historical performance and evaluations by specialists in each category. Some of the firms consulted were Data Resources Inc., a Lexington, Massachusetts, economic forecasting firm; Ibbotson Associates, Chicago financial analysts; and the investment banking firm of Salomon Brothers. The projections are not adjusted for inflation, which our consultants expected to range from 3 to 9 percent and to average roughly 5 percent.

Annuities

Annuities come in two main varieties — fixed and variable — but usually have one characteristic in common: high fees for withdrawing your money in the first seven years.

RATINGS OF ANNUITIES

Probable return on a typical stock-market *variable* annuity: 11 to 13 percent
Preservation of principal: 3
Liquidity: 2
Volatility: 3
Inflation protection: 4

Probable return on *fixed* annuities: about 10 percent
Preservation of principal: 4
Liquidity: 2
Volatility: 1
Inflation protection: 2

Investment-Grade Corporate Bonds

Newly issued corporates sell for face value. Discounted bonds sell for less than par because they were issued when interest rates were lower than they are when you buy them. You still get the equivalent of current yields because you pay less than the original purchase price, but you get back the full face value when the bond matures.

RATINGS OF INVESTMENT-GRADE CORPORATES

Probable return on an AAA 25-to-30-year bond: 8 to 13 percent
Preservation of principal: 4
Liquidity: 5
Volatility: 2
Inflation protection: 1

Lower-Grade Corporate Bonds

Unrated bonds and those graded below BBB are called junk bonds on Wall Street. They are higher yielding than their alphabetically superior cousins because they are riskier.

RATINGS OF LOWER-GRADE CORPORATE BONDS

Probable return on BB 20-year bonds: 11.5 to 14.5 percent
Preservation of principal: 3
Liquidity: 4

Volatility: 3
Inflation protection: 1

Convertible Bonds

Convertibles start out as bonds but convert profitably into common stock in the issuer's company if the share price climbs to a predetermined level.

RATINGS OF CONVERTIBLE BONDS

Probable yield on BBB 25-year bonds: 8 to 11 percent
Preservation of principal: 4
Liquidity: 5
Volatility: 3
Inflation protection: 3

Zero-Coupon Bonds

Zeros are heroes with IRA and Keogh investors because they let you lock in a fixed, long-term compounded interest rate. You can buy a six-month zero, a 30-year zero, and almost any maturity in between.

RATINGS OF ZERO-COUPON BONDS

Probable return on five-year Treasuries: 6.5 to 11.25 percent
Preservation of principal: 5
Liquidity: 5
Volatility: 3
Inflation protection: 1

Unit Trusts

While most unit trusts hold tax-free bonds, which don't belong in an IRA or Keogh, you also can invest in trusts made up of corporate bonds, government obligations, and combinations of these and other bonds.

RATINGS OF UNIT TRUSTS

Probable return on a 10- to 12-year government agency trust: 7.5 to 10.75 percent
Preservation of principal: 4
Liquidity: 5
Volatility: 2
Inflation protection: 1

Certificates of Deposit

More than half of all IRA dollars up to 1987 were invested in CDs. People clearly liked the security of principal and predictability of return. Most CDs are sold by banks, credit unions, and savings and loan associations and are federally insured up to $100,000. When you buy a CD, you agree to leave money on deposit for a specified period, as short as three months or as long as 10 years. In return, you are customarily paid a fixed rate for the duration of the investment.

RATINGS OF CDS

Probable return on a two-year CD: 6.25 to 10.25 percent
Preservation of principal: 5
Liquidity: 3
Volatility: 1
Inflation protection: 2

Gold

In spite of the romantic or aesthetic appeal of gold, there is not much room for it in your IRA or Keogh. For starters, the law prevents you from investing IRA money in any precious metal except gold or silver coins issued by the U.S. government. Then there is gold's volatility. The precious stuff rose from $175 an ounce in 1975 to an all-time high of $850 an ounce in January 1980, then fell back to the $300 to $450 level. That doesn't say much for gold's ability to preserve your principal. IRA and Keogh investors can have what some call the golden hedge by investing in the common stocks of companies that mine gold and other precious metals. You can buy shares in individual firms or in mutual funds that invest in them. Over a recent 10 years, the two best-performing gold funds were International Investors in New York City (800-221-2220), with an 8.5 percent sales charge, and Franklin Gold in San Mateo, California (800-632-2350), with a 7.25 percent load. Both usually invest heavily in South African mines, adding a political risk to the hazard of high volatility.

RATINGS OF GOLD-MINING STOCK

Probable return: widely variable
Preservation of principal: 1
Liquidity: 5
Volatility: 5
Inflation protection: 5

Treasury Notes

The customary minimum investment on these two- to 10-year government obligations is $1,000.

RATINGS OF TREASURY NOTES

Probable return on a five-year note: 6 to 11 percent
Preservation of principal: 5
Liquidity: 5
Volatility: 2
Inflation protection: 2

Treasury Bonds

With their 10- to 30-year maturities, Treasury bonds have the advantages and drawbacks that go along with a long life span. The minimum investment is $1,000.

RATINGS OF TREASURY BONDS

Probable return on a 20-year bond: 7 to 11 percent
Preservation of principal: 5
Liquidity: 5
Volatility: 2
Inflation protection: 1

Government Agency Issues

A whole family of non-Treasury U.S. government agency obligations is backed by a federal assurance that your principal will be repaid. Brokerages sell Treasury-backed real estate mortgage investment conduits (REMICs) for as little as $1,000. Mutual funds and unit trusts that invest in government agencies can also be bought for $1,000.

RATINGS OF GOVERNMENT AGENCY ISSUES

Probable return on a 20-year REMIC: 8.5 to 11.5 percent
Preservation of principal: 5
Liquidity: 5
Volatility: 2
Inflation protection: 2

Money-Market Accounts

Money-market funds, operated by brokerages and mutual-fund companies, and money-market deposit accounts, available at banks, credit unions, and savings and loans, pay yields that generally run three to five percentage points above the inflation rate.

RATINGS OF MONEY-MARKET ACCOUNTS

Probable return: 6.25 to 10.5 percent
Preservation of principal: 5
Liquidity: 5
Volatility: 1
Inflation protection: 3

Maximum Capital-Gains Mutual Funds

Maximum capital-gains funds try for high performance by investing in small, rapidly growing companies. They often go up faster in bull markets than such widely watched financial barometers as Standard & Poor's 500-stock index or the Dow Jones industrial average and fall harder when the market turns down.

RATINGS OF MAXIMUM CAPITAL-GAINS FUNDS

Probable return: 15 to 16 percent
Preservation of principal: 2

Liquidity: 5
Volatility: 4
Inflation protection: 4

Long-Term Growth Funds

The difference between maximum capital-gains funds and growth funds is often a matter of fine degree. The managers of long-term growth funds also seek capital appreciation, but they tend to put more emphasis on protecting shareholders' investments in weak markets.

RATINGS OF LONG-TERM GROWTH FUNDS

Probable return: 12 to 15 percent
Preservation of principal: 3
Liquidity: 5
Volatility: 3
Inflation protection: 4

Growth and Income Funds

The managers of these funds usually look for large, mature companies that pay high dividends but have the potential to provide investors with capital gains as well.

RATINGS OF GROWTH AND INCOME FUNDS

Probable return: 11 to 12 percent
Preservation of principal: 3
Liquidity: 5
Volatility: 3
Inflation protection: 4

Income Funds

These funds have high current income as their overriding objective. At any particular time, an income fund can be entirely invested in high-yielding stocks or in bonds or a mix of the two.

RATINGS OF INCOME FUNDS

Probable return: 9 to 12 percent
Preservation of principal: 3
Liquidity: 5
Volatility: 2
Inflation protection: 3

Balanced Funds

These funds divide their holdings between stocks and bonds according to set ratios, usually keeping 20 to 50 percent of their assets in interest-bearing securities. Most emphasize high income, but a few have growth and income, or growth alone, as a goal.

RATINGS OF BALANCED FUNDS

Probable return: 9 to 12 percent
Preservation of principal: 3
Liquidity: 5
Volatility: 2
Inflation protection: 3

Specialty Funds

Some specialty funds, those called sector funds, concentrate on stocks in such industries as health care or energy. Others focus on firms in the Far East or in Sunbelt areas of the United States. A few select securities not only on their financial merits but also according to perceptions of the issuer's social conscience. Many specialty funds move up and down faster than the market as a whole because they concentrate on a single type of stock.

RATINGS OF SPECIALTY FUNDS

Probable return: depends on type of fund
Preservation of principal: 1 to 4
Liquidity: 5
Volatility: 3 to 5
Inflation protection: 3 to 5

Real Estate Limited Partnerships

IRA and Keogh investors should limit their consideration to two types of income-oriented limited partnerships (see Chapter 39). The first is the more conservative choice: an insured first-mortgage loan partnership. In such deals, the general partners use investor capital to buy federally insured mortgages, thus providing almost certain preservation of your principal. If the mortgages are so-called participating loans, your guaranteed return can be augmented by rising rental income and gains on the sale of properties. That could boost your total return by an additional three or four percentage points.

The second type of partnership worth considering is one that buys such properties as office buildings, apartment projects, and shopping centers. Since mortgage-interest deductions would be wasted in a tax-deferred retirement plan, the sponsors pay cash for your real estate.

Choose only public partnerships, which are registered with the Securities and Exchange Commission and come with a prospectus. Consider only experienced general partners who manage their own properties and have consistently delivered average annual returns of 9 to 12 percent in past partnerships. Make sure the deal is structured fairly. All-cash partnerships should have front-end fees no greater than 15 percent of your original investment. Management fees shouldn't exceed 5 percent of annual rental income for residential properties, 6 percent for commercial buildings. Investors should be guaranteed a minimum cumulative 8 percent return each year before the general partner gets a share.

RATINGS OF REAL ESTATE PARTNERSHIPS

Probable return: 8 to 14 percent
Preservation of principal: 4
Liquidity: 1
Volatility: 2
Inflation protection: 5

Real Estate Investment Trusts

Because REITs are public companies that trade shares on a stock exchange or over the counter (see Chapter 39), they have a liquidity advantage over most types of real estate investments. By law REITs must pay out 95 percent of their income from rents or mortgages as dividends to shareholders. When properties held by the REIT are sold, gains are passed on to stockholders as special dividends or additional earnings per share. For IRAs and Keoghs look for REITs with a dividend-reinvestment program.

RATINGS OF REITS

Probable return: 8 to 14 percent
Preservation of principal: 4
Liquidity: 4
Volatility: 3
Inflation protection: 5

S&P's 500 Stocks

Investing in stocks can be a superb way to build your retirement fund. It is also a great way to diversify your retirement holdings, because stocks or shares of the mutual funds that invest in them are a crucial element in almost all well-balanced portfolios. The companies that make up the broad Standard & Poor's 500-stock index mirror the overall market. They are widely held shares of established companies in businesses ranging from financial services to heavy manufacturing.

Within the group are stocks to meet differing investment objectives. Stocks with high-dividend yields, such as utilities, would be appropriate for conservative investors who value current income over growth and who would feel uncomfortable merely waiting for a stock to appreciate. Blue-chip stocks such as IBM and General Electric suit a middle-of-the-road approach. They may not be the price-gain leaders in a bull market, and their dividends aren't the highest available, but they offer an appealing combination of current income and potential growth.

RATINGS OF S&P'S 500 STOCKS

Probable return: 11 to 12 percent
Preservation of principal: 3
Liquidity: 5
Volatility: 3
Inflation protection: 4

Emerging Growth Stocks

These are shares of companies that are expanding faster than the economy, often because they are pioneering new technologies or marketing attractive services (see Chapter 33). They are prized primarily for their potential for greater profitability, although they may have only meager current earnings per share and their dividends are small or nonexistent.

RATINGS OF EMERGING GROWTH STOCKS

Probable return: 15 to 16 percent
Preservation of principal: 2
Liquidity: 5
Volatility: 4
Inflation protection: 4

42

FINDING A STOCKBROKER TO YOUR TASTE

Most people maintain a businesslike attitude toward their lawyers or accountants, but mention stockbrokers and they become passionate. Their broker is a genius who has doubled the value of their portfolio, or he is a bum who collects commissions even as their losses mount. Sometimes in the space of just a few years, a broker can be first revered, then reviled by the same investor.

Whether he seeks out stocks for you or not, whether his advice makes money for you or not, your broker earns a commission every time you buy or sell. Accordingly, frequent trades are in his best financial interest although they may not be in yours. Recognizing that inherent conflict of interest is the beginning of a realistic brokerage relationship.

Basically, you can choose from four categories of brokerage firms: (1) the so-called national wirehouses such as Merrill Lynch, Paine Webber, Prudential-Bache, and Shearson Lehman Brothers, with networks of branches across the country; (2) regional firms such as A. G. Edwards & Sons in St. Louis, Piper Jaffray & Hopwood in Minneapolis, and Interstate Securities in Charlotte, North Carolina, which have offices throughout their areas; (3) small firms that have just one office in one city; (4) discounters — some nationwide, some local — that provide no research or advice but execute trades at reduced commissions. Increasingly, banks and thrift institutions also are offering discount brokerage services.

Discount brokers probably are not the best choice for neophytes, who need help and advice from a broker at least until they gain experience. Furthermore, small investors get little advantage from using discounters. Although commissions may be as much as 75 percent below regular brokerage rates on large trades, there is little or no saving on trades below $1,500 because of the minimums that discounters charge. Indeed, regular rates may be lower. For example, buying 10 shares of a $15 stock would cost you $15 in commissions at Dean Witter, compared with $20 to $40 at most discounters.

Full-Service Brokers

The big national firms offer the broadest range of services. Their analysts follow in detail from 300 to 1,200 companies. They can sell you certificates of deposit, limited partnerships, mutual funds, unit trusts, and annuities, as well as stocks and bonds. And you can invest your IRA or Keogh account with them in any of those securities. The disadvantage of the big firms is that you are likely to be treated more bureaucratically than at smaller brokerages.

Regional firms offer most of the services you can get from the wirehouses aside from their armies of analysts. The traditional strength of regionals has been in spotting little-known local companies that have gone on to be great winners. Clients who buy in before national analysts start recommending such stocks can profit handsomely. But regional firms are not necessarily more hospitable to small investors than the big national firms are.

Some, but not all, of the very small firms offer personalized service to small investors. Though these firms have tiny research budgets, they may be outstanding in one special area, such as small-company growth stocks. The Directory of Exceptional Stockbrokers ($19.95 from the Hirsch Organization, 6 Deer Trail, Old Tappan, New Jersey 07675), compiled in 1982, includes many people in small firms. At all brokerages, your account is protected up to $500,000 by the federally sponsored Securities Investor Protection Corporation (SIPC). Still, if you are considering a little-known firm, check its reputation with your banker, the Better Business Bureau, or your state securities agency. In the event a brokerage should fail, your assets could be tied up for months while SIPC sorts out the situation.

Even more important than the size of the firm is the broker who will handle your account. You will be relying on him to put your interest, if not ahead of his own, at least on a par with it. Because the world of the stock market sometimes calls for swift, difficult decisions, you need a broker who is unflappable, well informed, and experienced.

To conduct a successful search, most beginners have to give up their initial fantasies of what a broker will do. You can't expect him (or her:

women are beginning to make their mark here) to be a paragon of stock-picking sagacity who somehow will magically pluck one or two superperforming stocks from the more than 6,000 traded over the counter or on the New York and American exchanges. If a broker could do that, he wouldn't have to work. To be sure, there are brokers with proven records, but only a few have demonstrated a talent for making big gains for their clients over the long term. Those who have done so spend most of their time helping wealthy individuals whose accounts generate big commissions.

A smaller investor — and to most brokers any account under $50,000 is small — has little chance of becoming the client of a top performer. You might have an entrée to one if a wealthy relative or friend recommends you. Even then you cannot expect too much of the broker's time and attention. You shouldn't expect him to do your homework for you or to come up with the perfect investment for your particular situation on the basis of a short conversation. A young broker just starting out may be able to give you plenty of attention but obviously cannot offer much experience.

Instead of looking for someone who will tell you what to do, search for a broker who can use his knowledge and experience to help you make your own decisions. Assume that your broker will be only one of your sources of information. To make intelligent investment decisions, you must read financial publications and perhaps subscribe to an advisory service. Get samplings of research reports from branch offices of your broker-candidate's firm, not necessarily for investment advice but to learn the factors that analysts use to evaluate stocks. Whatever you do, don't rely on such reports for hot tips. Most of the news in them will be in the hands of the large institutional clients of the firm well before you see it, and they will already have acted on it.

Before making your choice, decide what and how you will trade. If you don't want to take too much risk, consider a broker who specializes in blue-chip investments. If you seek stocks with low price/earnings ratios, you need a broker willing to give you a computer-screened list of such stocks every month or so. You *don't* want a broker who calls you constantly. If you want to speculate, find a broker who will keep you informed of new issues and who will be available to help you make quick decisions. No broker is expert in all strategies or all the securities his firm sells. "If you find a broker who supposedly knows about every type of investment, run in the other direction as rapidly as you can," says George L. Ball, chairman of Prudential-Bache.

When you have your specifications clearly in mind, ask for recommendations from people whom you know to be successful in the market. But quiz your acquaintances closely and follow up only if their suggestions suit your needs. Some of the unhappiest investors are those who signed on with a friend's broker after a vague endorsement.

If referrals don't produce enough candidates, start a broader search. Leslie J. Silverstone, a Dean Witter branch manager in Washington, D.C., suggests writing a letter setting forth your financial circumstances and investment goals and sending it to the branch managers of several brokerage firms listed in the Yellow Pages. If you call or go to the office instead of writing, you will probably just be assigned to whichever customers' representative has been designated the "broker of the day."

When replies come in, arrange interviews with each prospect. Here are some crucial questions to ask:

How long have you been a broker?

Where do you get your information? From personal research? From the firm's analysts? Someone who combines the two deserves preference.

In what areas have you had your greatest success? Stocks? Options? Convertibles?

What is your biggest weakness? Candor counts.

Do you recommend a selling price at the time you suggest buying a stock? Not enough brokers do.

A conscientious broker will ask questions of you, too, to make sure he has a full picture of your finances. Almost any broker can point to big gains won for clients in bull markets. But as the highly successful contrarian investor Humphrey B. Neill counseled: "Don't confuse a bull market with brains." You want your broker to be able to spot signals warning of a market decline and to know what advice to give when sell-offs seem imminent.

As for that inherent conflict of interest — the fact that a broker profits from your trading whether you make money or not: if your broker pressures you more than you like, speak up. Weigh his commissions against your gains. If an order has not been executed, raise an objection immediately. Send it to the branch manager if you are not satisfied with your broker's response. If you are still dissatisfied, complain by letter directly to the head of the brokerage firm. If he fails to resolve the problem, you can take your grievance to arbitration or sue.

Even if you have no complaints, the time may come to seek out a second broker who is a specialist, assuming your firm cannot provide one. Or you might decide to change brokers altogether. If your representative keeps calling you with purported insider tips that you have told him you don't want, start looking for a new broker. Or if an annual review shows that your portfolio has done appreciably worse than the Standard & Poor's 500, that is reason to consider a switch. Editor Yale Hirsch of the Directory of Exceptional Brokers warns: "To find your handsome prince, you may have to kiss a lot of frogs."

Discount Brokers

Once you are confident of your own decisions and find yourself regularly making large trades, you might want to use a discount broker. Discounting, that honorable Main Street tradition, is finding itself very much at home on Wall Street. Since 1975, when stockbrokers were freed to set their own commission rates, discounters' numbers have grown to more than 125 independent firms plus an estimated 3,000 offices associated with banks.

Hefty commission savings are what brought active stock traders to the discounters. By defecting from the Merrill Lynches and Dean Witters and taking your patronage to a price cutter, you can often save 50 percent or more on trades of at least $8,000. And the appeal of discounters goes well beyond thrift. Many of them now offer IRAs, Keogh plans, mutual funds, and those one-stop, all-purpose financial smorgasbords, asset management accounts.

Still, discounters are limited in the kinds of business they handle. They seldom participate in the marketing of new issues, and most do not offer limited partnerships. If the availability of those investments is important to you, don't close your account with a traditional broker.

So seductive are the savings offered by discounters that you might find yourself changing your investment behavior to take advantage of them. You might also get smarter about the stock market. That doesn't mean you have to go it alone. The commission dollars you save with a discounter in just a few trades will pay for a subscription to an independent advisory newsletter. To choose among advisory services, consult their performance records, which are compiled and compared in the *Hulbert Financial Digest* (643 South Carolina Avenue, SE, Washington, D.C. 20003; $5 a copy).

Picking the right discounter gets a bit more complex. It is paramount to select a company that will still be around the next time the bears take over Wall Street, so that you don't risk having your account tied up by bankruptcy proceedings. If a firm has survived at least one long-term down market, you are probably safe.

The pursuit of the perfect discount broker is further complicated by the appearance of banks and insurance companies on the brokerage scene. The safe-haven reputation of banks alleviates some of the mistrust that many investors have of stockbrokers. Also appealing is the convenience of being able to transfer money automatically in or out of your checking or savings account.

But commission rates, not institutional affiliations, probably will be your chief consideration. Alas, gallons of midnight oil are required to illuminate the shadowy subject of how a discounter calculates his commissions. Figure 17 throws light on the rate structure. Generally, rates vary with the kind of trading you do. In the book *Seventy Percent Off! The Investor's Guide to Discount Brokerage Houses* (Facts on File, $24.95) author Mark Coler, president of Discount Brokerage Advisory Services, a consulting firm in New York City, separates discounters and their commission structures into two camps, which he calls value brokers and share brokers.

Value brokers figure their commissions as a percentage of the dollar value of each transaction. Their rate structure usually works out best for investors who deal in low-priced stocks or comparatively small numbers of shares. Rates don't stand still for long. But in 1984, for example, you would have paid an $81 commission on 200 shares bought at $40 a share through C. D. Anderson, a share broker in San Francisco. You would have paid only $41 at Brown & Company, a value broker in Boston.

In trades above $10,000 or so, dollar value loses its importance as a discount shopper's yardstick. Enter the share broker, who sweetens his discount the most when large numbers of shares are traded. This type of discounter works to the advantage of investors trading in lots of 500 shares or more and those dealing in high-priced shares. In 1984, you could have bought 300 shares of a $75 stock — a $22,500 transaction — for as little as $25 in commissions through a share broker. A value broker might have charged as much as $115.

Once you find a broker with a suitable commission scale, check out any additional services the firm may offer. For roughly the same cost, you might as well use a discounter that gives you the flexibility, for instance, to buy stock on margin.

A discounter, like a full-service broker, should pay you interest on cash in your account and give you stock quotes. When you phone in an order to buy or sell during market hours, at least two discount houses, Charles Schwab & Company and Rose & Company, will execute it immediately. Before you hang up, you will learn the price you paid or received — data you don't normally get as fast from regular brokers.

Figure 17. Finding the Lowest Fees for Your Trades

As this 1984 sampling shows, some discount brokers tend to base their commission schedules on the number of shares traded, while others peg theirs more to the dollar value of a transaction. The firms whose rates are compared are licensed to do business in most states, have Securities Investor Protection Corporation insurance of $500,000 per account, and allow margin and stock-option trading. At the time of our survey, many offered specialized services that set them apart. Most have only a handful of offices, but all provide nationwide toll-free phone numbers. The length of time a firm has been in business is one measure of its stability. If it was founded before 1982, the next bear market will not be its first.

Firm	*Basis of rate structure*	*Minimum fee per trade*	*Shares: 100 Share price: $20*	*Shares: 200 Share price: $40*	*Shares: 200 Share price: $75*	*Shares: 500 Share price: $50*	*Shares: 1,000 Share price: $30*
C.D. Anderson San Francisco 800-822-2222 Founded 1974	Number of shares traded	$40	$42	$81	$90	$132	$147
Marquette De Bary New York City 800-221-3305 Founded 1962	Total dollar value of trade	20	31	66	81	146	180
Brown & Company Boston 800-225-6707 Founded 1960	Dollar value and number of shares	25 plus 4¢ or more a share	30	41	41	65	95
Calvert Securities Bethesda, Maryland 800-368-2750 Founded 1976	Dollar value and number of shares	30	38	84	95	125	120

Kennedy Cabot Beverly Hills 800-252-0090 Founded 1960	Number of shares traded	20	30	76	93	187	95
Quick & Reilly New York City 800-221-5220 Founded 1974	Dollar value and number of shares	35	35	53	97	163	120
Rose & Company Chicago 800-621-3700 Founded 1972	Dollar value and number of shares	20 plus 5¢ a share	25	50	50	120	145
Charles Schwab & Company San Francisco 800-648-5300 Founded 1971	Total dollar value of trade	18	42	81	90	132	147
Whitehall Securities New York City 800-223-5023 Founded 1982	Number of shares traded	50	50	50	50	62	125
Typical full-service broker	Total dollar value of trade	Nominal	54	150	184	371	461

Investors usually prefer dealing with the same person each time they phone in a transaction. Many discounters offer you the choice of dealing with one representative or a team. A few offer full-fledged asset management accounts. Some of these services may be less important to you than others; choose a firm that fits you snugly.

On-Line Brokers

Shortly after David Francis of Novato, California, hooked his brokerage account to his personal computer, he ordered 200 shares of Security Pacific on margin at $48.75 per share. A few months later, with the price at $51.75, Security Pacific, a bank holding company, reported lower than expected earnings. Fearing the stock would tumble, Francis sat down at his PC and transmitted a stop-loss order to his broker, C. D. Anderson in San Francisco, to sell at $50.75. Anderson executed the trade when the stock fell the next day.

Francis gained only $76 after commissions and margin interest, but he had the consolation of watching Security Pacific fall to $41. "I had been investing for 30 years, but I had never put in a stop-loss order before I started trading on my computer," he said. "I always felt that brokers didn't want to be bothered. They told me that they would let me know if a stock started to sink. Well, they never did."

Computerized investing holds other charms for Francis. As a sixth-grade schoolteacher, he used to worry about finding time between classes to call his broker. Now he can send orders to Anderson after brokerage hours. Record keeping is not a chore anymore either, because his computer does all the work. With a few keystrokes, Francis can summon to the screen a list of his holdings and their current values. Whenever he sells a stock, the computer automatically displays his long- and short-term gain or loss. Low commissions are an added bonus.

Investing by computer — going on-line as it's called — is thus far the exclusive turf of discount brokers. One discounter, Spear Securities of Los Angeles, was created specifically for computerized stock trading. Another, Security Pacific Brokers, by coincidence is a subsidiary of the bank holding company that Francis bought and sold.

In 1986, barely past the dawn of on-line investing, there were at least seven services to choose from, according to your trading habits, your need for computerized record keeping, and the kind of financial information you want. To sign on you need, of course, a personal computer. Most popular makes will do, as long as they can run communications software that allows them to talk to the broker's computer. You also will have to buy a modem, which connects your computer to the telephone line. With an on-line account, you talk to a human only if something goes awry. To make paper copies of your portfolio status reports and financial facts from the broker's data base, you need a printer.

You might think that most on-line investors are fabulously wealthy and can spend their days watching the markets move. Not so, say brokers. Their wired-up clients tend to be too busy with their own professions during the day to call a broker, let alone monitor the market. They transmit 50 to 70 percent of their trading orders during evenings and weekends. Leonard Schwarz, vice president of marketing for Trade Plus, a company in Palo Alto, California, that developed on-line brokerage systems for Anderson and Fidelity, says, ''When we first offered our service through Anderson, orders came in at midnight on Saturday and I figured that people were showing off at cocktail parties. But Saturday night remains a busy trading time.''

By 1986 all but one of the on-line brokers immediately executed orders placed during market hours. The exception, Max Ule, the discount division of Ingham Becker & Company in New York City, accepted orders via personal computer only for execution the next business day. Immediate trades usually take two to five minutes, which is no improvement over phoning a broker. Under the rules of the Securities and Exchange Commission, electronic orders cannot be transmitted to the trading floor until they have been reviewed by your broker. If he has any question about an order, he phones you or sends a message to your computer before putting through the order. For example, a broker might want to know why an investor who never bought anything but blue chips in 100-share lots suddenly wants 5,000 shares of a highly speculative start-up company. Until the broker is sure that the order was sent correctly, he may delay executing it. Ordinarily, though, a confirmation soon appears on the investor's computer screen and another is sent by mail.

Brokers are working to hasten on-line order execution. A system called Fidelity Investors Express at Fidelity Investments, based in Boston, can tap information on each client's trading habits and his qualifications to buy and sell different types of securities. This makes it possible to meet SEC requirements yet execute trades instantly.

If you intend to trade during the day, you will want to know the price at which a security last traded. On-line brokers generally feed you prices that are 15 or 20 minutes old. To get current quotations from most of them costs a considerable sum — as much as $76.25 a month for all publicly traded stocks and options. However, Fidelity's system provides ''real time'' quotations from Dow Jones News Retrieval for $19.95 a month. Another on-line broker, Unified Management of Indianapolis, provides almost as fast a service at 8 cents per quote. When an investor asks his computer for a current price, a broker reads the request, gets the price from his Quotron machine, and electronically relays it to the client. Some other brokers alert investors before executing an order if the two prices differed significantly.

Trading is the meat of on-line brokerage, but record keeping and research round out the meal. The most complete record-keeping systems revolve around asset management accounts. If you open such an account with Unified Management in Indianapolis (800-862-7283), your computer will keep you apprised of your investments in Unified's family of no-load mutual funds. You can also view a list of the checks you have written on its money-market fund. If you code the checks, the program will sort them by type of expense: medical, charitable, and so on. You can even ask your computer once or twice a month whether you are breaking your budget. At the end of the year, you can print out a statement that categorizes your expenses and speeds the itemization of tax deductions.

On-line research reports can turn your computer into a one-stop investment center. What you get depends on which database comes with the service. One called CompuServe features information from Value Line and Standard & Poor's as well as news from the Associated Press. Some brokers offer similar data from the Source and their own databases.

Once you have figured out which on-line services you can use, compare costs. Most sponsors levy an initial fee and hourly rates for the time you accumulate on-line. Like telephone rates, hourly charges are highest during business hours. If you trade frequently, give equal weight to brokerage commissions.

V

LIVING WITH THE INCOME TAX

Before she went underground, Bunny was the kind of girl you would have wanted your son to marry: a music teacher at a college in New Jersey, a member of her church choir, a model citizen. But after she lost her job, she took to ripping off the government. On April 15, she failed to report to the Internal Revenue Service $7,000 that she had earned the previous year singing solos at her church, performing in a chorus at Carnegie Hall, and giving voice lessons at a private school. Bunny admitted to occasional twinges of remorse. "It's a shame I have to resort to all this subterfuge to make a living," she said.

By official and unofficial estimates, 20 million or more Americans make part or all of their income from the underground economy — a bustling and shadowy world where jobs, services, and business transactions are paid for in cash to avoid scrutiny by tax collectors. Subterranean commerce, once mainly the domain of prostitutes, pimps, drug dealers, loan sharks, and other criminals, now teems with otherwise law-abiding people who feel that they have been stung by high taxes. They fight back by using a variety of dodges to hide income from the IRS. They skim cash from their businesses, pad their expense accounts, barter their skills, or simply de-

mand payment in greenbacks instead of checks. The losses to the federal Treasury exceed $80 billion a year, according to an IRS reckoning made several years ago.

Advocates of tax reform foolishly hope that lowering rates, closing loopholes, and flattening the income brackets that determine everybody's rates will cause most members of the underground economy to surface and pay their taxes. But cheating the IRS has become the Great American Parlor Game. The very word "reform" makes tax-sensitive people bristle. The only action deserving of the word, they insist, would be to stop the government from taking money out of their paychecks.

Whether you condone it or despise it or do a little of both, the federal income tax manipulates your financial behavior now almost as much as it did before tax reform. It nudges you to own your home because the mortgage interest and property taxes are deductible. When you have paid off some of your mortgage, tax advantages are there again, egging you to use your equity as collateral for consumer loans, again because the interest is deductible. Meanwhile, tax considerations dictate to your boss which fringe benefits to pay you and which to avoid (the ones he can't claim as deductible business expenses). Whether to marry or live in sin has tax implications (sin is less taxing), as does whether to pay your ex-spouse alimony. The tax code whispers "give more" when the collection plate is passed in church. It screams "raise" when it is your bet in poker because gambling losses are deductible from gains. It meddles in your decision about when to schedule surgery and whether to incorporate your small business. In scores of other ways it stitches itself into the fabric of your life.

Besides being intrusive, the income tax keeps changing. How closely it will resemble the system described in this section of *The* Money *Book of Money* when you read it, nobody in the White House or the Capitol or the Treasury can possibly say. But unless you join the underground, you will be

paying your portion to the IRS every payday — or every three months if your tax is not withheld — for the rest of your life. You might as well pay the least you legitimately can. The next five chapters should aid you in that mission.

43

LEARNING THE CODE

Understanding the federal income tax laws is not a task to be left to accountants and lawyers. You can learn the rules of the game — complex and off-putting though they are — and then alter your borrowing, saving, and investment habits to take advantage of available deductions, credits, exemptions, exclusions, and other tax preferences. Figure 18, at the end of this chapter, takes you through the steps of estimating your next tax bill. But first, whether you do your own income tax or hire a tax preparer, you need to know how the income tax works.

Filing Status

This is the first question you are asked by Form 1040 in all its manifestations. When you file your return, you must choose one of five types of status: single, married filing jointly, married filing separately, head of household, or qualifying widow or widower with dependent child. The taxes you owe will be determined, in part, by the category you come under.

Married couples filing a joint return usually owe less tax than filers with the same income who come under a different status. On a taxable income of $32,000, for example, the tax owed for 1988 will be $5,093 if you are a married couple filing jointly, $5,853 if you file as a head of household, and $6,640 if you are single. Widows and widowers have to file as either single or married and filing jointly; it depends on when their spouse died. You can claim head-of-household status if you are single, widowed, or divorced and you pay more than 50 percent of the cost of keeping a residence for someone you claim as a dependent; that person can be your child, grandchild, parent, or some other close relative. Some married couples file separate returns because each wants to be responsible only for his or her own tax. But they pay the same tax as they would by filing jointly.

Gross Income

All your income that would be subject to taxes before you subtracted any deductions, adjustments, or exemptions is called gross income. It includes wages, salary, tips, interest, dividends, alimony, taxable pensions, rents, royalties, and most other money you earn by working or investing. Earnings that are not part of your gross income include interest on tax-exempt bonds and other nontaxable investments; certain death benefits; awards or insurance settlements you receive for personal injuries; claims paid by your health insurance company; tax-free gifts; and scholarships awarded to students working toward a degree and earmarked for tuition, course fees, books, supplies, and other educational materials. In more detail:

Capital gains. Understanding the rules affecting capital gains is extremely important to your money management. If you sell a capital asset — an investment in property such as stocks, corporate bonds, or real estate — for more than it cost you, the profit is taxable.

Capital losses. Assets you sell at a loss can be deducted from your capital gains. If you have more losses than gains in one year, you can deduct the net loss from your other income. But you cannot claim more than $3,000 of net loss in any one year. Instead, you must postpone taking deductions for the excess loss until future years.

In short, you cannot treat gains or losses as isolated events for tax purposes. You must offset the one against the other. And if you end up too big a loser, your deductible loss will be rationed out over more fortunate later years. Starting in 1988, the tax code makes no distinction between long-term gains or losses (most recently defined as those realized on assets owned more than six months) and short-term gains or losses. In 1987 the only distinction drawn is that long-term gains won't be taxed more than 28 percent, while other income may be taxed as much as 38.5 percent.

Adjusted Gross Income

After tallying your gross income, you can reduce it if you qualify for special kinds of deductions. The result is called your adjusted gross income (AGI). Deductions from gross income sometimes are especially valuable because AGI serves as a basis for other deductions. You cannot claim miscellaneous deductions unless they exceed 2 percent of your AGI or medical deductions unless they exceed 7.5 percent of it. Thus the smaller your AGI, the better your chance of getting those deductions. Here are the main adjustments to gross income.

Individual Retirement Accounts. Anyone who works for pay but is not covered by a pension plan can deduct contributions to an IRA up to the full limit of $2,000 a year. Married couples with two incomes can deduct up to $4,000, and couples with one paid spouse can deduct up to $2,250. If your income is not too high, you can deduct IRA contributions even though you are in a pension plan. Married people with a combined adjusted gross income no higher than $40,000 can deduct their full contributions, and so can single people earning $25,000 or less. Marrieds making between $40,000 and $50,000 and singles making $25,000 to $35,000 lose $200 of their IRA deduction for each $1,000 of additional income.

Keogh plans. If you are self-employed you can deduct contributions to a Keogh plan. The maximum contribution here is $30,000 or 20 percent of your net self-employment income, whichever is less.

Alimony. Alimony or spousal support that you pay is deductible from gross income, but child-support payments are not.

Limited partnership losses. Investors who bought shares in limited partnerships before the 1986 tax bill was signed into law can deduct 65 percent of the tax write-offs generated by a partnership in 1987, 40 percent of write-offs in 1988, 20 percent in 1989, 10 percent in 1990, and nothing after that. However, these "passive losses," as they are now designated, can be used to offset "passive income" from other limited partnerships.

Itemized Deductions

When you prepare your tax return, you can take the standard deduction, or you can deduct the larger amount that some people can claim by itemizing their deductible expenses on schedule A. For 1987 incomes, the standard deduction is $3,800 for married couples filing jointly. It is $2,570 for heads of households. And it is $1,900 for single filers and married people filing separate returns. Starting in 1988, the standard deduction rises to $5,000 for joint filers, $4,400 for heads of households, $3,000 for singles, and $2,500 for married people filing separately.

If you are at least 65 years old in 1987, you are entitled to the 1988 standard deduction applicable to your filing status. Furthermore, blind taxpayers of any age and 65-year-olds who are married get an additional $600 standard deduction. When a husband and wife are both at least 65, their extra deduction is $1,200. The added deduction for singles at that age is $750. Finally, anyone who is blind and past 65 gets both special deductions. Starting in 1989, all standard deductions rise annually with the consumer price index.

Medical and dental expenses. As mentioned earlier, you can deduct medical costs in excess of 7.5 percent of your adjusted gross income. Don't forget to include prescription drugs and insulin, as well as transportation costs to and from doctors' offices, hospitals, therapeutic centers, and other medical treatment facilities. Over-the-counter medicines, however, are not deductible, nor are expenses that were reimbursed by insurance or your employer.

State and local taxes. These include state and local income taxes and property taxes but not general sales taxes, which lost their deductible status in 1987.

Interest. You can deduct interest on mortgages financing the purchase of your primary residence and a second home. Interest on other loans using your house as collateral — second mortgages or home-equity loans — can also be written off, provided the amount of these loans is no greater than the price you paid for the property, plus the cost of any improvements. Interest on amounts in excess of that limit are fully deductible only if you use the borrowed money to pay for home improvements or educational or medical expenses.

Interest on larger second mortgages used to raise money for other purposes is subject to phaseout limitations that apply to all other consumer credit. The phaseout reduces your deductions on credit-card finance charges, car loans, student loans, and all other personal debts on the following schedule: you can deduct 65 percent of the consumer interest incurred in 1987, 40 percent in 1988, 20 percent in 1989, and 10 percent in 1990. The deduction ends after that.

If you borrow on margin from a broker or use credit from other sources to finance investments, the finance charges are deductible only to the extent of your total investment income — interest, dividends, and capital gains. You cannot write off interest on loans used to buy tax-exempt securities or interest on loans backed by securities if you use the money to buy something other than investments or a dwelling.

Charitable contributions. People who take the standard deduction cannot write off any part of their charitable contributions. For itemizers, gifts to religious, scientific, literary, and education groups qualify for this deduction, as do donations to nonprofit schools and hospitals. You also can itemize and deduct the value of clothing, household goods, books, magazine subscriptions, and other property that you donate. If you do volunteer work for a charity, you can deduct travel costs to meetings, fund raisers and such, at the rate of 12 cents a mile, plus parking fees and tolls. You cannot deduct the value of your work, gifts to individuals, or the price of raffle, bingo, or lottery tickets.

Charitable gifts of appreciated property in such forms as securities and real estate relieve you of any capital-gains tax you would have owed after selling those assets. The tax code also rewards you with deductions equal to the appraised value of the gifts. However, collector's items are deductible only if they are of use to the recipient: paintings given to a museum, religious artifacts to a church. You can claim, in any one year, donations of capital-gain property, as it is called, worth up to 30 percent of your adjusted gross income.

Casualty and theft losses. A deductible loss is one resulting from a sudden, unexpected, or unusual event. Robberies and property damage from hurricanes, floods, storms, and car wrecks generally qualify. But your loss has to be rather devastating and poorly insured if it is to produce a tax deduction. You cannot claim insured losses at all, and uncompensated losses are deductible only to the extent that they exceed 10 percent of your adjusted gross income plus $100.

Miscellaneous deductions. With a few exceptions, these items are deductible only to the extent that they exceed 2 percent of your adjusted gross income. First the main exceptions, to which the 2 percent floor does not apply:

• Moving expenses. You can deduct the full unreimbursed cost of moving your household to a new job location. To qualify for the deduction, your new workplace must be at least 35 miles farther from your old home than your former workplace was. You must work at least 39 weeks (78 weeks if you are self-employed) at the new location to deduct moving expenses.

• Employee business expenses. You can deduct in full business expenses that arise because you are physically handicapped.

Other miscellaneous deductions that can save you taxes — if they exceed the 2 percent limit — include unreimbursed expenses such as a car or personal computer if more than half of your use of it is for work; union and professional dues; employment agency fees; job uniforms; subscriptions to professional journals and trade publications; safe-deposit-box rentals; investment counseling and management fees; tax preparers' fees; the cost of income tax guides and professional advice on tax planning; and the cost of tuition and books if your employer requires you to take a course at your own expense or you attend a class to maintain or improve your job skills. However, in adding up your unreimbursed costs, you can include only 80 percent of the tab for business meals and entertainment, out-of-town trips, transportation between two job sites, and education-related travel.

Exemptions

Personal exemptions are close cousins of itemized deductions. On 1987 tax returns, an exemption is worth $1,900; in 1988, $1,950; and in 1989, $2,000. Starting in 1990, the $2,000 personal exemption will be adjusted for inflation.

You can claim exemptions for yourself, your spouse, and all children and other close relatives who qualify as your dependents. The IRS includes in its definition of dependent children those who live with their parents and are under 19 years old, those older than 19 with an annual income of less than $1,000, and full-time students regardless of income. Even married children can be claimed as dependents if they don't make enough money to file their own tax returns. Stepchildren, adopted children, foster children, and grandchildren who live with you all year can qualify. You can claim an exemption for a child or parent who didn't live with you during the year if you can prove you furnished more than half of his or her total support. In divorced families, the parent with whom the children live is ordinarily entitled to claim the dependency exemptions.

Beginning in 1988, however, people earning very high incomes lose at least part of their exemptions. The phaseout starts for married couples filing jointly when their taxable income reaches $149,250. This is done by raising their tax rate from 28 to 33 percent. Every $10,920 of additional taxable income in 1988 wipes out one exemption. And beginning in 1989, every extra $11,200 costs an exemption.

Taxable Income and Your Bracket

You find your taxable income by subtracting your deductions and exemptions from your adjusted gross income. Having pounded down the final figure as much as is legally possible with deductions and exemptions, you now turn to the tax-rate schedules in the Treasury Department instruction booklet to start tallying the total damage. Welcome to the land of the tax bracket. Before passage in 1986 of a simplified tax, brackets started at 11 percent and climbed in 13 or 14 steps to 50 percent. For 1987, the number of brackets is reduced to five, ranging from 11 to 38.5 percent. For 1988 and later, just two brackets remain, 15 percent and 28 percent, but a 5 percent surcharge on higher incomes creates a 33 percent bracket for a range of high incomes.

By no means all of your income is likely to be taxed at your top, or marginal, bracket rate. Some and perhaps most falls in the 15 percent bracket. If you earn enough, however, you will pay a flat tax of 28 percent on all your taxable income. For example, a couple with two children reach the 28 percent flat rate when their taxable income in 1988 reaches $192,930. Adjustments for inflation in later years almost certainly will boost that threshold.

The vast majority of people, though, pay the IRS a much smaller percentage of their taxable income than their marginal rate suggests. This effective rate, as it is called, is easy enough to figure out. You just divide the tax you owe by your taxable income. Take a couple with $40,000 of taxable income in 1988. They would owe a tax of $7,333. Divided by $40,000, that represents an effective rate of 18.3 percent — nothing to laugh about but well below the 28 percent top bracket.

It is important to know your marginal tax rate when making investment decisions. The closer you get to the 28 percent tax bracket or the surcharged 33 percent level, the more attention you should give to tax-saving investments such as municipal bonds. The couple with the taxable income of $40,000 wouldn't be pushed into the 33 percent bracket until their taxable income topped $71,900. But a single taxpayer would get there at $43,140.

Until 1987, anyone whose income had risen sharply from year to year could average his past four or five years of taxable income and perhaps reduce his obligation to the IRS. In lowering the top bracket, however, and adopting a three-bracket schedule, Congress killed that kind of income averaging.

Tax Credits

The most appealing type of write-off, tax credits are subtracted directly from your tax bill. While people in the 28 percent bracket save 28 cents on each dollar of deductions, they can slash $1 off their tax for each $1 of credits. Here are four kinds of tax credits that you might be able to claim.

Credit for child- and dependent-care expenses. To get this credit as a parent, you must be working for pay, looking for a job, or attending school full time, and your child or children must be under 15 years old. Married couples generally must file jointly to claim child-care costs. The credit is figured as a percentage of the first $2,400 of your expenses for one child or other dependent and the first $4,800 for two or more children.

The credit works on a sliding scale, from 30 percent of the allowable expense if your adjusted income is below $10,000, to 20 percent if it exceeds $28,000. So, for example, if your adjusted gross income is $30,000 and you paid $2,000 for child care, you can claim a credit of $400 — 20 percent of $2,000. The largest credit possible is $960.

Credit for the elderly and the permanently and totally disabled. If you are over 65 and have a low income, or if you are totally and permanently disabled, you may be able to claim this tax credit. The maximum credit is $750 for single taxpayers and $1,125 for couples.

Rehabilitation tax credit. If you plan to restore a business property that was built before 1936, you might be eligible to claim a tax credit of 10 percent of the rehabilitation costs. The IRS grants this rehabilitation tax credit only if you put more than $5,000 into the building over two consecutive years or will spend as much as the building is worth. The credit rises to 20 percent of rehabilitation costs if the U.S. Department of the Interior declares the building a certified historic structure.

Low-income housing credit. Investors who put money into the construction or rehabilitation of rental housing for the poor may be able to claim annual tax credits equal to 9 percent of their costs over the next 10 years. To give you a tax credit, the project must be under stringent rent controls, and a specified percentage of housing units must be occupied by tenants whose income is far below the median income for that area.

The Bottom Line

By the time a taxpayer with a robust income and an active investment life has reached the last line of his tax preparation, he will have compiled a stack of special forms high enough to warm the spirits of the stoniest CPA. But the end is nigh. Now you have only to subtract what you can from the tax amount you figured by using the rate schedule. First take away the withholdings and estimated payments the government already has collected from you. Then deduct any credits you were lucky or smart enough to have earned. The remainder is the tax you still owe, the bottom line — maybe.

The Alternative Minimum Tax

If the taxable income on your regular return has been sharply reduced by certain tax-sheltered investments and limited-partnership write-offs, you have to refigure your tax and perhaps pay a higher amount under a special formula known as the alternative minimum tax (AMT). In enacting this tax, Congress took aim at people who capitalized so heavily on loopholes — preferences, in the jargon of code writers — that they paid little or no income tax.

The AMT at first missed its mark. In 1983, for instance, about 30,000 taxpayers with incomes above $250,000 a year paid less than 5 percent of it in taxes; 25,000 paid only 5 to 10 percent. So the 1986 tax act clamps down even harder on tax preferences. For example, it requires you to refigure your tax if you claimed deductions for the appreciated value of artwork or other assets that you gave to charity. It makes you add back into your AMT calculations the interest you earned on tax-exempt municipal bonds issued after August 7, 1986, to finance private housing, student loans, industrial developments, and other nongovernmental activities. It counts as income the difference between what a corporate executive paid for his company's stock, which he bought by exercising an incentive stock option, and what the stock was worth on the market at that time — even though he has not sold the stock.

While putting items like these back into your income, the AMT denies you deductions for state and local taxes, miscellaneous itemized expenses, residential mortgage interest on loans larger than the price you paid for your house and its improvements, and medical expenses below 10 percent of your adjusted gross income. Furthermore, people with high incomes — $150,000 on joint returns, $125,000 on single returns, and $75,000 on returns of married people filing separately — lose 25 cents worth of their exemptions for every extra dollar of income. Thus it takes $8,000 of earnings above those levels to wipe out a $2,000 exemption.

The AMT is a flat 21 percent of the income to which such deductions and exclusions have been restored, after that income has been reduced by one large deduction — $20,000 if you are married and filing separately, $30,000 if you file singly, $40,000 if you file jointly. If 21 percent of the new total is more than your standard-form tax, including any credits, you have to pay the higher amount. Better luck next year: your unused credits carry over to then — or later if your sheltered income is too high again.

Figure 18. Projecting Your Next Tax Bill

People who would never think of glancing at their Form 1040 before mid-April may be better off estimating their next tax bill in advance. Such a projection could alert you to the tax consequences of an investment decision before you act. Or if something occurs to alter your financial situation — say an extraordinary medical expense or a bracket-busting bonus — a projection will tell you whether to expect a big refund or a big balance due. You might then reduce your withholdings accordingly — or start saving money to pay the IRS.

You can employ this worksheet to get a notion of what your tax liability will be in 1987, 1988, or later, using estimated income and deductions. For further instructions, see the accompanying text.

Regular Tax Computation

Estimated Income

1. Wages, salaries, tips, etc.	$______
2. Interest income	______
3. Dividends	______
4. Alimony received	______
5. Net business income or (loss)	______
6. Net capital gain or (loss up to $3,000)	______
7. Pension, annuity, IRA distributions	______
8. Scholarships, prizes, and grants (excluding tuition, fees, books, and equipment for study leading to a degree)	
9. Rents and royalties minus expenses	______
10. Net income from partnerships or rental property	______
11. Income from estates and trusts	______
12. Total income (add lines 1 through 11; where a number is negative, subtract it)	______

Adjustments

13. Keogh contributions	$______
14. Alimony paid	______
15. Net passive losses from limited partnerships (reduce by 35% for 1987, 60% for 1988, 80% for 1989, 90% for 1990, 100% after that)	______
16. Deductible IRA contributions	______
17. Adjusted gross income (subtract lines 13–16 from line 12)	______

Itemized Deductions

18. Medical expenses that exceed 7.5 percent of line 17 $________

19. State and local income and property taxes ________

20. Mortgage and investment interest ________

21. Other deductible interest expenses ________

22. Charitable contributions ________

23. Casualty and theft losses (to the extent that they exceed 10% of line 17 minus $100) ________

24. Miscellaneous deductions (fully deductible items plus others to the extent that they exceed 2 percent of line 17) ________

25. Total itemized deductions (add lines 18 through 24) ________

26. Standard deduction (starting in 1988, $5,000 if filing jointly, $4,400 if head of household, $3,000 if filing singly, $2,500 if married and filing separately; see text for 1987 standard deductions and extra deductions for the blind and those over 65 years old) ________

27. Enter the larger figure from line 25 or 26 ________

28. Exemptions ($1,900 per person in 1987, $1,950 in 1988, $2,000 in 1989, $2,000 plus inflation adjustments starting in 1990) ________

29. Total deductions and exemptions (add lines 27 and 28) ________

30. Taxable income (subtract line 29 from line 17) ________

31. Tax on amount on line 30 (from the 1987 or 1988 rate schedule on page 359) ________

For 1987 only: fill out the next four lines if you entered a capital gain on line 6 and your taxable income on line 30 exceeds $27,000 if you are single, $38,000 if you are a head of household, or $45,000 if you are married and filing jointly.

32. Special capital-gains tax for 1987 (multiply line 6 by .28) ________

33. Taxable income minus capital gain (subtract line 6 from line 30) ________

34. Tax on amount on line 33 (from the 1987 rate schedule) ________

35. 1987 tax before credits (add lines 32 and 34) ________

Credits

36. Investment tax credit (check with the sponsor of any limited partnership interest you acquired before October 22, 1986) $________

37. Child-care credit ________

38. Credit for the elderly and the permanently and totally disabled ____________
39. Rehabilitation tax credit ____________
40. Low-income housing credit ____________
41. Total credits (add lines 36 through 40) ____________
42. Your tax (line 31 or 35 minus line 41) ____________

TAX SCHEDULES FOR 1987, 1988, AND THEREAFTER

	If your taxable income on line 30 or 33 exceeds:	*You will pay:*	*Plus this percent of your taxable income that exceeds the amount in the first column:*
Singles			
1987	$0	$0	11.0%
	1,800	198	15.0
	16,800	2,448	28.0
	27,000	5,304	35.0
	54,000	14,754	38.5
1988 and thereafter	$0	$0	15.0%
	17,850	2,678	28.0
	43,140	9,759	33.0
	102,430 (102,480 after 1988)	28,681	28.0
Married Couples Filing Jointly			
1987	$0	$0	11.0%
	3,000	330	15.0
	28,000	4,080	28.0
	45,000	8,840	35.0
	90,000	24,590	38.5
1988 and thereafter	$0	$0	15.0
	29,750	4,463	28.0
	71,900	16,265	33.0
1988 only:	192,930	56,205	28.0[1]
1989 only:	193,490	56,389	28.0[2]
1990 and thereafter:	195,332	56,998	28.0[3]
Heads of Households			
1987	$0	$0	11.0%
	2,500	275	15.0
	23,000	3,350	28.0
	38,000	7,550	35.0
	80,000	22,250	38.5

	If your taxable income on line 30 or 33 exceeds:	You will pay:	Plus this percent of your taxable income that exceeds the amount in the first column:
1988 and thereafter	$0	$0	15.0%
	23,900	3,585	28.0
	61,650	14,155	33.0
1988 only:	145,630	41,868	28.0[4]
1989 only:	146,190	42,053	28.0[5]
1990 and thereafter:	148,032	42,661	28.0[6]

[1] Includes two exemptions. Add $10,920 to column 1 and $3,604 to column 2 for each additional exemption.
[2] Includes two exemptions. Add $11,200 to column 1 and $3,696 to column 2 for each additional exemption.
[3] Includes two exemptions. Add $12,121 to column 1 and $4,000 to column 2 for each additional exemption.
[4] Includes two exemptions. Add $10,920 to column 1 and $3,604 to column 2 for each additional exemption.
[5] Includes two exemptions. Add $11,200 to column 1 and $3,696 to column 2 for each additional exemption.
[6] Includes two exemptions. Add $12,121 to column 1 and $4,000 to column 2 for each additional exemption.

Alternative Minimum Tax Computation

1. Adjusted gross income (from line 17 on the regular tax worksheet on page 357) ________
2. Difference between market value and cost to you of any incentive stock options exercised ________
3. The following tax-shelter items:
   a. excess of accelerated over straight-line depreciation on real estate and leased equipment ________
   b. percentage depletion allowances on oil and gas wells ________
   c. intangible drilling costs ________
   d. mining exploration and development costs ________
   e. research and development costs ________
4. Tax-exempt interest on municipal bonds issued for private purposes ________
5. Value of appreciated property donated to charity ________
6. Exemptions equal to 25 cents for each dollar over $150,000 of joint adjusted gross income, $112,000 of single income, or $75,000 of income of married person filing separately
7. Total income subject to AMT before deductions and exclusion (add lines 1 through 6) ________
8. Medical deductions on line 18 that exceed 10 percent of adjusted gross income on line 17 ________

9. Interest deductions on lines 20 and 21 (excluding interest on the balance of a home equity loan in excess of the purchase price of your house plus the cost of improvements) __________
10. Charitable deductions on line 22 __________
11. Casualty and theft losses on line 23 __________
12. Exclusion ($30,000 if single, $40,000 if married and filing jointly)[1] __________
13. Total deductions and exclusion (add lines 8 through 12 above) __________
14. Income subject to AMT (line 7 minus line 13) __________
15. Alternative minimum tax (21% of line 14) __________

You have to pay the AMT if it is larger than the tax on line 42 of the regular tax form.

[1] These amounts are reduced by 25 cents for each $1 on line 7 above $150,000 for joint filers, $112,500 for singles, and $75,000 for marrieds filing separately.

44

YOUR TAX-ADVANTAGED DWELLING

Your house, condominium, or cooperative apartment can shelter you from taxes as well as from the elements. It provides you with deductions when you buy it, while you live in it, and when you sell it.

The breaks of home ownership begin even before you lasso a mortgage. If you must move because of your job, you can write off the cost of the mover except for amounts that your company reimburses (see Chapter 43). There is a $3,000 limit on deductions for other move-related expenses, such as traveling costs to find a new house.

Points you pay to a lender for a mortgage may be deducted as an interest expense on schedule A but only if lenders in your area usually charge points and they are competitive with those levied by others. Points are up-front fees; each point equals 1 percent of the amount you are about to borrow. If you pay, say, six points in a locality where two is average, only two points can be deducted. The IRS rarely demands proof of typical fees, but if points where you live are extraordinarily high, get a statement from the lender saying so. It will provide telling evidence in your defense in case the IRS audits your tax return. You cannot deduct points paid on Veterans Administration and Federal Housing Administration loans; to be deductible on other mortgages, points must be charged as a loan origination fee.

Settlement costs that are not deductible in buying a house can help reduce your tax on any capital gain when you sell it. Keep a record of such expenses as a professional house inspection, state real estate transfer taxes, county recorder's taxes paid at closing, and your attorney's fees. They can be counted as part of your original purchase price, the basis for figuring a taxable gain.

Once you own the house, the interest on your mortgage is likely to furnish your biggest annual tax saving. If you financed the purchase with a 30-year, $100,000 mortgage at 10 percent, your interest deduction in the first year would be nearly $10,000. The deductible amount declines very little during the early years of the mortgage. But if you still own the house after 25 years, you will be paying more principal than interest, so your tax break will be small. There is one other useful tax rule about interest. You cannot deduct prepaid mortgage interest, but you can claim January mortgage payments paid in December.

Property taxes, which typically equal 1.5 percent of a house's appraised value, are fully deductible each year. Condominium owners write off both the real estate taxes on their units and a proportionate share of the taxes paid on the common areas of their buildings. Owners of cooperative apartments can deduct their allocated portion of the co-op's property tax bill, unless it leases the land and building. Then there are no property taxes to deduct because the lessor pays them.

Repairs and improvements to your house usually cannot be written off. Expenses incurred to maintain a home office are fully deductible, however. What's more, you can claim as a business expense a modest amount of depreciation on the portion of your house that you use as an office. Say your house is worth $100,000 and in 1986 you started using 10 percent of the space in it for your business. Using straight-line depreciation over 27 years, you can claim annual depreciation of $10,000 divided by 27, or $370 a year. You also can deduct part of your homeowners insurance and utility bills. A snag may arise in getting the IRS to believe the office is legitimate. You have to prove that it is used regularly and exclusively for commerce. To qualify for the deduction, your home must be your primary business location or the place where you meet patients, clients, or customers.

If your house is burglarized or damaged, causing thousands of dollars worth of loss, you may be able to claim a deduction for the uninsured portion of the loss (see Chapter 43) and the cost of hiring an appraiser to assess the damage. The U.S. Tax Court has ruled that you can take this kind of deduction even if you choose not to file an insurance claim for fear that your homeowners insurance premium would rise.

Sheltering Yourself When You Sell

As one of your largest assets, your house may become a major tax liability when you sell it. The market value of most dwellings bought by Americans in the 1970s or earlier has multiplied handsomely.

In the 1980s real estate continued to appreciate, but unevenly, enriching homeowners in the Northeast, for example, while a housing recession depressed values in the Southwest. Any profit from the sale of your home is subject to taxation at your highest marginal rate as a capital gain. So 28 percent or even 33 percent of taxable appreciation may go to the U.S. Treasury and some more to your state revenue department. Perversely, though, you cannot claim a deduction if you sell the place at a loss.

When you do sell your house, you can reduce, postpone, or eliminate the capital-gains tax by several means. First of all, you can claim a deduction from your ordinary income for any penalty levied by a bank for paying off your mortgage early. Furthermore, in calculating your profit on the sale, you can adjust it downward by adding to your original purchase price the cost of all capital improvements you have made since you took possession, including additions, new bathrooms, triple-glazed windows, and the completion of unfinished rooms. Also add on the real estate agent's commission.

However, the chances are that you will be able to defer the capital-gains tax on your house permanently. IRS rules say that a homeowner may postpone paying the tax if he buys another house within two years and pays at least as much for it as he got for his old one. There is no limit to the number of times you can sell and buy again without paying tax on the accumulating gains. And if your last house is still in your possession when you die, the accrued gains will never be taxed as income.

Anyone aged 55 or older who has lived in the same house for at least three of the previous five years can exclude from the taxable gain as much as $125,000 of the profit from its sale. A married couple who own the house jointly can claim this tax break even if only one spouse meets both the age and residency tests. The exclusion is a once-in-a-lifetime break, however; conserve it if you anticipate getting a larger gain from another house sale in the future. You can take your time deciding. After you file your tax return for the year in which you sold your house, you get three years to notify the IRS that you are claiming the $125,000 exclusion.

Keep a file labeled ''House'' with your other tax records. Stuff into this file copies of the sales contracts for all homes you have bought and sold and receipts for any improvements and repairs you have made to them. Save papers that relate to casualty or theft losses. Preserving receipts and filing additional tax forms may seem a nuisance, but it will be your best defense in case of a tax audit. The resulting tax savings can more than compensate you for the bother.

45

FINDING A TAX ADVISER OR PREPARER

The only difference between a tax collector and a taxidermist, a former IRS commissioner once remarked, is that the taxidermist leaves the hide. In hopes of saving most of their skin — not to mention a month of Sundays — many taxpayers turn to professional tax preparers. The wizard they fancy, a grand master of deductions and world champion refund-getter, exists as a heroic possibility. What miracles he can perform! While you are busy earning your money — or better yet spending it — Supertaxman riffles through your receipts for overlooked deductions, pulls tax credits out of thin but perfectly legal air, shelters loads of income at a single stroke, and rolls over your money into tax-deferred accounts with the effortless grace of a master tumbler. You just breeze into his office some spring afternoon, sign the forms, and await your refund.

Loverly, no? But how do you find help like this? Or, putting aside the fantasy, where can you find someone who simply will save you the most on your taxes — safely — and cost you the least?

There are plenty of places to look; tax advice is a boom industry. Accountants, tax lawyers, financial planners, swarms of storefront seasonal workers, and, of course, your brother's wife's cousin who crunches on the IRS in his breakfast nook — all are eager to help you. Each holds out the alluring promise that he will save you more money than he charges you.

Storefront Chains

Begin by asking yourself how much help you need. If your tax profile is simple — say you are salaried, have less than $30,000 of income, maybe own a little stock and pay a mortgage — you should be able to handle the forms yourself with the help of a book. Or you can take them to one of the national storefront chains such as H&R Block or Beneficial Income Tax Service or to one of the large regional chains. Preparers who work at H&R Block — the largest of these organizations and the industry pacesetter — are not full-time employees, and many earn their living for a large part of the year at jobs unrelated to taxes. Yet most have tax experience from previous years, and all must pass a rigorous examination to assure Block of their familiarity with the main points of tax law.

Most tax professionals charge by the hour, but Block and the majority of other storefront chains set their fees according to the complexity of your taxes. The returns people present them with tend to be relatively simple and inexpensive to prepare; the average price of a Block return is only $45. Even at this price you get some salient services. If you are not satisfied with the person assigned to do your forms, you can interview Block preparers until you find one who suits you better. And if you are audited, the Block district manager will go with you to the IRS at no additional charge. But for those with more entangled finances — usually anyone earning over $30,000 a year — the $45 treatment may not do.

Accountants

Enter the tally man par excellence: the certified public accountant. No professional is, by training, better prepared to handle your taxes. Still, it is best to find a CPA who specializes in taxes rather than one who does general accounting. Because tax law is so complex and changes so often, you want someone who lives and breathes it all year. Every point that he doesn't have to go to his books to check while his meter is running will save you money.

Accountants charge $50 to $200 an hour, depending on the firm, the city, and the client. Merely having your forms filled out by a CPA probably will cost at least $300. But if your income is large enough to warrant an accountant's help, you will want more than that; you need tax planning. This requires an expert who, besides preparing your return, will provide you with strategies you can employ throughout the year. A few of the chains offer such service — Block does not — but their charges are often no lower than those of CPAs at accounting firms.

At Touche Ross, one of the Big Eight accounting firms, a typical package for a top-tax-bracket client would include estate as well as income-tax planning. The client would meet with one of the firm's partners, and his returns would be prepared by a staff accountant, checked by a manager, and finally reviewed by a partner. In addition, such a client would have four or five meetings with his own adviser during the year to work out new tax strategies. He would be called and told of any IRS ruling that might affect him. The client also gets monthly projections of his taxes for the year, along with an array of tax reports and newsletters. Such treatment generally costs more than $3,500 annually and sometimes can stray into the teens.

Four-figure fees are unthinkable for the majority of taxpayers. Yet most of the services are as necessary — in a scaled-down form — for a $50,000-a-year family as they are for a millionaire. An experienced CPA working with the resources of a small firm should be able to give you an approximation of this royal treatment for $300 to $600.

Some accountants specialize in the unique tax problems and possibilities of a particular profession. Jerry Sloane of Schwaeber & Sloane, an accounting firm in Great Neck, New York, specializes in airline pilots. Sloane's pilots can commute so cheaply over long distances that he often advises them to live in tax havens such as the Bahamas even though they are based in New York.

How do you find a specialist in your own line of work? Unfortunately, the American Institute of Certified Public Accountants discourages CPAs from advertising their specific areas of interest, so your best recourse is the grapevine. "We get our pilot business by word of mouth," says Sloane. "At 35,000 feet, after they have stopped talking about girls and where they're going to eat after they land, the next topic is always taxes."

Tax Attorneys

One type of professional who can chaperone you where even accountants fear to tread is the tax attorney. Practitioners of this specialty are great at handling tax problems related to divorce and the sale, purchase, or start-up of a business. In addition to their law degrees, most have formal training in accounting. Their fees run higher than accountants' — $200 an hour is typical. Consequently, for most people a CPA makes more sense as a primary adviser. But be sure that you choose an accountant who has a working relationship with a tax attorney for situations where legal counsel is needed.

Enrolled Agents

Tax preparers who have passed a special two-day examination administered by the IRS receive licenses as enrolled agents. The test is designed to challenge their knowledge of complicated tax regulations and accounting methods. Enrolled agents must take continuing education courses every year and must pass a license-renewal exam every three years. Like CPAs and lawyers, they can act as advocates for taxpayers before the IRS. They can also represent you in an administrative appeals process following an audit, though not in court. A commercial preparer, such as an H&R Block employee, can act as a witness at an audit but not as your legal representative.

Enrolled agents usually attract clients whose returns are complex enough to invite possible IRS audits. Examples might include people who have recently retired or divorced. There are about 30,000 enrolled agents; their fees are similar to those charged by CPAs. For a listing of the 4,500 members of the National Association of Enrolled Agents, write to the group at 5410 Grovesnor Lane, Bethesda, Maryland 20841, or phone 800-424-4339.

Evaluating Preparers

How can you judge the quality of tax help you will get from an adviser or firm you are considering? Ask what kind of clients the firm handles, to see if its members are experienced with people in your shoes. Beware of firms that operate on a pool arrangement in which your forms float from accountant to accountant, each of whom handles a few lines. Errors are less likely when one accountant is responsible for the entire return.

Listen to the questions the tax adviser asks you. If he neglects to inquire about the basics of your tax situation — do you own a home? have a Keogh plan? an IRA? — you know you have drawn a dud. Be particularly suspicious if he starts steering you into esoteric deals such as jojoba-bean partnerships without first establishing your needs. He may be trying to sell you a product rather than providing a service.

Limited partnerships, while they no longer do much to cut your taxable income, may be recommended to you by accountants or lawyers, as well as stockbrokers, as investments akin to tax-exempt bonds. Most financial planners specialize in selling partnership shares but don't have the broad tax knowledge of an accountant. All purveyors of partnerships except accountants routinely are paid commissions or fees on deals they sell you. Under the code of ethics of the American Institute of Certified Public Accountants, CPAs are forbidden to accept money from the sponsor for the sale of any investment. ''Still, some of them do,'' says William

Brennan, publisher of the prestigious monthly newsletter *Brennan Reports,* which covers tax shelters and tax planning.

The IRS is equipped with an arsenal of pain-inflicting penalties to punish those who try to deceive the tax man. Your tax adviser can be penalized along with you for aiding and abetting understatements. On the bright side, this could mean that he will go with you to the audit for free — it is his neck, too. Yet fear of penalization may also lead tax advisers to be more conservative in recommending artful deductions.

Self-Help

It pays to familiarize yourself with the rudiments of tax law so that you can participate knowingly in the preparation of your return with whomever you hire. A host of fine books stands ready to enlighten you. For those who want to understand the vagaries of the tax code, the best guide is the Research Institute of America's *Master Federal Tax Manual* (RIA, 111 Radio Circle, Mt. Kisco, New York 10549; $12.95 plus sales tax). A similar book, the *U.S. Master Tax Guide,* costs $14.50 and is published by Commerce Clearing House (4025 West Peterson Avenue, Chicago, Illinois 60646). Both of these lucid semiprofessional volumes cover basic corporate and individual tax law.

For a handy general treatment of personal income taxes, *Julian Block's Guide to Year-Round Tax Savings* (Dow Jones–Irwin; $10.95) is hard to beat. Clearly written and both wide and deep in its coverage, Block's book lends plain, authoritative wisdom to the average taxpayer. An ex-IRS investigator (no relation to H. or R. Block), the author keeps his advice safe. It won't replace an accountant, but it may help you decide whether you should replace yours. ''If you are paying someone $125 an hour to do your taxes, he should be familiar with all the points I make in my book just off the top of his head,'' Block says. ''If he isn't, find someone else.''

46

COPING WITH THE IRS: HOW TO COMPLAIN

Consider the experience of Joseph Mullaly, a Manhasset, New York, businessman. He spent about four months visiting IRS offices and making phone calls to explain a consolidation of his three small real estate and construction companies that should have cut his tax paperwork. ''I was amazed at the indifference I ran into,'' Mullaly said. ''The only thing they told me at the IRS was to hire an accountant — as if I were an idiot.'' Finally he took his complaint to his congressman, whose staff member referred it to a person in Mullaly's IRS district called a problem-resolution officer, or PRO. After that the matter was resolved so quickly and painlessly that, Mullaly says, ''it restored my faith in government.''

Considering that 180 million or so personal and business tax returns are processed each year by the IRS, it is hardly surprising that hundreds of thousands of misunderstandings and errors have to be dealt with or that many complaints get mishandled, leaving taxpayers with a taste of gall. Automated and systematized as it must be to handle the huge volume of returns, the IRS is vulnerable to the unusual. Anything that ceases to be routine, such as a garbled Social Security number or an error by a government clerk, can lead to months of frustration. Most often, a refund doesn't arrive. Other chronic problems: the refund is less than expected; instead of a refund, you get a bill for more taxes; bills keep arriving after you have paid your tax.

In the weeks and months after the tax-filing season ends, many people become embroiled in those and other controversies. If you are one of them, don't be too patient. Don't continue to hope that one more letter, with additional copies of all relevant documents, will unsnarl matters.

Unknown to most Americans, IRS guidelines say that after one attempt, you are entitled to the services of a PRO.

There were 80 of these merciful missionaries in 1986, one in each IRS district office and service center and seven at the regional level. You can get their phone numbers at any of those locations. Accountants and other tax preparers agree that a PRO can usually sweep away weeks or months of frustration and settle your problem efficiently and courteously. And if the logs are not unjammed in five working days, your PRO is supposed to advise you of the status of the matter and give you the name and phone number of someone down the line who is responsible for solving it. Meanwhile, the PRO stays on your case.

The IRS created this problem-resolution program several years ago under congressional pressure and put a Washington-based ombudsman in command of it. The man in charge in 1984, George O'Hanlon, said, "The long-range goal of any ombudsman, and my goal, is to work myself out of my job." He was in little danger of doing that. In 1983 O'Hanlon's small staff handled 312,000 cases. In 1985 the case load rose above 500,000.

The faith of many a taxpayer would be less severely tried if someone at the IRS had told him about the program. It is mentioned briefly in tax-return instruction booklets. In practice, however, Linda Martin, director of the problem-resolution staff, acknowledges, "Most individuals don't know we exist." She and her colleagues see themselves as taxpayer advocates. Their own gripe is that the people who most need help seldom complain. As Martin said, "The squeaky wheel gets greased, but what bothers me is that some people never squeak. They think the amount is too small, do not want to be bothered, or maybe are intimidated."

The way the IRS treats its overload of paperwork can be worse than intimidating. It is sometimes downright unfriendly. Alfred Yaude, a past chairman of the federal taxation committee of the National Society of Public Accountants, complains, "When we send a letter to the service, often nobody reads it."

Defending yourself in this morass may in the end require legal action. If you are at loggerheads with an IRS agent over, say, a disputed deduction, you can ask that your case be sent to the IRS appeals division. If you lose there, you have 90 days to take one of three further steps:

1. Withhold payment on a claim of less than $5,000 and take your case to the small-claims division of the Tax Court. There you can represent yourself, but if you lose you cannot appeal.
2. Pay a disputed tax of any amount and file for a refund with your IRS

office. If that is rejected, you can sue in U.S. District Court or Claims Court. But you will probably need a lawyer.

3. Sue the Commissioner of Internal Revenue in Tax Court without paying the tax in advance. Appeals from decisions in any formal court can go all the way to the Supreme Court.

To succeed in a conflict with the IRS, keep a file of all your tax records and correspondence. And do everything possible to get your case into problem resolution. Sometimes people cannot reach a PRO because phone lines are constantly busy or whoever answers is uncooperative. When that happens, it is time to call your congressman. Somebody on his staff can at least arouse the attention of balky IRS officials and get your case into the resolution system.

47

COPING WITH THE IRS: HOW TO HANDLE AN AUDIT

The notice begins, "We have selected your federal income tax return for the year shown below to examine the items listed at the end of this letter." The IRS is summoning you to an audit. If you are like most taxpayers, you will dread the prospect. Audits can be time-consuming, troublesome, and expensive. Three out of four people who go into them come out poorer. But audits also are infrequent. In 1985 only 13 nonbusiness returns and 24 corporate returns per thousand were chosen for this onerous process.

The IRS generally begins sending out audit notices in July of the year in which the returns in question are filed. The agency can audit a return up to 27 months after it was filed, but if you haven't heard from the IRS within a year and a half of the date you mailed in your forms, you probably won't be audited. All the same, protect yourself by keeping your back tax returns indefinitely and supporting tax documents for five years or so.

Whether or not your return will be audited depends mostly on how closely your data conform to a set of IRS formulas known as the Discriminate Function System, or DIF. Roughly 70 percent of returns audited are picked out by the DIF computer.

DIF compares certain deductions, credits, and exemptions with the norms for taxpayers at your level of income. Only the top IRS officials know precisely what variables are considered by DIF or how much importance each is assigned. But the IRS lets it be known that the higher your so-called total positive income — income before subtracting tax-shelter losses and other adjustments — the more likely you will be audited. That stands to reason. While public policy says all taxpayers should kick in their fair share, the IRS wants to collect the maximum revenues at the lowest cost. High-income people make greatest use of sophisticated tax breaks and thus are most likely to claim debatable write-offs. The denial of such deductions brings in more money than an equal effort would reap from challenging the write-offs of lower-income taxpayers.

The other returns audited are chosen by IRS computers and personnel for a variety of reasons. A few tax forms are pulled because they were filled out by people the IRS considers to be questionable preparers. That preparer list, too, is top secret. Other returns, called automatics, get singled out because they show deductions for nondeductible items. You might be called in for an audit, for example, if you claimed a capital loss on the sale of your personal residence. Some people get the hook merely because the returns of their business associates are under suspicion. Still others are audited because revenge-seeking or bounty-hunting ex-spouses squeal on them. In 1985 the IRS paid $853,690 to 350 people for tips that led its auditors to tax cheats. (However, more than 7,000 people that year sent in finger-pointing accusations.) Informants whose leads pay off are rewarded with 10 percent of the extra taxes collected.

A number of taxpayers fall victim to special IRS campaigns, such as the continuing vendetta against abusive tax shelters. Others are audited because the IRS has a hunch that they underreported their income. You can easily arouse suspicions at the IRS if, for example, you live in a wealthy neighborhood and report a conspicuously low income for such an address. Certain occupations make you vulnerable. Waiters, taxi drivers, beauticians, and others who get paid mostly in cash are potential audit targets. So are teachers; their returns frequently send up red flags at the IRS partly because many teachers travel abroad, and some of them unjustifiably deduct the cost of their trips. "I've seen returns of teachers who have listed their occupations as pedagogues and pedants to disguise themselves," says Mary Sprouse, a Los Angeles tax attorney who formerly ran audits in an IRS district office.

What to Do When the Notice Comes

If you get a letter saying your return will be audited, you generally have up to six weeks to get ready for a meeting. The IRS permits you to respond by mail if the deductions can be easily documented, but that is the exception.

The place to start mounting your defense is in the office of your tax preparer, who can advise you how to prove to the IRS that your write-offs are legitimate. This strategy session might cost you $100, but the investment should pay off, particularly if the meeting gives you the confidence to meet with the auditor on your own. The cost of paying your preparer to accompany you can easily run into hundreds of dollars. He will charge you his hourly rate, typically about $100, from the time he leaves his office until he returns. The audit itself might take only 45 minutes, but you would also have to pay for travel and waiting time.

On occasion, though, it is worth paying your tax preparer to be at your side during an audit. Beatrice Borscher of Baltimore couldn't persuade an auditor that in 1981 she provided enough financial support to her mother to claim her as a dependent. Two weeks later, her 1982 return was audited for the same reason. This time her son, Harvey Berger, a certified public accountant with the firm of Grant Thornton in Washington, D.C., went to the audit and more eloquently pleaded his mother's case. In 10 minutes he sustained the write-offs for both tax returns. In addition to supplying eloquence, a tax preparer can save you from blurting out information that might pique an auditor's curiosity. If you have too loose a tongue, it might even pay to send your preparer and not go along.

Whether or not you go to the audit, the most important factor in deciding the outcome will be the evidence supporting your deductions, credits, and exemptions. Receipts, bills, and diaries don't guarantee that you will salvage a write-off; the auditor still can throw out your deductions if he doesn't believe you are entitled to them. Such records, however, are the most persuasive exhibits you can lay before an examiner.

When receipts cannot be found, turn to secondary sources. For proof of a business meal, get your dining companion to give you a written statement describing the details of your get-together. A letter from your boss requiring you to own a computer could persuade an auditor that the machine was a deductible business expense. But the language should be forthright. A sentence saying "it would be desirable" for you to have a personal computer at home won't help your cause.

How to Behave at the Audit

Your attitude during the examination and the personal chemistry between you and the auditor will influence the outcome. Act belligerently and you will narrow your chances of victory. Joe Girard, author of several books on salesmanship, was an IRS audit target for 12 consecutive years. He has five audit taboos: don't speak loudly; don't smoke; don't wear tinted glasses, which make you look shifty; don't show up with dirty nails or hair; and don't wear jewelry that might cause the auditor to think your income is higher than you reported.

You will win favor by letting the auditor lead the discussion. Don't expect the two of you to become chummy, but if you do get along, he or she (most auditors who see taxpayers in IRS offices are women) might pass over an iffy deduction or suggest write-offs you missed. Curtis Mathis, general manager of a billboard company in Chicago, lost audit bouts for 1980 and 1981, when he spent much time on the road as a salesman for the firm. But his 1982 audit was handled by the same woman who examined his return the previous year. This time Mathis wowed her by pulling out an appointment book in which he had methodically recorded the expenses of driving his car on the job — a diary she had advised him to start the year before. The auditor was so pleased that she pointed out how he could claim an extra $1,312 in deductions from rental property he owned. The net result was a $190 refund.

Many, though not all, audit issues are negotiable. Randy Bruce Blaustein, author of *How to Do Business with the IRS: Taxpayer's Edition* (Prentice-Hall, $8.95), recommends asking your tax preparer before the audit how much of each write-off under review he thinks you will be able to keep. Then you will know which battles to fight and which to concede. Perhaps your disputed deductions arise from a trip that was part personal and part business. The preparer might say that in other audits he has attended, the examiners accepted about 65 percent of the cost of meals on the road as business expenses.

If you are not satisfied with the outcome of your audit, you can appeal on the spot to the examiner's supervisor. That official will review the case and come to his own conclusion. If you are still not pleased, you have 30 days to ask that your case be turned over to an appeals officer. You can telephone for an appointment unless the IRS says you owe $2,500 or more. In disputes over larger sums, you must make your request in writing, briefly outlining your arguments.

It can take several months to get a date with an appeals officer. Once you sit down with him, however, you might find him more willing to concede issues than your auditor was. In determining how much more tax, if any, you should pay, appeals officers, unlike auditors, are authorized to weigh the cost of waging a court battle with you. In 1983, appeals officers settled for an average of 41 cents on the dollar. But they are no patsies. Having come up through the ranks of IRS auditors, agents, or tax-law specialists, they may see through a ploy that a less experienced examiner would have missed. Appeals officers can also reopen issues closed by auditors and question deductions that weren't discussed in the first go-around. So appeal only if you are sure your case is as airtight as a mason jar.

When your audit is resolved, put together a folder containing all your IRS correspondence. This dossier could be especially helpful if you are an audit winner. You might have to step into the ring with the IRS again. If so, you can bring no better evidence that a deduction is legit than a letter from an auditor allowing the write-off on an earlier return.

Superaudits

Once every three years, 50,000 individual taxpayers are summoned at random for a superaudit of their previous year's returns under the Taxpayer Compliance Measurement Program, the IRS's main tool for keeping everybody honest. The purpose of the TCMP is to produce profiles of typical returns at various income levels. An audit by any other name would be far sweeter.

While conventional audits usually focus on a few items, TCMPs always require line-by-line scrutiny and complete documentation. They are time-consuming, arduous, and inflexible. Indeed, the pain of a TCMP usually is in the process, not the outcome. It is true that taxpayers whose returns deviate significantly from the norms generated by the TCMP model are then singled out for conventional audits. But half of those who go through a superaudit wind up owing no additional tax, and in recent years 7 or 8 percent actually got refunds.

The real cost can be calculated in time spent. It is not unusual for a superauditee to put in hundreds of hours searching for hard proof of exemptions and deductions — children's birth certificates, marriage licenses, $25 restaurant chits, receipts for magazine subscriptions, and insurance policies. Add to that the days or even weeks of face-to-face confrontations with the IRS agent. Once the IRS fingers you, it is free to examine your personal and business returns from several years past if an official suspects something fishy. A San Francisco businessman summoned to a superaudit in 1980 recalled: "I experienced fear, anger, betrayal, and, finally, acceptance — all the things that Dr. Elisabeth Kübler-Ross [the author and psychiatrist] identified with dying."

Even those who keep complete records may be surprised at the extent to which the IRS will nitpick in a TCMP audit. Al Hill, a San Diego mechanical engineer, spent three evenings putting every relevant receipt in a loose-leaf notebook whose pages corresponded to each line of his 1979 tax return. But even though Hill's binder contained the canceled check that proved he had paid the insurance policy premium for a rental property, the agent was not satisfied. He wanted to see the policy as well.

If you have the bad luck to be tagged for a superaudit, the first thing to do is examine your return and your records for potential trouble spots. Richard Weatherington, a tax consultant in Willow Springs, Missouri, advises calling credit-card companies right away to get copies of the misplaced receipts that you will need. You can get photocopies of canceled checks from your bank, which keeps them on microfilm. Unless you have substantiation for an expense, you probably will wind up paying more tax. If you have exaggerated expenses for an otherwise legitimate deduction, you may be able to make your transgression seem one of sloppiness rather than felonious intent. But the parent who claimed five dependents while having only two will have no case for absentmindedness. He may face a heavy penalty, though rarely a criminal one.

Taxpayers have the same rights in a TCMP audit as in a regular one. You can ask for a delay and request that the audit be done at your office or home. If you would rather the agent did not see your fancy digs, request a meeting at the IRS office. You can have an accountant or other professional represent you. Alas, the fee can range from hundreds to thousands of dollars, depending on how well organized your records are and how much time is involved.

Whether you need representation hinges on the complexity of your return and on your personality. Because the probe is so painstaking, it is easy to become frustrated with a persistent IRS agent. Your accountant can be a buffer. He can also buy you time. According to Thomas L. Dunn, a CPA and partner in the New York City office of Ernst & Whinney, "Your representative can plead ignorance in a clinch, giving both of you time to explain a disallowed deduction."

VI

THE NEW WORLD OF BANKING AND BORROWING

A bank used to be the place you went for a checking account, a savings account, or a loan. A brokerage house was where you went for stocks and bonds. As for department stores and food markets, their only financial services were charge accounts and check cashing. But in the brave new world of deregulation, bankers are trading stocks through brokerage affiliates, brokers are making loans, some retailers are doing both, and so many newcomers are crowding the financial services field that it's tough to tell the players apart. One thing is clear. Nearly every institution in the contest wants it all—to be your one-stop financial emporium, where you can go for everything from meat-and-potatoes checking accounts to epicurean-style investing.

Perhaps the single most potent symbol of the financial supermarket is the Cash Management Account pioneered by Merrill Lynch. The CMA and its clones at other brokerages, as well as at banks and mutual funds, let you write checks, issue you a national-brand credit card or debit card (a piece of plastic that immediately taps your brokerage account for payment), let you borrow against your investments, and automatically stow your investment income in a money-market fund.

Financial institutions keep grafting strange new fruit to their branches. At Goldome, a savings and loan group based in Buffalo, New York, you can buy real estate and several kinds of insurance. E. F. Hutton owns a bank in Delaware that is accessible to its brokerage customers across the country. Fidelity Investments, a big mutual-fund company in Boston, offers discount brokerage, checking accounts, and debit cards. Supermarket shoppers — the traditional kind — can buy insurance at Kroger's and use their credit cards to get cash from bank-owned automated teller machines (ATMs) at Safeway stores in California and Publix stores in Florida. Sears, Roebuck will sell you a house, a mortgage, a credit card, insurance, stocks, bonds, and mutual funds.

Is your bank still the best place for your checking account? Should you shop for a mortgage or a car loan there? Is it preferable to a brokerage firm for trading stocks? For many people the question is not which one bank to use but how many or whether to use a bank at all. This section is a guide to getting the most out of the new world of banking and borrowing. It also tells you how to groom your credit rating or, at worst, how to escape from the miasma of debt.

48

DO YOU STILL NEED YOUR BANK?

Given the *richesse* of financial services now available from nonbanks, does it still make sense to do business with a bank? The question has two maddeningly indefinitive answers: maybe and maybe not.

The all-purpose brokerage house tool, which Merrill Lynch calls a Cash Management Account and which is generically labeled an asset management account, dramatizes the banking alternatives. This package of financial services typically includes an account for trading stocks and receiving dividends, an account for buying stocks on margin, one or more money-market funds, a checking account, a debit or credit card, and a consolidated monthly statement of all activity. Some banks and mutual-fund groups duplicate those services and add their own extras. For example, plans such as Fidelity's USA account let you code checks for tax purposes in categories such as business travel and medical expenses.

Some sponsors of asset management accounts, especially brokerage firms, send two or three statements monthly in a head-scratching format. One of the most lucid statements comes with the Unisave account from Unified Management Corporation, a mutual-fund group in Indianapolis (800-862-7283). Along with check coding and other standard features, its statement separates out your brokerage commissions, gives a percentage breakdown of your stock holdings by type and industry, notes the latest price/earnings ratio of each stock, and even warns you when you have exceeded your average monthly outlay for a category of budgetary expenses.

Now that banks have been deregulated, some of them are offering their own asset management accounts. In New York City, for instance, Citibank's Focus account entitles holders to discount brokerage service, a checking account, several borrowing arrangements (including a line of credit), a debit card, and a card for Citibank's cash machines. However, most banks that introduced such accounts in the 1980s found them unprofitable and discontinued them, according to Robert Ladner, a market researcher with Behavioral Science Research Corporation in Coral Gables, Florida.

Do you really need any kind of asset management account? Probably you do. At some institutions you can open one by depositing as little as $5,000 in cash or securities ($1,000 at Unisave). Yearly fees, ranging from $50 to $150, could total less than the separate fees you currently pay for a checking account, credit cards, traveler's checks, and other services. And the convenience is unquestionable. "For people who own a number of stocks and bonds, there's no more dealing with shoeboxes full of itty-bitty pieces of paper," Ladner says. "Asset management accounts also eliminate the delay between receiving your securities-related checks and depositing them in the bank, so you earn money from the day a dividend is distributed or a stock is sold."

As to who offers the best asset management accounts, that depends largely on what you need. If you expect to borrow, a brokerage version may be the right choice; using your securities as collateral, you usually can get a loan for only one or two percentage points more than the prime rate — the rate banks charge their most creditworthy corporate customers. If you are trading stocks and feel you don't need a broker's advice, you will fare best with a discount brokerage account, either directly with the firm or through an affiliated bank or mutual fund.

Equipped with a broker's version of the asset management account, you could reduce your relationship with a bank. But cutting the ties completely would probably be unwise. The borrowing power of your brokerage asset management account is limited to half the value of your stocks, which probably would not be enough to finance a house, for instance. Moreover, a nearby bank branch is still the easiest place for most people to make deposits and cash checks.

Once you decide you still need a bank — and so far even most asset management account holders seem to think they do — give some thought to whether your present bank still wants you. If you have been standing in ever-longer teller lines or gaping in disbelief as checking-account fees double and redouble, the bank might be trying to tell you something: leave! For decades banks lost money on small accounts, but tradition dictated that one person be treated much like the next. Increasingly, however, the bankers are reserving the welcome mat for customers with incomes of $40,000 or more — sometimes much more — and hoping the masses will huddle on someone else's doorstep.

At Houston's Med Center Bank, for instance, customers with $100,000 or more in their accounts can charter the bank's six-passenger plane and crew for just the cost of the fuel. The bank will also order flowers, reserve theater tickets, and provide limos for big customers, many of whom are doctors. When checking-account balances drop below $1,000, the bank charges $12.50 a month, and it returns bounced checks with a Texas-size price tag of $30. Med Center Bank boasts that by targeting the upscale market and pricing services out of the reach of everyone else, it drove away half of its customers in a single year.

The so-called emerging affluent are the bull's-eye of another big marketing push. Mainly two-income couples of baby-boom vintage earning over $50,000, they are heavy consumers of financial services because of their enthusiasm for credit cards and their need for mortgages and life insurance as they start families. Banks eager to do business with Mr. and Mrs. Upscale are repackaging services and rejiggering fees. This so-called relationship banking consists mainly of asset management accounts, but at some banks you will face a far bolder proposition: the more business you bring, the better you will be treated. If your money-market account or Super-NOW balance exceeds $5,000 or so, you may earn a fraction of a point more interest than depositors with smaller balances. Citibank, for one, also lets customers with balances in excess of $25,000 use special, shorter teller lines. Keeping a pile of money at the same bank probably won't entitle you to a discount on a credit-card fee or a mortgage, but according to Robert L. Stevens, president of Bryn Mawr Trust in Pennsylvania, your interest rate might well be reduced on any kind of installment loan. Relationship banking does cost you something, however. If you use different banks, each for the most cost-efficient service it provides, you will be sure you are getting the best deals available.

Where should you bank if you are neither affluent nor demonstrably on your way to wealth? Income doesn't matter at credit unions because their charters prohibit them from creating classes of members. Although they cannot provide trust services or commercial loans, most credit unions offer the financial staples. And since they are not-for-profit organizations owned by their members, they generally charge less for services than banks do.

For many of the newer financial services, the question of whether to get them from a bank or some other source is often meaningless in itself. Consider the case of debit cards, on which purchases are deducted directly from an account balance rather than billed at the end of the month. Apart from possible differences in annual fees, one institution's debit card is much the same as another's.

The same standoff applies to automated teller machines. It used to make sense to choose a bank because it had ATMs all over town, and the two nationwide coalitions of banks, Cirrus and Plus, enabled customers of one bank to get cash from machines at other institutions. But Visa, MasterCard, and American Express are spinning their own cross-country ATM webs. As ATM networks spread, you will also have less need for traveler's checks, so don't be wooed to a bank — or to a broker's asset management account — solely on the promise of this decreasingly valuable benefit.

Announcements of the death of banks — put forth earnestly by the nonbank competition — are clearly premature. Pleads one banker, "Bear with us while we're under construction. Banking laws have changed so quickly that we need a little time to catch up." Some bank analysts say that once the construction is finished, the array of financial services available at most banks will be as resplendent and competitively priced as the comparable services of nonbanks.

During the catch-up period, you may want to stay with a bank simply because you trust it and feel comfortable there. As handy and economical as a broker's asset management account may be, dealing with a service rep at an 800 number will never give you the personal touches often available at a neighborhood bank — the willingness to cash out-of-town checks, the quick loan from a banker who knows you. As bank consultant Edward E. Furash says, "A decent relationship with a bank that understands your whole financial picture may be worth more than trying to get the last inch out of every dollar."

If you are unhappy with your bank — perhaps because it hasn't changed enough or has begun focusing on a group to which you don't belong — the aggressive competition in financial services leaves you with more options than ever before. You can assign your bank a large or small role in your financial affairs, but dismissing it altogether might be a mistake unless your borrowing and check-cashing needs are amply covered elsewhere.

49

HOW TO SAVE ON CHECKING

In recent years, only 4 percent of all banks and savings and loan associations have let you write as many checks as you would like each month for free; the other 96 percent levied monthly or per-check fees or both when your balance dipped below a stipulated minimum. Some charged you for checking, no matter what. Because service charges differ from bank to nearby bank in this highly competitive industry, it pays to shop and compare. If you lived in Washington, D.C., in 1986, for example, and wanted to open a NOW account, you would have needed to make an initial deposit of $2,000 at United National Bank of Washington. The account would have earned you a minimal 5.25 percent interest. Let your balance slip below $500, however, and you would have got no interest at all. And let it drop below $2,000 for just one day and you would have paid a $5 monthly fee plus 25 cents for each check you wrote. At Home Federal Savings & Loan, also in Washington, you could have opened the same kind of account with a $250 deposit and earned 5.5 percent interest. You would have paid a $5 fee only if your balance fell below that amount.

Over the course of a year, the quarters and dollars can add up. After surveying 73 banks and 69 S&Ls in April 1985, the Consumer Federation of America reported that a hypothetical customer with $300 to $500 in a NOW account (then subject to a 5.25 percent federal interest ceiling) would earn up to $11 or pay as much as $172 a year, depending on the bank. Clearly, it pays to understand the different kinds of checking accounts available in banks, credit unions, mutual funds, and asset management accounts.

Capitalize on two general rules when you shop for low-cost checking: S&Ls offer better deals than banks, and old-fashioned non-interest-bearing accounts are cheaper to maintain than bank NOW accounts. Traditional bank accounts and S&L NOWs let you have free checking with lower balances than bank NOW accounts permit: on average, it is $537 for S&Ls, $836 for non-interest-bearing accounts, and $1,800 for NOWs.

Those figures hold true only in banks that define monthly minimum balance as your average daily balance for the month. Some banks define it as your lowest balance for the month. When you are gathering information from different banking institutions, be sure to ask how minimum balances are calculated. At a few institutions, you risk double jeopardy. At last report, for example, Crocker National Bank in San Francisco slapped a $3.50 monthly fee plus 20 cents a check on accounts that fell below a $500 daily minimum or $1,000 monthly average balance. You should also find out how the bank determines applicable balances. New York City's Citibank tacked fees on regular NOW accounts when balances sank below $5,000, but that balance was calculated by adding up all of a customer's deposits, including CDs and IRAs.

You also need to know what it costs to slip under the minimum. Monthly fees range from $1 to $10, while per-check charges go from 15 to 50 cents. At many banks with graduated fee scales, the lower your balance falls, the higher the fees you will pay. When you bounce a check, banks add inflation to indignity: the cost varies from $5 to $30 and averages $13. Yet the Bank Administration Institute, an industry-sponsored organization, has found that the average total cost to a bank for processing a returned check is just $1.

Lest you believe that only deadbeats need worry about bouncing checks, heed this: your chances of writing a bad check increase with the length of time it takes a bank to credit deposits to your account. A survey done in 1985 by the U.S. Public Interest Research Group, covering 669 banks and S&Ls, revealed that more than half waited three to five business days before crediting their customers' accounts for deposits in the form of checks drawn on accounts at local banks. Three-quarters of the institutions waited more than a week to clear out-of-state checks, and 20 percent dawdled for more than two weeks. If you are unaware of such lags and depend on an uncleared check in your account to pay for a check that you have written, your own check will sometimes be rejected for insufficient funds.

The banking practice of withholding funds on deposited checks is hardly universal. For example, only one in five credit unions routinely delays crediting checks to members' accounts. In 1987 Congress was working hard on legislation to set limits on how long bankers can delay making money from checks available to customers who deposit them.

No-Frills Checking

If you don't want to keep enough cash in your checking account to escape fees, look for a bank that will give you a no-frills account. You pay a flat monthly fee no matter what your balance, but you may be restricted in the number of checks you can write per month and the number of deposits and withdrawals you can make at the teller's window. The idea is to encourage you to use an automated teller machine, to which you get unlimited access. Self-service checking account customers at Bank of America, for example, pay a $2 monthly fee and have no restrictions on the size of their balance or the number of checks they can write. But if they visit a human instead of a machine to make even one transaction, their monthly fee jumps to $5.

Another bit of austerity in this Bank of America account is the disappearance of canceled checks. You don't get them back with your monthly statement, and so you must rely on your check stubs or register as your record of whom you paid and how much. Within banking circles, this is called ''truncation,'' but for marketing purposes it gets a more up-beat label: ''safe-keeping.'' And indeed, all is not lost. The bank keeps microfilm copies of your checks for at least seven years. If you need evidence of payment of a disputed bill or tax deduction, the bank will send you free photocopies. But requests for more than two or three copies a month may cost you as much as $5 per check. At Valley National Bank in Phoenix, a pioneer of truncation, 70 percent of new customers choose it.

If you are under 19 or over 55, you may be able to find a bank that will waive your checking account fees. About a third of all banks and S&Ls offer free NOW accounts to both senior citizens and minors. Two-thirds of all banks have free non-interest-bearing checking accounts for seniors; 10 percent collect no fees from minors.

Credit unions can be a low-cost alternative to banks. Among those that let you write checks — called share drafts — 75 percent provide the service free. Most of the others waive fees if customers maintain an average monthly balance of $300. Additionally, credit unions generally pay 6 percent annual interest, which is a bit more than most banks pay. But now that banks are no longer protected by a federal ceiling on checking account interest rates, the comparison may change. Credit unions, however, have two major drawbacks. First of all, most of the 18,000 or so such institutions in the United States are open only to people who are associated with companies or community groups that sponsor the activity. Second, fewer than a third of credit unions offer share drafts.

Brokerage House Accounts

Asset management accounts that combine brokerage, checking, and credit services can also be used for checking in lieu of a bank, but their appeal is limited. You can write as many free checks as you like for any amount up to your available balance, but it usually takes $5,000 to $25,000 in cash and securities just to open an asset management account. Additionally, most sponsors assess annual management fees ranging from $25 to $100. When you consider these fees and the high initial deposits, you will probably conclude that setting up an account for the primary purpose of writing checks makes about as much sense as buying a microwave oven just to soften ice cream.

Money-market mutual funds are a third alternative to banks and S&Ls, but they have a serious flaw: most of the funds set a $250 or $500 minimum on each check you write, so you would end up buying a $1.50 money order every time you needed to pay a $23.98 telephone bill. Worse yet, mutual-fund managers are slower than bankers when it comes to letting you tap deposits. In most cases, they hold a deposit for two weeks before you can make a withdrawal.

50

SHOPPING FOR LOANS

Without dangerously exceeding their means, most Americans buy their cars on the installment plan and go in hock to finance their children's college educations. Almost everybody who owns a house needs a mortgage, and credit cards are very nearly indispensable in this fast-moving society — just try to rent a car without one. Whether you are using credit or not at any given moment, you should have enough borrowing power in reserve to raise a goodly sum if a serious need arises. You also should have a firm grasp on when to pay cash or postpone an expenditure.

The justification for most consumer credit is the present enjoyment of future earnings. If you have unused borrowing power, you will never have to endure the summer heat while saving up enough to buy an air conditioner. You won't have to drive an aging, unreliable car until you have amassed $10,000 or more to buy a new one. Buying now and paying later may tempt you in times of fast-rising prices even if you can pay cash. Lenders factor inflation into their interest rates, however, so the most you can hope to do is write off part of your borrowing cost as price protection and perhaps income tax savings. (If you itemize deductions, some of the finance charges on home equity loans are deductible expenses.) No matter how you figure it, credit has a real cost. It involves real risk, too. If you can't make the payments on time, your financial reputation will be damaged. The next time you need borrowing power, it probably won't be there.

Safe Debt Limits

Lenders are likely to judge your ability to repay your debts far less severely than the judgment you should impose on yourself. Their business is selling the use of their money, and they build a percentage of bad debts into their interest rates and customer screening process. When they have lots of money to lend, they market it vigorously, sometimes heedless of their customers' total burden of payments on earlier loans. For your own protection, give yourself the credit test in Figure 19 before assuming heavy new obligations.

Credit-Shopping Tools

Only 20 percent of borrowers compare lending rates at more than one source, according to a study published in the *Journal of Retail Banking*. Even people who shop compulsively for bargains don't always look for the lowest-cost loans. Yet shopping for money can really pay off. In 1984 the Purdue University Credit Research Center surveyed most kinds of consumer lenders: banks, credit unions, car dealers, and finance companies. It turned out that new-car loans in Illinois at that time cost anywhere from 9 to 25 percent. The difference in finance charges between those two rates is immense. At 9 percent, a four-year loan of $5,000 costs $972. At 25 percent, you pay $2,958.

To save hundreds and perhaps thousands of dollars by shopping around, make use of the tools provided under the federal Truth in Lending Act. It requires lenders to disclose easily comparable terms. The interest rate must be called the annual percentage rate, the interest in dollars must be labeled the finance charge, and credit contracts must display both those terms more prominently than any others. To make sure you stay within your self-imposed debt limit, look at another required number, the monthly payment. But don't use it for comparison shopping. By itself, the monthly payment conceals the cost of financing. Three variables determine what you pay for a loan: the amount you borrow, the annual percentage rate, and the *number* of monthly payments.

You also need to work your way through the maze of lenders and the variety of deals they offer. A dealer who is begging you to borrow does not necessarily give you a bargain. In 1985, rates on three-year installment loans at commercial banks and S&Ls ranged from 14.5 to 17 percent. At finance companies the same loans cost as much as 26 percent. Rates in general will fall and rise, but that differential is likely to persist.

Borrowing costs also vary according to the type of loan you want.

Figure 19. Your Self-Imposed Debt Limit

To take this test of your ability to assume more debt, first assemble your latest month's bills and payment books from lenders, credit-card companies, and stores where you have charge accounts. Cull out accounts that you habitually pay in full. For this analysis, they don't count. Also ignore mortgage payments on your home. Take only the bills on which your monthly installments include finance charges. Enter these accounts and their minimum monthly payments on the credit test list. Add them up.

Next, turn back to Figure 3 in Chapter 5, Your Cash-Flow Statement, and dig out your annual disposable income — the amount you had left last year after taxes. Divide that number by 12 to get your monthly disposable income after taxes. Then on line 3 set a manageable debt-payment limit for your circumstances — usually either 10 or 20 percent of your disposable income. The proper proportion is not chiseled in granite. You can choose a higher or lower limit than the one prescribed for people like you. But don't commit more than 25 percent of your take-home pay to nonmortgage debt repayments no matter how high your salary. Set your limit below the one suggested if being in debt makes you uneasy. By subtracting your total monthly debt payments from your debt limit, you will discover whether you have any unused borrowing power.

Loans and Charge Accounts	*Monthly Payments*
______________________	$__________
______________________	__________
______________________	__________
______________________	__________
______________________	__________
______________________	__________
______________________	__________
______________________	__________

1. Total monthly payments $__________
2. Your annual disposable income (from Figure 3 in Chapter 5), divided by 12 $__________
3. Total monthly payments you can safely handle $__________
   (If you are over 65 or the sole wage earner in your family or if the amount on line 2 is less than $2,000, enter 10 percent of line 2. If you and your spouse both work, or if you are under 35, or if line 2 is more than $2,000, enter 20 percent of line 2.)
4. Amount of room in your budget for additional debt or, if negative, amount of your current debt over the danger limit (line 3 minus line 1) $__________

Lenders usually charge you less interest on a secured loan — that is, one for which you put up collateral such as real estate or securities — than they do for an unsecured loan, where they rely for repayment on your income and your honest face.

No single institution will have the lowest rate for every type of borrowing. That is why you should canvass a number of different lenders when you are looking for money. The best place to start is where you keep your checking and savings accounts. Many banks have two rates — one for noncustomers and another as much as two percentage points lower for people who already have accounts. Moreover, a few thousand dollars sitting in a money-market account or an Individual Retirement Account may mean the difference between rejection and approval if your credit rating or income is marginal.

Shopping for a mortgage to buy a house raises a special set of choices, which are discussed in Chapter 51. For smaller, shorter-term loans that economists lump together as consumer credit, here is a rundown on where you can get the best terms.

Auto Loans

If you are financing a new car, you can often drive a better bargain on the showroom floor than at the bank. Thomas Cover, a spokesman for General Motors Acceptance Corporation, GM's financing division, can honestly say, "We're more flexible than other lenders because part of our mission is to get cars out the door." Such missionary zeal has driven U.S. auto makers to cut interest rates in half or eliminate finance charges altogether in the heat of inventory clearing. And banks are likely to add an expensive option to the standard equipment — "documentation" fees of $25 to $150.

Second Mortgages

If you have equity in real estate to put up as collateral for a loan, you can get a second mortgage. Lenders usually let you borrow as much as 70 to 80 percent of your equity. If your home is worth $125,000 and the balance on your first mortgage is $55,000, most banks will lend you at least $49,000.

Interest rates on second mortgages from banks and S&Ls run two to three percentage points more than on first mortgages. Some finance companies charge far higher. As is true of any loan secured by real estate, you also pay closing costs. The term of a second mortgage may be as short as five years, but 10 to 15 years is the norm. Second mortgages are popular with banks, S&Ls, and finance companies because of the relatively high interest rate and short maturity.

Be extra cautious if you are dealing with a mortgage broker — a company that matches borrowers and lenders. Some brokers charge homeowners exorbitant rates and fees by passing off commercial loans as second mortgages to get around state usury laws. Others dupe homeowners into signing over title to their property.

Home Equity Credit Lines

A variation on second mortgages is the home equity line of credit — a jumbo revolving-credit charge account secured by your house. Home equity lines, which are offered by many banks, S&Ls, and brokerage firms and by at least a few large credit unions, let you tap 70 to 80 percent of the equity in your home by writing checks or presenting a credit card. You pay interest only on the amount of money you draw against your credit limit.

Repayment terms are flexible. Most lenders give you 10 years to pay up. You may be required to make regular payments of principal and interest, or you may get the choice of paying only interest, with the principal due when the loan expires. However, you should be disciplined enough to make principal payments even if they are not required. If you are not so inclined, says bank consultant Edward Furash, "then you are better off with a second mortgage that has regularly scheduled payments."

Since lenders have your home as collateral, the rate they charge on home equity lines is lower than on most other types of borrowing. The interest floats one to two points over the prime rate and adjusts to that rate from month to month. If the prime is 7.5 percent, home equity rates of 8.5 to 9.5 percent will have an edge over second mortgages. But associated charges can be steep. Some lenders levy an application or origination fee in the form of points — as much as 3.5 percent of the amount of the credit line whether or not you borrow all of it. Additional closing costs can add $250 or so. On a $50,000 home equity line, that can mean paying $2,000 up front.

If you itemize deductions on your tax return, you get a special bonus with a home equity loan. While deductions for most other forms of interest are being phased out, interest on home equity loans remains deductible — up to a point. The deduction applies to interest on loans up to the price you paid for your house and for home improvements. You cannot deduct interest on loans backed by the gain in value of your house unless you use the money for education, medical bills, or home improvements.

The low rate of interest, the tax deduction, and the ease of access once you have been granted the loan may tempt you to use a home equity line of credit for all your borrowing needs. Resist! You should not nibble away at the equity in your home to spend a week of fun and sun in Acapulco. Use these loans for financing such things as home improvements or a child's education.

Secured Personal Loans

If you don't own a house or are reluctant to dip into your equity in the property, try for a loan that can be collateralized by other assets — certificates of deposit, perhaps, or stocks and bonds. Banks will lend against a CD and charge two to four percentage points above the rate they are paying on it. You can also borrow up to 70 percent of the market value of your securities at most banks. Some lenders charge a fixed rate for such loans, while others let their rate float over the prime. If you have a Focus account at Citibank in New York City — an account that ties together checking, savings, and brokerage services — you can borrow 70 percent of the market value of certain types of securities at rates that vary from one-half to one and three-quarters percentage points above prime, depending on the size of the loan.

You can borrow from your broker at still lower rates if you have a stash of stocks and bonds in a specialized broker-loan account. The interest is pegged to the call loan rate, which is the broker's borrowing cost from banks. Usually, the call rate is one-half to three-quarters of a percentage point below prime. A Flexible Credit Account at Merrill Lynch, for example, will let you borrow as much as 60 percent of the value of your stocks, 70 percent of your bonds, and 92 percent of your government securities. Depending on the amount borrowed — $25,000 was the minimum loan in 1986 — you will be charged three-quarters to two and one-quarter percentage points over the call rate.

Unsecured Personal Loans

Bargain rates on secured loans aren't much use if you have no acceptable collateral. Most of the time, however, banks and other lenders aggressively push unsecured lines of credit that typically give you access to $2,000 to $25,000. The actual amount you qualify for depends on your income, and you draw on the line by writing checks. You are charged interest on only the amount you have borrowed, and you usually have three years to repay the loan.

Although unsecured lines of credit often carry a fixed rate of interest, you can cut at least your initial cost by around two percentage points by shopping for a variable rate. An unsecured line generally costs one to three percentage points more than a secured line such as a home equity loan. The fees, however, are much lower because you pay no closing costs. There is usually an annual charge of up to $75 and a $150 application fee, but unsecured lines of credit can be cheaper than home equity lines for amounts under $10,000.

Credit Cards

Bank-issued credit cards often come with a line of credit that you can tap by writing a check. But this is not a good way to borrow because the rates run high. In 1986, annual percentage rates on bank cards usually ranged from 16 to 21 percent; and even when banks' money costs are tumbling, credit-card rates rarely budge. If you carry a balance of several thousand dollars on your credit cards month after month, you should switch to an unsecured line and pay off your credit-card balances. Over the course of a year you could save as much as $210 that way on a $3,000 debt.

In their eagerness to charge into interstate banking, many banks are wooing out-of-state customers by mail with preapproved credit-card application forms. All you have to do is ''sign here'' and your card arrives practically by return post. Banks are not the only ones pushing plastic. J. C. Penney issues MasterCard and Visa cards to its regular customers in several states through a Penney-owned limited-service bank in Delaware. Sears competes head to head with MasterCard and Visa with its Discover card.

Instead of courting you with lower rates, card issuers may try to wow you with packages of perks called enhancements. Some are glamorous. Customers who paid the $250 annual fee for the American Express Platinum Card in 1984 got a chance to fork over another $2,100 to attend Broadway's Tony awards and hobnob with theater luminaries at a weekend of dinners, parties, and shows. Most inducements are more mundane: discount shopping, toll-free message service, automobile road service, travel life insurance, and a credit-card registration service that will report lost or stolen cards and provide cash and airline tickets in emergencies.

Some enhancements may be included in your card's annual fee, but those with tangible value cost extra — typically $25 to $35 a year. Don't let these bells and whistles distract you from comparing the basic costs. To choose the best credit-card deal, home in on such terms as the interest rate on unpaid balances, the annual fee, and the free-ride period — the number of days between the time you buy something and the moment the interest meter starts ticking.

You may have to look outside your home state to get a bargain interest rate. In 1985, for instance, customers of Bankers Trust of South Carolina, in Columbia, were paying one of the highest rates in the nation — 22.2 percent. Right next door in North Carolina, state law prevented banks from charging more than 18 percent. Arkansas had the lowest rates because the state sets its interest ceiling five percentage points above the Federal Reserve's discount rate. That made the 1987 rate at Simmons First National Bank in Pine Bluff a mere 10.5 percent. Some Arkansas banks will issue cards nationwide. Simmons vice president John C. Ramer says that while his institution doesn't actively solicit out-of-state accounts, it will send an application to anyone who writes or phones for one (Simmons First National Bank, P.O. Box 6609, Pine Bluff, Arkansas 71601; 501-541-1272).

If you are a thrifty card carrier who pays off each month's balance in full, the annual percentage rate is academic. You get free credit except for the annual fee. Be sure you understand how you are billed for purchases, however. Some banks give you a grace period of up to 25 days during which you can pay your bill and incur no interest. But many assess interest from the day they receive your charge from the merchant. A few even calculate interest from the date of sale.

A handful of banks may still offer cards with no fee, but most charge $18 to $25 for plastic with credit lines of $500 to $3,500 and $30 to $50 for Gold MasterCards and Premier Visas, which give you heftier borrowing power of $5,000 to $50,000. Bankcard Holders of America, a consumer group, keeps a list of banks that charge low interest rates or issue no-fee cards nationally. For a copy send $2.95 to the organization at 333 Pennsylvania Avenue, SE, Washington, D.C. 20003.

You are not likely to find a card with no annual fee and a very low rate, so let your payment habits determine your choice. If you are a "revolver" — bankerese for someone who sends just the minimum monthly payment — look for a card with the lowest interest rate.

Debit Cards

You don't have to worry about interest charges at all if you use a debit card. This piece of plastic functions much like a credit card but with one important difference: when you make a purchase, the amount is immediately deducted from your checking account at the bank or your money-market fund at the brokerage firm. You don't get the free ride that goes with many credit cards.

A debit card can help impulse buyers to discipline themselves by limiting their spending to the funds they have on deposit, but such a card has two drawbacks. One is that you lose an effective weapon against shoddy goods and services. When you use a credit card in your state of residence or within 100 miles of home, you can withhold payment, putting pressure on the bank to intervene in your behalf. The other problem with debit cards concerns liability for bogus charges if your card is lost or stolen. Federal law limits your loss on a credit card to $50. Debit-card liability can run as high as $500 and, in rare instances, far higher. You have to treat your debit card like cash, not plastic.

51

GETTING THE BEST MORTGAGE

Choosing the right mortgage for your situation is not a simple matter of finding the lowest interest rate. You have to sort through a baffling variety of loans with varying rates, terms, and fees. This sort of proliferation tends to accelerate when interest rates ascend to double digits. In the early 1980s, for instance, Globe Mortgage Company of Hackensack, New Jersey, boasted of offering 28 different types of mortgages — "just like Howard Johnson's ice cream," said senior vice president James Richmond. A couple of years later, with rates inching below 10 percent, the selection narrowed noticeably. But it still wasn't much simpler to spot the best loan.

As you browse among mortgages, your attention will naturally be drawn to interest rates, both fixed and adjustable. On adjustable-rate mortgages, ARMs, your interest rate and monthly payments are linked to an index of rates and fluctuate in step with the movement of that index. At the outset the rate on an ARM will be at least a couple of percentage points below that on a conventional, fixed-rate mortgage. A year later, unless the index is down, your rate will automatically rise to the vicinity of fixed rates.

All else being equal, you would grab that lower rate, but nothing is equal in the mortgage market. Depending on whether your bank, savings and loan, or other lender wants to make fixed- or adjustable-rate loans, you will pay higher fees, in the form of points, for the type of deal the lender is least enthusiastic about. Each point equals 1 percent of the amount borrowed and is paid to the lender at the outset — up front, as they say in the lending business. One point on a $75,000 mortgage, for example, is $750 out of your pocket at the real estate closing.

The way to compare different types of loans is to have the lender figure out for you the annual percentage rate (APR), which includes points. For example, the APR could have told you which of the following two $80,000 mortgages offered in 1985 by a New York City savings bank was more attractive — a fixed rate at 12.875 percent with $1,600 in fees or an ARM at an introductory rate of 9.75 percent and 14 percent in the second year, with $2,000 in points up front. Answer: the fixed rate. Its effective rate is 13.26 percent vs. 13.63 for the adjustable.

Once you have put different mortgages on the same interest-rate footing, you will be able to judge the best one more accurately. However, the lender will often make the choice for you, basing it on your income, your current debt load, and the size loan you need. You may find that you cannot qualify for any kind of mortgage if the monthly payment, including principal, interest, taxes, and homeowners insurance, exceeds 25 percent of your gross monthly income. Moreover, lenders will usually turn you down if the loan leaves you committed to paying more than 33 percent of your gross income to service all of your long-term debts, including such obligations as alimony, car payments, and revolving credit-card balances. Let's say you want to buy a $100,000 house and have no other debts. You can borrow $80,000 for 30 years at a fixed rate of 10 percent if your annual income is more than $44,000.

Assuming you have a choice, how do you decide between a fixed-rate loan and an ARM? For an answer, take a look at both types of mortgage and the home buyers for whom each is best suited.

Fixed-Rate Loans

The virtue of a fixed-rate loan is implicit in the name: your mortgage costs are fixed. Such a loan is ideal for young couples who anticipate starting a family. They need to know what their monthly mortgage bill is going to be, particularly if one spouse's income might disappear with the arrival of children.

Not everyone who wants predictable housing expenses needs a 30-year loan, however. Shorter-term variations on the traditional fixed-rate mortgage — especially a 15-year version — are gaining a certain amount of popularity. Because bankers get nervous about making long-term commitments, they generally charge a lower rate on a 15-year loan. The spread is typically one-quarter to one-half a percentage point. Monthly payments on an $80,000 loan at 9.75 percent, let's say, for 15 years, would be $847 vs. $702 for 30 years at 10 percent. In exchange for the higher monthly payments, a borrower could save $100,000 in interest costs by paying off the mortgage much faster. The saving is deceptive, however. It omits from the equation the larger tax deductions that go with the heavier finance charges on a 30-year loan. It also overlooks the investment value of the considerable saving in monthly payments. With those factors favoring the long-term loan, the 15-year advantage dwindles or, if your investment results rival those from stocks in general recently, becomes a disadvantage.

Most people don't live in the same house long enough to retire their mortgage; in fact, houses are resold about every seven years on average. Even so, a 15-year borrower builds up more equity by the time he sells than a 30-year borrower does. For this reason, two-career couples who are reasonably confident that their income will rise might find a 15-year loan appealing. They would come away with more money for the down payment on their next house.

If you are an executive who is regularly bounced from place to place by his or her company, you could gamble on yet another variation of the fixed-rate mortgage — a three-year balloon loan. With that short a term you should be able to negotiate a reduction of one to two percentage points from the normal rate for 30-year fixed-rate mortgages. ''Smaller banks are the most likely to give you this kind of deal. It's used so frequently in financing small businesses that it's a familiar, comfortable product to them,'' says Barry Havemann, president of HSH Associates of Riverdale, New Jersey, a mortgage consulting firm.

The advantage of a balloon loan is that for three years you might lock in a lower rate than you would get on an adjustable loan. The drawback is that if you don't sell your house by the time the three years are up, you'll have to refinance your mortgage. Your lender will charge one to three points for that, and by then mortgage rates could be vying with the Voyager spacecraft to see which blasts out of the solar system first.

Adjustable-Rate Mortgages

Buyers who are scaling the income ladder or plan to move in three to five years can look beyond the predictability of fixed-rate mortgages to the short-term cash-flow benefit of adjustable-rate mortgages. Their strategy is to capitalize on discounted loan payments in the early years of an ARM and refinance their house at a fixed-rate loan later if the ARM proves too expensive. When mortgage rates are hovering in double digits, lenders set the initial interest on ARMs two to three points lower than their fixed rate to induce borrowers to take the risk that rates will rise.

Some homeowners have refinanced their fixed-rate loans with ARMs just to realize short-term savings. When Samuel Roberson decided in 1984 to remortgage his 78-year-old farmhouse in north Seattle to get some of his equity out of the house, he could have traded his 12 percent fixed-rate loan for one at 13.5 percent. Instead, he chose a one-year adjustable with an initial rate of 11 percent. Roberson figured he saved at least $2,000 in the first year alone even after closing costs, and he was able to invest his savings in high-yielding stocks and bonds. Roberson's ARM is convertible to a fixed mortgage at the prevailing rate at the time of each adjustment during the first five years of the loan. ''For five years, I'm really protected on interest rates,'' he observed with obvious satisfaction.

The call to ARMs is irresistible to someone who reckons that interest rates will fall. But even if rates go up, homeowners with rising incomes will be better off with a variable-rate loan as long as they are certain of moving within a couple of years and the mortgage contains no prepayment penalty. Since adjustable-rate loans are generally assumable by another buyer, whereas fixed-rate loans usually are not, your ARM also could make your house easier to sell.

Mortgage payments on an ARM go up or down by an amount based on two factors: the index to which the loan is tied and the lending institution's profit margin. Lenders peg adjustable loans to a variety of indexes, but by far the most common one tracks the yield of one-year Treasury notes. The mortgage interest rate adjusts every year, on the anniversary of the loan, in line with the average level of that yield over the previous month. The adjustment shows up as a reduction or increase in your monthly payment. Interest-rate fluctuations between your adjustments do not affect what you pay.

The one-year Treasury index can take rather sharp turns, which is fine when interest rates are dropping but not so nice when they are rising. A more sluggish index, such as the Federal Home Loan Bank Board's average contract rate on recently issued fixed-rate and variable mortgages, would provide better protection against rate increases. Alas, few lenders let you select an index. But at least make sure you know which one your mortgage will be tied to. If you can't get a satisfactory explanation of how the changes in the index will affect your loan, take your business elsewhere.

Changes in the index account for only part of each adjustment to your mortgage. To any increase — or decrease — in the index, lenders add their profit margin, which is typically 2 to 2.5 percent of the loan.

Here's how this works. The initial mortgage rate may have less to do with the underlying index than with competitive conditions. To get his share of business, the lender might quote an 8 percent adjustable rate while the Treasury note rate is 7.5 percent. (A couple of points up front will more than make up for any discount on the first-year interest charges.)

On the loan anniversary, however, your rate will rise even if the T-note rate has drifted down a bit. That's because the lender now adds his margin to the index and charges you the sum of the two. So the index may be standing just where it did when you bought the house, but the second-year rate will rise just the same from 7.5 percent to 9.5 or 10 percent, depending on the lender's margin.

In all years after that, the index alone will dictate your rate. All this is spelled out in your contract, although the lending officer may not have made it clear when he explained the terms.

Your lender does not want you to be completely at the mercy of interest-rate fluctuations. No one comes out ahead if you are so impoverished by untethered gyrations that you can't make your payments. That is why almost all new ARMs have limits, called caps, on the amount of each adjustment and on total increases in the rate during the life of your loan.

Two types of cap are treacherous, however. Watch out for one that limits increases in your payments while the interest rate on the mortgage is allowed to bob up and down. The result could be a debt that is growing instead of diminishing as you make payments. Also be wary of a cap that doesn't take effect with the first rate adjustment, which, as noted, may result in a much higher payment than an introductory teaser rate. The cap, if there is one, applies to that rate, not the teaser. Before you accept such a loan, advises Jane Greenstein, president of Mortgage Clearing House Inc., a mortgage shopper's consultation and placement service in New Hyde Park, New York, "make sure your current income is sufficient to handle the highest possible second-year payment."

Fortunately, ARMs have become nearly standardized. The vast majority are capped at two percentage points on yearly interest-rate changes up or down and at five points over the life of the loan. These caps shift more of the interest-rate risk back onto the shoulders of the lender.

Without the escape hatch of refinancing, however, an ARM still can be risky. Although bankers have become stricter about qualifying borrowers for ARMs, the lenders' guidelines are not based on a worst-case scenario. You are the one who has to figure out if you could cope with suddenly higher mortgage payments. One important defense is a provision in the loan contract that lets you trade your ARM for some sort of fixed-rate mortgage if rates rise to the point that you can't afford your payments or if you don't sell your house when you expect to. Refinancing, however, is expensive; you'll have to pay most of your closing costs all over again. Refinancing usually eats up 3 to 4 percent of your mortgage balance, or as much as $4,000 on a $100,000 loan.

Another option is conversion. If you are willing to pay a higher rate — sometimes one point more — some lenders may be willing to give you an ARM whose unpaid principal can be converted to a fixed-rate loan at the prevailing rate. Conversion is usually allowed during the first three to five years of the loan, typically at a cost of one point plus a small fee — at most $200. But the higher initial ARM rate could reduce the cost saving to the point where you would be as well off with a conventional mortgage — and save yourself considerable distress.

Shopping Aids

Armed with information about loans, you can mount your own search for funds. But rare is the shopper who self-confidently confronts lenders on their own territory. To get professional help in many metropolitan areas, you can turn to mortgage search and placement firms that survey the marketplace, then publish their findings about rates, terms and costs. Each week, for example, HSH Associates (10 Mead Avenue, Riverdale, New Jersey 07457) compiles data from lenders in most populous states in its home buyers' mortgage kit. The cost is $12 a copy. A more localized service, the Peeke Report (101 Chestnut Street, Gaithersburg, Maryland 20877; $20 a copy), covers Washington, D.C., plus sections of Florida, Maryland, and Virginia.

A number of other companies have computer networks that advertise the wares of participating mortgage lenders. Your real estate agent punches a few keys on a desktop terminal and up pops the most attractive available loan. This is known as computerized mortgage origination. In some cases, the computer not only sorts through various types of loans to come up with the best rate and terms for which you would qualify but also accepts your application, gives you a conditional commitment subject to a credit check, and processes the loan.

The convenience of borrowing by computer is very appealing, and the number of companies offering the service is increasing. But does electronic mortgage shopping live up to its promise? The answer is maybe. The computer can uncover attractive rates, but you may be able to do better on your own.

Bridge Loans

A familiar homeowners' dilemma: despite your best efforts to rid yourself of your old digs before you bought new ones, you own two homes. The people who sold you your new house insisted on an earlier closing date than the date you set with the people buying your old house. Your worst problem is not carrying costs — a month or two of double mortgage payments won't ruin you — but where to get the money you have to put down on your new house while your equity is still locked up in the old one.

The solution is a bridge, or swing, loan from a commercial or savings bank. This financing is designed to tide you over and typically takes the form of a 30- to 120-day personal loan secured by the equity in the old house or sometimes both houses. Interest rates run low — about two percentage points above the prime rate. Before a lending institution will advance you a bridge loan, though, it probably will insist that you have a firm, signed contract of sale on your present home.

Moral: Sell your present house before you buy a new one.

52

HOW TO KEEP A WELL-POLISHED CREDIT IMAGE

When you apply for a loan, credit card, or charge account, you are given an application form to fill out. The lender judges whether or not you are an acceptable credit risk from the information you provide and often from a report on you that is supplied by a credit bureau. In addition to a history of unblemished borrowing, loan officers look for evidence of financial stability: length of time on the job, level of skill or professional standing, infrequent changes of address. Your assets, such as real estate, stocks, bonds, and mutual funds, may help to elevate your credit standing.

In considering your application, the loan officer may want to know what the money is for, especially if you are trying to borrow $5,000 or more. Some lenders leave the yes or no decision to the interviewer and his superior, but most large lenders use computerized point-scoring systems.

Computerized judgments can be fickle. Let's say you move from Washington, D.C., to Minneapolis to begin a new job. Shortly after settling in, you stop at a local bank to apply for an auto loan and a Visa card. On both credit applications you are asked how long you have lived at your current address. Your response — less than six months —probably will hurt your chances of getting the auto loan but may help you with your Visa application. Yet if you had moved instead from Minneapolis to Washington, quite likely the D.C. bank wouldn't even consider your length of residence in deciding whether to grant you credit.

Such apparent contradictions are characteristic of credit scoring. Your desirability as a customer can vary from lender to lender, from city to city, and, in the case of at least one major retailer, Sears, from store to store in the same town. Creditors stamp their scoring schemes "top secret." Nevertheless, certain categories of information are known to count heavily. Learning what those categories are can help you fill out at least some sections of your credit application in a way that improves your odds of getting the card or loan you want.

All sorts of facts and alleged facts about you come into play in the scoring process. First you are awarded points for each of your answers to key questions on the credit application. Second, after the score on your application has been tallied, most lenders add or subtract points according to how much they esteem your credit bureau report. A pattern of delinquent payments can shift your application to the reject pile even if you have racked up enough points on your application to reach the approval level.

On a credit application, you may fill in dozens of blanks and answer enough questions to make you yearn for the simpler days of the Spanish Inquisition. Most of your answers go into the creditor's file for marketing purposes and record keeping. Only six to 12 questions figure in your score. They were selected by the scoring-system designer, who sometimes is the lender but usually is a consulting firm specializing in such projects. The selection is based on an analysis of the lender's past experience with credit customers.

If statistical analysis has shown that a significant number of those who proved to be bad credit risks were tenants rather than homeowners, you will be asked on your application whether you own or rent your residence. You will get more points for being an owner. If owners and renters are equally represented among the customers who had trouble paying their bills, that question probably won't be scored.

The greatest number of points hinge on the questions that have proved most effective in culling bad risks. Giving the "right" answer to a heavily weighted question could earn you as many as 75 points toward the 150 needed to make you eligible on a 250-point scale; questions that aren't considered strong predictors of bill-paying performance may carry a maximum of 10 points.

With secrecy tight, it is almost impossible to know precisely which pieces of information will carry the most weight. In the past, the most heavily scored characteristics have been the financial stability factors. But because scoring systems are continually reviewed and updated, they mirror changes in society. For instance, as more and more people hop from job to job and place to place, mobility becomes an unreliable predictor of creditworthiness. Some items that used to be weighted fairly heavily, such as the age of your car or whether you have a telephone at home, are rarely scored at all anymore. You are never scored on your race, religion, or sex because federal law prohibits lenders from discriminating on those grounds.

Here are some characteristics often included in scoring systems, along with tips on how lenders may judge you in each category.

Relationships with Other Creditors

In addition to your credit bureau report, you are scored on the number and types of charge cards or loans you list on your application. Some lenders award up to half the points you need for approval if you have had a loan or account with them in the past and have paid on schedule. You get the most points for travel-and-entertainment cards such as American Express and Diners Club, followed by bank credit cards and department store charge cards.

You score less highly for having borrowed from consumer loan companies, which are often lenders of last resort and inevitably take on a significant percentage of bad credit risks. Some systems give bonus points for not having that kind of debt. However, car manufacturers' captive finance companies don't carry the same stigma as consumer loan companies.

Without credit references to list on your application, you will have a tough time scoring well. "If a system consists of eight scoring items, at least two to three will relate to other credit relationships," says O. Davis Nelson, vice president of the Fair Isaac Company, scoring-system designers in San Rafael, California. "So you would have to score well in all the other areas to offset the points you would be lacking without a credit history."

Income

The higher your income, the more points you score. In most systems, however, income isn't as important a credit scoring measure as it once was. As one point-scoring consultant says, "Creditors now realize that someone who earns $40,000 isn't necessarily twice as creditworthy as someone who makes $20,000." When filling in your application, include all sources of income, such as alimony, child support, and investment income. But be prepared to provide proof that you earn what you say you do from such sources.

Debt-to-Income Ratio

If you are applying for a mortgage or installment loan, your debt-to-income ratio is more important than your level of income. Some bank credit-card issuers also emphasize this yardstick of your total indebtedness. Lenders aren't likely to approve your application if your fixed current obligations — mortgage or rent and other monthly payments such as auto loans — take more than 35 percent of your gross income.

Occupation

In most credit-scoring systems, your job will be put into one of roughly eight occupational categories: professional-technical, clerical, unskilled, and so forth. You will score higher if you are put in a category that suggests stability, responsibility, and a college education. "When filling out a credit application," says Catherine Stribling, vice president and senior loan officer at the Bank of Los Angeles, "make your job sound as executive-oriented as possible without distorting the truth. Saying you are an executive assistant will probably get you more points than describing yourself as a secretary."

Length of Time at Job and Residence

In rural areas and medium-size cities, creditors are likely to give more points for putting down roots than you would get in urban centers. If you live in an area with a transient population, such as Los Angeles or Washington, D.C., you probably won't even be scored on this criterion. The type of credit you are applying for can also determine how many points you get for staying put. Davis Nelson of Fair Isaac says, "People who apply for bank credit cards soon after making a move are often the best risks, probably because individuals who are sophisticated in handling their finances establish new credit relations shortly after they move." For installment loans, though, you will score more points the longer you have been at your current address.

Homeowner vs. Renter

As a rule you earn more points if you own your home than if you rent. In the early 1980s, however, the point gap narrowed, reflecting the plight of financially solid people who had been shut out of the housing market by lofty interest rates.

Bank Accounts

Maintaining a checking or savings account says less than it once did about your acceptability. Nonetheless, having either type of account can add points with potential creditors.

What to Do If You Get Turned Down

Do not give up hope if, at first, you are turned down for a loan or credit card. Even royalty doesn't always measure up. A news item a few years ago suggested that credit-scoring systems in the United Kingdom were so stringent that Prince Philip himself couldn't pass them. Thereupon, the head of Fair Isaac's European division decided to test the notion. He completed a sample credit application for the prince and scored it on six different systems the firm had developed for European clients. Prince Philip passed with ease on four of the applications — all for upscale retailers and credit cards. His Royal Highness barely scored above the approval mark on the fifth application, a low-scale retailer's, and he was rejected on the sixth, for a finance company.

Creditors must tell you why you were rejected, specifying the categories in which you scored lowest. You may be able to turn an initially negative decision into one that favors you by supplying additional information — explaining, say, to an auto-loan officer that your frequent relocations result from job transfers demanded by a fast-track executive training program in your company.

Similarly, if you strike out with one creditor, don't assume you will get the same response from another. Because scoring systems reflect each creditor's unique customer base, you, like Prince Philip, may score quite differently for an account at a discount outlet than at an upscale retailer. The more closely your profile matches that of the store's creditworthy customers, the better your chances are.

Most credit rejections don't come from quirky scoring systems but from genuine doubts about your ability to pay. Whether your problem is to repair a damaged credit profile or to establish your financial identity for the first time, you can usually ease your way into the money-lending system by doing the following.

Open checking and savings accounts. A bank, credit union, or savings and loan association will welcome you as a depositor even if it won't lend you money. Make deposits regularly. Never let a check bounce; you are trying to develop a happy relationship with the bank.

Take out a passbook loan. After you have deposited $500 to $1,000 in your savings account, borrow against it. Since the loan is backed by your own money, which is then frozen in your account, you can get this type of loan without question. The cost of borrowing won't be too much more than the interest your money is earning. Pay off the loan on a fixed, unswerving schedule. Ask a loan officer to report the loan and its prompt repayment to a major credit bureau.

Apply to your bank for a credit card. If you are turned down, offer to let the bank freeze $500 of your savings as a guarantee of repayment of your account. If you are a college student and the bank won't issue you a card, you can usually get one through the College Credit Card Corporation (2000 Market Street, Philadelphia, Pennsylvania 19103; 215-567-2100). Use your card but don't abuse it.

Apply for a department store charge account. Retailers are likely to be more receptive to first-time credit applicants than banks are. Charge purchases occasionally. Use revolving credit if you wish, but don't miss any payments.

Your Credit Bureau Report

While lenders guard their customized point-scoring systems as zealously as Coca-Cola Company protects its secret formula for Classic Coke, one crucial tool used in the scoring process — your credit bureau report — is as accessible to you as it is to creditors. You can enhance your standing with lenders by getting a copy of your report every couple of years and making sure the information on file is accurate and pertains to you. It is especially important to do this before applying for a home mortgage or other major financing.

To find out who has been keeping credit tabs on you, ask your bank or a retailer with whom you have an account for the name of the credit bureau it uses. Local credit bureaus collect information about your bill-paying habits and use the computer facilities of TRW Information Services, Equifax Services, and other national firms to store your history. If you move, your file will be transmitted to a bureau in your new town the first time you apply for credit there.

Credit bureaus are required by law to disclose to you the full contents of your report. They can enlighten you face to face or over the phone, or they can send you a copy of the report, which many bureaus prefer to do. They usually charge $10 for the information. However, if you have been turned down for credit during the previous 30 days because of your report, you can review it for free. (In New York and California, credit bureaus must send it in writing.) Creditors must give you the name and address of a credit bureau whose data contributed to your rejection or to a decision to lend you less than you requested.

Your credit report will list your payment history with all creditors that feed information to the bureau. If you hold an account jointly with your spouse, the payment record should be listed on your report as well as your partner's. Don't be surprised to find some of your accounts omitted. For example, American Express seldom supplies credit bureaus with information on its cardholders. Many oil companies that issue gasoline credit cards report only on delinquent accounts. And while house payments may represent the biggest chunk of your debt load, mortgage lenders seldom supply information to credit bureaus because creditors assume that you will meet those obligations even if you are behind on others.

Credit bureaus are not obliged to eradicate black marks against you for seven years. Most information in your report, however, has a much briefer life span than that. Walter Kurth, president of Associated Credit Bureaus, a national trade group, explains why: "Generally, the more recent the adverse credit history, the more weight it is given in determining creditworthiness. Conversely, an unblemished record over the past 24 months may very well outweigh an adverse item or two dating back four or five years." Some credit scars, however, linger much longer. A bankruptcy in which your debts were dismissed can, and in all probability will, stay on your record for 10 years.

By law, the bureau must investigate any errors you discover in your report. Then it must delete information that turns out to be mistaken and notify all lenders who received your report within the previous six months that erroneous material has been removed from your file. If the credit bureau's investigation doesn't uphold your side of the dispute, you are entitled to add to your file a short statement defending yourself. Future reports to prospective lenders must include your explanation.

Shady outfits describing themselves as credit clinics or credit repair shops are reaping high fees — sometimes $1,000 or more — on the strength of promises to clear people's records of blemishes. These operators take advantage of the public's right to dispute credit bureau information by deluging bureaus with requests for investigations. The sting works on the theory that the bureau will delete the data rather than go to the expense of checking it. But there is no assurance that such harassment will succeed in your case.

53

THE DEBT MONSTER

Before they had been married very long, Susan and Albert Bogert ran up bills of $20,000 on their 25 credit cards for trips to Hawaii and Saint Martin, plus clothing and furniture. They owed $300 a month in interest alone. Then things got really bad. Between the signing of the contract on a house they were buying in New Jersey and the closing date, a surge in interest rates hiked the monthly mortgage payment from $700 to $1,100. Despite their combined income of $45,000, the Bogerts were suddenly overwhelmed. They had fallen victim to America's love affair with credit.

Installment debt took off in the 1980s. By mid-decade the nation's buy-now-pay-later binge was pushing up the unpaid balance on all types of consumer loans by 20 percent a year. Consumers owed well over half a trillion dollars. The strain of this headlong borrowing was showing on family budgets. Delinquent loans had climbed steeply. More than 6 percent of home mortgage payments were a month or more overdue — the most ever. More and more families sought the advice of credit counselors. The National Foundation for Consumer Credit, which has more than 250 affiliated agencies around the United States, reported 10 to 15 percent increases in the number of people enrolling for counseling. As usual, most clients were experiencing temporary setbacks such as a job loss or disabling illness. But counselors were seeing many productive people who no longer could handle their credit burden. At Consumer Credit Counselors in San Francisco, nearly half of the clients were young managerial and professional workers with relatively high incomes.

Back in New Jersey the Bogerts, after seeking help from a credit counselor, realized that they had to boost their monthly take-home pay by $400 to meet their payments. Susan, a Xerox sales rep, took on a nighttime waitressing job, and they squeezed a boarder into their three-bedroom house. They threw away their credit cards, cut out costly vacations, shopped for secondhand clothing for their infant son, and put off replacing their 1976 Toyota and 1964 Valiant. In three years they cleared all their installment debts, even though Susan had quit full-time work to look after their 18-month-old son, and the family's income had slipped to $33,000.

Credit can help you make your dreams come true, or it can turn your life into a waking nightmare. You are most vulnerable if you have been hauling around debts for years, juggling payments, and staving off the inevitable day when you no longer can borrow new money to pay off old balances. You may never reach that extreme, but be on the lookout for these early symptoms:

1. You start using credit cards to pay for groceries and other necessities.
2. You use credit cards without keeping track of what you are spending.
3. You sweat it out when sales clerks call the credit-card company for clearance of your purchase.
4. You go on credit shopping sprees when you are angry or depressed.

When letters start coming from debt collectors, you know your troubles are grave. Don't let dunners scare you into hiding from your creditors. Deal with them in a responsible way. The first thing to do is admit to yourself that stopgaps will no longer stave off the problem. Increasing your debts any further is sheer folly. Take your credit cards out of your wallet or purse. If you cannot trust yourself not to use them again, destroy them as the Bogerts did. That's better in the long run than having them canceled by the store or bank.

If you cannot meet a bill payment, call and explain your financial situation to your creditor. Express your willingness to settle the debt as fast as you can. Creditors frequently will work with you. They may accept partial or delayed payments if they believe you will make good. To protect yourself, though, ask the creditor to put any revised payment plan in writing. Look for ways to reduce your living expenses. Dine out less often or forgo some entertainment. Drive your old car a little longer before trading it in, avoid shopping sprees, pay cash whenever possible.

Seeing a Credit Counselor

If all else fails, you may need to see a nonprofit credit counselor. The experience might be less traumatic than you think. To find the counseling agency nearest you, write or telephone the National Foundation for Consumer Credit (8701 Georgia Avenue, Silver Spring, Maryland 20910; 301-589-5600). Almost without exception, these organizations are preferable to for-profit credit counseling groups, which charge as much as $1,500. They are usually debt-consolidation firms, which make money by refinancing your debt at a higher rate. Extending credit to a heavy spender can be as dangerous as offering a drink to an alcoholic.

Founded in 1951, the National Foundation for Consumer Credit is supported financially by banks, department stores, the AFL–CIO, Family Service Association, the Legal Aid Society, the American Bar Association, and other organizations and businesses with an interest in helping people handle their debts. In 1984, counseling centers affiliated with the NFCC arranged the payment of bills totaling $117 million, up from $108 million in 1983.

When you sit down with your credit counselor, he or she will ask you for the latest bills or statements from all your creditors, the stubs from recent paychecks, and other financial intimacies. The expertise of counselors varies; they may have passed two days of tests administered by the NFCC, or they may have held jobs that offer comparable experience, such as bank lending officer or social worker. The counselor will review your cash flow, set up a budget, and help you decide whether you can handle your own bills. If things are rough enough, you may be put into a voluntary debt-repayment plan. Then you will normally turn over to the agency a monthly amount equal to one-thirtieth of your total indebtedness. The counselor may also recommend that you take a part-time job or sell some assets, depending on how severe your shortfall is.

The agency will notify your creditors that you have resolved to pay off your debts through its program, and creditors will be urged to suspend further interest charges; most will do so. In any event a good counselor will try to protect your interests by saving your car from repossession and shielding your wages from garnishment.

For the initial consultation, an NFCC agency may charge you as much as $50, though $10 to $20 is more usual. If you go into a debt-payment plan, you also will pay a fee of $10 to $20 a month; but no one is ever turned away for lack of the fee.

Personal Bankruptcy

About 10 percent of credit counseling clients are advised to seek a lawyer's help. Bankruptcy may be recommended in cases where clients would face garnishment and other hardships. In one form of bankruptcy, called Chapter 7 after a section of the federal bankruptcy law, the court distributes all but certain untouchable portions of your assets to your creditors and dismisses the rest of your debts — with some major exceptions. You remain responsible for alimony and child support obligations; state and federal taxes due for the past three years; student loans that came due in the past five years; luxury items costing more than $500 if they were bought less than 40 days before you filed for bankruptcy; and credit purchases of more than $1,000 that were made within 20 days of your bankruptcy petition.

State laws differ over the value of your assets that creditors cannot claim after you file for bankruptcy. At least a dozen states have adopted a model code that gives you an idea of what is likely to be protected where you live: you can keep up to $4,000 of the cash value and reinvested dividends of life insurance policies, $7,500 of the equity in your house, $750 worth of the tools or other implements of your trade, $500 worth of jewelry (the wedding ring provision), items of household property worth no more than $200 each, and a car worth no more than $1,200.

A less drastic form of bankruptcy, Chapter 13, is open to you if you have a steady income. The court protects your assets from seizure and gives you three to five years to pay off your debts under the supervision of a trustee, much as you would repay debts through a nonprofit credit counseling plan. Given the choice, you are better off with the credit counseling payment plan than with Chapter 13. Bankruptcy of any kind will seriously tarnish your credit record, not only depriving you of most sources of credit, but also making it more difficult for you to get car insurance because insurers peg bankrupt people as poor risks.

VII

INSURING AGAINST THE UNKINDEST CUTS

Suited up in 50 pounds of body-contoured metal, medieval knights looked formidable indeed. Yet the bulk often increased their vulnerability by restricting their movements. Even a Saint George should recognize that no protection is perfect and too much protection can weigh you down. It is wise to reconcile yourself to taking minor financial injuries out of your own hide. A well-designed insurance program protects you against disaster, not against the cost of every head cold or dented fender. Nor is insurance meant to be a consolation prize for misfortune. The purpose is to help you get back on your feet, not to improve your standard of living.

Reducing or avoiding obvious hazards should be the first step toward a properly structured program of risk management. It costs little or nothing to fasten your car seat belt, install smoke detectors in your home, and adopt a physical fitness routine. Such measures can save money as well as an-

guish by making you eligible for discounts on your insurance premiums. After that, you can cut costs by taking more risk on your own shoulders. The chief way to do so is by increasing the deductibles on your car and homeowners policies and by guarding against being overinsured, all the while securing your flanks against surprise attacks.

Take a hard look at your existing life, health, and disability insurance, including any group coverage you receive as an employee benefit, to see where your defenses require bolstering or exceed your needs. Most people have no idea of where their coverage overlaps or falls short.

In buying any kind of insurance, consider the advice of Professor Robert I. Mehr of the University of Illinois at Urbana-Champaign, coauthor of the classic text *Principles of Insurance:* "Don't risk more than you can afford to lose. But don't pay to insure what you can afford to risk." Following this guideline will make your insurance fit your needs instead of your nightmares.

54

THE BEST AUTO POLICIES

Maricelle Victoria, a medical secretary in San Francisco, cut the insurance bill on her 1982 Volkswagen convertible 30 percent by calling six companies and choosing the one with the lowest rate. Jay Bradley Myres, manager of the Chesapeake Bay Yacht Club in Easton, Maryland, saved 20 percent on the policy for his 1980 Toyota Corolla after calling several insurance agents. Mark Douglas, a draftsman in Norwalk, Connecticut, got quotes from only two insurers but still managed to slash the premium by 35 percent on his two cars, a 1963 Falcon and a 1983 Sentra.

Chances are, you can do at least as well. Profit margins and claims experience are so varied among insurers that the cost of identical coverage in many states varies by as much as 100 percent. In addition, if you get every discount you qualify for, you can pare your premium even further (as Figure 20 shows). ''The biggest mistake people make is that they simply take what they are persuaded to buy, not what they actually need,'' says Peter Hiam, the state insurance commissioner in Massachusetts.

Since their customers are often uninformed, insurance agents almost invariably push their standard, fully loaded (and fully priced) policy. The six basic types of coverage in the standard policy are bodily injury liability, property damage liability, collision, comprehensive (fire, theft, vandalism), uninsured motorist, and medical payments. Some of those coverages are essential and, indeed, compulsory. But most can be tailored to save you money, and you may be able to do without some of them and cut others to the bone.

Figure 20. The 10 Largest Car Insurers and Their Primary Discounts

When it comes to car insurance, hardly any two people pay exactly the same rate. The variables involve where you live, how you drive, who you are, what merits adorn and blemishes mar your driving record, and which company insures you. The motorist whom we have chosen to demonstrate the differences in rates and discounts at major companies is Mr. Middle American. He is 40 years old and a resident of Evanston, Illinois. He owns a new Buick Skylark, which he drives less than 10 miles each way to work. His coverage consists of bodily injury liability up to $100,000 per person and $300,000 per accident; property damage liability up to $50,000 per accident; $5,000 medical payments; full comprehensive; $200-deductible collision. The rates and discounts shown were current in 1986.

To qualify for these discounts, a driver or his car had to meet the following characteristics:

Good driver—no moving violations or insurance claims for four years.

Multicar—two or more vehicles insured with the same company.

Antitheft—interior hood lock, alarm, or a device that makes the ignition system inoperable.

Driver training—state- or county-certified course.

Insurer	*Typical annual rate*	*Good driving record*	*Multicar*	*Antitheft devices*	*Driver training*	*Senior citizen (age)*
USAA	$340	5%	20%	5% to 15%	up to 10%	5% (50 and over)
TRAVELERS	395	up to 20%	15% to 20%	5% to 20%	15%	5% (50–64) 5% to 15% (over 65)
GEICO	479	—	5% to 27%	5% to 10%	6% to 11%	up to 10% (over 50, pleasure driving only)
LIBERTY MUTUAL	487	—	10% to 20%	10% to 15%	10%	15% (55 and over)

FARMERS	582	20% to 23%	10% to 20%	5% to 15%	10%	—
NATIONWIDE	585	—	4% to 19%	—	—	7% to 11% (55 and over)
ALLSTATE	587	5% to 30%	up to 25%	5% to 30%	—	up to 10% (over 55 and retired)
STATE FARM	589	5% to 10%	10%	5% to 15%	10%	5% to 10% (65 and over)
AETNA	602	30%	20%	—	10%	10% (50 to 64) 20% (over 65)
USF&G	687	—	15% to 20%	5% to 15%	5% to 15%	10% to 20% (50 and over)

One coverage not to skimp on is bodily injury and property damage liability. If you — or anyone driving your car with your permission — is in an accident in which someone is killed or injured, this coverage pays your attorney's fee, court costs, and any judgments against you. Property damage liability covers damage you do to other people's property.

Most states require you to carry a minimum amount of bodily injury and property coverage. But the state-mandated minimums are far less than adequate for most drivers. Insurance agents and consumer groups say that the average driver should carry at least 100/300/50 coverage. That is, the policy would pay up to $100,000 for a single injury but no more than $300,000 for all injuries in any one accident, and up to $50,000 in property damage.

Once you have bought adequate bodily injury and property coverage, you can start looking for savings in the remainder of your auto policy:

Consider increasing collision and comprehensive deductibles. The deductible is the loss you agree to pay before the insurance kicks in. Increasing the deductible therefore lowers the premium. *Example:* by raising the deductible on your collision coverage from $100 to $500 — that is, by taking responsibility for $400 of additional risk — you can slash your premium about 35 percent. If you can afford a $1,000 deductible, you can save as much as 60 percent. Lesser savings are available on comprehensive coverage.

The odds are in your favor here. The Highway Loss Data Institute, an insurance industry group, estimates that in any given year only one car in 10 will be in an accident serious enough for the owner to file a collision claim. If your car is more than five years old, consider dropping collision and comprehensive. After five years, most American-made cars are worth no more than a third of their original value. That's the maximum your insurance company would pay if your car was totally wrecked.

Find a forgiving company. Ask the agents for several insurers how much their premium would rise if you filed an accident claim. Your survey may be enlightening. Nationwide Insurance, for instance, will hike its rate 30 percent in most states if you put in for more than $400. State Farm, the nation's largest car insurer, usually increases its premium 10 percent after the first $200 property damage claim. Some companies also increase their rates if you get more than one ticket for speeding or some other moving violation.

Check out the rates on a car before you buy it. The second largest insurer, Allstate, offers 25 to 55 percent discounts in most states on comprehensive and collision policies for cars that are least likely to be stolen or are cheapest to repair. It boosts rates by similar percentages on makes and models that are frequently ripped off or cost the most to repair. Other companies have similar programs.

Allstate's biggest discounts in recent years were on full-size sedans. Its largest surcharges applied to makes that thieves tend to covet, including BMW, Cadillac Eldorado, Chevrolet Camaro Z28, Chevrolet Corvette, Mazda RX7, Nissan 300ZX, Pontiac Firebird Trans Am, Porsche, Saab, and Volkswagen Scirocco.

Question your need for medical payments. This coverage pays a limited amount of medical expenses for people injured in your car. It duplicates coverage that most families already have in group health policies. The only reason to carry medical payments insurance in a car policy might be to fill gaps in your basic health coverage or to protect guest passengers.

Consider accepting the least possible personal injury protection. Several states require motorists to buy this form of no-fault coverage as a way of reducing court costs, speeding compensation, and lowering insurance rates. Personal injury protection pays medical costs and replaces lost wages of accident victims to a limited extent without proof of another driver's negligence. Many drivers with adequate health and disability plans can afford to accept the least no-fault coverage required. If you belong to a group health plan, ask your employee benefits office whether to take only the compulsory amount of personal injury protection.

Don't reject uninsured or underinsured motorist coverage. In case you are hurt by a hit-run driver or someone with little or no liability coverage, this section of your policy will pay up to $20,000 or $30,000 in compensation for the kinds of losses that are hard to measure in dollars — what lawyers call pain and suffering.

Spurn most optional coverages. They include payments for towing and labor, for stolen radios, and for a car rental while your heap is in the shop. A towing policy may run just $2 a year per car, but typically it covers only labor performed at the scene of a breakdown plus a fixed amount, usually $50, to have your car hauled away.

Once you understand your insurance options, you can start canvassing companies for price quotes. As a benchmark price, J. Robert Hunter, president of the National Insurance Consumer Organization, a nonprofit public interest group in Alexandria, Virginia, suggests getting your first quote from State Farm. In many parts of the country, State Farm charges among the lowest rates. It is, like Nationwide and Allstate, a so-called direct writer, which keeps a lid on costs by maintaining its own sales force. Agents for direct writers generally earn lower commissions than do independent agents, who sell insurance for a number of different companies. Cheapest of all are companies that sell insurance by mail and over toll-free telephone lines. One mail-order insurer, USAA (800-531-8080), writes auto insurance mainly for active or retired officers of the armed services. Another, Amica Mutual (800-242-6422), accepts only motorists who have good driving records and are recommended by its policyholders.

If you are unfamiliar with a firm offering attractively low rates, you can check its financial stability in *Best's Insurance Reports,* available at public libraries. Stick with property and casualty insurers rated A+. Cheap insurance from a company that goes broke is no bargain.

Just as important as an insurer's premium rates and financial stability is its reputation for service. Insurance departments in the larger states, including Illinois, New York, and Pennsylvania, publish lists of companies with the highest and lowest consumer-complaint ratios — total gripes against it divided by the number of its policies in force in the state. Of the ten largest insurers in Figure 20, the two with the lowest complaint ratios in Illinois in 1984 were State Farm and USAA. The two with the highest complaint ratios were Aetna and Liberty Mutual.

55

GUARDING YOUR CASTLE AGAINST CALAMITY

Ever since the Phoenix, England's first fire insurance company, began insuring private houses after the Great Fire of London in 1666, homeowners have grappled with the problem of protecting their property from disaster. Today's American homeowner can insure not only the structure but also its contents against fire, theft, and a wide range of other disasters. Tenants and condominium owners can buy coverage on their furnishings, decorations, and household goods. In addition, homeowners and tenants insurance includes personal-liability protection for injuries that visitors sustain on your premises and damage you may do to the property of others.

Homeowners insurance can be had in a basic stripped-down version that safeguards your castle only from named perils such as fire, windstorm, and hail. Or you can upgrade it to various degrees until it achieves the somewhat overstated status of all-risk coverage. At this "comprehensive" level you can collect claims for damage caused by burst water pipes or a collapsed roof, but you are still out in the cold if losses are caused by war, nuclear accident, earthquake, or, to the surprise of irate victims, flood. The insurance industry's latest and most encompassing policy, one called the Homeowners Program, provides more personal-liability protection than before and better coverage of such possessions as jewelry, furs, and computers used at home for business purposes. As a sensible economy, this form of policy raises the amount of loss you must pay out of your own pocket — the standard deductible — from $100 to $250.

The Dollar Amount You Need

The amount of homeowners insurance you should carry depends on replacement cost — what you would have to spend to rebuild your manse as it now stands. Don't confuse this concept with market value, or you could wind up seriously over- or underinsuring your dwelling. The replacement cost of a new house, for example, is typically only 75 percent of the purchase price. The land is indestructible and the foundation is nearly so; neither need be insured. Conversely, the replacement cost of a Victorian townhouse with carved mahogany banisters and ornate gingerbread woodwork can outstrip what the house would fetch if resold.

The cost-estimating forms that most insurers use to arrive at replacement value assess such factors as the soundness of construction, the number of rooms, and the quality of kitchen appliances and bathroom fixtures. This method is fine for the typical house; but if you own a custom-designed or period home, you should get a written estimate of its replacement cost from a real estate appraiser.

Insurance companies prefer that you insure your home for 100 percent of replacement cost. Total losses are rare, however, and you will be adequately compensated for partial damage with 80 percent coverage. Reducing your coverage to 80 percent of replacement value can lower premium costs as much as one-fifth.

Make sure your policy indexes the replacement cost to inflation. Sluggish real estate values might tempt you to forgo this extra protection, but that would be a big mistake. Replacement costs move independent of market value. From 1983 to 1985, residential construction costs climbed 9.8 percent, while the resale prices of houses rose 7.2 percent. If you make a substantial improvement to your house, raise your coverage to reflect the new replacement cost.

Covering Your Possessions

All homeowners policies insure your personal possessions, but important limits apply. Most contracts, including the Homeowners Program, restrict the total claim for personal possessions to half of the amount of coverage on the house itself. Insure your home for $120,000, and the most you can collect on the contents is $60,000. Moreover, you are reimbursed not for a destroyed item's replacement cost but for its actual cash value — replacement cost minus depreciation. A five-year-old TV that goes up in smoke might fetch only $100 instead of the $700 you paid for it or the price of the newest equivalent set.

To make sure you will be adequately reimbursed when you make a claim, add to your policy a replacement-cost endorsement for personal contents. Your yearly premium will go up 10 to 15 percent, but the extra protection is worth that. And to have enough coverage for a major disaster, raise the claim limit from 50 to 70 percent of the coverage on the house. Your premium will rise only about $1 per additional $1,000 in coverage.

A much lower reimbursement limit than actual cash value applies to jewelry, furs, silverware, and collectibles. If a thief makes off with your $5,000 diamond bracelet, the standard policy pays you only $500. The Homeowners Program policy raises the coverages on jewelry, furs, and negotiable securities to $1,000 and on gold and silverware to $2,500. A blanket endorsement can boost your protection up to a maximum of $10,000 for about $3 per $100 value of jewelry, $1 per $100 for furs, and 25 cents per $100 for fine art. Blanket coverage, however, may still have a limit for individual items. Therefore, valuables worth more than $2,500 should be itemized and insured individually. To support a claim, you need sales receipts and appraisals for all valuables that are covered by endorsements.

Liability Limits

Many older homeowners policies still have only $25,000 of liability coverage, although the Homeowners Program offers $100,000. Even that might not be enough. Raising your liability limit to $100,000 adds $10 a year to your premium, and $500,000 worth of protection adds $30.

Homeowners polices don't usually cover commercial activities. If you work part-time in your house, add an incidental business option to your policy. With it, you can insure up to $10,000 of business property for about $20 a year and extend your liability protection to the business. Many newer policies such as the Homeowners Program automatically cover up to $2,500 worth of business equipment used at home. But if your residence is also your primary place of business, you probably need the more expensive but more comprehensive Business Owners policy. Premiums start at $200 to $250 for $20,000 of property protection and $500,000 worth of liability insurance.

Where to Economize

The premiums can pile up when you shape your homeowners policy to your circumstances. One way to hold down costs is to take advantage of the special deals offered by most insurers. If your house was built in the past two years, you are eligible for a 20 percent new-home discount. The discount diminishes by three percentage points every two years. Installing dead bolts and smoke detectors can knock 5 percent off your annual premium cost. A telephonic home-protection system — fire and burglar alarms that report to a central station — lops off 20 percent. The discounts are cumulative. "If you have a new home with a central station alarm," says Bonnie McHenry, a homeowners insurance specialist at Aetna Life & Casualty, "you can save up to 40 percent."

Increase your deductible and you will also decrease your premium. Agree to absorb the first $250 of any loss instead of the standard $100 and you save 10 percent. Jump to a $500 deductible and you pocket 20 percent of the premium. If your budget can handle a $1,000 loss, make that 25 percent. Those whose finances are solid enough to absorb $2,500 or $5,000 hits can reduce premiums 30 or 35 percent.

Don't let the quest for savings lead you into the trap of choosing a low deductible and scrimping on the overall coverage. Countless homeowners, too concerned about getting reimbursed for minor losses, have given in to this temptation, leaving themselves dangerously underinsured against major risks.

Tenant and Condo Coverage

Four out of five renters carry no property or liability insurance. "Renters simply assume that their landlords have insurance," says Woody Widrow, director of the National Tenants Union, a lobbying group based in Orange, New Jersey. "They do. But it covers only the building, not a tenant's possessions or his liability to others." Similarly, many owners of cooperative apartments and condominiums believe that the policy bought by their cooperative corporation or condo association insures their possessions and provides liability protection. But those policies, too, generally apply only to the building's structure and to liability claims arising from mishaps in lobbies, elevators, and other shared areas. If you want liability protection or coverage for your personal effects, you have to buy it yourself.

Insurance packages for tenants are nearly identical to those for condominium and co-op dwellers. Like the policies that single-family homeowners buy, they do much more than simply protect against losses from burglary and fire.

Nevertheless, selecting the right policy can be tricky. Many plans have potentially nettlesome exclusions, and prices can vary from roughly $70 a year to $700 or so. The cost depends not only on the company you deal with and how much coverage you buy, but also on such factors as the construction of the building you live in and the incidence of crime in your city.

One of the first variables to consider is how much liability coverage you need. As with homeowners contracts, the liability limit can be boosted from $25,000 to $100,000 for $10 or so extra a year. If you have sizable assets or a big income to protect, increase your coverage even more.

Condominium owners should double-check their condo association's master policy to make sure its coverage extends to such items as kitchen cabinets, built-in appliances, bathroom fixtures, and wall and floor coverings that came with your unit. If not, you need to estimate the cost of replacing these articles to determine how much insurance you need. Improvements made to your apartment, including fancy wallpaper, marble tiling, or recessed lighting, are another matter. Condo policies typically cover only the first $1,000 worth of such improvements. Renters plans may have higher or lower limits, depending on the amount of coverage you buy. In either case, the limit can easily be raised, at a cost of about $3 a year for each $1,000 of alterations insured.

Once you know how much property coverage you need, the next step is to choose the kind of policy you want. A replacement-cost endorsement can be especially important for co-op and condo owners. Be sure to add that coverage under the "additions and alterations" or the "betterments and improvements" section of the policy if you renovate the kitchen or redo the bathroom. The premiums run 15 to 40 percent higher than for actual-cash-value policies, but they pay the entire cost of repairs or replacement. Many endorsements, however, won't guarantee more than 400 percent of an item's actual cash value.

Both replacement-cost and actual-cash-value policies pay for losses that arise from any of 18 named perils, including fire, smoke, riot, or frozen pipes. But unless you have an all-risk policy, you are not covered if someone spills a glass of Burgundy on your expensive white carpet. Such plans are available from only a handful of major insurers, including the Chubb Group and Fireman's Fund. All-risk policies are the top of the line and too pricey for most people. A standard $50,000 replacement-cost policy in 1986 for a condominium in Atlanta cost $556 from Chubb. A similar policy upgraded to cover all risks — including red wine on your white Persian carpet — lifted the annual premium to $755.

Taking Inventory

Those possessions of yours, whether in a house, condo, co-op, or rental apartment, may be worth more than you think. As an example, the average replacement value of the items in a two-bedroom apartment is about $25,000. To nail down the worth of your things in case your home is destroyed or badly damaged, you need detailed records.

Devise your own household inventory procedure or ask your insurance agent for a form. Another option is to describe your possessions on an audio cassette tape. Agents often suggest taking photos to support any written or tape-recorded inventory. Better yet, videotape your things with a VCR camera.

No matter which inventory method you choose, you should list where, when, and at what cost you purchased each item of value in your home. You should also estimate, item by item, how much you would have to pay today to replace your belongings. For particularly valuable items such as antiques and jewelry, get professional appraisals.

Keep all records, including bills of sale, in a safe place outside your home, preferably in a safe-deposit box. Receipts can be persuasive evidence of your buying habits. For instance, they can demonstrate to a skeptical insurance adjuster that you made a habit of buying all your shoes at Gucci.

Shopping for Price

Choose a homeowners or tenants insurance company just as you do an automobile policy (see Chapter 54). Stick with companies rated A+ by A. M. Best Company. To get benchmark prices, call an agent of the State Farm Insurance Company. Don't overlook discount insurers such as USAA, Colonial Penn, and Geico. (The same companies that write car insurance also write homeowners.) If you are content with the agency that sold you your car policy, keep life simple by giving your homeowners business to the same firm. It may even reward you with a 10 percent discount.

56

EXCESS LIABILITY: YOUR LAST BASTION AGAINST DAMAGE SUITS

Accidents happen, and when they do the law says that those who were to blame must pay the victims' financial losses. As a consequence, people who cause accidents through negligence can suffer grievous losses, too. That's why it is so important to choose high liability coverage in your car and homeowners policies. But at times their liability limits aren't high enough.

If you have substantial assets that could be seized by a court to pay off a judgment that exceeds your auto and homeowners coverage, you should almost certainly buy an additional excess liability policy, also known as an umbrella policy. It is designed to take over where your other coverage ends. A $1 million umbrella policy costs between $80 and $150 a year.

Jury Verdict Research in Solon, Ohio, a firm that keeps records of jury awards in personal-injury cases, reports that in recent years the average judgment for spinal fractures has ranged from $115,000 to $138,000. You can get that much insurance in a car policy, but what if the person tripped over a tricycle left by your child on your front walk? Homeowners policies seldom cover more than $100,000 — less than the average jury award and much less than many above-average ones. Except in commercial and professional liability cases, which have gotten completely out of hand, truly enormous judgments are rare. But they are increasing. In 1982 there were 30 jury awards of $1 million or more to individual auto accident victims in the United States. In 1983 there were 38, and in 1984 there were 50.

Even if your personal net worth is modest, you should consider buying an excess liability policy because a judgment against you could lay claim to your future income. James A. Robertson, an insurance consultant in Irvine, California, observes, "People tend to have an unrealistic idea of what is at stake. Almost anyone with a job has an asset that needs to be protected."

Excess liability policies, sold in amounts of $1 million and up, cover you for accidents you might either cause or be responsible for — if, for instance, your children were at fault. The premium depends on the company you select and on such factors as the number of cars and houses you own. The best contracts cover almost every kind of liability claim except those related to business activities, which your employer probably insures.

Since the excess liability policy takes over where auto or homeowners insurance ends, insurers will issue it only if you already have substantial primary coverage. Cigna, whose INA company pioneered the umbrella policy in the 1960s, insists that your car insurance include bodily injury coverage of $250,000 per injured person or $300,000 per accident. Adding the extra coverage will raise your auto premium by $20 to $80 a year.

As another precondition, Cigna and most other insurers demand that you carry $100,000 in comprehensive personal liability insurance in your homeowners policy. This protects you in case of mishaps that you or others in your household cause away from home, as well as accidents around your house. If one of your kids is on a ski trip and knocks down someone on the slopes, your homeowners insurance would pay damages awarded to the injured person. Increasing your homeowners liability from $25,000 to $100,000 adds roughly $10 to the annual premium.

The excess liability umbrella also gives you protection that you do not have in other policies. It covers your legal defense and any judgment or settlement if you are sued for libel, slander, or invasion of privacy. There is typically a deductible of $250, but attorneys' fees alone easily can exceed 10 times that amount.

Elected officials may have a particular need for excess liability insurance because their responsibilities and visibility make them open targets for lawsuits. In a New York State case, the widow of a teacher sued the members of her board of education and the superintendent of schools for $10,000 on the ground that they drove her husband to suicide. The school district's insurance did not cover board members individually, but one foresighted defendant had an excess liability policy with Aetna. The company provided his defense, which cost over $1,000, and he was absolved.

While every insurer supplies lawyers to represent its policyholders, some companies count the cost of defense as part of a policy's coverage limit. Policies differ in other respects, too. A few insurers prefer to indemnify you — that is, reimburse you for money you have already paid — rather than paying claims directly. Avoid such policies. Other questions you should ask:

Who is covered? Your policy should extend to everyone in your household who is related to you by blood, adoption, or marriage. That includes children away at school.

What kinds of liability are covered? In addition to physical injuries, most policies protect you against a potpourri of other claims: libel, slander, invasion of privacy, malicious prosecution, wrongful eviction, defamation of character, and discrimination.

In what circumstances do you have coverage? Not all umbrella policies protect you if you are sued while serving as an officer or trustee of a municipal, civic, charitable, or religious organization. Many companies are writing new exclusions into their policies. For example, Aetna, which paid for the New York State school trustee's defense, says it has abandoned the municipal liability field. You also may find it hard to get coverage as a member of a homeowners or condominium association or other less formal groups. Look for the policy with the fewest exclusions for participation in nonprofit organizations.

What if you caused an injury intentionally? Some companies consider extenuating circumstances. For instance, they will stand by you if you find kids vandalizing your house and in the act of stopping them you break an intruder's arm. The Travelers' policies seem to cover such situations with the words "bodily injury or property damage resulting from an insured's use of reasonable force to protect persons or property."

A sensible way to choose an excess liability policy is with the help of an independent insurance agent. He represents a number of companies and can help you sort through their policies, interpreting technical language. Choose the policy with the most extensive coverage. Three companies that insurance consultants believe have among the broadest policies are Crum & Forster, Kemper, and St. Paul Fire & Marine. St. Paul, however, will cover you only if you carry its car and homeowners policies.

People whose professional and personal lives blend should consider buying a type of commercial liability policy that covers them on and off the job. Lawyers and owners of small companies, for example, often take their business into social settings — on a tennis court, perhaps, or in a duck blind. Commercial liability insurance with an endorsement adding personal coverage would provide such people with gap-free protection. The premium starts at around $300.

One inescapable irony of excess liability insurance is that it not only protects against huge damage suits but also may provoke them. Claimants' attorneys have ways of finding out how much you are insured for. Louis Korecki, who is in charge of the Travelers' personal liability insurance, says, ''It's uncanny how often the verdict comes in exactly at the limit of the policy.''

57

LIFE INSURANCE: ENOUGH IS ENOUGH

Of all the varieties of coverage, life insurance is the hardest to gauge correctly. You have to estimate the income your family would need, and for how long, if a breadwinner died. This is an exercise in matching foreseeable dollars with unknowable future events. If no one is relying on you for financial support, you probably don't need any life insurance. As someone's provider, you may want coverage for only a limited period — until the kids finish college, say — or perhaps for the rest of your spouse's life.

People often compound the difficulty of judging their life insurance needs by regarding financial benefits as a way to make up for emotional losses. If you do that, you are throwing money away on more insurance than you really require. It is far better to invest the difference toward the purchase of things you will want if you live a normal life span — the much greater probability.

Agents have tables and formulas to help you determine your life insurance needs, but with patience and a hand-held calculator, you can do your own calculations using the worksheets in Figure 21 at the end of this chapter. Don't assume that your survivors can invest the entire proceeds of your insurance and live off just the income. Few people can afford that much insurance. Realistic planning should be based on the gradual use of the principal.

Even then, after adding in funeral expenses and estate settlement costs, a 40-year-old parent earning $45,000 a year could need more than $500,000 of insurance to protect his or her family. Social Security survivors benefits will replace some lost income; family savings and group life insurance at work will probably contribute, too. But unless your spouse has high earning power, you are still likely to need coverage in six figures.

Assumptions in the Worksheet

Money's approach to life insurance planning supposes that you spend one-third of your annual take-home pay on yourself, for food, clothing, commuting, entertainment, and other personal expenses, and on obligatory items including life insurance itself. The other two-thirds of your paycheck is what your family would need if you were to die. If you find that percentage too high or too low, use a figure (on line 2 of the worksheet) more in accord with your way of life.

This exercise assumes that you wish, at the very least, to provide money for living costs until your youngest child goes off to college. Whether to give your family support after that is a matter for discussion between spouses. Will the survivor want and be able to support himself or herself with no help from the other's estate? In two-career households, the answer may be a simple yes. But if one of you earns the bulk of the household income, the other may not be able to cling to your present standard of living without an insurance lifeline. One thing is clear: if you have children, each wage-earning parent should have insurance and should separately calculate how much is needed.

Base your figuring on the grim assumption — but the normal one for insurance purposes — that the person insured will die soon after insurance coverage begins. Make it your aim to preserve but not improve your family's living standard. Another crucial assumption is that your survivor would invest most or all of your lump-sum insurance payout and spend the principal gradually. Therefore, the raw amounts of money needed to accomplish insurance goals need some marinating. The worksheet and tables adjust long-term funding for a net annual return on investment of 2 percent. This conservatively allows for the inroads of taxes and inflation. It is the same return used in Chapter 24 for retirement planning. (Table A applies the 2 percent return to annual income needs; it is an annuity computation. Table B, for annuity funds that would not be needed for several years, reduces those sums to their present value, again assuming a 2 percent net return.)

You can fill out optional sections of the worksheet devoted to paying for the kids' college, supporting a spouse after child rearing, and establishing a spouse's retirement fund. Also called for is a fund for funeral expenses, medical bills, and other costs and obligations of your estate.

One year's take-home pay usually is more than ample to cover those items. Provide for less than that if you wish.

Having arrived at the maximum amount of money your family would need, you must take into account such existing sources of funds as savings, investments, and insurance policies now in force. You should also consider how much, if anything, your spouse might earn during the period you are providing for. To find out how much Social Security survivors income your spouse and children could expect to receive, use the Social Security worksheet and table of benefits (Table C). As the years pass, ask your district Social Security office for updated amounts.

What Kind of Policy to Buy

Once you decide how much insurance to buy, you must choose between a policy that doubles as a savings account — whole, universal, variable or adjustable life — and one that provides nothing but protection. That would be term insurance. The premiums for term coverage are low: about $200 a year buys $100,000 worth of annual renewable term at age 40 for a man, and about $175 buys that amount for a woman. By contrast, $100,000 of whole life generally costs at least $1,000 a year for either sex at age 40. But the comparison isn't quite that simple. The cost of term life rises as you grow older. Whole life has a fixed premium for as long as you keep the policy in force. Furthermore, universal life, the newest form of insurance-plus-savings account, combines some of the best attributes of term and whole life. These and other types of policies need a closer look.

Annual Renewable Term

Term insurance still provides protection at the lowest possible price. Premiums are modest while you are young, but rise inexorably to reflect the mortality odds that go with aging. In the most popular plan, annual renewable and convertible term, rates go up every year. However, the need for insurance is almost always greatest while your children are young and your assets are slim. Each year parents discharge some of their financial responsibilities. If they are planning properly, they put aside money regularly toward such objectives as college and retirement. In time, their insurance needs decline or disappear.

Like store-brand aspirin tablets, term policies sell at highly competitive prices, especially if you are buying a lot of coverage. Premiums vary with your age, sex, and, to some extent, your living habits, but male nonsmokers should be able to get $100,000 of term insurance for about $170 a year at age 30, $200 a year at 40, or $530 a year at 50. Women pay 10 to 20 percent less because they live longer; smokers generally have to pay 25 percent more than nonsmokers.

Never buy term insurance on the basis of the first-year premium alone because the step-ups over the years can distort price comparisons. Industry and consumer groups have developed more accurate cost indexes based on interest-adjusted long-term calculations. Two organizations rank insurers and their policies by cost analysis and publish the results periodically. Consumers Union ran a three-part report in its magazine, *Consumer Reports,* in June, July, and August 1986. (For copies send $12 to the Back Issue Department, *Consumer Reports,* P.O. Box 2485, Boulder, Colorado 80322.) The National Insurance Consumer Organization lists low-cost companies in a booklet, *How to Save Money on Life Insurance* ($7.25 from NICO, 121 North Payne Street, Alexandria, Virginia 22314).

Whole Life

While whole life insurance premiums never rise, that advantage is illusory. A large portion of the high premium goes into a cash reserve, which rises by a guaranteed amount each year. This reserve steadily reduces the company's risk by replacing insurance with the customer's own money. Year by year, you get less insurance for your fixed premium. However, the cash value of the policy, which belongs to you, keeps growing, tax-deferred. The unanswered question about whole life is how much interest the insurer is paying on your cash.

For most people who keep their policies in force, the cash reserve becomes a retirement fund. By surrendering the policy, you can retrieve a fair amount of money. It won't equal the policy's face value — the death benefit — but a whole life policy that you bought when you were 35 and kept up for 25 or 30 years is likely to have a cash surrender value of around two-thirds of its face value. What makes whole life resemble a savings account is the interest earned by your growing equity in the policy.

Although the return on your cash value is known only to the company, independent analysts surmise that whole life usually pays its policyholders little more than a passbook savings account, and then only after you have paid into a policy for many years. A few companies have started paying better returns, though still not disclosing the rate. A prominent example is Northwestern Mutual of Milwaukee.

Whole life has other disadvantages in cost and rigidity. There are heavy sales charges, typically 70 percent of the first-year premium plus 7.5 percent of each successive premium over the next nine years and lesser charges after that. And the vital terms of a standard contract are unchangeable. You cannot permanently withdraw any of the money and remain insured, although you can borrow it. Nor can you vary the premium or freely increase the insurance protection to suit your changing situation.

Adjustable Life

Whole life's reputation became so tarnished in the 1970s that a couple of companies introduced a mutation called adjustable life. It is a bit more flexible than whole life, and the company may disclose your rate of return on cash value.

Adjustable life was introduced by Minnesota Mutual Life of St. Paul; a similar policy is sold by the Principal Financial Group (formerly Bankers Life) of Des Moines, Iowa. These plans are designed to let you focus on the two essential questions of life insurance — how much coverage you need and how much you can afford to pay in premiums. A cost-of-living option gives policyholders up to age 55 a chance every three years to increase their coverage to correspond with changes in the consumer price index — up to a limit. The Principal's maximum each time is 20 percent of the face value or $20,000, whichever is less; Minnesota Mutual's is 20 percent or $30,000. No medical or other exam is needed for these increases.

You must, however, accept each cost-of-living increase to remain eligible for future increases. You would ordinarily pay a higher premium for expanded coverage, but with adjustable life you can keep payments the same by reducing the term of the coverage. As with whole life, sales commissions are onerous. But in a study commissioned some years ago by *Money,* the cost of the Minnesota Mutual and Bankers Life plans compared favorably with those of whole life at most other companies.

Universal Life

In 1980 a handful of relatively small companies addressed the problems of rigidity and a low rate of return by introducing a policy called universal life. It combines term insurance with a tax-deferred savings account that earns interest at money-market or bond-market rates — and it discloses those rates. Suddenly insurance began to make sense as more than bare-bones protection against your unexpected demise. Hundreds of insurers, major as well as minor, now sell universal life, and many of them push it hard.

At its best, universal life is among the most attractive of tax shelters — indeed, one of the few shelters left undisturbed by the 1986 tax overhaul. If you need a lot of life insurance, it is hard to think of a better way to get it and simultaneously put money aside for the children's education, a business venture, or even a dream cruise around the world.

With any kind of policy, you usually can reduce the amount of insurance as the years go by, but universal life lets you raise your premium and allocate an ever-increasing portion of it to tax-sheltered savings. Congress has put limits on the total savings you can shelter from taxes in universal life, relative to the insurance portion. But the limits are generous. For instance, a man aged 35 with $100,000 of insurance can amass, by the time he is 65, a cash value of as much as $666,666 without incurring tax liability. Policyholders who are on the verge of saving up more than that can either withdraw some cash from the policy or buy more insurance. Tax time does arrive, however, when you cash in the policy.

Many universal life plans come loaded with heavy commissions and other hidden costs. But worthy plans minimize sales charges and free you from the inflexible requirements of whole life. You can vary the amount you put into the investment account from year to year. You can decrease the size of your insurance premium when your household budget is pinched. You can even skip an occasional premium and pay your insurance out of the policy's investments. You can boost your coverage at will — if your health is unimpaired — simply by phoning the company for a form, though you may have to see a doctor if you want much more insurance. In the best universal life policies you can withdraw money from the savings account whenever you want without serious penalty.

The cost of the term insurance embodied in a universal life policy is hard to pin down. At first glance it seems competitive with annual term, but such a comparison ignores commissions. Are they part of the cost of the insurance, the cash account, or both? The companies do not say. In any case, the universal life agent gets a larger commission than the term agent. The money often comes out of an extra fee tacked onto the first-year premium.

The interest rate the company will pay you typically changes from year to year as a result of the insurer's investment success or in step with market interest rates. These changes are not announced very far in advance. Furthermore, the quoted rate often is not paid on all your cash value; the first $1,000 usually earns only 4 percent. Universal life also hits you with annual fees equal to 3 to 10 percent of each year's premium for the life of the policy. Many universal life policies give the company the right to slap heavy additional fees on withdrawals made in the first few years.

With all those nicks and scratches, it is not easy to tell which versions of universal life give decent rates of return. Fortunately, the National Insurance Consumer Organization has done legwork on many policies. James Hunt, a director of NICO and a former Vermont insurance commissioner, identified the best buy as the plan sold by USAA Life of San Antonio, Texas (800-531-8000). USAA Life is a subsidiary of the cooperative United Services Automobile Association, one of the nation's largest car insurers. Hunt found that its universal life policy, sold only by mail, had the lowest sales charge (a start-up fee of $50 plus 3 percent of each premium) and paid high interest as well. The only additional charge was $25 for each withdrawal of cash.

As second choices, Hunt recommended the universal life plan of Bankers National Life of Parsippany, New Jersey (800-631-0099; in New Jersey, 201-267-2540). The only sales charge is a $45 annual policy fee. That fee, plus a 2.5 percent state premium tax, is deducted from your cash value. The minimum policy size is $50,000.

A couple of cautionary notes. First, Hunt's study, like all insurance analyses, attempts to pin down a moving target. Competition can alter policy comparisons quickly. Review the terms when you phone the companies to make sure nothing has changed for the worse. Second, avoid any universal life policy with high surrender charges, sometimes called back-end loads. They are designed to discourage you from withdrawing your cash, which is exactly what you will want to do if the yield tumbles.

Variable Life

Variable life insurance hitches an old-fashioned buggy called whole life to the hard-charging but unpredictable stock market. You can take the investment reins in your own hands and, with skill and luck, outrace stodgy bond yields and that old devil inflation. In a typical plan, you can also try to time the stock market, switching between stocks and bonds and the money market. Or you can diversify into fixed proportions of all three. Whichever way you choose to do it, your gains if any will be tax-deferred.

With this freedom and flexibility go considerable risks. The cash value of your policy — and its death benefit — can plummet as well as soar. Despite the hazards inherent in investing in securities, however, the policy never loses sight of its primary objective: to protect your family from the financial consequences of your death. The amount payable to your beneficiary if you die cannot sink below the face value of the policy you initially purchased.

Variable life comes as a variant of whole life and as a version of universal life and single-premium life (see below). With whole life, funds earmarked for cash reserves go into the insurance company's gigantic general investment pot, consisting largely of bonds and mortgages. With variable life, your funds are kept separate from the company's general portfolio. Cash values don't increase at a fixed rate but fluctuate daily with the value of the securities in your account. These, of course, can shrink as well as grow.

Some insurers selling variable whole life offer more investment choices than others. Equitable Life of New York, the first company to market the plan, has just two portfolios in 1986, a stock fund and a money-market fund. You are permitted two switches between them each year. Metropolitan Life, New York Life, and Provident Mutual, which also offer two or more portfolios, allow four moves a year; Monarch Life allows five.

Most insurers manage the various portfolios themselves, but an increasing number hire outsiders to do it. For instance, Provident Mutual's equity fund is run by Shearson Lehman Brothers. Monarch, a leading writer of variable life, has two groups of funds, one directed by Merrill Lynch and the other by Oppenheimer Management Corporation. Between them, they offer 12 investment portfolios and zero-coupon-bond unit trusts with a full range of maturity dates. Other insurers offering variable life include Bankers Security of Washington, D.C., Massachusetts Mutual, the New England, and the Prudential.

Prudential, the leader in universal variable life, manages its plan's five portfolios and offers to apportion your account among them according to its investment managers' judgment of market conditions. Predicting market turns is at best guesswork, but an educated guess by experts is likely to be right more often than an uninformed one. Prudential's policy is selling so well that other big insurers have introduced rival plans. Universal variable life is shaping up as the most popular stock-market-related policy. As the competition to sell it heats up, agents' commissions are likely to grow. Prudential's strategy is to keep your costs low if you stay with the plan but penalize you with a back-end load if you let your policy lapse within 10 years.

At times when investments in a variable life policy enjoy healthy growth, some of the increase in cash value goes to buy more life insurance. That enables not only the cash value but also the death benefit to rise. Yet the guarantee of at least as much insurance as you initially bought keeps your dependents reasonably well protected against wrong investment decisions. That is essential because your survivors won't be able to wait, as investors can, for stocks or bonds to recover from a serious sinking spell.

The policyholder who lives to enjoy the fruits of his variable life investment gets no guaranteed amount of cash. The risk is his, rather than the insurer's. In return, there is greater growth potential. If you accept the premise that returns from stocks, bonds, or money-market funds will exceed inflation or keep pace with it, variable life answers a major criticism of whole life: that inflation plays a cruel joke on people who rely on the purchasing power of fixed cash values and death benefits that may not be needed until far in the future.

Variable life also shares with whole life three important tax advantages. First, earnings generated by the policy are not taxed while the policy remains in force. Second, when you cash in the policy, only the amount that exceeds the sum of premiums paid over the years is taxable. Third, the death benefit is not taxable as income. It is added to the policyholder's estate, where assets up to $600,000 are free of federal estate tax (see Chapter 28).

Variable life makes sense only if you are fairly certain you will keep the policy in force for at least 10 years to take fullest advantage of the possible growth in cash value. Whether as whole or universal life, variable's high fees and commissions eat into the early cash buildup. Even after 15 or 20 years, the fees charged by some insurers would reduce a 12 percent annual gain on investments by two or three percentage points.

You need to have faith in your own investment acumen or your insurer's if you choose variable life. Also keep in mind that while you can pick your type of investment, managers chosen by the insurance company still select the underlying securities. Most companies have not offered policies long enough to compile significant track records.

Single-Premium Life

Under most circumstances it is foolish to pay for insurance in a lump sum up front. If you die shortly after insuring yourself, your beneficiaries will get far less money than if you had put a smaller premium into a conventional contract that you pay for a year at a time. Yet many people in the mid-1980s were pouring anywhere from $5,000 to $1 million at one clip into suddenly popular single-premium life insurance policies. And for good reason: today's single-premium policies are designed as protection against taxes instead of against death. They are tax-sheltered investments that take fullest possible advantage of the tax deferral of the earnings being generated inside your policy.

"I'd guess 99 percent of people who buy single-premium insurance do so for tax purposes and 1 percent buy it for insurance," says David Watts, director of the insurance portfolio division of Scudder Stevens & Clark, a large mutual-fund management firm. Companies that sell single-premium contracts therefore try to keep the guaranteed death benefit to the legal minimum. For example, a 60-year-old who pays a $10,000 single premium might get a mere $30,000 of insurance.

Since the whole emphasis is on investment, insurers have no hesitation about telling you the rate of return on the cash value. Single-premium whole life, the prototype policy, pays a fixed yield for a specified time, generally one to three years. The gross return in early 1987 was 8 to 9 percent. However, the policy is likely to guarantee you no more than 4 percent; thus, if interest rates take a dive, so does the yield.

Your net return will be much less than your gross, especially when the policy is new and being charged for sales commissions. The insurer also subtracts from your income its own expenses, state taxes, and a small amount for insurance costs. Taking all expenses into account, analysts in 1987 mentioned policies from Equitable Life Assurance Society, Fidelity Bankers Life, and Life of Virgina as among the best contracts available.

In addition to single-premium whole life, some companies sell variable life plans. Not even a nominal rate of return is guaranteed. But you can have your premium invested in mutual funds that are managed exclusively for policyholders: portfolios of stocks, bonds, and money-market securities, to any of which you can allot part or all of your money. You can also switch investments from fund to fund in an effort to time the markets. Some single-premium variable policies worth considering, according to analysts, are those from Guardian, Monarch, and Provident Mutual.

Tax reform gave single-premium life a huge boost in sales. With one premium — just about as large a one as you care to invest — going to work for you immediately, you can pile up a lot more untaxed compound interest than you get from the slow buildup of yearly $2,000 contributions to an Individual Retirement Account. An even greater selling point is the access you get to this investment income without loss of coverage. Single-premium life offers what amounts to tax-free, interest-free loans that you need not repay.

Here's how the loans work. The company declares a borrowing rate but instead of billing you for the money deducts an equal amount from your investment earnings. In 1987, for example, it was common for insurers to charge 7 percent interest and credit your account with 7 percent earnings. If you want to borrow some of your premium, you can do that, too. In that case, you actually have to hand over some interest, but only at a rate of 2 to 4 percent a year.

Don't invest in a single-premium policy expecting to withdraw much money in the first few years. So many dollars of your early earnings are drained away to pay off commission costs that your investment growth gets off to a slow start. Furthermore, don't plan on ever cashing in your policy. In the first several years, surrender charges will cost you part of your premium as a penalty — usually 9 percent of it the first year and one percentage point less in each of several succeeding years. Once you have generated a nice pile of earnings, however, and there are no more surrender charges, cashing in the policy will cost you a bundle in taxes. And if you have already borrowed most of your earnings, you will be committing tax suicide, because no money will be left in the policy to pay the IRS. Make up your mind that single-premium life is for life.

If you expect to take advantage of the loan privilege, buy only a policy that guarantees zero net interest on borrowed earnings and no more than 2 percent interest on borrowed premium money. Avoid any policy that extends the surrender charge beyond the first seven years. Finally, before signing up, check with the insurance agent or your accountant for possible changes in tax law. Congress might have changed its mind by then and decided that interest-free loans and low-interest loans should be treated as taxable income.

Figure 21. Life Insurance Planning Worksheet

By filling in the blanks, you can get a firm fix on how much more life insurance you need. Two-career couples should calculate their coverages separately in the columns provided. The worksheet following this one helps you to estimate Social Security survivors benefits, a major contributor to almost everyone's life insurance coverage. You can use this planning method to insure just the living and college expenses of your dependent children, or you can calculate additional insurance funds for the post–child-rearing years of your spouse. Those years are divided into two periods, before and after your spouse's 60th birthday. At 60, she or he could start collecting Social Security survivors retirement income. The retirement fund computation provides the amount of income you have planned even if your spouse lives to be 100.

Current Living Expenses

	Wife	*Husband*
1. Your annual take-home pay	$________	$________
2. Amount used for family living expenses (two-thirds of line 1 or see the text)	$________	$________
3. Number of years remaining before your youngest child's 18th birthday	________	________
4. Total living expenses (line 3 times line 2)	$________	$________
COLLEGE FUND		
5. Number of children you expect to send to college	________	
6. Estimated four-year college costs per child, in current dollars (see Figure 6, Chapter 18)	$________	
7. Total college cost (line 6 times line 5; if both spouses work, divide the total cost in proportion to your salaries)	$________	$________
8. Total living and college expenses during child-rearing years (line 4 plus line 7)	$________	$________
AVAILABLE INCOME		
9. Total Social Security survivors benefits before your youngest child's 18th birthday (from line 4 or line 9 of the Social Security Worksheet, page 453)	$________	$________
10. Total net living and college expenses (line 8 minus line 9)	$________	$________
11. Years remaining before all of your children complete college (ordinarily the number on line 3 plus 4 years)	________	________

	Wife	Husband
12. Average annual amount needed (line 10 divided by line 11)	$______	$______
13. Lump sum that, if invested and drawn upon as needed, would provide the annual amount on line 12 for the number of years on line 11 (factor from Table A times $1,000)	$______	$______

OPTION A: ADDITIONAL LIVING EXPENSES FOR YOUR SPOUSE FROM THE END OF CHILD-REARING TO AGE 60

	Wife	Husband
14. Annual living expenses (suggestion: half of the amount on line 2)	$______	$______
15. Number of years before your youngest child's 16th birthday	______	______
16. Number of years remaining before your spouse could receive Social Security survivors retirement benefits (60 minus your spouse's present age minus the number of years on line 15)	______	______
17. Lump sum that, if invested and drawn upon as needed, would provide the annual amount on line 14 for the number of years on line 16 (factor from Table A times $1,000)	$______	$______
18. Lump sum that, if invested now, would provide the amount on line 17 (multiply line 17 by the factor from Table B for the number of years on line 15)	$______	$______

OPTION B: ADDITIONAL LIVING EXPENSES FOR YOUR SPOUSE AFTER AGE 60

	Wife	Husband
19. Annual living expenses (from line 14)	$______	$______
20. Annual Social Security survivors benefit (from Table C on page 454) plus any other pension benefits already earned	$______	$______
21. Net annual expenses needed (line 19 minus line 20)	$______	$______
22. Lump sum that, if invested and drawn upon as needed, would provide the annual amount on line 21 (factor for 40 years from Table A times $1,000)	$______	$______

	Wife	*Husband*
23. Number of years remaining before your spouse would be eligible for Social Security retirement benefits (60 minus your spouse's present age)	$______	$______
24. Lump sum that, if invested now, would provide the annual amount on line 21 (multiply line 22 by the factor from Table B for the years on line 23)	$______	$______

The Final Reckoning

	Wife	*Husband*
25. Total amount needed now (line 13 plus line 18 plus line 24)	$______	$______
26. Funeral and estate costs (these typically equal one year's take-home pay, the amount on line 1)	$______	$______
27. Amount your family would need at your death (line 25 plus line 26)	$______	$______
28. Present life insurance coverage	$______	$______
29. Your current net worth, excluding your dwelling and personal property (from Figure 1, Chapter 3)	$______	$______
30. Additional coverage needed (line 27 minus lines 28 and 29). A negative result means you are overinsured.	$______	$______

TABLE A

The values in this table are called annuity values. They are based on the assumption that annual income would be drawn from a fund at the beginning of each year for the number of years in the left-hand column. The amounts remaining on deposit would compound at an inflation-adjusted after-tax rate of return of 2 percent per year.

To calculate the lump sums needed in lines 13, 17, and 22 of the Life Insurance Planning Worksheet, look on the top line of the table for the annual amount nearest

Years	*$5,000*	*$10,000*	*$15,000*	*$20,000*	*$25,000*	*$30,000*	*$35,000*
5	24	48	71	95	118	142	166
6	29	57	85	113	141	169	197
7	33	65	98	130	163	195	227
8	37	74	111	147	184	221	257
9	41	82	123	164	205	245	286
10	45	90	135	180	225	270	315
11	49	98	147	196	245	294	343
12	53	106	159	212	265	318	370
13	57	114	170	227	284	340	397
14	61	121	182	242	303	363	424
15	65	129	193	257	321	385	449
16	68	136	204	272	339	407	475
17	72	143	214	286	357	428	500
18	75	150	225	300	374	449	524
19	79	157	235	313	391	469	548
20	82	164	245	327	408	490	571
21	85	170	255	340	425	510	594
22	89	177	265	353	441	529	617
25	100	199	299	398	498	597	697
30	114	228	343	457	571	685	800
35	127	255	382	510	637	765	892
40	140	279	419	558	698	837	977
45	150	301	451	602	752	902	1053
50	160	321	481	641	801	962	1122

to your goal. Go down that column to the number of years your survivors would need the income. Multiply the factor for that number of years by $1,000. Beyond 22 years of child rearing, the factors are given in five-year intervals. In planning your life insurance, it is best to err on the high side; so choose the next highest interval to the one you're looking for and the next highest annual amount on the top line.

$40,000	*$45,000*	*$50,000*	*$55,000*	*$60,000*	*$65,000*	*$70,000*	*$75,000*
189	213	236	260	283	307	331	354
225	253	281	309	337	365	393	421
260	292	325	357	390	422	454	487
294	331	367	404	441	477	514	551
327	368	408	449	490	531	571	612
360	405	450	495	540	585	629	674
391	440	489	538	587	636	685	734
423	476	529	582	635	688	740	793
454	510	567	624	680	737	794	850
484	545	605	666	726	787	847	908
513	578	642	706	770	834	898	962
543	611	678	746	814	882	950	1017
571	642	713	785	856	927	999	1077
599	674	748	823	898	973	1048	1122
626	704	782	860	938	1016	1095	1173
653	734	816	898	979	1061	1142	1224
679	764	849	934	1019	1104	1188	1273
705	793	881	969	1057	1145	1233	1321
797	896	996	1095	1195	1294	1394	1494
914	1028	1142	1256	1371	1485	1599	1713
1020	1147	1275	1402	1530	1657	1785	1912
1116	1256	1395	1535	1674	1814	1953	2093
1203	1354	1504	1654	1805	1955	2106	2256
1282	1442	1603	1763	1923	2083	2244	2404

Table B

Insurance funds that your beneficiary will not start using for at least five years after your death should be reduced to their present value on the assumption that they will earn interest in the meantime. In this table a 2 percent return after taxes and inflation is used to make the adjustment. Use these present value factors to figure the lump sums on lines 18 and 24 of the Life Insurance Planning Worksheet.

Number of years	*Present value factor*
5	.91
10	.82
15	.74
20	.67
25	.61
30	.55
35	.50
40	.45
45	.41
50	.37

Figuring Your Social Security Survivors Benefits

The children of parents covered by Social Security get monthly income from the system if a parent dies while one or more children are under the age of 18. Children still in high school at 18 qualify for one additional year of benefits, and children who become totally and permanently disabled before age 22 get benefits for life. A spouse who stays home to care for the children can also receive benefits while any child is under 16. However, there is a ceiling amount, called the maximum family benefit. It has the effect of ruling out income for a spouse with more than two children under 16. Starting at the age of 60, a surviving spouse is eligible for lifetime retirement income.

All these benefits add up to a large life insurance policy, but one in which the face value declines month by month. You can't pin down this value with great accuracy, but by putting a reasonable estimate on it, you can save yourself from buying more life insurance than you need. The first section of this worksheet is designed for spouses who would expect to take a job or keep the one they have if their mate died while the children were young. The second section is for spouses who would stay home to take care of the kids. Choose either set of benefits and enter the total value on line 9 of the Life Insurance Planning Worksheet.

	Wife	*Husband*
BENEFITS FOR CHILDREN ONLY		
1. The average age of your children under 18 (their total ages divided by the number of children)	________	________

	Wife	Husband
2. The number of years of benefits (18 minus line 1)	________	________
3. The children's annual benefits (the number of children times the benefit for one child from Table C on page 454, or the maximum family benefit from Table C, whichever is less)	$________	________
4. The total benefit for children under 18 (line 2 times line 3). Enter this amount on line 9 of the Life Insurance Planning Worksheet.	$________	$________

BENEFITS FOR A NONWORKING SPOUSE AND CHILDREN

	Wife	Husband
1. The average age of your children under age 16 (their total ages divided by the number of children)	________	________
2. The number of years of benefits (16 minus line 1)	________	________
3. The number of beneficiaries (children under 16 plus 1)	________	________
4. The annual benefit (line 3 times the benefit for one child from Table C, or the maximum family benefit, whichever is less)	$________	$________
5. The total benefit for a spouse and one or more children under 16 (line 2 times line 4)	$________	$________
6. The annual benefit per child (from Table C)	$________	$________
7. The total annual benefit (number of children under age 18 times line 6 or the maximum family benefit, whichever is less)	$________	$________
8. The total benefit for children aged 16 to 18 (2 times line 7)	$________	$________
9. The total survivors benefits during child-rearing (line 5 plus line 8). Enter this amount on line 9 of the Life Insurance Planning Worksheet.	$________	$________

TABLE C

SOCIAL SECURITY SURVIVORS BENEFITS: 1985 ANNUAL INCOME

		The benefits if your present annual earnings are:				
Your present age	*Beneficiaries*	*$10,000*	*$16,000*	*$23,000*	*$31,000*	*$40,000 or more*
63–64	Spouse at age 60	$3,363	$4,573	$5,791	$6,117	$6,255
	Child	3,528	4,788	6,072	6,420	6,564
	Maximum benefit	7,644	11,880	14,172	14,964	15,300
56–62	Spouse at age 60	3,432	4,650	5,860	6,212	6,341
	Child	3,600	4,872	6,144	6,516	6,648
	Maximum benefit	7,812	12,024	14,340	15,192	15,516
51–55	Spouse at age 60	3,432	4,650	5,885	6,255	6,392
	Child	3,600	4,884	6,180	6,552	6,708
	Maximum benefit	7,812	12,024	14,400	15,300	15,636
46–50	Spouse at age 60	3,432	4,650	5,980	6,358	6,538
	Child	3,600	4,884	6,264	6,672	6,852
	Maximum benefit	7,812	12,024	14,628	15,552	15,996
41–45	Spouse at age 60	3,432	4,659	6,049	6,512	6,744
	Child	3,600	4,884	6,336	6,828	7,080
	Maximum benefit	7,812	12,048	14,796	15,936	16,500
31–40	Spouse at age 60	3,432	4,667	6,066	6,778	7,259
	Child	3,600	4,896	6,360	7,104	7,608
	Maximum benefit	7,812	12,060	14,844	16,584	17,760
Under 31	Spouse at age 60	3,483	4,745	6,118	6,898	7,782
	Child	3,648	4,968	6,408	7,236	8,160
	Maximum benefit	8,004	12,204	14,964	16,872	19,044

Source: *1985 Guide to Social Security* by Dale R. Detlefs (William M. Mercer-Meidinger, Inc., Louisville, Kentucky, 1984).

58

A HEALTH INSURANCE CHECKUP

Shopping for health care once was easy. Your doctor told you what you needed, and your insurance company paid the bills. Since most Americans — nearly 85 percent by recent count — have health insurance coverage, few people worried about costs, least of all physicians. Unrestrained by normal market forces, the cost of following doctors' orders outraced the consumer price index, making health care a bigger business than national defense. Insurance companies quietly raised their premiums to pay larger claims; corporations, which pick up the tab for most health insurance, passed along the increased cost to the consumer in the form of higher prices. But when imports began pricing U.S. goods out of the market — especially big-ticket items like cars — manufacturers broke their silence. At Ford Motor Company, for instance, the employee-insurance manager got the attention of the press when he declared that a doubling of medical premiums for salaried workers in the five years to 1983 had added $300 to the price of every Ford car.

The spotlight then fell on low-price alternatives to the traditional private doctor and full-service hospital. Among the most popular substitutes are health maintenance organizations and various forms of nonhospital treatment, such as outpatient surgery. These options allow insurers to create policies that reward efforts to control costs without necessarily sacrificing care. Employers in turn can modify their coverage so that employees will think more carefully about their choices.

Even if your own company still provides a traditional medical plan, you may be faced with some changes in your coverage before long. Ruth Stack, director of the National Association of Employers on Health Care

Alternatives, reported in 1986 that at least 90 percent of all large companies had redesigned their health plans or were in the process of doing so. Here are some of the choices you are likely to be offered.

Outpatient Surgery

Nearly half of all surgery is performed on patients who can return home the same day. Surgical lasers reduce hazardous bleeding, and gentler anesthetics eliminate hours of grogginess and nausea. As a result, hernia repair, vasectomy, cataract removal, and many other routine procedures can be done safely and efficiently on an outpatient basis for most healthy people. Same-day operations are performed at hospital-affiliated clinics, independent surgical centers, and doctors' offices. Though chances of complications are less than one percent, most clinics have emergency-admission arrangements with nearby hospitals. Doctors' fees are usually the same wherever an operation is performed, but other costs run 40 to 60 percent less than for a similar operation in a hospital because the overhead in a clinic is lower and there are no room charges.

Nonhospital Care

More and more medical services are being separated from hospital settings. Some emergency-room treatment and many recuperative services don't need the vast, and vastly expensive, resources of a fully equipped hospital. Well-documented studies have shown that 43 percent of emergency-room visits aren't medically urgent and 30 percent of hospital care is unnecessary.

Home Health Care

Nursing and other therapeutic services have grown rapidly. Profit-making and nonprofit agencies offer physical, speech, and occupational therapy in the patient's home, as well as supplying medical equipment and providing medical social services. There were 3,627 Medicare-approved home-care agencies in 1983 and more than 5,000 in 1986.

Employee Incentives

Many group health policies reward employees for taking an active role in managing their medical costs. For example, employees of Foote Cone & Belding, an advertising agency, are encouraged to audit their bills. If they spot an overcharge, the company will split the savings with them or pay them $25, whichever is greater.

Until 1983, Foote Cone employees were covered for 100 percent of most hospital costs and 80 percent of doctor bills. Faced with having to raise employee contributions by 30 percent to maintain that coverage, the ad agency decided to rewrite its health benefits. Only 80 percent of the hospital charges are now reimbursed until a year's out-of-pocket costs reach $3,000 per family or $1,500 per person, but there is complete coverage for a wide variety of nonhospital treatment, including outpatient surgery and hospice care for the terminally ill. Insurance also picks up 80 percent of surgeons' fees, but only when a second opinion verifies the need for an elective operation. Otherwise, payment is 50 percent. Paul Sollitto, vice president for compensation and benefits, explained the objective: ''The idea was to make the employees better shoppers for medical care and still provide for catastrophic illness.''

Teachers and other employees of Mendocino County, California, schools can earn up to $500 a year by staying well. The school district pays the $500 deductible on each staff member's medical insurance plan and educates him or her about good health habits. If an employee doesn't use up the deductible in any year, the unspent portion is put into an account in his name. When he leaves his job, he takes that money with him. Ed Nickerman, an assistant superintendent, claims his employees have the lowest health costs in the county.

Diagnosing Your Protection

Whether your medical costs are covered by group insurance or by a policy you bought as an individual, you probably can choose between two types of protection: a conventional plan, which reimburses you or your medical providers for part of the costs you have run up, and a prepaid plan provided by a health maintenance organization. By giving the policy you have or are considering a thorough examination, you can diagnose its weaknesses and perhaps patch them up.

On your job, begin your checkup by getting a summary of policy benefits from your company's personnel department. If that does not answer all your questions, ask your personnel department for a copy of the insurance contract. You may need help in deciphering it, which you should be able to get from officials at your firm or the insurance company. People who are self-employed and covered by individual policies or group plans sponsored by trade and professional groups can get similar information from the sponsoring organization or insurance company. The language and format of policies differ, but they usually provide the same general information.

Conventional Reimbursement Plans

Here is a checklist of items that you should scrutinize especially carefully.

Outpatient benefits. After you have paid a yearly deductible amount, almost all major medical policies cover 80 percent of your bills for doctors' appointments, prescription drugs, lab tests, private nurses, and other out-of-hospital care. Deductibles vary from $50 to $500 a year. You cannot buy additional insurance to reduce a deductible, so if yours is high, you have no choice but to budget for it.

Hospital benefits. If you are hospitalized, most policies still pay 100 percent of the cost of your stay in a semiprivate room for a specified number of days, typically 120. After that, some policies pick up 80 percent of the charges. Otherwise, you can buy a supplementary individual major-medical policy from one of the big insurance companies. Aetna Life & Casualty, for example, offers a plan with a $300 deductible that pays 80 percent of your additional medical bills up to $1,000 or $2,000 and 100 percent above that. Premiums depend on your age and where you live. The company provided this 1986 example. A couple in their early thirties choose a plan that switches to 100 percent reimbursement when their own costs exceed $2,000. If they live in Chicago, their premium is $3,448 a year; in rural Cedar Falls, Iowa, it is $2,708.

Medical and surgical benefits. After you have paid the deductible, most policies reimburse you for 80 percent of your doctor's "reasonable and customary charges" — that is, the going rate in your area for medical treatment. But some plans pay only specified amounts for surgery. For example, until Monsanto Chemical upgraded its group coverage in 1986, the policy reimbursed employees for $529 of the fee for an appendectomy, even though the operation cost up to $1,000 in some cities. Fixed payouts leave you vulnerable to rising medical costs. For added protection here, too, you can buy an individual major-medical policy. Don't waste your money, though, on so-called dread-disease policies, which insure you against a specific illness such as cancer. These policies make no more sense than insuring only the transmission on your car.

Maximum benefits. Most policies set a limit on your lifetime benefit — some as low as $25,000, others as high as $1 million. The Health Insurance Association of America recommends $250,000 for each person covered by a policy. If you feel ill at ease with your plan's maximum, you can supplement it at relatively low cost. Many authorities on insurance argue against supplementing your existing insurance with an indemnity policy, which pays a fixed amount, say $50, for every day you are hospitalized. Such policies pay nothing toward the sometimes painful price of outpatient treatment.

Stop-loss protection. In group plans, this clause typically limits your out-of-pocket medical expenses in any year to $1,000 for one person or $2,200 for a family. Above that, the insurer pays 100 percent of your medical bills. Against the trend to leaner group coverage, this protection so far has grown in popularity because of its comparatively low cost; for example, Prudential's rates in 1986 were $117 a year for a single worker and $250 for a family of four.

Dental care. Group plans increasingly include dental care. You can buy dental coverage on your own, but it is expensive. Mutual of Omaha, for instance, charges about $600 a year for a family of four. Its policy has a $25 deductible and severely limits payment — for instance, to $18 for a filling, which on average costs $35.

Health Maintenance Organizations (HMOs)

With traditional health plans, you pick your own doctor, pay as you go, and seek reimbursement from your insurance company. In a health maintenance organization you or your employer pays an annual fee in return for which the plan's own doctors — and usually they alone — handle almost all your health needs. In 1985, nearly 19 million Americans belonged to about 400 HMOs in the United States — more than three times as many members and twice as many plans as in 1975. HMOs, a quarter of which are run on a for-profit basis, operate in more than 200 cities and are within reach of most of the U.S. population. Eager to keep medical care costs down, Congress has given seed money to HMOs, and companies trying to save on health insurance premiums have urged their employees to sign up. In many cities you have a choice among plans.

There are two basic types of HMO. More than half are group practices with centralized facilities. The others are individual-practice plans, in which the HMO is a network of doctors who maintain their own offices. Your doctor may already work part-time for such a plan. Both types of HMO generally preserve the traditional arrangement of one patient, one physician. When you enroll, you either pick your doctor from a list or have one assigned to you. If you don't like that doctor, you can choose again. An advantage of group HMOs is that they have a built-in quality-control mechanism. Because your medical records are in one place, every doctor you see can refer to them.

Whichever form they take, HMOs are not for everybody. It is hardly worth giving up a good doctor-patient relationship just to join a prepaid plan or to change over to an HMO whose nearest doctor or medical center is far from your home. Also, people who do a lot of traveling or who have children away at college might find a fee-for-service plan more convenient.

The main reason for joining an HMO is the simple prospect of saving money at no threat to your health. The average monthly HMO premium in 1986 was $212 per family, $164 per couple, and $75 per single person. Traditional coverage cost slightly less but was also less comprehensive. In an HMO the sum total of premium payments and out-of-pocket patient costs may be 10 to 40 percent less because HMOs typically have no deductibles and cover a higher percentage of surgical and hospital costs than traditional major-medical policies do. Another potential saving with HMOs is time: you won't encounter the paperwork and reimbursement delay that come when you see your pay-as-you-go doctor and file a claim with your insurance company.

Where you most want your health care to measure up is, of course, in quality. Studies by the American Medical Association and the Johns Hopkins University have shown that medical care in HMOs generally is at least as good as in traditional settings. But HMOs, like doctors and hospitals, range from superlative to poor. Because you will be signing up for a year at a time, you should bring more effort to the decision than you would in choosing a doctor.

The scrutiny you give an HMO might begin at the administration office. Ask whether the organization is federally qualified, which means that it offers a specific group of services. About two-thirds of all HMOs qualify. But you should not automatically dismiss a plan that doesn't have the label. Many conscientious outfits abide by the rules of the agency in their state that regulates HMOs. Ask the HMO for the name of the agency and call to find out about a plan's reputation. Another positive sign is an HMO's membership in the Group Health Association of America, a self-policing trade organization that sets medical and financial standards for its 126 member plans.

In evaluating an HMO, find out who provides treatment under what circumstances. Many HMOs spare their doctors — and hold down costs — by relying heavily on nurses and other medical aides to handle minor medical matters. If the plan you are considering uses a lot of assistants, be sure you always have the right to see a doctor.

HMOs also save money by sending patients to hospitals as seldom as possible. Some HMOs — notably the nation's two largest, Kaiser-Permanente in Oakland, California, and HIP, the Health Insurance Plan of Greater New York — have their own hospitals. More commonly, you go to a hospital affiliated with the plan. HMOs keep their hospital costs low by several means. A prominent one is reducing the length of stay. An independent 10-year study of the Group Health Cooperative of Puget Sound, a large Seattle plan, found that members spent 40 percent fewer days in the hospital in a year than a similar group of patients did under traditional care.

For some people a troubling drawback of HMOs is the restrictions on the use of non-HMO care. Generally, you can see a doctor who is not on the HMO's roster only if the group can't provide the specialty you need and one of the HMO's doctors gives you the referral. The same rules apply to a patient's request for a second opinion on the necessity of surgery. This restriction may represent a conflict of interest: a second doctor at an HMO is less likely to challenge a staff colleague than an outside specialist might be. In sizing up a plan, get an explanation of its policy on outside care; do not enroll unless you feel comfortable with the rules.

In medical emergencies, your HMO covers the cost of treatment when you are out of town or out of the country. Often an HMO operates on a lenient definition of what is reimbursable. If you are traveling and your child comes down with fever, for example, see a doctor and the HMO will pay. For nonemergency treatment you pick up the bill unless you go to an HMO that has reciprocal arrangements with your organization. So ask for a list of plans that swap visiting privileges with yours.

An important feature of HMOs is signaled in their name: health maintenance. HMOs make a particular point of emphasizing preventive care, and they surpass conventional insurance in covering checkups and other medical exams for adults and children. Many plans also sponsor health education classes and exercise clinics.

Prospective members sometimes need to look beyond their own health to that of the plan itself. By 1986, 27 of the nation's 352 active federally qualified HMOs had lost that status, most of them on grounds of financial mismanagement. Federally qualified HMOs must carry insurance or cash reserves to protect the members from a plan's insolvency. At an HMO that is not qualified, find out from the state HMO regulatory agency whether the organization is financially sound. Your risk is least if it has been in existence at least three years or has the support of a large insurance company. And ask who pays your bills if the plan folds.

An HMO Checklist

Since HMOs vary so widely in quality, here are five questions that can help you discover how well-equipped a local plan is to keep you healthy — and happy — if you join:

How can I be sure I will get topnotch care? The most reliable sign of quality is a satisfied membership. Consult enrolled friends or coworkers about how they rate the plan. Ask for a roster of the HMO's staff, with specialties and credentials. A majority of the doctors should be certified by national boards in their medical specialties and the rest should be eligible to become so. Federally qualified HMOs are required to invite their members to complain or make suggestions. Ask the HMO what some typical gripes are and how they are being resolved.

Where do I go if I need to be hospitalized? There is good reason to reject an HMO if its hospital has a poor reputation or is too far from your home.

What happens if I need emergency or after-hours care? Have the HMO spell out its procedures. Can you get prompt nighttime help at an HMO office or over the phone?

What are my out-of-pocket expenses likely to be? If the HMO's annual premium is higher than the one for conventional medical insurance, your employer may expect you to make up the difference. Many HMOs also charge $2 to $3 for each office visit, as well as fees for filling prescriptions and doing other services.

How long must I wait to get an appointment and to see a doctor once I have arrived in the waiting room? HMOs have a vested interest in saving patients' time, and punctuality is a sign of a well-run group. You shouldn't join an HMO unless it guarantees that a doctor will see you the same day you call in sick. Find out whether patients can expect to spend less than 30 minutes in the waiting room and whether they can get an appointment within two months for a checkup or other nonurgent care.

Health Plan Gaps and Weak Points

In analyzing any health insurance plan, whether major medical or HMO, you will discover gaps and weaknesses that can't be filled at any price. Major medical almost always excludes routine physical exams and vaccinations. Neither type of coverage is likely to pay for cosmetic surgery unrelated to an accident. Insurance rarely pays more than 50 percent of the cost of mental illness; some plans also limit payments for psychiatric care to $1,000 a year.

Two-career couples with different employers have two policies to study for shortcomings — hers and his. In addition to gaps in their coverage, they may discover bonuses. The strengths of one policy may make up for the weaknesses of the other, thus making supplementary insurance unnecessary.

If you retire before age 65, make sure you are still covered under your group plan; if not, you will have to buy a policy of your own, and that won't be easy. The best insurance companies are abandoning the market for individual policies on the ground that they can't make a profit from them. (Long-term coverage in nursing homes is an even more serious problem; for solutions see Chapter 23.) Similarly, if you quit your job, ask that your coverage be continued. Most employers keep their policies in force for 30 to 90 days after someone leaves voluntarily. Under a law in effect since 1986, employers with more than 20 workers have to offer to continue group health coverage for 18 months for people they fire. The policy must be identical to the company plan, except that ex-employees who accept the protection must pay the premiums. If you quit your job, however, you must fend for yourself. You can buy a stopgap policy for two to six months from any of two dozen firms, including Aetna, State Farm, and Travelers. To give you an idea of the cost: in 1986 the premium for State Farm's two-month policy for a 42-year-old couple with two children was $370 in Chicago and $175 in rural Kansas.

The same 1986 law that requires companies to extend coverage to people they lay off also protects family members covered by a group health plan if the worker dies. In that case, the survivors are entitled to group coverage at their own expense for the next 36 months. The law gives equal protection to divorced spouses and to dependent children when they reach the age at which the group plan no longer covers them, usually 23 for students and 19 for nonstudents. When family group coverage lapses for a child, it also can be converted, in many cases, to an individual policy, though in this case the benefits probably will fall far short of those being replaced.

The self-employed have two options. One is to join a group plan through a union, trade association, or professional society. The other is to buy a policy that a handful of companies sell exclusively to the self-employed. For example, Sentry Insurance has a combined life and health policy. For the minimum $10,000 of life insurance but medical benefits up to $1 million, the premium for a couple rises with age, from about $1,300 a year at age 30 to $3,500 at 64. There is a $100 deductible.

If analyzing your health coverage seems too complicated a chore, you can get help from Mediform (St. Alexis Medical Arts Center, Room 210,

5109 Broadway, Cleveland, Ohio 44127). The firm also will double-check your insurance claims to make sure you get everything you are entitled to under your policy. Mediform's hourly fee is a stiff $50, but its specialists can often review a policy or claim in 30 minutes, in which case they will charge you only $25.

59

INCOME WHILE YOU ARE DOWN

What are the chances that a serious illness or injury will knock you out of work for months or even years? Rather long, you might think, especially if you are young and healthy. Quite the contrary: the odds are uncomfortably short. About a quarter of all people age 50 will be incapacitated for six months or longer before they reach 65. To anyone whose income stops when he cannot work, a long-term disability becomes calamitous. Yet most Americans are woefully unprotected against the financial consequences.

Your first line of defense, Social Security, has stringent eligibility rules. You must be totally disabled to collect. Also, you must wait at least six months — often much longer — for the first check to arrive. If you do qualify, the government is supposed to pay you for as long as you are out of action. In 1986 the maximum disability benefit for a worker with a family was $1,727 a month. But in practice, disabled people by the thousands have lost their benefits under cost-cutting drives in recent years and have had to hire lawyers in the struggle to get payments restored.

For most disabilities your own income-replacement insurance is a more reliable bastion. About 20 million people have disability coverage, two-thirds of them in group policies sponsored by their employers. That leaves nearly 80 percent of the working population unprotected. A disability-income policy worthy of the name will cost at least a few hundred dollars a year and possibly $1,000 or more. It can replace either a little or a lot of your salary for anywhere from a few months to the rest of your life. If you choose a policy carelessly, you may consign yourself to many years of hardship. If you choose wisely, you may count it a blessing.

What you should aim for is enough coverage from all sources to let you cling to your present standard of living. Social Security is structured to replace more income for people at relatively low salary levels than for those with high incomes. For anyone earning more than about $45,000, private disability insurance is especially important.

The first step in deciding how much coverage you need is to add up all other potential sources of disability income. You may find some unexpected ones. After Gregory Van Kirk, a service adviser at a Seattle car dealership, fractured his neck in an auto accident in 1982, he discovered four disability policies he didn't know he had. His no-fault auto insurance paid him $800 a month for one year. A $3,500 bank loan included disability insurance equal to the monthly payments until the debt was paid, and a provision called the disability waiver in each of his two life insurance policies took care of their premiums, a total of $38.90 a month.

The most important decision in shopping for a policy is to choose the right company. Gerald Parker, a Greenwich, Connecticut, consultant to insurance companies, offers this caution: ''If you become disabled, you are going to have a relationship that may last for years. And a lot rides on how the company interprets certain sections of your policy.''

A few companies write most of the high-quality individual disability policies. The leaders include Equitable of New York, Guardian, Massachusetts Mutual, Minnesota Mutual, Monarch, Northwestern Mutual, Paul Revere, and Provident Life & Accident. All offer first-rate policies, as do a score of competitors, but not for everybody: Northwestern and Provident slant their policies to high-income executives and professionals. Mutual of Omaha aims more at the blue-collar market. Insurers that cater to people in a wide range of occupations are likely to withhold certain highly desirable benefits from blue-collar people. At Monarch, for example, only two top-level categories of white-collar applicants qualify for a provision that continues to pay benefits while you ease back to work at part salary.

Within occupational limits, a trustworthy and experienced insurance broker can help you tailor your policy to your financial situation. Here are the main features and what you should aim for.

Monthly Benefits

Try to replace 60 percent of your current earnings before taxes. That should be enough to maintain most of your spending power, especially since disability benefits are tax-free if you have paid for your own insurance. If your employer paid the bill, however, the benefits are taxable.

Length of Benefits

How long you are likely to be incapacitated is an imponderable. If you are one of those sidelined for 90 days or more, chances are about nine out of 10 that you will be back to work within a year. The odds of being out much longer are statistically slim; less than 5 percent of long-term disabilities last for as long as five years. Therefore, many insurance professionals advocate a short period of benefits. It is true that you can save hundreds of dollars a year in premiums by settling for five years of income instead of benefits until age 65. But doing so violates rule number one about insurance: that it protect your family from the worst disasters.

Waiting Period

A better way to reduce premiums is to lengthen the number of weeks you have to be disabled before the policy starts paying — the "waiting period." As is stressed elsewhere in this book, your first bulwark against disability should be a cash emergency fund large enough to replace three to six months of take-home pay. The longer you can postpone insurance benefits, the more you save on premiums. A policy that costs $1,200 with a one-month waiting period costs about $850 if you can hold out for three months.

Definition of Disability

Physical limitations often are subjective; you may judge yourself to be completely incapacitated while the insurance company insists you can drag yourself back to the office. "Over the years, our industry has always had trouble defining total disability in a way that was satisfactory to the consumer," concedes Charles Soule, executive vice president of Paul Revere. To collect disability payments in 1960, says Soule, you usually had to be unable to do any job for which your education, training, or experience fitted you. If partial paralysis from a stroke kept a surgeon out of the operating room but did not prevent him from doing consultations in his office, his benefits stopped. Under the terms of many policies today, that surgeon would continue to collect insurance. Such a policy specifies that you are disabled if you cannot pursue your "own occupation."

An equally acceptable definition of disability focuses on the underlying issue: lost income. If a disabled person returns to the job while recuperating but earns less than before because he can't yet work full-tilt or full-time, he can continue getting partial insurance payments, called "residual benefits." Say a sales manager who is drawing $2,000 in monthly insurance benefits because of a heart attack gradually resumes his duties. If at first he earns 50 percent of his prior salary, he still gets half of his insurance payments, $1,000 a month. Residual benefits can be especially important if you are self-employed and cannot count on anyone to pick up the slack at the office. The chance to make a slow comeback can save you from overtaxing yourself.

Sickness vs. Injury

Buy a policy that covers all types of disabilities. Your loss of income will be the same whether you are laid up by sickness or injury and whether or not you are in the hospital. Some weasel-worded contracts give the company an out by saying you are disabled only if confined to hospital or home. Once the claims investigator spots you taking a wobbly walk around the block, he can cut off all benefits.

Renewability

Two things you don't want an insurer to do after you have bought a policy are raise your premiums or cancel your coverage. Some inexpensive policies let the company do either. Any disability contract worth considering should be at least "guaranteed renewable." In such a policy the company can increase your premium, but only if it does the same for a large group of policyholders with some common characteristics: residency in the same state, for instance. The best type of policy goes by the key word "noncancelable." It both guarantees renewal and freezes the premium at its original level for as long as you keep the insurance. The premium is only a little higher than for a guaranteed renewable policy.

Easing the Cost

Cost may become the ultimate determinant. If the coverage you want is more expensive than you can afford, there may be attractive alternatives. Applicants can pay less now by agreeing to pay more later. Using what is called a step-rate premium, a man or woman age 25 who is beginning a managerial career can buy coverage of $1,000 a month to age 65 in

Monarch's noncancelable policy, with a 90-day waiting period and residual benefits, for a premium of $238 a year. When he or she reaches age 35, the cost rises permanently to $420 a year.

Monarch's unisex premium rates were something of a breakthrough in the 1980s. At all companies until then, women paid much more for disability coverage, especially in their thirties, than men did. Now the major disability companies all have unisex rates.

One of the best ways to reduce cost and preserve your desired level of benefits is to make an agreement with the insurance company that you will forgo part of the insurance if you qualify for Social Security or workers compensation. Let's say your policy normally would pay $2,500 a month, but you start getting $750 a month from Social Security. Then the insurance company can cut its contribution to $1,750. Such an arrangement in a noncancelable Paul Revere policy with residual benefits would reduce the annual premium for a male executive or professional age 40 from $1,087 to $914.

With benefits carefully coordinated, you won't be enriched by a disabling illness or injury, but neither will you be impoverished or made insurance-poor in the likelier event that you get through life unscathed.

VIII THE CONSUMMATE CONSUMER

You want to buy something. You pay the price. It's that simple. Or is it? Why, then, can you buy an Arrow shirt for $22.95 at a department store and for $13.95 at the discounter next door? Knowing how prices are set and where money goes once it leaves the warm confines of your pocket may improve your shopping skills.

Several economic ingredients contributed to a discount boom in the 1980s: excessive retail inventories; lower prices for raw materials, energy, and labor; advances in technology; and for a while a muscular dollar in world markets. Sometimes it seemed that everything was on sale. List prices became meaningless numbers. Discount prices, deep or shallow, became the true retail prices.

Longer-term trends also accounted for the phenomenon. Prominent among them was the coming of age of the baby boomers, who have been more willing than their parents were to patronize discount and off-price stores. According to pollster and social researcher Daniel Yankelovich, baby boomers have a calculating, highly competitive psychology. "They have a more conditional loyalty, whether it be to the job, the brands, the retail outlets, or the marriage," he says.

"Hold on there," entrepreneurial types reply. They depict

themselves as the major force prompting new ways of selling. "Consumers are robotic — they take their direction from the stores," says Eugene Ferkauf, founder of E. J. Korvette, one of the original discount chains. "The real changes come from the appearance of very smart retailers."

Whether the customers make the stores or the stores make the customers, the plain fact of the matter is that the various types of discount and off-price retailers have been experiencing boom times. Discount stores pay full wholesale prices for the things they buy, but they keep overhead low and make greater use of private labels. They can consistently sell their goods at 15 to 30 percent below the price for comparable items at department stores. Off-price stores buy stock at a lower wholesale price than department stores because they pay manufacturers within 10 to 30 days, commit to buy months in advance, and make none of the ancillary demands (such as credit for money spent on advertising or the right to return unsold merchandise) that department stores do. As a result, their prices range anywhere from 25 to 60 percent less than the largely fictitious list price.

Discount stores such as K Mart and Wal-Mart gained revenues at a 20 percent annual rate from 1970 to 1985, roughly twice that of department stores. Off-price stores such as Marshall's, T. J. Maxx, and Loehmann's captured 5 to 6 percent of the market for apparel retailing, according to Arthur B. Britten, a New York City consultant who worked for Loehmann's for 19 years. "A lot of analysts believe the off-prices will be up to a 20 percent share of the market by 1990," he adds. Indeed, specialized shopping centers devoted entirely to off-price stores and manufacturers' factory outlets grew from 54 in 1980 to more than 300 five years later.

The spectacular growth of discounters and off-pricers scarcely exhausts the new sources of bargain merchandise. Members-only shopping marts located in airplane hangarlike buildings and better known as warehouse clubs are among the deepest discounters. By 1985 nearly a dozen warehouse clubs with more than 70 outlets in 16 states were merchandising at prices between wholesale and retail. Discount retailing in other guises — catalogue showrooms and mail-order businesses — were expanding, while the ultimate low-overhead discounters — street vendors — hawked their wares to an increasingly upscale clientele.

With all this competition, how are department stores coping? Simple. They, too, are marking down prices like mad. It is not unusual for the toniest establishments — Gump's in San Francisco, I. Magnin in Chicago, Bloomingdale's in New York — to have something substantial on sale at 25 to 30 percent off every week. The department stores have some advantages of their own. They get special treatment from manufacturers: first crack at the best-selling designs and the guarantee of a full range of sizes and colors. "The thing you always have to remember is that without on-price there's no off-price," says Howard Davidowitz, a New York City retailing consultant. "The day Bloomingdale's stops buying from a supplier, the off-pricers lose interest in the stuff, too."

60

SECRETS OF BLACK-BELT SHOPPERS

Full retail prices can be divided roughly fifty-fifty. Half of what you spend covers the cost of making the item; the other half covers the cost of getting it and you together at the cash register. Your attention as a consumer should focus on the second half — the part known as the markup. This is the retailer's selling cost plus his projected profit. It will vary from one product to another and from one variety of store to another. Knowing what play the retailer has in a price can help you size up how good a sale really is. An auto dealer marks up cars only 11 to 18 percent, but by getting him to shave a few points you will spare yourself substantial dollars. A jewelry store, on the other hand, can mark up its wares as much as 300 percent. Therefore, a big store that does a brisk business in baubles can afford to offer a better price than a small shop with a slow turnover.

Finding out the markup on a specific item is a little like trying to crack the formula of Chanel No. 5. As a rule, turnover of goods correlates with markups. Cans of peas turn over every few days and have a low markup, say 20 percent, while the sterling-silver cutlery you use to scoop them up has a high one, up to 55 percent.

Department stores try to charge twice the wholesale price, which is called a keystone markup. On some imported goods and private-label merchandise, they will tack on an additional 10 percent or more. That allows them the option of selling at half off and still making money. Discounters like K Mart have lower selling costs and consequently a lower markup than department stores — about 40 percent — but rarely carry the same items. Off-pricers buy the same merchandise as department stores and mark it up the least, roughly 35 percent.

Within the same store, the markup can vary from one category of goods to another. For example, one-third off a pair of shoes with a keystone markup may not be as good a value as 25 percent off a toaster. That's because small appliances have markups of less than 30 percent, among the lowest in a department store.

The fun for the shopper really begins when the store starts offering markdowns on its markup. What is left, the difference between the actual selling price and the wholesale price, is called the gross margin. This figure is most telling, but is closely guarded by retailers. For example, costume jewelry and designer ready-to-wear clothes have roughly the same markup — 53 percent — but the jewelry has a gross margin of about 50 percent, whereas the fashions have less than 30 percent. Discount-determined shoppers can conclude that meaty reductions abound for the high-fashion clothes but seldom for faux pearls.

Another element in pricing is "Wow" content. Retail consultant Howard Davidowitz explains: "That's when a customer falls in love with a product and will pay anything for it. If he wants a sweater for warmth, he will pay only so much. If he wants a sweater that says, 'Wow,' he is likely to pay far more."

Needless to say, "Wow" content holds no sway over the consummate consumer. If ceremonial honors were bestowed for inspired shopping, the following four martial artists of the marketplace would all merit black-belt standing.

Psychological Warfare: Gary Berg

"I research everything so that I'm on solid ground when I start bargaining," declares Gary Berg, a financial planner who lives in Pleasant Hill, California, near San Francisco. This scholarly endeavor pays off. In 1984 Berg and his wife Lois spent a hefty $42,400 to buy two cars and a 19-foot speedboat — but that was $7,000 less than three battle-weary retailers would have liked.

Such savings are the rewards of pitting dealer against dealer with Machiavellian aplomb. Berg's guiding principles:

Know precisely what you want — make, model, and frills — before you start comparing prices.

Divide your opponents. Get competing prices from a number of sources.

Always give an inch. An inflexible position tends to undermine your psychological advantage.

When Gary set out to buy those three major items — a used BMW 528i, a new GMC four-wheel-drive vehicle and a Centurion ski boat — he employed his tactics with precision. First he rallied his financial forces. "I put my calculator on the desk, get out the Yellow Pages, and start calling banks to compare interest rates. Once I find the right loan, I have one less thing to worry about while I dicker over price."

Then Berg gets tough. "What dealers hate most is when you bargain them down and then tell them you're going to compare their price to those at other dealerships — I never say which one."

Next Berg turns up the pressure. "I tell them I will definitely buy from someone within the next 48 hours, but I'll check back with them before I sign. Of course, then you've got to be ready to buy; otherwise you have just wasted everyone's time. So when one dealer came down $2,000 on the GMC, I jumped."

According to Berg, you have to be willing to give a little yourself. "If you become belligerent, retailers will walk away from you. So always leave the door open; leave them a small profit. I knew, for example, that the wholesale Blue Book value of the used BMW was $11,800, but the salesman dug in his heels at $12,600. That meant an $800 profit for him, but it was 14 percent off the asking price, so I bought it."

When Berg went shopping for the boat, he found that many dealers refused to budge from the full $17,900 price. "I didn't create a scene at all, although I knew that was top dollar," he says. Calm but persistent, Berg kept shopping and bought the dream boat from a hungrier dealer for $15,500.

Let the Postman Do the Walking: Roger Horchow

Mail-order mogul Roger Horchow practices what he peddles. The quintessential Ivy Leaguer (Yale, 1950), he does most of his personal shopping by mail. He sends for his Oxford shirts from Brooks Brothers, his loafers and slacks from L.L. Bean, and his underwear and socks from Joseph Banks. His ties and sports shirts are strictly Horchow, which offers a variety of luxury items.

His advice for shopping mail order:

Shop from familiar catalogues.
Always buy with a credit card.
Avoid firms without toll-free numbers.

Horchow cautions that the mail-order field is booby-trapped with firms that don't stay in business long enough to fill their orders. Sometimes he checks with the Better Business Bureau in the city given as the company's address. The best catalogues, he says, have toll-free numbers for shoppers to order items as well as another number for them to inquire or complain about orders. Reputable mail-order companies always refund your money if you are not satisfied.

Why the credit-card requirement? Credit-card companies, Horchow explains, always investigate the merchants they deal with. Also, when you use a card, you might have additional recourse in case the merchandise arrives damaged.

When he buys in stores, Horchow tries to negotiate. "I used to be shy and embarrassed about bargaining," he admits, "but I've found a polite way to do it." He always tries to get the seller to set the price first. Then he asks if there might be some accommodation for paying in cash or with traveler's checks or for taking the items with him rather than having them sent. Often there is.

Ties are a big catalogue item, and Horchow demands the best quality. He insists that his ties be handmade and lined to the tip to preserve their shape. A handmade silk tie, he notes, has a string on the underside that straightens out wrinkles when you pull it. Even when it is made with the finest silk, a tie should not cost more than $30, Horchow says. "After that, you are just paying for a designer name, and that's ridiculous."

Untortured by the Racks: Susan Dresner

Susan Dresner darts through the busy communal dressing room of a New York City discount store to an unoccupied corner, where she deposits her coat, briefcase, and other paraphernalia. She then steams onto the sales floor, bypassing other customers who, in varying states of undress, are soliciting opinions on clothes they are trying on. "If they ask my advice, I tell them I charge $50 an hour," Dresner says. As the founder of Successful Ways & Means, she helps individual clients — largely executive women — to adopt a style of dress and shop for clothes.

Dresner teaches her clients to save not only money but time. "I tell them if they aren't buying 75 percent of what they take into the dressing room, they aren't screening well enough." She has honed a rack routine designed to separate promising pieces from clothing catastrophes long before she slips them on. Her pointers:

First consider the fabric and workmanship — what goes into a garment is the true tip-off to its quality.

Then examine the label, not for the designer name but for the country of origin.

Look at the price tag last, and measure it in cost per wearing.

According to Dresner, Italy and then France produce the finest men's and women's clothes. The West Germans and Scandinavians also have been turning out well-made garments at reasonable prices. Ireland, she says, is the sleeper in the fashion crowd. ''Today Ireland is doing more than the preppy sweaters and tartan skirts that were always a tremendous value.''

Dresner steers her female customers away from tailored dress-for-success suits and in general warns against department stores and discount chains with central buying offices. For more distinctive clothes for less money, she patronizes smaller off-price shops where the owner scouts manufacturers for the best deals on unique merchandise.

Timing is important. Dresner shops these stores just as she would their full-price cousins — August for fall-winter clothes and March for spring-summer apparel. ''Buy what you like immediately; pick up bargains later. Don't wait till the end of the season for what nobody else wants,'' says Dresner. ''By and large, leftovers are losers.'' She violates her department store dictum only when it comes to designer ready-to-wear. Fashionable stores often carry the most prestigious names to build their own image rather than their bottom line. At the end of a season, when they must move out the old line, prices often slip below cost.

For couture quality at discount prices, Dresner suggests resale shops. Unlike thrift stores, these profit-making businesses are more likely to select the finest offerings to recycle. Dresner's rule of resale: shoot for the big-ticket items — like formal wear that originally cost thousands of dollars.

Four-Star Food Buyer: Kaye Neil Noble

The neighborhood for Kaye Noble is an increasingly upscale area on Manhattan's Upper West Side honeycombed with supermarkets, delicatessens, greengrocers, fish stores, butcher shops, and bakeries. For years a cookbook researcher, Noble is so skilled a shopper that even the food merchants are impressed. Her butcher, Walter ''Frenchy'' Trcak, declares, ''It's a pleasure to serve a customer who really knows her way around the meat counter.''

Noble's recipe for getting the best food buys:

Know your neighborhood stores — and be known in them.
Snap up only the "specials" that are truly special.
Shop for what is in season — and bear in mind that almost every product has a season.
Shop new stores — the latest store to open often has the lowest prices.

Noble begins a characteristic morning's shopping trip at the supermarket, where Frenchy will bone and cut up large pieces of meat free of charge, saving her some 10 cents a pound. Leaving an order for a pork roast (on special at $1.69 a pound), she moves on to a delicatessen whose cheese seller can tell her what is in season and therefore cheaper — French Camembert, since it is spring, just as Swiss Vacherin will be in the fall. She drops into a health store to buy brown rice at 49 cents a pound. Testing her belief that the newcomers will often offer the best prices, she makes her last stop at a new fish market. Sure enough, she finds delectably pale pink, fresh-looking shad roe there for $4 a pair — roughly half the going rate.

Like all smart shoppers in towns with ethnic enclaves, Noble looks for discounts aimed at subgroups within her city's population. She gets corned beef on sale before St. Patrick's Day, brisket of beef during Jewish High Holy Days, ricotta and mozzarella cheese on the eve of Italian festivals. Her spices come from a Greek store that sells them out of burlap bags ("the smallest amount you can buy is a quarter of a pound, which I split with a friend"), and she gets fresh baby eels at a Hispanic market.

Noble's shopping choices are based on her love of food and cooking as well as on price. She will buy the best grade of potatoes for baking but gets a cheaper variety to use in vichyssoise. She likes such gourmet vegetables as watercress, bean sprouts, and red pepper but avoids wasting them by getting just the amount she needs at supermarket salad bars.

61

A CAR SHOPPER'S GUIDE

The purchase of a new or used car is usually not just a single transaction but as many as four separate deals: on the car you are buying, the trade-in, the financing, and the insurance. The salesperson's most profitable strategy is to wrap all four into one package. At not-too-scrupulous dealerships, the sales force plays a highly polished game of getting out of you as large a monthly payment as possible.

Your own best strategy is to unbundle the four components and negotiate them one by one — not always at the showroom. In fact, make it a point never to include insurance in your financing deal. Insure the car elsewhere (see Chapter 54). Refuse credit life and disability insurance even though the loan officer or car salesman raises his eyebrows and says, "But everybody takes it." This coverage of the unpaid balance on your loan, if you die or become disabled, not only protects the lending institution but also adds generously to its profit. When wrapped into an installment sale, credit life insurance can be extremely high-priced.

The Price

When you are ready to buy a car, first choose the make and model you want and decide how you want it equipped; then shop and negotiate. The best deals are not those you find but those you make. In the haggling process, an indispensable fact for the buyer to know is the dealer's cost. It defines the rock-bottom price you can expect to pay. You might think dealer's cost would be a deep trade secret; in fact, it is readily available. One inexpensive and accessible source is Edmund's *New Car Prices,* a $3.50 Dell paperback, which is updated frequently.

Add up the dealer's cost for your car and all the options you intend to order. Then start negotiating. Unless your favorite make and model is in short supply, you will have plenty of room to bargain. Peg your opening bid $125 to $200 above cost. Sticker prices — the itemized prices that dealers must paste on the car window — run $500 to $4,500 over cost. On domestic cars, your goal should be to pay $200 to $500 as the dealer markup. Allow imported-car dealers at least $500.

You may not have to haggle at all at six mass-marketing General Motors dealers. They sell all their cars at cost plus $49. (That is not their only profit: General Motors pays all dealers a 3 percent rebate on sales.) The six maverick dealers are Ande Chevrolet & Olds in Lawrenceburg, Indiana; Buckles Motors in Urbana, Ohio; Klick-Lewis Chevrolet in Palmyra, Pennsylvania; Murphy Chevrolet in Bergenfield, New Jersey; Pattison Chevrolet in Logansport, Louisiana; and Porter Chevrolet in Cambridge, Massachusetts.

Or you can hire others to haggle for you, through an automobile broker or buying service. For example, Nationwide in Southfield, Michigan, and Brown-Clarkson in Redwood City, California, order through networks of dealers at prices as low as $50 above cost. In the buying service category, Car/Puter (800-221-4001; in New York, 800-522-5104) charges $20 to refer you to the nearest of some 475 dealers that have promised to give Car/Puter clients low prices — typically $50 to $150 over cost on domestic cars and as low as $400 over cost on imports.

The Trade-in

Assuming you have a car to swap, prepare ahead by looking up its current market value. Your bank's loan department probably subscribes to the monthly *N.A.D.A. Official Used Car Guide* (better known as the Blue Book), which lists average trade-in and retail prices of most models manufactured in the past seven years. While you're at it, ask the loan office for the bank's annual percentage rates on car loans (new or used, as the case may be) for three, four, and five years. But don't apply for a loan just yet. Don't even mention monthly payments to the car dealer. If the salesperson brings up payments, say that you will talk financing later. Look for telltale signs of a high-pressure sales operation: you are handed over to several different salespeople; you are left alone for long periods in a sales booth; the salesperson keeps changing the price for no apparent reason. These may be attempts to eavesdrop or wear you down. Walk out of the place if you suspect they're giving you the treatment.

After you hear what seems like a firm price on the car, ask about the allowance on your old car. Don't expect a dealer to offer more than trade-in value, but use the combined offer — purchase price less trade-in — as a bargaining chip with other dealers. In the end you may want to find your own buyer if the dealer's trade-in allowance falls far below Blue Book value.

The Financing

Now you are ready to discuss financing. By negotiating the price of the car in advance and pinning down the dealer to a firm offer, you have thus far avoided attempts to pack the deal with unwanted accessories and other extras. More important, you have prevented the salesperson from obscuring the purchase price in a welter of other terms. All new-car dealers have standing arrangements with an auto manufacturer's finance company or a bank to handle customer loans. Dealers make part of their profit that way. You may get a better loan from them than from your own bank, especially when car makers are offering low-interest deals to pep up sales. But don't sign an installment sales contract yet. First shop at other banks and your credit union, if you belong to one. Check out home equity loans as well as car loans. You are likely to find rates lower on credit secured by your house, but these rates are variable. In times of rising interest rates your monthly payments can get out of hand. (For more on home equity loans, see Chapter 50.)

When average new-car prices climbed over the $10,000 mark, many buyers found the monthly payments on traditional three-year loans to be more than they could afford. Therefore, four-, five-, and six-year loans have become common. According to standard wisdom, extending payments is unwise because it makes financing more expensive in the long run. This is true enough; finance charges mount with every additional month of maturity. But there is more to the story. A study by *Money* found that if inflation is adding 6 percent or more a year to car prices and if interest can be deducted from your taxable income (as it can with home equity loans), the true cost of borrowing remains almost the same whether the loan is for three years or five years. Just make sure that your auto outlasts your loan. If you have to buy a new car before the old one is paid for, you will run head-on into a debt overload.

The Down Payment

One reason to accept a car dealer's trade-in offer may be that you don't have enough cash for a down payment. In typical financing deals, you have to put down about 20 percent of the purchase price. The trade-in allowance on your old car often provides enough money for the down payment. If you have no trade-in, raising the down payment may be a hurdle, but it is not insurmountable. Some banks will lend you the full price of a car, although they are likely to add a percentage point to their regular interest rate. A much more popular solution is to lease a new car rather than finance it. Over the life of a loan, leasing usually costs a little more than financing, but one month's rent is the only down payment.

How Long to Keep Your Car

Curbstone wisdom has it that cars should be traded in after four years or 60,000 miles to avoid major problems. But if you are set on saving money, then age or a magic number on the odometer should take a back seat. The case for keeping an old car going was convincingly made a few years ago in a study by Runzheimer & Company, corporate consultants specializing in transportation analysis. The prices are archaic now, but the result is not.

The study begins with identical four-year-old compact cars. One, it is assumed, will be driven for another four years. The other is traded in for a more fuel-efficient model with the $2,811 proceeds used as a down payment on the $8,872 new car; the difference is made up with a 10-percent-interest car loan. The new car saves its owner some $730 on gasoline and $540 on repairs needed to keep the old car running over the next four years. But the $7,380 total monthly loan payments vastly outweigh those savings.

Insurance premiums also eat up more of the new-car owner's money. Since his auto is more valuable, he spends a total of $147 more to cover it for the four years. That assumes the drivers of both cars have kept their collision and theft policies in force. But many people drop such coverage after paying off their car loans, further reducing the cost of owning an old car.

Finally, some hidden costs take their toll when trade-in time comes. The value of a new car drops much more sharply in the first four years than in the second four. Typically, 30 percent of its worth evaporates in the first year. Depreciation then starts to decelerate. After four years the car may retain half of its value, and after eight years it still will have some worth. In four years the newer model can be traded in for about $4,400, while the old one is worth perhaps $400. But the new-car owner's $4,000 advantage has been eclipsed by the costs of buying and insuring the car. In all, the owner who keeps his four-year-old car on the road ends up $2,200 ahead. And that doesn't count the money he might have earned from investing the money he saved.

Granted, car owning is not solely a matter of dollars and cents. For some, their wheels are a status symbol; for others, newness buys relief from worries about getting stuck in a clunker far from home or wasting precious time at the repair shop. Then, too, Robert Kastengren, Runzheimer's transportation division director, noted, ''Many Americans simply get sick of driving the same car, and they don't care if it costs a lot more to drive a new one.''

For motorists who place pocketbook over pride, here are guidelines for keeping a jalopy purring:

Maintain the car faithfully. Use a knowledgeable mechanic. See that brakes, tires, and steering stay in top condition.

Keep the body clean and well waxed. This can prevent rusting. In high-pollution areas, garage your car as much as possible.

Consider renting a car for longer trips. You may be satisfied with your older car's performance on its daily rounds but reluctant to push it to its limits. If so, an occasional rental can stall off the ultimate trip to a new-car dealer.

Review repair records regularly. If costs climb sharply, ask your mechanic what is likely to go next and the cost of fixing it.

James Noonan, executive vice president of Peterson Howell & Heather, a large car-leasing company in Baltimore, says, ''Statistics show that you can safely avoid most major expenses — except for new tires and a battery — if you trade in a car before 55,000 miles.'' But his statistics are based on both well-maintained and poorly maintained cars. Noonan and other automotive professionals concede that most autos can reach 100,000 miles without facing transmission overhauls and other costly repairs so long as drivers consistently heed the maintenance instructions in their owner's manual.

62

GAINING THROUGH COMPLAINING

Though he called them ''tigers, not daughters'' and bitched about them for an entire five acts, King Lear never made the girls shape up; in the end, they drove him crazy. But when Henry II complained, ''Who will free me from this turbulent priest?'' that monarch got results. In no time at all, courtiers snatched Thomas à Becket and did him in. Why did one complaint fail while the other succeeded? In large part because Lear only moaned and groaned, while Henry left no doubt of what he wanted.

Modern-day consumers with less than regal beefs about unreliable products, snarled-up computers, immobile bureaucrats, and snooty clerks would do well to follow Henry's example. Take it from Kelly Cullins, former national manager of AutoCAP, a trade group that handles thousands of complaints from car owners: ''Lots of people gripe just to get something off their chests, but demanding a specific remedy is much more effective.''

The art of complaining is easy to learn. Any good gripe — whether made in person, by phone or in writing — has five simple elements:

A clear statement of the problem — for example, ''Your bank mistakenly debited my checking account for $12,000.''

Facts that back up the story — receipts, names, and titles of people dealt with, a chronology of the untoward events.

A request for redress — correction of a bill, a refund, repairs, or, if you are merely ticked off, an apology.

A deadline — by which time your problem *must* be solved.

A threat — some credible reprisal that you are prepared to carry out if things don't go your way.

The last is most important. Though customer relations specialists deny it, threats work. But what could you, the lowly *emptor,* possibly say to a powerful company? Take a cue from Ralph Charell, author of *Satisfaction Guaranteed* (Linden Press, $14.95) and the world's most successful complainer, according to the *Guinness Book of World Records.* Charell recounts:

> I once had an absolutely awful stay at a resort hotel in the Bahamas, which I happened to know was owned by a huge conglomerate. I made a list of my complaints and brought them to the manager but was making no headway. Frustrated, I wondered aloud if the chairman of the conglomerate knew the hotel was being run this way. The name was hardly out of my mouth before the manager asked me, as a personal favor, to permit him to cancel the bill.

Here is a rundown of less veiled threats that are effective and won't get you in trouble with the law.

You will stop payment. Carry out this threat and the company will either negotiate the issue or sue for payment. But by law it cannot blacken your credit record or set collection-agency goons on you until you admit — or a judge or jury decides — that you owe a just debt to the firm.

You will end your patronage. Money talks. As the head of customer service at Bloomingdale's in New York City put it awhile ago, "If a customer has spent $30,000 to $40,000 in the store in the past 10 years, I will try to settle his complaint right away."

You will tell other people how badly you have been treated. Word of mouth can kill sales as effectively as it builds them. The bigger the stink you can create, the more potent the threat. A few years ago, a man who led a Boy Scout troop telephoned Safeway, the grocery chain, to protest his local supermarket's installation of video games, which he viewed as a corrupting influence. When he threatened to mobilize his troop to picket the store, the vision of fresh-scrubbed boys marching on Safeway persuaded company executives to remove the machines.

It is true that some companies are out of range of such attacks. "You can't threaten to go to our competitors, heh-heh," says John Dillon, director of customer services for Con Edison, the metropolitan New York electric company that local folks love to hate. When dealing with utilities and other unrepentant businesses, your best tactic is to say that you will take your complaint to higher authorities. Among them are industry associations, Better Business Bureaus, and government regulatory bodies, especially those that can withhold rate increases.

If all else fails, you can threaten a lawsuit, but you had better bring money. Donald Brown, a lawyer in Torrance, California, sued Alpha Beta grocery stores when a clerk impudently and loudly announced to other customers that the check Brown had presented would bounce. In court, Brown claimed that he had been slandered and emotionally injured. He won $1,000 in damages and court costs. His son, also an attorney, represented him without fee, but Brown estimates that nonlawyers would have had to pay $10,000 in legal fees.

A truly artful complainer can combine a threat with a pathetic appeal for sympathy — sometimes to great effect. Take the case of the young Houston couple who received a cheap camera instead of the microwave oven they were promised for visiting vacation homesites in Tyler, Texas. They succeeded in getting the company to make its offer good by penning a heartrending description of how they suffered while waiting for their premium outside the land development office: "It was a cold day with a bitter wind. There was no seating available and hundreds of people were waiting. We had a baby of 11 months with us who eventually screamed from cold and hunger. But we waited three hours because we thought the oven would be worth it." At the bottom of the letter, they noted that they were sending a carbon to the Better Business Bureau.

Speaking Out

The pen is mightier than the spoken word. Face-to-face kvetching often fails because you take out your anger on a clerk or bank teller who doesn't have the power to correct a problem. Still and all, advises Ralph Charell, the supergriper:

> If you have a routine complaint that needs only a routine solution — say you were overcharged on a department store credit card — then give the usual customer relations channels the first crack at your complaint. But if you want something unusual, no one in these departments will have the authority to give it to you. You have to finesse them and find someone who does, the person I call Mr. or Ms. Big.
>
> First I call the chief operator on the corporation's switchboard. It is that person's job to know who is where and how the company is organized. In the briefest, most general way, tell the chief operator the nature of the problem and ask who would be the best person to help you. If you sound upbeat, pleasant, and not likely to burden her with your problem, she will cooperate. Also try to find out who Mr. or Ms. Big reports to.

Why should Mr. or Ms. Big bother with a consumer complaint? Won't the secretary simply bounce you back to the customer relations department? Charell's reply:

> One technique is to call person to person, which you can do even locally in most places by going through the telephone company operator. By interposing the operator as a third party, I make my call sound more urgent. And it's harder for Mr. or Ms. Big's secretary to screen the call. She obviously can't quiz the operator about what my call is in regard to. If she still balks, I tell her that Mr. Big could easily handle my call, but if he doesn't want to be bothered, would she please transfer my call to Mr. Bigger? The secretary knows that the last thing Mr. Big wants is to bother his boss with a routine matter he tried to evade.

Once you get Mr. or Ms. Big on the wire, be as sweet as you can be. "Emphasize that you have always liked his company, you plan to buy from him in the future, and in fact you like everything about his company except this one unusual but easily corrected problem," says Charell. "If he doesn't seem to sympathize with you, make it clear that you know you have recourse, that he is not the highest authority in the world. In the nicest possible way, introduce the possibility of turning to his corporate superior or an outside authority like the local bureau of consumer affairs."

A successful face-to-face technique developed by specialists in assertiveness training is called the broken record. You drive your listener to distraction by repeating ad nauseam your problem and your request for redress in a helpful and unctuous manner. Let's say you take a defective watch back to a store, but the department manager tells you that returns aren't accepted after 90 days.

You counter, "I understand your position, but the watch never worked so I expect a refund."

He replies, "It's against store policy."

You say, "Of course, stores have to have policies for such matters, but the watch has always been defective and I think I should get my money back."

After 20 minutes of such slippery responses, any red-blooded manager is going to snap something like, "Customers break their own watches and then expect us to take them back." You must ignore insults, stick to the point, and answer sympathetically: "Some people may do that, but *my* watch *never* worked, and I'm sure I am entitled to a refund."

You can take passive resistance one step further by announcing, fortissimo, "I'm not moving until you straighten this out." Other customers quickly leave this unpleasant scene, and a smart shopkeeper will do almost anything just to get rid of you.

Putting It in Writing

If palavering doesn't get your problem resolved, escalate to a letter. Launch your missive directly at the head of the company. He probably won't even read it, but an aide may bump it down to a subordinate with a note that says, "The boss wants you to take care of this." Such a command is often enough to turn the laziest employee into a dynamo.

Many company presidents send complaints to their customer relations department, where scores of employees pore over letters that are often boring, vague, abusive, and longer than *The Forsyte Saga*. So you have to make your letter stand out. A Pennsylvania housewife sent Ford Motor Company's owner-director, Ned Smith, a 12-page comic book she had drawn, showing how repair problems with her Pinto strained her marriage. Smith returned a comic book of his own called "Captain Pinto to the Rescue" — and Ford fixed the car.

Normally, though, a letter in plain, forceful English will suffice. Richard Viguerie, who raises funds for conservative causes by direct-mail advertising, has letter writing down to a science. The first or "lead" paragraph, he says, should be brief — no more than two sentences of 10 to 15 words each — and should summarize the problem in a dramatic way. *Example:* "I am distressed by a billing problem that your company refuses to correct." Almost as important is the P.S. Tests have proved that a P.S. is one of the first things people read. "You want to make a statement that will get someone to read the rest of the letter," says Viguerie. The P.S. may be the best place for your deadline and your threat. "P.S. If I do not hear from your bank by Friday, May 28, I shall be compelled to [pick one] take my account elsewhere / notify the state banking commission / take this matter up with my lawyer."

In the paragraph after the lead, compliment the company. Try something like, "Over the years, I have been delighted with the appliances I have bought from Super Duper Products." Elaborate a bit. "Your digital readout food scale and rotary-spin electric toothbrush are joys to own." Then, in the next paragraph, go in for the kill: "So you can imagine my dismay when my Super Duper Mama Mia Rigatoni Maker (Model No. 230-1142-Z) turned out to be a dud."

Move on to the facts, but omit unnecessary details such as what your Aunt Effie had to say and how many times the phone rang before a company representative picked it up. Since most people only scan letters, you should state your demand twice — in the second sentence and at the end.

Try to establish a relationship with your reader to gain empathy. Viguerie suggests a sentence such as: ''I am in business, too, and I would be upset to learn that one of my customers had been treated as poorly as I have been.'' John Zyrkowski of Pittsburgh used this technique effectively after being bumped from first class to business class on an overbooked Qantas flight. He got a refund for the difference in fare but felt he had been rudely treated by cabin attendants, so he shot off a letter to the chairman of the airline. Zyrkowski's executive position — he was then a vice president of a multinational construction equipment firm — allowed him to pontificate: ''I think this incident contains important lessons for your organization.'' Of course, his threat — ''to tell my people not to fly on your airline'' — probably carried more influence. The chairman apologized and offered Zyrkowski a first-class seat for the price of a business-section ticket the next time he flew Qantas.

If your complaint doesn't bring immediate results, step up your demands. For example, in a phone call you might remark, ''See here! Miss Simpson in customer relations told me on April 1 that my flincher gear would arrive on the fourth. It is now May 3 and no flincher gear. I think you should compensate me for this intolerable delay by including a free harvest-gold dustcover with the order.'' If you keep raising the ante, management tends to become more eager to settle.

Finding the Right Referee

When right reason fails, you will probably find yourself entertaining the idea of a suit. For consumer complaints, small-claims courts run by state or local judicial systems have long been the courts of first resort. The maximum claim ranges from $200 in some rural counties of Washington and Georgia to $5,000 in Albuquerque. These courts are supposed to be simple, straightforward, and free of lawyers. But in many cities, consumers suing businesses in small-claims courts find themselves facing lawyers hired by the defendants and long delays. Moreover, laymen often do not know how to collect court judgments and get no help from court officials. Exceptions include New York City and California, which provide counseling services for small-claims courts, and Chicago, which has a *pro se* court — Latin for ''for himself'' — that bans lawyers for plaintiffs. Many major cities also have landlord-tenant courts, which are supposed to be quick, simple, and cheap. But they, too, sometimes are dominated by lawyers.

Many consumers have another place to turn: state and local organizations. Government agencies obviously have the most authority but may be strapped for funds. Private alternatives include the Better Business Bureau, which offers mediation and arbitration services to consumers at most of its 157 independent local affiliates. In addition, several industries have set up consumer action panels (CAPs) of their own to arbitrate disputes between consumers and businesses. There are AutoCAP, MACAP (major appliances), FICAP (for the furniture industry), and even ThanaCAP (for undertakers). These panels typically consist of industry representatives, technical experts, and consumer advocates. However, the more militant consumer groups, such as Ralph Nader's Public Citizen and the National Consumers League, are suspicious of the industry-sponsored organizations.

Arbitration and mediation services have special appeal if you don't want to alienate the other party permanently. Privacy is an added benefit of resolving a case out of court. So is the flexibility of the remedies. Courts award money damages; they generally cannot order a contractor to fix a leaky roof. The big obstacle is getting the other party to go along. Your opponent may simply not want to. He may be in the thrall of a lawyer who knows only litigation and wants to keep his meter running as long as possible. A deep-pocket defendant may want to deal with motions, interrogatories, and depositions to wear down a poorer plaintiff. And the defendant's lawyer may want a naive jury that can be manipulated with courtroom trickery and histrionics. Attempts to divert medical malpractice cases from the courts to mediation and arbitration boards have largely failed, in part because plaintiffs' lawyers want to pull the heartstrings of juries and in part because of the need for expert witnesses.

Further, in the case of arbitration there is a loophole: state arbitration statutes that allow the parties to appeal in court if there were procedural errors in the arbitration process. Usually, however, even a contentious loser accepts an arbitrator's decision.

APPENDIX: SEVENTY ESSENTIAL ADDRESSES

THIS LIST OF addresses and phone numbers will give you quick access to the best information and sources of help around the United States on such practical matters as how to find a knowledgeable broker or where to complain when you discover that your new car is a $12,000 lemon. If you are just starting out as an investor, you can use the list to find out about investment clubs. If you are a bank depositor aching to blow the whistle on a deceptive ad, you can learn where to direct your shrill. The list will enable you, as well, to do prudent research before buying a product or investing in an unfamiliar security.

Autos

AutoCAP, *8400 Westpark Drive, McLean, Virginia 22102; 703-821-7144*

Administers about 50 car-owner complaint-mediation services around the country — some in cities, others operating statewide. If the dealer who sold you a car won't stand behind it as stoutly as he should, you need help from AutoCAP, short for Automotive Consumer Action Program, sponsored by the National Automobile Dealers Association.

Insurance Institute for Highway Safety, *Communications Department, Watergate 600, Suite 300, Washington, D.C. 20037; 202-333-0770*

Supplies information on the crashworthiness, collision claims, and theft histories of various models of automobiles, plus performance records of such products as children's car seats.

National Highway Traffic Safety Administration, U.S. Department of Transportation, *400 Seventh Street, SW, Washington, D.C. 20590; 800-424-9393 or 202-366-0123*

Gives out information on such safety subjects as auto recalls and defective tires.

Banking

Comptroller of the Currency, *Consumer Activities Division, Washington, D.C. 20219; 202-447-1600*

Deals with consumer complaints and enforces Truth in Lending regulations at national banks — those with ''National'' in their names or the initials N.A., for ''National Association,'' after their names.

Federal Deposit Insurance Corporation, *Office of Consumer Affairs, 550 17th Street, NW, Washington, D.C. 20429; 202-393-8400*

Handles consumer complaints and enforces Truth in Lending regulations at federally insured state banks.

Federal Home Loan Bank Board, *Office of the Secretary, 1700 G Street, NW, Washington, D.C. 20552; 202-377-6000*

Handles consumer complaints and enforces Truth in Lending regulations at federally chartered savings and loan groups.

Federal Reserve Board, *Division of Consumer and Community Affairs, 20th and C Streets, NW, Washington, D.C. 20551; 202-452-3946*

Handles consumer complaints and enforces Truth in Lending regulations at state-chartered banks that are members of the Federal Reserve System. The Fed writes regulations to carry out Truth in Lending, Equal Credit Opportunity, and other consumer protection laws involving credit. (*See also* Credit.) The Federal Reserve System itself consists of 12 districts with banks in Atlanta, Boston, Chicago, Cleveland, Dallas, Kansas City, Minneapolis, New York City, Philadelphia, Richmond, St. Louis, and San Francisco. To save brokerage fees, you can go to any of these district banks to buy newly issued Treasury securities on days when they are being auctioned.

Collectibles

Appraisers Association of America, *60 East 42nd Street, Suite 2505, New York, New York 10165; 212-867-9775*

Issues a list of appraisers with their specialties. Being overinsured can be just as expensive as being underinsured. So all valuables should be properly appraised.

Christie's, *502 Park Avenue, New York, New York 10022; 212-546-1000*

Sotheby's, *1334 York Avenue, New York, New York 10021; 212-606-7000*

Offer free evaluation services in addition to selling many types of art and antiques at auction. Christie's and Sotheby's are the two leading names in the business. Call either firm for an appointment with a specialist or write, enclosing a photograph of the work you want evaluated.

R. M. Smythe & Company, *24 Broadway, New York, New York 10004; 212-943-1880*

Evaluates antique stock or bond certificates for a $25 appraisal fee. This firm does research on both domestic and foreign certificates and will auction them for you as well.

Credit

Associated Credit Bureaus, *P.O. Box 218300, Houston, Texas 77218; 713-492-8155*

Handles complaints about credit bureaus.

Federal Trade Commission, *Bureau of Consumer Protection, Pennsylvania Avenue at Sixth Street, NW, Washington, D.C. 20580; 202-523-3727*

Enforces the Truth in Lending Act against such violators as car dealers that don't make full disclosure of their interest rates for loans, and stores and mail-order houses that engage in unfair sales practices or deceptive advertising. (*See also* Banking.)

Credit Unions

Credit Union National Association, *Public Relations Department, P.O. Box 431, Madison, Wisconsin 53701; 608-231-4000*

Tells you everything you want to know about both state and federal credit unions — what they are, how to find one near you, how to organize one.

National Credit Union Administration, *Office of Public and Congressional Affairs, 1776 G Street, NW, Washington, D.C. 20456; 202-357-1050*

Regulates federally chartered credit unions and offers help in organizing a credit union or affiliating with an existing one. For more information, check with the regional office in Atlanta, Austin, Boston, Chicago, San Francisco, or Washington, D.C.

Dispute Settlement

American Arbitration Association, *140 West 51st Street, New York, New York 10020; 212-484-4000*

Gives you an alternative to taking civil disputes to court. The AAA has more than 25 regional offices, which arbitrate issues ranging from spats between live-in lovers to minority-group charges of discrimination. Fees for arbitration are 3 percent of claims up to $10,000 and lower percentages for larger amounts; for mediation, $250 for claims up to $100,000.

American Bar Association, *Standing Committee on Dispute Resolution, 1800 M Street, NW, Washington, D.C. 20036; 202-331-2258*

Provides a list of about 200 dispute resolution centers throughout the country.

Major Appliance Consumer Action Panel (MACAP), *20 North Wacker Drive, Chicago, Illinois 60606; 800-621-0477*

Mediates irreconcilable customer complaints against major appliance dealers, service agencies, and manufacturers. MACAP is an independent nonprofit review board established by its industry. (For a complete list of consumer action panels, *see* the next entry.)

Consumer Information Center, *Pueblo, Colorado 81009*

Distributes free of charge the *Consumers' Resource Handbook,* prepared by the U.S. Office of Consumer Affairs. This publication includes a list of all consumer complaint forums, from consumer action panels to Better Business Bureaus.

Education

American College Testing Program, *P.O. Box 168, Iowa City, Iowa 52243; 319-337-1000*

Through its Student Need Analysis Service, helps you make out a family financial statement to learn how much aid you can expect to get toward a child's college costs. Also available: general information about sources of financial aid and how to apply for it.

The College Board, *45 Columbus Avenue, New York, New York 10023-6917; 212-713-8000*

Through its public affairs department, provides general information on financial aid and college costs. The College Board also helps guide applicants to advanced-placement courses and exams.

The Experiment in International Living, *Kipling Road, Brattleboro, Vermont 05301; 802-257-7751*

Arranges for high school and college students as well as adults to spend a term or a summer abroad studying and staying with a foreign family.

U.S. Department of Education, *Student Information Center, P.O. Box 84, Washington, D.C. 20044; 301-984-4070*

Gives out general information about government sources of student financial aid and offers a useful free publication, *The Student Guide: Five Federal Financial Aid Programs.*

Entrepreneurs

International Franchise Association, *1350 New York Avenue, NW, Suite 900, Washington, D.C. 20005; 202-628-8000*

Offers information on franchising, including a step-by-step guide to evaluating franchises. Also available: a list of association members, giving details of types of business, history, cash required, and qualifications required of prospective franchisees. There are more than 600 members in 50 industries from business services to pet shops.

Small Business Administration, *1441 L Street, NW, Washington, D.C. 20416; SBA answer desk, 800-368-5855*

Answers questions on how to start a small business, training courses available, special programs for women and veterans, as well as financial assistance. Since most of the programs are administered by field offices, the desk will direct you to the right person and district.

The SBA's Office of Advocacy represents small-business interests before government agencies on regulatory issues and federal laws and helps you deal with government red tape.

U.S. Department of Commerce, *Andrew Kostecka, Industry Commodity Specialist, 14 Constitution Avenue, Room 1110, Washington, D.C. 20230; 202-377-0342*

Compiles general franchise information and statistics. Two annual publications are of particular interest: the *Franchise Opportunities Handbook* ($15 a copy) and *Franchising in the Economy* ($4.50). Both are available from the Superintendent of Documents, U.S. Government Printing Office, Washington, D.C. 20402.

Financial Planning

Institute of Certified Financial Planners, *2 Denver Highlands, 10065 East Harvard Avenue, Suite 320, Denver, Colorado 80231-5942; 303-751-7600*

Will send a list of members in your area. Members have passed courses given by the College for Financial Planning and are entitled to use the designation CFP after their names.

International Association for Financial Planning, *2 Concourse Parkway, Suite 800, Atlanta, Georgia 30328; 800-241-2148; 404-395-1605*

Will send you a list of members in your zip code area. Ask for its Registry of Financial Planning Practitioners, which lists only those IAFP members who have planning experience and specialized training and have passed the registry's examination.

National Center for Financial Education, *50 Fremont Street, 31st Floor, San Francisco, California 94105; 415-777-0460*

Educates and motivates people to save, invest, and plan for their financial future. For a $50 annual fee, this nonprofit membership organization sends you a monthly newsletter, a quarterly magazine, and a variety of services to help you get started.

Funerals

Continental Association of Funeral and Memorial Societies, *2001 S Street, NW, Suite 530, Washington, D.C. 20009; 202-745-0634*

Offers guidance on joining a memorial society providing low-cost funerals and information on the pros and cons of funeral prepayment plans.

Federal Trade Commission, *Funeral Rule Coordinator, Division of Enforcement, Washington, D.C. 20580; 202-376-2863*

Receives complaints about funeral directors who misrepresent services and products or won't give you a complete breakdown of prices. Although the FTC cannot represent individual consumers, it can issue cease-and-desist orders and in extreme cases may take persistent violators to federal court, where they face fines of up to $10,000 for each offense.

ThanaCAP, *11121 West Oklahoma Avenue, Milwaukee, Wisconsin 53227; 414-541-7925*

Mediates between consumers and undertakers. This panel is funded by the National Funeral Directors Association, but its members are all consumer advocates unaffiliated with the industry.

Futures

Chicago Board of Trade, *Office of Investigations and Audits, 141 West Jackson Boulevard, Chicago, Illinois 60604; 312-435-3650*

Trades futures contracts and options for four commodity groups: the grains (corn, wheat, oats, and soybean products), precious metals (one-kilo gold contracts and 1,000-ounce silver contracts), financial instruments (Treasury bonds and notes, a municipal bond index, Ginnie Maes), and stock indexes (NASDAQ, Major Market). If you encounter problems trading any of these, you can complain to the Office of Investigations and Audits, provided your broker is a member of this exchange. If you are seeking monetary adjustment, you also can use the board's arbitration service.

Chicago Mercantile Exchange, *30 South Wacker Drive, Chicago, Illinois 60606; 312-930-1000*

Trades in foreign currency futures and options, short-term interest rates, stock indexes, lumber, and livestock. If you need advice or arbitration, or are just confused, call the Merc at the above number. For market information call 312-930-8282.

Commodity Exchange Inc., *Public Relations Department, 4 World Trade Center, New York, New York 10048; 212-938-2958*

Trades in gold, silver, copper, and aluminum futures, as well as in options on gold, silver, and copper futures. The Comex helps investors with questions or problems concerning all these commodities. Also available are brochures explaining the intricacies of commodity trading and a list of member firms.

Commodity Futures Trading Commission, *Enforcement Division, 2033 K Street, NW, Washington, D.C. 20581; 202-254-7424*

Takes complaints involving fraud, unauthorized trading, and other shady practices. To confirm whether a commodity firm or an individual broker is registered with the commission — an important indication of good faith in doing business — call the National Futures Association at 800-621-3570. To seek reparation (an alternative to litigation) or to find out whether the commission or another customer has filed complaints, call the reparation section at 202-254-5008 or write R. Britt Lenz, Director of Complaints, at the address above.

National Futures Association, *Arbitration Administrator, 200 West Madison Street, Suite 1600, Chicago, Illinois 60606; 312-781-1300*

Resolves disputes on futures transactions and options involving NFA members. Also can audit members to make sure they are in compliance with NFA standards.

Giving

National Charities Information Bureau, *19 Union Square West, New York, New York 10003-3395; 212-929-6300*

Provides reports on up to three organizations, detailing how much they spend on charitable activities and how much on administration. Before giving to a charitable institution, it is an excellent idea to find out how carefully the organization is spending the funds it raises. On written request, the bureau also will send you its *Wise Giving Guide,* which lists 400 national nonprofit organizations.

Philanthropic Advisory Service, Council of Better Business Bureaus, *1515 Wilson Boulevard, Arlington, Virginia 22209; 703-276-0133*

Collects and disseminates data on how 7,000 charitable organizations spend their money. Publishes and sells for $1 a bimonthly list of charities, identifying those that meet — and don't meet — Better Business Bureau standards.

Insurance

American Council of Life Insurance, *Information Services, 1850 K Street, NW, Washington, D.C. 20006; 800-423-8000*

Will send you general information or answers to questions about life and health insurance. If you have a complaint, the council will direct you to the government agency with jurisdiction over the matter.

Insurance Information Institute, *110 William Street, New York, New York 10038; 800-221-4954*

Provides general information and answers questions on property and casualty insurance. If the institute can't help you, it will try to refer you to someone who can.

National Insurance Consumer Organization, *121 North Payne Street, Alexandria, Virginia 22314; 703-549-8050*

A nonprofit membership organization ($25 a year, tax deductible) set up to educate insurance buyers. Will calculate the real rate of return on your cash-value life insurance policy. Publications include *How to Save Money on Life Insurance* ($7.25); *Buyers Guide to Insurance: What Companies Won't Tell You* ($2 plus a self-addressed stamped envelope); and a bimonthly newsletter.

Investment Advisers

Select Information Exchange, *2095 Broadway, Suite 404, New York, New York 10023; 212-874-6408*

Offers a free catalogue describing the 800 investment advisory newsletters that SIE represents as a subscription agency. It lets you choose sampler packages of newsletters that you can take for short trials. The basic package: 20 newsletters for one to five issues, depending upon frequency of publication, for $11.95. If you decide to subscribe to one of them, this fee will be applied to the price.

American Association of Individual Investors, *612 North Michigan Avenue, Suite 317, Chicago, Illinois 60611; 312-280-0170*

Supplies its members with a variety of self-help investment publications and organizes seminars in cities around the country. This is a fine outfit to join if you want to learn how to invest.

National Association of Investment Clubs, *1515 East 11 Mile Road, Royal Oak, Michigan 48067; 313-543-0612*

Sends information on how to form an investment club and supplies clubs that join the association with information on how to invest.

Jewelry

American Gem Society, *5901 West Third Street, Los Angeles, California 90036-2898; 213-936-4367*

Can refer you to reputable jewelers and appraisers in your vicinity. This nonprofit organization offers two free publications: *The American Gem Society Consumer Kit,* which includes a listing of the society's 3,000 member firms in the United States and Canada; and *Diamonds . . . Facts and Fallacies,* a purchasing guide.

Legal Services

Academy of Family Mediators, *P.O. Box 4686, Greenwich, Connecticut 06830; 203-629-8049*

Makes referrals to hundreds of divorce mediators throughout the country.

American Bar Association, *American Bar Center, 750 North Lake Shore Drive, Chicago, Illinois 60611; 312-988-5000*

Offers consumer information on such subjects as choosing a lawyer and the legal aspects of marriage, consumer credit, and bankruptcy. To tap into the lawyer referral service, you have to go through your nearest city, county, or state bar association.

National Resource Center for Consumers of Legal Services, *124D East Broad Street, Falls Church, Virginia 22046; 703-536-8700*

Will help you with broad legal questions, including how to shop for a lawyer and how to complain about an incompetent one. But this research and education center cannot provide individual advice.

Mutual Funds

Investment Company Institute, *1600 M Street, NW, Suite 600, Washington, D.C. 20036; 202-293-7700*

Distributes a $1 directory of its 1,500 mutual-fund members, load and no-load, with details about each. Also available: a 16mm film on mutual funds; video tapes, films, and booklets covering such topics as money-market funds, IRAs, and saving for college.

No-Load Mutual Fund Association, *11 Penn Plaza, Suite 2204, New York, New York 10001; 212-563-4540*

Offers *The Investors Guide and Directory to Mutual Funds* ($5), listing more than 400 funds that market shares by mail and phone and therefore have minimal sales charges or none at all — no-load or low-load funds.

Real Estate

Home Owners Warranty, *2000 L Street, NW, Washington, D.C. 20036; eastern region, 800-241-9260; western region, 800-433-7657*

Fosters high-quality construction. The 12,000 builders that belong to HOW are required to follow approved standards and carry 10-year protection against major structural defects on the houses they build. Write for a list of HOW members in your area. Phone for a free brochure on how to maintain your house and remodel it.

National Association of Home Builders, *Department of Consumer Affairs, 15th and M Streets, NW, Washington, D.C. 20005; 202-822-0409*

Tries to speed settlement of disputes over construction quality between buyers and member builders but acts only on written requests. Enclose copies of documentation, such as checks and warranties. If your problem is outside the association's jurisdiction, it will refer you to the proper authority.

Retirement

National Council on the Aging, *600 Maryland Avenue, SW, West Wing 100, Washington, D.C. 20024; 202-479-1200*

Takes stands on issues and will send you information on national laws that affect older Americans. Among its interests: Social Security, nursing care, senior citizen centers, health and housing, and employment for the elderly.

American Association of Retired Persons, *1909 K Street, NW, Washington, D.C. 20049; 202-872-4700*

Provides its members with such services as group health insurance, car and homeowners insurance, a nonprofit mail-order pharmacy, a travel bureau, and a money-market fund. Discounts on car rentals and hotel rooms are also available. The AARP advocates legislation for older people at the state and federal levels; through 3,300 local chapters, it develops community programs on health, crime prevention, and driver improvement. As a $5-a-year member you also get a monthly news bulletin, a bimonthly magazine, *Modern Maturity,* and other publications.

Securities

National Association of Securities Dealers, *Customer Complaint Department, 1735 K Street, NW, Washington, D.C. 20006; 202-728-8217; Arbitration Department, 2 World Trade Center, 98th floor, New York, New York 10048; 212-839-6251*

Fields investors' complaints at 14 district offices. Call the Washington number to find the office nearest you, the New York number if you are considering taking action against a broker or his firm.

Securities and Exchange Commission, *Office of Consumer Affairs and Information Services, 450 Fifth Street, NW, Washington, D.C. 20549; 202-272-7440*

Considers complaints about brokers, stock exchanges, and corporate issuers of stocks and bonds. Subjects can range from delays in receiving dividends or stock certificates to allegations of fraud or misrepresentation. The SEC also operates public reference libraries in Washington, D.C., New York City, and Chicago, where you can find all the financial reports that corporations are required to file with the commission. Copies are available on written request for a small charge.

Securities Investor Protection Corporation, *900 17th Street, NW, Suite 800, Washington, D.C. 20006; 202-223-8400*

Protects the cash and securities that customers of brokerage firms insured by SIPC (pronounced *sip*-ic) keep on deposit with those firms. Most securities dealers and brokerage houses belong to this government-fostered agency, which promises reimbursement for losses as high as $500,000 per account, including $100,000 of cash deposits. Compensation funds come mainly from assessments against member securities firms.

Standard & Poor's Corporation, *25 Broadway, New York, New York 10004; 212-208-8000*

Value Line, *711 Third Avenue, New York, New York 10017; 212-687-3965*

Compile basic reference material for investors. Among other publications, S&P offers *The Outlook* ($207 a year) and the *Security Owner's Stock Guide* ($84 a year). Value Line's flagship is the three-part weekly *Investment Survey*, which includes stock selections, commentary on the stock-market outlook, and financial data on companies. These publications may be available at your broker's office or public library.

Stock Exchanges

American Stock Exchange, *86 Trinity Place, New York, New York 10006; 212-306-1000*

Provides information about the stocks traded on this exchange and puts you in touch with its arbitration department if you wish to complain about member brokers. For *The Fact Book,* a $3 annual statistical review of the exchange, write to the Publications Department, Seventh Floor.

Chicago Board Options Exchange, *400 South La Salle Street, Chicago, Illinois 60605; 312-786-5600*

Distributes free pamphlets on how to trade options. Phone to find out when the CBOE Investors' Roadshow — free seminars on options strategies — will come to a city near you.

New York Stock Exchange, *11 Wall Street, New York, New York 10005; 212-656-3000*

Through its publication division, offers an Investors Information Kit for $4. It consists of four pamphlets: *Understanding Stocks and Bonds, Getting Help When You Invest, Understanding Financial Statements,* and a *Glossary*. For problems with brokers, address inquiries to the arbitration department.

Taxes

Internal Revenue Service, *800-424-1040*

Handles your tax problems through its local offices. Phone your district director or ask for the problem resolution officer (PRO). If you believe that your accountant is guilty of any type of professional misconduct, get in touch with Leslie S. Shapiro, Director of Practice, Internal Revenue Service, 1111 Constitution Avenue, NW, Washington, D.C. 20224; 202-535-6787.

U.S. Tax Court, *400 Second Street, NW, Washington, D.C. 20217; 202-376-2754*

Hears cases in which taxpayers may represent themselves. The clerk of the court will send you a package of materials, including all the necessary forms, a list of cities where the court sits, and a booklet explaining small tax case procedure in lay terms.

Travel

American Society of Travel Agents, *Consumer Affairs Department, 4400 MacArthur Boulevard, NW, Washington, D.C. 20007; 202-965-7520*

Will try to assist with travel problems. If you have a gripe about your travel agent, ASTA will help mediate the dispute.

Department of Transportation, *Office of Community and Consumer Affairs, Office of the Assistant Secretary for Governmental Affairs, Washington, D.C. 20590; 202-366-2220*

Enforces airline regulations and handles complaints about failure to honor paid reservations (called "bumping"), lost luggage, deceptive practices, nonsmoking rules.

Federal Aviation Administration, *800 Independence Avenue, SW, Washington, D.C. 20591; 202-426-8521*

Sets safety standards for aircraft construction and maintenance and operates airport control towers. Inquire at this agency of the Department of Transportation about airline safety, airport noise, and other environmental problems caused by commercial aviation.

International Airline Passengers Association, *Consumer Affairs Division, P.O. Box 660074, Dallas, Texas 75266; 800-527-5888 or 214-520-1070*

Provides such services as travel insurance and hotel and car-rental discounts, lobbies in Washington for air safety and airline-related consumer protection.

This organization for travelers has more than 100,000 members in 175 countries. Members' requests get priority, but nonmembers also can get help. For consumer concerns such as overbooking or lost luggage, address the Dallas office. To report safety problems, write or call IAPA, Group Aerotech Operation, P.O. Box 23079, Washington, D.C. 20024; 703-920-1704.

Treasury Securities

Department of the Treasury, *Bureau of the Public Debt, Department F, Washington, D.C. 20239-1200; 202-287-4113*

Answers questions about investing in Treasury bills, notes, and bonds. You can also get brochures on the various Treasury securities.

U.S. Savings Bonds

Department of the Treasury, *U.S. Savings Bond Division, 1111 20th Street, NW, Washington, D.C. 20226; 202-634-5377*

Gives general information and answers questions about such problems as replacing lost bonds. But try your bank first.

INDEX

ABCS (agency-backed compounded securities), 303
Abdoo, Brian, 284
Academy of Family Mediators, 142, 499
accountants. *See* tax advisers
Addiss, William, 304
adjustable-rate mortgages (ARM). *See* mortgages
advance/decline line, 261
Advanced Micro Devices, 254
Aetna Life & Casualty, 424, 428, 432, 433, 458, 463; Variable Fund, 171
AFA Financial (investments), 278, 279
AFL-CIO, 414; *Guide to Union Sponsored Scholarships, Awards and Student Financial Aid,* 124
age: checking account fees, 387; insurance, 67, 98, 151, 163, 437–438, 463; IRA withdrawals, 179–181; life expectancy, 156, 163, 165, 180–181, 438; of majority, 114, 191, 218; retirement, 156, 159–164; senior discounts, 163; tax credits, 351, 355, 364; U.S. population, 148–149, 251, 253. *See also* children; parents; retirement plans
AGI (adjusted gross income). *See* income
Agriculture, U.S. Department of, 96
Alden, Philip, 130
Alex. Brown & Sons, 313
alimony. *See* divorce
Allmon, Charles, 255
alternative minimum tax (AMT), 356, 360–361
AMCOL Development Group, 107
American Academy of Matrimonial Lawyers, 134
American Arbitration Association, 142, 494
American Association of Individual Investors, 224, 499
American Association of Retired Persons, 501
American Bar Association, 71, 414, 495, 500
American Capital Pace fund, 58
American College for insurance professionals, 44
American College of Probate Counsel, 202
American College Testing Program, 118, 495
American Council of Life Insurance, 498
American Council on Education, 116
American Express, 229, 395, 411
American Gem Society, 499
American Institute of Certified Public Accountants, 367, 368
American Legion scholarships, 124
American Medical Association, 460
American Society of Appraisers, 11
American Society of Travel Agents, 503
American Stock Exchange, 283, 285, 502
American Stores, 275
Amica Mutual insurance company, 424
annual percentage rate (APR), 399
annuities, 174; cash value, 10, 450–451; fixed and variable, 170–172, 323–324; and IRAs, 169, 323–324; joint-and-survivor, 74, 159, 176; lifetime, types of, 176–177; vs. lump sum, 175–176, 177–179
Apple Computer, 225, 244, 249
appliances, complaints about, 495
appraisals. *See* commissions and fees; valuables
Appraisers Association of America, 11, 493
Arbel, Avner, 250, 255
arbitrageurs, 265, 271–275 *passim,* 280

armed forces: survivors' benefits, 33, 188. *See also* mortgages (VA)
Armstrong, Alexandra, 87, 88
art and artifacts. *See* valuables
Asset Analysis Focus newsletter, 246
asset management accounts. *See* brokers
assets: hidden (company), 246–247; "wasting," 12, 229. *See also* cash; inventories
Associated Credit Bureaus, 411, 494
Associated Press, 344
AT&T, 159, 229
auctions: art and antique, 493–494; bond and stock, 239–240, 292, 493
Auerbach, Marshall J., 76
Austin, Douglas, 275
AutoCAP (Automotive Consumer Action Program), 485, 491, 492
automated teller machines (ATMs). *See* banks
automobile insurance, 419–424, 430, 483; bankruptcy and, 415; disability, 466, 480; excess liability, 431, 432; high-risk premium, 67, 73, 98; table, 420–421
automobiles: budget and, 31; cash value, 11; complaints, 485, 492–493, 494; loans, 351, 390, 392, 481, 482–483; mileage allowance, 352; shopping for, 476, 480–484
Avon Products, 249

baby boomers, 1, 160, 383, 471
Baker, William R., 252
balance sheet: corporate, analysis of, 270; personal, 8, 9–12; worksheet, 13–15
Ball, George L., 336
balloon loan, 400
Bank Administration Institute, 386
Bankcard Holders of America, 396
Bankers National Life, 441
Bank of Los Angeles, 408
bankruptcy. *See* debts, personal
banks, 379–380; asset management accounts, 381–382; automated teller machines, 380, 384, 387; as brokers, 168, 339, 379, 382; complaints about, 493; credit cards of, 395–396, 407, 410; department-store- or broker-owned, 236, 240, 380, 395; joint accounts, 71, 75, 235; loans, 392, 393, 394, 409; relationship banking, 382–384, 409. *See also* certificates of deposit; checking accounts; credit unions; interest rates; loans; money-market funds; savings; savings and loan associations; trusts
Barnett, Rosalind, 184
Barron's, 54, 265
Baskin, Henry, 79
Bass brothers, 243
Battle for Investment Survival, The (Loeb), 225
Beatrice Foods, 271
Beckerman, David, 131
Behavioral Science Research Corporation, 382
Belli, Melvin M., 69
Beneficial Finance savings plan, 240, 241
Beneficial Income Tax Service, 366
beneficiary: change of, 74, 76, 209, 220; as executor, 217; IRA or pension plan, 139, 159, 181, 193; trust, 195, 197–199, 200. *See also* Social Security benefits
Berg, Gary, 475–476
Berger, Harvey, 375
Berkshire Hathaway, 243
Berkus, Barry, 106
Berry, Burton, 58, 60
Best, A. M., *Best's Insurance Reports,* 170, 171, 424, 430
beta rating, 279. *See also* volatility
Better Business Bureau, 335, 477, 486, 491, 495, 498
biotechnology, 253
birth certificates, 181, 188
Blaustein, Randy Bruce, 376
blindness, and tax deduction, 351
blind pools, 313
Block, H&R, 366, 368
Block, Julian, 369
Blue Cross/Blue Shield, 150. *See also* health insurance
Blume, Marshall, 56, 289
Boesky, Ivan, 271, 273
bond funds. *See* mutual funds
bonds: ABCS, 303; appraisal of old certificates, 494; capital gains on, 227, 231; convertible, 231, 291, 325; "deep discount," 288; defined, 287; interest rates and, 58, 59, 230, 287–288, 291, 301; mortgage-revenue, 305–310; put, 300–301; safety/risk of, 173, 287–295 *passim,* 299, 302, 303, (rated) 324–325; steady-state, 300–304; taxable/tax-exempt, 120, 288–291, 293–295, 300, 349 (*see also* municipal bonds); and warrants, 229; zero-coupon, 114, 301–304, 325. *See also* corporate bonds; Treasury securities
book value (of company), 246
borrowing. *See* debts, personal; loans
Boston Company Advisors, 262
Boyar, Mark, 246
Brazelton, Dr. T. Berry, 101
Brennan, William, *Brennan Reports,* 368–369
bridge loans, 404
Britten, Arthur B., 472
brokers: asset management accounts, 237, 338, 342, 344, 379–380, 381–384, 388; automobile, 481; banking services by, 379, 381; banks and insurance companies as, 168, 339, 379, 382; borrowing from, 394; and CDs, 239; and complaint mediation, 497–498, 501; and conflict of interest, 52, 337; discount, 47, 168, 334–335, 338–342,

380, 382, (on-line) 342–344; full-service, 335–338; how to choose, 334–344; and IRAs, Keogh plans, 168, 169, 335, 338; mortgage, 393; share, 339; value, 339. *See also* commissions and fees
Bryn Mawr Trust, 383
Buck Consultants, 129n, 183
budgeting. *See* financial planning
Buffett, Warren E., 242–243
Bugen, David, 46–47
Bunn, Jeffrey, 318
Bush, Julian, 209
business: commercial liability insurance, 433; expenses, handicapped employee deduction, 352; home, 363, 427; starting own, 126–127, 257, 495–496
business cycles, 259, 266
Butcher & Singer, 114–115, 286, 289
buybacks, 276. *See also* takeovers
Buyers Guide to Insurance: What Companies Won't Tell You, 499
Buying Treasury Securities at Federal Reserve Banks, 240
buyouts. *See* takeovers
bypass trusts. *See* trusts

Caine, Lynn, 186, 189
calls, 229–230; bonds and, 288, 291, 292, 294, 297, 304; call loan rate, 394; selling (and buying), 282–283
cancer research, 253
capital gains, 56, 173, 227, 231; mutual funds, 328–329; tax deductions, 352, 356; and taxes, 6, 91, 139, 178, 228, 273, 275, 287, 349, 364
capital losses, 228, 283, 349, 364, 374
Cardwell, Robert, 279
Career and Family Institute, 82
career-average pension plan, 159
careers. *See* jobs
Carl, Bernard, 309
Car/Puter, 481
Carter, Donald C., and Carter Organization, 276
Carter, Jimmy, 266
Carter Financial Management, 96
Carter Hawley Hale, 274
cash: -assets ratio (mutual funds), 261, 264; reserve, *see* emergency fund; turning assets into (liquidity), 10–12, 115, 131, 173, 192, 235, 322–333 *passim,* 438 (*see also* insurance); unreported income, *see* income
cash flow: company, 247 (*see also* debt-to-equity ratio); personal, 27, 28, 86, 150, 163, (worksheet), 23–26; rental property, 318, 320
Cash Management Account (CMA), 379, 381
Catalyst (organization), 98
CATS. *See* Treasury securities
CDA Investment Technologies, 51, 52
Census Bureau, U.S., 63, 68, 143, 253
Central Maine Power, 278
certificates of deposit (CDs), 4, 98, 115, 163, 189, 237–239; brokered, 239; cashing in, 10, 173, 322; as collateral, 394; finance company sales, 240–241; interest rates, 236, 238, 239, 240; in IRAs, 168, 238, 323, 326; rated, 326; zero, 303
Certified Financial Planner (CFP) program, 44
certified public accountants (CPAs). *See* tax advisers
Charell, Ralph, 486, 487–488
charge accounts, 87, 407, 410
charitable remainder, charitable lead trusts, 211–212
charities: contributions to, 86; deductions for, 192, 211–212, 351–352, 356; information about, 498; in will, 216
Chartered Financial Consultant (ChFC), curriculum, 44
Chase Manhattan Bank, 187
Chasen, Nancy, 150
checking accounts, 380, 385–388; asset management, 237, 380, 381–382, 384, 388; bad checks, 386, 409; balances, 385, 386, 387; joint, 86; money-market, 236, 388; NOW, Super-NOW, 383, 385–386, 387
Chicago Board of Trade, 497
Chicago Board Options Exchange (CBOE), 283, 502
Chicago Mercantile Exchange, 497
children: adopted, 215; bank/checking accounts for, 235, 387; in blended family, 144–147; careers compatible with, 83–84, 93–95; cost of raising, 63, 84, 85, 94–99, 101 (*see also* education costs); day care for, 84–85, 93–95, 97, 98, 100–103, 251, 355; dependent, defined, 353; divorce and, *see* divorce; gifts to, 113–114 (*see also* inheritance; trusts); guardianship of, *see* guardianship; interest of, in stock market, 280; life insurance for, 90; of POSSLQs, 68–69, 73, 74; Social Security/insurance benefits for, 74, 90, 452–454, 463. *See also* students
Child Study Center (Yale), 85
Child Trends (organization), 84
Christie's (auctions), 493
Cigna insurance, 432
CIM (computer-integrated manufacturing), 252
Citibank, Citicorp, 168, 301, 382, 383, 386, 394
Clarke, Janet, 273
Clifford trust. *See* trusts
Clinical Register (National Association of Social Workers), 155
closing costs. *See* home ownership
CMA (Cash Management Account), 379, 381
cohabitation contracts, 69–70, 71–72

Cohen, Martin, 312, 313
Coler, Mark, 339
collectibles. *See* valuables
College Board, The, 495
College Credit Card Corporation, 410
College for Financial Planning, 44, 496
College Money Handbook, The, 119–120
College Scholarship Service, 118
college tuition. *See* education costs
College Work-Study (aid program), 117
Collingwood, Charles, 213
Colonial Penn Insurance Company, 430
Columbus Mutual Life, 171
Commerce, U.S. Department of, 496
Commerce Clearing House, 369
commissions and fees: annuities and bond mutual funds, 172, 299; appraisal, 139, 140, 217, 363, 494; asset management, 237, 382, 388; automobile broker, 481; checking account, 385–386, 387; computer analysis, 244; credit card, report or counseling, 383, 395–396, 410, 411, 414; deductible, 353; dividend reinvestment, 279, 280; divorce mediator, 141; "documentation," 392; family counseling, 151; financial planner, 45–47, 51, 52–53, 59, 60, 368; insurance, 440–441, (analysis of) 463–464; IRA maintenance or startup, 167, 168; legal, 77, 151, 195–196, 214, 318, 362; private investigator, 188; real estate agent, 321, 331, 364; stockbroker, 240, 298, 302, 334–339 *passim,* 344, (table) 340–341; tax return preparation/defense, 366–367, 369, 375, 378; trust drafting, trustee, unit trust, 194, 200, 295, 296
commodities, 232, 497–498
Commodity Exchange Inc., 497
Commodity Futures Trading Commission, 498
community property. *See* joint ownership
Comparative Annuity Reports, 171
complaints, 485–491; auto insurance, 424; to IRS, 370–372; mediation services, 491, 492–503
Comptroller of the Currency, U.S., 200, 493
CompuServe data base, 344
computer(s), 254, 425; and credit applications, 405; DIF, in tax audit, 373; and growth stocks, 250, 251–252; mortgage origination by, 403; on-line investing by, 342–344; software for, 244, 252; stock analysis by, 244, 246, 270, 336
Computer Directions Advisers, 248
Computer Pictures Corporation, 127
Compu-Val Management Associates, 51
condominiums. *See* home ownership
Connon, Laura, 202
conservatorship, 151, 196, 218. *See also* guardianship
consumer action panels (CAPs), 491, 495, 497
Consumer Affairs, U.S. Office of, 495
Consumer: Credit Counselors, 412; Expenditure Survey, 64; Federation of America, 385; Information Center, 495
consumer loan companies, 407
consumer price index. *See* inflation
Consumers' Resource Handbook, 495
Consumers Union and *Consumer Reports,* 438
Continental Association of Funeral and Memorial Societies, 497
Control Data Corporation, 94
conversion price, 291
convertible bonds. *See* bonds
convertible trust, 197
Cooper, Peter, 303
cooperative apartments. *See* home ownership
Coping (Yates), 189
Corbett, Clare, 156
Cornfeld, Bernard, 60
corporate bonds, 58, 173, 174, 222, 298; industrials, 288–289; junk, 58–59, 271, 289–291, 304, 324–325; rated, 324–325; return on, 4, 58, 230, 288–289, 291, 294, 298–299, 324; utilities, 228–229, 277–278, 288–289; zero, 303. *See also* bonds
Corporation Records (Standard & Poor's), 256
cost-averaging, 281–282
cost of living. *See* inflation
Cover, Thomas, 392
credit, 412; credit record, 92, 109, 389, 392, 405–411, 415; limit on (in budgeting), 27, 28, 87, 390, (worksheet) 391; phaseout limitations (tax deduction), 351; refusal of, 409–410; shopping for, 389–397; for two-income families, 86, 87; for women, 92, 185. *See also* debts, personal; loans
credit bureaus, 410–411, 494
credit cards, 237, 397, 477; and ATMs, 384; avoidance of use, 27, 413; bank-, broker- or retailer-issued, 240, 380, 381, 393, 395–396, 407, 410; finance charges, 87, 351, 383, 395–396; joint vs. separate, 71, 92; record of, 33
credit counselors, 86, 412, 414
Credit Union National Association, 494
credit unions, 168, 235, 383, 386, 387–388, 409, 494
Crittenden, Alan, and *Crittenden Report,* 311
crowd psychology, 260, 261
Crowell, Richard A., 262
Crum & Forster, 433
Cullins, Kelly, 485
current ratio, 246. *See also* debt-to-equity ratio

Dacey, Norman, 201
Daniele, Anthony R., 80
Daniels, George, 53, 55
Dankenbring, James, 186

Data Resources Inc., 253, 323
Davidowitz, Howard, 473, 475
day care. *See* children
Dean Witter, 335, 337, 338
death certificate, need for, 188
death tax. *See* estates
Deaton, Virginia, 189
debit cards, 380, 381, 383–384, 396–397
debts, personal: bankruptcy, 411, 415, 500; deduction limitations, 351; excessive, 27, 85–87, 412–413; -income ratio, 408; installment, 27, 390, 408, 412; joint accounts and, 71; limits on, 390, (worksheet) 391; liquidation of, 27–28, 87; working wives' assumption of, 92. *See also* credit; loans
debt-to-equity ratio (of company), 244, 246, 256, 270, 279, 285–286, 289
defense spending, 251
deficit spending, 5
defined-benefit/defined-contribution plan. *See* pension plans
dental expenses and insurance, 351, 459
department stores. *See* retailers
dependents. *See* income tax
depreciation: automobile, 484; home office, 363; real estate, 110, 312, 313
devaluation, 3–4. *See also* inflation
Diamonds . . . Facts and Fallacies, 499
DIF (Discriminate Function System), 373. *See also* tax audits
Dillon, John, 486
Directory of Exceptional Stockbrokers, 335, 338
disability/handicap: Social Security benefits, 91, 465, 466, 469; tax deductions/credits, 351, 352, 355; trusts, 198–199
disability-income insurance, 66–67, 91, 222, 465–469, 480
Discount Brokerage Advisory Services, 339
discount brokers. *See* brokers
discount stores. *See* retailers
discretionary account, 50
Disney, Walt, Productions, 243–244, 271
dispute settlement. *See* complaints
diversification: mutual fund, 56, 58, 59, 225; personal investment, 12, 114, 222, 243, 255, 284, 332, (by bond maturity) 295, (by industry) 227, (inflation and) 323; REIT lack of, 313
dividends, 4, 56, 228, 230; automatic reinvestment, 56, 279–280, 332; real estate income as, 311, 314–315, 331–332; taxes on, 229, 349; trusting in, 277–279
divorce: alimony, 79, 135, 145, 407, 415, (tax status) 136–137, 166, 349, 350; attorneys and mediators, 140–142, 499; child custody and support, 73, 79, 92, 141, 145, 407, 415, (guardianship) 219, (tax status) 136–137, 350, 353; and income tax, 91, 348, 367, 368; prenuptial contracts, 77, 78, 79, 80, 140; property division, 77–78, 91–92, 134–136; settlement worksheet, 138; Social Security/insurance benefits, 162, 181, 463; wills, 153, 220; working wives, 92, 135–136. *See also* separation
DM Data, 252
"documentation" fees (auto loans), 392
Dodd, David, 242
"do-it-yourself": investment, 499; prenuptial contract, 80; student aid, 117, 119; tax return preparation, 369; trusts, 201–202; wills, 201, 214
dollar: cost-averaging, 281–282; devaluation, 3–4 (*see also* inflation)
Don't Miss Out: The Ambitious Student's Guide to Financial Aid (Leider and Leider), 119
Dorfman, Lisa, 254
Douglas Austin & Associates, 275
Dow Jones: *Dow Theory Forecasts* newsletter, 278; industrial average, 5, 53, 54, 258, 261, 279, 328; News Retrieval, 343; utility average, 278
down payment: automobile, 483; house, *see* home ownership
Dresner, Susan, 477–478
Drexel Burnham Lambert High Interest Trust Shares (HITS), 290–291
DuCanto, Joseph N., 140
Dunn, Thomas L., 378

eating out. *See* food
Economic Recovery Tax Act (1981), 5, 114, 191, 320
Edelstein, Saul, 141
Education, U.S. Department of, 495
education costs, 86, 98; of degree, 97, 111–115, 123–124; need-analysis formula and Service, 118–119, 121, 495; planning for, 57, 88, 90, 111–115, 302, 303, 440, (worksheet) 112; scholarships, 117, 118, 124–125, (taxable/nontaxable) 124, 349; student loans, 109, 116–125, 415, 495, (crib sheet) 122–123
Egan, Peter, 128
Eisenhower, Dwight, 266
Elefant, Marcia, 192
Elks (organization) scholarships, 124
emergency fund, 8, 12, 28, 87, 91, 98, 222, 234
employee stock-ownership plan (ESOP), 130–131, 132
energy crisis. *See* oil embargo and prices
entrepreneurs, 495–496. *See also* business
Equal Credit Opportunity, 493
Equifax Services, 410
Equitable Capital Management, 162
Equitable of New York, 466

equity: company, return on, 247–248, 256 (*see also* debt-to-equity ratio); personal, *see* loans (home-equity); mortgages (shared-equity)
Ernst & Whinney, 378
Esmark takeover, 271
ESOP (employee stock-ownership plan), 130–131, 132
Estate Planning for the Elderly Client (Schlesinger), 153
estates: death/estate taxes, 91, 113, 147, 153, 191–192, 193–194, 203–212, 443, (worksheet) 204–206; executors of, 147, 153, 213, 217–218; planning, 152–153, 190–202, 203–212. *See also* inheritance; wills
Evans, Elliot L., 69
Evans, Richard, 278
Experiment in International Living, The, 495

Fact Book, The (American Stock Exchange), 502
Fahey, Msgr. Charles, 148, 154
Fain, Harry, 134
Fair Isaac Company, 407, 408, 409
family: blended, 143–147; in buying first house, 109–110. *See also* children; married couples; parents; two-income families
Family Service Association of America, 154, 414
Fannie Mae (Federal National Mortgage Association), 303, 305–306, 308–309
fear. *See* risk
Federal Aviation Administration, 503
Federal Council on Aging, 148
Federal Deposit Insurance Corporation (FDIC), 235, 239, 303, 493
Federal Home Loan: Bank Board, 401, 493; Mortgage Corporation, *see* Freddie Mac
Federal Housing Administration (FHA). *See* mortgages
Federal National Mortgage Association. *See* Fannie Mae
Federal Reserve Board, 3, 4, 5, 51, 260, 396, 493; banks, 240, 260, 292
Federal Savings and Loan Insurance Corporation (FSLIC), 235, 239, 303
Federal Trade Commission, 494, 497
Feeney, John, 224
fees. *See* commissions and fees
Felder, Raoul Lionel, 71
Feldman, Stan, 252
Fenimore Asset Management, 51
Ferkauf, Eugene, 472
Ferraro, Geraldine, 196
Ferris, Robert D., 280
fiber optics, 252–253
FICAP (Furniture Industry Consumer Action Panel), 491
Fidelity Investments, 280; Equity Income, 58; Flexible Bond, 298; High Income, 298; Investors Express, 343; Magellan, 89; USA account, 381
Fieldman, Leon, 146
Fields, W. C., 7
FIFO accounting, 246
finance companies, 236, 240, 390, 392, 393, 407
Financial Aids for Higher Education (Keeslar), 125
Financial Management Consultants, 45
financial planning, 496; aging parents' care, 149–155; blended family, 145–147; budgeting, 8, 21–31, 65, 86–87, 98–99, 381, (models) 29–31; choice and use of financial planners, 41–49, 51–55, 499; and divorce, 136; goals, 8, 16–20, 47–48, 50, 57, 88, 111, 145, 222, (worksheet) 18; income tax, 366–367; independence, 126–133; retirement, 155–174, (worksheet) 164–165. *See also* commissions and fees; education costs; estates
financial records, 32–33, 153–154, 186, 201, 410, 414; computerized, 342; contracts, 70; for insurance purposes, 11, 427, 430; of taxes and for tax purposes, 27, 362, 364, 372, 373, 375, 376, 387; worksheets, 34–39. *See also* inventories
Financial Strategies Inc., 28
Finkelstein, Bernard, 195
First Boston bank, 309
First Variable Annuity "A," 171
Fishman, Barbara, 145–146
Fitzgerald, John, 200
fixed-income: investments, 114, 130, 157, 163, 259, 288, 291; pension plan, 172
fixed interest rates. *See* interest rates
fixed-premium insurance, 438
Fleck, Judge Charles J., 135
food: children's, 97; convenience, 85, 87; eating out, 64, 85, 86, 87; shopping for, 478–479
Foote Cone & Belding, 456–457
Ford Motor Company, 455, 489
Fortune 500 companies, 130, 248
forward averaging, 169, 178–179, 356
401(k) plan. *See* salary reduction or withholding plan
Franchise Opportunities Handbook, 496
Franchising in the Economy, 496
Frank, Robert, 313
Franklin, Benjamin, 1–2
Franklin Gold Fund, 326
Freddie Mac (Federal Home Loan Mortgage Corporation), 303, 305–306, 308–309
Frederic, Duane E., 280
Freed, Doris Jonas, 68
Free to All (Student Guide), 118n

FREITs (finite-life real estate investment trusts), 312–313
Friedman, Milton, 259
Friedman, W. Robert, Jr., 253
Fund Exchange newsletter, 268
Fundline newsletter, 268
FundTrust, 60
''Fund Watch.'' *See Money* magazine
funerals, 66, 153, 217, 436, 497
Furash, Edward E., 384, 393
Furman Selz Mager Dietz & Birney, 60
futures, 232, 233, 497–498

Gaining on the Market (Rolo), 225
Gardner, Richard A., 218
Geico insurance, 430
General American Life, 171
General Electric, 229, 249, 332
General Motors, 481; Acceptance Corporation, 392
geriatric care, 253. *See also* age; parents; retirement plans
German, Tim, 107
Getting Help When You Invest, 502
gifts and gift tax, 76, 113–114, 136, 153, 191–192, 210–212, 349; state tax, 206, 207; wills and, 216–217. *See also* inheritance
Ginnie Maes (GNMA mortgage certificates), 173, 303, 305, 306–308, 309, 497; in bond funds, 59, 297, 299
G.J.G. Inc., 55
Globe Mortgage Company, 398
GNMA mortgage certificates. *See* Ginnie Maes
goals. *See* financial planning
gold. *See* precious metals
Goldome (savings and loan group), 380
Goodkin, Sanford, 105
Goodman, Gary, 55
Gordon Jewelry Company, 247
government agency issues: bonds, bond funds, 177, 299; rated, 328. *See also* Treasury securities
Government National Mortgage Corporation. *See* Ginnie Maes
Graduate, The (film), 254
Graham, Benjamin, 225, 242, 243, 244, 246
Grant Thornton (CPA firm), 375
Granville, Joseph E., 261
Great American Life, 171
Great American Reserve, 171
Great Depression, 5, 260. *See also* recessions
Green, Howard, 319
''greenmail,'' 271
Greenspan Advisory, 273
Greenstein, Jane, 109, 402
Group Health: Association of America, 460; Cooperative of Puget Sound, 461
Growth Fund Guide newsletter, 268
Growth Stock Outlook newsletter, 255
growth strategies, growth funds, growth stocks. *See* investment strategies; mutual funds; stocks
guaranteed income contract, 130, 176
Guaranteed Student Loans (GSL), 117, 121
Guarantee Security Life, 171
Guardian insurance, 466
guardianship: of children, 33, 113, 191, 197, 199, 213, 218–219; of handicapped, 199; of parent, 151, 199. *See also* conservatorship; power of attorney
Guide to Understanding Your Pension Plan, A (Pension Rights Center), 157
Guinness Book of World Records, 486

handicap. *See* disability/handicap
Hanks, Dave, 252
H&R Block. *See* Block, H&R
Harrison, Ellen, 217
Harvard University, 125, 224
Havemann, Barry, 400
head-of-household, 113, 348–349, 350
Heady, Robert K., 236, 238
Health and Human Services, U.S. Department of, 101
health insurance, 455–464; auto insurance and, 423; Blue Cross-Blue Shield, 150; child-related, 90–91, 96; claims, 349; dental care, 459; for elderly, 150–152, 163; for married/two-income couples, 76, 90–91, 463; Medicare, 150, 151, 163, 456; POSSLQs and, 68, 73; for singles, 66, 67
Health Insurance Association of America, 458
health maintenance organizations (HMOs), 459–462
health services (as investment), 253
hedging. *See* inflation; investment strategies
Hedlund, Randy, 45, 46
Heine, Leonard, 248
Herzfeld, Thomas, 299
Hewitt Associates, 128, 132
Hewlett-Packard, 94
Hiam, Peter, 419
high-tech. *See* technology
Highway Loss Data Institute, 422
Hirsch, Michael, 60
Hirsch, Yale, and Hirsch Organization, 335, 338
Hoffman, Dustin, 254
home business. *See* business
home-equity loans. *See* loans
homemaker helpers, 254
home ownership: as asset, 150; burglary or damage, *see* loss; buying first house, 104–110; condominiums/cooperative apartments, 65, 104–105, 363, 425, 428–429, 433; and credit record, 109, 408; down payment and closing costs, 108–110, 132, 317–318, 362, 392, 393; joint, vs. tenants

home ownership (*cont.*)
in common, 76, 145; maintenance, repairs, improvement, 105, 110, 351, 363, 364, 426, 429; for "mingles" (unmarried couples), 71–72; selling house, 363–364. *See also* loans (home-equity); mortgages; real estate; tex credits/deductions
homeowners insurance, 11, 73, 318, 425–430, 431; deductible, 363
Home Owners Warranty, 500
Hoover, Herbert, 266
Horchow, Roger, 476–477
Horwitz, Merle, 71, 73
hostile bids, 274. *See also* takeovers
Household Finance savings plan, 240
Household Financial Services, 241
housing: cost of, 28, 64, 163; low-income tax credit, 355. *See also* home ownership; mortgages; real estate; rentals
Housing and Urban Development, U.S. Department of, 108
Howard Weil Labouisse & Friedrichs, 226
How to Avoid Probate! (Dacey), 201
How to Beat the Market with High-Performance Generic Stocks Your Broker Won't Tell You About (Arbel), 250
How to Do Business with the IRS: Taxpayer's Edition (Blaustein), 376
How to Make Your Real Estate Fortune (Zick), 320
How to Save Money on Life Insurance, 438, 499
HSH Associates, 400, 403
Hughes, Charles G., Jr., 90
Hulbert Financial Digest, 338
Hunt, James, 441
Hunter, J. Robert, 423
Hutton, E. F., 177, 301, 304, 380; Bond & Income Series, 298; National Municipal fund, 300

Ibbotson Associates, 58, 323
IBM, 94, 159, 226, 229, 244, 249, 332
Ihara, Toni, 70
income: averaging, 354 (*see also* forward averaging); and credit rating, 407–408; gross and adjusted gross (AGI), 182, 349–350, 353, 355; scholarship money as, 124; unreported taxable, 5, 26, 345–346, 374
Income & Safety newsletter, 237
income funds and stocks. *See* mutual funds; stocks
income tax: alternative minimum (AMT), 356; avoidance of, 5, 26, 345–346, 356, 372 (*see also* tax shelters); "bracket creep," 4; brackets established (1986), 6, 87, 137, 354; and dependents, 72, 148–149, 349, 353, 355; estimating (worksheet), 357–361; filing status, 348–349; and financial goals, 19–20; joint payment, 65, 72, 113, 146, 182, 348–356 *passim;* preparation and defense of return, 355, 365–369, 370–372, 502 (*see also* tax audits); singles vs. married couples, 62, 65–66, 72, 87, 146, 348–356 *passim;* state and local, 351, 356, 363; withheld, *see* salary reduction or withholding plan (401[k]); W-2 statements, 27, 181, 182. *See also* capital gains; tax credits/deductions; tax deferral; tax exemptions
Income Without Taxes (Richelson), 295
index: and mortgage, 401–402; options, *see* options
Indicator Digest newsletter, 279
Individual Asset Planning Corporation, 46
Individual Retirement Account. *See* IRA
industrials. *See* corporate bonds
inflation, 3–6, 234, 251, 354; and annuities, 178; and bonds, 230, 287; and car prices, 482; consumer price index (cost of living), 4, 17, 161, 182, 301, 439, (and income tax) 351, 353; in election years, 266; and financial goals, 17, 19; hedges against, 163, 173, 174, 232, 314, 323–333 *passim;* and insurance coverage, 426, 443; and interest rates, 4, 234, 260, 389, 398, (short- vs. long-term) 114–115, 287, 323; and retirement, 163, 182
Ingham Becker & Company, 343
inheritance: by children (and of former marriage), 73, 77, 144, 145, 147, 191, 209, 215; disinheritance, 214–215; divorce and, 136; POSSLQs and, 68, 69, 73–74. *See also* estates; widows/widowers; wills
installment debt. *See* debts, personal
Institute for Social Research, 84, 85
Institute of Certified Financial Planners, 44, 496
insurance: cash value of policy, 10, 115, 139, 211, 438–444 *passim,* 452; information about, 498–499; insured losses, 352; mortgage, 90, 189; record of policies, 33; settlements, nontaxable, 349; for singles and POSSLQs, 66–67, 68, 73–74; tenants, 73, 425, 428–430; transfer of policy ownership, 211; for two-income families, 90–91, 437, 463; on valuables, 425, 427. *See also* automobile insurance; disability-income insurance; health insurance; homeowners insurance; liability insurance; life insurance
insurance companies as brokers, 339
Insurance Information Institute, 498
Insurance Institute for Highway Safety, 492
insured bonds. *See* municipal bonds (munis)
Integrated Resources Equity Corporation, 16
Intelligent Investor, The (Graham), 225
interest: deductible, *see* tax credits/deductions;

taxable and nontaxable, 349, 351, 356. *See also* interest rates
interest rates, 222; bond, *see* bonds; checking account, 383, 385, 387; credit card/charge account, 87, 395–396; fixed, 4, 287, 323, 394, 395, 399–400 (*see also* inflation); "floating," 301, 393, 394; on insurance premiums, 439, 440–441; and mortgage securities, 305–308; savings and CD, 234–241; student loan, 117–118, 120, 121, 123; and Treasury issues, 5, 236, 292; turning points in, as market indicators, 259–260; variation in, among lenders, 383, 390, 392–393. *See also* mortgages
Interior, U.S. Department of the, 355
Internal Revenue Code (reformed). *See* Tax Reform Act (1986)
Internal Revenue Service (IRS), 169; PROs (problem-resolution officers), 370–372, 502. *See also* income tax; tax audits
International Airline Passengers Association, 503
International Association for Financial Planning, 44, 496
International Franchise Association, 495–496
International Harvester, 288
International Investors, 326
International Society of Preretirement Planners, 156
inter vivos (living) trust. *See* trusts
intestacy laws. *See* wills
inventories: assets and liabilities, 11–12, 75, 222, (of aging parents) 149–150, (in divorce) 139, (worksheet) 13–15; financial documents, 32–33; possessions, 430. *See also* financial records
investment clubs, 223–224
Investment Company Institute, 264, 500
Investment Directions Associates, 53
investment managers. *See* financial planning
investment strategies, 223–233; buy-and-hold, 226, 258, 282, 296; clubs, seminars and courses for, 223–225; defensive, 277–286; for growth, 249–257 (*see also* mutual funds; stocks); hedging, 277, 282–286, 301 (*see also* inflation); marginal tax rate and, 354; presidential elections and, 265–267; record of, for survivor, 33; retirement, 322–333 (*see also* retirement plans); takeover targets, 269–276, 290 (*see also* takeovers); timing the market, 58, 258–268, (worksheet) 262–264; value investing, 242–248, (worksheet) 245, when to sell, 257, 274, 275–276, 284–286. *See also* financial planning; risk; savings
Investor Access Corporation, 280
Investors Guide and Directory to Mutual Funds, The, 500
IRA (Individual Retirement Account), 5, 156, 235, 240, 267, 392, 444; brokers and, 168, 335, 338; cash value of, 11; CDs in, 168, 238, 323, 326; corporate bonds in, 288, 298, 304; eligibility for, 6, 66, 166–167, 350; investments not permitted in, 167; investor's guide to, 322–333; lump sums rolled over into, 176, 178, 179, 180; maintenance or startup fees for, 167, 168; for married couples/two-income families, 88, 166, 167, 235, 350; maximum contribution to, 322n; mutual funds for, 57, 60, 168, 298; real estate trusts/partnerships for, 314, 331; for singles, 66, 167, 350; and tax deductions, 5, 88, 137, 167–168, 350; withdrawal from, 109, 167, 169, 178, 179–181; zero bonds in, 302, 304. *See also* pension plans; retirement plans
It's Your Choice (Nelson), 153
ITT, 278

Jacobs, Beverly S., 278, 279
Jacobs, Irwin, 243
Janke, Kenneth, 222
Janus fund, 58
Jewel Company, 275
jewelry, 499. *See also* valuables
Jewish Theological Seminary of America, 148
jobs: career-switching, 126, 157; job-hopping, 132–133, 157; part-time, 157; supplementing Social Security benefits, 162, 175, 182–183
Johns Hopkins University, 224, 460
joint-and-survivor annuity. *See* annuities
joint income tax. *See* income tax
joint life-expectancy calculation, 181
joint ownership (community property); bank accounts/credit cards, 71, 75, 86, 92, 235; divorce, 77–78, 91, 135–136; right of survivorship, 76, 144–145, 191, 193–194, 207, 214; sale of house, 364; vs. tenancy in common, 76, 145; for unmarried couples, 71
Jones, Betty D., 16
Journal of Retail Banking, 390
Julian Block's Guide to Year-Round Tax Savings (Block), 369
junk bonds. *See* corporate bonds
junk REMICs, 309
Jury Verdict Research, 431
Juster, F. Thomas, 84

Kalil, James, Sr., 51
Kalin, Sharon, 274, 276
Kalish, Jerry, 159
Kass, Benny L., and Kass & Skalet, 320
Kastengren, Robert, 484
Keeslar, Oreon, 125
Keim, Donald, 289

Kellner, George A., and Kellner DiLeo & Company, 274
Kemper (insurance), 433
Keogh plan, 45, 66, 88, 156, 170; brokers and, 169, 335, 338; investment funds for, 57, 288, 302, 304, 314, (guide to) 322–333; maximum contribution to, 322n, 350; tax deductions under, 169, 350; withdrawal from, 169, 178. *See also* pension plans; retirement plans
Keynes, John Maynard, 5
Kidder Peabody, 303
King Drew Medical Center, 100
Kirsch, Charlotte, 185, 186, 189
Kniffin, Robert, 127
Knight, Dick, 90
Knight Insurance Agency, 123
Knights of Columbus scholarships, 124
Kodak (Eastman Kodak), 249
Kohlberg Kravis Roberts, 271
Koons, William, 140
Korczyk, Sophie, 133
Korecki, Louis, 434
Korvette, E. J., 472
Krause, Lawrence A., 149
Kroger's, 380
Kurth, Walter, 411
Kushner, Greg, 179

Labor Statistics, Bureau of, 64
Lachman, Leanne, 315
Ladenburg Thalmann & Company, 255
Ladner, Robert, 382
Langer, Judith, 64, 83
Lanyi, Andrew, 255, 256, 257
LaRossa, Ralph, 99
Lebenthal, Jim, and Lebenthal & Company, 297
Legal Aid Society, 414
legal services, 499–500. *See also* commissions and fees
Leider, Robert and Anna, 119
Leightman, Stephen, 111
Lenz, R. Britt, 498
Leonetti & Associates, 45
Leuthold, Steven, 289
leveraged buyout. *See* takeovers
Levine, Andrew C., 110
Lexington GNMA Income Fund, 308
liabilities. *See* inventories
liability insurance: automobile, 422, 423; excess (personal and commercial), 431–434; homeowners/tenant, 427, 428–429
Libbey, Pat, 82
Liberty Mutual insurance, 424
life expectancy. *See* age
life insurance, 222, 435–445; adjustable, 439; for children, 90; credit, in buying car, 480; cutback in later years, 151, 163, 437; lump sum payments, 185, 436; for married couples, 90, 147, 151, 436–437; ownership of policy transferred, 211; planning worksheet, 447–454; single-premium, 443–445; for singles and POSSLQs, 66, 73–74; taxability of proceeds, 147, 192, 209–210, 443; term, 147, 437–438, 439, 440; universal, 10, 115, 439–441; variable, 441–443, 444; whole, 10, 151, 438–439, 442, 443. *See also* insurance
life insurance trust, irrevocable, 209
Life of Georgia, 171
life-prolonging measures, 153
LIFO accounting, 246–247
Limited, The, hostile bid by, 274
limited partnerships. *See* real estate limited partnerships
LION bonds, 302. *See also* bonds
Lipper Analytical Services, 59, 171–172
liquidity. *See* cash
Liquidity Fund Investment Corporation, 139
living together. *See* POSSLQs
Living Together Kit, The (Warner and Ihara), 70
living trust, living wills. *See* trusts; wills
load mutual funds. *See* mutual funds
loans, 389–397; auto, *see* automobiles; balloon, 400; bridge, 404; consumer loan companies, 407; fixed-rate, 399–400; home-equity, 121, 346, 351, 389, 392–394, 482; installment, 390, 408, 412; passbook, 409–410; personal (secured vs. unsecured), 392, 394–395; refusal of, 409–410; against retirement plans, 132; single-premium life insurance, 444–445; student, *see* education costs. *See also* credit; debts, personal; finance companies; interest rates; mortgages
Loans for Parents, 117, 121
Loeb, Gerald M., 225
Longden, Clair, 114–115
loss: casualty, theft, damage, 352, 363, 364; credit/debit card, 397; deductible, 425; records of, 364. *See also* capital losses; tax credits/deductions
Love Is Love But Business Is Business: The Essential Guide to Living Together (Horwitz), 71
lump-sum payments, 169, 175–180 *passim,* 185, 436

MACAP (Major Appliance Consumer Action Panel), 491, 495
McClelland, Dale E., 126
McDonald's, 227
McElwain, Robert, 53
McGee, Judith Headington, 21
McHenry, Bonnie, 428
MacNeill, David W., 266
McNellis, Richard T., 46

mail-order houses, 476–477
Major Market index, 283, 497
Makin, Malcolm A., 48, 89
Malcolm, Bill, 73, 74
Mamis, Justin and Robert, 284
Manufacturers Hanover Bank, 302
margin, 232; buying or borrowing on, 233, 351, 381
Markle, Alvin, 289
markups, 474–475; automobile, 481
marriage certificate, 33, 181, 188
married couples: blended family, 143–147; budget, 31, (worksheets) 29–31; income tax, 62, 65, 72, 87, 146, 348–349, 355, 356; IRAs for, *see* IRA; marital deduction, 76, 91, 153, 192, 203, 208–209, 210; and net worth, goals, 9, 16; sale of jointly owned house, 364; Social Security/pension benefits, 74, 159, 162, 166, 187–188, 193, 435, 437, 452–454; spousal remainder trust, 114; standard deduction, 350; tax credit for child/dependent expenses, 101, 355; wills, 76, 214, 220. *See also* children; life insurance; parents; prenuptial agreements; two-income families; widows/widowers
Martin, Linda, 371
Marvin, Lee, 69
Massachusetts Capital Development fund, 89
Massachusetts Mutual insurance, 466
Massachusetts Securities Division, 45
Master Federal Tax Manual, 369
maternity/paternity leave, 94, 95, 97, 98, 158
Max Ule, 343
Mead, Margaret, 63
Meals on Wheels, 154
Med Center Bank, 383
Medicaid, 149, 152, 198
medical and dental expenses, 132, 350, 351, 356
medical insurance, Medicare. *See* health insurance
Mediform (coverage analysis), 463–464
Mehr, Robert I., 418
memory chips, 254
Merck pharmaceuticals, 94, 229
mergers and "mergerspeak." *See* takeovers
Merrill Lynch, 301, 302, 334, 338, 442; Capital Markets, 290; Cash Management Account, 379, 381; Financial Pathfinder, 47; Flexible Credit Account, 394
Metz, Michael, 243, 247
MidAmerica Exchange, 232
Mihaly, Orestes, 45
Milbank, Jeremiah III, and Milbank Tanaka & Associates, 53, 55
mileage allowance deduction, 352
military service benefits. *See* armed forces
Milling, Donna, 110, 321
Milne, Ann, 141
"mingles," 71
Minnesota Mining & Manufacturing (3M), 95
Minnesota Mutual insurance, 466
minors. *See* age; children
Mirontschuk, Victor, 106
mobile homes, 108. *See also* home ownership
Modern Maturity magazine, 501
Monarch insurance, 466, 469
monetarism, 4, 5
Money magazine, 1, 93, 225, 323, 436, 439, 482; financial recommendations, 28, 65, 89; "Fund Watch" column, 59, 114, 160
money-market funds, 130, 168, 173, 235, 266, 381, 392; automatic investment in, 380; bank deposit/checking accounts, 234, 236, 383, 388; as emergency reserve, 88, 89, 93, 189; insurers', 442; and interest rates, 4, 234, 236, 237, 240, 328; rated, 328; tax-exempt, 237; transfer of, 57, 58, 60, 267. *See also* mutual funds
Montgomery Securities, 253
Moody's, 288, 297, 310; *OTC Industrial Manual,* 256
Moore, Kristin, 84
Morgan, Gwen, 102
Morgan, James, 85
Morgan Guaranty bank, 302
Morgan Lewis & Bockius, 217
Morris, William, 145
Mortgage Clearing House, Inc., 109, 402
mortgages, 398–404; applying for, 410; brokers, 393; consultants, 320; deductibility of interest, *see* tax credits/deductions; FHA, 108, 109, 231, 306, 308, 362; mobile home, 108; mortgage insurance, 90, 189; overdue (1980s), 412; points (surcharges) on, 317–318, 362, 393, 398–399; prepayment of, 307, 309, (penalty for) 364; rates, 31, 104, 105, 109, 231, 393, (adjustable [ARM]) 398–399, 400–403; second, 314, 351, 392–393; shared-equity, 320; Veterans Administration, 108, 109, 231, 306, 308, 362
mortgage securities. *See* Fannie Mae; Freddie Mac; Ginnie Maes
mortgage trusts (REITs), 314
moving expenses, 352, 362
Mulder, James C., 154
Muldoon, Kathleen, 96
municipal bonds (munis), 168, 298, 299, 497; insured, 294, 295; safety of/yield from, 173, 293–295, 303–304; special tax on, 182, 356; unit trust, 295–297; zero-coupon, 114, 301, 303–304. *See also* bonds; trusts
Murphy fund (Harvard), 125
mutual funds, 56–60; asset management accounts, 380, 381, 388; balanced, 330; for beginning investors, 42, 56, 58, 225, 226, (how to choose and switch) 59–60, 267,

mutual funds (*cont.*)
298; bond, 58–59, 291, 297–299, (closed-end) 298–299, (tax-free) 114, 299–300; cash-assets ratio, 261, 264; conversion to cash, 10; discount brokers and, 338; gold investments by, 173, 268, 326; government bond funds, 299, 328; growth/growth and income/income, 52, 57, 157, 266, (rated) 329–330; and IRAs, 57, 60, 168, 298; load and no-load, 58, 59, 60, 258, 281, 292, 298, 299, 307; maximum capital-gains, 328–329; money-market, 57, 60, 222, 234, 235, 236–237, 388; mortgage investments by, 307, 308; newsletters and information, 267–268, 500; sector (specialty), 57, 268, 330; services offered by, 380; types of, 57–58
Mutual Fund Specialist newsletter, 268
Mutual of Omaha insurance, 466
Mutual Shares fund, 58
Myers, Albert, 157

N.A.D.A. Official Used Car Guide (Blue Book), 11, 481, 482
Nader, Ralph, 1, 491
NASDAQ, 497
National Association(s): of Employers on Health Care Alternatives, 455–456; of Enrolled Agents, 368; of Home Builders, 500; of Investment Clubs, 222, 223, 499; of Personal Financial Advisers, 45; of Securities Dealers, 501; of Social Workers, 155
National Automobile Dealers Association, 11, 492
National Benefit Services, 159
National Center for Financial Education, 496
National Charities Information Bureau, 498
National Consumers League, 491
National Council on the Aging, 501
National Credit Union Administration, 494; Share Insurance Fund, 235
National Foundation for Consumer Credit (NFCC), 412, 414
National Funeral Directors Association, 497
National Futures Association, 498
National Highway Traffic Safety Administration, 492
National Institutes of Health, 96, 252
National Insurance Consumer Organization, 423, 438, 441, 499
National Life Variable Annuity Account, 171
National Merit Scholarships, 124
National Personnel Records Center, 188
National Resource Center for Consumers of Legal Services, 500
National Securities Real Estate Stock Fund, 312
National Society of Public Accountants, 371
National Tenants Union, 428
Navy, U.S.: child care program, 95
Need A Lift? (American Legion), 124
need-analysis formula. *See* education costs
Neill, Humphrey B., 260, 261, 337
Nelson, O. Davis, 407, 408
Nelson, Thomas C., 153
net worth: company, *see* equity; personal, 9–12, 80, (worksheet) 13–15 (*see also* inventories)
Neuberger & Berman Partners Fund, 58
New Car Prices (Edmund), 481
New York State Securities Bureau, 45
New York Stock Exchange, 283, 285, 502. *See also* stock market
Nicholas Fund, 58
Nickerman, Ed, 457
''Nifty Fifty,'' 249
Nissenbaum, Gerald L., 80
Nixon, Richard M., 3, 4, 266
Noble, Kaye Neil, 478–479
No Load Fund Investor newsletter, 59, 268
*Noload Fund*X* newsletter, 58, 59
No-Load Mutual Fund Association, 500
no-load mutual funds. *See* mutual funds
nonprofit institutions: annuities taxed, 179
Noonan, James, 484
North American Capital Management, 53
Northwestern Mutual Life, 466; ''C'' Bond, 172
NOW accounts. *See* checking accounts

O'Brien, John, 304
O'Brien, Michael, 290
O'Dea, Thomas, 321
O'Hanlon, George, 371
oil embargo and prices, 3, 4, 260; and energy crisis, 288–289
Omohundro, Richard, 290
Onassis, Jacqueline Kennedy, 215
100 Highest Yields newsletter, 236, 238
on-line investing. *See* computer(s)
Oppenheimer & Company, 243, 247, 274, 290; Management Corporation, 442
options, 229–230, 282–283, 497; index, 229, 283–284; stock, 128, 139, 356
organ donations, 153, 217
Organization of Petroleum Exporting Countries (OPEC), 3, 4
OTC Industrial Manual (Moody's), 256
Outlook, The (Standard & Poor's), 225, 502
ownership rights: prenuptial contract and, 77–78. *See also* joint ownership (community property)

Pacific Gas & Electric, 288
Paine Webber, 53, 284, 334
Paley, William S., 213
''palimony,'' 69
Pallas Financial Services, 267

Pan-American Life, 171
Parco, Vincent, 188
Parent Loans for Undergraduate Students (PLUS). *See* Loans for Parents
parents: care/support of, 16, 17, 148–155, 199, 353; single, 101, 113; tax credits for, 355; working, *see* two-income families. *See also* children; family; widows/widowers
Parker, Gerald, 466
Parker, Glen King, 237
partnerships. *See* real estate limited partnerships
part-time work, 157
passbook loans, 409–410
pass-through certificates, 306, 308, 309
paternity leave. *See* maternity/paternity leave
Patient Investor newsletter, 255, 256, 257
Paul Revere insurance, 466, 467, 469
P/E. *See* price/earnings (P/E) ratio
Peat Marwick Mitchell, 133, 186
Peeke Report, 403
Pell (student) Grants, 117
Penney, J. C., 240, 395
Pennsylvania Family Partnership Loan, 120
Pennsylvania Mutual Fund, 247
pension plans, 156–170; beneficiary, 159, 193, (divorce and) 139; career-average, 159; cash value, 11, 139; defined-benefit/contribution, 169, 172, 322n; evaluated, 157–160, 166; and pension management, 172–174; and POSSLQs, 73–74; taxed, 179, 349; for two-income families, 88; vested, 11, 132, 157, 158, 160. *See also* annuities; IRA (Individual Retirement Account); Keogh plan; retirement plans; Social Security benefits
Perkins, Carl D., National Direct Student Loans, 117
Peterson Howell & Heather, 484
Phiel, Ruth, 317, 319
Philanthropic Advisory Service, 498
Philip, Prince, 409
Pickering, Dr. Larry, 102
"pickup" taxes, 206. *See also* estates
plastics, 251, 254–255
Pleck, Joseph H., 84
points. *See* mortgages
Polaroid, 286
Policy Wise (Chasen), 150
politics: and stock market, 265–267
population. *See* age; baby boomers
portfolios: growth stocks, how to assemble, 255–257; junk-bond, 59, 289–291; municipal bond, 295. *See also* diversification; mutual funds
POSSLQs, 68–74
poverty level, 92, 253, 355
power of attorney, 73, 151, 153, 197. *See also* guardianship
precious metals: cash value, 10; futures, 497; gold prices, 3, 326; gold standard, 4; as inflation hedge, 173, 174, 327, (risk) 178, 232; and IRA or Keogh, 167, 326; mutual funds investment in, 173, 268, 326. *See also* valuables
prenuptial agreements, 75–80, 140, 144, 215
presidential elections, 265–267
price/earnings (P/E) ratio, 248, 256, 257, 285, 313
Price Waterhouse, 179
principal: payment of, on home-equity loan, 393; preservation of, 322–333 *passim;* safety of IRA, 168
Principal Financial Group, 439
Principles of Insurance (Mehr), 418
private investigators, 188
PRO (problem resolution officer), 370–372, 502
probate. *See* wills
Procter & Gamble, 94, 289
Professional Insurance Agents Association of Connecticut, 73
profit-sharing plans, 128, 130, 176, (table) 129; anticipated, 166; borrowing against, 109, 132; POSSLQ as beneficiary, 73; as tax shelter, withdrawal from, 88
property tax: deductibility, 86, 109, 346, 351, 363; prepayment, in buying house, 318
Provident Life & Accident insurance, 466
Prudential-Bache Securities, 111, 334, 336
psychiatric care, 462
Public Citizen consumer group, 491
Public Interest Research Group, U.S., 386
Publix stores, 380
Puerto Rican tax-exempt bonds, 297
Purdue University Credit Research Center, 390
Putnam, Thomas, 51
puts, 229, 230, 283; put bonds, 300–301

QTIP trust, 209. *See also* trusts
Quanex Corporation, 227
Quinn, Jane Bryant, 83

Ramer, John C., 396
Raymond James & Associates, 89
Rea, James B., 244
Reagan, Ronald, and Reaganomics, 3, 5, 6, 251, 266, 314; budget cuts, 116, 120
real estate, 231; agent's commission, 321, 331, 364; backyard investing, 316–321; cash value, 10–11; information about home building, 500; rehabilitation tax credit, 315, 355; risk with, 178, 363–364. *See also* home ownership; housing; mortgages; rentals
real estate investment trusts. *See* REITs
Real Estate Investors, Inc., 110
Real Estate Investors' Monthly, 316

real estate limited partnerships, 88, 139, 231, 314–315, 368; cash value, 11; commission, 47; losses, 350; rated, 331
real estate mortgage investment conduit. *See* REMIC
Real Estate Research Corporation, 315
recessions, 5, 87, 259, 266, 364
record-keeping. *See* financial records
Reed, John T., 316
Registry of Financial Planning Practitioners, 44
REITs (real estate investment trusts), 231, 311–315, 331–332
REMIC (real estate mortgage investment conduit), 309, 328
rentals: income from, 311–315, 318, 319–320, 321, 331, 349; low-income, tax credit for, 355; parents as landlords, 110; selection of tenants, 321; singles and, 64
Republic National Bank, 60
Research Institute of America, 369
Reserve Officer Training Corps, 125
Resource Management, 72
retailers: bank-owning, 236, 240, 380, 395; charge accounts, 407, 410; department stores, 240, 410, 473, 474, 478; discount/off-price stores, 471–473, 474–475, 477, 478; mail-order, 476–477; resale shops, 478; and shopping, 474–479
retirement, 501; age at, 156, 159–164; and group insurance, 463; tax choices of, 175–183. *See also* retirement plans
Retirement Equity Act, 139
retirement plans, 156–174; changes in (1981 and after), 6; for self-employed, 66, 88, 169, 322n; for singles, 66; worksheet, 164–165. *See also* IRA (Individual Retirement Account); Keogh plan; pension plans; Social Security benefits; withdrawal penalties
revocable/irrevocable living trusts. *See* trusts
Rhea, Rev. John, 148
Richelson, Hildy, 295
Richmond, James, 398
risk, 239, 277–278, 322; age and, 173; bonds and, 289–290, 291, 294; circumstances and, 17, 57; credit and, 389; fear of/tolerance for, 7–8, 19, 133, 222, 238, 281, (choice of adviser and) 50, 54; and insurance, 418; in investing lump sum, 178
Risk Arbitrage Monitor, 274, 276
Robertson, James A., 432
Robinson-Humphrey/Shearson American Express, 53
Rogers, John, 255, 257
Rolo, Charles J., 225
Roosevelt, Franklin D., 266
Rose & Company, 339
Rosenfeld, Eric, 275
royalties, 140, 349
Royce, Charles, and Royce Value Fund, 247
Rukeyser, Louis, 226, 233
Runzheimer & Company, 483, 484

Safeco Municipal fund, 300
safe-deposit box, 33, 214, 430
Safeway stores, 380
St. Paul Fire & Marine, 433
salary reduction or withholding plan (402[k]), 66, 88, 109, 130, 131–132
sales receipts, 427. *See also* financial records
sales tax, 351
Salo, Ann, 218
Salomon Brothers, 302, 304, 309, 323
Sanders, W. J. III, 254
Satisfaction Guaranteed (Charell), 486
savings, 234–241; budgeting for, 21, 27–28, 86, 87; company-sponsored/payroll savings plans, 11, 28, 88, 128, 131, 157, 179, (evaluation of) 160, 166, (table) 129; department-store plans, 240; vs. investing, 234; retirement, 157. *See also* banks
savings and loan (S&L) associations, 168, 235–239 *passim,* 380, 390, 392, 393; checking accounts, 386, 387
Savings Bonds, U.S. *See* Treasury securities
Schabacker Investment Management, 298
Schachter, Rabbi Stanley, 148
Schlesinger, Sanford, 153, 198, 199
scholarships. *See* education costs
Schorr, Eugene, 186
Schwab, Charles, & Company, 60, 168, 339
Schwaeber & Sloane, 367
Schwarz, Leonard, 343
Scudder Stevens & Clark, 444; Target Fund, 292
Sears, Roebuck & Co., 240, 380, 395, 405
Seattle Public Library, 225
sector funds. *See* mutual funds
securities, 227–233, 501–502; as collateral, 394; mortgage, *see* Fannie Mae; Freddie Mac; Ginnie Maes. *See also* bonds; futures; mutual funds; stocks; Treasury securities
Securities and Exchange Commission (SEC), 44, 53, 139, 314, 331, 343, 501
securities and margin account, 237
Securities Investor Protection Corporation (SIPC), 335, 501
Security Analysis (Graham and Dodd), 242
Security Owner's Stock Guide, 256, 502
Security Pacific, 342
Select Information Exchange, 499
self-employment: estate planning, 201; health and disability insurance, 457, 463, 468; moving expenses, 352; retirement plans, 66, 88, 169, 322n (*see also* Keogh plan); Social Security taxes, 183
self-help. *See* "do-it-yourself"

semiconductors, 254
Senft, Dexter, 309
Sentry Insurance, 463
separation, POSSLQs and, 69, 71–72. *See also* divorce
Services Unlimited, 254
Sestina, John, 46
Seventy Percent Off! The Investor's Guide to Discount Brokerage Houses (Coler), 339
Shapiro, Leslie S., 502
share brokers. *See* brokers
shared-equity financing, 320–321
share drafts, 387–388
Sharkey, Eileen, 49, 114, 150
Shea & Gould, 209
Shearson Lehman Brothers, 334, 442
shopping. *See* automobiles; credit; retailers
short selling, 264–265
silver. *See* precious metals
Silverstone, Leslie J., 337
Silverstone, Robert, 224
Simmons First National Bank, 396
single parents, 101, 113
singles, 63–67; budget, 65, (worksheet) 29; income tax, 62, 65–66, 72, 146, 348, 350, 351, 356; insurance problems, 66–67, 68, 73–74; and IRAs, 66, 167, 350. *See also* POSSLQs
Skadden Arps Slate Meagher & Flom, 215
Sloane, Jerry, 367
Small Business Administration, 496
small-claims courts, 490–491
SMB Financial Planning, 46
Smith, Allen, 101
Smith, Ned, 489
smokers, and life insurance, 438
Smythe, R. M. & Company, 494
Social Security benefits, 132–133, 154, 156, 157, 160–162, 163; for disability, 91, 465, 469; for divorced spouse, 162, 181; enrolling for, 181–182, 187–188; integrated with pension or insurance, 159, 166, 469; POSSLQs and, 74; retirement, 166, (table) 161; survivors', 74, 90, 187–188, 435, 437, 452–454; tax on, 182; for working wife, 87; working to supplement, 162, 175, 182–183
Social Security number: for child, 113; of deceased spouse, 188
Social Security taxes (FICA), 87, 100, 183
Sollitto, Paul, 457
Sonny Mae (State of New York Mortgage Agency), 310
Soroptimists scholarships, 124
Sotheby's (auctions), 493
Soule, Charles, 467
Spear Securities, 342
specialty (sector) funds. *See* mutual funds
spousal remainder trust, 114
spouse employment assistance program (SEAP, Navy), 95
"sprinkling provision." *See* trusts
Sprouse, Mary, 374
Sputnik, 3
Stack, Ruth, 455
Standard & Poor's (S&P): bond ratings, 288, 294, 296, 297, 303; index (500), 51, 53, 160, 171, 260, 311, 328, 338, 344, (futures on) 232, (P/E of) 248, (rated) 332; index (100), 283–284; publications, 225, 256, 502; Stockpak II (computer program), 244
Starner, Margaret, 89
state-aid education programs, 120, 121
state and local taxes, 364; estate, 193, 203, 206–207, 210. *See also* tax credits/deductions; tax exemptions
State Farm Insurance Company, 423, 424, 430, 463
State of New York Mortgage Agency (Sonny Mae), 310
Stearns, Peter, 156
Steelcase (furniture manufacturers), 94–95
Stein, Edward I., 136
Steinberg, Allen, 132
Steinberg, Saul, 243, 271
Stein Roe Managed Municipal fund, 300
Stepfamily Association of America, 143
Stevens, Robert L., 383
stockbrokers. *See* brokers
Stock Exchange information, 502
Stock Guide, 256, 502
stock market: children's interest in, 280; crash (1973–74), 261; economy and, 259, 266; forecasting, four approaches to, 259–267. *See also* Dow Jones; investment strategies; Standard & Poor's (S&P)
Stock Market Strategy (Crowell), 262
stock options. *See* options
stock plans. *See* employee stock-ownership plan (ESOP)
Stock Reports (Standard & Poor's), 225
stocks: appraisal of old certificates, 494; beginners' choice, 222, 226–227; blue-chip, 157, 173, 174, 178, 229, 332, 336; vs. bonds, 58; common, 227–229, 259, 266, (conversion to) 231, 291, 325; computer-analyzed, 244, 246, 270, 336; defensive, 54; evaluation of, 244–248, (worksheet) 245; growth, 52, 228–229, 249–257, 332–333; income, 228–229; net current asset value, 246; penny, 226; preferred, 230, 231, 291; and warrants, 229
Stolper, Michael, and Stolper & Company, 52, 53
Strebel, Paul, 250
Stribling, Catherine, 408
Stride Rite (shoe manufacturer), 95
strike price, 282, 283, 284

STRIPS. *See* Treasury securities
Strong Total Return fund, 58
Strum, Gary, 177
Student Guide, The: Five Federal Financial Aid Programs, 495
students, 463; credit cards for, 410. *See also* education costs
Successful Ways & Means, 477
Success Over Sixty (Myers), 157
supermarkets, 380. *See also* retailers
Supplemental Loans for Students, 117–118, 121
Supplemental Security Income (SSI), 152, 198
Supplementary Educational Opportunity Grants, 117
surgery, 456, 457, 458, 460, 462
survivorship, right of. *See* widows/widowers
Survivor's Manual, A (Kirsch), 185, 189
Switch Fund Advisory newsletter, 268

takeovers, 243, 247, 269–276, 289, 290; leveraged buyouts, 243, 270, 271, 273, 289, 290; mergers, 243, 270, 271–274; ''mergerspeak,'' 272–273; tender offers, 271, 275–276
Tandy Corporation, 131, 225
tax advisers: accountants as, 175, 179, 180, 366–367, 368, 369, 378; choosing, 365–369
tax audits, 373–378; appeal of, 376–377; financial records for, 362, 364, 372, 374–376, 387; tax advisers and, 366, 368, 369, 374–375, 376, 378; TCMP, 377–378
tax brackets. *See* income tax
Tax Court, U.S., 363, 371–372, 502–503
tax credits/deductions, 354, (worksheet) 358–359; alimony, 136–137, 350; alternative minimum tax (AMT) and, 356, 360–361; casualty, theft, damage, 352, 363, 364; charity, 192, 211–212, 351–352, 356; child/dependent care, 101, 355; depreciation, 110, 312, 313, 363; elderly or disabled, 351, 352, 355, 364; home office expenses, 363; home ownership and, 65, 88, 109, 346, 362–364; IRAs and, 5, 88, 137, 167–168, 350; IRS challenge of, 375 (*see also* tax audits); itemized vs. standard, 350–353; Keogh plan, 169, 350; loan interest, 121, 351, 389, 393–394, 482; low-income housing, 355; marital, 76, 91, 153, 192, 203, 208, 210; medical expense, 350, 351, 356; mortgage interest and points, 88, 105, 312, 313, 331, 346, 351, 362–363, 400; moving expense, 352, 362; real estate rehabilitation, 315, 355; state and local taxes (property, income), 88, 109, 346, 351, 356, 363
tax deferral: EE bonds, 293; forward averaging, 169, 178–179, 356; life insurance, 439–440, 444; savings/retirement plans, 66, 128, 132, 167–168, 178–179, 180, 331; trust income and gifts, 114, 210
tax exemptions: bond funds, 114, 299–300, 310; gift/estate/trust, 153, 191–192, 209, 443; life insurance proceeds, 147, 192, 209–210, 443; money-market funds, 237; personal, 353; Social Security benefits, 163, 182; state and local, 72, 237, 239, 291, 293, 297, 310; ''waste'' of, 168–169, 187, 331. *See also* municipal bonds (munis)
taxes. *See* estates; gifts and gift tax; income tax; property tax; sales tax; state and local taxes
Taxpayer Compliance Measurement Program (TCMP), 377–378
tax reform, 346
Tax Reform Act (1986), 3, 6, 88, 109, 112–113, 121, 314; and bonds (municipal, mortgage-revenue), 293, 309, 310; and IRAs, 137, 167; and long-term capital gains, 139, 228, 287; penalties on withdrawals, 131–132, 178–179; singles under, 62, 65, 72; and tax deferral, 128, 178–179, 440; and tax preferences (loopholes), 356
tax shelters: average taxpayer use of, 5, 19, 88; for children, 113; home ownership, 65, 88, 346, 362–364; IRS suspicions of, 374; limits on, 356, 440. *See also* IRA (Individual Retirement Account); profit-sharing plans; real estate limited partnerships; salary reduction or withholding plan (401[k]); savings; tax deferral
teachers, 179, 374, 457
technology, 251–253, 254–355. *See also* computer(s)
Telephone Switch Newsletter, 268
tenancy in common. *See* home ownership
tenants. *See* insurance; rentals
tender offers. *See* takeovers
testamentary trust. *See* trusts
ThanaCAP (consumer action panel), 491, 497
Theos Foundation, 189
3M, 95
TIGRs. *See* Treasury securities
tips, as income, 349
title search, 318
Toomey-Ryan, Paula, 162
Touche Ross, 366
Towers Perrin Forster & Crosby, 129n, 130
Trade Plus, 343
tranches (REMIC issues), 309
Transportation, U.S. Department of, 492, 503
travel, information and complaint mediation, 503
traveler's checks, 384
Travelers Insurance Company, 433, 434, 463
Treasury, U.S. Department of the, 503

Treasury securities (bonds, bills, notes), 118, 163, 222, 266, 503; cashing in, 173, 235; CATS, STRIPS, TIGRs, 302; futures, 232, 497; index, 401, 402; in mutual funds, 58, 59, 297, 328; purchase of, 239–240, 292, 493, 503; safety of, 19, 174, 235–240 *passim,* 291–292, 298, 299, 322, 327; Savings Bonds, 114, 239, 240, (cash value) 10, (EE & HH) 115, 292–293, 301, (lost) 503; yield on, 5, 19, 240, 292–293, 307, 309, 327; zero-coupon, 304. *See also* Ginnie Maes
trusts: bank trust departments, 52, 200–201, 229; bypass, 208, 209; charitable remainder/lead, 211–212; for children, 147, 191, 197–198, 218; choice of trustee, 196, 199–201, 218; Clifford (short-term), 113, 114; "do-it-yourself," 201–202; general power of appointment, 209; for handicapped, 198–199; irrevocable life insurance, 209; living (*inter vivos;* revocable and irrevocable), 152, 194–196, 201, 207, 209; marital deduction, 192, 203, 208–209, 210; QTIP, 209; real estate investment, *see* REITs; spousal remainder, 114; "sprinkling provision" in, 198, 199; standby or convertible, 197; testamentary, 147, 152–153, 194–201 *passim,* 207–210, 211; unit, 290, 295–297, 299, 307, 308, 328, (rated) 325–326, (zero-coupon) 304
Truth in Lending Act, 390, 493, 494
TRW Information Services, 410
Twentieth Century Select fund, 58
two-income families, 28, 32, 72, 81–92, 383; budgeting, 85–87, (worksheets) 29–30; child care, 93–95, 96–97 (*see also* children); insurance, 90–91, 437, 463; IRAs, 88, 166, 235, 350; loans, 400

Ufford, Charles W., Jr., 215
Understanding Financial Statements, 502
Understanding Stocks and Bonds, 502
Unger, Michael, 45
Unified Management Corporation, 344; Unisave account, 381, 382
Uniform Gifts to Minors Act, 113–114
Uniform Marriage and Divorce Act, 134–135
Unionmutual Life, 171
United Nations World Assembly on Aging, 148
unit trusts. *See* trusts
unmarried couples, 68–74
Urban Institute, 81
USAA (United Services Automobile Association) insurance, 424, 430, 441
USAA Income Fund, 308
U.S. Master Tax Guide, 369
utility bills (deductible), 363
utility issues. *See* corporate bonds

valuables, 139; appraisals and insurance, 11, 425, 427, 493–494, 499; art and artifacts (capital gains on), 352, 356; in IRA, 167; sales charges on, 47. *See also* precious metals
value brokers, 339
value investing, 242–248, (worksheet) 245
Value Line: stocks, 244, 247; Tax Exempt High Yield mutual funds, 114
Value Line Investment Survey, 225, 244, 245, 256, 279, 344, 502
Van der Linden, Bernard, 226
Van Eaton, Bryan M., 184
Vanguard Fixed Income-GNMA funds, 299, 307
Venture Muni Plus mutual funds, 114
Verrill, Phillip R., 267
vested plans. *See* pension plans
Veterans Administration (VA), 188. *See also* mortgages
Vietnam War, 3–4
Viguerie, Richard, 489, 490
volatility, 279, 286, 323–333 *passim*
Volcker, Paul, 5

wages and salary, 4, 5, 349. *See also* salary reduction or withholding plan (401[k])
Walker, Lewis, and Walker Cogswell & Company, 16
Wall Street Journal, 240, 244, 264, 265, 299
"Wall Street Week" (TV program), 226
warehouse clubs, 472–473
Warner, Ralph, 70
warrants, 229
Watts, David, 444
Weatherington, Richard, 378
Weinger, Norman, 243
Weinstein, Vivian, 100
Weitzman, Lenore, 136
Wellesley College Center for Research on Women, 84, 184
Westbrook, Paul, 183
What Do You Do Now?, 189
When to Sell (Mamis and Mamis), 284
White, Theodore, 213
Widow (Caine), 189
widows/widowers, 74, 184–189; filing status, 348; right of survivorship, 76, 144–145, 191, 193–194, 207, 214. *See also* estates; inheritance; trusts; wills
Widrow, Woody, 428
Williams, Fred, 65
Willis, Catherine W., 187
wills, 76, 186, 190–191, 213–220; and aging parents, 152, 153–154; "do-it-yourself," 201, 214; and intestacy laws, 191, 214, 215; invalidated, 220; living, 153; and POSSLQs, 73–74; "pour-over," 196; and probate, 190, 192–193, 195–196, 197, 217,

wills (*cont.*)
219; stepparents', 147. *See also* estates; inheritance
Wise Giving Guide, 498
withdrawal penalties: annuity, 171, 323; CD, 238; IRA/retirement plan, 109, 131–132, 167, 169, 171, 175, 179–181
women: credit for, 92, 185; and divorce, 92, 134–135; and insurance, 67, 73, 90, 437–438, 469; Social Security for, 162; in work force, 28, 81, 84, 92, 98–99, 251. *See also* two-income families; widows/widowers
Women for Rent, 254
working parents. *See* two-income families
World Bank zero issue, 303
W-2 statements. *See* income tax

Xerox, 249, 285

Yaeger, Norma, 52
Yale University Child Study Center, 85
Yankelovich, Daniel, 471
Yashewski, Richard, 286
Yates, Martha, 189
Yaude, Alfred, 371
Young, Richard C., and Young Research & Publishing, 290

Zabalaoui, Judith, 72
Zaccaro, John, 196
zero-coupon bonds. *See* bonds
Zick, Bernard Hale, 320, 321